I0028900

Digital Currency Embedded In

Identities of All Society Members

II

Guoping Jie

Digital Currency Embedded In Identities Of All Society Members II

First Edition

Copyright © 2017 by Guoping Jie

All rights reserved.

ISBN-10: 0995820333

ISBN-13: 978-0-9958203-3-3 (Guoping Jie)

www.mathaccounting.com

Acknowledgements

I wish to take this opportunity to sincerely thank OSAP system (Canada) which gave me a chance to study.

Guoping Jie

Graduated from the Beijing University of Aeronautics and Astronautics, I immediately went to The National University of Defense Technology in Changsha, China. Three years later, I got my master degree and went to Shanghai XinLi Machinery Factory where I design and develop motors as an engineer. In 2005, I immigrated to Canada after having worked for many years. In 2007, I entered the Centennial College in Toronto, Canada to study accounting. During two years, I had had some thoughts about mathematical accounting and its software. I went to the York University in Toronto, Canada in 2009 and graduated with the Honors BAS four years later. After having taken many years to research and develop mathematical accounting model and its MathAccounting software, I opened the Foreverr MathAccounting Software Company Ltd. in February, 2015 (www.mathaccounting.com).

For relaxation, I enjoy reading, driving, and travelling.

ABSTRACT

The digital currency may have other definition. However, I give the digital currency a new definition in this book. Based on the MathAccounting software, the digital currency is the electric extension of the traditional money. The most advantage of the MathAccounting software is that it can embed an identity ID into every dollar in the process of money circulation regardless of the cash receipts and the cash payments. Because all members of the society in the world will touch money, all identity IDs of society members can be embedded in the money. Embedding an identity ID into the money can be achieved by adding the three-level subaccount to existing multi-subaccount name of the parent account "Cash". Namely, the "MultiSubaccount Name" form of the "Cash" is the "Identity ID < Cash receipts from xxx or Cash payments for (to) xxx < Financial activities or Investment activities or Operating activities" in the MathAccounting software. I have developed two models of the simple digital currency and the mixed digital currency. The MathAccounting software is the technical support and security of the two models. The Simple digital currency means that there is not any paper money in the process of money circulation. Obviously, it is an ideal society and the MathAccounting software will be a perfect solution of the digital currency. The most advantage of digital currency is that the Tax Bureau can get the cash flows statement of an organization or company by data which is provided by other related organizations or companies. In this situation, drawing up false accounts, tax evasion, and money laundering will be impossible to occur. The mixed digital currency means that there is some paper money in the process of money circulation. In this situation, the MathAccounting software is also a good solution and the possibility of drawing up false accounts, tax evasion, and money laundering is very small. Moreover, taking some measures and doing analysis can prevent them to occur.

Keywords: digital currency, MathAccounting software, social member rank, simple digital currency model, and mixed digital currency model

x

Contents

Chapter 3

Social Members Accounting Fiscal Years

In this chapter, the accounting fiscal years of ten organizations (plus an abstract organization of the Cash Management Center) will be discussed and entered into themselves databases. All individuals' information in this accounting fiscal year will be included in the organizations, so financial information of all social members will be recoded and discussed in detail. In addition, I make the following hypothesises in the Chapter 3.

- The Accrued interest payable and the Interest expenses accounts all have multi-subaccounts in the Chapter 2. However, the detail multi-subaccounts information of the Cash is more necessary than the Accrued interest payable and the Interest expenses accounts in this book, so the multi-subaccount name forms of the Accrued interest payable and the Interest expenses accounts are the "n" for simplification.

- The Travelling expenses account only includes travel allowance and the Other expenses account only includes the meals expenses. In addition, the income of the travel allowance is not taxable income.

- I have built the detailed three-level subaccount names of the Cash account in the previous Converting Multi-Subaccount Names Tables in the Chapter2. Now, the three-level subaccount names of the Cash account is the "Member ID-symbol-related parent account name or its first word <" for simplification.

- The details of the meals should not be recorded by the customer's organization and should be recorded by product supplier's organization. However, for explaining their corresponding relationship and decreasing mistakes in writing, I also write the details of the meals in transaction explanation of the customer's organization.

- I first enter the transactions (exception of the last transaction of recording tax expenses) of one organization (not including the Business Bank1 and the Business Bank2) and then enter all deposit transactions of this organization in a fiscal year. Then, I enter the Business Bank1's or the Business Bank2's transactions and the deposit transactions. Last, I enter the transactions of recording tax expenses for all organizations.

- For the Business bank1 and the Business bank2, the multi-subaccount name of the Deposit payable account is the "n" now. The balance of the Deposit payable account is equal to the sum of balances of all customers' accounts (including secondary accounts).

3.1 Central Bank

The Central Bank includes an abstract organization of the Cash Management Center, so the Central Bank has two financial statements which will be respectively discussed below.

3.1.1 Cash Management Center

3.1.1.1 An Accounting Fiscal Year of the Cash Management Center

In the new fiscal year, the Cash Management Center (CMC) occurs the following transactions.

- On January 2, 2016, the Cash Management Center pays the money to governments at all levels (including the Central Bank) according to the planned national budgets. Here, the three-level subaccount names of the Cash account all are the "ID-n-Budgets". There are the following four transaction sub-equations, seeing the table in the Figure 3.1-1.

Order	Government Names	Amount	Sub-equations	Cash Multi-Subaccounts
1	Central Bank	85000	Cash (1): -85000 = Tax receipts payable (2): -85000	88-654301-n-budgets < Cash payments of national budgets < Operating activities

2	Government1	90000	Cash (1): -90000 = Tax receipts payable (2): -90000	88-654302-n-budgets < Cash payments of national budgets < Operating activities
3	Tax Bureau	95000	Cash (1): -95000 = Tax receipts payable (2): -95000	88-654303-n-budgets < Cash payments of national budgets < Operating activities
4	Cash Management Center	2062.66	0 = Tax receipts payable (2): -2062.66 + National capital (3): 2062.66	-
5	**Total**	**272062.66**	-	-

Figure 3.1-1   Detail Information of Planned National Budgets

- On January 31, 2016, the Cash Management Center records a transaction of the Accrued interest payable account and the Interest expenses account (one-level subaccount "Bond01-interest") about the Bond01. The transaction sub-equation is:

0 = Accrued interest payable (2): 200 + Interest expenses (5): -200

- On February 28, 2016, the Cash Management Center records the transaction of the Accrued interest payable account and the Interest expenses account about the Bond01 repeatedly.

- On March 31, 2016, the Cash Management Center records the transaction of the Accrued interest payable account and the Interest expenses account about the Bond01 repeatedly.

- On April 30, 2016, the Cash Management Center records the transaction of the Accrued interest payable account and the Interest expenses account about the Bond01 repeatedly.

- On May 31, 2016, the Cash Management Center records the transaction of the Accrued interest payable account and the Interest expenses account about the Bond01 repeatedly.

- On June 1, 2016, the Cash Management Center purchases one Bond23 (three years, 4.5% annually, pay at end of each year) for -$25,000 from the Business Bank2. The multi-subaccount name of the Cash account and transaction sub-equation respectively are:

88-654305-n-investment bond23 < Cash payments for investments < Investing activities

Cash (1): -25000 + Bonds (1): 25000 = 0

- On June 30, 2016, the Cash Management Center records the transaction of the Accrued interest payable account and the Interest expenses account about the Bond01 repeatedly.

- On July 31, 2016, the Cash Management Center records the transaction of the Accrued interest payable account and the Interest expenses account about the Bond01 repeatedly.

- On August 31, 2016, the Cash Management Center records the transaction of the Accrued interest payable account and the Interest expenses account about the Bond01 repeatedly.

- On September 30, 2016, the Cash Management Center records the transaction of the Accrued interest payable account and the Interest expenses account about the Bond01 repeatedly.

- On October 31, 2016, the Cash Management Center records the transaction of the Accrued interest payable account and the Interest expenses account about the Bond01 repeatedly.

- On November 30, 2016, the Cash Management Center records the transaction of the Accrued interest payable account and the Interest expenses account about the Bond01 repeatedly.

- On December 31, 2016, the Cash Management Center records the transaction of the Accrued interest payable account and the Interest expenses account about the Bond01 repeatedly.

- On the same day, the Cash Management Center pays cash -$2,400 for the balance of the Accrued interest payable account for the Bond01 to the bond holders. Here, the transaction is put in the financial activities and the three-level sub-account names are different from other organizations or companies. Later, the same transactions for other organizations or companies are put in the operating activities. The twelve multi-subaccount names of the Cash account and three transaction sub-equations respectively are:

909876501-t-interest expenses < Cash payments for issued bond interest < Financial activities

909865302-t-interest expenses < Cash payments for issued bond interest < Financial activities

909865303-t-interest expenses < Cash payments for issued bond interest < Financial activities

909865307-t-interest expenses < Cash payments for issued bond interest < Financial activities

909865309-t-interest expenses < Cash payments for issued bond interest < Financial activities

909865310-t-interest expenses < Cash payments for issued bond interest < Financial activities

909865311-t-interest expenses < Cash payments for issued bond interest < Financial activities

909865312-t-interest expenses < Cash payments for issued bond interest < Financial activities

909865315-t-interest expenses < Cash payments for issued bond interest < Financial activities

909865316-t-interest expenses < Cash payments for issued bond interest < Financial activities

909865321-t-interest expenses < Cash payments for issued bond interest < Financial activities

909865322-t-interest expenses < Cash payments for issued bond interest < Financial activities

Cash (1): -200 + Cash (1): -200 + Cash (1): -200 + Cash (1): -200 = Accrued interest payable (2): 200 + Accrued interest payable (2): 200 + Accrued interest payable (2): 200 + Accrued interest payable (2): 200

Cash (1): -200 + Cash (1): -200 + Cash (1): -200 + Cash (1): -200 = Accrued interest payable (2): 200 + Accrued interest payable (2): 200 + Accrued interest payable (2): 200 + Accrued interest payable (2): 200

Cash (1): -200 + Cash (1): -200 + Cash (1): -200 + Cash (1): -200 = Accrued interest payable (2): 200 + Accrued interest payable (2): 200 + Accrued interest payable (2): 200 + Accrued interest payable (2): 200

- On the same day, the Cash Management Center pays -$2,500 cash to the Business Bank1 for the administrative fee (Bank fee expenses). The multi-subaccount name of the Cash account is:

  88-654304-t-bank fee expenses < Cash payments to Business banks < Operating activities

- On the same day, the Cash Management Center receives cash $656.25 from the Business Bank2 for investment interest of the Bond23. The multi-subaccount name of the Cash account and transaction sub-equation respectively are:

  88-654305-c-investment income < Cash receipts from investments < Investing activities

  Cash (1): 656.25 = Investment incomes (4): 656.25

- On the same day, the Cash Management Center records the Tax expenses $0 and the Tax payable $0. Because tax rate is zero, the amount of the Tax expenses is also zero. The multi-subaccount name forms of the Tax expenses and the Tax payable accounts all are the 'n'. The transaction sub-equation is:

  0 = Tax payable (2): 0 + Tax expenses (5): 0

So far, I have entered all transactions in the fiscal year 2016. After clicking the

"IncomeStatement" box and answer the "Yes" for new fiscal year, I can get balance sheet of the Cash Management Center the last.

3.1.1.2 Brief Summary of Cash Management Center

The Figure 3.1-2 on the next page shows two sums and all cash transactions of the Cash Management Center by using of SQL Server query. As a closed system based on the MathAccounting software, the sum0 should be equal to zero. However, the individuals are not responsible for recording any transaction, so the sum0 ($2,400) is the sum of the amounts that the some individuals received from the Cash Management Center. If the sum0 is negative, then it is sum of the amounts that individuals paid to the Cash Management Center. The opposite value ($758,814.45) of the sum1 (-$758,814.45) is the balance of the Cash account of the Cash Management Center on December 31, 2016. It is also the balance of the deposit of the Cash Management Center in the Business Bank1 on December 31, 2016.

The Figure 3.1-3, which follows the Figure 3.1-2, shows the Cash Management Center cash flows statement. From the Figure 3.1-3, the cash balance at the ending of this fiscal year is also $758,814.45, which is the same as the sum1's opposite amount in the Figure 3.1-2.

The Figure 3.1-4, which follows the Figure 3.1-3, shows the Cash Management Center cash account table. From the Figure 3.1-4, the cash balance at the ending of this fiscal year is also $758,814.45, which is the same as the sum1's opposite amount in the Figure 3.1-2.

The Figure 3.1-5, which follows the Figure 3.1-4, shows the Cash Management Center income statement. From the Figure 3.1-5, the amount of the earnings before income taxes is -$4,243.75 and the amount of the tax expenses is zero, so the amount of the net earnings of the Cash Management Center in this fiscal year is also -$4,243.75.

The following Figure 3.1-6, which follows the Figure 3.1-5, shows the Central Bank balance sheet. From the Figure 3.1-6, the amount of total assets is $783,814.45, and the amount of the total liabilities and the shareholders' equity is also $783,814.45.

```
SQLQuery3.sql - LIU...SS.dcj021 (sa (56))*    SQLQuery2.sql - LIU...SS.dcj100 (sa (53))*    SQLQuery1.sql - LIU...SS.dcj100 (sa (52))*  ×
```

```sql
use dcj100
select sum(amount) as sum0 from CashByMembers where IDM='88-654300' and TransDate between '2016-01-01' and '2016-12-31'
select sum(amount) as sum1 from CashByMembers where IDM='88-654300' and Symbol = 'd'
select * from CashByMembers where Recorder='88-654300' order by TransDate
```

100 % ▾

Results | Messages

	sum0
1	2400.00

	sum1
1	-758814.45

	IDM	Amount	Symbol	MultiSubaccount	Recorder	TransDate
1	909876501	-5000.00	i	909876503-i-bond01 < Cash receipts from issued bonds < Financial activities	88-654300	2015-12-31
2	909876502	-5000.00	i	909876502-i-bond01 < Cash receipts from issued bonds < Financial activities	88-654300	2015-12-31
3	909876503	-5000.00	i	909876503-i-bond01 < Cash receipts from issued bonds < Financial activities	88-654300	2015-12-31
4	909876507	-5000.00	i	909876507-i-bond01 < Cash receipts from issued bonds < Financial activities	88-654300	2015-12-31
5	909876509	-5000.00	i	909876509-i-bond01 < Cash receipts from issued bonds < Financial activities	88-654300	2015-12-31
6	909876510	-5000.00	i	909876510-i-bond01 < Cash receipts from issued bonds < Financial activities	88-654300	2015-12-31
7	909876511	-5000.00	i	909876511-i-bond01 < Cash receipts from issued bonds < Financial activities	88-654300	2015-12-31
8	909876512	-5000.00	i	909876512-i-bond01 < Cash receipts from issued bonds < Financial activities	88-654300	2015-12-31
9	909876515	-5000.00	i	909876515-i-bond01 < Cash receipts from issued bonds < Financial activities	88-654300	2015-12-31
10	909876516	-5000.00	i	909876516-i-bond01 < Cash receipts from issued bonds < Financial activities	88-654300	2015-12-31
11	909876521	-5000.00	i	909876521-i-bond01 < Cash receipts from issued bonds < Financial activities	88-654300	2015-12-31
12	909876522	-5000.00	i	909876522-i-bond01 < Cash receipts from issued bonds < Financial activities	88-654300	2015-12-31
13		-2000000.00		Cash receipts from issued money < Financial activities	88-654300	2015-12-31
14		-726395.54		Cash receipts from public markets < Operating activities	88-654300	2015-12-31
15		2000000.00		Cash payments to public markets < Operating activities	88-654300	2015-12-31
16		400.00		Cash payments for operating expenses < Operating activities	88-654300	2015-12-31
17	88-654303	-34112.53	c	88-654303-c-tax < Cash receipts from public markets-tax < Financial activities	88-654300	2015-12-31
18	88-654303	-31671.27	c	88-654303-c-tax < Cash receipts from public markets-tax < Financial activities	88-654300	2015-12-31
19	88-654303	-52674.38	c	88-654303-c-tax < Cash receipts from public markets-tax < Financial activities	88-654300	2015-12-31
20	88-654303	-71318.63	c	88-654303-c-tax < Cash receipts from public markets-tax < Financial activities	88-654300	2015-12-31
21	88-654303	-51453.71	c	88-654303-c-tax < Cash receipts from public markets-tax < Financial activities	88-654300	2015-12-31
22	88-654303	-20752.91	c	88-654303-c-tax < Cash receipts from public markets-tax < Financial activities	88-654300	2015-12-31
23	88-654303	-10079.23	c	88-654303-c-tax < Cash receipts from public markets-tax < Financial activities	88-654300	2015-12-31
24	88-654301	85000.00	n	88-654301-n-budgets < Cash payments of national budgets < Operating activities	88-654300	2016-01-02

	IDM	Amount	Symbol	MultiSubaccount	Recorder	TransDate
25	88-654302	90000.00	n	88-654302-n-budgets < Cash payments of national budgets < Operating activities	88-654300	2016-01-02
26	88-654303	95000.00	n	88-654303-n-budgets < Cash payments of national budgets < Operating activities	88-654300	2016-01-02
27	88-654305	25000.00	n	88-654305-n-investment bond81 < Cash payments for investments < Investing activities	88-654300	2016-06-01
28	909876501	200.00	t	909876501-t-interest expenses < Cash payments for issued bond interest < Financial activities	88-654300	2016-12-31
29	909876502	200.00	t	909876502-t-interest expenses < Cash payments for issued bond interest < Financial activities	88-654300	2016-12-31
30	909876503	200.00	t	909876503-t-interest expenses < Cash payments for issued bond interest < Financial activities	88-654300	2016-12-31
31	909876507	200.00	t	909876507-t-interest expenses < Cash payments for issued bond interest < Financial activities	88-654300	2016-12-31
32	909876509	200.00	t	909876509-t-interest expenses < Cash payments for issued bond interest < Financial activities	88-654300	2016-12-31
33	909876510	200.00	t	909876510-t-interest expenses < Cash payments for issued bond interest < Financial activities	88-654300	2016-12-31
34	909876511	200.00	t	909876511-t-interest expenses < Cash payments for issued bond interest < Financial activities	88-654300	2016-12-31
35	909876512	200.00	t	909876512-t-interest expenses < Cash payments for issued bond interest < Financial activities	88-654300	2016-12-31
36	909876515	200.00	t	909876515-t-interest expenses < Cash payments for issued bond interest < Financial activities	88-654300	2016-12-31
37	909876516	200.00	t	909876516-t-interest expenses < Cash payments for issued bond interest < Financial activities	88-654300	2016-12-31
38	909876521	200.00	t	909876521-t-interest expenses < Cash payments for issued bond interest < Financial activities	88-654300	2016-12-31
39	909876522	200.00	t	909876522-t-interest expenses < Cash payments for issued bond interest < Financial activities	88-654300	2016-12-31
40	88-654304	2500.00	t	88-654304-t-bank fee expenses < Cash payments to Business banks < Operating activities	88-654300	2016-12-31
41	88-654305	-656.25	c	88-654305-c-investment income < Cash receipts from investments < Investing activities	88-654300	2016-12-31

Query executed successfully.

Figure 3.1-2   CMC Received or Paid by Other Members

Cash Flow Statement

Cash Flows Statement Year Ended 2016-12-31	
Operating activities	
Cash payments of national budgets	-$270,000.00
Cash payments to Business banks	-$2,500.00
Net cash provided by Operating activities	-$272,500.00
Investing activities	
Cash payments for investments	-$25,000.00
Cash receipts from investments	$656.25
Net cash provided by Investing activities	-$24,343.75
Financial activities	
Cash payments for issued bond interest	-$2,400.00
Net cash provided by Financial activities	-$2,400.00
Net change in cash	-$299,243.75
Cash, Begining	$1,058,058.20
Cash, Ending	$758,814.45

Figure 3.1-3   CMC Cash Flows Statement

Cash

ID	Multi-Name	Amount	Balance	General ID	Transaction Date
1	909876501-i-bond01 < Cash receipts from issued bonds < Financial activities	$5,000.00	$5,000.00	3	2015-12-31
2	909876502-i-bond01 < Cash receipts from issued bonds < Financial activities	$5,000.00	$10,000.00	3	2015-12-31
3	909876503-i-bond01 < Cash receipts from issued bonds < Financial activities	$5,000.00	$15,000.00	3	2015-12-31
4	909876507-i-bond01 < Cash receipts from issued bonds < Financial activities	$5,000.00	$20,000.00	3	2015-12-31
5	909876509-i-bond01 < Cash receipts from issued bonds < Financial activities	$5,000.00	$25,000.00	3	2015-12-31
6	909876510-i-bond01 < Cash receipts from issued bonds < Financial activities	$5,000.00	$30,000.00	3	2015-12-31
7	909876511-i-bond01 < Cash receipts from issued bonds < Financial activities	$5,000.00	$35,000.00	4	2015-12-31
8	909876512-i-bond01 < Cash receipts from issued bonds < Financial activities	$5,000.00	$40,000.00	4	2015-12-31
9	909876515-i-bond01 < Cash receipts from issued bonds < Financial activities	$5,000.00	$45,000.00	4	2015-12-31
10	909876516-i-bond01 < Cash receipts from issued bonds < Financial activities	$5,000.00	$50,000.00	4	2015-12-31
11	909876521-i-bond01 < Cash receipts from issued bonds < Financial activities	$5,000.00	$55,000.00	4	2015-12-31
12	909876522-i-bond01 < Cash receipts from issued bonds < Financial activities	$5,000.00	$60,000.00	4	2015-12-31
13	Cash receipts from issued money < Financial activities	$2,000,000.00	$2,060,000.00	5	2015-12-31
14	Cash receipts from public markets < Operating activities	$726,395.54	$2,786,395.54	5	2015-12-31
15	Cash payments to public markets < Operating activities	-$2,000,000.00	$786,395.54	5	2015-12-31
16	Cash payments for operating expenses < Operating activities	-$400.00	$785,995.54	5	2015-12-31
17	88-654303-c-tax < Cash receipts from public markets-tax < Financial activities	$34,112.53	$820,108.07	6	2015-12-31
18	88-654303-c-tax < Cash receipts from public markets-tax < Financial activities	$31,671.27	$851,779.34	6	2015-12-31
19	88-654303-c-tax < Cash receipts from public markets-tax < Financial activities	$52,674.38	$904,453.72	6	2015-12-31
20	88-654303-c-tax < Cash receipts from public markets-tax < Financial activities	$71,318.63	$975,772.35	6	2015-12-31
21	88-654303-c-tax < Cash receipts from public markets-tax < Financial activities	$51,453.71	$1,027,226.06	6	2015-12-31
22	88-654303-c-tax < Cash receipts from public markets-tax < Financial activities	$20,752.91	$1,047,978.97	6	2015-12-31
23	88-654303-c-tax < Cash receipts from public markets-tax < Financial activities	$10,079.23	$1,058,058.20	6	2015-12-31
24	88-654301-n-budgets < Cash payments of national budgets < Operating acti...	-$85,000.00	$973,058.20	8	2016-01-02

Figure 3.1-4   CMC Cash Account Table (Continue)

Cash

ID	Multi-Name	Amount	Balance	General ID	Transaction Date
20	88-654303-c-tax < Cash receipts from public markets-tax < Financial activities	$71,318.63	$975,772.35	6	2015-12-31
21	88-654303-c-tax < Cash receipts from public markets-tax < Financial activities	$51,453.71	$1,027,226.06	6	2015-12-31
22	88-654303-c-tax < Cash receipts from public markets-tax < Financial activities	$20,752.91	$1,047,978.97	6	2015-12-31
23	88-654303-c-tax < Cash receipts from public markets-tax < Financial activities	$10,079.23	$1,058,058.20	6	2015-12-31
24	88-654301-n-budgets < Cash payments of national budgets < Operating acti...	-$85,000.00	$973,058.20	8	2016-01-02
25	88-654302-n-budgets < Cash payments of national budgets < Operating acti...	-$90,000.00	$883,058.20	9	2016-01-02
26	88-654303-n-budgets < Cash payments of national budgets < Operating acti...	-$95,000.00	$788,058.20	10	2016-01-02
27	88-654305-n-investment bond81 < Cash payments for investments < Investi...	-$25,000.00	$763,058.20	17	2016-06-01
28	909876501-t-interest expenses < Cash payments for issued bond interest < ...	-$200.00	$762,858.20	25	2016-12-31
29	909876502-t-interest expenses < Cash payments for issued bond interest < ...	-$200.00	$762,658.20	25	2016-12-31
30	909876503-t-interest expenses < Cash payments for issued bond interest < ...	-$200.00	$762,458.20	25	2016-12-31
31	909876507-t-interest expenses < Cash payments for issued bond interest < ...	-$200.00	$762,258.20	25	2016-12-31
32	909876509-t-interest expenses < Cash payments for issued bond interest < ...	-$200.00	$762,058.20	26	2016-12-31
33	909876510-t-interest expenses < Cash payments for issued bond interest < ...	-$200.00	$761,858.20	26	2016-12-31
34	909876511-t-interest expenses < Cash payments for issued bond interest < ...	-$200.00	$761,658.20	26	2016-12-31
35	909876512-t-interest expenses < Cash payments for issued bond interest < ...	-$200.00	$761,458.20	26	2016-12-31
36	909876515-t-interest expenses < Cash payments for issued bond interest < ...	-$200.00	$761,258.20	27	2016-12-31
37	909876516-t-interest expenses < Cash payments for issued bond interest < ...	-$200.00	$761,058.20	27	2016-12-31
38	909876521-t-interest expenses < Cash payments for issued bond interest < ...	-$200.00	$760,858.20	27	2016-12-31
39	909876522-t-interest expenses < Cash payments for issued bond interest < ...	-$200.00	$760,658.20	27	2016-12-31
40	88-654304-t-bank fee expenses < Cash payments to Business banks < Oper...	-$2,500.00	$758,158.20	28	2016-12-31
41	88-654305-c-investment income < Cash receipts from investments < Investin...	$656.25	$788,814.45	29	2016-12-31

Figure 3.1-4   CMC Cash Account Table

Income Statement

Year ended: 12/31/2016	
Revenues	
Sales	$0.00
Cost	
Cost of goods sold	$0.00
Gross Margin	$0.00
Operating and administrative expenses	
Interest expenses	-$2,400.00
Bank fee expenses	-$2,500.00
Tax expenses	$0.00
Other income	
Investment income	$656.25
Earnings Before Income Taxes	-$4,243.75
Net Earnings	-$4,243.75
Retained Earnings.Begining	$0.00
Retained Earnings.Ending	-$4,243.75

Figure 3.1-5   CMC Income Statement

Balance Sheet

As at 12/31/2016	
ASSETS	
Current assets	
Cash	$758,814.45
Account receivable	$0.00
	$758,814.45
Long term investments	
Bonds	$25,000.00
Equipment	
Vehicle	$0.00
Accumulated amortization: Vehicle	$0.00
	$0.00
Total Assets	$783,814.45
LIABILITIES	
Current liabilities	
Tax receipts payable	$0.00
Accrued interest payable	$0.00
Account payable	$0.00
Tax payable	$0.00
	$0.00
Long term liabilities	
Bonds payable	$60,000.00
Total Liability	$60,000.00
SHAREHOLDERS' EQUITY	

SHAREHOLDERS' EQUITY	
Owners capital	
National capital	$728,058.20
Retined earnings	-$4,243.75
Accumulated other comprehensive income	$0.00
Total Shareholders' Equity	$723,814.45
Total Liabilities and Shareholders' Equity	$783,814.45

Figure 3.1-6 CMC Balance Sheet Statement

3.1.2 Central Bank

3.1.2.1 An Accounting Fiscal Year of the Central Bank

In the new fiscal year, the Central Bank occurs the following transactions.

- On January 2, 2016, the Central Bank receives cash $85,000 from the Cash

Management Center for the planned national budgets. Here, I presume that the received cash is revenue (sales) of the Central Bank. Of course, you can set it as other account, such as the Budgets payable account and merge it into the Retained earnings or Budgets capital at the end of each fiscal year. The multi-subaccount name of the Cash account and the transaction sub-equation respectively are:

88-654300-c-budgets < Cash receipts from national budgets < Financial activities

Cash (1): 85000 = Sales (received budgets) (4): 85000

- On January 21, 2016, the Central Bank pays -$176.56 cash to A1 (SIN: 909876501) for the Travelling expenses (travel allowance) $137.56 and the Other expenses (meals: food422: $13 + food613: $26) $39. The two multi-subaccount names of the Cash account and the transaction sub-equation respectively are:

909876501-n-travelling < Cash payments for operating expenses < Operating activities

909876501-n-other < Cash payments for operating expenses < Operating activities

Cash (1): -137.56 + Cash (1): -39 = Travelling expenses (5): -137.56 + other expenses (5): -39

Here, the A1's cash receipts of the Travelling expenses and the Other expenses all are no tax payable income. Moreover, the their amounts have been recorded in detail in the two accounts of the Travelling expenses and the Other expenses, so the two multi-subaccount names of the Cash account can merge into a multi-subaccount name. The multi-subaccount name of the Cash account and the transaction sub-equation respectively are:

909876501-n-operating expenses < Cash payments for operating expenses < Operating activities

Cash (1): -176.56 = Travelling expenses (5): -137.56 + other expenses (5): -39

- On January 31, 2016, the Central Bank pays two employees' salary expenses for cash -$5,650. The two multi-subaccount names of the Cash account and the transaction sub-equation respectively are:

  909876501-t-salary < Cash payments for opcrating expenses < Operating activities

  909876502-t-salary < Cash payments for operating expenses < Operating activities

  Cash (1): -2800 + Cash (1): -2850 = Salary expenses (5): -2800 + Salary expenses (5): -2850

  Here, the salary expenses of the A1 and the A2 have been recorded in the three-level subaccounts of the Cash account, so I presume that the multi-subaccount name of the Salary expenses account is "no". The two multi-subaccount names of the Salary expenses account can merge into a multi-subaccount name. The transaction sub-equation is:

  Cash (1): -2800 + Cash (1): -2850 = Salary expenses (5): -5560

- On February 13, 2016, the Central Bank pays -$800 cash to Company1 (phone number: 123456784) with the General ID 1 and pays $200 cash to Company3 (phone number: 123456782) with the General ID 1. The two multi-subaccount names of the Cash account and the transaction sub-equation respectively are:

  88-654306-t-machinery < Cash payments for machinery < Operating activities

  88-654308-t-operating expenses < Cash payments for operating expenses < Operating activities

  Cash (1): -800 + Cash (1): -200 = Account payable (2): -800 + Account payable (2): -200

- On February 22, 2016, the Central Bank purchases the following supplies (inventories) $5,600 from the Company3 (phone number: 123456782) with the General ID 9 for cash -$3,600 and other on credit. The multi-subaccount name is set as the "n" for simplification.

Inven111 < Inven11 < Inven1: 10*40

Inven112 < Inven11 < Inven1: 40*40

Inven221 < Inven22 < Inven2: 30*40

Inven222 < Inven22 < Inven2: 50*40

PPGH parts < ASD parts < Inven2: 2*200

The multi-subaccount name of the Cash account and transaction sub-equation respectively are:

88-654308-t-supplies < Cash payments to suppliers < Operating activities

Cash (1): -3600 + Supplies (1): 5600 = Account payable (2): 2000

- On February 28, 2016, the Central Bank pays two employees' salary expenses for cash -$5,650 repeatedly.

- On March 25, 2016, the Central Bank pays -$600 cash to Company1 (phone number: 123456784) with the General ID 1. The multi-subaccount name of the Cash account and the transaction sub-equation respectively are:

88-654306-t-machinery < Cash payments for machinery < Operating activities

Cash (1): -600 = Account payable (2): -600

- On March 28, 2016, the Central Bank pays -$459.61 cash to A2 (SIN: 909876502) for the Travelling expenses (travel allowance) $387.61 and the Other expenses (meals: food111: $10 + food214: $11 + food312: $24 + food321: $27) $72. The multi-subaccount name of the Cash account and the transaction sub-equation respectively are:

909876502-n-operating expenses < Cash payments for operating expenses < Operating activities

Cash (1): -459.61 = Travelling expenses (5): -387.61 + other expenses (5): -72

- On March 31, 2016, the Central Bank pays two employees' salary expenses for cash -$5,650 repeatedly.

- On April 19, 2016, the Central Bank pays -$159.78 cash to A2 (SIN: 909876502) for the Travelling expenses (travel allowance) $109.78 and the Other expenses (meals: food611: $20 + food614: $30) $50.

- On April 30, 2016, the Central Bank pays two employees' salary expenses for cash $5,650 repeatedly.

- On April 30, 2016, the Central Bank records the Amortization expenses $983.34 of a computer server1 ($466.67, four months), a computer1 ($266.67, four months), and a computer2 ($250, four months). The transaction sub-equation is:

  Accumulated amortization: Computer (1): -466.67 + Accumulated amortization: Computer (1): -266.67 + Accumulated amortization: Computer (1): -250 = Amortization expenses (5): -466.67 + Amortization expenses (5): -266.67 + Amortization expenses (5): -250

- On April 30, 2016, the Central Bank cancels the balances of the Computer account and the Accumulated amortization: Computer account because these computers have used for two years. The transaction sub-equation is:

  Computer (1): -2800 + Computer (1): -1600 + Computer (1): -1500 + Accumulated amortization: Computer (1): 2800 + Accumulated amortization: Computer (1): 1600 + Accumulated amortization: Computer (1): 1500 = 0

- On May 1, 2016, the Central Bank purchases a new computer server1, a new computer1, and a new computer2 for cash -$1,900 and other on credit $4,000 from the Company1 (phone number: 123456784) with the General ID 18. The multi-subaccount name of the Cash account and the transaction sub-equation respectively are:

  88-654306-t-machinery < Cash payments for machinery < Operating activities

Cash (1): -1900 + Company (1): 2800 + Company (1): 1600 + Company (1): 1500
= Account payable (2): 4000

- On May 16, 2016, the Central Bank purchases supplies from the Proprietorship2 for cash -$316 ($14*10 + $16*11). The multi-subaccount name of the Cash account and the transaction sub-equation respectively are:

  88-654310-t-supplies < Cash payments to supplies < Operating activities

  Cash (1): -316 + Supplies (1): 316 = 0

- On May 31, 2016, the Central Bank pays two employees' salary expenses for cash - $5,650 repeatedly.

- On June 1, 2016, the Central Bank purchases one Bond23 (three years, 4.5% annually, pay at end of each year) for -$5,000 from the Business Bank2. The multi-subaccount name of the Cash account and the transaction sub-equation respectively are:

  88-654305-n-Bonds < Cash payments for investments < Investing activities

  Cash (1): -5000 + Bonds (1): 5000 = 0

- On June 22, 2016, the Central Bank pays -$477.25 cash to A2 (SIN: 909876502) for the Travelling expenses (travel allowance) $341.25 and the Other expenses (meals: food522: $13*4 + food622: $28*3) $136.

- On June 30, 2016, the Central Bank pays two employees' salary expenses for cash - $5,650 repeatedly.

- On July 31, 2016, the Central Bank pays two employees' salary expenses for cash - $5,650 repeatedly.

- On August 14, 2016, the Central Bank purchases two service packages (Truck1- Service package1 < Truck-service < Vehicle-service for cash -$550 and Car1- Service package3 < Car-service < Vehicle-service for cash -$490) for cash -$1,040 from the Company1. The multi-subaccount name of the Cash account and the transaction sub-equation respectively are:

88-654306-t-service packages < Cash payments to suppliers < Operating activities

Cash (1): -1040 = Service package expenses (5): -550 + Service package expenses (5): =490

- On August 31, 2016, the Central Bank pays two employees' salary expenses for cash -$5,650 repeatedly.
- On September 7, 2016, the Central Bank pays -$233.16 cash to A2 (SIN: 909876502) for the Travelling expenses (travel allowance) $174.16 and the Other expenses (meals: food514: $11*3 + food621: $26) $59.
- On September 30, 2016, the Central Bank pays two employees' salary expenses for cash -$5,650 repeatedly.
- On October 31, 2016, the Central Bank pays two employees' salary expenses for cash -$5,650 repeatedly.
- On November 30, 2016, the Central Bank pays two employees' salary expenses for cash -$5,650 repeatedly.
- On December 11, 2016, Central Bank pays -$552.37 cash to A1 (SIN: 909876501) for the Travelling expenses (travel allowance) $432.37 and the Other expenses (meals: food43: $14*3 + food44: $15*2 + food612: $24*2) $120.
- On December 31, 2016, the Central Bank pays two employees' salary expenses for cash -$5,650 repeatedly.
- On the same day, the Central Bank receives cash $131.25 from the Business Bank2 for investment interest of the Bond23. The multi-subaccount name of the Cash account and transaction sub-equation respectively are:

  88-654305-c-investment income < Cash receipts from investments < Investing activities

  Cash (1): 131.25 = Investment incomes (4): 131.25

- On the same day, the Central Bank receives cash $120 from the Business Bank2 for primary deposit interest. The multi-subaccount name of the Cash account and transaction sub-equation respectively are:

88-654305-c-deposit interest income < Cash receipts from deposit interest < Financial activities

Cash (1): 120 = Deposit interest incomes (4):120

- On the same day, the Central Bank records the Vehicle's amortization expenses -$17,000 one year (5 years, straight line). The transaction sub-equation is:

Accumulated amortization: Vehicle (1): -9000 + Accumulated amortization: Vehicle (1): -8000 = Amortization expenses (5): -9000 + Amortization expenses (5): -8000

- On the same day, the Central Bank records the Computer's amortization expenses $1,966.66 eight months (2 years, straight line) which includes a new computer server1 ($933.33), a new computer1 ($533.33), and a new computer2 ($500). The transaction sub-equation is:

Accumulated amortization: Computer (1): -933.33 + Accumulated amortization: Computer (1): -533.33 + Accumulated amortization: Computer (1): -500 = Amortization expenses (5): -933.33 + Amortization expenses (5): -533.33 + Amortization expenses (5): -500

- On the same day, the Central Bank records the Office supplies expenses -$5,935.72. The transaction sub-equation is:

Supplies (1): -5935.72 = Office supplies expenses (5): -5935.72

- On the same day, the Central Bank pays cash $3,500 to the Company1 (phone number: 123456784) with the General ID 18. The multi-subaccount name of the Cash account and the transaction sub-equation respectively are:

88-654306-t-machinery < Cash payments for machinery < Operating activities

Cash (1): -3500 = Account payable (2): -3500

- On the same day, the Central Bank records the Tax expenses $0 and the Tax payable $0. Because tax rate is zero, the amount of the Tax expenses is also zero. The multi-subaccount name forms of the Tax expenses and the Tax payable accounts all are the 'n'. The transaction sub-equation is:

  0 = Tax payable (2): 0 + Tax expenses (5): 0

So far, I have entered all transactions in the fiscal year 2016. After getting the Income Statement and clicking the "Yes" button for new fiscal year, I can get the Balance Sheet of the Central Bank.

3.1.2.2 Brief Summary of the Central Bank

The Figure 3.1-7 on the next pages shows two sums and all cash transactions of the Central Bank by using of SQL Server query. As a closed system based on the MathAccounting software, the sum0 should be equal to zero. However, the individuals are not responsible for recording any transaction, so the sum0 ($69,858.73) is the sum of the amounts that the individuals received from the Central Bank. If the sum0 is negative, then it is sum of the amounts that some individuals paid to the Central Bank. The opposite value ($2,527.17) of the sum1 (-$2,527.17) is the balance of the Cash account of the Central Bank on December 31, 2016. It is also the balance of the deposits of the Central Bank in the Business Bank2 on December 31, 2016.

```
SQLQuery10.sql - LI...ESS.dcj100 (sa (52))*  ×
use dcj100
select sum(amount) as sum0 from CashByMembers where IDM='88-654301' and TransDate between '2016-01-01' and '2016-12-31'
select sum(amount) as sum1 from CashByMembers where IDM='88-654301' and Symbol = 'd'
select * from CashByMembers where Recorder='88-654301' order by TransDate
```

100 % ▾

Results Messages

	sum0
1	69858.73

	sum1
1	-2527.17

	IDM	Amount	Symbol	MultiSubaccount	Recorder	TransDate
1	88-654300	-1600.00	c	88-654300-c-budgets < Cash receipts from central bank budgets < Financial activities	88-654301	2015-12-31
2	88-654306	45000.00	t	88-654306-t-truck1 < Cash payments for machinery < Operating activities	88-654301	2015-12-31
3	88-654306	40000.00	t	88-654306-t-car1 < Cash payments for machinery < Operating activities	88-654301	2015-12-31
4	88-654306	2800.00	t	88-654306-t-computer server1 < Cash payments for machinery < Operating activities	88-654301	2015-12-31
5	88-654306	1600.00	t	88-654306-t-computer1 < Cash payments for machinery < Operating activities	88-654301	2015-12-31
6	88-654306	1500.00	t	88-654306-t-computer2 < Cash payments for machinery < Operating activities	88-654301	2015-12-31
7	88-654300	-639270.84	c	88-654300-c-budgets < Cash receipts from central bank budgets < Financial activities	88-654301	2015-12-31
8		197854.41		Cash payments for operating expenses < Operating activities	88-654301	2015-12-31
9		196722.75		Cash payments for operating expenses < Operating activities	88-654301	2015-12-31
10		195432.19		Cash payments for operating expenses < Operating activities	88-654301	2015-12-31
11	88-654300	3287.50	c	88-654300-c-budgets < Cash receipts from central bank budgets < Financial activities	88-654301	2015-12-31
12	88-654300	-47416.66	c	88-654300-c-budgets < Cash receipts from central bank budgets < Financial activities	88-654301	2015-12-31
13	88-654300	-85000.00	c	88-654300-c-budgets < Cash receipts from central bank budgets < Financial activities	88-654301	2016-01-02
14	9098765...	176.56	n	909876501-n-operating expenses < Cash payments for operating expenses < Operating activities	88-654301	2016-01-21
15	9098765...	2800.00	t	909876501-t-salary < Cash payments for operating expenses < Operating activities	88-654301	2016-01-31
16	9098765...	2850.00	t	909876502-t-salary < Cash payments for operating expenses < Operating activities	88-654301	2016-01-31
17	88-654306	800.00	t	88-654306-t-machinery < Cash payments for machinery < Operating activities	88-654301	2016-02-13
18	88-654308	200.00	t	88-654308-t-operating expenses < Cash payments for operating expenses < Operating activities	88-654301	2016-02-13
19	88-654308	3600.00	t	88-654308-t-supplies < Cash payments to suppliers < Operating activities	88-654301	2016-02-22
20	9098765...	2800.00	t	909876501-t-salary < Cash payments for operating expenses < Operating activities	88-654301	2016-02-28
21	9098765...	2850.00	t	909876502-t-salary < Cash payments for operating expenses < Operating activities	88-654301	2016-02-28
22	88-654306	600.00	t	88-654306-t-machinery < Cash payments for machinery < Operating activities	88-654301	2016-03-25
23	9098765...	459.61	n	909876502-n-operating expenses < Cash payments for operating expenses < Operating activities	88-654301	2016-03-28
24	9098765...	2800.00	t	909876501-t-salary < Cash payments for operating expenses < Operating activities	88-654301	2016-03-31

	IDM	Amount	Symbol	MultiSubaccount	Recorder	TransDate
25	9098765...	2850.00	t	909876502-t-salary < Cash payments for operating expenses < Operating activities	88-654301	2016-03-31
26	9098765...	159.78	n	909876502-n-operating expenses < Cash payments for operating expenses < Operating activities	88-654301	2016-04-19
27	9098765...	2800.00	t	909876501-t-salary < Cash payments for operating expenses < Operating activities	88-654301	2016-04-30
28	9098765...	2850.00	t	909876502-t-salary < Cash payments for operating expenses < Operating activities	88-654301	2016-04-30
29	88-654306	1900.00	t	88-654306-t-machinery < Cash payments for machinery < Operating activities	88-654301	2016-05-01
30	88-654310	316.00	t	88-654310-t-supplies < Cash payments to supplies < Operating activities	88-654301	2016-05-16
31	9098765...	2800.00	t	909876501-t-salary < Cash payments for operating expenses < Operating activities	88-654301	2016-05-31
32	9098765...	2850.00	t	909876502-t-salary < Cash payments for operating expenses < Operating activities	88-654301	2016-05-31
33	88-654305	5000.00	n	88-654305-n-Bonds < Cash payments for investments < Investing activities	88-654301	2016-06-01
34	9098765...	477.25	n	909876502-n-operating expenses < Cash payments for operating expenses < Operating activities	88-654301	2016-06-22
35	9098765...	2800.00	t	909876501-t-salary < Cash payments for operating expenses < Operating activities	88-654301	2016-06-30
36	9098765...	2850.00	t	909876502-t-salary < Cash payments for operating expenses < Operating activities	88-654301	2016-06-30
37	9098765...	2800.00	t	909876501-t-salary < Cash payments for operating expenses < Operating activities	88-654301	2016-07-31
38	9098765...	2850.00	t	909876502-t-salary < Cash payments for operating expenses < Operating activities	88-654301	2016-07-31
39	88-654306	1040.00	t	88-654306-t-service packages < Cash payments to suppliers < Operating activities	88-654301	2016-08-14
40	9098765...	2800.00	t	909876501-t-salary < Cash payments for operating expenses < Operating activities	88-654301	2016-08-31
41	9098765...	2850.00	t	909876502-t-salary < Cash payments for operating expenses < Operating activities	88-654301	2016-08-31
42	9098765...	233.16	n	909876502-n-operating expenses < Cash payments for operating expenses < Operating activities	88-654301	2016-09-07
43	9098765...	2800.00	t	909876501-t-salary < Cash payments for operating expenses < Operating activities	88-654301	2016-09-30
44	9098765...	2850.00	t	909876502-t-salary < Cash payments for operating expenses < Operating activities	88-654301	2016-09-30
45	9098765...	2800.00	t	909876501-t-salary < Cash payments for operating expenses < Operating activities	88-654301	2016-10-31
46	9098765...	2850.00	t	909876502-t-salary < Cash payments for operating expenses < Operating activities	88-654301	2016-10-31
47	9098765...	2800.00	t	909876501-t-salary < Cash payments for operating expenses < Operating activities	88-654301	2016-11-30
48	9098765...	2850.00	t	909876502-t-salary < Cash payments for operating expenses < Operating activities	88-654301	2016-11-30

Figure 3.1-7   Central Bank Cash Received or Paid by Other Members (Continue)

49	9098765...	552.37	n	909876501-n-operating expenses < Cash payments for operating expenses < Operating activities	88-654301	2016-12-11
50	9098765...	2800.00	t	909876501-t-salary < Cash payments for operating expenses < Operating activities	88-654301	2016-12-31
51	9098765...	2850.00	t	909876502-t-salary < Cash payments for operating expenses < Operating activities	88-654301	2016-12-31
52	88-654305	-131.25	c	88-654305-c-investment income < Cash receipts from investments < Investing activities	88-654301	2016-12-31
53	88-654305	-120.00	c	88-654305-c-deposit interest income < Cash receipts from deposit interest < Financial activities	88-654301	2016-12-31
54	88-654306	3500.00	t	88-654306-t-machinery < Cash payments for machinery < Operating activities	88-654301	2016-12-31

Query executed successfully.

Figure 3.1-7   Central Bank Cash Received or Paid by Other Members

The Figure 3.1-8 on the next pages shows two sums and all cash transactions of the individual A1 (SIN: 909876501) by using of SQL Server query. As a closed system based on the MathAccounting software, the sum0 should be equal to zero because all transactions of every individual have been recorded by related organizations or companies. In addition, the sum0 can also be used as a checked standard. If the sum0 is not equal to zero, then there must be some mistakes in this individual's transactions. The opposite value of the sum1 is the sum of balances of the deposits of the individual A1 (SIN: 909876501) in the Business Bank1 and the Business Bank2 on December 31, 2016. From the Figure 3.1-8, the sum0's and sum1's opposite value are $0 and $14,810.18 (= $13,870.03 + $940.15) respectively.

The Figure 3.1-9 shows two sums and all cash transactions of the individual A2 (SIN: 909876502) by using of SQL Server query. As a closed system based on the MathAccounting software, the sum0 should be equal to zero. The opposite value of the sum1 is the sum of balances of the deposits of the individual A2 (SIN: 909876502) in the Business Bank1 and the Business Bank2 on December 31, 2016. From the Figure 3.1-9, the sum0's and sum1's opposite value are $0 and $36,017.46 (= $19,516.91 + $16,500.55) respectively.

SQLQuery3.sql - not connected* | SQLQuery2.sql - LIU...SS.dcj100 (sa (52))* ✕ | SQLQuery1.sql - LIU...SS.dcj100 (sa (53))*

```
use dcj100
select sum(amount) as sum0 from CashByMembers where IDM='909876501' and TransDate between '2016-01-01' and '2016-12-31'
select sum(amount) as sum1 from CashByMembers where IDM='909876501' and Symbol = 'd'
select * from CashByMembers where IDM='909876501' and TransDate between '2016-01-01' and '2016-12-31' order by TransDate
```

100 % ▾

▦ Results   ▯ Messages

	sum0
1	0.00

	sum1
1	-14810.18

	IDM	Amount	Symbol	MultiSubaccount	Recorder	TransDate
1	909876501	-10000.00	d	909876501-d-deposits < Cash receipts from customers deposits < Operating activities	88-654304	2016-01-10
2	909876501	10000.00	d	909876501-d-deposits < Cash receipts from customers deposits < Operating activities	88-654305	2016-01-10
3	909876501	-20000.00	d	909876501-d-deposits < Cash receipts from customers deposits < Operating activities	88-654305	2016-01-10
4	909876501	20000.00	d	909876501-d-deposits < Cash receipts from customers deposits < Operating activities	88-654304	2016-01-10
5	909876501	-39.00	c	909876501-c-customers < Cash receipts from customers < Operating activities	88-654310	2016-01-18
6	909876501	39.00	d	909876501-d-deposits < Cash receipts from customers deposits < Operating activities	88-654304	2016-01-18
7	909876501	-176.56	d	909876501-d-deposits < Cash receipts from customers deposits < Operating activities	88-654304	2016-01-21
8	909876501	176.56	n	909876501-n-operating expenses < Cash payments for operating expenses < Operating activities	88-654301	2016-01-21
9	909876501	2800.00	t	909876501-t-salary < Cash payments for operating expenses < Operating activities	88-654301	2016-01-31
10	909876501	-2800.00	d	909876501-d-deposits < Cash receipts from customers deposits < Operating activities	88-654304	2016-01-31
11	909876501	-10790.00	c	909876501-c-customers < Cash receipts from customers < Operating activities	88-654310	2016-01-31
12	909876501	-14560.00	c	909876501-c-customers < Cash receipts from customers < Operating activities	88-654309	2016-01-31
13	909876501	14560.00	d	909876501-d-deposits < Cash receipts from customers deposits < Operating activities	88-654304	2016-01-31
14	909876501	10790.00	d	909876501-d-deposits < Cash receipts from customers deposits < Operating activities	88-654305	2016-01-31
15	909876501	-2800.00	d	909876501-d-deposits < Cash receipts from customers deposits < Operating activities	88-654304	2016-02-28
16	909876501	2800.00	t	909876501-t-salary < Cash payments for operating expenses < Operating activities	88-654301	2016-02-28
17	909876501	2800.00	t	909876501-t-salary < Cash payments for operating expenses < Operating activities	88-654301	2016-03-31
18	909876501	-2800.00	d	909876501-d-deposits < Cash receipts from customers deposits < Operating activities	88-654304	2016-03-31
19	909876501	-310.00	c	909876501-c-customers < Cash receipts from customers < Operating activities	88-654307	2016-04-12
20	909876501	310.00	d	909876501-d-deposits < Cash receipts from customers deposits < Operating activities	88-654304	2016-04-12
21	909876501	2800.00	t	909876501-t-salary < Cash payments for operating expenses < Operating activities	88-654301	2016-04-30
22	909876501	-2800.00	d	909876501-d-deposits < Cash receipts from customers deposits < Operating activities	88-654304	2016-04-30
23	909876501	-2800.00	d	909876501-d-deposits < Cash receipts from customers deposits < Operating activities	88-654304	2016-05-31
24	909876501	2800.00	t	909876501-t-salary < Cash payments for operating expenses < Operating activities	88-654301	2016-05-31
25	909876501	2800.00	t	909876501-t-salary < Cash payments for operating expenses < Operating activities	88-654301	2016-06-30
26	909876501	-2800.00	d	909876501-d-deposits < Cash receipts from customers deposits < Operating activities	88-654304	2016-06-30
27	909876501	-2800.00	d	909876501-d-deposits < Cash receipts from customers deposits < Operating activities	88-654304	2016-07-31
28	909876501	2800.00	t	909876501-t-salary < Cash payments for operating expenses < Operating activities	88-654301	2016-07-31
29	909876501	11050.00	d	909876501-d-deposits < Cash receipts from customers deposits < Operating activities	88-654304	2016-07-31
30	909876501	10270.00	d	909876501-d-deposits < Cash receipts from customers deposits < Operating activities	88-654305	2016-07-31
31	909876501	-10270.00	c	909876501-c-customers < Cash receipts from customers < Operating activities	88-654309	2016-07-31
32	909876501	-11050.00	c	909876501-c-customers < Cash receipts from customers < Operating activities	88-654310	2016-07-31
33	909876501	-1600.00	c	909876501-c-customers < Cash receipts from customers < Operating activities	88-654306	2016-08-02
34	909876501	1600.00	d	909876501-d-deposits < Cash receipts from customers deposits < Operating activities	88-654304	2018-08-02
35	909876501	2800.00	t	909876501-t-salary < Cash payments for operating expenses < Operating activities	88-654301	2018-08-31
36	909876501	-2800.00	d	909876501-d-deposits < Cash receipts from customers deposits < Operating activities	88-654304	2016-08-31
37	909876501	-2800.00	d	909876501-d-deposits < Cash receipts from customers deposits < Operating activities	88-654304	2016-09-30
38	909876501	2800.00	t	909876501-t-salary < Cash payments for operating expenses < Operating activities	88-654301	2016-09-30
39	909876501	2800.00	t	909876501-t-salary < Cash payments for operating expenses < Operating activities	88-654301	2016-10-31
40	909876501	-2800.00	d	909876501-d-deposits < Cash receipts from customers deposits < Operating activities	88-654304	2016-10-31
41	909876501	-2800.00	d	909876501-d-deposits < Cash receipts from customers deposits < Operating activities	88-654304	2016-11-30
42	909876501	2800.00	t	909876501-t-salary < Cash payments for operating expenses < Operating activities	88-654301	2016-11-30
43	909876501	120.00	d	909876501-d-deposits < Cash receipts from customers deposits < Operating activities	88-654304	2016-12-08
44	909876501	-120.00	c	909876501-c-customers < Cash receipts from customers < Operating activities	88-654310	2016-12-08
45	909876501	-552.37	d	909876501-d-deposits < Cash receipts from customers deposits < Operating activities	88-654304	2016-12-11
46	909876501	552.37	n	909876501-n-operating expenses < Cash payments for operating expenses < Operating activities	88-654301	2016-12-11
47	909876501	2800.00	t	909876501-t-salary < Cash payments for operating expenses < Operating activities	88-654301	2016-12-31
48	909876501	-138.00	d	909876501-d-deposits < Cash receipts from customers deposits < Operating activities	88-654304	2016-12-31

Figure 3.1-8   Central Bank Cash Received or Paid by A1 (Continue)

49	909876501	138.00	t	909876501-t-bond interest < Cash payments to bond holders < Operating activities	88-654308	2016-12-31
50	909876501	288.00	t	909876501-t-bond interest < Cash payments to bond holders< Operating activities	88-654308	2016-12-31
51	909876501	-288.00	d	909876501-d-deposits < Cash receipts from customers deposits < Operating activities	88-654304	2016-12-31
52	909876501	-2800.00	d	909876501-d-deposits < Cash receipts from customers deposits < Operating activities	88-654304	2016-12-31
53	909876501	-200.00	d	909876501-d-deposits < Cash receipts from customers deposits < Operating activities	88-654304	2016-12-31
54	909876501	364.00	t	909876501-t-bond interest < Cash payments to bond holders < Operating activities	88-654310	2016-12-31
55	909876501	-364.00	d	909876501-d-deposits < Cash receipts from customers deposits < Operating activities	88-654304	2016-12-31
56	909876501	210.00	t	909876501-t-bond interest < Cash payments to bond holders< Operating activities	88-654304	2016-12-31
57	909876501	-210.00	d	909876501-d-deposits < Cash receipts from customers deposits < Operating activities	88-654304	2016-12-31
58	909876501	120.00	t	909876501-t-deposit interest expenses < Cash payments for operating expenses < Operating act...	88-654304	2016-12-31
59	909876501	-120.00	d	909876501-d-deposits < Cash receipts from customers deposits < Operating activities	88-654304	2016-12-31
60	909876501	200.00	t	909876501-t-interest expenses < Cash payments for issued bond interest < Financial activities	88-654300	2016-12-31

Query executed successfully.

Figure 3.1-8   Central Bank Cash Received or Paid by A1

SQLQuery3.sql - not connected*   SQLQuery2.sql - LIU...SS.dcj100 (sa (54))*   ×   SQLQuery1.sql - not connected*

```
use dcj100
select sum(amount) as sum0 from CashByMembers where IDM='909876502' and TransDate between '2016-01-01' and '2016-12-31'
select sum(amount) as sum1 from CashByMembers where IDM='909876502' and Symbol = 'd'
select * from CashByMembers where IDM='909876502' and TransDate between '2016-01-01' and '2016-12-31' order by TransDate
```

100 %   ▾

Results   Messages

	sum0
1	0.00

	sum1
1	-36017.46

	IDM	Amount	Symbol	MultiSubaccount	Recorder	TransDate
1	909876502	2850.00	t	909876502-t-salary < Cash payments for operating expenses < Operating activities	88-654301	2016-01-31
2	909876502	-2850.00	d	909876502-d-deposits < Cash receipts from customers deposits < Operating activities	88-654304	2016-01-31
3	909876502	-13000.00	c	909876502-c-customers < Cash receipts from customers < Operating activities	88-654309	2016-01-31
4	909876502	13000.00	d	909876502-d-deposits < Cash receipts from customers deposits < Operating activities	88-654304	2016-01-31
5	909876502	-2850.00	d	909876502-d-deposits < Cash receipts from customers deposits < Operating activities	88-654304	2016-02-28
6	909876502	2850.00	t	909876502-t-salary < Cash payments for operating expenses < Operating activities	88-654301	2016-02-28
7	909876502	900.00	d	909876502-d-deposits < Cash receipts from customers deposits < Operating activities	88-654304	2016-03-24
8	909876502	-3500.00	c	909876502-c-customers < Cash receipts from customers < Operating activities	88-654308	2016-03-24
9	909876502	2600.00	d	909876502-d-deposits < Cash receipts from customers deposits < Operating activities	88-654304	2016-03-24
10	909876502	-72.00	c	909876502-c-customers < Cash receipts from customers < Operating activities	88-654309	2016-03-26
11	909876502	72.00	d	909876502-d-deposits < Cash receipts from customers deposits < Operating activities	88-654304	2016-03-26
12	909876502	-72.00	d	909876502-d-deposits < Cash receipts from customers deposits < Operating activities	88-654304	2016-03-26
13	909876502	72.00	d	909876502-d-deposits < Cash receipts from customers deposits < Operating activities	88-654304	2016-03-26
14	909876502	-459.61	d	909876502-d-deposits < Cash receipts from customers deposits < Operating activities	88-654304	2016-03-28
15	909876502	459.61	n	909876502-n-operating expenses < Cash payments for operating expenses < Operating activities	88-654301	2016-03-28
16	909876502	2850.00	t	909876502-t-salary < Cash payments for operating expenses < Operating activities	88-654301	2016-03-31
17	909876502	-2850.00	d	909876502-d-deposits < Cash receipts from customers deposits < Operating activities	88-654304	2016-03-31
18	909876502	50.00	d	909876502-d-deposits < Cash receipts from customers deposits < Operating activities	88-654304	2016-04-15
19	909876502	-50.00	c	909876502-c-customers < Cash receipts from customers < Operating activities	88-654310	2016-04-15
20	909876502	-159.78	d	909876502-d-deposits < Cash receipts from customers deposits < Operating activities	88-654304	2016-04-19
21	909876502	159.78	n	909876502-n-operating expenses < Cash payments for operating expenses < Operating activities	88-654301	2016-04-19
22	909876502	2850.00	t	909876502-t-salary < Cash payments for operating expenses < Operating activities	88-654301	2016-04-30
23	909876502	-2850.00	d	909876502-d-deposits < Cash receipts from customers deposits < Operating activities	88-654304	2016-04-30
24	909876502	-2850.00	d	909876502-d-deposits < Cash receipts from customers deposits < Operating activities	88-654304	2016-05-31

Figure 3.1-9   Central Bank Cash Received or Paid by A2 (Continue)

	IDM	Amount	Symbol	MultiSubaccount	Recorder	TransDate
25	909876502	2850.00	t	909876502-t-salary < Cash payments for operating expenses < Operating activities	88-654301	2016-05-31
26	909876502	136.00	d	909876502-d-deposits < Cash receipts from customers deposits < Operating activities	88-654304	2016-06-18
27	909876502	-136.00	c	909876502-c-customers < Cash receipts from customers < Operating activities	88-654310	2016-06-18
28	909876502	-477.25	d	909876502-d-deposits < Cash receipts from customers deposits < Operating activities	88-654304	2016-06-22
29	909876502	477.25	n	909876502-n-operating expenses < Cash payments for operating expenses < Operating activities	88-654301	2016-06-22
30	909876502	2850.00	t	909876502-t-salary < Cash payments for operating expenses < Operating activities	88-654301	2016-06-30
31	909876502	-2850.00	d	909876502-d-deposits < Cash receipts from customers deposits < Operating activities	88-654304	2016-06-30
32	909876502	-2850.00	d	909876502-d-deposits < Cash receipts from customers deposits < Operating activities	88-654304	2016-07-31
33	909876502	2850.00	t	909876502-t-salary < Cash payments for operating expenses < Operating activities	88-654301	2016-07-31
34	909876502	-11180.00	c	909876502-c-customers < Cash receipts from customers < Operating activities	88-654310	2016-07-31
35	909876502	11180.00	d	909876502-d-deposits < Cash receipts from customers deposits < Operating activities	88-654304	2016-07-31
36	909876502	2850.00	t	909876502-t-salary < Cash payments for operating expenses < Operating activities	88-654301	2016-08-31
37	909876502	-2850.00	d	909876502-d-deposits < Cash receipts from customers deposits < Operating activities	88-654304	2016-08-31
38	909876502	59.00	d	909876502-d-deposits < Cash receipts from customers deposits < Operating activities	88-654304	2016-09-05
39	909876502	-59.00	c	909876502-c-customers < Cash receipts from customers < Operating activities	88-654310	2016-09-05
40	909876502	-233.16	d	909876502-d-deposits < Cash receipts from customers deposits < Operating activities	88-654304	2016-09-07
41	909876502	233.16	n	909876502-n-operating expenses < Cash payments for operating expenses < Operating activities	88-654301	2016-09-07
42	909876502	2850.00	t	909876502-t-salary < Cash payments for operating expenses < Operating activities	88-654301	2016-09-30
43	909876502	-2850.00	d	909876502-d-deposits < Cash receipts from customers deposits < Operating activities	88-654304	2016-09-30
44	909876502	-2850.00	d	909876502-d-deposits < Cash receipts from customers deposits < Operating activities	88-654304	2016-10-31
45	909876502	2850.00	t	909876502-t-salary < Cash payments for operating expenses < Operating activities	88-654301	2016-10-31
46	909876502	2850.00	t	909876502-t-salary < Cash payments for operating expenses < Operating activities	88-654301	2016-11-30
47	909876502	-2850.00	d	909876502-d-deposits < Cash receipts from customers deposits < Operating activities	88-654304	2016-11-30
48	909876502	-1400.00	c	909876502-c-customers < Cash receipts from customers < Operating activities	88-654306	2016-12-22
49	909876502	1400.00	d	909876502-d-deposits < Cash receipts from customers deposits < Operating activities	88-654304	2016-12-22
50	909876502	-276.00	d	909876502-d-deposits < Cash receipts from customers deposits < Operating activities	88-654304	2016-12-31
51	909876502	276.00	t	909876502-t-bond interest < Cash payments to bond holders < Operating activities	88-654306	2016-12-31
52	909876502	-192.00	d	909876502-d-deposits < Cash receipts from customers deposits < Operating activities	88-654304	2016-12-31
53	909876502	192.00	t	909876502-t-bond interest < Cash payments to bond holders< Operating activities	88-654308	2016-12-31
54	909876502	312.00	t	909876502-t-bond interest < Cash payments to bond holders < Operating activities	88-654310	2016-12-31
55	909876502	200.00	t	909876502-t-interest expenses < Cash payments for issued bond interest < Financial activities	88-654300	2016-12-31
56	909876502	-312.00	d	909876502-d-deposits < Cash receipts from customers deposits < Operating activities	88-654304	2016-12-31
57	909876502	84.00	t	909876502-t-bond interest < Cash payments to bond holders< Operating activities	88-654304	2016-12-31
58	909876502	-84.00	d	909876502-d-deposits < Cash receipts from customers deposits < Operating activities	88-654304	2016-12-31
59	909876502	120.00	t	909876502-t-deposit interest expenses < Cash payments for operating expenses < Operating ac...	88-654304	2016-12-31
60	909876502	-120.00	d	909876502-d-deposits < Cash receipts from customers deposits < Operating activities	88-654304	2016-12-31
61	909876502	-2850.00	d	909876502-d-deposits < Cash receipts from customers deposits < Operating activities	88-654304	2016-12-31
62	909876502	-200.00	d	909876502-d-deposits < Cash receipts from customers deposits < Operating activities	88-654304	2016-12-31
63	909876502	2850.00	t	909876502-t-salary < Cash payments for operating expenses < Operating activities	88-654301	2016-12-31

Query executed successfully.

Figure 3.1-9   Central Bank Cash Received or Paid by A2

By using of same method, I can respectively get the sums of the balances of all other individuals' deposits in the Business Bank1 and the Business Bank2 on December 31, 2016, seeing the Figure 3.11-1 on the page 580.

The Figure 3.1-10 on the next page shows the Central Bank cash flows statement. From the Figure 3.1-10, the cash balance at the ending of this fiscal year is also $2,527.17, which is the same as the sum1's opposite amount in the Figure 3.1-7.

Cash Flow Statement

Cash Flows Statement Year Ended 2016-12-31	
Operating activities	
Cash payments for machinery	-$6,800.00
Cash payments for operating expenses	-$70,058.73
Cash payments to suppliers	-$4,640.00
Cash payments to supplies	-$316.00
Net cash provided by Operating activities	-$81,814.73
Investing activities	
Cash payments for investments	-$5,000.00
Cash receipts from investments	$131.25
Net cash provided by Investing activities	-$4,868.75
Financial activities	
Cash receipts from central bank budgets	$85,000.00
Cash receipts from deposit interest	$120.00
Net cash provided by Financial activities	$85,120.00
Net change in cash	-$1,563.48
Cash, Begining	$4,090.65
Cash, Ending	$2,527.17

Figure 3.1-10   Central Bank Cash Flows Statement

The Figure 3.1-11 on the next pages shows the Central Bank cash account table. From the Figure 3.1-11, the cash balance on December 31, 2016 is also $2,527.17, which is the same as the sum1's opposite amount in the Figure 3.1-7.

Cash

ID	Multi-Name	Amount	Balance	General ID	Transaction Date
1	88-654300-c-budgets < Cash receipts from central bank budgets < Fina...	$1,600.00	$1,600.00	1	2015-12-31
2	88-654306-t-truck1 < Cash payments for machinery < Operating activities	-$45,000.00	-$43,400.00	2	2015-12-31
3	88-654306-t-car1 < Cash payments for machinery < Operating activities	-$40,000.00	-$83,400.00	2	2015-12-31
4	88-654306-t-computer server1 < Cash payments for machinery < Opera...	-$2,800.00	-$86,200.00	2	2015-12-31
5	88-654306-t-computer1 < Cash payments for machinery < Operating ac...	-$1,600.00	-$87,800.00	2	2015-12-31
6	88-654306-t-computer2 < Cash payments for machinery < Operating ac...	-$1,500.00	-$89,300.00	2	2015-12-31
7	88-654300-c-budgets < Cash receipts from central bank budgets < Fina...	$639,270.84	$549,970.84	3	2015-12-31
8	Cash payments for operating expenses < Operating activities	-$197,854.41	$352,116.43	3	2015-12-31
9	Cash payments for operating expenses < Operating activities	-$196,722.75	$155,393.68	3	2015-12-31
10	Cash payments for operating expenses < Operating activities	-$195,432.19	-$40,038.51	3	2015-12-31
11	88-654300-c-budgets < Cash receipts from central bank budgets < Fina...	-$3,287.50	-$43,326.01	3	2015-12-31
12	88-654300-c-budgets < Cash receipts from central bank budgets < Fina...	$47,416.66	$4,090.65	4	2015-12-31
13	88-654300-c-budgets < Cash receipts from central bank budgets < Fina...	$85,000.00	$89,090.65	5	2016-01-02
14	909876501-n-operating expenses < Cash payments for operating expe...	-$176.56	$88,914.09	6	2016-01-21
15	909876501-t-salary < Cash payments for operating expenses < Operati...	-$2,800.00	$86,114.09	7	2016-01-31
16	909876502-t-salary < Cash payments for operating expenses < Operati...	-$2,850.00	$83,264.09	7	2016-01-31
17	88-654306-t-machinery < Cash payments for machinery < Operating act...	-$800.00	$82,464.09	8	2016-02-13
18	88-654308-t-operating expenses < Cash payments for operating expen...	-$200.00	$82,264.09	8	2016-02-13
19	88-654308-t-supplies < Cash payments to suppliers < Operating activities	-$3,600.00	$78,664.09	9	2016-02-22
20	909876501-t-salary < Cash payments for operating expenses < Operati...	-$2,800.00	$75,864.09	10	2016-02-28
21	909876502-t-salary < Cash payments for operating expenses < Operati...	-$2,850.00	$73,014.09	10	2016-02-28
22	88-654306-t-machinery < Cash payments for machinery < Operating act...	-$600.00	$72,414.09	11	2016-03-25
23	909876502-n-operating expenses < Cash payments for operating expe...	-$459.61	$71,954.48	12	2016-03-28
24	909876501-t-salary < Cash payments for operating expenses < Operati...	-$2,800.00	$69,154.48	13	2016-03-31
25	909876502-t-salary < Cash payments for operating expenses < Operati...	-$2,850.00	$66,304.48	13	2016-03-31
26	909876502-n-operating expenses < Cash payments for operating expe...	-$159.78	$66,144.70	14	2016-04-19
27	909876501-t-salary < Cash payments for operating expenses < Operati...	-$2,800.00	$63,344.70	15	2016-04-30
28	909876502-t-salary < Cash payments for operating expenses < Operati...	-$2,850.00	$60,494.70	15	2016-04-30
29	88-654306-t-machinery < Cash payments for machinery < Operating act...	-$1,900.00	$58,594.70	18	2016-05-01
30	88-654310-t-supplies < Cash payments to supplies < Operating activities	-$316.00	$58,278.70	19	2016-05-16
31	909876501-t-salary < Cash payments for operating expenses < Operati...	-$2,800.00	$55,478.70	20	2016-05-31
32	909876502-t-salary < Cash payments for operating expenses < Operati...	-$2,850.00	$52,628.70	20	2016-05-31
33	88-654305-n-Bonds < Cash payments for investments < Investing activit...	-$5,000.00	$47,628.70	21	2016-06-01
34	909876502-n-operating expenses < Cash payments for operating expe...	-$477.25	$47,151.45	22	2016-06-22
35	909876501-t-salary < Cash payments for operating expenses < Operati...	-$2,800.00	$44,351.45	23	2016-06-30
36	909876502-t-salary < Cash payments for operating expenses < Operati...	-$2,850.00	$41,501.45	23	2016-06-30
37	909876501-t-salary < Cash payments for operating expenses < Operati...	-$2,800.00	$38,701.45	24	2016-07-31
38	909876502-t-salary < Cash payments for operating expenses < Operati...	-$2,850.00	$35,851.45	24	2016-07-31
39	88-654306-t-service packages < Cash payments to suppliers < Operatin...	-$1,040.00	$34,811.45	25	2016-08-14
40	909876501-t-salary < Cash payments for operating expenses < Operati...	-$2,800.00	$32,011.45	26	2016-08-31
41	909876502-t-salary < Cash payments for operating expenses < Operati...	-$2,850.00	$29,161.45	26	2016-08-31
42	909876502-n-operating expenses < Cash payments for operating expe...	-$233.16	$28,928.29	27	2016-09-07
43	909876501-t-salary < Cash payments for operating expenses < Operati...	-$2,800.00	$26,128.29	28	2016-09-30
44	909876502-t-salary < Cash payments for operating expenses < Operati...	-$2,850.00	$23,278.29	28	2016-09-30
45	909876501-t-salary < Cash payments for operating expenses < Operati...	-$2,800.00	$20,478.29	29	2016-10-31
46	909876502-t-salary < Cash payments for operating expenses < Operati...	-$2,850.00	$17,628.29	29	2016-10-31
47	909876501-t-salary < Cash payments for operating expenses < Operati...	-$2,800.00	$14,828.29	30	2016-11-30

Figure 3.1-11   Central Bank Cash Account Table (Continue)

48	909876502-t-salary < Cash payments for operating expenses < Operati...	-$2,850.00	$11,978.29	30	2016-11-30
49	909876501-n-operating expenses < Cash payments for operating expe...	-$552.37	$11,425.92	31	2016-12-11
50	909876501-t-salary < Cash payments for operating expenses < Operati...	-$2,800.00	$8,625.92	32	2016-12-31
51	909876502-t-salary < Cash payments for operating expenses < Operati...	-$2,850.00	$5,775.92	32	2016-12-31
52	88-654305-c-investment income < Cash receipts from investments < Inv...	$131.25	$5,907.17	33	2016-12-31
53	88-654305-c-deposit interest income < Cash receipts from deposit inter...	$120.00	$6,027.17	35	2016-12-31
54	88-654306-t-machinery < Cash payments for machinery < Operating act...	-$3,500.00	$2,527.17	38	2016-12-31

Figure 3.1-11　Central Bank Cash Account Table

The following Figure 3.1-12 shows the Central Bank income statement. From the Figure 3.1-12, the amount of the earnings before income taxes is -$11,533.20 and the amount of the tax expenses is zero, so the amount of the net earnings of the Central Bank in this fiscal year is also -$11,533.20.

Income Statement

	Year ended: 12/31/2016	
Revenues		
Sales (received budgets)		$85,000.00
Cost		
Cost of goods sold		$0.00
Gross Margin		$85,000.00
Operating and administrative expenses		
Travelling expenses		-$1,582.73
Other expenses		-$476.00
Office supplies expenses		-$5,935.72
Salary expenses		-$67,800.00
Service package expenses		-$1,040.00
Amortization expenses		-$19,950.00
Tax expenses		$0.00
Other income		
Investment incomes		$131.25
Deposits interest income		$120.00
Earnings Before Income Taxes		-$11,533.20
Net Earnings		-$11,533.20
Retained Earnings,Begining		$0.00
Retained Earnings,Ending		-$11,533.20

Figure 3.1-12　Central Bank Income Statement

The following Figure 3.1-13 shows the Central Bank balance sheet. From the Figure 3.1-13, the amount of total assets is $37,112.32, and the amount of the total liabilities and the shareholders' equity is also $37,112.32.

Balance Sheet

	As at 12/31/2016	
ASSETS		
Current assets		
Cash		$2,527.17
Supplies		$151.81
Account receivable		$0.00
		$2,678.98
Long term investments		
Bonds		$5,000.00
Equipment		
Vehicle		$85,000.00
Accumulated amortization: Vehicle		-$59,500.00
Computer		$5,900.00
Accumulated amortization: Computer		-$1,966.66
		$29,433.34
Total Assets		$37,112.32
LIABILITIES		
Current liabilities		
Account payable		$2,500.00
Tax payable		$0.00
		$2,500.00
Total Liability		$2,500.00
SHAREHOLDERS' EQUITY		
Owners capital		

SHAREHOLDERS' EQUITY		
Owners capital		
Budgets capital		$46,145.52
Retined earnings		-$11,533.20
Accumulated other comprehensive income		$0.00
Total Shareholders' Equity		$34,612.32
Total Liabilities and Shareholders' Equity		$37,112.32

Figure 3.1-13   Central Bank Balance Sheet Statement

3.2 Government1

3.2.1 An Accounting Fiscal Year of the Government1

In the new fiscal year, the Government1 occurs the following transactions.

- On January 2, 2016, the Government1 receives cash $90,000 from the Cash Management Center for the planned national budgets. The multi-subaccount name of the Cash account and the transaction sub-equation respectively are:

  88-654300-c-budgets < Cash receipts from national budgets < Financial activities

  Cash (1): 90000 = Sales (received budgets) (4): 90000

- On January 9, 2016, the Government1 pays -$307.23 cash to A3 (SIN: 909876503) for the Travelling expenses (travel allowance) $199.23 and the Other expenses (meals: food113: $12*4 + food322: $30*2) $108. The multi-subaccount name of the Cash account and the transaction sub-equation respectively are:

  909876503-n-operating expenses < Cash payments for operating expenses < Operating activities

  Cash (1): -307.23 = Travelling expenses (5): -199.23 + other expenses (5): -108

- On January 31, 2016, the Government1 pays two employees' salary expenses for cash -$5,660. The two multi-subaccount names of the Cash account and the transaction sub-equation respectively are:

  909876503-t-salary < Cash payments for operating expenses < Operating activities
  909876504-t-salary < Cash payments for operating expenses < Operating activities

  Cash (1): -2810 + Cash (1): -2850 = Salary expenses (5): -5660

- On February 21, 2016, the Government1 pays -$500 cash to Company2 (phone number: 123456783) with the General ID 1. The multi-subaccount name of the Cash account and the transaction sub-equation respectively are:

  88-654307-t-machinery < Cash payments for machinery < Operating activities

Cash (1): -500 = Account payable (2): -500

- On February 28, 2016, the Government1 pays two employees' salary expenses for cash -$5,660 repeatedly.

- On February 28, 2016, the Government1 pays -$295.17 cash to A3 (SIN: 909876503) for the Travelling expenses (travel allowance) $196.17 and the Other expenses (meals: food123: $15*3 + food321: $27*2) $99.

- On March 22, 2016, the Government1 pays -$558.34 cash to A4 (SIN: 909876504) for the Travelling expenses (travel allowance) $386.34 and the Other expenses (meals: food112: $11*2 + food213: $10*3 + food322: $30*4) $172.

- On March 31, 2016, the Government1 pays two employees' salary expenses for cash -$5,660 repeatedly.

- On April 24, 2016, the Government1 pays -$283.53 cash to A4 (SIN: 909876504) for the Travelling expenses (travel allowance) $183.53 and the Other expenses (meals: food612: $24*2 + food621: $26*2) $100.

- On April 30, 2016, the Government1 pays two employees' salary expenses for cash -$5,660 repeatedly.

- On April 30, 2016, the Government1 purchases supplies $330 ($14*11 + $16*11) from the Proprietorship2 (phone number: 123456780) for cash -$330. The multi-subaccount name of the Cash account and the transaction sub-equation respectively are:

  88-654310-t-supplies < Cash payments for operating expenses < Operating activities

  Cash (1): -330 + Supplies (1): 330 = 0

- On April 30, 2016, the Government1 purchases one service packages (Computer server1 - Service package6 < Computer server-service < Computer-service) for cash -$60 from the Company1. The multi-subaccount name of the Cash account and the transaction sub-equation respectively are:

88-654306-t-service packages < Cash payments for operating expenses <
Operating activities

Cash (1): -60 = Service package expenses (5): -60

- On May 1, 2016, the Government1 purchases a new Car1 for cash -$8,000 and other on credit $32,000 from the Company1 (phone number: 123456784) with the General ID xx. The multi-subaccount name of the Cash account and the transaction sub-equation respectively are:

  88-654306-t-machinery < Cash payments for machinery < Operating activities

  Cash (1): -8000 + Vehicle (1): 40000 = Account payable (2): 32000

- On May 16, 2016, the Government1 pays -$415.97 cash to A3 (SIN: 909876503) for the Travelling expenses (travel allowance) $310.97 and the Other expenses (meals: food123: $15*3 + food311: $20*3) $105.

- On May 31, 2016, the Government1 pays two employees' salary expenses for cash -$5,660 repeatedly.

- On June 1, 2016, the Government1 purchases one Bond23 (three years, 4.5% annually, pay at end of each year) for $5,000 from the Business Bank2. The multi-subaccount name of the Cash account and the transaction sub-equation respectively are:

  88-654305-n-bonds < Cash payments for investments < Investing activities

  Cash (1): -5000 + Bonds (1): 5000 = 0

- On June 17, 2016, the Government1 pays -$272.59 cash to A3 (SIN: 909876503) for the Travelling expenses (travel allowance) $179.59 and the Other expenses (meals: food44: $15*3 + food53: $16*3) $93.

- On June 30, 2016, the Central Bank pays two employees' salary expenses for cash -

$5,660 repeatedly.

- On July 19, 2016, the Government1 pays -$336.87 cash to A4 (SIN: 909876504) for the Travelling expenses (travel allowance) $224.87 and the Other expenses (meals: food211: $8*6 + food23: $16*4) $112.

- On July 31, 2016, the Government1 pays two employees' salary expenses for cash $5,660 repeatedly.

- On August 13, 2016, the Government1 pays -$481.11 cash to A3 (SIN: 909876503) for the Travelling expenses (travel allowance) $331.11 and the Other expenses (meals: food212: $9*6 + food312: $24*4) $150.

- On August 31, 2016, the Government1 pays two employees' salary expenses for cash -$5,660 repeatedly.

- On September 7, 2016, the Government1 pays -$384.46 cash to A4 (SIN: 909876504) for the Travelling expenses (travel allowance) $298.46 and the Other expenses (meals: food513: $10*3 + food622: $28*2) $86.

- On September 25, 2016, the Government1 purchases the following supplies (inventories) $4,200 from the Company3 (phone number: 123456782) for cash -$3,200 and other on credit.

    Inven111 < Inven11 < Inven1: 10*30

    Inven112 < Inven11 < Inven1: 40*30

    Inven221 < Inven22 < Inven2: 30*30

    Inven222 < Inven22 < Inven2: 50*30

    PPGH parts < ASD parts < Inven2: 2*150

    The multi-subaccount name of the Cash account and transaction sub-equation respectively are:

     88-654308-t-supplies < Cash payments to suppliers < Operating activities

     Cash (1): -3200 + Supplies (1): 4200 = Account payable (2): 1000

- On September 30, 2016, the Government1 pays two employees' salary expenses for cash -$5,660 repeatedly.

- On October 3, 2016, the Government1 purchases two service packages (Truck2-Service package2 < Truck-service < Vehicle-service for cash -$500 and Car1-Service package3 < Car-service < Vehicle-service for cash -$490) for cash -$990 from the Company1. The multi-subaccount name of the Cash account and the transaction sub-equation respectively are:

  88-654306-t-service packages < Cash payments for operating expenses < Operating activities

  Cash (1): -990 = Service package expenses (5): -500 + Service package expenses (5):-490

- On October 24, 2016, the Government1 pays -$377.77 cash to A3 (SIN: 909876503) for the Travelling expenses (travel allowance) $256.77 and the Other expenses (meals: food213: $10*4 + food321: $27*3) $121.

- On October 31, 2016, the Government1 pays two employees' salary expenses for cash -$5,660 repeatedly.

- On November 14, 2016, the Government1 pays -$375.39 cash to A4 (SIN: 909876504) for the Travelling expenses (travel allowance) $290.39 and the Other expenses (meals: food514: $11*3 + food613: $26*2) $85.

- On November 30, 2016, the Government1 pays two employees' salary expenses for cash -$5,660 repeatedly.

- On December 23, 2016, the Government1 pays -$514.62 cash to A3 (SIN: 909876503) for the Travelling expenses (travel allowance) $385.62 and the Other expenses (meals: food221: $12*3 + food222: $13*3 + food321: $27*2) $129.

- On December 30, 2016, the Government1 pays cash -$2,000 to the Company1 (phone number: 123456784) with the General ID 18. The multi-subaccount name of the Cash account and the transaction sub-equation respectively are:

  88-654306-t-machinery < Cash payments for machinery < Operating activities

  Cash (1): -2000 = Account payable (2): -2000

Here, I made a mistake. I enter the amount -$4,000 for the Cash account and the amount -$4,000 for the Account payable account into the database dcj03, so I enter following transaction sub-equation with the General ID 18 into the database dcj03 to correct this mistake on December 31, 2016.

Cash (1): 2000 = Account payable (2): 2000

- On December 31, 2016, the Government1 pays two employees' salary expenses for cash -$5,660 repeatedly.
- On the same day, the Government1 receives cash $240 from the Business Bank1 for investment interest of the Bond11. The multi-subaccount name of the Cash account and transaction sub-equation respectively are:

  88-654304-c-investment income < Cash receipts from investments < Investing activities

  Cash (1): 240 = Investment incomes (4):240

- On the same day, the Government1 receives $500.25 (cash $369 for investment interest of the Bond21and cash $131.25 for investment interest of the Bond23) from the Business Bank2. The multi-subaccount name of the Cash account and transaction sub-equation respectively are:

  88-654305-c-investment income < Cash receipts from investments < Investing activities

  Cash (1): 500.25 = Investment incomes (4): 369 + Investment incomes (4): 131.25

- On the same day, the Government1 receives cash $120 from the Business Bank1 for primary deposit interest. The multi-subaccount name of the Cash account and transaction sub-equation respectively are:

  88-654304-c-deposit interest income < Cash receipts from deposit interest <

Financial activities

Cash (1): 120 = Deposit interest incomes (4):120

- On the same day, the Government1 records the Office supplies expenses -$4,577.33. The transaction sub-equation is:

  Supplies (1): -4577.33 = Office supplies expenses (5): -4577.33

- On the same day, the Government1 records the Vehicle's amortization expenses -$17,000 one year (5 years, straight line). The transaction sub-equation is:

  Accumulated amortization: Vehicle (1): -8000 + Accumulated amortization: Vehicle (1): -8000 + Accumulated amortization: Vehicle (1): -5333.33 = Amortization expenses (5): -8000 + Amortization expenses (5): -8000 + Amortization expenses (5): -5333.33

- On the same day, the Government1 records the Computer's amortization expenses $2,950 eight months (2 years, straight line) which includes a new computer server1 ($1,400), a new computer1 ($800), and a new computer2 ($750). The transaction sub-equation is:

  Accumulated amortization: Computer (1): -1400 + Accumulated amortization: Computer (1): -800 + Accumulated amortization: Computer (1): -750 = Amortization expenses (5): -1400 + Amortization expenses (5): -800 + Amortization expenses (5): -750

- On the same day, the Government1 records the Tax expenses $0 and the Tax payable $0. Because tax rate is zero, the amount of the Tax expenses is also zero. The multi-subaccount name forms of the Tax expenses and the Tax payable accounts all are the 'n'. The transaction sub-equation is:

$$0 = \text{Tax payable (2): 0 + Tax expenses (5): 0}$$

So far, I have entered all transactions in the fiscal year 2016. After getting the Income Statement and clicking the "Yes" button for new fiscal year, I can get the Balance Sheet of the Government1.

3.2.2 Brief Summary of the Government1

The Figure 3.2-1 on this page and the next page shows two sums and all cash transactions of the Government1 by using of SQL Server query. As a closed system based on the MathAccounting software, the sum0 should be equal to zero. However, the individuals are not responsible for recording any transaction, so the sum0 ($72,223.05) is the sum of the amounts that the some individuals received from the Government1. If the sum0 is negative, then it is sum of the amounts that individuals paid to the Government1. The opposite value ($156.39) of the sum1 (-$156.39) is the balance of the Cash account of the Government1 on December 31, 2016. It is also the sum of the balances of the deposits of the Government1 in the Business Bak1 ($146.31) and the Business Bak2 ($10.08) on December 31, 2016.

```
SQLQuery11.sql - LI...ESS.dcj100 (sa (53))*  ×
use dcj100
  select sum(amount) as sum0 from CashByMembers where IDM='88-654302' and TransDate between '2016-01-01' and '2016-12-31'
  select sum(amount) as sum1 from CashByMembers where IDM='88-654302' and Symbol = 'd'
select * from CashByMembers where Recorder='88-654302' and TransDate between '2016-01-01' and '2016-12-31'
  order by TransDate
100 %  ▾
Results   Messages
      sum0
  1   72223.05

      sum1
  1   -156.39
```

	IDM	Amount	Symbol	MultiSubaccount	Recorder	TransDate
1	88-654300	-90000.00	c	88-654300-c-budgets < Cash receipts from national budgets < Financial activities	88-654302	2016-01-02
2	909876503	307.23	n	909876503-n-operating expenses < Cash payments for operating expenses < Operating activities	88-654302	2016-01-09
3	909876503	2810.00	t	909876503-t-salary < Cash payments for operating expenses < Operating activities	88-654302	2016-01-31
4	909876504	2850.00	t	909876504-t-salary < Cash payments for operating expenses < Operating activities	88-654302	2016-01-31
5	88-654307	500.00	t	88-654307-t-machinery < Cash payments for machinery < Operating activities	88-654302	2016-02-21
6	909876503	2810.00	t	909876503-t-salary < Cash payments for operating expenses < Operating activities	88-654302	2016-02-28
7	909876504	2850.00	t	909876504-t-salary < Cash payments for operating expenses < Operating activities	88-654302	2016-02-28
8	909876503	295.17	n	909876503-n-operating expenses < Cash payments for operating expenses < Operating activities	88-654302	2016-02-28
9	909876504	558.34	n	909876504-n-operating expenses < Cash payments for operating expenses < Operating activities	88-654302	2016-03-28
10	909876503	2810.00	t	909876503-t-salary < Cash payments for operating expenses < Operating activities	88-654302	2016-03-31
11	909876504	2850.00	t	909876504-t-salary < Cash payments for operating expenses < Operating activities	88-654302	2016-03-31
12	909876504	283.53	n	909876504-n-operating expenses < Cash payments for operating expenses < Operating activities	88-654302	2016-04-24
13	909876503	2810.00	t	909876503-t-salary < Cash payments for operating expenses < Operating activities	88-654302	2016-04-30

Figure 3.2-1   Government1 Received or Paid by Other Members (Continue)

	IDM	Amount	Symbol	MultiSubaccount	Recorder	TransDate
14	909876504	2850.00	t	909876504-t-salary < Cash payments for operating expenses < Operating activities	88-654302	2016-04-30
15	88-654310	330.00	t	88-654310-t-supplies < Cash payments for operating expenses < Operating activities	88-654302	2016-04-30
16	88-654306	60.00	t	88-654306-t-service packages < Cash payments for operating expenses < Operating activities	88-654302	2016-04-30
17	88-654306	8000.00	t	88-654306-t-machinery < Cash payments for machinery < Operating activities	88-654302	2016-05-01
18	909876503	415.97	n	909876503-n-operating expenses < Cash payments for operating expenses < Operating activities	88-654302	2016-05-16
19	909876503	2810.00	t	909876503-t-salary < Cash payments for operating expenses < Operating activities	88-654302	2016-05-31
20	909876504	2850.00	t	909876504-t-salary < Cash payments for operating expenses < Operating activities	88-654302	2016-05-31
21	88-654305	5000.00	n	88-654305-n-bonds < Cash payments for investments < Investing activities	88-654302	2016-06-01
22	909876503	272.59	n	909876503-n-operating expenses < Cash payments for operating expenses < Operating activities	88-654302	2016-06-17
23	909876503	2810.00	t	909876503-t-salary < Cash payments for operating expenses < Operating activities	88-654302	2016-06-30
24	909876504	2850.00	t	909876504-t-salary < Cash payments for operating expenses < Operating activities	88-654302	2016-06-30
25	909876504	336.87	n	909876504-n-operating expenses < Cash payments for operating expenses < Operating activities	88-654302	2016-07-19
26	909876503	2810.00	t	909876503-t-salary < Cash payments for operating expenses < Operating activities	88-654302	2016-07-31
27	909876504	2850.00	t	909876504-t-salary < Cash payments for operating expenses < Operating activities	88-654302	2016-07-31
28	909876503	481.11	n	909876503-n-operating expenses < Cash payments for operating expenses < Operating activities	88-654302	2016-08-13
29	909876503	2810.00	t	909876503-t-salary < Cash payments for operating expenses < Operating activities	88-654302	2016-08-31
30	909876504	2850.00	t	909876504-t-salary < Cash payments for operating expenses < Operating activities	88-654302	2016-08-31
31	909876504	384.46	n	909876504-n-operating expenses < Cash payments for operating expenses < Operating activities	88-654302	2016-09-07
32	88-654308	3200.00	t	88-654308-t-supplies < Cash payments to suppliers < Operating activities	88-654302	2016-09-25
33	909876503	2810.00	t	909876503-t-salary < Cash payments for operating expenses < Operating activities	88-654302	2016-09-30
34	909876504	2850.00	t	909876504-t-salary < Cash payments for operating expenses < Operating activities	88-654302	2016-09-30
35	88-654306	990.00	t	88-654306-t-service packages < Cash payments for operating expenses < Operating activities	88-654302	2016-10-03
36	909876503	377.77	n	909876503-n-operating expenses < Cash payments for operating expenses < Operating activities	88-654302	2016-10-24
37	909876503	2810.00	t	909876503-t-salary < Cash payments for operating expenses < Operating activities	88-654302	2016-10-31
38	909876504	2850.00	t	909876504-t-salary < Cash payments for operating expenses < Operating activities	88-654302	2016-10-31
39	909876504	375.39	n	909876504-n-operating expenses < Cash payments for operating expenses < Operating activities	88-654302	2016-11-14
40	909876503	2810.00	t	909876503-t-salary < Cash payments for operating expenses < Operating activities	88-654302	2016-11-30
41	909876504	2850.00	t	909876504-t-salary < Cash payments for operating expenses < Operating activities	88-654302	2016-11-30
42	909876503	514.62	n	909876503-n-operating expenses < Cash payments for operating expenses < Operating activities	88-654302	2016-12-23
43	88-654306	4000.00	t	88-654306-t-machinery < Cash payments for machinery < Operating activities	88-654302	2016-12-30
44	909876503	2810.00	t	909876503-t-salary < Cash payments for operating expenses < Operating activities	88-654302	2016-12-31
45	909876504	2850.00	t	909876504-t-salary < Cash payments for operating expenses < Operating activities	88-654302	2016-12-31
46	88-654304	-240.00	c	88-654304-c-investment income < Cash receipts from investments < Investing activities	88-654302	2016-12-31
47	88-654305	-500.25	c	88-654305-c-investment income < Cash receipts from investments < Investing activities	88-654302	2016-12-31
48	88-654304	-120.00	c	88-654304-c-deposit interest income < Cash receipts from deposit interest < Financial activities	88-654302	2016-12-31
49	88-654306	-2000.00	t	88-654306-t-machinery < Cash payments for machinery < Operating activities	88-654302	2016-12-31

Query executed successfully.

Figure 3.2-1   Government1 Cash Received or Paid by Other Members

The Figure 3.2-2 on the next page shows the Government1 cash flows statement. From the Figure 3.2-2, the cash balance at the ending of this fiscal year is also $156.39, which is the same as the sum1's opposite amount in the Figure 3.2-1.

The Figure 3.2-3 on the next pages shows the Government1 cash account table between 2016-01-02 and 2016-12-31. From the Figure 3.2-3, the cash balance on December 31, 2016 is also $156.39, which is the same as the sum1's opposite amount in the Figure 3.2-1.

Cash Flow Statement

Cash Flows Statement Year Ended 2016-12-31	
Operating activities	
Cash payments for machinery	-$10,500.00
Cash payments for operating expenses	-$73,903.05
Cash payments to suppliers	-$3,200.00
Net cash provided by Operating activities	-$87,603.05
Investing activities	
Cash payments for investments	-$5,000.00
Cash receipts from investments	$740.25
Net cash provided by Investing activities	-$4,259.75
Financial activities	
Cash receipts from deposit interest	$120.00
Cash receipts from national budgets	$90,000.00
Net cash provided by Financial activities	$90,120.00
Net change in cash	-$1,742.80
Cash, Begining	$1,899.19
Cash, Ending	$156.39

Figure 3.2-2   Government1 Cash Flows Statement

Cash

ID	Multi-Name	Amount	Balance	General ID	Transaction Date
15	88-654301-c-budgets < Cash receipts from central bank budgets < Fina...	$37,229.16	$1,899.19	5	2015-12-31
16	88-654300-c-budgets < Cash receipts from national budgets < Financial...	$90,000.00	$91,899.19	6	2016-01-02
17	909876503-n-operating expenses < Cash payments for operating expe...	-$307.23	$91,591.96	7	2016-01-09
18	909876503-t-salary < Cash payments for operating expenses < Operati...	-$2,810.00	$88,781.96	8	2016-01-31
19	909876504-t-salary < Cash payments for operating expenses < Operati...	-$2,850.00	$85,931.96	8	2016-01-31
20	88-654307-t-machinery < Cash payments for machinery < Operating act...	-$500.00	$85,431.96	9	2016-02-21
21	909876503-t-salary < Cash payments for operating expenses < Operati...	-$2,810.00	$82,621.96	10	2016-02-28
22	909876504-t-salary < Cash payments for operating expenses < Operati...	-$2,850.00	$79,771.96	10	2016-02-28
23	909876503-n-operating expenses < Cash payments for operating expe...	-$295.17	$79,476.79	11	2016-02-28
24	909876504-n-operating expenses < Cash payments for operating expe...	-$558.34	$78,918.45	12	2016-03-28
25	909876503-t-salary < Cash payments for operating expenses < Operati...	-$2,810.00	$76,108.45	13	2016-03-31
26	909876504-t-salary < Cash payments for operating expenses < Operati...	-$2,850.00	$73,258.45	13	2016-03-31
27	909876504-n-operating expenses < Cash payments for operating expe...	-$283.53	$72,974.92	14	2016-04-24
28	909876503-t-salary < Cash payments for operating expenses < Operati...	-$2,810.00	$70,164.92	15	2016-04-30
29	909876504-t-salary < Cash payments for operating expenses < Operati...	-$2,850.00	$67,314.92	15	2016-04-30
30	88-654310-t-supplies < Cash payments for operating expenses < Opera...	-$330.00	$66,984.92	16	2016-04-30
31	88-654306-t-service packages < Cash payments for operating expenses...	-$60.00	$66,924.92	17	2016-04-30
32	88-654306-t-machinery < Cash payments for machinery < Operating act...	-$8,000.00	$58,924.92	18	2016-05-01
33	909876503-n-operating expenses < Cash payments for operating expe...	-$415.97	$58,508.95	19	2016-05-16
34	909876503-t-salary < Cash payments for operating expenses < Operati...	-$2,810.00	$55,698.95	20	2016-05-31
35	909876504-t-salary < Cash payments for operating expenses < Operati...	-$2,850.00	$52,848.95	20	2016-05-31
36	88-654305-n-bonds < Cash payments for investments < Investing activiti...	-$5,000.00	$47,848.95	21	2016-06-01

Figure 3.2-3   Government1 Cash Account Table (Continue)

ID	Multi-Name	Amount	Balance	General ID	Transaction Date
37	909876503-n-operating expenses < Cash payments for operating expe...	-$272.59	$47,576.36	22	2016-06-17
38	909876503-t-salary < Cash payments for operating expenses < Operati...	-$2,810.00	$44,766.36	23	2016-06-30
39	909876504-t-salary < Cash payments for operating expenses < Operati...	-$2,850.00	$41,916.36	23	2016-06-30
40	909876504-n-operating expenses < Cash payments for operating expe...	-$336.87	$41,579.49	24	2016-07-19
41	909876503-t-salary < Cash payments for operating expenses < Operati...	-$2,810.00	$38,769.49	25	2016-07-31
42	909876504-t-salary < Cash payments for operating expenses < Operati...	-$2,850.00	$35,919.49	25	2016-07-31
43	909876503-n-operating expenses < Cash payments for operating expe...	-$481.11	$35,438.38	26	2016-08-13
44	909876503-t-salary < Cash payments for operating expenses < Operati...	-$2,810.00	$32,628.38	27	2016-08-31
45	909876504-t-salary < Cash payments for operating expenses < Operati...	-$2,850.00	$29,778.38	27	2016-08-31
46	909876504-n-operating expenses < Cash payments for operating expe...	-$384.46	$29,393.92	28	2016-09-07
47	88-654308-t-supplies < Cash payments to suppliers < Operating activities	-$3,200.00	$26,193.92	29	2016-09-25
48	909876503-t-salary < Cash payments for operating expenses < Operati...	-$2,810.00	$23,383.92	30	2016-09-30
49	909876504-t-salary < Cash payments for operating expenses < Operati...	-$2,850.00	$20,533.92	30	2016-09-30
50	88-654306-t-service packages < Cash payments for operating expenses...	-$990.00	$19,543.92	31	2016-10-03
51	909876503-n-operating expenses < Cash payments for operating expe...	-$377.77	$19,166.15	32	2016-10-24
52	909876503-t-salary < Cash payments for operating expenses < Operati...	-$2,810.00	$16,356.15	33	2016-10-31
53	909876504-t-salary < Cash payments for operating expenses < Operati...	-$2,850.00	$13,506.15	33	2016-10-31
54	909876504-n-operating expenses < Cash payments for operating expe...	-$375.39	$13,130.76	34	2016-11-14
55	909876503-t-salary < Cash payments for operating expenses < Operati...	-$2,810.00	$10,320.76	35	2016-11-30
56	909876504-t-salary < Cash payments for operating expenses < Operati...	-$2,850.00	$7,470.76	35	2016-11-30
57	909876503-n-operating expenses < Cash payments for operating expe...	-$514.62	$6,956.14	36	2016-12-23
58	88-654306-t-machinery < Cash payments for machinery < Operating act...	-$4,000.00	$2,956.14	37	2016-12-30
59	909876503-t-salary < Cash payments for operating expenses < Operati...	-$2,810.00	$146.14	38	2016-12-31
60	909876504-t-salary < Cash payments for operating expenses < Operati...	-$2,850.00	-$2,703.86	38	2016-12-31
61	88-654304-c-investment income < Cash receipts from investments < Inv...	$240.00	-$2,463.86	39	2016-12-31
62	88-654305-c-investment income < Cash receipts from investments < Inv...	$500.25	-$1,963.61	40	2016-12-31
63	88-654304-c-deposit interest income < Cash receipts from deposit inter...	$120.00	-$1,843.61	41	2016-12-31
64	88-654306-t-machinery < Cash payments for machinery < Operating act...	$2,000.00	$156.39	44	2016-12-31

Figure 3.2-3   Government1 Cash Account Table

The Figure 3.2-4 on the next page shows the Government1 income statement. From the Figure 3.2-4, the amount of the earnings before income taxes is -$11,573.46 and the amount of the tax expenses is zero, so the amount of the net earnings of the Government1 in this fiscal year is also -$11,573.46.

Income Statement

	Year ended: 12/31/2016	
Revenues		
Sales (received budgets)		$90,000.00
Cost		
Cost of goods sold		$0.00
Gross Margin		$90,000.00
Operating and administrative expenses		
Travelling expenses		-$3,243.05
Other expenses		-$1,360.00
Office supplies expenses		-$4,577.33
Salary expenses		-$67,920.00
Amortization expenses		-$24,283.33
Service package expenses		-$1,050.00
Tax expenses		$0.00
Other income		
Investment incomes		$740.25
Deposits interest income		$120.00
Earnings Before Income Taxes		-$11,573.46
Net Earnings		-$11,573.46
Retained Earnings,Begining		$0.00
Retained Earnings,Ending		-$11,573.46

Figure 3.2-4   Government1 Income Statement

The Figure 3.2-5 on next page shows the Government1 balance sheet. From the Figure 3.2-5, the amount of total assets is $84,619.43, and the amount of the total liabilities and the shareholders' equity is also $84,619.43.

Balance Sheet

As at 12/31/2016	
ASSETS	
Current assets	
Cash	$156.39
Supplies	$75.53
Account receivable	$0.00
	$231.92
Long term investments	
Bonds	$20,000.00
Equipment	
Vehicle	$120,000.00
Accumulated amortization: Vehicle	-$57,333.33
Computer	$5,900.00
Accumulated amortization: Computer	-$4,179.16
	$64,387.51
Total Assets	$84,619.43
LIABILITIES	
Current liabilities	
Account payable	$31,000.00
Tax payable	$0.00
	$31,000.00
Total Liability	$31,000.00
SHAREHOLDERS' EQUITY	
Owners capital	

SHAREHOLDERS' EQUITY	
Owners capital	
Budgets capital	$65,192.89
Retined earnings	-$11,573.46
Accumulated other comprehensive income	$0.00
Total Shareholders' Equity	$53,619.43
Total Liabilities and Shareholders' Equity	$84,619.43

Figure 3.2-5 Government1 Balance Sheet Statement

3.3 Tax Bureau

3.3.1 An Accounting Fiscal Year of the Tax Bureau

In the new fiscal year, the Tax Bureau occurs the following transactions.

- On January 2, 2016, the Tax Bureau receives cash $95,000 from the Cash Management Center for the planned national budgets. The multi-subaccount name of the Cash account and the transaction sub-equation respectively are:

88-654303-c-budgets < Cash receipts from national budgets < Financial activities

Cash (1): 95000 = Sales (received budgets) (4): 95000

- On January 12, 2016, the Tax Bureau pays -$283.71 cash to A5 (SIN: 909876505) for the Travelling expenses (travel allowance) $185.71 and the Other expenses (meals: food214: $11*4 + food321: $27*2) $98. The multi-subaccount name of the Cash account and the transaction sub-equation respectively are:

909876505-n-operating expenses < Cash payments for operating expenses < Operating activities

Cash (1): -283.71 = Travelling expenses (5): -199.23 + other expenses (5): -108

- On January 12, 2016, the Tax Bureau pays -$277.71 cash to A6 (SIN: 909876506) for the Travelling expenses (travel allowance) $185.71 and the Other expenses (meals: food112: $11*4 + food23: $16*3) $92. The multi-subaccount name of the Cash account and the transaction sub-equation respectively are:

909876506-n-operating expenses < Cash payments for operating expenses < Operating activities

Cash (1): -277.71 = Travelling expenses (5): -199.23 + other expenses (5): -108

- On January 13, 2016, the Tax Bureau purchases one service packages (Computer server1- Service package6 < Computer server-service < Computer-service) for cash -$60 from the Company1. The multi-subaccount name of the Cash account and the transaction sub-equation respectively are:

88-654306-t-service packages < Cash payments for operating expenses < Operating activities

Cash (1): -60 = Service package expenses (5): -60

- On January 31, 2016, the Tax Bureau pays two employees' salary expenses for cash -$5,670. The two multi-subaccount names of the Cash account and the transaction sub-equation respectively are:

    909876505-t-salary < Cash payments for operating expenses < Operating activities
    909876506-t-salary < Cash payments for operating expenses < Operating activities

    Cash (1): -2810 + Cash (1): -2860 = Salary expenses (5): -5670

- On February 2, 2016, the Tax Bureau pays -$500 cash to Company1 (phone number: 123456784) with the General ID 1. The multi-subaccount name of the Cash account and the transaction sub-equation respectively are:

    88-654306-t-machinery < Cash payments for machinery < Operating activities

    Cash (1): -500 = Account payable (2): -500

- On February 11, 2016, the Tax Bureau pays -$400 cash to Company2 (phone number: 123456083) with the General ID 1. The multi-subaccount name of the Cash account and the transaction sub-equation respectively are:

    88-654307-t-machinery < Cash payments for machinery < Operating activities

    Cash (1): -400 = Account payable (2): -400

- On February 23, 2016, the Tax Bureau pays -$300 cash to Company3 (phone number: 123456782) with the General ID 1. The multi-subaccount name of the Cash account and the transaction sub-equation respectively are:

    88-654308-t-operating expenses < Cash payments for operating expenses < Operating activities

    Cash (1): -300 = Account payable (2): -300

- On February 26, 2016, the Tax Bureau pays -$335.63 cash to A5 (SIN: 909876505)

for the Travelling expenses (travel allowance) -$225.63 and the Other expenses (meals: food122: $14*4 + food321: $27*2) -$110.

- On February 28, 2016, the Tax Bureau pays two employees' salary expenses for cash $5,670 repeatedly.

- On March 12, 2016, the Tax Bureau pays -$419.99 cash to A6 (SIN: 909876506) for the Travelling expenses (travel allowance) -$296.99 and the Other expenses (meals: food214: $11*3 + food322: $30*3) -$123.

- On March 31, 2016, the Tax Bureau pays two employees' salary expenses for cash $5,670 repeatedly.

- On April 16, 2016, the Tax Bureau pays -$358.13 cash to A5 (SIN: 909876505) for the Travelling expenses (travel allowance) $246.13 and the Other expenses (meals: food613: $26*2 + food614: $30*2) $112.

- On April 30, 2016, the Tax Bureau pays two employees' salary expenses for cash -$5,670 repeatedly.

- On May 8, 2016, the Tax Bureau purchases supplies $300 ($14*10 + $16*10) from the Proprietorship2 for cash -$300. The multi-subaccount name of the Cash account and the transaction sub-equation respectively are:

  88-654310-t-supplies < Cash payments for operating expenses < Operating activities

  Cash (1): -300 + Supplies (1): 300 = 0

- On May 16, 2016, the Tax Bureau pays -$443.18 cash to A6 (SIN: 909876506) for the Travelling expenses (travel allowance) $331.18 and the Other expenses (meals: food121: $13*4 + food311: $20*3) $112.

- On May 31, 2016, the Tax Bureau pays two employees' salary expenses for cash -$5,670 repeatedly.

- On June 1, 2016, the Tax Bureau purchases one Bond23 (three years, 4.5% annually, pay at end of each year) for -$5,000 from the Business Bank2. The multi-subaccount name of the Cash account and the transaction sub-equation respectively are:

88-654305-n-Bonds < Cash payments for investments < Investing activities

Cash (1): -5000 + Bonds (1): 5000 = 0

- On June 20, 2016, the Tax Bureau pays -$364.55 cash to A5 (SIN: 909876505) for the Travelling expenses (travel allowance) $271.55 and the Other expenses (meals: food514: $11*3 + food611: $20*3) $93.
- On June 20, 2016, the Tax Bureau pays -$361.55 cash to A6 (SIN: 909876506) for the Travelling expenses (travel allowance) $271.55 and the Other expenses (meals: food513: $10*3 + food611: $20*3) $90.
- On June 29, 2016, the Tax Bureau purchases the following supplies (inventories) - $4,740 from the Company3 (phone number: 123456782) for cash -$2,000 and other on credit.

Inven121 < Inven12 < Inven1: 0.8*300

Inven122 < Inven12 < Inven1: 50*30

Inven21 < Inven2: 30*30

Inven221 < Inven22 < Inven2: 30*30

PPUK parts < ASD parts < Inven2: 40*30

The multi-subaccount name of the Cash account and transaction sub-equation respectively are:

88-654308-t-supplies < Cash payments to suppliers < Operating activities

Cash (1): -2000 + Supplies (1): 4740 = Account payable (2): 2740

- On June 30, 2016, the Tax Bureau pays two employees' salary expenses for cash $5,670 repeatedly.
- On July 24, 2016, the Tax Bureau pays -$317.22 cash to A5 (SIN: 909876505) for the Travelling expenses (travel allowance) $212.22 and the Other expenses (meals: food212: $9*5 + food311: $20*3) $105.

- On July 31, 2016, the Tax Bureau pays two employees' salary expenses for cash - $5,670 repeatedly.

- On August 11, 2016, the Tax Bureau pays -$395.47 cash to A6 (SIN: 909876506) for the Travelling expenses (travel allowance) $281.47 and the Other expenses (meals: food513: $10*5 + food53: $16*4) $114.

- On August 31, 2016, the Tax Bureau pays two employees' salary expenses for cash - $5,670 repeatedly.

- On September 17, 2016, the Tax Bureau pays -$399.36 cash to A6 (SIN: 909876506) for the Travelling expenses (travel allowance) $294.36 and the Other expenses (meals: food514: $11*3 + food612: $24*3) $105.

- On September 30, 2016, the Tax Bureau pays two employees' salary expenses for cash -$5,670 repeatedly.

- On September 30, 2016, the Tax Bureau records the Amortization expenses $2,212.5 of a computer server1 ($1,050, nine months), a computer1 ($600, nine months), and a computer2 ($562.5, nine months). The transaction sub-equation is:

  Accumulated amortization: Computer (1): -1050 + Accumulated amortization: Computer (1): -600 + Accumulated amortization: Computer (1): -562.5 = Amortization expenses (5): -1050 + Amortization expenses (5): -600 + Amortization expenses (5): -562.5

- On September 30, 2016, the Tax Bureau cancels the balances of the Computer account and the Accumulated amortization: Computer account because these computers have used for two years. The transaction sub-equation is:

  Computer (1): -2800 + Computer (1): -1600 + Computer (1): -1500 + Accumulated amortization: Computer (1): 2800 + Accumulated amortization: Computer (1): 1600 + Accumulated amortization: Computer (1): 1500 = 0

- On October 1, 2016, the Tax Bureau purchases a new computer server1, a new computer1, and a new computer2 for cash -$2,400 and other on credit $3,500 with the General ID 37 from the Company1. The multi-subaccount name of the Cash account and the transaction sub-equation respectively are:

88-654306-t-computer < Cash payments for machinery < Operating activities

Cash (1): -2400 + Company (1): 2800 + Company (1): 1600 + Company (1): 1500 = Account payable (2): 3500

- On October 3, 2016, the Tax Bureau purchases one Truck2 part1 for cash -$4,500 and other on credit $4,000 from the Company2 (123456783). Here, the parts are not as the equipment but as the Vehicle part expenses (Operating and administrative expenses) for simplification. The following is the same as this. The multi-subaccount name of the Cash account and the transaction sub-equation respectively are:

88-654307-t- part activities < Cash payments for operating activities < Operating activities

Cash (1): -4500 = Account payable (2): 4000 + Vehicle part expenses (5): -8500

- On October 25, 2016, the Tax Bureau pays -$369.53 cash to A5 (SIN: 909876508) for the Travelling expenses (travel allowance) $253.53 and the Other expenses (meals: food214: $11*4 + food312: $24*3) $116.
- On October 31, 2016, the Tax Bureau pays two employees' salary expenses for cash -$5,670 repeatedly.
- On November 18, 2016, the Tax Bureau pays -$388.19 cash to A6 (SIN: 909876506) for the Travelling expenses (travel allowance) $295.19 and the Other expenses (meals: food121: $13*3 + food321: $27*2) $93.
- On November 19, 2016, the Tax Bureau purchases three service packages (Truck2-Service package2 for cash -$500, Car1- Service package3 for cash -$490, and Car3-Service package5 for cash -$410) for cash -$1,400 from the Company1. The multi-subaccount name of the Cash account and the transaction sub-equation respectively

are:

88-654306-t-service packages < Cash payments for operating expenses <
Operating activities

Cash (1): -1400 = Service package expenses (5): -500 + Service package expenses
(5): -490 + Service package expenses (5): -410

- On November 30, 2016, the Tax Bureau pays two employees' salary expenses for
  cash -$5,670 repeatedly.

- On December 28, 2016, the Tax Bureau pays -$664.58 cash to A5 (SIN: 909876505)
  for the Travelling expenses (travel allowance) $472.58 and the Other expenses
  (meals: food111: $10*6 + food213: $10*6 + food312: $24*3) $192.

- On December 28, 2016, the Tax Bureau pays -$670.58 cash to A6 (SIN: 909876506)
  for the Travelling expenses (travel allowance) $472.58 and the Other expenses
  (meals: food113: $12*6 + food214: $11*6 + food311: $20*3) $198.

- On December 28, 2016, the Tax Bureau pays -$2,500 cash to Company3 (phone
  number: 123456782) with the General ID 27.

- On December 29, 2016, the Tax Bureau pays -$2,400 cash to Company1 (phone
  number: 123456784) with the General ID 37. The multi-subaccount name of the
  Cash account is:

  88-654306-t-machinery < Cash payments for machinery < Operating activities

- On December 31, 2016, the Tax Bureau pays two employees' salary expenses for
  cash -$5,670 repeatedly.

- On the same day, the Tax Bureau receives cash $200 from the Business Bank1 for
  investment interest of the Bond11. The multi-subaccount name of the Cash account
  and transaction sub-equation respectively are:

  88-654304-c-investment income < Cash receipts from investments < Investing
  activities

  Cash (1): 200 = Investment incomes (4):200

- On the same day, the Tax Bureau receives cash $459.25 ($328 for investment interest of the Bond21and cash $131.25 for investment interest of the Bond23) from the Business Bank2. The multi-subaccount name of the Cash account and transaction sub-equation respectively are:

  88-654305-c-investment income < Cash receipts from investments < Investing activities

  Cash (1): 459.25 = Investment incomes (4): 328 + Investment incomes (4): 131.25

- On the same day, the Tax Bureau receives cash $120 from the Business Bank1 for primary deposit interest. The multi-subaccount name of the Cash account and transaction sub-equation respectively are:

  88-654304-c-deposit interest income < Cash receipts from deposit interest < Financial activities

  Cash (1): 120 = Deposit interest incomes (4):120

- On the same day, the Tax Bureau records the Office supplies expenses -$5,171.46. The transaction sub-equation is:

  Supplies (1): -5171.46 = Office supplies expenses (5): -5171.46

- On the same day, the Tax Bureau records the Vehicle's amortization expenses -$23,600 one year (5 years, straight line). The transaction sub-equation is:

  Accumulated amortization: Vehicle (1): -8000 + Accumulated amortization: Vehicle (1): -8000 + Accumulated amortization: Vehicle (1): -7600 = Amortization expenses (5): -8000 + Amortization expenses (5): -8000 + Amortization expenses (5): -7600

- On the same day, the Tax Bureau records the Computer's amortization expenses

$737.5 three months (2 years, straight line) which includes a new computer server1 ($350), a new computer1 ($200), and a new computer2 ($187.5). The transaction sub-equation is:

Accumulated amortization: Computer (1): -350 + Accumulated amortization: Computer (1): -200 + Accumulated amortization: Computer (1): -187.5 = Amortization expenses (5): -350 + Amortization expenses (5): -200 + Amortization expenses (5): -187.5

- On the same day, the Tax Bureau records the Tax expenses $0 and the Tax payable $0. Because tax rate is zero, the amount of the Tax expenses is also zero. The multi-subaccount name forms of the Tax expenses and the Tax payable accounts all are the 'n'. The transaction sub-equation is:

0 = Tax payable (2): 0 + Tax expenses (5): 0

So far, I have entered all transactions in the fiscal year 2016. After getting the Income Statement and clicking the "Yes" button for new fiscal year, I can get the Balance Sheet of the Tax Bureau.

In the new fiscal year, the Tax Bureau will record the following transactions.
- On January 2, 2017, the Tax Bureau receives cash $0 from the Business Bank1 for the Taxation. The multi-subaccount name of the Cash account is:
  88-654304-c-Tax < Cash receipts from taxation < Financial activities
- On the same day, the Tax Bureau receives cash $0 from the Business Bank2 for the Taxation. The multi-subaccount name of the Cash account is:
  88-654305-c-Tax < Cash receipts from taxation < Financial activities
- On the same day, the Tax Bureau receives cash $8,694.39 from the Company1 for the Taxation. The multi-subaccount name of the Cash account and transaction sub-equation respectively are:
  88-654306-c-Tax < Cash receipts from taxation < Financial activities

Cash (1): 8,694.39 = Tax receipts payable (2): 8,694.39

- On the same day, the Tax Bureau receives cash $0 from the Company2 for the Taxation. The multi-subaccount name of the Cash account is:

    88-654307-c-Tax < Cash receipts from taxation < Financial activities

- On the same day, the Tax Bureau receives cash $3,555.43 from the Company3 for the Taxation. The multi-subaccount name of the Cash account is:

    88-654308-c-Tax < Cash receipts from taxation < Financial activities

- On the same day, the Tax Bureau receives cash $34,827.41 from the Proprietorship1 for the Taxation. The multi-subaccount name of the Cash account is:

    88-654309-c-Tax < Cash receipts from taxation < Financial activities

- On the same day, the Tax Bureau receives cash $22,373.43 from the Proprietorship2 for the Taxation. The multi-subaccount name of the Cash account is:

    88-654310-c-Tax < Cash receipts from taxation < Financial activities

- On the same day, the Tax Bureau receives total cash $89,014.80 from the individual A1 to the individual A25 for the Taxation respectively. The multi-subaccount names of the Cash account are:

    909876501-c-Tax < Cash receipts from taxation < Financial activities
    909876525-c-Tax < Cash receipts from taxation < Financial activities

- On the same day, the Tax Bureau pays the balance $158,465.46 of the Tax receipts payable account to the Cash Management Center. The multi-subaccount name of the Cash account and transaction sub-equation respectively are:

    88-654300-n-tax < Cash payments to center < Financial activities

    Cash (1): -158465.46 = Tax receipts payable (2): -158465.46

3.3.2 Brief Summary of the Tax Bureau

The Figure 3.3-1 shows two sums and all cash transactions of the Tax Bureau by using of

SQL Server query. As a closed system based on the MathAccounting software, the sum0 should be equal to zero. However, the individuals are not responsible for recording any transaction, so the sum0 ($74,089.38) is the sum of the amounts that the individuals received from the Tax Bureau. If the sum0 is negative, then it is sum of the amounts that individuals paid to the Tax Bureau. The opposite value ($2,051.55) of the sum1 (-$2,051.55) is the balance of the Cash account of the Tax Bureau on December 31, 2016. It is also the sum of the balances of the deposits of the Tax Bureau in the Business Bak1 ($933.59) and the Business Bak2 ($1,117.96) on December 31, 2016.

Figure 3.3-1   Tax Bureau Received or Paid by Other Members (Continue)

	IDM	Amount	Symbol	MultiSubaccount	Recorder	TransDate
24	909876505	364.55	n	909876505-n-operating expenses < Cash payments for operating expenses < Operating activities	88-654303	2016-06-20
25	909876506	361.55	n	909876506-n-operating expenses < Cash payments for operating expenses < Operating activities	88-654303	2016-06-20
26	88-654308	2000.00	t	88-654308-t-supplies < Cash payments to suppliers < Operating activities	88-654303	2016-06-29
27	909876505	2810.00	t	909876505-t-salary < Cash payments for operating expenses < Operating activities	88-654303	2016-06-30
28	909876506	2860.00	t	909876506-t-salary < Cash payments for operating expenses < Operating activities	88-654303	2016-06-30
29	909876505	317.22	n	909876505-n-operating expenses < Cash payments for operating expenses < Operating activities	88-654303	2016-07-24
30	909876505	2810.00	t	909876505-t-salary < Cash payments for operating expenses < Operating activities	88-654303	2016-07-31
31	909876506	2860.00	t	909876506-t-salary < Cash payments for operating expenses < Operating activities	88-654303	2016-07-31
32	909876506	395.47	n	909876506-n-operating expenses < Cash payments for operating expenses < Operating activities	88-654303	2016-08-11
33	909876505	2810.00	t	909876505-t-salary < Cash payments for operating expenses < Operating activities	88-654303	2016-08-31
34	909876506	2860.00	t	909876506-t-salary < Cash payments for operating expenses < Operating activities	88-654303	2016-08-31
35	909876506	399.36	n	909876506-n-operating expenses < Cash payments for operating expenses < Operating activities	88-654303	2016-09-17
36	909876505	2810.00	t	909876505-t-salary < Cash payments for operating expenses < Operating activities	88-654303	2016-09-30
37	909876506	2860.00	t	909876506-t-salary < Cash payments for operating expenses < Operating activities	88-654303	2016-09-30
38	88-654306	2400.00	t	88-654306-t-computer < Cash payments for machinery < Operating activities	88-654303	2016-10-01
39	88-654307	4500.00	t	88-654307-t- part activities < Cash payments for operating activities < Operating activities	88-654303	2016-10-03
40	909876505	369.53	n	909876505-n-operating expenses < Cash payments for operating expenses < Operating activities	88-654303	2016-10-25
41	909876505	2810.00	t	909876505-t-salary < Cash payments for operating expenses < Operating activities	88-654303	2016-10-31
42	909876506	2860.00	t	909876506-t-salary < Cash payments for operating expenses < Operating activities	88-654303	2016-10-31
43	909876506	388.19	n	909876506-n-operating expenses < Cash payments for operating expenses < Operating activities	88-654303	2016-11-18
44	88-654306	1400.00	t	88-654306-t-service packages < Cash payments for operating expenses < Operating activities	88-654303	2016-11-19
45	909876505	2810.00	t	909876505-t-salary < Cash payments for operating expenses < Operating activities	88-654303	2016-11-30
46	909876506	2860.00	t	909876506-t-salary < Cash payments for operating expenses < Operating activities	88-654303	2016-11-30
47	909876505	664.58	n	909876505-n-operating expenses < Cash payments for operating expenses < Operating activities	88-654303	2016-12-28
48	909876506	670.58	n	909876506-n-operating expenses < Cash payments for operating expenses < Operating activities	88-654303	2016-12-28
49	88-654308	2500.00	t	88-654308-t-supplies < Cash payments to suppliers < Operating activities	88-654303	2016-12-28
50	88-654306	2400.00	t	88-654306-t-computer < Cash payments for machinery < Operating activities	88-654303	2016-12-29
51	909876505	2810.00	t	909876505-t-salary < Cash payments for operating expenses < Operating activities	88-654303	2016-12-31
52	909876506	2860.00	t	909876506-t-salary < Cash payments for operating expenses < Operating activities	88-654303	2016-12-31
53	88-654304	-200.00	c	88-654304-c-investment income < Cash receipts from investments < Investing activities	88-654303	2016-12-31
54	88-654305	-459.25	c	88-654305-c-investment income < Cash receipts from investments < Investing activities	88-654303	2016-12-31
55	88-654304	-120.00	c	88-654304-c-deposit interest income < Cash receipts from deposit interest < Financial activities	88-654303	2016-12-31

Query executed successfully.

Figure 3.3-1   Tax Bureau Cash Received or Paid by Other Members

The Figure 3.3-2 on the next page shows the Tax Bureau cash flows statement. From the Figure 3.3-2, the cash balance at the ending of this fiscal year is also $2,051.55, which is the same as the sum1's opposite amount in the Figure 3.3-1.

The Figure 3.3-3, which follows the Figure 3.3-2, shows the Tax Bureau cash account table between 2016-01-02 and 2016-12-31. From the Figure 3.3-3, the cash balance on December 31, 2016 is also $2,051.55, which is the same as the sum1's opposite amount in the Figure 3.3-1.

Cash Flow Statement

Cash Flows Statement Year Ended 2016-12-31	
Operating activities	
Cash payments for machinery	-$6,000.00
Cash payments for operating activities	-$4,500.00
Cash payments for operating expenses	-$75,849.38
Cash payments to suppliers	-$4,500.00
Net cash provided by Operating activities	-$90,849.38
Investing activities	
Cash payments for investments	-$5,000.00
Cash receipts from investments	$659.25
Net cash provided by Investing activities	-$4,340.75
Financial activities	
Cash receipts from deposit interest	$120.00
Cash receipts from national budgets	$95,000.00
Net cash provided by Financial activities	$95,120.00
Net change in cash	-$70.13
Cash, Begining	$2,121.68
Cash, Ending	$2,051.55

Figure 3.3-2   Tax Bureau Cash Flows Statement

Cash

ID	Multi-Name	Amount	Balance	General ID	Transaction Date
24	88-654300-c-budgets < Cash receipts from center < Financial activities	$47,354.17	$2,121.68	6	2015-12-31
25	88-654300-c-budgets < Cash receipts from national budgets < Financial...	$95,000.00	$97,121.68	7	2016-01-02
26	909876505-n-operating expenses < Cash payments for operating expe...	-$283.71	$96,837.97	8	2016-01-12
27	909876506-n-operating expenses < Cash payments for operating expe...	-$277.71	$96,560.26	9	2016-01-12
28	88-654306-t-service packages < Cash payments for operating expenses...	-$60.00	$96,500.26	10	2016-01-13
29	909876505-t-salary < Cash payments for operating expenses < Operati...	-$2,810.00	$93,690.26	11	2016-01-31
30	909876506-t-salary < Cash payments for operating expenses < Operati...	-$2,860.00	$90,830.26	11	2016-01-31
31	88-654306-t-machinery < Cash payments for machinery < Operating act...	-$500.00	$90,330.26	12	2016-02-02
32	88-654307-t-machinery < Cash payments for machinery < Operating act...	-$400.00	$89,930.26	13	2016-02-11
33	88-654308-t-machinery < Cash payments for machinery < Operating act...	-$300.00	$89,630.26	14	2016-02-23
34	909876505-n-operating expenses < Cash payments for operating expe...	-$335.63	$89,294.63	15	2016-02-26
35	909876505-t-salary < Cash payments for operating expenses < Operati...	-$2,810.00	$86,484.63	16	2016-02-28
36	909876506-t-salary < Cash payments for operating expenses < Operati...	-$2,860.00	$83,624.63	16	2016-02-28
37	909876506-n-operating expenses < Cash payments for operating expe...	-$419.99	$83,204.64	17	2016-03-12
38	909876505-t-salary < Cash payments for operating expenses < Operati...	-$2,810.00	$80,394.64	18	2016-03-31
39	909876506-t-salary < Cash payments for operating expenses < Operati...	-$2,860.00	$77,534.64	18	2016-03-31
40	909876505-n-operating expenses < Cash payments for operating expe...	-$358.13	$77,176.51	19	2016-04-16
41	909876505-t-salary < Cash payments for operating expenses < Operati...	-$2,810.00	$74,366.51	20	2016-04-30
42	909876505-t-salary < Cash payments for operating expenses < Operati...	-$2,860.00	$71,506.51	20	2016-04-30
43	88-654310-t-supplies < Cash payments for operating expenses < Opera...	-$300.00	$71,206.51	21	2016-05-08
44	909876506-n-operating expenses < Cash payments for operating expe...	-$443.18	$70,763.33	22	2016-06-16
45	909876505-t-salary < Cash payments for operating expenses < Operati...	-$2,810.00	$67,953.33	23	2016-05-31

Figure 3.3-3   Tax Bureau Cash Account Table (Continue)

ID	Multi-Name	Amount	Balance	General ID	Transaction Date
46	909876506-t-salary < Cash payments for operating expenses < Operati...	-$2,860.00	$65,093.33	23	2016-05-31
47	88-654305-n-Bonds < Cash payments for investments < Investing activiti...	-$5,000.00	$60,093.33	24	2016-06-01
48	909876505-n-operating expenses < Cash payments for operating expe...	-$364.55	$59,728.78	25	2016-06-20
49	909876506-n-operating expenses < Cash payments for operating expe...	-$361.55	$59,367.23	26	2016-06-20
50	88-654308-t-supplies < Cash payments to suppliers < Operating activities	-$2,000.00	$57,367.23	27	2016-06-29
51	909876505-t-salary < Cash payments for operating expenses < Operati...	-$2,810.00	$54,557.23	28	2016-06-30
52	909876506-t-salary < Cash payments for operating expenses < Operati...	-$2,860.00	$51,697.23	28	2016-06-30
53	909876505-n-operating expenses < Cash payments for operating expe...	-$317.22	$51,380.01	29	2016-07-24
54	909876505-t-salary < Cash payments for operating expenses < Operati...	-$2,810.00	$48,570.01	30	2016-07-31
55	909876506-t-salary < Cash payments for operating expenses < Operati...	-$2,860.00	$45,710.01	30	2016-07-31
56	909876506-n-operating expenses < Cash payments for operating expe...	-$395.47	$45,314.54	31	2016-08-11
57	909876505-t-salary < Cash payments for operating expenses < Operati...	-$2,810.00	$42,504.54	32	2016-08-31
58	909876506-t-salary < Cash payments for operating expenses < Operati...	-$2,860.00	$39,644.54	32	2016-08-31
59	909876506-n-operating expenses < Cash payments for operating expe...	-$399.36	$39,245.18	33	2016-09-17
60	909876505-t-salary < Cash payments for operating expenses < Operati...	-$2,810.00	$36,435.18	34	2016-09-30
61	909876506-t-salary < Cash payments for operating expenses < Operati...	-$2,860.00	$33,575.18	34	2016-09-30
62	88-654306-t-computer < Cash payments for machinery < Operating acti...	-$2,400.00	$31,175.18	37	2016-10-01
63	88-654307-t- part activities < Cash payments for operating activities < O...	-$4,500.00	$26,675.18	38	2016-10-03
64	909876505-n-operating expenses < Cash payments for operating expe...	-$369.53	$26,305.65	39	2016-10-25
65	909876505-t-salary < Cash payments for operating expenses < Operati...	-$2,810.00	$23,495.65	40	2016-10-31
66	909876506-t-salary < Cash payments for operating expenses < Operati...	-$2,860.00	$20,635.65	40	2016-10-31
67	909876506-n-operating expenses < Cash payments for operating expe...	-$388.19	$20,247.46	41	2016-11-18
68	88-654306-t-service packages < Cash payments for operating expense...	-$1,400.00	$18,847.46	42	2016-11-19
69	909876505-t-salary < Cash payments for operating expenses < Operati...	-$2,810.00	$16,037.46	43	2016-11-30
70	909876506-t-salary < Cash payments for operating expenses < Operati...	-$2,860.00	$13,177.46	43	2016-11-30
71	909876505-n-operating expenses < Cash payments for operating expe...	-$664.58	$12,512.88	44	2016-12-28
72	909876506-n-operating expenses < Cash payments for operating expe...	-$670.58	$11,842.30	45	2016-12-28
73	88-654308-t-supplies < Cash payments to suppliers < Operating activities	-$2,500.00	$9,342.30	46	2016-12-28
74	88-654306-t-computer < Cash payments for machinery < Operating acti...	-$2,400.00	$6,942.30	47	2016-12-29
75	909876505-t-salary < Cash payments for operating expenses < Operati...	-$2,810.00	$4,132.30	48	2016-12-31
76	909876506-t-salary < Cash payments for operating expenses < Operati...	-$2,860.00	$1,272.30	48	2016-12-31
77	88-654304-c-investment income < Cash receipts from investments < Inv...	$200.00	$1,472.30	49	2016-12-31
78	88-654305-c-investment income < Cash receipts from investments < Inv...	$459.25	$1,931.55	50	2016-12-31
79	88-654304-c-deposit interest income < Cash receipts from deposit inter...	$120.00	$2,051.55	51	2016-12-31

Figure 3.3-3   Tax Bureau Cash Account Table

The Figure 3.3-4 on the next page shows the Tax Bureau income statement. From the Figure 3.3-4, the amount of the earnings before income taxes is -$19,991.59 and the amount of the tax expenses is zero, so the amount of the net earnings of the Tax Bureau in this fiscal year is also -$19,991.59.

The Figure 3.3-5 on next pages shows the Tax Bureau balance sheet. From the Figure 3.3-5, the amount of total assets is $37,112.32, and the amount of the total liabilities and the shareholders' equity is also $37,112.32.

Income Statement

	Year ended: 12/31/2016	
Revenues		
Sales (received budgets)		$95,000.00
Cost		
Cost of goods sold		$0.00
Gross Margin		$95,000.00
Operating and administrative expenses		
Travelling expenses		-$4,296.38
Other expenses		-$1,753.00
Office supplies expenses		-$5,171.46
Salary expenses		-$68,040.00
Amortization expenses		-$26,550.00
Vehicle part expenses		-$8,500.00
Service package expenses		-$1,460.00
Tax expenses		$0.00
Other income		
Investment incomes		$659.25
Deposit interest incomes		$120.00
Earnings Before Income Taxes		-$19,991.59
Net Earnings		-$19,991.59
Retained Earnings,Begining		$0.00
Retained Earnings,Ending		-$19,991.59

Figure 3.3-4   Tax Bureau Income Statement

Balance Sheet

	As at 12/31/2016	
ASSETS		
Current assets		
Cash		$2,051.55
Supplies		$35.32
Account receivable		$0.00
		$2,086.87
Long term investments		
Bonds		$18,000.00
Equipment		
Vehicle		$118,000.00
Accumulated amortization: Vehicle		-$67,266.67
Computer		$5,900.00
Accumulated amortization: Computer		-$737.50
		$55,895.83
Total Assets		$75,982.70

Figure 3.3-5   Tax Bureau Balance Sheet Statement (Continue)

LIABILITIES	
Current liabilities	
Account payable	$5,340.00
Tax payable	$0.00
	$5,340.00
Total Liability	$5,340.00
SHAREHOLDERS' EQUITY	
Owners capital	
Budgets capital	$90,634.29
Retined earnings	-$19,991.59
Accumulated other comprehensive income	$0.00
Total Shareholders' Equity	$70,642.70
Total Liabilities and Shareholders' Equity	$75,982.70

Figure 3.3-5   Tax Bureau Balance Sheet Statement

3.4 Business Bank1

The Business Bank1 has two class of transactions. One is itself transaction; another is only transaction of other organizations and individuals' deposit change. The transactions itself are first recorded. After that, the transactions of other organizations and individuals are recorded according to other organization's names.

3.4.1 An Accounting Fiscal Year of the Business Bank1

In the new fiscal year, the Business Bank1 occurs the following two class of transactions: the Business Bank2 itself transactions and the customer deposit transactions.

3.4.1.1 Business Bank1 Itself Transactions

- On January 2, 2016, the Business Bank1 purchases the supplies $162 (supplies1 $14*7 and supplies2 $16*4) from the Proprietorship2 (phone number: 123456080) for cash -$162. The multi-subaccount name of the Cash account and transaction sub-equation respectively are:

    88-654310-t-supplies < Cash payments for operating expenscs < Operating activities

- On January 10, 2016, A1 transfers $10,000 to his or her second account in the Business Bank2. The multi-subaccount name of the Cash account and the transaction sub-equation are respectively:

  909876501-d-deposits < Cash receipts from customers deposits < Operating

  Cash (1): -10000 = Deposits payable (2): -10000

- On January 13, 2016, the Business Bank1 purchases the following supplies (inventories) -$4,660 from the Company3 (phone number: 123456782) for cash - $2,000 and other on credit. Here, the supplies will be recorded as the Office supplies expenses for simplification.

  Inven121 < Inven12 < Inven1: 0.8*200

  Inven122 < Inven12 < Inven1: 50*30

  Inven21 < Inven2: 30*30

  Inven221 < Inven22 < Inven2: 30*30

  PPUK parts < ASD parts < Inven2: 40*30

  The multi-subaccount name of the Cash account and transaction sub-equation respectively are:

  88-654308-t-suppliers < Cash payments to suppliers < Operating activities

  Cash (1): -2000 = Account payable (2): 2660 + Office supplies expenses (5): - 4660

- On January 18, 2016, the Business Bank1 pays -$148.78 cash to A8 (SIN: 909876508) for the Travelling expenses (travel allowance) $91.78 and the Other expenses (meals: food321: $27*1 + food322: $30*1) $57. The multi-subaccount name of the Cash account and transaction sub-equation are respectively:

  909876508-n-operating expenses < Cash payments for operating expenses < Operating activities

  Cash (1): -148.78 = Travelling expenses (5): -91.78 + other expenses (5): 57

The twin multi-subaccount name of the Cash account and the twin transaction sub-equation are respectively:

909876508-d-deposits < Cash receipts from customers deposits < Operating

Cash (1): 148.78 = Deposits payable (2): 148.78

- On January 23, 2016, the Business Bank1 pays -$179.59 cash to A7 (SIN: 909876507) for the Travelling expenses (travel allowance) $97.59 and the Other expenses (meals: food613: $26*2 + food614: $30*1) $82.

- On January 26, 2016, A12 receives cash $13,000 from his or her primary account in the Business Bank2. The multi-subaccount name of the Cash account and the transaction sub-equation are respectively:

909876512-d-deposits < Cash receipts from customers deposits < Operating

Cash (1): 13000 = Deposits payable (2): 13000

- On February 26, 2016, the Business Bank1 purchases one Car1 part2 from the Company2 (phone number: 123456783) for cash $5200 and other on credit. The multi-subaccount name of the Cash account and transaction sub-equation respectively are:

88-654307-t-supplies < Cash payments for operating expenses < Operating activities

Cash (1): -5200 = Account payable (2): 2000 + Vehicle part expenses (5): -7200

- On January 27, 2016, the Business Bank1 pays -$232.31 cash to A9 (SIN: 909876509) for the Travelling expenses (travel allowance) $132.31 and the Other expenses (meals: food311: $20*2 + food322: $30*2) $100.

- On January 31, 2016, the Business Bank1 pays three employees' salary expenses for cash -$8,660. The two multi-subaccount names of the Cash account and the transaction sub-equation respectively are:

909876507-t-salary < Cash payments for operating expenses < Operating activities

909876508-t-salary < Cash payments for operating expenses < Operating activities

909876509-t-salary < Cash payments for operating expenses < Operating activities

Cash (1): -3000 + Cash (1): -2910 + Cash (1): 2750 = Salary expenses (5): -8660

The twin three multi-subaccount names of the Cash account and the twin transaction sub-equation are respectively:

88-654307-d-deposits < Cash receipts from customers deposits < Operating activities

88-654308-d-deposits < Cash receipts from customers deposits < Operating activities

88-654309-d-deposits < Cash receipts from customers deposits < Operating activities

Cash (1): 3000 + Cash (1): 2910 + Cash (1): 2750 = Deposits payable (2): 3000 + Deposits payable (2): 2910 + Deposits payable (2): 2750

- On February 1, 2016, the Business Bank1 purchases one Car2 $39,000 from the Company1 (phone number: 123456784) for cash -$19,000 and other on credit. The multi-subaccount name of the Cash account and transaction sub-equation respectively are:

  88-654306-t-machinery < Cash payments for machinery < Operating activities

  Cash (1): -19000 + Vehicle (1): 39000 = Account payable (2): 20000

- On February 21, 2016, the Business Bank1 pays -$290.33 cash to A9 (SIN: 909876509) for the Travelling expenses (travel allowance) $178.33 and the Other expenses (meals: food611: $20*3 + food621: $26*2) $112.

- On February 24, 2016, the Business Bank1 pays -$226.44 cash to A8 (SIN: 909876508) for the Travelling expenses (travel allowance) $130.44 and the Other expenses (meals: food611: $20*2 + food622: $28*2) $96.

- On February 28, 2016, the Business Bank1 pays three employees' salary expenses for cash -$8,660 repeatedly.

- On March 20, 2016, the Business Bank1 pays -$252.59 cash to A9 (SIN: 909876509) for the Travelling expenses (travel allowance) $148.59 and the Other expenses (meals: food53: $16*3 + food622: $28*2) $104.

- On March 24, 2016, the Business Bank1 pays -$226.44 cash to A7 (SIN: 909876500) for the Travelling expenses (travel allowance) $130.44 and the Other expenses (meals: food611: $20*2 + food622: $28*2) $96.

- On March 29, 2016, the Business Bank1 pays -$148.93 cash to A8 (SIN: 909876508) for the Travelling expenses (travel allowance) $97.93 and the Other expenses (meals: food312: $24*1 + food321: $27*1) $51.

- On March 31, 2016, the Business Bank1 pays three employees' salary expenses for cash -$8,660 repeatedly.

- On April 8, 2016, the Business Bank1 pays -$255.17 cash to A9 (SIN: 909876509) for the Travelling expenses (travel allowance) $147.17 and the Other expenses (meals: food613: $26*2 + food622: $28*2) $108.

- On April 29, 2016, the Business Bank1 pays -$219.94 cash to A7 (SIN: 909876507) for the Travelling expenses (travel allowance) $117.94 and the Other expenses (meals: food312: $24*2 + food321: $27*2) $102.

- On April 30, 2016, the Business Bank1 pays three employees' salary expenses for cash -$8,660 repeatedly.

- On May 14, 2016, the Business Bank1 pays -$263.47 cash to A9 (SIN: 909876509) for the Travelling expenses (travel allowance) $151.47 and the Other expenses (meals: food222: $13*4 + food311: $20*3) $112.

- On May 31, 2016, the Business Bank1 pays three employees' salary expenses for cash -$8,660 repeatedly.

- On June 5, 2016, the Business Bank1 pays -$153.37 cash to A8 (SIN: 909876508) for the Travelling expenses (travel allowance) $99.37 and the Other expenses (meals: food613: $26*1 + food622: $28*1) $54.

- On June 16, 2016, the Business Bank1 pays -$229.58 cash to A9 (SIN: 909876509) for the Travelling expenses (travel allowance) $133.58 and the Other expenses (meals: food23: $16*3 + food312: $24*2) $96.

- On June 30, 2016, the Business Bank1 pays three employees' salary expenses for cash -$8,660 repeatedly.

- On July 4, 2016, the Business Bank1 pays -$279.41 cash to A9 (SIN: 909876509) for the Travelling expenses (travel allowance) $162.41 and the Other expenses (meals: food44: $15*3 + food612: $24*3) $117.

- On July 31, 2016, the Business Bank1 pays three employees' salary expenses for cash -$8,660 repeatedly.

- On July 31, 2016, the Business Bank1 records the Amortization expenses $1,633.33 of a computer server2 (-$787.5, seven months), a computer2 (-$437.5, seven months), and a computer3 (-$408.33, seven months). The transaction sub-equation is:

  Accumulated amortization: Computer (1): -787.5 + Accumulated amortization: Computer (1): -437.5 + Accumulated amortization: Computer (1): -408.33 = Amortization expenses (5): -787.5 + Amortization expenses (5): -437.5 + Amortization expenses (5): -408.33

- On July 31, 2016, the Business Bank1 cancels the balances of the Computer account and the Accumulated amortization: Computer account because these computers have used for two years. The transaction sub-equation is:

  Computer (1): -2700 + Computer (1): -1500 + Computer (1): -1400 + Accumulated amortization: Computer (1): 2700 + Accumulated amortization: Computer (1): 1500 + Accumulated amortization: Computer (1): 1400 = 0

- On August 1, 2016, the Business Bank1 purchases one Computer server1 $2,800, one Computer1 $1,600, and one Computer2 $1,500 from the Company1 (phone number: 123456784) for cash -$5,000 and other on credit. The multi-subaccount name of the Cash account and transaction sub-equation respectively are:

  88-654306-t-machinery < Cash payments for machinery < Operating activities

  Cash (1): -5000 + Computer (1): 2800 + Computer (1): 1600 + Computer (1): 1500 = Account payable (2): 900

- On August 14, 2016, the Business Bank1 pays -$284.33 cash to A9 (SIN: 909876509) for the Travelling expenses (travel allowance) $166.33 and the Other expenses (meals: food611: $20*2 + food621: $26*3) $118.

- On August 17, 2016, the Business Bank1 pays -$142.72 cash to A8 (SIN: 909876508) for the Travelling expenses (travel allowance) $90.72 and the Other expenses (meals: food514: $11*2 + food614: $30*1) $52.

- On August 31, 2016, the Business Bank1 pays three employees' salary expenses for cash -$8,660 repeatedly.

- On September 9, 2016, the Business Bank1 pays -$191.51 cash to A7 (SIN: 909876507) for the Travelling expenses (travel allowance) $101.51 and the Other expenses (meals: food43: $14*3 + food612: $24*2) $90.

- On September 12, 2016, the Business Bank1 pays -$18,000 cash to the Company1 (phone number: 123456784) with the General ID 900. The multi-subaccount name of the Cash account is:

  88-654306-t-machinery < Cash payments for machinery < Operating activities

- On September 19, 2016, the Business Bank1 pays -$261.35 cash to A9 (SIN: 909876509) for the Travelling expenses (travel allowance) $149.35 and the Other expenses (meals: food222: $13*4 + food322: $30*2) $112.

- On September 30 2016, the Business Bank1 pays three employees' salary expenses for cash -$8,660 repeatedly.

- On October 10, 2016, the Business Bank1 pays -$157.94 cash to A8 (SIN: 909876508) for the Travelling expenses (travel allowance) $101.94 and the Other expenses (meals: food511: $8*3 + food53: $16*2) $56.

- On October 18, 2016, the Business Bank1 pays -$2,660 cash to the Company3 (phone number: 123456782) with the General ID 890. The multi-subaccount name of the Cash account and transaction sub-equation respectively are:

  88-654308-t-suppliers < Cash payments to suppliers < Operating activities

- On October 25, 2016, the Business Bank1 pays -$268.73 cash to A9 (SIN: 909876509) for the Travelling expenses (travel allowance) $154.73 and the Other expenses (meals: food123: $15*4 + food321: $27*2) $114.

- On October 31, 2016, the Business Bank1 pays three employees' salary expenses for cash -$8,660 repeatedly.

- On November 18, 2016, the Business Bank1 pays -$286.66 cash to A9 (SIN: 909876509) for the Travelling expenses (travel allowance) $162.66 and the Other expenses (meals: food53: $16*4 + food614: $30*2) $124.

- On November 30, 2016, the Business Bank1 pays three employees' salary expenses for cash -$8,660 repeatedly.

- On December 11, 2016, the Business Bank1 pays -$1,500 cash to the Company1 (phone number: 123456784) with the General ID 900 (-$600) and the General ID 940 (-$900). The multi-subaccount name of the Cash account is:

  88-654306-t-machinery < Cash payments for machinery < Operating activities

- On December 17, 2016, the Business Bank1 pays -$220.85 cash to A9 (SIN: 909876509) for the Travelling expenses (travel allowance) $121.85 and the Other expenses (meals: food222: $13*3 + food311: $20*3) $99.

- On December 28, 2016, the Business Bank1 pays -$238.88 cash to A7 (SIN: 909876507) for the Travelling expenses (travel allowance) $130.88 and the Other expenses (meals: food53: $16*3 + food614: $30*2) $108.

- On December 30, 2016, the Business Bank1 pays -$1,400 cash to the Company1 (phone number: 123456784) with the General ID 900. The multi-subaccount name of the Cash account is:

88-654306-t-suppliers < Cash payments to suppliers < Operating activities

- On December 31, 2016, the Business Bank1 receives cash $38,650 from the Company1 for interest income $22,500 of the Note11 ($250,000, 9%) and interest income $16,150 of the Note15 ($170,000, 9.5%). Here, the interest incomes of the notes are recorded as the Sales (notes interest) account for the Business Banks. The multi-subaccount name of the Cash account and transaction sub-equation respectively are:

88-654306-c-customers < Cash receipts from customers < Operating activities

Cash (1): 38650 = Sales (notes interest) (4): 22500 + Sales (notes interest) (4): 16150

- On December 31, 2016, the Business Bank1 receives cash $35,600 ($12,600 + $23,000) from the Company2 for interest income of the Note12 ($140,000, 9%) and the Note14 ($250,000, 9.2%). The multi-subaccount name of the Cash account is:
88-654307-c-customers < Cash receipts from customers < Operating activities

- On December 31, 2016, the Business Bank1 receives cash $18,000 from the Company3 for interest income of the Note13 ($200,000, 9%). The multi-subaccount name of the Cash account is:

88-654308-c-customers < Cash receipts from customers < Operating activities

- On December 31, 2016, the Business Bank1 receives cash $2,500 from the Cash Management Center for bank fee income. The multi-subaccount name of the Cash account and transaction sub-equation respectively are:

88-654300-t-bank fee income < Cash receipts from customers < Operating activities

- On December 31, the Business Bank1 pays -$2,400 cash to the bond holders for the Bond interest expenses of the Bond11 (one-level subaccount "Bond11-interest"). Here, there is some twin transactions for its individuals whose primary accounts (seeing the Figure 2.1-3 on the page 13) are opened in the Business Bank1, and other individuals are recorded in the Business Bank2. The twin transactions for its organization customers have been recorded by these related organizations. Therefore, the multi-subaccount names of the Cash account and the transaction sub-equations respectively are:

88-654302-t-bond interest < Cash payments to bond holders< Operating activities

88-654303-t-bond interest < Cash payments to bond holders< Operating activities

88-654305-t-bond interest < Cash payments to bond holders< Operating activities

88-654306-t-bond interest < Cash payments to bond holders< Operating activities

88-654308-t-bond interest < Cash payments to bond holders< Operating activities

88-654309-t-bond interest < Cash payments to bond holders< Operating activities

909876507-t-bond interest < Cash payments to bond holders< Operating activities

909876509-t-bond interest < Cash payments to bond holders< Operating activities

909876513-t-bond interest < Cash payments to bond holders< Operating activities

909876514-t-bond interest < Cash payments to bond holders< Operating activities

Cash (1): -240 + Cash (1): -200 + Cash (1): -280 + Cash (1): -400 + Cash (1): -320 + Cash (1): -200 + Cash (1): -360 + Cash (1): -240 = Bond interest expenses (5): -2240

Cash (1): -120 + Cash (1): -40 = Bond interest expenses (5): -160

The twin transaction sub-equation for 909876507, 909876509, 909876513, and 909876514 is:

Cash (1): 360 + Cash (1): 240 + Cash (1): 120 + Cash (1): 40 = Deposits payable (2): 360 + Deposits payable (2): 240 + Deposits payable (2): 120 + Deposits payable (2):40

- On the same day, the Business Bank1 pays -$1,680 cash to the bond holders for the Bond interest expenses of the Bond12 (one-level subaccount "Bond12-interest"). Here, there is some twin transactions for the individuals whose primary accounts (seeing the Figure 2.1-3 on the page 13) are opened in the Business Bank1, and other individuals are recorded in the Business Bank2. Therefore, the multi-subaccount names of the Cash account and the transaction sub-equation respectively are:

88-654305-t-bond interest< Cash payments to bond holders< Operating activities

88-654307-t-bond interest< Cash payments to bond holders< Operating activities

88-654309-t-bond interest< Cash payments to bond holders< Operating activities

88-654310-t-bond interest< Cash payments to bond holders< Operating activities

909876501-t-bond interest< Cash payments to bond holders< Operating activities

909876502-t-bond interest< Cash payments to bond holders< Operating activities

909876504-t-bond interest< Cash payments to bond holders< Operating activities

909876521-t-bond interest< Cash payments to bond holders< Operating activities

Cash (1): -126 + Cash (1): -336 + Cash (1): -126 + Cash (1): -252 + Cash (1): -210 + Cash (1): -84 + Cash (1): -294 + Cash (1): -252 = Bond interest expenses (5): -1680

The twin transaction sub-equation for 909876501, 909876502, and 909876504 is:

Cash (1): 210 + Cash (1): 84 + Cash (1): 294 = Deposits payable (2): 210 + Deposits payable (2): 84 + Deposits payable (2): 294

- On the same day, the Business Bank1 pays -$2,250 cash to the bond holders for the Bond interest expenses of the Bond13 (one-level subaccount "Bond13-interest"). Here, there is some twin transactions for the individuals whose primary accounts (seeing the Figure 2.1-3 on the page 13) are opened in the Business Bank1, and other individuals are recorded in the Business Bank2. Therefore, the multi-subaccount names of the Cash account and the transaction sub-equations respectively are:

88-654305-t-bond interest< Cash payments to bond holders< Operating activities

88-654306-t-bond interest< Cash payments to bond holders< Operating activities

88-654309-t-bond interest< Cash payments to bond holders< Operating activities

909876503-t-bond interest< Cash payments to bond holders< Operating activities

909876505-t-bond interest< Cash payments to bond holders< Operating activities

909876506-t-bond interest< Cash payments to bond holders< Operating activities

909876515-t-bond interest< Cash payments to bond holders< Operating activities

909876517-t-bond interest< Cash payments to bond holders< Operating activities

909876518-t-bond interest< Cash payments to bond holders< Operating activities

909876519-t-bond interest< Cash payments to bond holders< Operating activities

909876521-t-bond interest< Cash payments to bond holders< Operating activities

Cash (1): -270 + Cash (1): -135 + Cash (1): -90 + Cash (1): -270 + Cash (1): -180 + Cash (1): -315 + Cash (1): -180 + Cash (1): -225 + Cash (1): -135 = Bond interest expenses (5): -1800

Cash (1): -270 + Cash (1): -180 = Bond interest expenses (5): -450

The twin transaction sub-equation for the individual 909876503, 909876505, 909876506, 909876515, and 909876518 is:

Cash (1): 270 + Cash (1): 180 + Cash (1): 315 + Cash (1): 180 + Cash (1): 135 = Deposits payable (2): 270 + Deposits payable (2): 180 + Deposits payable (2): 315 + Deposits payable (2): 180 + Deposits payable (2): 135

- On the same day, the Business Bank1 pays cash -$2,400 to its customers (not including itself) for primary deposit interest (interest expenses). Here, the Deposit interest expenses are recorded as the one-level subaccount of the Cost of notes interest parent account for the Business Banks. In addition, there is some twin transactions for its individuals whose primary accounts (seeing the Figure 2.1-3 on the page 13) are opened in the Business Bank1, and other individuals are recorded in the Business Bank2. The twin transactions for its organization customers have been recorded by these related organizations. The multi-subaccount names of the Cash account and transaction sub-equation respectively are:

88-654302-t-deposit interest expenses < Cash payments for operating expenses < Operating activities

88-654303-t-deposit interest expenses < Cash payments for operating expenses < Operating activities

88-654306-t-deposit interest expenses < Cash payments for operating expenses < Operating activities

88-654309-t-deposit interest expenses < Cash payments for operating expenses < Operating activities

909876501-t-deposit interest expenses < Cash payments for operating expenses < Operating activities

909876502-t-deposit interest expenses < Cash payments for operating expenses < Operating activities

909876503-t-deposit interest expenses < Cash payments for operating expenses < Operating activities

909876504-t-deposit interest expenses < Cash payments for operating expenses < Operating activities

909876505-t-deposit interest expenses < Cash payments for operating expenses < Operating activities

909876506-t-deposit interest expenses < Cash payments for operating expenses < Operating activities

909876507-t-deposit interest expenses < Cash payments for operating expenses < Operating activities

909876508-t-deposit interest expenses < Cash payments for operating expenses < Operating activities

909876509-t-deposit interest expenses < Cash payments for operating expenses < Operating activities

909876513-t-deposit interest expenses < Cash payments for operating expenses < Operating activities

909876514-t-deposit interest expenses < Cash payments for operating expenses <

Operating activities

909876515-t-deposit interest expenses < Cash payments for operating expenses < Operating activities

909876516-t-deposit interest expenses < Cash payments for operating expenses < Operating activities

909876518-t-deposit interest expenses < Cash payments for operating expenses < Operating activities

909876524-t-deposit interest expenses < Cash payments for operating expenses < Operating activities

909876525-t-deposit interest expenses < Cash payments for operating expenses < Operating activities

Cash (1): -120 + Cash (1): -120 + Cash (1): -120 + Cash (1): -120 + Cash (1): -120 + Cash (1): -120 + Cash (1): -120 + Cash (1): -120 + Cash (1): -120 = Cost of notes interest (5): -1080

Cash (1): -120 + Cash (1): -120 + Cash (1): -120 + Cash (1): -120 + Cash (1): -120 + Cash (1): -120 + Cash (1): -120 + Cash (1): -120 + Cash (1): -120 = Cost of notes interest (5): -1080

Cash (1): -120 + Cash (1): -120 = Cost of notes interest (5): -240

The twin transaction sub-equations for the above individuals are:

Cash (1): 120 + Cash (1): 120 + Cash (1): 120 + Cash (1): 120 + Cash (1): 120 = Deposits payable (2): 120 + Deposits payable (2): 120 + Deposits payable (2): 120 + Deposits payable (2): 120 + Deposits payable (2): 120

Cash (1): 120 + Cash (1): 120 + Cash (1): 120 + Cash (1): 120 + Cash (1): 120 = Deposits payable (2): 120 + Deposits payable (2): 120 + Deposits payable (2): 120 + Deposits payable (2): 120 + Deposits payable (2): 120

Cash (1): 120 + Cash (1): 120 + Cash (1): 120 + Cash (1): 120 + Cash (1): 120 =
Deposits payable (2): 120 + Deposits payable (2): 120 + Deposits payable (2): 120
+ Deposits payable (2): 120 + Deposits payable (2): 120

Cash (1): 120 = Deposits payable (2): 120

- On the same day, the Business Bank1 receives cash $466 (= $246 + $220) for
  investment interest of the Bond21 ($6,000) and the Bond22 ($5,000) from the
  Business Bank2. The multi-subaccount name of the Cash account and transaction
  sub-equation respectively are:

  88-654305-c-investment income < Cash receipts from investments < Investing
  activities

  Cash (1): 466 = Investment incomes (4):246 + Investment incomes (4): 220

- On December 31, 2016, the Business Bank1 pays three employees' salary expenses
  for cash -$8,660 repeatedly.
- On the same day, the Business Bank1 records the Office supplies expenses -$213.95.
  The transaction sub-equation is:

  Supplies (1): -213.95 = Office supplies expenses (5): -213.95

- On the same day, the Business Bank1 records the Vehicle's amortization expenses -
  $22,100 (5 years, straight line) which includes a Truck1 ($9,000, one year), a
  Car1($8,000, one year), and a new Car2 ($7,150, eleven months). The two
  transaction sub-equations are:

  Accumulated amortization: Vehicle (1): -9000 + Accumulated amortization:
  Vehicle (1): -8000 + Accumulated amortization: Vehicle (1): 7150 = Amortization
  expenses (5): -9000 + Amortization expenses (5): -8000 + Amortization expenses

(5): -7150

- On the same day, the Business Bank1 records the Computer's amortization expenses $1,229.16 five months (2 years, straight line) which includes a new computer server1 ($583.33), a new computer1 ($333.33), and a new computer2 ($312.5). The transaction sub-equation is:

  Accumulated amortization: Computer (1): -583.33 + Accumulated amortization: Computer (1): -333.33 + Accumulated amortization: Computer (1): -312.5 = Amortization expenses (5): -583.33 + Amortization expenses (5): -333.33 + Amortization expenses (5): -312.5

- On December 31, the Business Bank1 records the Tax expenses $0 and the Tax payable $0. The multi-subaccount name forms of the Tax expenses and the Tax payable accounts all are the 'n'. The transaction sub-equation is:

  0 = Tax payable (2): 0 + Tax expenses (5): 0

So far, I have entered all transactions of the Business Bank1 in the fiscal year 2016. After getting the Income Statement and clicking the "Yes" button for new fiscal year, I can get the Balance Sheet of the Business Bank1.

3.4.1.2 Customer Deposit Transactions

The followings is a list of all deposit transactions which are ordered by organizations or companies.

- **Cash Management Center.**
- On January 2, 2016, the Cash Management Center's cash deposit decreases $85,000. Please pay attention. This transaction is not the Business Bank1's transaction and is only an intermediate process between the Cash Management Center and the Central Bank. Therefore, the ID in three level subaccount of the Cash account is the Cash Management Center itself. In fact, the transaction can be recorded by various bank

cards and internet automatically. For simplification, the multi-subaccount name form of the Deposits payable account is the 'n'. The multi-subaccount name of the Cash account and transaction sub-equation respectively are:

88-654300-d-deposits < Cash receipts from customers deposits < Operating activities

Cash (1): -85000 = Deposits payable (2): -85000 = 0

- On January 2, 2016, the Cash Management Center's cash deposit decreases -$90,000 and -$95,000 respectively. The two multi-subaccount name of the Cash account and transaction sub-equation respectively are:

  88-654300-d-deposits < Cash receipts from customers deposits < Operating activities

  Cash (1): -185000 = Deposits payable (2): -185000

- On June 1, 2016, the Cash Management Center's cash deposit decreases -$25,000.
- On December 31, 2016, the Cash Management Center's cash deposit decreases - $2,400.
- On December 31, 2016, individual A1's cash deposit increases $200.
- On December 31, 2016, individual A2's cash deposit increases $200.
- On December 31, 2016, individual A3's cash deposit increases $200.
- On December 31, 2016, individual A7's cash deposit increases $200.
- On December 31, 2016, individual A9's cash deposit increases $200
- On December 31, 2016, individual A15's cash deposit increases $200.
- On December 31, 2016, individual A16's cash deposit increases $200.
- On December 31, 2016, the Cash Management Center's cash deposit decreases - $2,500.
- On December 31, 2016, the Cash Management Center's cash deposit increases $656.25.

- On December 31, 2016, the Cash Management Center's cash deposit increases $xxx.

- **Central Bank.**

- On January 18, 2016, the A1's cash deposit decreases -$39.

- On January 21, 2016, the A1's cash deposit increases $176.56.

- On January 31, 2016, the A1's cash deposit increases $2,800.

- On January 31, 2016, the A2's cash deposit increases $2,850.

- On February 28, 2016, the A1's cash deposit increases $2,800.

- On February 28, 2016, the A2's cash deposit increases $2,850.

- On March 26, 2016, the A2's cash deposit decreases -$72.

- On March 28, 2016, the A2's cash deposit increases $459.61.

- On March 31, 2016, the A1's cash deposit increases $2,800.

- On March 31, 2016, the A2's cash deposit increases $2,850.

- On April 15, 2016, the A2's cash deposit decreases -$50.

- On April 19, 2016, the A2's cash deposit increases $159.78.

- On April 30, 2016, the A1's cash deposit increases $2,800.

- On April 30, 2016, the A2's cash deposit increases $2,850.

- On May 31, 2016, the A1's cash deposit increases $2,800.

- On May 31, 2016, the A2's cash deposit increases $2,850.

- On June 18, 2016, the A2's cash deposit decreases -$136.

- On June 22, 2016, the A2's cash deposit increases $477.25.

- On June 30, 2016, the A1's cash deposit increases $2,800.

- On June 30, 2016, the A2's cash deposit increases $2,850.

- On July 31, 2016, the A1's cash deposit increases $2,800.

- On July 31, 2016, the A2's cash deposit increases $2,850.

- On August 31, 2016, the A1's cash deposit increases $2,800.

- On August 31, 2016, the A2's cash deposit increases $2,850.

- On September 5, 2016, the A2's cash deposit decreases -$59.

- On September 7, 2016, the A2's cash deposit increases $233.16.

- On September 30, 2016, the A1's cash deposit increases $2,800.

- On September 30, 2016, the A2's cash deposit increases $2,850.

- On October 31, 2016, the A1's cash deposit increases $2,800.

- On October 31, 2016, the A2's cash deposit increases $2,850.

- On November 30, 2016, the A1's cash deposit increases $2,800.

- On November 30, 2016, the A2's cash deposit increases $2,850.

- On December 8, 2016, the A1's cash deposit decreases -$120.

- On December 11, 2016, the A2's cash deposit increases $233.16.

- On December 31, 2016, the A1's cash deposit increases $2,800.

- On December 31, 2016, the A2's cash deposit increases $2,850.

- **Government1.**

- On January 2, 2016, the Government1's cash deposit increases $90,000. The multi-subaccount name of the Cash account and transaction sub-equation respectively are:
  88-654302-d-deposits < Cash receipts from customers deposits < Operating activities

  Cash (1): 90000 = Deposits payable (2): 90000 = 0

- On January 6, 2016, the A3's cash deposit decreases -$108.

- On January 9, 2016, the Government1's cash deposit decreases -$307.23.

- On January 9, 2016, the A3's cash deposit increases $307.23.

- On January 15, 2016, the Government1's cash deposit increases $600.

- On January 31, 2016, the Government1's cash deposit decreases -$5,660.

- On January 31, 2016, the A3's cash deposit increases $2,810.

- On January 31, 2016, the A4's cash deposit increases $2,850.

- On February 21, 2016, the Government1's cash deposit decreases -$500.

- On February 25, 2016, the A3's cash deposit decreases -$99.

- On February 28, 2016, the Government1's cash deposit decreases -$5,660.

- On February 28, 2016, the A3's cash deposit increases $2,810.

- On February 28, 2016, the A4's cash deposit increases $2,850.

- On February 28, 2016, the Government1's cash deposit decreases -$295.17.

- On February 28, 2016, the A3's cash deposit increases $295.17.

- On March 19, 2016, the A4's cash deposit decreases -$172.

- On March 22, 2016, the Government1's cash deposit decreases -$558.34.

- On March 22, 2016, the A4's cash deposit increases $558.34.

- On March 31, 2016, the Government1's cash deposit decreases -$5,660.

- On March 31, 2016, the A3's cash deposit increases $2,810.

- On March 31, 2016, the A4's cash deposit increases $2,850.

- On April 20, 2016, the A4's cash deposit decreases -$100.

- On April 24, 2016, the Government1's cash deposit decreases -$283.53.

- On April 24, 2016, the A4's cash deposit increases $283.53.

- On April 30, 2016, the Government1's cash deposit decreases -$5,660.

- On April 30, 2016, the A3's cash deposit increases $2,810.

- On April 30, 2016, the A4's cash deposit increases $2,850.

- On April 30, 2016, the Government1's cash deposit decreases -$330.

- On April 30, 2016, the Government1's cash deposit decreases -$60.

- On May 1, 2016, the Government1's cash deposit decreases -$8,000.

- On May 14, 2016, the A3's cash deposit decreases -$105.

- On May 16, 2016, the Government1's cash deposit decreases -$415.97.

- On May 16, 2016, the A3's cash deposit increases $415.97.

- On May 31, 2016, the Government1's cash deposit decreases -$5,660.

- On May 31, 2016, the A3's cash deposit increases $2,810.

- On May 31, 2016, the A4's cash deposit increases $2,850.

- On June 1, 2016, the Government1's cash deposit decreases -$5,000.

- On June 15, 2016, the A3's cash deposit decreases -$93.

- On June 17, 2016, the Government1's cash deposit decreases -$272.59.

- On June 17, 2016, the A3's cash deposit increases $272.59.

- On June 30, 2016, the Government1's cash deposit decreases -$5,660.

- On June 30, 2016, the A3's cash deposit increases $2,810.

- On June 30, 2016, the A4's cash deposit increases $2,850.

- On July 16, 2016, the A4's cash deposit decreases -$112.

- On July 19, 2016, the Government1's cash deposit decreases -$336.87.

- On July 19, 2016, the A4's cash deposit increases $336.87.

- On July 31, the Government1's cash deposit decreases -$5,660.

- On July 31, 2016, the A3's cash deposit increases $2,810.

- On July 31, 2016, the A4's cash deposit increases $2,850.

- On August 10, 2016, the A3's cash deposit decreases -$150.

- On August 13, 2016, the Government1's cash deposit decreases -$481.11.

- On August 13, 2016, the A3's cash deposit increases $481.11.

- On August 31, the Government1's cash deposit decreases -$5,660.

- On August 31, 2016, the A3's cash deposit increases $2,810.

- On August 31, 2016, the A4's cash deposit increases $2,850.

- On September 5, 2016, the A4's cash deposit decreases -$86.

- On September 7, 2016, the Government1's cash deposit decreases -$384.46.

- On September 7, 2016, the A4's cash deposit increases $384.46.

- On September 25, 2016, the Government1's cash deposit decreases -$3,200.

- On September 30, the Government1's cash deposit decreases -$5,660.

- On September 30, 2016, the A3's cash deposit increases $2,810.

- On September 30, 2016, the A4's cash deposit increases $2,850.

- On October 3, the Government1's cash deposit decreases -$990.

- On October 21, 2016, the A3's cash deposit decreases -$121.

- On October 24, 2016, the Government1's cash deposit decreases -$377.77.

- On October 24, 2016, the A3's cash deposit increases $377.77.

- On October 31, the Government1's cash deposit decreases -$5,660.

- On October 31, 2016, the A3's cash deposit increases $2,810.

- On October 31, 2016, the A4's cash deposit increases $2,850.

- On November 11, 2016, the A4's cash deposit decreases -$85.

- On November 14, 2016, the Government1's cash deposit decreases -$375.39.

- On November 14, 2016, the A4's cash deposit increases $375.39.

- On November 30, the Government1's cash deposit decreases -$5,660.

- On November 30, 2016, the A3's cash deposit increases $2,810.

- On November 30, 2016, the A4's cash deposit increases $2,850.

- On December 20, 2016, the A3's cash deposit decreases -$129.

- On December 23, 2016, the Government1's cash deposit decreases -$514.62.

- On December 23, 2016, the A3's cash deposit increases $514.62.

- On December 30, the Government1's cash deposit decreases -$2,000.

- On December 31, the Government1's cash deposit decreases -$5,660.

- On December 31, 2016, the A3's cash deposit increases $2,810.

- On December 31, 2016, the A4's cash deposit increases $2,850.

- On December 31, 2016, the Government1's cash deposit increases $240.

- On December 31, 2016, the Government1's cash deposit increases $500.25.

- On December 31, 2016, the Government1's cash deposit increases $120.

- **Tax Bureau.**

- On January 2, 2016, the Tax Bureau's cash deposit increases $95,000. The multi-subaccount name of the Cash account and transaction sub-equation respectively are: 88-654303-d-deposits < Cash receipts from customers deposits < Operating activities

  Cash (1): 95000 = Deposits payable (2): 95000 = 0

- On January 10, 2016, the A5's cash deposit decreases -$98.

- On January 10, 2016, the A6's cash deposit decreases -$92.

- On January 12, 2016, the Tax Bureau's cash deposit decreases -$283.71.

- On January 12, 2016, the A5's cash deposit increases $283.71.

- On January 12, 2016, the Tax Bureau's cash deposit decreases -$277.71.

- On January 12, 2016, the A6's cash deposit increases $277.71.

- On January 13, 2016, the Tax Bureau's cash deposit decreases -$60.

- On January 31, 2016, the Tax Bureau's cash deposit decreases -$5,670.

- On January 31, 2016, the A5's cash deposit increases $2,810.

- On January 31, 2016, the A6's cash deposit increases $2,860.

- On February 2, 2016, the Tax Bureau's cash deposit decreases -$500.

- On February 11, 2016, the Tax Bureau's cash deposit decreases -$400.

- On February 23, 2016, the Tax Bureau's cash deposit decreases -$300.

- On February 24, 2016, the A5's cash deposit decreases -$110.

- On February 26, 2016, the Tax Bureau's cash deposit decreases -$335.63.

- On February 26, 2016, the A5's cash deposit increases $335.63.

- On February 28, 2016, the Tax Bureau's cash deposit decreases -$5,670.

- On February 28, 2016, the A5's cash deposit increases $2,810.

- On February 28, 2016, the A6's cash deposit increases $2,860.

- On March 10, 2016, the A6's cash deposit decreases -$123.

- On March 12, 2016, the Tax Bureau's cash deposit decreases -$419.99.

- On March 12, 2016, the A6's cash deposit increases $419.99.

- On March 31, 2016, the Tax Bureau's cash deposit decreases -$5,670.

- On March 31, 2016, the A5's cash deposit increases $2,810.

- On March 31, 2016, the A6's cash deposit increases $2,860.

- On April 13, 2016, the A5's cash deposit decreases -$112.

- On April 16, 2016, the Tax Bureau's cash deposit decreases -$358.13.

- On April 16, 2016, the A5's cash deposit increases $358.13.

- On April 30, 2016, the Tax Bureau's cash deposit decreases -$5,670.

- On April 30, 2016, the A5's cash deposit increases $2,810.

- On April 30, 2016, the A6's cash deposit increases $2,860.

- On May 8, 2016, the Tax Bureau's cash deposit decreases -$300.

- On May 13, 2016, the A6's cash deposit decreases -$112.

- On May 16, 2016, the Tax Bureau's cash deposit decreases -$443.18.

- On May 16, 2016, the A6's cash deposit increases $443.18.

- On May 31, 2016, the Tax Bureau's cash deposit decreases -$5,670.

- On May 31, 2016, the A5's cash deposit increases $2,810.

- On May 31, 2016, the A6's cash deposit increases $2,860.

- On June 1, 2016, the Tax Bureau's cash deposit decreases -$5,000.

- On June 17, 2016, the A5's cash deposit decreases -$93.

- On June 17, 2016, the A6's cash deposit decreases -$90.

- On June 20, 2016, the Tax Bureau's cash deposit decreases -$364.55.

- On June 20, 2016, the A5's cash deposit increases $364.55.

- On June 20, 2016, the Tax Bureau's cash deposit decreases -$361.55.

- On June 20, 2016, the A6's cash deposit increases $361.55.

- On June 29, 2016, the Tax Bureau's cash deposit decreases -$2,000.

- On June 30, 2016, the Tax Bureau's cash deposit decreases -$5,670.

- On June 30, 2016, the A5's cash deposit increases $2,810.

- On June 30, 2016, the A6's cash deposit increases $2,860.

- On July 22, 2016, the A5's cash deposit decreases -$105.

- On July 24, 2016, the Tax Bureau's cash deposit decreases -$317.22.

- On July 24, 2016, the A5's cash deposit increases $317.22.

- On July 31, 2016, the Tax Bureau's cash deposit decreases -$5,670.

- On July 31, 2016, the A5's cash deposit increases $2,810.

- On July 31, 2016, the A6's cash deposit increases $2,860.

- On August 9, 2016, the A6's cash deposit decreases -$114.

- On August 11, 2016, the Tax Bureau's cash deposit decreases -$395.47.

- On August 11, 2016, the A6's cash deposit increases $395.47.

- On August 31, 2016, the Tax Bureau's cash deposit decreases -$5,670.

- On August 31, 2016, the A5's cash deposit increases $2,810.

- On August 31, 2016, the A6's cash deposit increases $2,860.

- On September 15, 2016, the A6's cash deposit decreases -$105.

- On September 17, 2016, the Tax Bureau's cash deposit decreases -$399.36.

- On September 17, 2016, the A6's cash deposit increases $399.36.

- On September 30, 2016, the Tax Bureau's cash deposit decreases -$5,670.

- On September 30, 2016, the A5's cash deposit increases $2,810.

- On September 30, 2016, the A6's cash deposit increases $2,860.

- On October 1, 2016, the Tax Bureau's cash deposit decreases -$2,400.

- On October 3, 2016, the Tax Bureau's cash deposit decreases -$4,500.

- On October 22, 2016, the A5's cash deposit decreases -$116.

- On October 25, 2016, the Tax Bureau's cash deposit decreases -$369.53.

- On October 25, 2016, the A5's cash deposit increases $369.53.

- On October 31, 2016, the Tax Bureau's cash deposit decreases -$5,670.

- On October 31, 2016, the A5's cash deposit increases $2,810.

- On October 31, 2016, the A6's cash deposit increases $2,860.

- On November 15, 2016, the A6's cash deposit decreases -$93.

- On November 18, 2016, the Tax Bureau's cash deposit decreases -$388.19.

- On November 18, 2016, the A6's cash deposit increases $388.19.

- On November 19, 2016, the Tax Bureau's cash deposit decreases -$1,400.

- On November 30, 2016, the Tax Bureau's cash deposit decreases -$5,670.

- On November 30, 2016, the A5's cash deposit increases $2,810.

- On November 30, 2016, the A6's cash deposit increases $2,860.

- On December 26, 2016, the A5's cash deposit decreases -$192.

- On December 26, 2016, the A6's cash deposit decreases -$198.

- On December 28, 2016, the Tax Bureau's cash deposit decreases -$664.58.

- On December 28, 2016, the A5's cash deposit increases $664.58.

- On December 28, 2016, the Tax Bureau's cash deposit decreases -$670.58.

- On December 28, 2016, the A6's cash deposit increases $670.58.

- On December 28, 2016, the Tax Bureau's cash deposit decreases -$2500.

- On December 29, 2016, the Tax Bureau's cash deposit decreases -$2400.

- On December 31, 2016, the Tax Bureau's cash deposit decreases -$5,670.

- On December 31, 2016, the A5's cash deposit increases $2,810.

- On December 31, 2016, the A6's cash deposit increases $2,860.

- On December 31, 2016, the Tax Bureau's cash deposit increases $200.

- On December 31, 2016, the Tax Bureau's cash deposit increases $459.25.

- On December 31, 2016, the Tax Bureau's cash deposit increases $120.

- On December 31, 2016, the Tax Bureau's cash deposit increases $x1.

- On December 31, 2016, the Tax Bureau's cash deposit increases $x2.

- On December 31, 2016, the Tax Bureau's cash deposit increases $x3.

- On December 31, 2016, the Tax Bureau's cash deposit increases $x4.

- On December 31, 2016, the Tax Bureau's cash deposit increases $x5.

- On December 31, 2016, the Tax Bureau's cash deposit increases $x6.

- On December 31, 2016, the Tax Bureau's cash deposit increases $x7.

- On December 31, 2016, the Tax Bureau's cash deposit decreases -$XX.

- **Company1.**
- On January 2, 2016, the Company1's cash deposit decreases -$500.

- On January 13, 2016, the Company1's cash deposit increases $60.

- On January 14, 2016, the Company1's cash deposit decreases -$11,000.

- On January 14, 2016, the Company1's cash deposit decreases -$8,000.

- On January 15, 2016, the Company1's cash deposit decreases -$415.67.

- On January 15, 2016, the A13's cash deposit increases $415.67.

- On January 16, 2016, the Company1's cash deposit decreases -$42.12.

- On January 16, 2016, the A15's cash deposit increases $42.12.

- On January 31, 2016, the Company1's cash deposit decreases -$2,040.

- On January 31, 2016, the Company1's cash deposit decreases -$1,000.

- On January 31, 2016, the Company1's cash deposit decreases -$8,400.

- On January 31, 2016, the A14's cash deposit increases $2,900.

- On January 31, 2016, the A13's cash deposit increases $2,600.

- On January 31, 2016, the A15's cash deposit increases $2,900.

- On February 1, 2016, the Company1's cash deposit increases $19,000.

- On February 1, 2016, the Company1's cash deposit increases $28,000.

- On February 1, 2016, the Company1's cash deposit increases $30,000.

- On February 1, 2016, the Company1's cash deposit decreases -$49.68.

- On February 1, 2016, the A14's cash deposit increases $49.68.

- On February 2, 2016, the Company1's cash deposit increases $500.

- On February 13, 2016, the Company1's cash deposit increases $800.

- On February 20, 2016, the Company1's cash deposit decreases -$557.83.

- On February 20, 2016, the A13's cash deposit increases $557.83.

- On February 25, 2016, the Company1's cash deposit increases $600.

- On February 27, 2016, the Company1's cash deposit increases $900.

- On February 28, 2016, the Company1's cash deposit decreases -$8,400.

- On February 28, 2016, the A14's cash deposit increases $2,900.

- On February 28, 2016, the A13's cash deposit increases $2,600.

- On February 28, 2016, the A15's cash deposit increases $2,900.

- On March 1, 2016, the Company1's cash deposit increases $19,000.

- On March 4, 2016, the Company1's cash deposit decreases -$2,400.

- On March 4, 2016, the Company1's cash deposit decreases -$1,600.

- On March 6, 2016, the Company1's cash deposit increases $1,000.

- On March 9, 2016, the Company1's cash deposit increases $2,000.

- On March 23, 2016, the Company1's cash deposit decreases -$516.37.

- On March 23, 2016, the A13's cash deposit increases $516.37.

- On March 25, 2016, the Company1's cash deposit increases $600.

- On March 30, 2016, the Company1's cash deposit decreases -$239.73.

- On March 30, 2016, the A14's cash deposit increases $239.73.

- On March 31, 2016, the Company1's cash deposit decreases -$8,400.

- On March 31, 2016, the A14's cash deposit increases $2,900.

- On March 31, 2016, the A13's cash deposit increases $2,600.

- On March 31, 2016, the A15's cash deposit increases $2,900.

- On April 12, 2016, the Company1's cash deposit decreases -$1,000.

- On April 28, 2016, the Company1's cash deposit decreases -$717.38.

- On April 28, 2016, the A13's cash deposit increases $717.38.

- On April 29, 2016, the Company1's cash deposit decreases -$1,000.

- On April 30, 2016, the Company1's cash deposit increases $60.

- On April 30, 2016, the Company1's cash deposit decreases -$8,400.

- On April 30, 2016, the A14's cash deposit increases $2,900.

- On April 30, 2016, the A13's cash deposit increases $2,600.

- On April 30, 2016, the A15's cash deposit increases $2,900.

- On May 1, 2016, the Company1's cash deposit increases $1,900.

- On May 1, 2016, the Company1's cash deposit increases $8,000.

- On May 1, 2016, the Company1's cash deposit decreases -$15,000.

- On May 1, 2016, the Company1's cash deposit decreases -$3,250.

- On May 1, 2016, the Company1's cash deposit decreases -$2,300.

- On May 24, 2016, the Company1's cash deposit decreases -$623.75.

- On May 24, 2016, the A13's cash deposit increases $623.75.

- On May 31, 2016, the Company1's cash deposit decreases -$8,400.

- On May 31, 2016, the A14's cash deposit increases $2,900.

- On May 31, 2016, the A13's cash deposit increases $2,600.

- On May 31, 2016, the A15's cash deposit increases $2,900.

- On June 1, 2016, the Company1's cash deposit increases $3,000.

- On June 10, 2016, the Company1's cash deposit decreases -$15,000.

- On June 12, 2016, the Company1's cash deposit decreases -$64,000.

- On June 23, 2016, the Company1's cash deposit decreases -$580.91.

- On June 23, 2016, the A13's cash deposit increases $580.91.

- On June 30, 2016, the Company1's cash deposit decreases -$8,400.

- On June 30, 2016, the A14's cash deposit increases $2,900.

- On June 30, 2016, the A13's cash deposit increases $2,600.

- On June 30, 2016, the A15's cash deposit increases $2,900.

- On July 7, 2016, the Company1's cash deposit decreases -$442.56.

- On July 7, 2016, the A14's cash deposit increases $442.56.

- On July 19, 2016, the Company1's cash deposit increases $1,300.

- On July 19, 2016, the A8's cash deposit decreases -$1,300.

- On July 25, 2016, the Company1's cash deposit decreases -$487.84.

- On July 25, 2016, the A13's cash deposit increases $487.84.

- On July 31, 2016, the Company1's cash deposit decreases -$8,400.

- On July 31, 2016, the A14's cash deposit increases $2,900.

- On July 31, 2016, the A13's cash deposit increases $2,600.

- On July 31, 2016, the A15's cash deposit increases $2,900.

- On August 1, 2016, the Company1's cash deposit increases $5,000.

- On August 1, 2016, the Company1's cash deposit increases $38,000.

- On August 1, 2016, the A16's cash deposit decreases -$10,000.

- On August 1, 2016, the A23's cash deposit decreases -$11,500.

- On August 1, 2016, the Company1's cash deposit increases $3,000.

- On August 2, 2016, the Company1's cash deposit increases $1,600.

- On August 2, 2016, the A1's cash deposit decreases -$1,600.

- On August 3, 2016, the Company1's cash deposit decreases -$12,000.

- On August 10, 2016, the Company1's cash deposit increases $1,500.

- On August 14, 2016, the Company1's cash deposit increases $1,040.

- On August 17, 2016, the Company1's cash deposit decreases -$386.36.

- On August 17, 2016, the A15's cash deposit increases $386.36.

- On August 25, 2016, the Company1's cash deposit decreases -$501.22.

- On August 25, 2016, the A13's cash deposit increases $501.22.

- On August 31, 2016, the Company1's cash deposit decreases -$8,400.

- On August 31, 2016, the A14's cash deposit increases $2,900.

- On August 31, 2016, the A13's cash deposit increases $2,600.

- On August 31, 2016, the A15's cash deposit increases $2,900.

- On September 2, 2016, the Company1's cash deposit increases $18,000.

- On September 12, 2016, the Company1's cash deposit increases $18,000.

- On September 13, 2016, the Company1's cash deposit decreases -$25,000.

- On September 14, 2016, the Company1's cash deposit decreases -$10,000.

- On September 26, 2016, the Company1's cash deposit increases $17,000.

- On September 26, 2016, the Company1's cash deposit decreases -$8,000.

- On September 28, 2016, the Company1's cash deposit decreases -$658.33.

- On September 28, 2016, the A13's cash deposit increases $658.33.

- On September 30, 2016, the Company1's cash deposit decreases -$8,400.

- On September 30, 2016, the A14's cash deposit increases $2,900.

- On September 30, 2016, the A13's cash deposit increases $2,600.

- On September 30, 2016, the A15's cash deposit increases $2,900.

- On October 1, 2016, the Company1's cash deposit increases $2,400.

- On October 1, 2016, the Company1's cash deposit increases $5,000.

- On October 1, 2016, the Company1's cash deposit increases $5,500.

- On October 3, 2016, the Company1's cash deposit increases $990.

- On October 5, 2016, the Company1's cash deposit increases $39,000.

- On October 5, 2016, the A13's cash deposit decreases -$10,000.

- On October 5, 2016, the A25's cash deposit decreases -$10,500.

- On October 7, 2016, the Company1's cash deposit decreases -$392.36.

- On October 7, 2016, the A15's cash deposit increases $392.36.

- On October 27, 2016, the Company1's cash deposit decreases -$607.57.

- On October 27, 2016, the A13's cash deposit increases $607.57.

- On October 31, 2016, the Company1's cash deposit decreases -$8,400.

- On October 31, 2016, the A14's cash deposit increases $2,900.

- On October 31, 2016, the A13's cash deposit increases $2,600.

- On October 31, 2016, the A15's cash deposit increases $2,900.

- On November 5, 2016, the Company1's cash deposit increases $2,900.

- On November 19, 2016, the Company1's cash deposit decreases -$551.13.

- On November 19, 2016, the A13's cash deposit increases $551.13.

- On November 19, 2016, the Company1's cash deposit increases $1,400.

- On November 19, 2016, the Company1's cash deposit decreases -$401.13.

- On November 19, 2016, the A15's cash deposit increases $401.13.

- On November 29, 2016, the Company1's cash deposit decreases -$14,420.

- On November 29, 2016, the Company1's cash deposit decreases -$3,000.

- On November 29, 2016, the Company1's cash deposit increases $1,500.

- On November 29, 2016, the A4's cash deposit decreases -$1,500.

- On November 30, 2016, the Company1's cash deposit increases $1,500.

- On November 30, 2016, the A18's cash deposit decreases -$1,500.

- On November 30, 2016, the Company1's cash deposit increases $1,300.

- On November 30, 2016, the A6's cash deposit decreases -$1,300.

- On November 30, 2016, the Company1's cash deposit decreases -$8,400.

- On November 30, 2016, the A14's cash deposit increases $2,900.

- On November 30, 2016, the A13's cash deposit increases $2,600.

- On November 30, 2016, the A15's cash deposit increases $2,900.

- On December 1, 2016, the Company1's cash deposit increases $5.000.

- On December 10, 2016, the Company1's cash deposit increases $1,600.

- On December 10, 2016, the A24's cash deposit decreases -$1,600.

- On December 11, 2016, the Company1's cash deposit increases $1,500.

- On December 16, 2016, the Company1's cash deposit decreases -$638.34.

- On December 16, 2016, the A13's cash deposit increases $638.34.

- On December 19, 2016, the Company1's cash deposit increases $1,600.

- On December 19, 2016, the Company1's cash deposit increases $2,800.

- On December 22, 2016, the Company1's cash deposit increases $1,400.

- On December 22, 2016, the A2's cash deposit decreases -$1,400.

- On December 23, 2016, the Company1's cash deposit decreases -$444.45.

- On December 23, 2016, the A14's cash deposit increases $444.45.

- On December 23, 2016, the Company1's cash deposit decreases -$5,500.

- On December 23, 2016, the Company1's cash deposit decreases -$18,000.

- On December 29, 2016, the Company1's cash deposit increases $2,400.

- On December 29, 2016, the Company1's cash deposit increases $10,000.

- On December 29, 2016, the Company1's cash deposit increases $27,000.

- On December 29, 2016, the Company1's cash deposit decreases -$39,700.

- On December 30, 2016, the Company1's cash deposit increases $2,000.

- On December 30, 2016, the Company1's cash deposit increases $1,400.

- On December 31, 2016, the Company1's cash deposit increases $3,500.

- On December 31, 2016, the Company1's cash deposit increases $40,000.

- On December 31, 2016, the A7's cash deposit decreases -$40,000.

- On December 31, 2016, the Company1's cash deposit increases $40,000.

- On December 31, 2016, the Company1's cash deposit decreases -$8,400.

- On December 31, 2016, the A14's cash deposit increases $2,900.

- On December 31, 2016, the A13's cash deposit increases $2,600.

- On December 31, 2016, the A15's cash deposit increases $2,900.

- On December 31, 2016, the Company1's cash deposit increases $38,000.

- On December 31, 2016, the A24's cash deposit decreases -$38,000.

- On December 31, 2016, the Company1's cash deposit decreases -$55,000.

- On December 31, 2016, the Company1's cash deposit decreases -$22,500.

- On December 31, 2016, the Company1's cash deposit decreases -$16,150.

- On December 31, 2016, the Company1's cash deposit decreases -$19,800.

- On December 31, 2016, the Company1's cash deposit decreases -$230.

- On December 31, 2016, the Company1's cash deposit decreases -$138.

- On December 31, 2016, the A1's cash deposit increases $138.

- On December 31, 2016, the Company1's cash deposit decreases -$276.

- On December 31, 2016, the A2's cash deposit increases $276.

- On December 31, 2016, the Company1's cash deposit decreases -$230.

- On December 31, 2016, the A8's cash deposit increases $230.

- On December 31, 2016, the Company1's cash deposit decreases -$322.

- On December 31, 2016, the Company1's cash deposit decreases -$92.

- On December 31, 2016, the A14's cash deposit increases $92.

- On December 31, 2016, the Company1's cash deposit decreases -$184.

- On December 31, 2016, the A16's cash deposit increases $184.

- On December 31, 2016, the Company1's cash deposit decreases -$92.

- On December 31, 2016, the A18's cash deposit increases $92.

- On December 31, 2016, the Company1's cash deposit decreases -$138.

- On December 31, 2016, the Company1's cash deposit decreases -$230.

- On December 31, 2016, the Company1's cash deposit decreases -$138.

- On December 31, 2016, the A24's cash deposit increases $138.

- On December 31, 2016, the Company1's cash deposit decreases -$230.

- On December 31, 2016, the A25's cash deposit increases $230.

- On December 31, 2016, the Company1's cash deposit increases $400.

- On December 31, 2016, the Company1's cash deposit increases $135.

- On December 31, 2016, the Company1's cash deposit increases $369.

- On December 31, 2016, the Company1's cash deposit increases $120.

- **Company2.**

- On January 12, 2016, the A25's cash deposit decreases -$360.

- On January 15, 2016, the A16's cash deposit increases $411.32.

- On January 30, 2016, the A18's cash deposit increases $379.78.

- On January 31, 2016, the A16's cash deposit increases $2,610.

- On January 31, 2016, the A18's cash deposit increases $2,880.

- On February 20, 2016, the A16's cash deposit increases $557.83.

- On February 28, 2016, the A16's cash deposit increases $2,610.

- On February 28, 2016, the A18's cash deposit increases $2,880.

- On March 1, 2016, the A18's cash deposit increases $221.16.

- On March 23, 2016, the A16's cash deposit increases $347.65.

- On March 31, 2016, the A16's cash deposit increases $2,610.

- On March 31, 2016, the A18's cash deposit increases $2,880.

- On April 12, 2016, the A1's cash deposit decreases -$310.

- On April 26, 2016, the A16's cash deposit increases $369.88.

- On April 30, 2016, the A16's cash deposit increases $2,610.

- On April 30, 2016, the A18's cash deposit increases $2,880.

- On May 2, 2016, the A18's cash deposit increases $307.09.

- On May 3, 2016, the A13's cash deposit decreases -$290.

- On May 24, 2016, the A16's cash deposit increases $366.59.

- On May 31, 2016, the A16's cash deposit increases $2,610.

- On May 31, 2016, the A18's cash deposit increases $2,880.

- On June 23, 2016, the A16's cash deposit increases $362.81.

- On June 30, 2016, the A16's cash deposit increases $2,610.

- On June 30, 2016, the A18's cash deposit increases $2,880.

- On July 11, 2016, the A5's cash deposit decreases -$290.

- On July 13, 2016, the A7's cash deposit decreases -$320.

- On July 27, 2016, the A16's cash deposit increases $307.41.

- On July 31, 2016, the A16's cash deposit increases $2,610.

- On July 31, 2016, the A18's cash deposit increases $2,880.

- On August 23, 2016, the A16's cash deposit increases $392.33.

- On August 31, 2016, the A16's cash deposit increases $2,610.

- On August 31, 2016, the A18's cash deposit increases $2,880.

- On September 28, 2016, the A16's cash deposit increases $410.89.

- On September 30, 2016, the A16's cash deposit increases $2,610.

- On September 30, 2016, the A18's cash deposit increases $2,880.

- On October 6, 2016, the A18's cash deposit increases $377.63.

- On October 27, 2016, the A16's cash deposit increases $396.27.

- On October 31, 2016, the A16's cash deposit increases $2,610.

- On October 31, 2016, the A18's cash deposit increases $2,880.

- On November 19, 2016, the A16's cash deposit increases $399.28.

- On November 20, 2016, the A18's cash deposit decreases -$360.

- On November 30, 2016, the A16's cash deposit increases $2,610.

- On November 30, 2016, the A18's cash deposit increases $2,880.

- On December 17, 2016, the A16's cash deposit increases $395.88.

- On December 20, 2016, the A18's cash deposit increases $424.37.

- On December 31, 2016, the A16's cash deposit increases $2,610.

- On December 31, 2016, the A18's cash deposit increases $2,880.

- On December 31, 2016, the A4's cash deposit increases $188.

- On December 31, 2016, the A5's cash deposit increases $94.

- On December 31, 2016, the A6's cash deposit increases $47

- On December 31, 2016, the A13's cash deposit increases $235.

- On December 31, 2016, the A15's cash deposit increases $94.

- On December 31, 2016, the A24's cash deposit increases $235.

- On December 31, 2016, the A25's cash deposit increases $94.

- **Company3.**
- On January 31, 2016, the A6's cash deposit decreases -$350
- On February 1, 2016, the A24's cash deposit decreases -$10,010.
- On February 1, 2016, the A25's cash deposit decreases -$10,270.
- On March 24, 2016, the A2's cash deposit decreases -$3,500.
- On July 11, 2016, the A4's cash deposit decreases -$250.
- On August 13, 2016, the A13's cash deposit decreases -$700.
- On September 4, 2016, the A18's cash deposit decreases -$520.
- On October 3, 2016, the A15's cash deposit decreases -$550.
- On November 20, 2016, the A6's cash deposit decreases -$640.
- On December 31, 2016, the A1's cash deposit increases $288.
- On December 31, 2016, the A2's cash deposit increases $192.
- On December 31, 2016, the A3's cash deposit increases $336.
- On December 31, 2016, the A7's cash deposit increases $288.
- On December 31, 2016, the A8's cash deposit increases $192.
- On December 31, 2016, the A9's cash deposit increases $240.
- On December 31, 2016, the A14's cash deposit increases $240.
- On December 31, 2016, the A16's cash deposit increases $336.
- On December 31, 2016, the A18's cash deposit increases $288.

- **Proprietorship1.**
- On January 2, 2016, the Proprietorship1's cash deposit decreases -$450.
- On January 2, 2016, the Proprietorship1's cash deposit decreases -$10,000.
- On January 3, 2016, the Proprietorship1's cash deposit increases $9,300.
- On January 6, 2016, the Proprietorship1's cash deposit increases $108.
- On January 10, 2016, the Proprietorship1's cash deposit increases $98.
- On January 10, 2016, the Proprietorship1's cash deposit increases $92.
- On January 13, 2016, the Proprietorship1's cash deposit decreases -$150.

- On January 13, 2016, the Proprietorship1's cash deposit increases $20.

- On January 13, 2016, the A15's cash deposit decreases -$20.

- On January 13, 2016, the Proprietorship1's cash deposit increases $192.

- On January 13, 2016, the A16's cash deposit decreases -$192.

- On January 16, 2016, the Proprietorship1's cash deposit increases $57.

- On January 16, 2016, the A8's cash deposit decreases -$57.

- On January 16, 2016, the Proprietorship1's cash deposit increases $44.

- On January 18, 2016, the Proprietorship1's cash deposit increases $51.

- On January 18, 2016, the Proprietorship1's cash deposit decreases -$153.87.

- On January 19, 2016, the Proprietorship1's cash deposit increases $57.

- On January 19, 2016, the A25's cash deposit decreases -$57.

- On January 25, 2016, the Proprietorship1's cash deposit increases $100.

- On January 25, 2016, the A9's cash deposit decreases -$100.

- On January 26, 2016, the Proprietorship1's cash deposit increases $1,300.

- On January 27, 2016, the Proprietorship1's cash deposit decreases -$250.

- On January 27, 2016, the Proprietorship1's cash deposit increases $57.

- On January 28, 2016, the Proprietorship1's cash deposit increases $144.

- On January 28, 2016, the A18's cash deposit decreases -$144.

- On January 28, 2016, the Proprietorship1's cash deposit increases $42.

- On January 28, 2016, the Proprietorship1's cash deposit increases $44.

- On January 30, 2016, the Proprietorship1's cash deposit increases $500.

- On January 30, 2016, the Proprietorship1's cash deposit decreases -$145.54.

- On January 31, 2016, the Proprietorship1's cash deposit increases $2,040.

- On January 31, 2016, the Proprietorship1's cash deposit decreases -$5,670.

- On January 31, 2016, the Proprietorship1's cash deposit increases $10,400.

- On January 31, 2016, the A12 (secondary card)'s cash deposit decreases -$10,400.

- On January 31, 2016, the Proprietorship1's cash deposit increases $14,560.

- On January 31, 2016, the A1's cash deposit decreases -$14,560.

- On January 31, 2016, the Proprietorship1's cash deposit increases $13,000.

- On January 31, 2016, the A2's cash deposit decreases -$13,000.

- On January 31, 2016, the Proprietorship1's cash deposit increases $13,130.

- On January 31, 2016, the A3's cash deposit decreases -$13,130.

- On January 31, 2016, the Proprietorship1's cash deposit increases $14,430.

- On January 31, 2016, the A4's cash deposit decreases -$14,430.

- On January 31, 2016, the Proprietorship1's cash deposit increases $14,170.

- On January 31, 2016, the A5's cash deposit decreases -$14,170.

- On January 31, 2016, the Proprietorship1's cash deposit increases $12,610.

- On January 31, 2016, the A6's cash deposit decreases -$12,610.

- On January 31, 2016, the Proprietorship1's cash deposit increases $12,400.

- On January 31, 2016, the A7's cash deposit decreases -$12,400.

- On January 31, 2016, the Proprietorship1's cash deposit increases $13,000.

- On January 31, 2016, the A8's cash deposit decreases -$13,000.

- On January 31, 2016, the Proprietorship1's cash deposit increases $18,460.

- On January 31, 2016, the A9's cash deposit decreases -$18,460.

- On January 31, 2016, the Proprietorship1's cash deposit increases $13,900.

- On January 31, 2016, the Proprietorship1's cash deposit increases $14,430.

- On January 31, 2016, the Proprietorship1's cash deposit increases $14,560.

- On January 31, 2016, the Proprietorship1's cash deposit increases $18,460.

- On January 31, 2016, the A13's cash deposit decreases -$18,460.

- On February 1, 2016, the Proprietorship1's cash deposit decreases -$28,000.

- On February 17, 2016, the Proprietorship1's cash deposit increases $310.

- On February 17, 2016, the A13's cash deposit decreases -$310.

- On February 20, 2016, the Proprietorship1's cash deposit increases $400.

- On February 21, 2016, the Proprietorship1's cash deposit decreases -$300.

- On February 23, 2016, the Proprietorship1's cash deposit increases $124.

- On February 24, 2016, the Proprietorship1's cash deposit increases $110.

- On February 25, 2016, the Proprietorship1's cash deposit increases $99.

- On February 28, 2016, the Proprietorship1's cash deposit increases $102.

- On February 28, 2016, the A18's cash deposit decreases -$102.

- On February 28, 2016, the Proprietorship1's cash deposit increases $102.

- On February 28, 2016, the Proprietorship1's cash deposit decreases -$5,670.

- On March 6, 2016, the Proprietorship1's cash deposit decreases -$1,000.

- On March 7, 2016, the Proprietorship1's cash deposit increases $78.

- On March 7, 2016, the A25's cash deposit decreases -$78.

- On March 10, 2016, the Proprietorship1's cash deposit increases $123.

- On March 11, 2016, the Proprietorship1's cash deposit increases $50.

- On March 19, 2016, the Proprietorship1's cash deposit increases $172.

- On March 23, 2016, the Proprietorship1's cash deposit decreases -$159.45.

- On March 26, 2016, the Proprietorship1's cash deposit increases $72.

- On March 27, 2016, the Proprietorship1's cash deposit increases $51.

- On March 27, 2016, the A8's cash deposit decreases -$51.

- On March 31, 2016, the Proprietorship1's cash deposit decreases -$5,670.

- On April 13, 2016, the Proprietorship1's cash deposit increases $69.

- On April 22, 2016, the Proprietorship1's cash deposit increases $75.

- On April 22, 2016, the A24's cash deposit decreases -$75.

- On April 24, 2016, the Proprietorship1's cash deposit increases $156.

- On April 24, 2016, the A16's cash deposit decreases -$156.

- On April 24, 2016, the Proprietorship1's cash deposit increases $78.

- On April 27, 2016, the Proprietorship1's cash deposit increases $102.

- On April 27, 2016, the A7's cash deposit decreases -$102.

- On April 29, 2016, the Proprietorship1's cash deposit decreases -$5,000.

- On April 30, 2016, the Proprietorship1's cash deposit decreases -$5,670.

- On May 1, 2016, the Proprietorship1's cash deposit decreases -$800.

- On May 1, 2016, the Proprietorship1's cash deposit decreases -$5,000.

- On May 1, 2016, the Proprietorship1's cash deposit increases $3,250.

- On May 1, 2016, the Proprietorship1's cash deposit increases $9,000.

- On May 1, 2016, the Proprietorship1's cash deposit increases $90.

- On May 1, 2016, the A18's cash deposit decreases -$90.

- On May 1, 2016, the Proprietorship1's cash deposit increases $50.

- On May 12, 2016, the Proprietorship1's cash deposit increases $112.

- On May 12, 2016, the A9's cash deposit decreases -$112.

- On May 12, 2016, the Proprietorship1's cash deposit increases $50.

- On May 13, 2016, the Proprietorship1's cash deposit increases $112.

- On May 14, 2016, the Proprietorship1's cash deposit decreases -$166.23.

- On May 14, 2016, the Proprietorship1's cash deposit increases $105.

- On May 20, 2016, the Proprietorship1's cash deposit increases $56.

- On May 22, 2016, the Proprietorship1's cash deposit increases $403.

- On May 22, 2016, the A13's cash deposit decreases -$403.

- On May 22, 2016, the Proprietorship1's cash deposit increases $155.

- On May 22, 2016, the A16's cash deposit decreases -$155.

- On May 22, 2016, the Proprietorship1's cash deposit increases $138.

- On May 24, 2016, the Proprietorship1's cash deposit decreases -$176.95.

- On May 31, 2016, the Proprietorship1's cash deposit decreases -$5,670.

- On June 14, 2016, the Proprietorship1's cash deposit increases $96.

- On June 14, 2016, the A9's cash deposit decreases -$96.

- On June 16, 2016, the Proprietorship1's cash deposit increases $300.

- On June 18, 2016, the Proprietorship1's cash deposit increases $109.

- On June 20, 2016, the Proprietorship1's cash deposit increases $310.

- On June 20, 2016, the A13's cash deposit decreases -$310.

- On June 20, 2016, the Proprietorship1's cash deposit increases $163.

- On June 20, 2016, the A16's cash deposit decreases -$163.

- On June 21, 2016, the Proprietorship1's cash deposit increases $108

- On June 23, 2016, the Proprietorship1's cash deposit decreases -$157.37.

- On June 30, 2016, the Proprietorship1's cash deposit decreases -$5,670.

- On July 4, 2016, the Proprietorship1's cash deposit decreases -$55,000.

- On July 5, 2016, the Proprietorship1's cash deposit increases $180.

- On July 5, 2016, the A14's cash deposit decreases -$180.

- On July 16, 2016, the Proprietorship1's cash deposit increases $112.

- On July 21, 2016, the Proprietorship1's cash deposit increases $125.

- On July 22, 2016, the Proprietorship1's cash deposit increases $302.

- On July 22, 2016, the A13's cash deposit decreases -$302.

- On July 22, 2016, the Proprietorship1's cash deposit increases $105.

- On July 25, 2016, the Proprietorship1's cash deposit increases $118.

- On July 25, 2016, the A16's cash deposit decreases -$118.

- On July 25, 2016, the Proprietorship1's cash deposit increases $88.

- On July 25, 2016, the Proprietorship1's cash deposit increases $64.

- On July 27, 2016, the Proprietorship1's cash deposit decreases -$187.55.

- On July 31, 2016, the Proprietorship1's cash deposit decreases -$5,670.

- On July 31, 2016, the Proprietorship1's cash deposit increases $10,270.

- On July 31, 2016, the Proprietorship1's cash deposit increases $18,460.

- On July 31, 2016, the A14's cash deposit decreases -$18,460.

- On July 31, 2016, the Proprietorship1's cash deposit increases $18,200.

- On July 31, 2016, the A15's cash deposit decreases -$18,200.

- On July 31, 2016, the Proprietorship1's cash deposit increases $18,720.

- On July 31, 2016, the A16's cash deposit decreases -$18,720.

- On July 31, 2016, the Proprietorship1's cash deposit increases $17,940.

- On July 31, 2016, the Proprietorship1's cash deposit increases $18,460.

- On July 31, 2016, the A18's cash deposit decreases -$18,460.

- On July 31, 2016, the Proprietorship1's cash deposit increases $18,590.

- On July 31, 2016, the Proprietorship1's cash deposit increases $10,400.

- On July 31, 2016, the Proprietorship1's cash deposit increases $10,660.

- On July 31, 2016, the Proprietorship1's cash deposit increases $10,530.

- On July 31, 2016, the Proprietorship1's cash deposit increases $11,050.

- On July 31, 2016, the Proprietorship1's cash deposit increases $11,570.

- On July 31, 2016, the A24's cash deposit decreases -$11,570.

- On July 31, 2016, the Proprietorship1's cash deposit increases $12,090.

- On July 31, 2016, the A25's cash deposit decreases -$12,090.

- On August 10, 2016, the Proprietorship1's cash deposit increases $150.

- On August 14, 2016, the Proprietorship1's cash deposit increases $120.

- On August 17, 2016, the Proprietorship1's cash deposit decreases -$65,000.

- On August 17, 2016, the Proprietorship1's cash deposit increases $63.

- On August 20, 2016, the Proprietorship1's cash deposit increases $162.

- On August 20, 2016, the A16's cash deposit decreases -$162.

- On August 21, 2016, the Proprietorship1's cash deposit increases $78.

- On August 22, 2016, the Proprietorship1's cash deposit increases $112.

- On August 22, 2016, the Proprietorship1's cash deposit increases $312.

- On August 22, 2016, the A13's cash deposit decreases -$312.

- On August 23, 2016, the Proprietorship1's cash deposit decreases -$166.18.

- On August 31, 2016, the Proprietorship1's cash deposit decreases -$5,670.

- On September 15, 2016, the Proprietorship1's cash deposit increases $300.

- On September 17, 2016, the Proprietorship1's cash deposit increases $112.

- On September 17, 2016, the A9's cash deposit decreases -$112.

- On September 17, 2016, the Proprietorship1's cash deposit increases $104.

- On September 19, 2016, the Proprietorship1's cash deposit increases $99.

- On September 19, 2016, the A24's cash deposit decreases -$99.

- On September 26, 2016, the Proprietorship1's cash deposit increases $451.

- On September 26, 2016, the A13's cash deposit decreases -$451.

- On September 26, 2016, the Proprietorship1's cash deposit decreases -$1,800.

- On September 26, 2016, the Proprietorship1's cash deposit increases $183.

- On September 26, 2016, the A16's cash deposit decreases -$183.

- On September 26, 2016, the Proprietorship1's cash deposit increases $87.

- On September 30, 2016, the Proprietorship1's cash deposit decreases -$5,670.

- On October 1, 2016, the Proprietorship1's cash deposit decreases -$5,500.

- On October 8, 2016, the Proprietorship1's cash deposit decreases -$168.73.

- On October 12, 2016, the Proprietorship1's cash deposit decreases -$31,000.

- On October 16, 2016, the Proprietorship1's cash deposit increases $108.

- On October 21, 2016, the Proprietorship1's cash deposit increases $121.

- On October 22, 2016, the Proprietorship1's cash deposit increases $116.

- On October 22, 2016, the Proprietorship1's cash deposit increases $114.

- On October 22, 2016, the A9's cash deposit decreases -$114.

- On October 24, 2016, the Proprietorship1's cash deposit increases $383.

- On October 24, 2016, the A13's cash deposit decreases -$383.

- On October 25, 2016, the Proprietorship1's cash deposit increases $25,000.

- On October 25, 2016, the Proprietorship1's cash deposit increases $174.

- On October 25, 2016, the A16's cash deposit decreases -$174.

- On October 25, 2016, the Proprietorship1's cash deposit increases $90.

- On October 31, 2016, the Proprietorship1's cash deposit decreases -$5,670.

- On November 15, 2016, the Proprietorship1's cash deposit increases $93.

- On November 15, 2016, the Proprietorship1's cash deposit increases $361.

- On November 15, 2016, the A13's cash deposit decreases -$361.

- On November 17, 2016, the Proprietorship1's cash deposit increases $184.

- On November 17, 2016, the A16's cash deposit decreases -$184.

- On November 17, 2016, the Proprietorship1's cash deposit increases $87.

- On November 19, 2016, the Proprietorship1's cash deposit increases $100.

- On November 19, 2016, the Proprietorship1's cash deposit decreases -$177.16.

- On November 30, 2016, the Proprietorship1's cash deposit decreases -$5,670.

- On December 13, 2016, the Proprietorship1's cash deposit increases $413.

- On December 13, 2016, the A13's cash deposit decreases -$413.

- On December 15, 2016, the Proprietorship1's cash deposit increases $99.

- On December 15, 2016, the A9's cash deposit decreases -$99.

- On December 15, 2016, the Proprietorship1's cash deposit increases $104.

- On December 15, 2016, the Proprietorship1's cash deposit increases $74.

- On December 15, 2016, the Proprietorship1's cash deposit increases $174.

- On December 15, 2016, the A16's cash deposit decreases -$174.

- On December 17, 2016, the Proprietorship1's cash deposit decreases -$207.52.

- On December 19, 2016, the Proprietorship1's cash deposit decreases -$198.35.

- On December 20, 2016, the Proprietorship1's cash deposit increases $129.

- On December 23, 2016, the Proprietorship1's cash deposit increases $18,000.

- On December 26, 2016, the Proprietorship1's cash deposit increases $192.

- On December 26, 2016, the Proprietorship1's cash deposit increases $198.

- On December 27, 2016, the Proprietorship1's cash deposit increases $125.

- On December 29, 2016, the Proprietorship1's cash deposit decreases -$10,000.

- On December 31, 2016, the Proprietorship1's cash deposit decreases -$4,300.

- On December 31, 2016, the Proprietorship1's cash deposit decreases -$5,670.

- On December 31, 2016, the Proprietorship1's cash deposit decreases -$11,280.

- On December 31, 2016, the Proprietorship1's cash deposit decreases -$2,500.

- On December 31, 2016, the A4's cash deposit increases $150.

- On December 31, 2016, the A5's cash deposit increases $200.

- On December 31, 2016, the A6's cash deposit increases $250.

- On December 31, 2016, the A8's cash deposit increases $100.

- On December 31, 2016, the A13's cash deposit increases $250.

- On December 31, 2016, the A15's cash deposit increases $200.

- On December 31, 2016, the A16's cash deposit increases $100.

- On December 31, 2016, the A18's cash deposit increases $150.

- On December 31, 2016, the Proprietorship1's cash deposit increases $416.

- On December 31, 2016, the Proprietorship1's cash deposit increases $352.

- On December 31, 2016, the Proprietorship1's cash deposit increases $120.

- **Proprietorship2.**

- On January 12, 2016, the A24's cash deposit decreases -$118.

- On January 13, 2016, the A13's cash deposit decreases -$208.

- On January 14, 2016, the A24's cash deposit increases $255.37.

- On January 15, 2016, the A11's cash deposit decreases -$54.

- On January 20, 2016, the A7's cash deposit decreases -$82.

- On January 21, 2016, the A25's cash deposit increases $149.65.

- On January 31, 2016, the A14's cash deposit decreases -$24.

- On January 31, 2016, the A24's cash deposit increases $2,870.

- On January 31, 2016, the A25's cash deposit increases $2,790.

- On January 31, 2016, the A14's cash deposit decreases -$10,920.

- On January 31, 2016, the A15's cash deposit decreases -$11,050.

- On January 31, 2016, the A16's cash deposit decreases -$11,180.

- On January 31, 2016, the A18's cash deposit decreases -$11,830.

- On January 31, 2016, the A24's cash deposit decreases -$10,010.

- On January 31, 2016, the A25's cash deposit decreases -$10,270.

- On February 6, 2016, the A12's cash deposit decreases -$116 (second card).

- On February 17, 2016, the A16's cash deposit decreases -$310.

- On February 19, 2016, the A9's cash deposit decreases -$112.

- On February 22, 2016, the A8's cash deposit decreases -$96.

- On February 23, 2016, the A24's cash deposit decreases -$62.

- On February 25, 2016, the A24's cash deposit increases $187.84.

- On February 28, 2016, the A24's cash deposit increases $2,870.

- On February 28, 2016, the A25's cash deposit increases $2,790.

- On March 7, 2016, the A12's cash deposit decreases -$100.

- On March 7, 2016, the A25's cash deposit increases $201.66.

- On March 18, 2016, the A9's cash deposit decreases -$104.

- On March 20, 2016, the A13's cash deposit decreases -$290.

- On March 20, 2016, the A16's cash deposit decreases -$131.

- On March 22, 2016, the A7's cash deposit decreases -$96.

- On March 25, 2016, the A25's cash deposit decreases -$70.

- On March 27, 2016, the A25's cash deposit increases $191.43.

- On March 28, 2016, the A14's cash deposit decreases -$84.

- On March 31, 2016, the A24's cash deposit increases $2,870.

- On March 31, 2016, the A25's cash deposit increases $2,790.

- On April 6, 2016, the A9's cash deposit decreases -$108.

- On April 24, 2016, the A24's cash deposit increases $236.37.

- On April 26, 2016, the A13's cash deposit decreases -$470.

- On April 30, 2016, the A24's cash deposit increases $2,870.

- On April 30, 2016, the A25's cash deposit increases $2,790.

- On May 15, 2016, the A24's cash deposit decreases -$78.

- On May 17, 2016, the A24's cash deposit increases $210.77.

- On May 31, 2016, the A24's cash deposit increases $2,870.

- On May 31, 2016, the A25's cash deposit increases $2,790.

- On June 3, 2016, the A8's cash deposit decreases -$54.

- On June 17, 2016, the A24's cash deposit decreases -$74.

- On June 19, 2016, the A24's cash deposit increases $196.83.

- On June 30, 2016, the A24's cash deposit increases $2,870.

- On June 30, 2016, the A25's cash deposit increases $2,790.

- On July 2, 2016, the A9's cash deposit decreases -$117.

- On July 21, 2016, the A25's cash deposit decreases -$108.

- On July 23, 2016, the A25's cash deposit increases $251.19.

- On July 31, 2016, the A24's cash deposit increases $2,870.

- On July 31, 2016, the A25's cash deposit increases $2,790.

- On July 31, 2016, the A12's cash deposit decreases -$10,920.

- On July 31, 2016, the A1's cash deposit decreases -$11,050.

- On July 31, 2016, the A2's cash deposit decreases -$11,180.

- On July 31, 2016, the A3's cash deposit decreases -$11,310.

- On July 31, 2016, the A4's cash deposit decreases -$11,440.

- On July 31, 2016, the A5's cash deposit decreases -$11,830.

- On July 31, 2016, the A6's cash deposit decreases -$10,790.

- On July 31, 2016, the A7's cash deposit decreases -$11,310.

- On July 31, 2016, the A8's cash deposit decreases -$11,570.

- On July 31, 2016, the A9's cash deposit decreases -$12,090.

- On July 31, 2016, the A13's cash deposit decreases -$11,830.

- On August 12, 2016, the A9's cash deposit decreases -$118.

- On August 14, 2016, the A15's cash deposit decreases -$123.

- On August 15, 2016, the A8's cash deposit decreases -$52.

- On August 16, 2016, the A24's cash deposit decreases -$74.

- On August 18, 2016, the A24's cash deposit increases $203.47.

- On August 31, 2016, the A24's cash deposit increases $2,870.

- On August 31, 2016, the A25's cash deposit increases $2,790.

- On September 7, 2016, the A7's cash deposit decreases -$90.

- On September 21, 2016, the A24's cash deposit increases $256.18.

- On September 30, 2016, the A24's cash deposit increases $2,870.

- On September 30, 2016, the A25's cash deposit increases $2,790.

- On October 3, 2016, the A15's cash deposit decreases -$129.

- On October 4, 2016, the A18's cash deposit decreases -$117.

- On October 6, 2016, the A22's cash deposit decreases -$54 (second card).

- On October 8, 2016, the A8's cash deposit decreases -$56.

- On October 16, 2016, the A24's cash deposit decreases -$86.

- On October 18, 2016, the A24's cash deposit increases $228.66.

- On October 31, 2016, the A24's cash deposit increases $2,870.

- On October 31, 2016, the A25's cash deposit increases $2,790.

- On November 16, 2016, the A9's cash deposit decreases -$124.

- On November 16, 2016, the A15's cash deposit decreases -$132.

- On November 18, 2016, the A24's cash deposit decreases -$86.

- On November 20, 2016, the A24's cash deposit increases $204.61.

- On November 30, 2016, the A24's cash deposit increases $2,870.

- On November 30, 2016, the A25's cash deposit increases $2,790.

- On December 15, 2016, the A24's cash deposit decreases -$108.

- On December 17, 2016, the A24's cash deposit increases $277.93.

- On December 18, 2016, the A18's cash deposit decreases -$144.

- On December 18, 2016, the A25's cash deposit decreases -$98.

- On December 20, 2016, the A14's cash deposit decreases -$162.

- On December 20, 2016, the A25's cash deposit increases $249.51.

- On December 26, 2016, the A7's cash deposit decreases -$108.

- On December 31, 2016, the A24's cash deposit increases $2,870.

- On December 31, 2016, the A25's cash deposit increases $2,790.

- On December 31, 2016, the A1's cash deposit increases $364.

- On December 31, 2016, the A2's cash deposit increases $312.

- On December 31, 2016, the A4's cash deposit increases $260.

- On December 31, 2016, the A7's cash deposit increases $312.

- On December 31, 2016, the A9's cash deposit increases $312.

- On December 31, 2016, the A16's cash deposit increases $364.

- On December 31, 2016, the A18's cash deposit increases $312.

- On December 31, 2016, the A4's cash deposit increases $220.

- On December 31, 2016, the A5's cash deposit increases $275.

- On December 31, 2016, the A6's cash deposit increases $330.

- On December 31, 2016, the A8's cash deposit increases $275.

- On December 31, 2016, the A13's cash deposit increases $220.

- On December 31, 2016, the A15's cash deposit increases $275.

- On December 31, 2016, the A16's cash deposit increases $330.

- On December 31, 2016, the A18's cash deposit increases $220.

- **Business Bank2.**

- On December 31, 2016, the A7's cash deposit increases $164.

- On December 31, 2016, the A9's cash deposit increases $246.

- On December 31, 2016, the A13's cash deposit increases $123.

- On December 31, 2016, the A14's cash deposit increases $205.

- On December 31, 2016, the A18's cash deposit increases $123.

- On December 31, 2016, the A3's cash deposit increases $264.

- On December 31, 2016, the A4's cash deposit increases $308.

- On December 31, 2016, the A6's cash deposit increases $264.

3.4.2 Brief Summary of the Business Bank1

The Figure 3.4-1 shows two sums and all cash transactions of the Business Bank1 itself by using of SQL Server query. In other words, there is not any cash transaction with the symbol "d" in the Figure 3.4-1. As a closed system based on the MathAccounting software, the sum0 should be equal to zero. However, the individuals are not responsible for recording any transaction, so the sum0 ($36,839) is the sum of the amounts that the individuals received from the Business Bank1. If the sum0 is negative, then it is sum of the amounts that individuals paid to the Business Bank1. The opposite value ($1,339,882.49) of the sum1 (-$1,339,882.49) is the sum of the Cash accounts of all organizations or companies on December 31, 2016. It is also the sum of their deposits in the Business Bak1 and the Business Bank2 on December 31, 2016.

```
SQLQuery14.sql - LI...ESS.dcj100 (sa (53))*    SQLQuery13.sql - LI...ESS.dcj100 (sa (52))*  ×

  ⊟use dcj100
   select sum(amount) as sum0 from CashByMembers where IDM='88-654304' and TransDate between '2016-01-01' and '2016-12-31'
   select sum(amount) as sum1 from CashByMembers where Symbol = 'd' and IDM like '%-%'
  ⊟select * from CashByMembers where Recorder='88-654304' and Symbol not like 'd' and
        TransDate between '2016-01-01' and '2016-12-31' order by TransDate
100 %  ▾
```

Results | Messages

	sum0
1	36839.00

	sum1
1	-1339882.49

	IDM	Amount	Symbol	MultiSubaccount	Recorder	TransDate
1	88-654310	162.00	t	88-654310-t-supplies < Cash payments for operating expenses < Operating activities	88-654304	2016-01-02
2	88-654308	2000.00	t	88-654308-t-suppliers < Cash payments to suppliers < Operating activities	88-654304	2016-01-13
3	909876508	148.78	n	909876508-n-operating expenses < Cash payments for operating expenses < Operating activities	88-654304	2016-01-18
4	909876507	179.59	n	909876507-n-operating expenses < Cash payments for operating expenses < Operating activities	88-654304	2016-01-23
5	909876509	232.31	n	909876509-n-operating expenses < Cash payments for operating expenses < Operating activities	88-654304	2016-01-27
6	909876507	3000.00	t	909876507-t-salary < Cash payments for operating expenses < Operating activities	88-654304	2016-01-31
7	909876508	2910.00	t	909876508-t-salary < Cash payments for operating expenses < Operating activities	88-654304	2016-01-31
8	909876509	2750.00	t	909876509-t-salary < Cash payments for operating expenses < Operating activities	88-654304	2016-01-31
9	88-654306	19000.00	t	88-654306-t-machinery < Cash payments for machinery < Operating activities	88-654304	2016-02-01
10	909876509	290.33	n	909876509-n-operating expenses < Cash payments for operating expenses < Operating activities	88-654304	2016-02-21
11	909876508	226.44	n	909876508-n-operating expenses < Cash payments for operating expenses < Operating activities	88-654304	2016-02-24
12	88-654307	5200.00	t	88-654307-t-supplies < Cash payments for operating expenses < Operating activities	88-654304	2016-02-26
13	909876507	3000.00	t	909876507-t-salary < Cash payments for operating expenses < Operating activities	88-654304	2016-02-28
14	909876508	2910.00	t	909876508-t-salary < Cash payments for operating expenses < Operating activities	88-654304	2016-02-28
15	909876509	2750.00	t	909876509-t-salary < Cash payments for operating expenses < Operating activities	88-654304	2016-02-28
16	909876509	252.59	n	909876509-n-operating expenses < Cash payments for operating expenses < Operating activities	88-654304	2016-03-20
17	909876507	226.44	n	909876507-n-operating expenses < Cash payments for operating expenses < Operating activities	88-654304	2016-03-24
18	909876508	148.93	n	909876508-n-operating expenses < Cash payments for operating expenses < Operating activities	88-654304	2016-03-29
19	909876507	3000.00	t	909876507-t-salary < Cash payments for operating expenses < Operating activities	88-654304	2016-03-31
20	909876508	2910.00	t	909876508-t-salary < Cash payments for operating expenses < Operating activities	88-654304	2016-03-31
21	909876509	2750.00	t	909876509-t-salary < Cash payments for operating expenses < Operating activities	88-654304	2016-03-31
22	909876509	255.17	n	909876509-n-operating expenses < Cash payments for operating expenses < Operating activities	88-654304	2016-04-08
23	909876507	219.94	n	909876507-n-operating expenses < Cash payments for operating expenses < Operating activities	88-654304	2016-04-29

Figure 3.4-1   Business Bank1Cash Received or Paid by Other Members (Continue)

	IDM	Amount	Symbol	MultiSubaccount	Recorder	TransDate
24	909876507	3000.00	t	909876507-t-salary < Cash payments for operating expenses < Operating activities	88-654304	2016-04-30
25	909876508	2910.00	t	909876508-t-salary < Cash payments for operating expenses < Operating activities	88-654304	2016-04-30
26	909876509	2750.00	t	909876509-t-salary < Cash payments for operating expenses < Operating activities	88-654304	2016-04-30
27	909876509	263.47	n	909876509-n-operating expenses < Cash payments for operating expenses < Operating activities	88-654304	2016-05-14
28	909876507	3000.00	t	909876507-t-salary < Cash payments for operating expenses < Operating activities	88-654304	2016-05-31
29	909876508	2910.00	t	909876508-t-salary < Cash payments for operating expenses < Operating activities	88-654304	2016-05-31
30	909876509	2750.00	t	909876509-t-salary < Cash payments for operating expenses < Operating activities	88-654304	2016-05-31
31	909876508	153.37	n	909876508-n-operating expenses < Cash payments for operating expenses < Operating activities	88-654304	2016-06-05
32	909876509	229.58	n	909876509-n-operating expenses < Cash payments for operating expenses < Operating activities	88-654304	2016-06-16
33	909876507	3000.00	t	909876507-t-salary < Cash payments for operating expenses < Operating activities	88-654304	2016-06-30
34	909876508	2910.00	t	909876508-t-salary < Cash payments for operating expenses < Operating activities	88-654304	2016-06-30
35	909876509	2750.00	t	909876509-t-salary < Cash payments for operating expenses < Operating activities	88-654304	2016-06-30
36	909876509	279.41	n	909876509-n-operating expenses < Cash payments for operating expenses < Operating activities	88-654304	2016-07-04
37	909876507	3000.00	t	909876507-t-salary < Cash payments for operating expenses < Operating activities	88-654304	2016-07-31
38	909876508	2910.00	t	909876508-t-salary < Cash payments for operating expenses < Operating activities	88-654304	2016-07-31
39	909876509	2750.00	t	909876509-t-salary < Cash payments for operating expenses < Operating activities	88-654304	2016-07-31
40	88-654306	5000.00	t	88-654306-t-machinery < Cash payments for machinery < Operating activities	88-654304	2016-08-01
41	909876509	284.33	n	909876509-n-operating expenses < Cash payments for operating expenses < Operating activities	88-654304	2016-08-14
42	909876508	142.72	n	909876508-n-operating expenses < Cash payments for operating expenses < Operating activities	88-654304	2016-08-17
43	909876507	3000.00	t	909876507-t-salary < Cash payments for operating expenses < Operating activities	88-654304	2016-08-31
44	909876508	2910.00	t	909876508-t-salary < Cash payments for operating expenses < Operating activities	88-654304	2016-08-31
45	909876509	2750.00	t	909876509-t-salary < Cash payments for operating expenses < Operating activities	88-654304	2016-08-31
46	909876507	191.51	n	909876507-n-operating expenses < Cash payments for operating expenses < Operating activities	88-654304	2016-09-09
47	88-654306	18000.00	t	88-654306-t-machinery < Cash payments for machinery < Operating activities	88-654304	2016-09-12
48	909876509	261.35	n	909876509-n-operating expenses < Cash payments for operating expenses < Operating activities	88-654304	2016-09-19
49	909876507	3000.00	t	909876507-t-salary < Cash payments for operating expenses < Operating activities	88-654304	2016-09-30
50	909876508	2910.00	t	909876508-t-salary < Cash payments for operating expenses < Operating activities	88-654304	2016-09-30
51	909876509	2750.00	t	909876509-t-salary < Cash payments for operating expenses < Operating activities	88-654304	2016-09-30

	IDM	Amount	Symbol	MultiSubaccount	Recorder	TransDate
52	909876508	157.94	n	909876508-n-operating expenses < Cash payments for operating expenses < Operating activities	88-654304	2016-10-10
53	909876509	268.73	n	909876509-n-operating expenses < Cash payments for operating expenses < Operating activities	88-654304	2016-10-25
54	909876507	3000.00	t	909876507-t-salary < Cash payments for operating expenses < Operating activities	88-654304	2016-10-31
55	909876508	2910.00	t	909876508-t-salary < Cash payments for operating expenses < Operating activities	88-654304	2016-10-31
56	909876509	2750.00	t	909876509-t-salary < Cash payments for operating expenses < Operating activities	88-654304	2016-10-31
57	909876509	286.66	n	909876509-n-operating expenses < Cash payments for operating expenses < Operating activities	88-654304	2016-11-18
58	909876507	3000.00	t	909876507-t-salary < Cash payments for operating expenses < Operating activities	88-654304	2016-11-30
59	909876508	2910.00	t	909876508-t-salary < Cash payments for operating expenses < Operating activities	88-654304	2016-11-30
60	909876509	2750.00	t	909876509-t-salary < Cash payments for operating expenses < Operating activities	88-654304	2016-11-30
61	88-654306	1500.00	t	88-654306-t-machinery < Cash payments for machinery < Operating activities	88-654304	2016-12-11
62	909876509	220.85	n	909876509-n-operating expenses < Cash payments for operating expenses < Operating activities	88-654304	2016-12-17
63	909876507	238.88	n	909876507-n-operating expenses < Cash payments for operating expenses < Operating activities	88-654304	2016-12-28
64	88-654306	1400.00	t	88-654306-t-suppliers < Cash payments to suppliers < Operating activities	88-654304	2016-12-30
65	88-654306	-38650.00	c	88-654306-c-customers < Cash receipts from customers < Operating activities	88-654304	2016-12-31
66	88-654307	-35600.00	c	88-654307-c-customers < Cash receipts from customers < Operating activities	88-654304	2016-12-31
67	88-654308	-18000.00	c	88-654308-c-customers < Cash receipts from customers < Operating activities	88-654304	2016-12-31
68	88-654300	-2500.00	t	88-654300-t-bank fee income < Cash receipts from customers < Operating activities	88-654304	2016-12-31
69	88-654302	240.00	t	88-654302-t-bond interest < Cash payments to bond holders< Operating activities	88-654304	2016-12-31
70	88-654303	200.00	t	88-654303-t-bond interest < Cash payments to bond holders< Operating activities	88-654304	2016-12-31
71	88-654305	280.00	t	88-654305-t-bond interest < Cash payments to bond holders< Operating activities	88-654304	2016-12-31
72	88-654306	400.00	t	88-654306-t-bond interest < Cash payments to bond holders< Operating activities	88-654304	2016-12-31
73	88-654308	320.00	t	88-654308-t-bond interest < Cash payments to bond holders< Operating activities	88-654304	2016-12-31
74	88-654309	200.00	t	88-654309-t-bond interest < Cash payments to bond holders< Operating activities	88-654304	2016-12-31
75	909876507	360.00	t	909876507-t-bond interest < Cash payments to bond holders< Operating activities	88-654304	2016-12-31
76	909876509	240.00	t	909876509-t-bond interest < Cash payments to bond holders< Operating activities	88-654304	2016-12-31
77	909876513	120.00	t	909876513-t-bond interest < Cash payments to bond holders< Operating activities	88-654304	2016-12-31
78	909876514	40.00	t	909876514-t-bond interest < Cash payments to bond holders< Operating activities	88-654304	2016-12-31
79	88-654305	126.00	t	88-654305-t-bond interest < Cash payments to bond holders< Operating activities	88-654304	2016-12-31

Figure 3.4-1   Business Bank1Cash Received or Paid by Other Members (Continue)

	IDM	Amount	Symbol	MultiSubaccount	Recorder	TransDate
80	88-654307	336.00	t	88-654307-t-bond interest < Cash payments to bond holders< Operating activities	88-654304	2016-12-31
81	88-654309	126.00	t	88-654309-t-bond interest < Cash payments to bond holders< Operating activities	88-654304	2016-12-31
82	88-654310	252.00	t	88-654310-t-bond interest < Cash payments to bond holders< Operating activities	88-654304	2016-12-31
83	909876501	210.00	t	909876501-t-bond interest < Cash payments to bond holders< Operating activities	88-654304	2016-12-31
84	909876502	84.00	t	909876502-t-bond interest < Cash payments to bond holders< Operating activities	88-654304	2016-12-31
85	909876504	294.00	t	909876504-t-bond interest < Cash payments to bond holders< Operating activities	88-654304	2016-12-31
86	909876521	252.00	t	909876521-t-bond interest < Cash payments to bond holders< Operating activities	88-654304	2016-12-31
87	88-654305	270.00	t	88-654305-t-bond interest < Cash payments to bond holders< Operating activities	88-654304	2016-12-31
88	88-654306	135.00	t	88-654306-t-bond interest < Cash payments to bond holders< Operating activities	88-654304	2016-12-31
89	88-654309	90.00	t	88-654309-t-bond interest < Cash payments to bond holders< Operating activities	88-654304	2016-12-31
90	909876503	270.00	t	909876503-t-bond interest < Cash payments to bond holders< Operating activities	88-654304	2016-12-31
91	909876505	180.00	t	909876505-t-bond interest < Cash payments to bond holders< Operating activities	88-654304	2016-12-31
92	909876506	315.00	t	909876506-t-bond interest < Cash payments to bond holders< Operating activities	88-654304	2016-12-31
93	909876515	180.00	t	909876515-t-bond interest < Cash payments to bond holders< Operating activities	88-654304	2016-12-31
94	909876517	225.00	t	909876517-t-bond interest < Cash payments to bond holders< Operating activities	88-654304	2016-12-31
95	909876518	135.00	t	909876518-t-bond interest < Cash payments to bond holders< Operating activities	88-654304	2016-12-31
96	909876519	270.00	t	909876519-t-bond interest < Cash payments to bond holders< Operating activities	88-654304	2016-12-31
97	909876521	180.00	t	909876521-t-bond interest < Cash payments to bond holders< Operating activities	88-654304	2016-12-31
98	88-654302	120.00	t	88-654302-t-deposit interest expenses < Cash payments for operating expenses < Operating act...	88-654304	2016-12-31
99	88-654303	120.00	t	88-654303-t-deposit interest expenses < Cash payments for operating expenses < Operating act...	88-654304	2016-12-31
100	88-654306	120.00	t	88-654306-t-deposit interest expenses < Cash payments for operating expenses < Operating act...	88-654304	2016-12-31
101	88-654309	120.00	t	88-654309-t-deposit interest expenses < Cash payments for operating expenses < Operating act...	88-654304	2016-12-31
102	909876501	120.00	t	909876501-t-deposit interest expenses < Cash payments for operating expenses < Operating ac...	88-654304	2016-12-31
103	909876502	120.00	t	909876502-t-deposit interest expenses < Cash payments for operating expenses < Operating ac...	88-654304	2016-12-31
104	909876503	120.00	t	909876503-t-deposit interest expenses < Cash payments for operating expenses < Operating ac...	88-654304	2016-12-31
105	909876504	120.00	t	909876504-t-deposit interest expenses < Cash payments for operating expenses < Operating ac...	88-654304	2016-12-31
106	909876505	120.00	t	909876505-t-deposit interest expenses < Cash payments for operating expenses < Operating ac...	88-654304	2016-12-31
107	909876506	120.00	t	909876506-t-deposit interest expenses < Cash payments for operating expenses < Operating ac...	88-654304	2016-12-31

	IDM	Amount	Symbol	MultiSubaccount	Recorder	TransDate
94	909876517	225.00	t	909876517-t-bond interest < Cash payments to bond holders< Operating activities	88-654304	2016-12-31
95	909876518	135.00	t	909876518-t-bond interest < Cash payments to bond holders< Operating activities	88-654304	2016-12-31
96	909876519	270.00	t	909876519-t-bond interest < Cash payments to bond holders< Operating activities	88-654304	2016-12-31
97	909876521	180.00	t	909876521-t-bond interest < Cash payments to bond holders< Operating activities	88-654304	2016-12-31
98	88-654302	120.00	t	88-654302-t-deposit interest expenses < Cash payments for operating expenses < Operating act...	88-654304	2016-12-31
99	88-654303	120.00	t	88-654303-t-deposit interest expenses < Cash payments for operating expenses < Operating act...	88-654304	2016-12-31
100	88-654306	120.00	t	88-654306-t-deposit interest expenses < Cash payments for operating expenses < Operating act...	88-654304	2016-12-31
101	88-654309	120.00	t	88-654309-t-deposit interest expenses < Cash payments for operating expenses < Operating act...	88-654304	2016-12-31
102	909876501	120.00	t	909876501-t-deposit interest expenses < Cash payments for operating expenses < Operating ac...	88-654304	2016-12-31
103	909876502	120.00	t	909876502-t-deposit interest expenses < Cash payments for operating expenses < Operating ac...	88-654304	2016-12-31
104	909876503	120.00	t	909876503-t-deposit interest expenses < Cash payments for operating expenses < Operating ac...	88-654304	2016-12-31
105	909876504	120.00	t	909876504-t-deposit interest expenses < Cash payments for operating expenses < Operating ac...	88-654304	2016-12-31
106	909876505	120.00	t	909876505-t-deposit interest expenses < Cash payments for operating expenses < Operating ac...	88-654304	2016-12-31
107	909876506	120.00	t	909876506-t-deposit interest expenses < Cash payments for operating expenses < Operating ac...	88-654304	2016-12-31
108	909876507	120.00	t	909876507-t-deposit interest expenses < Cash payments for operating expenses < Operating ac...	88-654304	2016-12-31
109	909876508	120.00	t	909876508-t-deposit interest expenses < Cash payments for operating expenses < Operating ac...	88-654304	2016-12-31
110	909876509	120.00	t	909876509-t-deposit interest expenses < Cash payments for operating expenses < Operating ac...	88-654304	2016-12-31
111	909876513	120.00	t	909876513-t-deposit interest expenses < Cash payments for operating expenses < Operating ac...	88-654304	2016-12-31
112	909876514	120.00	t	909876514-t-deposit interest expenses < Cash payments for operating expenses < Operating ac...	88-654304	2016-12-31
113	909876515	120.00	t	909876515-t-deposit interest expenses < Cash payments for operating expenses < Operating ac...	88-654304	2016-12-31
114	909876516	120.00	t	909876516-t-deposit interest expenses < Cash payments for operating expenses < Operating ac...	88-654304	2016-12-31
115	909876518	120.00	t	909876518-t-deposit interest expenses < Cash payments for operating expenses < Operating ac...	88-654304	2016-12-31
116	909876524	120.00	t	909876524-t-deposit interest expenses < Cash payments for operating expenses < Operating ac...	88-654304	2016-12-31
117	909876525	120.00	t	909876525-t-deposit interest expenses < Cash payments for operating expenses < Operating ac...	88-654304	2016-12-31
118	909876507	3000.00	t	909876507-t-salary < Cash payments for operating expenses < Operating activities	88-654304	2016-12-31
119	909876508	2910.00	t	909876508-t-salary < Cash payments for operating expenses < Operating activities	88-654304	2016-12-31
120	909876509	2750.00	t	909876509-t-salary < Cash payments for operating expenses < Operating activities	88-654304	2016-12-31
121	88-654305	-466.00	c	88-654305-c-investment income < Cash receipts from investments < Investing activities	88-654304	2016-12-31

Query executed successfully.

Figure 3.4-1　Business Bank1 Cash Received or Paid by Other Members

The following Figure 3.4-2 shows the Business Bank1 cash flows statement. From the Figure 3.4-2, the cash balance at the ending of this fiscal year is $1,364,039.73.

Cash Flow Statement

Cash Flows Statement Year Ended 2016-12-31	
Operating activities	
Cash payments for machinery	-$43,500.00
Cash payments for operating expenses	-$116,841.32
Cash payments to bond holders	-$6,330.00
Cash payments to suppliers	-$6,060.00
Cash receipts from customers	$94,750.00
Cash receipts from customers deposits	-$34,800.44
Net cash provided by Operating activities	-$112,781.76
Investing activities	
Cash receipts from investments	$466.00
Net cash provided by Investing activities	$466.00
Financial activities	
Net cash provided by Financial activities	$0.00
Net change in cash	-$112,315.76
Cash, Begining	$1,476,355.49
Cash, Ending	$1,364,039.73

Figure 3.4-2   Business Bank1 Cash Flows Statement

The Figure 3.4-3 on the next pages shows the Business Bank1 cash account table between 2016-01-02 and 2016-12-31. From the Figure 3.4-3, the cash balance on December 31, 2016 is also $1,364,039.73, which is the same as the sum1 in the Figure 3.4-2.

The Figure 3.4-4, which follows the Figure 3.4-3, shows the Business Bank1 income statement. From the Figure 3.4-4, the amount of the earnings before income taxes is -$61,679.76 and the amount of the tax expenses is zero, so the amount of the net earnings of the Business Bank1 in this fiscal year is also -$61,679.76.

Cash

	ID	Multi-Name	Amount	Balance	General ID	Transaction Date
▶	214	88-654302-d-deposits < Cash receipts from customers deposits < Oper...	$120.00	$1,453,664.74	139	2016-12-31
	215	88-654303-d-deposits < Cash receipts from customers deposits < Oper...	$95,000.00	$1,548,664.74	140	2016-01-02
	216	909876505-d-deposits < Cash receipts from customers deposits < Oper...	-$98.00	$1,548,566.74	141	2016-01-10
	217	909876506-d-deposits < Cash receipts from customers deposits < Oper...	-$92.00	$1,548,474.74	142	2016-01-10
	218	88-654303-d-deposits < Cash receipts from customers deposits < Oper...	-$283.71	$1,548,191.03	143	2016-01-12
	219	909876505-d-deposits < Cash receipts from customers deposits < Oper...	$283.71	$1,548,474.74	144	2016-01-12
	220	88-654303-d-deposits < Cash receipts from customers deposits < Oper...	-$277.71	$1,548,197.03	145	2016-01-12
	221	909876506-d-deposits < Cash receipts from customers deposits < Oper...	$277.71	$1,548,474.74	146	2016-01-12
	222	88-654303-d-deposits < Cash receipts from customers deposits < Oper...	-$60.00	$1,548,414.74	147	2016-01-13
	223	88-654303-d-deposits < Cash receipts from customers deposits < Oper...	-$5,670.00	$1,542,744.74	148	2016-01-31
	224	909876505-d-deposits < Cash receipts from customers deposits < Oper...	$2,810.00	$1,545,554.74	149	2016-01-31
	225	909876506-d-deposits < Cash receipts from customers deposits < Oper...	$2,860.00	$1,548,414.74	150	2016-01-31
	226	88-654303-d-deposits < Cash receipts from customers deposits < Oper...	-$500.00	$1,547,914.74	151	2016-02-02
	227	88-654303-d-deposits < Cash receipts from customers deposits < Oper...	-$400.00	$1,547,514.74	152	2016-02-11
	228	88-654303-d-deposits < Cash receipts from customers deposits < Oper...	-$300.00	$1,547,214.74	153	2016-02-23
	229	909876505-d-deposits < Cash receipts from customers deposits < Oper...	-$110.00	$1,547,104.74	154	2016-02-24
	230	88-654303-d-deposits < Cash receipts from customers deposits < Oper...	-$335.63	$1,546,769.11	155	2016-02-26
	231	909876505-d-deposits < Cash receipts from customers deposits < Oper...	$335.63	$1,547,104.74	156	2016-02-26
	232	88-654303-d-deposits < Cash receipts from customers deposits < Oper...	-$5,670.00	$1,541,434.74	157	2016-02-28
	233	909876505-d-deposits < Cash receipts from customers deposits < Oper...	$2,810.00	$1,544,244.74	158	2016-02-28
	234	909876506-d-deposits < Cash receipts from customers deposits < Oper...	$2,860.00	$1,547,104.74	159	2016-02-28
	235	909876506-d-deposits < Cash receipts from customers deposits < Oper...	-$123.00	$1,546,981.74	160	2016-03-10
	236	88-654303-d-deposits < Cash receipts from customers deposits < Oper...	-$419.99	$1,546,561.75	161	2016-03-12
	237	909876506-d-deposits < Cash receipts from customers deposits < Oper...	$419.99	$1,546,981.74	162	2016-03-12

	ID	Multi-Name	Amount	Balance	General ID	Transaction Date
	1188	909876503-d-deposits < Cash receipts from customers deposits < Oper...	$150.00	$1,368,621.23	1010	2016-08-10
	1189	909876503-d-deposits < Cash receipts from customers deposits < Oper...	$121.00	$1,368,742.23	1011	2016-10-21
	1190	909876503-d-deposits < Cash receipts from customers deposits < Oper...	$129.00	$1,368,871.23	1012	2016-12-20
	1191	909876504-d-deposits < Cash receipts from customers deposits < Oper...	$172.00	$1,369,043.23	1013	2016-03-19
	1192	909876504-d-deposits < Cash receipts from customers deposits < Oper...	$112.00	$1,369,155.23	1014	2016-07-16
	1193	909876506-d-deposits < Cash receipts from customers deposits < Oper...	-$450.00	$1,368,705.23	1015	2016-01-31
	1194	909876506-d-deposits < Cash receipts from customers deposits < Oper...	$92.00	$1,368,797.23	1016	2016-01-10
	1195	909876506-d-deposits < Cash receipts from customers deposits < Oper...	$123.00	$1,368,920.23	1017	2016-03-10
	1196	909876506-d-deposits < Cash receipts from customers deposits < Oper...	$112.00	$1,369,032.23	1018	2016-05-13
	1197	909876506-d-deposits < Cash receipts from customers deposits < Oper...	$93.00	$1,369,125.23	1019	2016-11-15
	1198	909876506-d-deposits < Cash receipts from customers deposits < Oper...	$198.00	$1,369,323.23	1020	2016-12-26
	1199	909876505-d-deposits < Cash receipts from customers deposits < Oper...	$98.00	$1,369,421.23	1021	2016-01-10
	1200	909876505-d-deposits < Cash receipts from customers deposits < Oper...	$110.00	$1,369,531.23	1022	2016-02-24
	1201	909876505-d-deposits < Cash receipts from customers deposits < Oper...	$105.00	$1,369,636.23	1023	2016-07-22
	1202	909876505-d-deposits < Cash receipts from customers deposits < Oper...	$116.00	$1,369,752.23	1024	2016-10-22
	1203	909876505-d-deposits < Cash receipts from customers deposits < Oper...	$192.00	$1,369,944.23	1025	2016-12-26
	1204	909876509-d-deposits < Cash receipts from customers deposits < Oper...	-$112.00	$1,369,832.23	1026	2016-09-17
	1205	909876513-d-deposits < Cash receipts from customers deposits < Oper...	$717.38	$1,370,549.61	1027	2016-04-28
	1206	909876515-d-deposits < Cash receipts from customers deposits < Oper...	$42.12	$1,370,591.73	1028	2016-01-16
	1207	909876518-d-deposits < Cash receipts from customers deposits < Oper...	$48.00	$1,370,639.73	1029	2016-12-31
	1208	88-654307-t-supplies < Cash payments for operating expenses < Opera...	-$5,200.00	$1,365,439.73	1031	2016-02-26
	1209	88-654306-t-suppliers < Cash payments to suppliers < Operating activiti...	-$1,400.00	$1,364,039.73	1032	2016-12-30

Figure 3.4-3   Business Bank1 Cash Account Table

Income Statement

Year ended: 12/31/2016	
Revenues	
Sales (notes interest)	$92,250.00
Cost	
Cost of notes interest	-$2,400.00
Gross Margin	$89,850.00
Operating and administrative expenses	
Travelling expenses	-$2,999.32
Other expenses	-$2,160.00
Office supplies expenses	-$4,873.95
Salary expenses	-$103,920.00
Vehicle part expenses	-$7,200.00
Bond interest expenses	-$6,330.00
Amortization expenses	-$27,012.49
Other income	
Investment incomes	$466.00
Deposits fee incomes	$2,500.00
Earnings Before Income Taxes	-$61,679.76
Tax	
Tax expenses	$0.00
Net Earnings	-$61,679.76
Retained Earnings,Begining	$0.00
Retained Earnings,Ending	-$61,679.76

Figure 3.4-4   Business Bank1 Income Statement

The Figure 3.4-5 on next page shows the Business Bank1 balance sheet. From the Figure 3.4-5, the amount of total assets is $2,456,694.26, and the amount of the total liabilities and the shareholders' equity is also $2,456,694.26.

Balance Sheet

	As at 12/31/2016
ASSETS	
Current assets	
Cash	$1,364,039.73
Supplies	$50.36
Notes receivable	$1,010,000.00
Account receivable	$0.00
	$2,374,090.09
Long term investments	
Bonds	$11,000.00
Equipment	
Vehicle	$124,000.00
Accumulated amortization: Vehicle	-$57,066.67
Computer	$5,900.00
Accumulated amortization: Computer	-$1,229.16
	$71,604.17
Total Assets	$2,456,694.26
LIABILITIES	
Current liabilities	
Account payable	$2,000.00
Deposits payable	$1,360,804.20
Tax payable	$0.00
	$1,362,804.20
Long term liabilities	
Bonds payable	$150,000.00
Total Liability	$1,512,804.20
SHAREHOLDERS' EQUITY	
Owners capital	
Share capital	$1,000,000.00
Retained earnings (Conversion)	$5,569.82
	$1,005,569.82
Retined earnings	-$61,679.76
Accumulated other comprehensive income	$0.00
Total Shareholders' Equity	$943,890.06
Total Liabilities and Shareholders' Equity	$2,456,694.26

Figure 3.4-5   Business Bank1 Balance Sheet Statement

3.5 Business Bank2

The Business Bank2 has also two class of transactions. One is itself transaction; another is only transaction of other organizations and individuals' deposit change. The transactions itself are first recorded. After that, the transactions of other organizations and individuals are recorded according to other organization's names.

3.5.1 An Accounting Fiscal Year of the Business Bank2

In the new fiscal year, the Business Bank2 occurs the two class of transactions: the Business Bank2 itself transactions and the customer deposit transactions.

3.5.1.1 Business Bank2 Itself Transactions

- On January 2, 2016, the Business Bank2 purchases the supplies $186 (supplies1 $14*3 and supplies2 $16*9) from the Proprietorship2 (phone number: 123456780) for cash -$186. The multi-subaccount name of the Cash account is:

  88-654310-t-supplies < Cash payments for operating expenses < Operating activities

- On January 10, 2016, A1 receives cash $10,000 from A1's primary account in the Business Bank1. The multi-subaccount name of the Cash account and the transaction sub-equation are respectively:

  909876501-d-deposits < Cash receipts from customers deposits < Operating

  Cash (1): 10000 = Deposits payable (2): 10000

- On January 15, 2016, Government1 transfers $600 from the Business Bank2 to its primary account in the Business Bank1. The multi-subaccount name of the Cash account and the transaction sub-equation are respectively:

  88-654302-d-deposits < Cash receipts from customers deposits < Operating activities

  Cash (1): -600 = Deposits payable (2): -600

- On January 17, 2016, the Business Bank2 pays -$144.36 cash to A11 (SIN: 909876511) for the Travelling expenses (travel allowance) $90.36 and the Other expenses (meals: food621: $26*1 + food622: $28*1) $54. The multi-subaccount name of the Cash account and transaction sub-equation are respectively:

  909876511-n-operating expenses < Cash payments for operating expenses < Operating activities

  Cash (1): -144.36 = Travelling expenses (5): -90.36 + other expenses (5): 54

  The twin multi-subaccount name of the Cash account and the twin transaction sub-equation are respectively:

  88-654311-d-deposits < Cash receipts from customers deposits < Operating

  Cash (1): 144.36 = Deposits payable (2): 144.36

- On January 24, 2016, the Business Bank2 pays -$265.94 cash to A12 (SIN: 909876512) for the Travelling expenses (travel allowance) $145.94 and the Other expenses (meals: food53: $16*4 + food622: $28*2) $120.

- On January 26, 2016, A12 transfers $13,000 to his or her second account in the Business Bank1. The multi-subaccount name of the Cash account and the transaction sub-equation are respectively:

  909876512-d-deposits < Cash receipts from customers deposits < Operating

  Cash (1): -13000 = Deposits payable (2): -13000

- On January 29, 2016, the Business Bank2 pays -$158.67 cash to A10 (SIN: 909876510) for the Travelling expenses (travel allowance) $101.67 and the Other expenses (meals: food321: $27*1 + food322: $30*1) $57.

- On January 31, 2016, the Business Bank2 pays three employees' salary expenses for cash -$8,640. The three multi-subaccount names of the Cash account and the transaction sub-equation respectively are:

909876510-t-salary < Cash payments for operating expenses < Operating activities

909876511-t-salary < Cash payments for operating expenses < Operating activities

909876512-t-salary < Cash payments for operating expenses < Operating activities

Cash (1): -3000 + Cash (1): -2900 + Cash (1): -2740 = Salary expenses (5): -8640

The twin three multi-subaccount names of the Cash account and the twin transaction sub-equation are respectively:

88-654310-d-deposits < Cash receipts from customers deposits < Operating activities

88-654311-d-deposits < Cash receipts from customers deposits < Operating activities

88-654312-d-deposits < Cash receipts from customers deposits < Operating activities

Cash (1): 3000 + Cash (1): 2900 + Cash (1): 2740 = Deposits payable (2): 3000 + Deposits payable (2): 2900 + Deposits payable (2): 2740

- On February 8, 2016, the Business Bank2 pays -$272.76 cash to A12 (SIN: 909876512) for the Travelling expenses (travel allowance) $156.76 and the Other expenses (meals: food611: $20*3 + food622: $28*2) $116.
- On February 28, 2016, the Business Bank2 pays three employees' salary expenses for cash $8,640 repeatedly.
- On March 1, 2016, the Business Bank2 purchases one Car2 $39,000from the Company1 (phone number: 123456084) for cash -$19,000 and other on credit. The multi-subaccount name of the Cash account and transaction sub-equation respectively are:

88-654306-t-machinery < Cash payments for machinery < Operating activities

Cash (1): -19000 + Vehicle (1): 39000 = Account payable (2): 20000

- On March 9, 2016, the Business Bank2 pays -$247.59 cash to A12 (SIN: 909876512) for the Travelling expenses (travel allowance) $147.59 and the Other expenses (meals: food521: $12*4 + food621: $26*2) $100.

- On March 13, 2016, the Business Bank2 pays -$149.61 cash to A11 (SIN: 909876511) for the Travelling expenses (travel allowance) $99.61 and the Other expenses (meals: food111: $10*2 + food322: $30*1) $50.

- On March 31, 2016, the Business Bank2 pays three employees' salary expenses for cash $8,640 repeatedly.

- On April 6, 2016, the Business Bank2 purchases the following supplies (inventories) -$2,200 from the Company3 (phone number: 123456782) for cash -$1,500 and other on credit. Here, the supplies will be recorded as the Office supplies expenses for simplification.

Inven111 < Inven11 < Inven1: 10*10

Inven112 < Inven11 < Inven1: 40*10

Inven221 < Inven22 < Inven2: 30*20

Inven222 < Inven22 < Inven2: 50*20

PPGH parts < ASD parts < Inven2: 2*50

The multi-subaccount name of the Cash account and transaction sub-equation respectively are:

88-654308-t-suppliers < Cash payments to suppliers < Operating activities

Cash (1): -1500 = Account payable (2): 700 + Office supplies expenses (5): -2200

- On April 15, 2016, the Business Bank2 pays -$172.53 cash to A11 (SIN: 909876511) for the Travelling expenses (travel allowance) -$103.53 and the Other expenses (meals: food222: $13*3 + food322: $30*1) $69.

- On April 19, 2016, the Business Bank2 pays -$288.24 cash to A12 (SIN: 909876512) for the Travelling expenses (travel allowance) $168.24 and the Other expenses meals: food53: $16*4 + food622: $28*2) $120.

- On April 30, 2016, the Business Bank2 pays three employees' salary expenses for cash -$8,640 repeatedly.

- On May 22, 2016, the Business Bank2 pays -$159.22 cash to A11 (SIN: 909876511) for the Travelling expenses (travel allowance) $103.22 and the Other expenses (meals: food121: $13*2 + food322: $30*1) $56.

- On May 26, 2016, the Business Bank2 pays -$273.52 cash to A12 (SIN: 909876512) for the Travelling expenses (travel allowance) $165.52 and the Other expenses (meals: food522: $13*4 + food622: $28*2) $108.

- On May 31, 2016, the Business Bank2 pays three employees' salary expenses for cash -$8,640 repeatedly.

- On June 1, 2016, the Business Bank2 issues one Bond23 $40,000 (three years, 4.5% annually, pay at end of each year), seeing the following Figure 3.5-1.

Order	Bond	Amount	Term	Purchaser Name	Identity
1	Bond23	25000	June 1, 2016, three years, 4.5% annually, pay at end of each year	Cash Management Center	88-654300
2	Bond23	5000	June 1, 2016, three years, 4.5% annually, pay at end of each year	Central Bank	88-654301
3	Bond23	5000	June 1, 2016, three years, 4.5% annually, pay at end of each year	Government1	88-654302
4	Bond23	5000	June 1, 2016, three years, 4.5% annually, pay at end of each year	Tax Bureau	88-654303
9	**Total**	**40000**			

Figure 3.5-1 Business Bank2 Issued Bond Information Table

The multi-subaccount name of the Cash account and transaction sub-equation respectively are:

88-654300-i-bond23 < Cash receipts from issued bonds < Financial activities

88-654301-i-bond23 < Cash receipts from issued bonds < Financial activities

88-654302-i-bond23 < Cash receipts from issued bonds < Financial activities

88-654303-i-bond23 < Cash receipts from issued bonds < Financial activities

Cash (1): 25000 + Cash (1): 5000 + Cash (1): 5000 + Cash (1): 5000 = Bonds payable (2): 25000 + Bonds payable (2): 5000 + Bonds payable (2): 5000 + Bonds payable (2): 5000

- On June 21, 2016, the Business Bank2 pays -$278.54 cash to A12 (SIN: 909876512) for the Travelling expenses (travel allowance) $169.54 and the Other expenses (meals: food214: $11*5 + food321: $27*2) $109.

- On June 30, 2016, the Business Bank2 pays three employees' salary expenses for cash -$8,640 repeatedly.

- On July 11, 2016, the Business Bank2 pays -$187.57 cash to A11 (SIN: 909876511) for the Travelling expenses (travel allowance) $113.57 and the Other expenses (meals: food612: $24*2 + food621: $26*1) $74.

- On July 23, 2016, the Business Bank2 pays -$308.39 cash to A12 (SIN: 909876512) for the Travelling expenses (travel allowance) $183.39 and the Other expenses (meals: food222: $13*5 + food322: $30*2) $125.

- On July 31, 2016, the Business Bank2 pays three employees' salary expenses for cash -$8,640 repeatedly.

- On August 19, 2016, the Business Bank2 pays -$161.88 cash to A10 (SIN: 909876510) for the Travelling expenses (travel allowance) $98.88 and the Other expenses (meals: food221: $12*3 + food321: $27*1) $63.

- On August 24, 2016, the Business Bank2 pays -$267.61 cash to A12 (SIN: 909876512) for the Travelling expenses (travel allowance) $155.61 and the Other expenses (meals: food23: $16*4 + food312: $24*2) $112.

- On August 31, 2016, the Business Bank2 pays three employees' salary expenses for cash -$8,640 repeatedly.

- On September 19, 2016, the Business Bank2 pays -$251.18 cash to A12 (SIN: 909876512) for the Travelling expenses (travel allowance) $147.18 and the Other expenses (meals: food213: $10*5 + food321: $27*2) $104.

- On September 26, 2016, the Business Bank2 pays -$17,000 cash to the Company1 (phone number: 123456784) with the General ID 635. The multi-subaccount name of the Cash account is:

  88-654306-t-machinery < Cash payments for machinery < Operating activities

- On September 30 2016, the Business Bank2 pays three employees' salary expenses for cash -$8,640 repeatedly.

- On September 30, 2016, the Business Bank2 records the Amortization expenses - $2,212.5 of a computer server1 (-$1,050, nine months), a computer1 (-$600, nine months), and a computer2 (-$562.5, nine months). The transaction sub-equation is:

  Accumulated amortization: Computer (1): -1050 + Accumulated amortization: Computer (1): -600 + Accumulated amortization: Computer (1): -562.5 = Amortization expenses (5): -1050 + Amortization expenses (5): -600 + Amortization expenses (5): -562.5

- On September 30, 2016, the Business Bank2 cancels the balances of the Computer account and the Accumulated amortization: Computer account because these computers have used for two years. The transaction sub-equation is:

  Computer (1): -2800 + Computer (1): -1600 + Computer (1): -1500 + Accumulated amortization: Computer (1): 2800 + Accumulated amortization: Computer (1): 1600 + Accumulated amortization: Computer (1): 1500 = 0

- On October 1, 2016, the Business Bank2 purchases one Computer server1 $2,800, one Computer1 $1,600, and one Computer2 $1,500 from the Company1 (phone number: 123456784) for cash -$5,000 and other on credit. The multi-subaccount name of the Cash account and transaction sub-equation respectively are:

  88-654306-t-machinery < Cash payments for machinery < Operating activities

  Cash (1): -5000 + Computer (1): 2800 + Computer (1): 1600 + Computer (1):

1500 = Account payable (2): 900

- On October 18, 2016, the Business Bank2 pays -$260.75 cash to A12 (SIN: 909876512) for the Travelling expenses (travel allowance) $152.75 and the Other expenses (meals: food123: $15*4 + food23: $16*3) $108.

- On October 31, 2016, the Business Bank2 pays three employees' salary expenses for cash -$8,640 repeatedly.

- On November 3, 2016, the Business Bank2 pays -$161.42 cash to A11 (SIN: 909876511) for the Travelling expenses (travel allowance) $100.42 and the Other expenses (meals: food514: $11*3 + food622: $28*1) $61.

- On November 21, 2016, the Business Bank2 pays -$250.43 cash to A12 (SIN: 909876512) for the Travelling expenses (travel allowance) $150.43 and the Other expenses (meals: food113: $12*5 + food311: $20*2) $100.

- On November 30, 2016, the Business Bank2 pays three employees' salary expenses for cash -$8,640 repeatedly.

- On December 4, 2016, the Business Bank2 pays -$152.24 cash to A10 (SIN: 909876510) for the Travelling expenses (travel allowance) $76.24 and the Other expenses (meals: food612: $24*2 + food622: $28*1) $76.

- On December 19, 2016, the Business Bank2 pays -$2,800 cash to the Company1 (phone number: 123456784) with the General ID 635. The multi-subaccount name of the Cash account is:

  88-654306-t-machinery < Cash payments for machinery < Operating activities

- On December 29, 2016, the Business Bank2 pays -$302.36 cash to A12 (SIN: 909876512) for the Travelling expenses (travel allowance) $177.36 and the Other expenses (meals: food222: $13*5 + food322: $30*2) $125.

- On December 31, 2016, the Business Bank2 receives cash $19,800 from the Company1 for interest income of the Note21 ($220,000, 9%). Here, the interest incomes of the notes are recorded as the Sales (notes interest) account for the Business Banks. The multi-subaccount name of the Cash account and transaction sub-equation respectively are:

88-654306-c-customers < Cash receipts from customers < Operating activities

Cash (1): 19800 = Sales (notes interest) (4): 19800

- On December 31, 2016, the Business Bank2 receives cash $21,600 from the Company2 for interest income of the Note22 ($240,000, 9%).
- On December 31, 2016, the Business Bank2 receives cash $34,400 ($16,200 + $18,200) from the Company3 for interest income of the Note23 ($180,000), 9% and Note24 ($200,000, 9.1%).
- On December 31, 2016, the Business Bank2 receives cash $11,280 from the Proprietorship1 for interest income of the Note25 ($120,000, 9.4%).
- On the same day, the Business Bank2 receives cash $676 (= $280 + $126 + $270) for investment interest of the Bond11 ($7,000), Bond12 ($3,000), and the Bond13 ($6,000) from the Business Bank1. The multi-subaccount name of the Cash account and transaction sub-equation respectively are:

  88-654304-c-investment income < Cash receipts from investments < Investing activities

  Cash (1): 676 = Investment incomes (4):280 + Investment incomes (4): 126 + Investment incomes (4): 270

- On the same day, the Business Bank2 receives cash $230 for investment interest of the Bond31 ($5,000) from the Company1. The multi-subaccount name of the Cash account and transaction sub-equation respectively are:

  88-654306-c-investment income < Cash receipts from investments < Investing activities

  Cash (1): 230 = Investment incomes (4): 230

- On the same day, the Business Bank2 receives cash $376 for investment interest of the Bond41 ($8,000) from the Company2. The multi-subaccount name of the Cash account and transaction sub-equation respectively are:

88-654307-c-investment income < Cash receipts from investments < Investing activities

Cash (1): 376 = Investment incomes (4): 376

- On December 31, the Business Bank2 pays -$3,280 cash to the bond holders for the Bond interest expenses of the Bond21 (one-level subaccount "Bond21-interest"). Here, there is some twin transactions for the individuals whose primary accounts (seeing the Figure 2.1-3 on the page 13) are opened in the Business Bank2, and other individuals are recorded in the Business Bank1. Therefore, the multi-subaccount names of the Cash account and the transaction sub-equations respectively are:

  88-654302-t-bond interest< Cash payments to bond holders< Operating activities
  88-654303-t-bond interest< Cash payments to bond holders< Operating activities
  88-654304-t-bond interest< Cash payments to bond holders< Operating activities
  88-654306-t-bond interest< Cash payments to bond holders< Operating activities
  88-654308-t-bond interest< Cash payments to bond holders< Operating activities
  88-654310-t-bond interest< Cash payments to bond holders< Operating activities
  909876507-t-bond interest< Cash payments to bond holders< Operating activities
  909876509-t-bond interest< Cash payments to bond holders< Operating activities
  909876513-t-bond interest< Cash payments to bond holders< Operating activities
  909876514-t-bond interest< Cash payments to bond holders< Operating activities
  909876518-t-bond interest< Cash payments to bond holders< Operating activities
  909876520-t-bond interest< Cash payments to bond holders< Operating activities

  Cash (1): -369 + Cash (1): -328 + Cash (1): -246 + Cash (1): -369 + Cash (1): -492 + Cash (1): -287 + Cash (1): -164 + Cash (1): -246 = Bond interest expenses (5): -2501

Cash (1): -123 + Cash (1): -205 + Cash (1): -123 + Cash (1): -328 = Bond interest expenses (5): -779

The twin transaction sub-equation for the A20 (SIN: 909876520) is:

Cash (1): 328 = Deposits payable (2): 328

- On the same day, the Business Bank2 pays -$2,640 cash to the bond holders for the Bond interest expenses of the Bond22 (one-level subaccount "Bond22-interest"). Here, there is some twin transactions for the individuals whose primary accounts (seeing the Figure 2.1-3 on the page 13) are opened in the Business Bank2, and other individuals are recorded in the Business Bank1. Therefore, the multi-subaccount names of the Cash account and the transaction sub-equations respectively are:

  88-654304-t-bond interest< Cash payments to bond holders< Operating activities
  88-654307-t-bond interest< Cash payments to bond holders< Operating activities
  88-654309-t-bond interest< Cash payments to bond holders< Operating activities
  88-654310-t-bond interest< Cash payments to bond holders< Operating activities
  909876503-t-bond interest< Cash payments to bond holders< Operating activities
  909876504-t-bond interest< Cash payments to bond holders< Operating activities
  909876506-t-bond interest< Cash payments to bond holders< Operating activities
  909876511-t-bond interest< Cash payments to bond holders< Operating activities
  909876519-t-bond interest< Cash payments to bond holders< Operating activities
  909876520-t-bond interest< Cash payments to bond holders< Operating activities

Cash (1): -220 + Cash (1): -264 + Cash (1): -352 + Cash (1): -176 + Cash (1): -264 + Cash (1): -308 + Cash (1): -264 + Cash (1): -352 + Cash (1): -132 = Bond interest expenses (5): -2332

Cash (1): -308 = Bond interest expenses (5): -308

The twin transaction sub-equation for 909876511, 909876519, and 909876520 is:

Cash (1): 352 + Cash (1): 132 + Cash (1): 308 = Deposits payable (2): 352 + Deposits payable (2): 132 + Deposits payable (2): 308

- On the same day, the Business Bank2 pays -$1,050 cash to the bond holders for the Bond interest expenses of the Bond23 (one-level subaccount "Bond23-interest"). The multi-subaccount names of the Cash account and the transaction sub-equations respectively are:

   88-654300-t-bond interest < Cash payments to bond holders< Operating activities
   88-654301-t-bond interest < Cash payments to bond holders< Operating activities
   88-654302-t-bond interest < Cash payments to bond holders< Operating activities
   88-654303-t-bond interest < Cash payments to bond holders< Operating activities

   Cash (1): -656.25 + Cash (1): -131.25 + Cash (1): -131.25 + Cash (1): -131.25 = Bond interest expenses (5): -1050

- On the same day, the Business Bank2 pays cash -$1,560 to its customers (not including itself) for primary deposit interest (interest expenses). Here, the Deposit interest expenses are recorded as the one-level subaccount of the Cost of notes interest account for the Business Banks. In addition, there is some twin transactions for its individuals whose primary accounts (seeing the Figure 2.1-3 on the page 13) are opened in the Business Bank2, and other individuals are recorded in the Business Bank1. The twin transactions for its organization customers have been recorded by these related organizations. The multi-subaccount names of the Cash account and transaction sub-equations respectively are:

   88-654301-t-deposit interest expenses < Cash payments for operating expenses < Operating activities
   88-654307-t-deposit interest expenses < Cash payments for operating expenses < Operating activities
   88-654308-t-deposit interest expenses < Cash payments for operating expenses <

Operating activities

88-654310-t-deposit interest expenses < Cash payments for operating expenses < Operating activities

909876510-t-deposit interest expenses < Cash payments for operating expenses < Operating activities

909876511-t-deposit interest expenses < Cash payments for operating expenses < Operating activities

909876512-t-deposit interest expenses < Cash payments for operating expenses < Operating activities

909876517-t-deposit interest expenses < Cash payments for operating expenses < Operating activities

909876519-t-deposit interest expenses < Cash payments for operating expenses < Operating activities

909876520-t-deposit interest expenses < Cash payments for operating expenses < Operating activities

909876521-t-deposit interest expenses < Cash payments for operating expenses < Operating activities

909876522-t-deposit interest expenses < Cash payments for operating expenses < Operating activities

909876523-t-deposit interest expenses < Cash payments for operating expenses < Operating activities

Cash (1): -120 + Cash (1): -120 + Cash (1): -120 + Cash (1): -120 + Cash (1): -120 + Cash (1): -120 + Cash (1): -120 + Cash (1): -120 + Cash (1): -120 = Cost of notes interest (5): -1080

Cash (1): -120 + Cash (1): -120 + Cash (1): -120 + Cash (1): -120 = Cost of notes interest (5): -480

The twin transaction sub-equations for the above individuals (A10, A11, A12, A17, A19, A20, A21, A22, and A23) are:

Cash (1): 120 + Cash (1): 120 + Cash (1): 120 + Cash (1): 120 + Cash (1): 120 = Deposits payable (2): 120 + Deposits payable (2): 120 + Deposits payable (2): 120 + Deposits payable (2): 120 + Deposits payable (2): 120

Cash (1): 120 + Cash (1): 120 + Cash (1): 120 + Cash (1): 120 = Deposits payable (2): 120 + Deposits payable (2): 120 + Deposits payable (2): 120 + Deposits payable (2): 120

- On December 31, 2016, the Business Bank2 pays three employees' salary expenses for cash -$8,640 repeatedly.

- On the same day, the Business Bank2 records the Office supplies expenses -$215.77. The transaction sub-equation is:

Supplies (1): -215.77 = Office supplies expenses (5): -215.77

- On the same day, the Business Bank2 records the Vehicle's amortization expenses -$22,100 (5 years, straight line) which includes a Truck2 ($8,000, one year), a Car3($7,600, one year), and a new Car2 ($6,500, ten months). The two transaction sub-equations are:

Accumulated amortization: Vehicle (1): -8000 + Accumulated amortization: Vehicle (1): -7600 + Accumulated amortization: Vehicle (1): -6500 = Amortization expenses (5): -8000 + Amortization expenses (5): -7600 + Amortization expenses (5): -6500

- On the same day, the Business Bank2 records the Computer's amortization expenses $245.84 three months (2 years, straight line) which includes a new computer server1 ($350), a new computer1 ($200), and a new computer2 ($62.5). The transaction sub-equation is:

Accumulated amortization: Computer (1): -350 + Accumulated amortization: Computer (1): -200 + Accumulated amortization: Computer (1): -187.5 = Amortization expenses (5): -350 + Amortization expenses (5): -200 + Amortization expenses (5): -187.5

- On December 31, the Business Bank2 records the Tax expenses $0 and the Tax payable $0. The multi-subaccount name forms of the Tax expenses and the Tax payable accounts all are the 'n'. The transaction sub-equation is:

  0 = Tax payable (2): 0 + Tax expenses (5): 0

So far, I have entered all transactions of the Business Bank2 in the fiscal year 2016. After getting the Income Statement and clicking the "Yes" button for new fiscal year, I can get the Balance Sheet of the Business Bank2.

3.5.1.2 Customer Deposit Transactions

The followings is a list of all deposit transactions which are ordered by organizations or companies in the Business Bank2.

- **Cash Management Center.**
- On December 31, 2016, individual A10's cash deposit increases $200.
- On December 31, 2016, individual A11's cash deposit increases $200.
- On December 31, 2016, individual A12's cash deposit increases $200.
- On December 31, 2016, individual A21's cash deposit increases $200.
- On December 31, 2016, individual A22's cash deposit increases $200.

- **Central Bank.**
- On January 2, 2016, the Central Bank's cash deposit increases $85,000. The multi-subaccount name of the Cash account and transaction sub-equation respectively are:

  88-654301-d-deposits < Cash receipts from customers deposits < Operating

activities

Cash (1): 85000 = Deposits payable (2): 85000 = 0

- On January 21, 2016, the Central Bank's cash deposit decreases -$176.56.
- On January 31, 2016, the Central Bank's cash deposit decreases -$5,650.
- On February 13, 2016, the Central Bank's cash deposit decreases -$800.
- On February 13, 2016, the Central Bank's cash deposit decreases -$200.
- On February 22, 2016, the Central Bank's cash deposit decreases -$3,600.
- On February 28, 2016, the Central Bank's cash deposit decreases -$5,650.
- On March 25, 2016, the Central Bank's cash deposit decreases -$600.
- On March 28, 2016, the Central Bank's cash deposit decreases -$459.61.
- On March 31, 2016, the Central Bank's cash deposit decreases -$5,650.
- On April 19, 2016, the Central Bank's cash deposit decreases -$159.78.
- On April 30, 2016, the Central Bank's cash deposit decreases -$5,650.
- On May 1, 2016, the Central Bank's cash deposit decreases -$1,900.
- On May 16, 2016, the Central Bank's cash deposit decreases -$316.
- On May 31, 2016, the Central Bank's cash deposit decreases -$5,650.
- On June 1, 2016, the Central Bank's cash deposit decreases -$5,000.
- On June 22, 2016, the Central Bank's cash deposit decreases -$477.25.
- On June 30, 2016, the Central Bank's cash deposit decreases -$5,650.
- On July 31, 2016, the Central Bank's cash deposit decreases -$5,650.
- On August 14, 2016, the Central Bank's cash deposit decreases -$1,040.
- On August 31, 2016, the Central Bank's cash deposit decreases -$5,650.
- On September 7, 2016, the Central Bank's cash deposit decreases -$233.16.
- On September 30, 2016, the Central Bank's cash deposit decreases -$5,650.
- On October 31, 2016, the Central Bank's cash deposit decreases -$5,650.
- On November 30, 2016, the Central Bank's cash deposit decreases -$5,650.
- On December 11, 2016, the Central Bank's cash deposit decreases -$552.37.

- On December 31, 2016, the Central Bank's cash deposit decreases -$5,650.

- On December 31, 2016, the Central Bank's cash deposit increases $131.25.

- On December 31, 2016, the Central Bank's cash deposit increases $120.

- On December 31, 2016, the Central Bank's cash deposit decreases -$3,500.

- **Company1.**

- On August 1, 2016, individual A16's cash deposit decreases -$11,000.

- On August 1, 2016, the A23's cash deposit decreases -$5,500.

- On August 10, 2016, the A11's cash deposit decreases -$1,500.

- On October 5, 2016, the A13's cash deposit decreases -$11,500.

- On October 5, 2016, the A25's cash deposit decreases -$7,000.

- On December 19, 2016, the A22's cash deposit decreases -$1,600.

- On December 31, 2016, the A10's cash deposit decreases -$40,000.

- On December 31, 2016, the A11's cash deposit increases $322.

- On December 31, 2016, the A21's cash deposit increases $138.

- On December 31, 2016, the A22's cash deposit increases $230.

- **Company2.**

- On January 2, 2016, the Company2's cash deposit decreases -$500.

- On January 12, 2016, the Company2's cash deposit increases $360.

- On January 14, 2016, the Company2's cash deposit increases $11,000.

- On January 15, 2016, the Company2's cash deposit decreases -$5000.

- On January 15, 2016, the Company2's cash deposit decreases -$411.32.

- On January 18, 2016, the Company2's cash deposit decreases -$112.57.

- On January 18, 2016, the A17's cash deposit increases $112.57.

- On January 24, 2016, the Company2's cash deposit increases $600.

- On January 27, 2016, the Company2's cash deposit increases $250.

- On January 28, 2016, the Company2's cash deposit increases $7000.

- On January 30, 2016, the Company2's cash deposit decreases -$379.78.

- On January 30, 2016, the Company2's cash deposit decreases -$500.

- On January 30, 2016, the Company2's cash deposit decreases -$300.

- On January 31, 2016, the Company2's cash deposit decreases -$8,380.

- On January 31, 2016, the A17's cash deposit increases $2,890.

- On February 11, 2016, the Company2's cash deposit increases $400.

- On February 20, 2016, the Company2's cash deposit decreases -$557.83.

- On February 21, 2016, the Company2's cash deposit increases $500.

- On February 25, 2016, the Company2's cash deposit decreases -$600.

- On February 26, 2016, the Company2's cash deposit increases $5200.

- On February 28, 2016, the Company2's cash deposit decreases -$8,380.

- On February 28, 2016, the A17's cash deposit increases $2,890.

- On March 1, 2016, the Company2's cash deposit decreases -$221.16.

- On March 4, 2016, the Company2's cash deposit increases $2,400.

- On March 23, 2016, the Company2's cash deposit decreases -$347.65.

- On March 26, 2016, the Company2's cash deposit decreases -$253.93.

- On March 26, 2016, the A17's cash deposit increases $253.93.

- On March 30, 2016, the Company2's cash deposit decreases -$700.

- On March 31, 2016, the Company2's cash deposit decreases -$8,380.

- On March 31, 2016, the A17's cash deposit increases $2,890.

- On April 12, 2016, the Company2's cash deposit increases $310.

- On April 26, 2016, the Company2's cash deposit decreases -$369.88.

- On April 29, 2016, the Company2's cash deposit increases $5,000.

- On April 30, 2016, the Company2's cash deposit decreases -$8,380.

- On April 30, 2016, the A17's cash deposit increases $2,890.

- On May 1, 2016, the Company2's cash deposit increases $15,000.

- On May 2, 2016, the Company2's cash deposit decreases -$307.09.

- On May 3, 2016, the Company2's cash deposit increases $290.

- On May 24, 2016, the Company2's cash deposit decreases -$366.59.

- On May 31, 2016, the Company2's cash deposit decreases -$8,380.

- On May 31, 2016, the A17's cash deposit increases $2,890.

- On June 12, 2016, the Company2's cash deposit increases $64,000.

- On June 14, 2016, the Company2's cash deposit decreases -$255.54.

- On June 14, 2016, the A17's cash deposit increases $255.54.

- On June 23, 2016, the Company2's cash deposit decreases -$362.81.

- On June 30, 2016, the Company2's cash deposit decreases -$8,380.

- On June 30, 2016, the A17's cash deposit increases $2,890.

- On July 11, 2016, the Company2's cash deposit increases $290.

- On July 13, 2016, the Company2's cash deposit increases $320.

- On July 27, 2016, the Company2's cash deposit decreases -$307.41.

- On July 31, 2016, the Company2's cash deposit decreases -$8,380.

- On July 31, 2016, the A17's cash deposit increases $2,890.

- On August 1, 2016, the Company2's cash deposit decreases -$3,000.

- On August 3, 2016, the Company2's cash deposit increases $12,000.

- On August 13, 2016, the Company2's cash deposit increases $360.

- On August 13, 2016, the A11's cash deposit decreases -$360.

- On August 16, 2016, the Company2's cash deposit decreases -$373.77.

- On August 16, 2016, the A17's cash deposit increases $373.77.

- On August 23, 2016, the Company2's cash deposit decreases -$392.33.

- On August 31, 2016, the Company2's cash deposit decreases -$8,380.

- On August 31, 2016, the A17's cash deposit increases $2,890.

- On September 3, 2016, the Company2's cash deposit increases $310.

- On September 3, 2016, the A19's cash deposit decreases -$310.

- On September 10, 2016, the Company2's cash deposit increases $320.

- On September 10, 2016, the A22's cash deposit decreases -$320.

- On September 12, 2016, the Company2's cash deposit increases $4,000.

- On September 14, 2016, the Company2's cash deposit decreases -$380.

- On September 14, 2016, the Company2's cash deposit increases $10,000.

- On September 26, 2016, the Company2's cash deposit increases $1,800.

- On September 28, 2016, the Company2's cash deposit decreases -$410.89.

- On September 30, 2016, the Company2's cash deposit decreases -$8,380.

- On September 30, 2016, the A17's cash deposit increases $2,890.

- On October 3, 2016, the Company2's cash deposit increases $4,500.

- On October 6, 2016, the Company2's cash deposit decreases -$377.63.

- On October 27, 2016, the Company2's cash deposit decreases -$396.27.

- On October 31, 2016, the Company2's cash deposit decreases -$8,380.

- On October 31, 2016, the A17's cash deposit increases $2,890.

- On November 19, 2016, the Company2's cash deposit decreases -$399.28.

- On November 20, 2016, the Company2's cash deposit increases $360.

- On November 29, 2016, the Company2's cash deposit increases $14,420.

- On November 30, 2016, the Company2's cash deposit decreases -$8,380.

- On November 30, 2016, the A17's cash deposit increases $2,890.

- On December 17, 2016, the Company2's cash deposit decreases -$395.88.

- On December 20, 2016, the Company2's cash deposit decreases -$424.37.

- On December 29, 2016, the Company2's cash deposit increases $39,700.

- On December 30, 2016, the Company2's cash deposit decreases -$600.

- On December 31, 2016, the Company2's cash deposit increases $55,000.

- On December 31, 2016, the Company2's cash deposit decreases -$8,380.

- On December 31, 2016, the A17's cash deposit increases $2,890.

- On December 31, 2016, the Company2's cash deposit decreases -$35,600.

- On December 31, 2016, the Company2's cash deposit decreases -$21,600.

- On December 31, 2016, the Company2's cash deposit decreases -$1,880 (total amount of Bond41).

- On December 31, 2016, the A10's cash deposit increases $141.

- On December 31, 2016, the A19's cash deposit increases $141.

- On December 31, 2016, the A20's cash deposit increases $94.

- On December 31, 2016, the A23's cash deposit increases $141.

- On December 31, 2016, the Company2's cash deposit increases $336.

- On December 31, 2016, the Company2's cash deposit increases $264.

- On December 31, 2016, the Company2's cash deposit increases $120.

- **Company3.**

- On January 2, 2016, the Company3's cash deposit decreases -$400.

- On January 2, 2016, the Company3's cash deposit increases $10,000.

- On January 2, 2016, the Company3's cash deposit increases $8,000.

- On January 3, 2016, the Company3's cash deposit decreases -$9,300.

- On January 3, 2016, the Company3's cash deposit decreases -$6,000.

- On January 13, 2016, the Company3's cash deposit increases $150.

- On January 13, 2016, the Company3's cash deposit increases $2,000.

- On January 14, 2016, the Company3's cash deposit increases $8,000.

- On January 15, 2016, the Company3's cash deposit increases $5,000.

- On January 18, 2016, the Company3's cash deposit decreases -$261.26.

- On January 18, 2016, the A19's cash deposit increases $261.26.

- On January 19, 2016, the Company3's cash deposit decreases -$143.68.

- On January 19, 2016, the A20's cash deposit increases $143.68.

- On January 23, 2016, the Company3's cash deposit increases $230.

- On January 23, 2016, the A22's cash deposit decreases -$230.

- On January 24, 2016, the Company3's cash deposit decreases -$600.

- On January 26, 2016, the Company3's cash deposit decreases -$1,300.

- On January 26, 2016, the Company3's cash deposit decreases -$800.

- On January 28, 2016, the Company3's cash deposit increases $200.

- On January 28, 2016, the Company3's cash deposit decreases -$7,000.

- On January 30, 2016, the Company3's cash deposit decreases -$143.33.

- On January 30, 2016, the A21's cash deposit increases $143.33.

- On January 31, 2016, the Company3's cash deposit increases $350.

- On January 31, 2016, the Company3's cash deposit decreases -$8,370.

- On January 31, 2016, the A20's cash deposit increases $2,880.

- On January 31, 2016, the A19's cash deposit increases $2,700.

- On January 31, 2016, the A21's cash deposit increases $2,790.

- On February 13, 2016, the Company3's cash deposit increases $200.

- On February 22, 2016, the Company3's cash deposit increases $1,500.

- On February 23, 2016, the Company3's cash deposit increases $300.

- On February 25, 2016, the Company3's cash deposit decreases -$339.49.

- On February 25, 2016, the A19's cash deposit increases $339.49.

- On February 27, 2016, the Company3's cash deposit decreases -$900.

- On February 27, 2016, the Company3's cash deposit increases $1,050.

- On February 27, 2016, the A23's cash deposit decreases -$1,050.

- On February 28, 2016, the Company3's cash deposit decreases -$8,370.

- On February 28, 2016, the A20's cash deposit increases $2,880.

- On February 28, 2016, the A19's cash deposit increases $2,700.

- On February 28, 2016, the A21's cash deposit increases $2,790.

- On March 1, 2016, the Company3's cash deposit decreases -$225.64.

- On March 1, 2016, the A21's cash deposit increases $225.64.

- On March 4, 2016, the Company3's cash deposit increases $1,600.

- On March 23, 2016, the Company3's cash deposit decreases -$198.56.

- On March 23, 2016, the A19's cash deposit increases $198.56.

- On March 24, 2016, the Company3's cash deposit increases $3,500.

- On March 30, 2016, the Company3's cash deposit increases $700.

- On March 31, 2016, the Company3's cash deposit decreases -$8,370.

- On March 31, 2016, the A20's cash deposit increases $2,880.

- On March 31, 2016, the A19's cash deposit increases $2,700.

- On March 31, 2016, the A21's cash deposit increases $2,790.

- On April 6, 2016, the Company3's cash deposit increases $1,500.

- On April 14, 2016, the Company3's cash deposit increases $4,160.

- On April 14, 2016, the A10's cash deposit decreases -$4,160.

- On April 26, 2016, the Company3's cash deposit decreases -$236.37.

- On April 26, 2016, the A19's cash deposit increases $236.37.

- On April 30, 2016, the Company3's cash deposit decreases -$8,370.

- On April 30, 2016, the A20's cash deposit increases $2,880.

- On April 30, 2016, the A19's cash deposit increases $2,700.

- On April 30, 2016, the A21's cash deposit increases $2,790.

- On May 2, 2016, the Company3's cash deposit decreases -$167.19.

- On May 2, 2016, the A21's cash deposit increases $167.19.

- On May 3, 2016, the Company3's cash deposit increases $880.

- On May 24, 2016, the Company3's cash deposit decreases -$339.55.

- On May 24, 2016, the A19's cash deposit increases $339.55.

- On May 31, 2016, the Company3's cash deposit decreases -$8,370.

- On May 31, 2016, the A20's cash deposit increases $2,880.

- On May 31, 2016, the A19's cash deposit increases $2,700.

- On May 31, 2016, the A21's cash deposit increases $2,790.

- On June 1, 2016, the Company3's cash deposit decreases -$3000.

- On June 10, 2016, the Company3's cash deposit increases $15,000.

- On June 14, 2016, the Company3's cash deposit decreases -$193.49.

- On June 14, 2016, the A20's cash deposit increases $193.49.

- On June 16, 2016, the Company3's cash deposit decreases -$300.

- On June 23, 2016, the Company3's cash deposit decreases -$254.33.

- On June 23, 2016, the A19's cash deposit increases $254.33.

- On June 29, 2016, the Company3's cash deposit increases $2,000.

- On June 30, 2016, the Company3's cash deposit decreases -$8,370.

- On June 30, 2016, the A20's cash deposit increases $2,880.

- On June 30, 2016, the A19's cash deposit increases $2,700.

- On June 30, 2016, the A21's cash deposit increases $2,790.

- On July 3, 2016, the Company3's cash deposit increases $53,000.

- On July 4, 2016, the Company3's cash deposit increases $55,000.

- On July 11, 2016, the Company3's cash deposit increases $250.

- On July 13, 2016, the Company3's cash deposit increases $780.

- On July 13, 2016, the A21's cash deposit decreases -$780.

- On July16, 2016, the Company3's cash deposit decreases -$13,000.

- On July 27, 2016, the Company3's cash deposit decreases -$221.14.

- On July 27, 2016, the A19's cash deposit increases $221.14.

- On July 31, 2016, the Company3's cash deposit decreases -$8,370.

- On July 31, 2016, the A20's cash deposit increases $2,880.

- On July 31, 2016, the A19's cash deposit increases $2,700.

- On July 31, 2016, the A21's cash deposit increases $2,790.

- On August 3, 2016, the Company3's cash deposit increases $550.

- On August 3, 2016, the A17's cash deposit decreases -$550.

- On August 13, 2016, the Company3's cash deposit increases $700.

- On August 15, 2016, the Company3's cash deposit increases $66,000.

- On August 17, 2016, the Company3's cash deposit increases $65,000.

- On August 23, 2016, the Company3's cash deposit decreases -$208.31.

- On August 23, 2016, the A19's cash deposit increases $208.31.

- On August 31, 2016, the Company3's cash deposit decreases -$8,370.

- On August 31, 2016, the A20's cash deposit increases $2,880.

- On August 31, 2016, the A19's cash deposit increases $2,700.

- On August 31, 2016, the A21's cash deposit increases $2,790.

- On September 4, 2016, the Company3's cash deposit increases $520.

- On September 10, 2016, the Company3's cash deposit increases $550.

- On September 10, 2016, the A23's cash deposit decreases -$550.

- On September 12, 2016, the Company3's cash deposit decreases -$4,000.

- On September 13, 2016, the Company3's cash deposit increases $25,000.

- On September 15, 2016, the Company3's cash deposit decreases -$300.

- On September 25, 2016, the Company3's cash deposit increases $3,200.

- On September 26, 2016, the Company3's cash deposit increases $8,000.

- On September 28, 2016, the Company3's cash deposit decreases -$214.84.

- On September 28, 2016, the A19's cash deposit increases $214.84.

- On September 30, 2016, the Company3's cash deposit decreases -$8,370.

- On September 30, 2016, the A20's cash deposit increases $2,880.

- On September 30, 2016, the A19's cash deposit increases $2,700.

- On September 30, 2016, the A21's cash deposit increases $2,790.

- On October 3, 2016, the Company3's cash deposit increases $550.

- On October 8, 2016, the Company3's cash deposit decreases -$218.66.

- On October 8, 2016, the A21's cash deposit increases $218.66.

- On October 11, 2016, the Company3's cash deposit increases $41,000.

- On October 12, 2016, the Company3's cash deposit increases $31,000.

- On October 18, 2016, the Company3's cash deposit increases $2,660.

- On October 25, 2016, the Company3's cash deposit decreases -$25,000.

- On October 27, 2016, the Company3's cash deposit decreases -$242.23.

- On October 27, 2016, the A19's cash deposit increases $242.23.

- On October 31, 2016, the Company3's cash deposit decreases -$8,370.

- On October 31, 2016, the A20's cash deposit increases $2,880.

- On October 31, 2016, the A19's cash deposit increases $2,700.

- On October 31, 2016, the A21's cash deposit increases $2,790.

- On November 5, 2016, the Company3's cash deposit decreases -$2,900.

- On November 17, 2016, the A19's cash deposit decreases -$87.

- On November 19, 2016, the Company3's cash deposit decreases -$223.61.

- On November 19, 2016, the A19's cash deposit increases $223.61.

- On November 20, 2016, the Company3's cash deposit increases $640.

- On November 29, 2016, the Company3's cash deposit increases $3,000.

- On November 30, 2016, the Company3's cash deposit decreases -$8,370.

- On November 30, 2016, the A20's cash deposit increases $2,880.

- On November 30, 2016, the A19's cash deposit increases $2,700.

- On November 30, 2016, the A21's cash deposit increases $2,790.

- On December 17, 2016, the Company3's cash deposit decreases -$272.78.

- On December 17, 2016, the A19's cash deposit increases $272.78.

- On December 20, 2016, the Company3's cash deposit decreases -$248.53.

- On December 20, 2016, the A21's cash deposit increases $248.53.

- On December 28, 2016, the Company3's cash deposit increases $2,500.

- On December 30, 2016, the Company3's cash deposit increases $600.

- On December 31, 2016, the Company3's cash deposit decreases -$8,370.

- On December 31, 2016, the A20's cash deposit increases $2,880.

- On December 31, 2016, the A19's cash deposit increases $2,700.

- On December 31, 2016, the A21's cash deposit increases $2,790.

- On December 31, 2016, the Company3's cash deposit decreases -$18,000.

- On December 31, 2016, the Company3's cash deposit decreases -$16,200.

- On December 31, 2016, the Company3's cash deposit decreases -$18,200.

- On December 31, 2016, the Company3's cash deposit decreases -$288 (actually enter total $3,840).

- On December 31, 2016, the Company3's cash deposit decreases -$192.

- On December 31, 2016, the Company3's cash deposit decreases -$336.

- On December 31, 2016, the Company3's cash deposit decreases -$88.

- On December 31, 2016, the Company3's cash deposit decreases -$192.

- On December 31, 2016, the Company3's cash deposit decreases -$240.

- On December 31, 2016, the Company3's cash deposit decreases -$192.

- On December 31, 2016, the A11's cash deposit increases $192.

- On December 31, 2016, the Company3's cash deposit decreases -$384.

- On December 31, 2016, the A12's cash deposit increases $384.

- On December 31, 2016, the Company3's cash deposit decreases -$240.

- On December 31, 2016, the Company3's cash deposit decreases -$336.

- On December 31, 2016, the Company3's cash deposit decreases -$240.

- On December 31, 2016, the A17's cash deposit increases $240.

- On December 31, 2016, the Company3's cash deposit decreases -$288.

- On December 31, 2016, the Company3's cash deposit decreases -$192.

- On December 31, 2016, the A21's cash deposit increases $192.

- On December 31, 2016, the Company3's cash deposit decreases -$288.

- On December 31, 2016, the A22's cash deposit increases $288.

- On December 31, 2016, the Company3's cash deposit increases $320.

- On December 31, 2016, the Company3's cash deposit increases $492.

- On December 31, 2016, the Company3's cash deposit increases $120.

- **Proprietorship1.**

- On January 16, 2016, individual A17's cash deposit decreases -$44.

- On January 18, 2016, the A20's cash deposit decreases -$51.

- On January 18, 2016, the A22's cash deposit increases $153.87.

- On January 27, 2016, the A10's cash deposit decreases -$57.

- On January 28, 2016, the A21's cash deposit decreases -$42.

- On January 28, 2016, the A23's cash deposit decreases -$44.

- On January 30, 2016, the A23's cash deposit increases $145.54.

- On January 31, 2016, the A22's cash deposit increases $2,870.

- On January 31, 2016, the A23's cash deposit increases $2,800.

- On January 31, 2016, the A10's cash deposit decreases -$13,900.

- On January 31, 2016, the A11's cash deposit decreases -$14,430.

- On January 31, 2016, the A12's cash deposit decreases -$14,560.

- On February 23, 2016, the A19's cash deposit decreases -$124.

- On February 28, 2016, the A21's cash deposit decreases -$102.

- On February 28, 2016, the A22's cash deposit increases $2,870.

- On February 28, 2016, the A23's cash deposit increases $2,800.

- On March 11 2016, the A11's cash deposit decreases -$50.

- On March 23, 2016, the A22's cash deposit increases $159.45.

- On March 31, 2016, the A22's cash deposit increases $2,870.

- On March 31, 2016, the A23's cash deposit increases $2,800.

- On April 13, 2016, the A11's cash deposit decreases -$69.

- On April 24, 2016, the A19's cash deposit decreases -$78.

- On April 30, 2016, the A22's cash deposit increases $2,870.

- On April 30, 2016, the A23's cash deposit increases $2,800.

- On May 1, 2016, the A21's cash deposit decreases -$50.

- On May 12, 2016, the A23's cash deposit decreases -$50.

- On May 14, 2016, the A23's cash deposit increases $166.23.

- On May 20, 2016, the A11's cash deposit decreases -$56.

- On May 22, 2016, the A19's cash deposit decreases -$138.

- On May 24, 2016, the A22's cash deposit increases $176.95.

- On May 31, 2016, the A22's cash deposit increases $2,870.

- On May 31, 2016, the A23's cash deposit increases $2,800.

- On June 18, 2016, the A12's cash deposit decreases -$109.

- On June 21, 2016, the A19's cash deposit decreases -$108.

- On June 23, 2016, the A22's cash deposit increases $157.37.

- On June 30, 2016, the A22's cash deposit increases $2,870.

- On June 30, 2016, the A23's cash deposit increases $2,800.

- On July 21, 2016, the A12's cash deposit decreases -$125.

- On July 25, 2016, the A19's cash deposit decreases -$88.

- On July 25, 2016, the A23's cash deposit decreases -$64.

- On July 27, 2016, the A23's cash deposit increases $187.55.

- On July 31, 2016, the A22's cash deposit increases $2,870.

- On July 31, 2016, the A23's cash deposit increases $2,800.

- On July 31, 2016, the A1 (secondary card)'s cash deposit decreases -$10,270.

- On July 31, 2016, the A17's cash deposit decreases -$17,940.

- On July 31, 2016, the A19's cash deposit decreases -$18,590.

- On July 31, 2016, the A20's cash deposit decreases -$10,400.

- On July 31, 2016, the A21's cash deposit decreases -$10,660.

- On July 31, 2016, the A22's cash deposit decreases -$10,530.

- On July 31, 2016, the A23's cash deposit decreases -$11,050.

- On August 14, 2016, the A17's cash deposit decreases -$120.

- On August 17, 2016, the A10's cash deposit decreases -$63.

- On August 21, 2016, the A19's cash deposit decreases -$78.

- On August 22, 2016, the A12's cash deposit decreases -$112.

- On August 23, 2016, the A22's cash deposit increases $166.18.

- On August 31, 2016, the A22's cash deposit increases $2,870.

- On August 31, 2016, the A23's cash deposit increases $2,800.

- On September 17, 2016, the A12's cash deposit decreases -$104.

- On September 26, 2016, the A19's cash deposit decreases -$87.

- On September 30, 2016, the A22's cash deposit increases $2,870.

- On September 30, 2016, the A23's cash deposit increases $2,800.

- On October 8, 2016, the A22's cash deposit increases $168.73.

- On October 16, 2016, the A12's cash deposit decreases -$108.

- On October 25, 2016, the A19's cash deposit decreases -$90.

- On October 31, 2016, the A22's cash deposit increases $2,870.

- On October 31, 2016, the A23's cash deposit increases $2,800.

- On November 17, 2016, the A19's cash deposit decreases -$87.

- On November 19, 2016, the A12's cash deposit decreases -$100.

- On November 19, 2016, the A22's cash deposit increases $177.16.

- On November 30, 2016, the A22's cash deposit increases $2,870.

- On November 30, 2016, the A23's cash deposit increases $2,800.

- On December 15, 2016, the A19's cash deposit decreases -$104.

- On December 15, 2016, the A23's cash deposit decreases -$74.

- On December 17, 2016, the A23's cash deposit increases $207.52.

- On December 19, 2016, the A22's cash deposit increases $198.35.

- On December 27, 2016, the A12's cash deposit decreases -$125.

- On December 31, 2016, the A22's cash deposit increases $2,870.

- On December 31, 2016, the A23's cash deposit increases $2,800.

- On December 31, 2016, the A10's cash deposit increases $150.

- On December 31, 2016, the A17's cash deposit increases $250.

- On December 31, 2016, the A19's cash deposit increases $250.

- On December 31, 2016, the A20's cash deposit increases $150.

- On December 31, 2016, the A21's cash deposit increases $200.

- On December 31, 2016, the A22's cash deposit increases $100.

- **Proprietorship2.**
- On January 2, 2016, the Proprietorship2's cash deposit increases $400.

- On January 2, 2016, the Proprietorship2's cash deposit increases $500.

- On January 2, 2016, the Proprietorship2's cash deposit increases $450.

- On January 2, 2016, the Proprietorship2's cash deposit decreases -$8,000.

- On January 2, 2016, the Proprietorship2's cash deposit increases $500.

- On January 3, 2016, the Proprietorship2's cash deposit increases $6,000.

- On January 12, 2016, the Proprietorship2's cash deposit increases $118.

- On January 13, 2016, the Proprietorship2's cash deposit increases $208.

- On January 14, 2016, the Proprietorship2's cash deposit decreases -$255.37.

- On January 15, 2016, the Proprietorship2's cash deposit increases $54.

- On January 16, 2016, the Proprietorship2's cash deposit increases $122.

- On January 16, 2016, the A19's cash deposit decreases -$122.

- On January 16, 2016, the Proprietorship2's cash deposit increases $48.

- On January 16, 2016, the A22's cash deposit decreases -$48.

- On January 18, 2016, the Proprietorship2's cash deposit increases $39.

- On January 20, 2016, the Proprietorship2's cash deposit increases $82.

- On January 21, 2016, the Proprietorship2's cash deposit decreases -$149.65.

- On January 22, 2016, the Proprietorship2's cash deposit increases $120.

- On January 22, 2016, the A12's cash deposit decreases -$120.

- On January 26, 2016, the Proprietorship2's cash deposit increases $800.

- On January 28, 2016, the Proprietorship2's cash deposit decreases -$200.

- On January 30, 2016, the Proprietorship2's cash deposit increases $300.

- On January 31, 2016, the Proprietorship2's cash deposit increases $1,000.

- On January 31, 2016, the Proprietorship2's cash deposit increases $24.

- On January 31, 2016, the Proprietorship2's cash deposit decreases -$5,660.

- On January 31, 2016, the Proprietorship2's cash deposit increases $10,790.

- On January 31, 2016, the A1's cash deposit decreases -$10,790.

- On January 31, 2016, the Proprietorship2's cash deposit increases $10,920.

- On January 31, 2016, the Proprietorship2's cash deposit increases $11,050.

- On January 31, 2016, the Proprietorship2's cash deposit increases $11,180.

- On January 31, 2016, the Proprietorship2's cash deposit increases $10,270.

- On January 31, 2016, the A17's cash deposit decreases -$10,270.

- On January 31, 2016, the Proprietorship2's cash deposit increases $11,830.

- On January 31, 2016, the Proprietorship2's cash deposit increases $11,570.

- On January 31, 2016, the A19's cash deposit decreases -$11,570.

- On January 31, 2016, the Proprietorship2's cash deposit increases $12,090.

- On January 31, 2016, the A20's cash deposit decreases -$12,090.

- On January 31, 2016, the Proprietorship2's cash deposit increases $12,870.

- On January 31, 2016, the A21's cash deposit decreases -$12,870.

- On January 31, 2016, the Proprietorship2's cash deposit increases $10,790.

- On January 31, 2016, the A22's cash deposit decreases -$10,790.

- On January 31, 2016, the Proprietorship2's cash deposit increases $12,350.

- On January 31, 2016, the A23's cash deposit decreases -$12,350.

- On January 31, 2016, the Proprietorship2's cash deposit increases $10,010.

- On January 31, 2016, the Proprietorship2's cash deposit increases $10,270.

- On February 1, 2016, the Proprietorship2's cash deposit decreases -$30,000.

- On February 6, 2016, the Proprietorship2's cash deposit increases $116.

- On February 17, 2016, the Proprietorship2's cash deposit increases $310.

- On February 19, 2016, the Proprietorship2's cash deposit increases $112.

- On February 20, 2016, the Proprietorship2's cash deposit decreases -$400.

- On February 21, 2016, the Proprietorship2's cash deposit increases $300.

- On February 22, 2016, the Proprietorship2's cash deposit increases $96.

- On February 23, 2016, the Proprietorship2's cash deposit increases $62.

- On February 25, 2016, the Proprietorship2's cash deposit decreases -$187.84.

- On February 28, 2016, the Proprietorship2's cash deposit decreases -$5,660.

- On March 7, 2016, the Proprietorship2's cash deposit increases $100.

- On March 7, 2016, the Proprietorship2's cash deposit decreases -$201.66.

- On March 9, 2016, the Proprietorship2's cash deposit decreases -$2,000.

- On March 18, 2016, the Proprietorship2's cash deposit increases $104.

- On March 20, 2016, the Proprietorship2's cash deposit increases $290.

- On March 20, 2016, the Proprietorship2's cash deposit increases $131.

- On March 21, 2016, the Proprietorship2's cash deposit increases $73.

- On March 21, 2016, the A19's cash deposit decreases -$73.

- On March 21, 2016, the Proprietorship2's cash deposit increases $58.

- On March 21, 2016, the A22's cash deposit decreases -$58.

- On March 22, 2016, the Proprietorship2's cash deposit increases $96.

- On March 24, 2016, the Proprietorship2's cash deposit increases $87.

- On March 24, 2016, the A17's cash deposit decreases -$87.

- On March 25, 2016, the Proprietorship2's cash deposit increases $70.

- On March 27, 2016, the Proprietorship2's cash deposit decreases -$191.43.

- On March 28, 2016, the Proprietorship2's cash deposit increases $84.

- On March 31, 2016, the Proprietorship2's cash deposit decreases -$5,660.

- On April 6, 2016, the Proprietorship2's cash deposit increases $108.

- On April 12, 2016, the Proprietorship2's cash deposit increases $1,000.

- On April 13, 2016, the Proprietorship2's cash deposit increases $112.

- On April 15, 2016, the Proprietorship2's cash deposit increases $50.

- On April 17, 2016, the Proprietorship2's cash deposit increases $120.

- On April 17, 2016, the A12's cash deposit decreases -$120.

- On April 20, 2016, the Proprietorship2's cash deposit increases $100.

- On April 24, 2016, the Proprietorship2's cash deposit decreases -$236.37.

- On April 26, 2016, the Proprietorship2's cash deposit increases $470.

- On April 29, 2016, the Proprietorship2's cash deposit increases $1,000.

- On April 30, 2016, the Proprietorship2's cash deposit increases $330.

- On April 30, 2016, the Proprietorship2's cash deposit decreases -$5,660.

- On May 1, 2016, the Proprietorship2's cash deposit decreases -$9,000.

- On May 1, 2016, the Proprietorship2's cash deposit increases $2,300.

- On May 1, 2016, the Proprietorship2's cash deposit increases $5,000.

- On May 1, 2016, the Proprietorship2's cash deposit increases $800.

- On May 8, 2016, the Proprietorship2's cash deposit increases $300.

- On May 15, 2016, the Proprietorship2's cash deposit increases $78.

- On May 16, 2016, the Proprietorship2's cash deposit increases $316.

- On May 17, 2016, the Proprietorship2's cash deposit decreases -$210.77.

- On May 22, 2016, the Proprietorship2's cash deposit increases $56.

- On May 22, 2016, the A22's cash deposit decreases -$56.

- On May 24, 2016, the Proprietorship2's cash deposit increases $108.

- On May 24, 2016, the A12's cash deposit decreases -$108.

- On May 31, 2016, the Proprietorship2's cash deposit decreases -$5,660.

- On June 3, 2016, the Proprietorship2's cash deposit increases $54.

- On June 12, 2016, the Proprietorship2's cash deposit increases $68.

- On June 12, 2016, the A17's cash deposit decreases -$68.

- On June 12, 2016, the Proprietorship2's cash deposit increases $68.

- On June 12, 2016, the A20's cash deposit decreases -$68.

- On June 15, 2016, the Proprietorship2's cash deposit increases $93.

- On June 17, 2016, the Proprietorship2's cash deposit increases $93.

- On June 17, 2016, the Proprietorship2's cash deposit increases $90.

- On June 17, 2016, the Proprietorship2's cash deposit increases $74.

- On June 18, 2016, the Proprietorship2's cash deposit increases $136.

- On June 19, 2016, the Proprietorship2's cash deposit decreases -$196.83.

- On June 21, 2016, the Proprietorship2's cash deposit increases $48.

- On June 21, 2016, the A22's cash deposit decreases -$48.

- On June 30, 2016, the Proprietorship2's cash deposit decreases -$5,660.

- On July 2, 2016, the Proprietorship2's cash deposit increases $117.

- On July 3, 2016, the Proprietorship2's cash deposit decreases -$53,000.

- On July 9, 2016, the Proprietorship2's cash deposit increases $74.

- On July 9, 2016, the A11's cash deposit decreases -$74.

- On July 16, 2016, the Proprietorship2's cash deposit increases $13,000.

- On July 21, 2016, the Proprietorship2's cash deposit increases $108.

- On July 23, 2016, the Proprietorship2's cash deposit decreases -$251.19.

- On July 31, 2016, the Proprietorship2's cash deposit decreases -$5,660.

- On July 31, 2016, the Proprietorship2's cash deposit increases $10,920.

- On July 31, 2016, the Proprietorship2's cash deposit increases $11,050.

- On July 31, 2016, the Proprietorship2's cash deposit increases $11,180.

- On July 31, 2016, the Proprietorship2's cash deposit increases $11,310.

- On July 31, 2016, the Proprietorship2's cash deposit increases $11,440.

- On July 31, 2016, the Proprietorship2's cash deposit increases $11,830.

- On July 31, 2016, the Proprietorship2's cash deposit increases $10,790.

- On July 31, 2016, the Proprietorship2's cash deposit increases $11,310.

- On July 31, 2016, the Proprietorship2's cash deposit increases $11,570.

- On July 31, 2016, the Proprietorship2's cash deposit increases $12,090.

- On July 31, 2016, the Proprietorship2's cash deposit increases $11,570.

- On July 31, 2016, the A10's cash deposit decreases -$11,570.

- On July 31, 2016, the Proprietorship2's cash deposit increases $10,270.

- On July 31, 2016, the A11's cash deposit decreases -$10,270.

- On July 31, 2016, the Proprietorship2's cash deposit increases $11,830.

- On July 31, 2016, the A12's cash deposit decreases -$11,830.

- On July 31, 2016, the Proprietorship2's cash deposit increases $11,830.

- On August 9, 2016, the Proprietorship2's cash deposit increases $114.

- On August 12, 2016, the Proprietorship2's cash deposit increases $118.

- On August 14, 2016, the Proprietorship2's cash deposit increases $123.

- On August 15, 2016, the Proprietorship2's cash deposit decreases -$66,000.

- On August 15, 2016, the Proprietorship2's cash deposit increases $52.

- On August 16, 2016, the Proprietorship2's cash deposit increases $74.

- On August 18, 2016, the Proprietorship2's cash deposit decreases -$203.47.

- On August 21, 2016, the Proprietorship2's cash deposit increases $56.

- On August 21, 2016, the A22's cash deposit decreases -$56.

- On August 31, 2016, the Proprietorship2's cash deposit decreases -$5,660.

- On September 2, 2016, the Proprietorship2's cash deposit decreases -$18,000.

- On September 5, 2016, the Proprietorship2's cash deposit increases $59.

- On September 5, 2016, the Proprietorship2's cash deposit increases $86.

- On September 7, 2016, the Proprietorship2's cash deposit increases $90.

- On September 14, 2016, the Proprietorship2's cash deposit increases $380.

- On September 15, 2016, the Proprietorship2's cash deposit increases $105.

- On September 21, 2016, the Proprietorship2's cash deposit decreases -$256.18.

- On September 30, 2016, the Proprietorship2's cash deposit decreases -$5,660.

- On October 3, 2016, the Proprietorship2's cash deposit increases $129.

- On October 4, 2016, the Proprietorship2's cash deposit increases $117.

- On October 6, 2016, the Proprietorship2's cash deposit increases $78.

- On October 6, 2016, the A21's cash deposit decreases -$78.

- On October 6, 2016, the Proprietorship2's cash deposit increases $54.

- On October 8, 2016, the Proprietorship2's cash deposit increases $56.

- On October 11, 2016, the Proprietorship2's cash deposit decreases -$41,000.

- On October 16, 2016, the Proprietorship2's cash deposit increases $86.

- On October 18, 2016, the Proprietorship2's cash deposit decreases -$228.66.

- On October 31, 2016, the Proprietorship2's cash deposit decreases -$5,660.

- On November 1, 2016, the Proprietorship2's cash deposit increases $61.

- On November 1, 2016, the A11's cash deposit decreases -$61.

- On November 11, 2016, the Proprietorship2's cash deposit increases $85.

- On November 16, 2016, the Proprietorship2's cash deposit increases $124.

- On November 16, 2016, the Proprietorship2's cash deposit increases $132.

- On November 18, 2016, the Proprietorship2's cash deposit increases $86.

- On October 20, 2016, the Proprietorship2's cash deposit decreases -$204.61.

- On November 30, 2016, the Proprietorship2's cash deposit decreases -$5,660.

- On December 1, 2016, the Proprietorship2's cash deposit decreases -$5,000.

- On December 2, 2016, the Proprietorship2's cash deposit increases $76.

- On December 2, 2016, the A10's cash deposit decreases -$76.

- On December 8, 2016, the Proprietorship2's cash deposit increases $120.

- On December 15, 2016, the Proprietorship2's cash deposit increases $108.

- On December 17, 2016, the Proprietorship2's cash deposit decreases -$277.93.

- On December 17, 2016, the Proprietorship2's cash deposit increases $68.

- On December 17, 2016, the A22's cash deposit decreases -$68.

- On December 18, 2016, the Proprietorship2's cash deposit increases $144.

- On December 18, 2016, the Proprietorship2's cash deposit increases $88.

- On December 18, 2016, the A21's cash deposit decreases -$88.

- On December 18, 2016, the Proprietorship2's cash deposit increases $98.

- On December 20, 2016, the Proprietorship2's cash deposit increases $162.

- On December 20, 2016, the Proprietorship2's cash deposit decreases -$249.51.

- On December 23, 2016, the Proprietorship2's cash deposit increases $5,500.

- On December 26, 2016, the Proprietorship2's cash deposit increases $108.

- On December 29, 2016, the Proprietorship2's cash deposit decreases -$27,000.

- On December 31, 2016, the Proprietorship2's cash deposit increases $4,300.

- On December 31, 2016, the Proprietorship2's cash deposit decreases -$5,660.

- On December 31, 2016, the Proprietorship2's cash deposit decreases -$3,640 (total amount).

- On December 31, 2016, the A11's cash deposit increases $260.

- On December 31, 2016, the A12's cash deposit increases $208.

- On December 31, 2016, the A17's cash deposit increases $260.

- On December 31, 2016, the A19's cash deposit increases $260.

- On December 31, 2016, the A20's cash deposit increases $416.

- On December 31, 2016, the Proprietorship2's cash deposit decreases -$2,750 (total amount).

- On December 31, 2016, the A10's cash deposit increases $330.

- On December 31, 2016, the A17's cash deposit increases $275.

- On December 31, 2016, the Proprietorship2's cash deposit increases $252.

- On December 31, 2016, the Proprietorship2's cash deposit increases $463.

- On December 31, 2016, the Proprietorship2's cash deposit increases $120.

- **Business Bank1.**
- On December 31, 2016, the A21's cash deposit increases $252.
- On December 31, 2016, the A17's cash deposit increases $225.
- On December 31, 2016, the A19's cash deposit increases $270.
- On December 31, 2016, the A21's cash deposit increases $180.

3.5.2 Brief Summary of the Business Bank2

The Figure 3.5-2 shows two sums and all cash transactions of the Business Bank2 itself by using of SQL Server query. In other words, there is not any cash transaction with the symbol "d" in the Figure 3.5-2. As a closed system based on the MathAccounting software, the sum0 should be equal to zero. However, the individuals are not responsible for recording any transaction, so the sum0 ($78,243) is the sum of the amounts that the individuals received from the Business Bank2. If the sum0 is negative, then it is sum of the amounts that individuals paid to the Business Bank2. The opposite value ($687,829.61) of the sum1 (-$687,829.61) is the sum of the deposit accounts of all individuals in the Business Bak1 and the Business Bank2on December 31, 2016.

The Figure 3.5-3, which follows the Figure 3.5-2, shows the Business Bank2 cash account table between 2016-01-02 and 2016-12-31. From the Figure 3.5-3, the cash balance on December 31, 2016 is $635,960.27.

The Figure 3.5-4, which follows the Figure 3.5-3, shows the Business Bank2 income statement. From the Figure 3.5-4, the amount of the earnings before income taxes is -$56,028.58 and the amount of the tax expenses is zero, so the amount of the net earnings of the Business Bank2 in this fiscal year is also -$56,028.58.

SQLQuery14.sql - LI...ESS.dcj100 (sa (53))*   SQLQuery13.sql - LI...ESS.dcj100 (sa (52))*   ×

```sql
use dcj100
select sum(amount) as sum0 from CashByMembers where IDM='88-654305' and TransDate between '2016-01-01' and '2016-12-31'
select sum(amount) as sum1 from CashByMembers where Symbol = 'd' and IDM not like '%-%'
select * from CashByMembers where Recorder='88-654305' and Symbol not like 'd' and
    TransDate between '2016-01-01' and '2016-12-31' order by TransDate
```

100 % ▾

Results   Messages

	sum0
1	78243.00

	sum1
1	-687829.61

	IDM	Amount	Symbol	MultiSubaccount	Recorder	TransDate
1	88-654310	186.00	t	88-654310-t-supplies < Cash payments for operating expenses < Operating activities	88-654305	2016-01-02
2	909876511	144.36	n	909876511-n-operating expenses < Cash payments for operating expenses < Operating activities	88-654305	2016-01-17
3	909876512	265.94	n	909876512-n-operating expenses < Cash payments for operating expenses < Operating activities	88-654305	2016-01-24
4	909876510	158.67	n	909876510-n-operating expenses < Cash payments for operating expenses < Operating activities	88-654305	2016-01-29
5	909876510	3000.00	t	909876510-t-salary < Cash payments for operating expenses < Operating activities	88-654305	2016-01-31
6	909876511	2900.00	t	909876511-t-salary < Cash payments for operating expenses < Operating activities	88-654305	2016-01-31
7	909876512	2740.00	t	909876512-t-salary < Cash payments for operating expenses < Operating activities	88-654305	2016-01-31
8	909876512	272.76	n	909876512-n-operating < Cash payments for operating expenses < Operating activities	88-654305	2016-02-08
9	909876510	3000.00	t	909876510-t-salary < Cash payments for operating expenses < Operating activities	88-654305	2016-02-28
10	909876511	2900.00	t	909876511-t-salary < Cash payments for operating expenses < Operating activities	88-654305	2016-02-28
11	909876512	2740.00	t	909876512-t-salary < Cash payments for operating expenses < Operating activities	88-654305	2016-02-28
12	88-654306	19000.00	t	88-654306-t-machinery < Cash payments for machinery < Operating activities	88-654305	2016-03-01
13	909876512	247.59	n	909876512-n-operating < Cash payments for operating expenses < Operating activities	88-654305	2016-03-09
14	909876511	149.61	n	909876511-n-operating expenses < Cash payments for operating expenses < Operating activities	88-654305	2016-03-13
15	909876510	3000.00	t	909876510-t-salary < Cash payments for operating expenses < Operating activities	88-654305	2016-03-31
16	909876511	2900.00	t	909876511-t-salary < Cash payments for operating expenses < Operating activities	88-654305	2016-03-31
17	909876512	2740.00	t	909876512-t-salary < Cash payments for operating expenses < Operating activities	88-654305	2016-03-31
18	88-654308	1500.00	t	88-654308-t-suppliers < Cash payments to suppliers < Operating activities	88-654305	2016-04-06
19	909876511	172.53	n	909876511-n-operating < Cash payments for operating expenses < Operating activities	88-654305	2016-04-15
20	909876512	288.24	n	909876512-n-operating < Cash payments for operating expenses < Operating activities	88-654305	2016-04-19
21	909876510	3000.00	t	909876510-t-salary < Cash payments for operating expenses < Operating activities	88-654305	2016-04-30
22	909876511	2900.00	t	909876511-t-salary < Cash payments for operating expenses < Operating activities	88-654305	2016-04-30
23	909876512	2740.00	t	909876512-t-salary < Cash payments for operating expenses < Operating activities	88-654305	2016-04-30

	IDM	Amount	Symbol	MultiSubaccount	Recorder	TransDate
24	909876511	159.22	n	909876511-n expenses < Cash payments for operating expenses < Operating activities	88-654305	2016-05-22
25	909876512	273.52	n	909876512-n-operating < Cash payments for operating expenses < Operating activities	88-654305	2016-05-26
26	909876510	3000.00	t	909876510-t-salary < Cash payments for operating expenses < Operating activities	88-654305	2016-05-31
27	909876511	2900.00	t	909876511-t-salary < Cash payments for operating expenses < Operating activities	88-654305	2016-05-31
28	909876512	2740.00	t	909876512-t-salary < Cash payments for operating expenses < Operating activities	88-654305	2016-05-31
29	88-654300	-25000.00	i	88-654300-i-bond23 < Cash receipts from issued bonds < Financial activities	88-654305	2016-06-01
30	88-654301	-5000.00	i	88-654301-i-bond23 < Cash receipts from issued bonds < Financial activities	88-654305	2016-06-01
31	88-654302	-5000.00	i	88-654302-i-bond23 < Cash receipts from issued bonds < Financial activities	88-654305	2016-06-01
32	88-654303	-5000.00	i	88-654303-i-bond23 < Cash receipts from issued bonds < Financial activities	88-654305	2016-06-01
33	909876512	278.54	n	909876512-n-operating < Cash payments for operating expenses < Operating activities	88-654305	2016-06-21
34	909876510	3000.00	t	909876510-t-salary < Cash payments for operating expenses < Operating activities	88-654305	2016-06-30
35	909876511	2900.00	t	909876511-t-salary < Cash payments for operating expenses < Operating activities	88-654305	2016-06-30
36	909876512	2740.00	t	909876512-t-salary < Cash payments for operating expenses < Operating activities	88-654305	2016-06-30
37	909876511	187.57	n	909876511-n-operating < Cash payments for operating expenses < Operating activities	88-654305	2016-07-11
38	909876512	308.39	n	909876512-n-operating < Cash payments for operating expenses < Operating activities	88-654305	2016-07-23
39	909876510	3000.00	t	909876510-t-salary < Cash payments for operating expenses < Operating activities	88-654305	2016-07-31
40	909876511	2900.00	t	909876511-t-salary < Cash payments for operating expenses < Operating activities	88-654305	2016-07-31
41	909876512	2740.00	t	909876512-t-salary < Cash payments for operating expenses < Operating activities	88-654305	2016-07-31
42	909876510	161.88	n	909876510-n-operating < Cash payments for operating expenses < Operating activities	88-654305	2016-08-19
43	909876512	267.61	n	909876512-n-operating < Cash payments for operating expenses < Operating activities	88-654305	2016-08-24
44	909876510	3000.00	t	909876510-t-salary < Cash payments for operating expenses < Operating activities	88-654305	2016-08-31
45	909876511	2900.00	t	909876511-t-salary < Cash payments for operating expenses < Operating activities	88-654305	2016-08-31
46	909876512	2740.00	t	909876512-t-salary < Cash payments for operating expenses < Operating activities	88-654305	2016-08-31
47	909876512	251.18	n	909876512-n-operating < Cash payments for operating expenses < Operating activities	88-654305	2016-09-19
48	88-654306	17000.00	t	88-654306-t-machinery < Cash payments for machinery < Operating activities	88-654305	2016-09-26
49	909876510	3000.00	t	909876510-t-salary < Cash payments for operating expenses < Operating activities	88-654305	2016-09-30
50	909876511	2900.00	t	909876511-t-salary < Cash payments for operating expenses < Operating activities	88-654305	2016-09-30
51	909876512	2740.00	t	909876512-t-salary < Cash payments for operating expenses < Operating activities	88-654305	2016-09-30

Figure 3.5-2   Business Bank1Cash Received or Paid by Other Members (Continue)

	IDM	Amount	Symbol	MultiSubaccount	Recorder	TransDate
52	88-654306	5000.00	t	88-654306-t-machinery < Cash payments for machinery < Operating activities	88-654306	2016-10-01
53	909876512	260.75	n	909876512-n-operating expenses < Cash payments for operating expenses < Operating activities	88-654305	2016-10-18
54	909876510	3000.00	t	909876510-t-salary < Cash payments for operating expenses < Operating activities	88-654305	2016-10-31
55	909876511	2900.00	t	909876511-t-salary < Cash payments for operating expenses < Operating activities	88-654305	2016-10-31
56	909876512	2740.00	t	909876512-t-salary < Cash payments for operating expenses < Operating activities	88-654305	2016-10-31
57	909876511	161.42	n	909876511-n-operating expenses < Cash payments for operating expenses < Operating activities	88-654305	2016-11-03
58	909876512	250.43	n	909876512-n-operating expenses < Cash payments for operating expenses < Operating activities	88-654305	2016-11-21
59	909876510	3000.00	t	909876510-t-salary < Cash payments for operating expenses < Operating activities	88-654305	2016-11-30
60	909876511	2900.00	t	909876511-t-salary < Cash payments for operating expenses < Operating activities	88-654305	2016-11-30
61	909876512	2740.00	t	909876512-t-salary < Cash payments for operating expenses < Operating activities	88-654305	2016-11-30
62	909876510	152.24	n	909876510-n-operating expenses < Cash payments for operating expenses < Operating activities	88-654305	2016-12-04
63	88-654306	2800.00	t	88-654306-t-machinery < Cash payments for machinery < Operating activities	88-654305	2016-12-19
64	909876512	302.36	n	909876512-n-operating expenses < Cash payments for operating expenses < Operating activities	88-654305	2016-12-29
65	88-654306	-19800.00	c	88-654306-c-customers < Cash receipts from customers < Operating activities	88-654305	2016-12-31
66	88-654307	-21600.00	c	88-654307-c-customers < Cash receipts from customers < Operating activities	88-654305	2016-12-31
67	88-654308	-34400.00	c	88-654308-c-customers < Cash receipts from customers < Operating activities	88-654305	2016-12-31
68	88-654309	-11280.00	c	88-654309-c-customers < Cash receipts from customers < Operating activities	88-654305	2016-12-31
69	88-654304	-676.00	c	88-654304-c-investment income < Cash receipts from investments < Investing activities	88-654305	2016-12-31
70	88-654306	-230.00	c	88-654306-c-investment income < Cash receipts from investments < Investing activities	88-654305	2016-12-31
71	88-654307	-376.00	c	88-654307-c-investment income < Cash receipts from investments < Investing activities	88-654305	2016-12-31
72	88-654302	369.00	t	88-654302-t-bond interest< Cash payments to bond holders< Operating activities	88-654305	2016-12-31
73	88-654303	328.00	t	88-654303-t-bond interest< Cash payments to bond holders< Operating activities	88-654305	2016-12-31
74	88-654304	246.00	t	88-654304-t-bond interest< Cash payments to bond holders< Operating activities	88-654305	2016-12-31
75	88-654306	369.00	t	88-654306-t-bond interest< Cash payments to bond holders< Operating activities	88-654305	2016-12-31
76	88-654308	492.00	t	88-654308-t-bond interest< Cash payments to bond holders< Operating activities	88-654305	2016-12-31
77	88-654310	287.00	t	88-654310-t-bond interest< Cash payments to bond holders< Operating activities	88-654305	2016-12-31
78	909876507	164.00	t	909876507-t-bond interest< Cash payments to bond holders< Operating activities	88-654305	2016-12-31
79	909876509	246.00	t	909876509-t-bond interest< Cash payments to bond holders< Operating activities	88-654305	2016-12-31
80	909876513	123.00	t	909876513-t-bond interest< Cash payments to bond holders< Operating activities	88-654305	2016-12-31
81	909876514	205.00	t	909876514-t-bond interest< Cash payments to bond holders< Operating activities	88-654305	2016-12-31
82	909876518	123.00	t	909876518-t-bond interest< Cash payments to bond holders< Operating activities	88-654305	2016-12-31
83	909876520	328.00	t	909876520-t-bond interest< Cash payments to bond holders< Operating activities	88-654305	2016-12-31
84	88-654304	220.00	t	88-654304-t-bond interest< Cash payments to bond holders< Operating activities	88-654305	2016-12-31
85	88-654307	264.00	t	88-654307-t-bond interest< Cash payments to bond holders< Operating activities	88-654305	2016-12-31
86	88-654309	352.00	t	88-654309-t-bond interest< Cash payments to bond holders< Operating activities	88-654305	2016-12-31
87	88-654310	176.00	t	88-654310-t-bond interest< Cash payments to bond holders< Operating activities	88-654305	2016-12-31
88	909876503	264.00	t	909876503-t-bond interest< Cash payments to bond holders< Operating activities	88-654305	2016-12-31
89	909876504	308.00	t	909876504-t-bond interest< Cash payments to bond holders< Operating activities	88-654305	2016-12-31
90	909876506	264.00	t	909876506-t-bond interest< Cash payments to bond holders< Operating activities	88-654305	2016-12-31
91	909876511	352.00	t	909876511-t-bond interest< Cash payments to bond holders< Operating activities	88-654305	2016-12-31
92	909876519	132.00	t	909876519-t-bond interest< Cash payments to bond holders< Operating activities	88-654305	2016-12-31
93	909876520	308.00	t	909876520-t-bond interest< Cash payments to bond holders< Operating activities	88-654305	2016-12-31
94	88-654300	656.25	t	88-654300-t-bond interest < Cash payments to bond holders< Operating activities	88-654305	2016-12-31
95	88-654301	131.25	t	88-654301-t-bond interest < Cash payments to bond holders< Operating activities	88-654305	2016-12-31
96	88-654302	131.25	t	88-654302-t-bond interest< Cash payments to bond holders< Operating activities	88-654305	2016-12-31
97	88-654303	131.25	t	88-654303-t-bond interest< Cash payments to bond holders< Operating activities	88-654305	2016-12-31
98	88-654301	120.00	t	88-654301-t-deposit interest expenses < Cash payments for operating expenses < Operating act...	88-654305	2016-12-31
99	88-654307	120.00	t	88-654307-t-deposit interest expenses < Cash payments for operating expenses < Operating act...	88-654305	2016-12-31
100	88-654308	120.00	t	88-654308-t-deposit interest expenses < Cash payments for operating expenses < Operating act...	88-654305	2016-12-31
101	88-654310	120.00	t	88-654310-t-deposit interest expenses < Cash payments for operating expenses < Operating act...	88-654305	2016-12-31
102	909876510	120.00	t	909876510-t-deposit interest expenses < Cash payments for operating expenses < Operating ac...	88-654305	2016-12-31
103	909876511	120.00	t	909876511-t-deposit interest expenses < Cash payments for operating expenses < Operating ac...	88-654305	2016-12-31
104	909876512	120.00	t	909876512-t-deposit interest expenses < Cash payments for operating expenses < Operating ac...	88-654305	2016-12-31
105	909876517	120.00	t	909876517-t-deposit interest expenses < Cash payments for operating expenses < Operating ac...	88-654305	2016-12-31
106	909876519	120.00	t	909876519-t-deposit interest expenses < Cash payments for operating expenses < Operating ac...	88-654305	2016-12-31
107	909876520	120.00	t	909876520-t-deposit interest expenses < Cash payments for operating expenses < Operating ac...	88-654305	2016-12-31
108	909876521	120.00	t	909876521-t-deposit interest expenses < Cash payments for operating expenses < Operating ac...	88-654305	2016-12-31
109	909876522	120.00	t	909876522-t-deposit interest expenses < Cash payments for operating expenses < Operating ac...	88-654305	2016-12-31
110	909876523	120.00	t	909876523-t-deposit interest expenses < Cash payments for operating expenses < Operating ac...	88-654305	2016-12-31
111	909876510	3000.00	t	909876510-t-salary < Cash payments for operating expenses < Operating activities	88-654305	2016-12-31
112	909876511	2900.00	t	909876511-t-salary < Cash payments for operating expenses < Operating activities	88-654305	2016-12-31
113	909876512	2740.00	t	909876512-t-salary < Cash payments for operating expenses < Operating activities	88-654305	2016-12-31

Query executed successfully.

Figure 3.5-2   Business Bank2 Cash Received or Paid by Other Members

366

Cash

ID	Multi-Name	Amount	Balance	General ID	Transaction Date
83	909876511-i-owners < Cash receipts from owners < Financial activities	$138,793.85	$390,884.49	18	2015-12-31
84	88-654301-d-deposits < Cash receipts from customers deposits < Opera...	$85,000.00	$475,884.49	19	2016-01-02
85	88-654301-d-deposits < Cash receipts from customers deposits < Opera...	-$176.56	$475,707.93	20	2016-01-21
86	88-654301-d-deposits < Cash receipts from customers deposits < Opera...	-$5,650.00	$470,057.93	21	2016-01-31
87	88-654301-d-deposits < Cash receipts from customers deposits < Opera...	-$800.00	$469,257.93	22	2016-02-13
88	88-654301-d-deposits < Cash receipts from customers deposits < Opera...	-$200.00	$469,057.93	23	2016-02-13
89	88-654301-d-deposits < Cash receipts from customers deposits < Opera...	-$3,600.00	$465,457.93	24	2016-02-22
90	88-654301-d-deposits < Cash receipts from customers deposits < Opera...	-$5,650.00	$459,807.93	25	2016-02-28
91	88-654301-d-deposits < Cash receipts from customers deposits < Opera...	-$600.00	$459,207.93	26	2016-03-25
92	88-654301-d-deposits < Cash receipts from customers deposits < Opera...	-$459.61	$458,748.32	27	2016-03-28
93	88-654301-d-deposits < Cash receipts from customers deposits < Opera...	-$5,650.00	$453,098.32	28	2016-03-31
94	88-654301-d-deposits < Cash receipts from customers deposits < Opera...	-$159.78	$452,938.54	29	2016-04-19
95	88-654301-d-deposits < Cash receipts from customers deposits < Opera...	-$5,650.00	$447,288.54	30	2016-04-30
96	88-654301-d-deposits < Cash receipts from customers deposits < Opera...	-$1,900.00	$445,388.54	31	2016-05-01
97	88-654301-d-deposits < Cash receipts from customers deposits < Opera...	-$316.00	$445,072.54	32	2016-05-16
98	88-654301-d-deposits < Cash receipts from customers deposits < Opera...	-$5,650.00	$439,422.54	33	2016-05-31
99	88-654301-d-deposits < Cash receipts from customers deposits < Opera...	-$5,000.00	$434,422.54	34	2016-06-01
100	88-654301-d-deposits < Cash receipts from customers deposits < Opera...	-$477.25	$433,945.29	35	2016-06-22
101	88-654301-d-deposits < Cash receipts from customers deposits < Opera...	-$5,650.00	$428,295.29	36	2016-06-30
102	88-654301-d-deposits < Cash receipts from customers deposits < Opera...	-$5,650.00	$422,645.29	37	2016-07-31
103	88-654301-d-deposits < Cash receipts from customers deposits < Opera...	-$1,040.00	$421,605.29	38	2016-08-14
104	88-654301-d-deposits < Cash receipts from customers deposits < Opera...	-$5,650.00	$415,955.29	39	2016-08-31
105	88-654301-d-deposits < Cash receipts from customers deposits < Opera...	-$233.16	$415,722.13	40	2016-09-07
106	88-654301-d-deposits < Cash receipts from customers deposits < Opera...	-$5,650.00	$410,072.13	41	2016-09-30
855	909876510-d-deposits < Cash receipts from customers deposits < Oper...	$120.00	$638,552.27	711	2016-12-31
856	909876511-d-deposits < Cash receipts from customers deposits < Oper...	$120.00	$638,672.27	711	2016-12-31
857	909876512-d-deposits < Cash receipts from customers deposits < Oper...	$120.00	$638,792.27	711	2016-12-31
858	909876517-d-deposits < Cash receipts from customers deposits < Oper...	$120.00	$638,912.27	711	2016-12-31
859	909876519-d-deposits < Cash receipts from customers deposits < Oper...	$120.00	$639,032.27	711	2016-12-31
860	909876520-d-deposits < Cash receipts from customers deposits < Oper...	$120.00	$639,152.27	712	2016-12-31
861	909876521-d-deposits < Cash receipts from customers deposits < Oper...	$120.00	$639,272.27	712	2016-12-31
862	909876522-d-deposits < Cash receipts from customers deposits < Oper...	$120.00	$639,392.27	712	2016-12-31
863	909876523-d-deposits < Cash receipts from customers deposits < Oper...	$120.00	$639,512.27	712	2016-12-31
864	909876510-t-salary < Cash payments for operating expenses < Operatin...	-$3,000.00	$636,512.27	713	2016-12-31
865	909876511-t-salary < Cash payments for operating expenses < Operatin...	-$2,900.00	$633,612.27	713	2016-12-31
866	909876512-t-salary < Cash payments for operating expenses < Operatin...	-$2,740.00	$630,872.27	713	2016-12-31
867	909876510-d-deposits < Cash receipts from customers deposits < Oper...	$3,000.00	$633,872.27	714	2016-12-31
868	909876511-d-deposits < Cash receipts from customers deposits < Oper...	$2,900.00	$636,772.27	714	2016-12-31
869	909876512-d-deposits < Cash receipts from customers deposits < Oper...	$2,740.00	$639,512.27	714	2016-12-31
870	909876501-d-deposits < Cash receipts from customers deposits < Oper...	$20,000.00	$659,512.27	718	2016-01-10
871	909876512-d-deposits < Cash receipts from customers deposits < Oper...	-$26,000.00	$633,512.27	719	2016-01-26
872	88-654308-d-deposits < Cash receipts from customers deposits < Opera...	$2,100.00	$635,612.27	720	2016-02-22
873	88-654310-d-deposits < Cash receipts from customers deposits < Opera...	$162.00	$635,774.27	721	2016-01-02
874	88-654310-d-deposits < Cash receipts from customers deposits < Opera...	$186.00	$635,960.27	722	2016-01-02
875	909876521-d-deposits < Cash receipts from customers deposits < Oper...	$138.00	$636,098.27	723	2016-12-31
876	909876511-d-deposits < Cash receipts from customers deposits < Oper...	-$138.00	$635,960.27	723	2016-12-31

Figure 3.5-3   Business Bank2 Cash Account Table

Income Statement

	Year ended: 12/31/2016
Revenues	
Sales (notes interest)	$87,080.00
Cost	
Cost of notes interest	-$1,560.00
Gross Margin	$85,520.00
Operating and administrative expenses	
Travelling expenses	-$2,807.81
Other expenses	-$1,907.00
Office supplies expenses	-$2,415.77
Salary expenses	-$103,680.00
Bond interest expenses	-$6,970.00
Amortization expenses	-$25,050.00
Other income	
Investment incomes	$1,282.00
qazxs	$0.00
Earnings Before Income Taxes	-$56,028.58
Tax	
Tax expenses	$0.00
Net Earnings	-$56,028.58
Retained Earnings,Begining	$0.00
Retained Earnings,Ending	-$56,028.58

Figure 3.5-4   Business Bank2 Income Statement

The Figure 3.5-5 on the next page shows the Business Bank2 balance sheet. From the Figure 3.5-5, the amount of total assets is $1,697,010.49, and the amount of the total liabilities and the shareholders' equity is also $1,697,010.49.

As at 12/31/2016	
ASSETS	
Current assets	
Cash	$635,960.27
Supplies	$54.39
Notes receivable	$960,000.00
Account receivable	$0.00
	$1,596,014.66
Long term investments	
Bonds	$29,000.00
Equipment	
Vehicle	$117,000.00
Accumulated amortization: Vehicle	-$50,166.67
Computer	$5,900.00
Accumulated amortization: Computer	-$737.50
	$71,995.83
Total Assets	$1,697,010.49
LIABILITIES	
Current liabilities	
Deposits payable	$666,907.90
Account payable	$1,800.00
Tax payable	$0.00
	$668,707.90
Long term liabilities	
Bonds payable	$180,000.00
Total Liability	$848,707.90
SHAREHOLDERS' EQUITY	
Owners capital	
Share capital	$900,000.00
Retained earnings (Conversion)	$4,331.17
	$904,331.17
Retined earnings	-$56,028.58
Accumulated other comprehensive income	$0.00
Total Shareholders' Equity	$848,302.59
Total Liabilities and Shareholders' Equity	$1,697,010.49

Figure 3.5-5   Business Bank2 Balance Sheet Statement

In addition, the Figure 3.5-6 on the next page shows the Reference table of the Business Bank2. You can compare this Reference table with the Income Statement in the Figure 3.5-4 and the Balance Sheet in the Figure 3.5-4. Actually, the Reference table is the combination of the Income Statement and the Balance Sheet.

Name	Row	Balance
Current assets	103	
Cash	104	$635,960.27
Supplies	106	$54.39
Notes receivable	112	$960,000.00
Account receivable	114	$0.00
Long term investments	141	
Bonds	143	$29,000.00
Equipment	171	
Vehicle	172	$117,000.00
Accumulated amortization: Vehicle	173	-$50,166.67
Computer	174	$5,900.00
Accumulated amortization: Computer	175	-$737.50
Current liabilities	203	
Deposits payable	206	$666,907.90
Account payable	210	$1,800.00
Tax payable	211	$0.00
Long term liabilities	251	
Bonds payable	252	$180,000.00
Owners capital	303	
Share capital	304	$900,000.00
Retained earnings (Conversion)	306	$4,331.17
Revenues	403	
Sales (notes interest)	404	$87,080.00
Cost	431	
Cost of notes interest	432	-$1,560.00

Name	Row	Balance
Cost	431	
Cost of notes interest	432	-$1,560.00
Operating and administrative expenses	453	
Travelling expenses	454	-$2,807.81
Other expenses	456	-$1,907.00
Office supplies expenses	458	-$2,415.77
Salary expenses	460	-$103,680.00
Bond interest expenses	462	-$6,970.00
Amortization expenses	464	-$25,050.00
Other income	475	
Investment incomes	476	$1,282.00
Tax	600	
Tax expenses	602	$0.00

Figure 3.5-6   Business Bank2 Reference Table

3.6 Company1

3.6.1 An Accounting Fiscal Year of the Company1

In the new fiscal year, the Company1 occurs the following transactions.

- On January 2, 2016, the Company1 purchases the supplies $1,500 ($14*50 + $16*50) from the Proprietorship2 (phone number: 123456080) for cash -$500 and other on credit. The multi-subaccount name of the Cash account and transaction sub-equation respectively are:

   88-654310-t-supplies < Cash payments for operating expenses < Operating activities

   Cash (1): -500 + Supplies (1): 1500 = Account payable (2): 1000

- On January 2, 2016, the Company1 transfers the supplies $1,200 to the Cost of goods manufactured to satisfy the need of producing. The transaction sub-equation is:

   Supplies (1): -1200 = Cost of goods manufactured (5): -1200

- On January 2, 2016, the Company1 transfers the following inventories $5,652 to the Cost of goods manufactured account to satisfy the need of producing.

   Inven111 < Inven11 < Inven1: -10*15

   Inven112 < Inven11 < Inven1: -40*20

   Inven121 < Inven12 < Inven1: -0.8*60

   Inven122 < Inven12 < Inven1: -50*6

   Inven21 < Inven2: -30*20

   Inven221 < Inven22 < Inven2: -30*10

   Inven222 < Inven22 < Inven2: -50*10

   PPUK parts < ASD parts < Inven2: -40*10

   PPGH parts < ASD parts < Inven2: -2*100

   Inven31 < Inven3: -10*10

   Inven32 < Inven3: -50*6

Inven331 < Inven33 < Inven3: -20*10

Inven332 < Inven33 < Inven3: -45*10

HGFCVB parts < QASXC parts < Inven3: -10*2

PPGHUP parts < ASDUP parts < Inven3: -20*10

Inven411 < Inven41 < Inven4: -5*22

Inven412 < Inven41 < Inven4: -18.5*4

TTTCU parts < TTT parts < Inven4: -20*25

RRRHJK parts < Inven4: -20*20

The three transaction sub-equations are respectively:

Inventory (1): -10*15 + Inventory (1): -40*20 + Inventory (1): -0.8*60 + Inventory (1): -50*6 + Inventory (1): -30*20 + Inventory (1): -30*10 + Inventory (1): -50*10 + Inventory (1): -40*10 + Inventory (1): -2*100 = Cost of goods manufactured (5): -3298

Inventory (1): -10*10 + Inventory (1): -50*6 + Inventory (1): -20*10 + Inventory (1): -45*10 + Inventory (1): -10*2 + Inventory (1): -20*10 + Inventory (1): -5*22 + Inventory (1): -18.5*4 = Cost of goods manufactured (5): -1454

Inventory (1): -20*25 + Inventory (1): -20*20 = Cost of goods manufactured (5): -900

- On January 13, 2016, the Company1 sells one Computer server1- Service package6 to the Tax Bureau (phone number: 123456787) for cash $60. The multi-subaccount name of the Cash account and transaction sub-equation respectively are:

  88-654303-c-customers < Cash receipts from customers < Operating activities

  Cash (1): 60 = Service package incomes (4): 60

- On January 14, 2016, the Company1 pays -$11,000 cash to the Company2 (phone number: 123456083) with the General ID 3. The multi-subaccount name of the Cash account and transaction sub-equation respectively are:

88-654307-t-suppliers < Cash payments to suppliers < Operating activities

Cash (1): -11000 = Account payable (2): -11000

- On January 14, 2016, the Company1 pays -$8,000 cash to the Company3 (phone number: 123456082) with the General ID 3. The multi-subaccount name of the Cash account and transaction sub-equation respectively are:

  88-654308-t-suppliers < Cash payments to suppliers < Operating activities

  Cash (1): -8000 = Account payable (2): -8000

- On January 15, 2016, the Company1 pays -$415.67 cash to A13 (SIN: 909876513) for the Travelling expenses (travel allowance) $207.67 and the Other expenses (meals: food514: $11*8 + food614: $30*4) $208. The multi-subaccount name of the Cash account and the transaction sub-equation respectively are:

  909876513-n-operating expenses < Cash payments for operating expenses < Operating activities

  Cash (1): -415.67 = Travelling expenses (5): -207.67 + other expenses (5): -208

- On January 16, 2016, the Company1 pays -$42.12 cash to A15 (SIN: 909876515) for the Travelling expenses (travel allowance) $22.12 and the Other expenses (meals: food311: $20*1) $20.

- On January 31, 2016, the Company1 pays -$2,040 cash to the Proprietorship1 (phone number: 123456081) with the General ID 3. The multi-subaccount name of the Cash account and transaction sub-equation respectively are:

  88-654309-t-suppliers < Cash payments to suppliers < Operating activities

  Cash (1): -2040 = Account payable (2): -2040

- On January 31, 2016, the Company1 pays -$1,000 cash to the Proprietorship2 (phone number: 123456080) with the General ID 3. The multi-subaccount name of the Cash account and transaction sub-equation respectively are:

88-654310-t-suppliers < Cash payments to suppliers < Operating activities

Cash (1): -1000 = Account payable (2): -1000

- On January 31, 2016, the Company1 pays three employees' salary expenses for cash -$8,400. The two multi-subaccount names of the Cash account and the transaction sub-equation respectively are:

  909876514-t-salary < Cash payments for operating expenses < Operating activities

  909876513-t-CGM < Cash payments for operating expenses < Operating activities

  909876515-t-CGM < Cash payments for operating expenses < Operating activities

  Cash (1): -2900 + Cash (1): -2600 + Cash (1): -2900 = Salary expenses (5): -2900 + Cost of goods manufactured (5): -2600 + Cost of goods manufactured (5): -2900

- On February 1, 2016, the Company1 sells one Car2 $39,000 (cost: $27,000) to the Business Bank1 (phone number: 123456786) for cash $19,000 and other on credit. The multi-subaccount name of the Cash account and transaction sub-equation respectively are:

  88-654304-c-customers < Cash receipts from customers < Operating activities

  Cash (1): 19000 + Account receivable (1): 20000 + Inventory (1): -27000 = Sales (4): 39000 + Cost of goods sold (5): -27000

- On February 1, 2016, the Company1 sells one Car3 $38,000 (cost: $26,000) to the Proprietorship1 (phone number: 123456781) for cash $28,000 and other on credit. The multi-subaccount name of the Cash account and transaction sub-equation respectively are:

  88-654309-c-customers < Cash receipts from customers < Operating activities

Cash (1): 28000 + Account receivable (1): 10000 + Inventory (1): -26000 = Sales (4): 38000 + Cost of goods sold (5): -26000

- On February 1, 2016, the Company1 sells one Car3 $38,000 (cost: $26,000) to the Proprietorship2 (phone number: 123456780) for cash $30,000 and other on credit. The multi-subaccount name of the Cash account is:

  88-654310-c-customers < Cash receipts from customers < Operating activities

- On February 1, 2016, the Company1 pays -$49.68 cash to A14 (SIN: 909876514) for the Travelling expenses (travel allowance) $25.68 and the Other expenses (meals: food612: $24*1) $24.

- On February 2, 2016, the Company1 receives $500 cash from the Tax Bureau (phone number: 123456787) with the General ID 3. The multi-subaccount name of the Cash account and transaction sub-equation respectively are:

  88-654303-c-customers < Cash receipts from customers < Operating activities

  Cash (1): -500 + Account receivable (2): -500 = 0

- On February 13, 2016, the Company1 receives $800 cash from the Central Bank (phone number: 123456789) with the General ID 3. The multi-subaccount name of the Cash account and transaction sub-equation respectively are:

  88-654301-c-customers < Cash receipts from customers < Operating activities

  Cash (1): 800 + Account receivable (2): -800 = 0

- On February 20, 2016, the Company1 pays -$557.83 cash to A13 (SIN: 909876513) for the Travelling expenses (travel allowance) $247.83 and the Other expenses (meals: food23: $16*10 + food322: $30*5) $310.

- On February 25, 2016, the Company1 receives $600 cash from the Company2 (phone number: 123456783) with the General ID 3. The multi-subaccount name of the Cash account and transaction sub-equation respectively are:

  88-654307-c-customers < Cash receipts from customers < Operating activities

Cash (1): -600 + Account receivable (2): -600 = 0

- On February 27, 2016, the Company1 receives $900 cash from the Company3 (phone number: 123456782) with the General ID 3. The multi-subaccount name of the Cash account and transaction sub-equation respectively are:

    88-654308-c-customers < Cash receipts from customers < Operating activities

    Cash (1): -900 + Account receivable (2): -900 = 0

- On February 28, 2016, the Company1 pays three employees' salary expenses for cash $8,400. The two multi-subaccount names of the Cash account and the transaction sub-equation respectively are:

    909876514-t-salary < Cash payments for operating expenses < Operating activities
    909876513-t-CGM < Cash payments for operating expenses < Operating activities
    909876515-t-CGM < Cash payments for operating expenses < Operating activities

    Cash (1): -2900 + Cash (1): -2600 + Cash (1): -2900 = Salary expenses (5): -2900 + Cost of goods manufactured (5): -2600 + Cost of goods manufactured (5):-2900

- On March 1, 2016, the Company1 sells one Car2 $39,000 to the Business Bank2 (phone number: 123456785) for cash $19000 and other on credit. The multi-subaccount name of the Cash account and transaction sub-equation respectively are:

    88-654305-c-customers < Cash receipts from customers < Operating activities

    Cash (1): 19000 + Account receivable (1): 20000 + Inventory (1): -27000 = Sales (4): 39000 + Cost of goods sold (5): -27000

- On March 4, 2016, the Company1 pays -$2,400 cash to the Company2 (phone number: 123456083) with the General ID 3. The multi-subaccount name of the Cash account and transaction sub-equation respectively are:

    88-654307-t-suppliers < Cash payments to suppliers < Operating activities

Cash (1): -2400 = Account payable (2): -2400

- On March 4, 2016, the Company1 pays -$1,600 cash to the Company3 (phone number: 123456082) with the General ID 3. The multi-subaccount name of the Cash account and transaction sub-equation respectively are:

  88-654308-t-suppliers < Cash payments to suppliers < Operating activities

  Cash (1): -1600 = Account payable (2): -1600

- On March 4, 2016, the Company1 transfers the following inventories $2,010 to the Cost of goods manufactured account to satisfy the producing need.

  Inven111 < Inven11 < Inven1: -10*40

  Inven112 < Inven11 < Inven1: -40*20

  Inven121 < Inven12 < Inven1: -0.8*100

  Inven122 < Inven12 < Inven1: -50*8

  Inven21 < Inven2: -30*5

  Inven332 < Inven33 < Inven3: -45*2

  HGFCVB parts < QASXC parts < Inven3: -10*3

  PPGHUP parts < ASDUP parts < Inven3: -20*2

  Inven411 < Inven41 < Inven4: -5*4

  The three transaction sub-equations are respectively:

  Inventory (1): -10*40 + Inventory (1): -40*20 + Inventory (1): -0.8*100 + Inventory (1): -50*8 + Inventory (1): -30*5 + Inventory (1): -45*2 + Inventory (1): -10*3 + Inventory (1): -20*2 + Inventory (1): -5*4 = Cost of goods manufactured (5): -2010

- On March 6, 2016, the Company1 receives $1,000 cash from the Proprietorship1 (phone number: 123456781) with the General ID 3. The multi-subaccount name of the Cash account and transaction sub-equation respectively are:

88-654309-c-customers < Cash receipts from customers < Operating activities

Cash (1): -1000 + Account receivable (2): -1000 = 0

- On March 9, 2016, the Company1 receives $2,000 cash from the Proprietorship2 (phone number: 123456780) with the General ID 3. The multi-subaccount name of the Cash account and transaction sub-equation respectively are:

  88-654310-c-customers < Cash receipts from customers < Operating activities

  Cash (1): -2000 + Account receivable (2): -2000 = 0

- On March 23, 2016, the Company1 pays -$516.37 cash to A13 (SIN: 909876513) for the Travelling expenses (travel allowance) $226.37 and the Other expenses (meals: food44: $15*10 + food622: $28*5) $290.

- On March 25, 2016, the Company1 receives $600 cash from the Central Bank (phone number: 123456789) with the General ID 3. The multi-subaccount name of the Cash account and transaction sub-equation respectively are:

  88-654301-c-customers < Cash receipts from customers < Operating activities

  Cash (1): -600 + Account receivable (2): -600 = 0

- On March 30, 2016, the Company1 pays -$239.73 cash to A14 (SIN: 909876514) for the Travelling expenses (travel allowance) $155.73 and the Other expenses (meals: food521: $12*3 + food612: $24*2) $84.

- On March 31, 2016, the Company1 pays three employees' salary expenses for cash -$8,400 repeatedly.

- On April 12, 2016, the Company1 purchases the supplies $3,000 ($14*100 + $16*100) from the Proprietorship2 (phone number: 123456080) for cash -$1000 and other on credit. The multi-subaccount name of the Cash account and transaction sub-equation respectively are:

  88-654310-t-supplies < Cash payments for operating expenses < Operating

activities

Cash (1): -1000 + Supplies (1): 3000 = Account payable (2): 2000

- On April 28, 2016, the Company1 pays -$717.38 cash to A13 (SIN: 909876513) for the Travelling expenses (travel allowance) $247.38 and the Other expenses (meals: food422: $13*10 + food612: $24*5 +food613: $26*5 + food614: $30*3) $470.

- On April 29, 2016, the Company1 pays -$1,000 cash to the Proprietorship2 (phone number: 123456080) with the General ID 17. The multi-subaccount name of the Cash account is:

  88-654310-t-suppliers < Cash payments to suppliers < Operating activities

- On April 30, 2016, the Company1 sells one Computer server1- Serving package6 to the Government1 (phone number: 123456788) for cash $60. The multi-subaccount name of the Cash account and transaction sub-equation respectively are:

  88-654302-c-customers < Cash receipts from customers < Operating activities

  Cash (1): 60 = Service package income (4): 60

- On April 30, 2016, the Company1 pays three employees' salary expenses for cash - $8,400 repeatedly.

- On April 30, 2016, the Company1 has completed all products of the Working-in-process inventory account. If all general parts have just been consumed and the supplies has rest $148.65, the rest supplies must be returned to the Supplies account from the Cost of goods manufactured account. The transaction sub-equation is:

  Supplies (1): 148.65 = Cost of goods manufactured (5): 148.65

- On April 30, 2016, the Company1 transfers the balance of the Cost of goods manufactured account to the Working-in-process inventory account. The Cost of goods manufactured account has four subaccounts of the "Supplies expenses", the "909876513-salary < Sales department-salary < Salary expenses", the "909876515-

salary < Product department-salary < Salary expenses", and the "General parts expenses". Their balances are -$1,051.35, -$10,400, -$11,600, and -$7,662 respectively. The two transaction sub-equations are:

Working-in-process inventory (1): 4127.09*2 + Working-in-process inventory (1): 2136.26*3 + Working-in-process inventory (1): 1012.67*2 + Working-in-process inventory (1): 2450.19*2 + Working-in-process inventory (1): 1587.83*3 = Cost of goods manufactured (5): 1051.35 + Cost of goods manufactured (5): 10400 + Cost of goods manufactured (5): 11600 + Cost of goods manufactured (5): 3300.82

Working-in-process inventory (1): 43.55*4 + Working-in-process inventory (1): 23.71*4 + Working-in-process inventory (1): 54.88*10 + Working-in-process inventory (1): 102.88*10 + Working-in-process inventory (1): 97.72*12 + Working-in-process inventory (1): 89.46*15 = Cost of goods manufactured (5): 4361.18

- On April 30, 2016, the Company1 transfers the balance of the Working-in-process inventory account to the Inventory account. The three transaction sub-equations are:

Working-in-process inventory (1): -33700*2 + Working-in-process inventory (1): -30000*3 + Working-in-process inventory (1): -28000*2 + Working-in-process inventory (1): -27000*2 + Working-in-process inventory (1): -26000*3 + Inventory (1): 33700*2 + Inventory (1): 30000*3 + Inventory (1): 28000*2 + Inventory (1): 27000*2 + Inventory (1): 26000*3 = 0

Working-in-process inventory (1): -1600*4 + Working-in-process inventory (1): -1500*4 + Working-in-process inventory (1): -1000*10 + Working-in-process inventory (1): -920*10 + Working-in-process inventory (1): -830*12 + Inventory (1): 1600*4 + Inventory (1): 1500*4 + Inventory (1): 1000*10 + Inventory (1): 920*10 + Inventory (1): 830*12 = 0

Working-in-process inventory (1): -770*15 + Inventory (1): 770*15 = 0

- On May 1, 2016, the Company1 sells one Computer server1, one Computer1, and one Computer2 to the Central Bank (phone number: 123456789) for cash $1900 and other on credit. The multi-subaccount name of the Cash account and transaction sub-equation respectively are:

  88-654301-c-customers < Cash receipts from customers < Operating activities

  Cash (1): 1900 + Account receivable (1): 4000 + Inventory (1): -1600 + Inventory (1): -1000+ Inventory (1): -920 = Sales (4): 5900 + Cost of goods sold (5): -3520

- On May 1, 2016, the Company1 sells one Car1 $40,000 to the Government1 (phone number: 123456788) for cash $8000 and other on credit. The multi-subaccount name of the Cash account and transaction sub-equation respectively are:

  88-654302-c-customers < Cash receipts from customers < Operating activities

  Cash (1): 8000 + Account receivable (1): 32000 + Inventory (1): -28000 = Sales (4): 40000 + Cost of goods sold (5): -28000

- On May 1, 2016, the Company1 plans to produce the following products in the following Figure 3.6-1.

Order	Product (the Lowest-level Subaccount) Names	Multi-subaccount Names	Costs	Amount
1	Truck1	Truck1 < Truck < Vehicle	33700.00	1
2	Truck2	Truck2 < Truck < Vehicle	30000.00	1
3	Car1	Car1 < Car < Vehicle	28000.00	4
4	Car2	Car2 < Car < Vehicle	27000.00	4
5	Car3	Car3 < Car < Vehicle	26000.00	4
6	Computer server1	Computer server1 < Computer server < Computer	1600 00	5
7	Computer server2	Computer server2 < Computer server < Computer	1500.00	5
8	Computer1	Computer1 < Computer	1000.00	15

9	Computer2	Computer2 < Computer	920.00	15
10	Computer3	Computer3 < Computer	830.00	15
11	Computer4	Computer4 < Computer	770.00	15

Figure 3.6-1   Company1 Producing Plan Table

Therefore, the Company1 purchases following inventories $216,420 from the Company2 (phone number: 123456083) for -$15,000 cash and other on credit.

Car1 part1 < Car1 parts < Vehicle parts: 8300*3

Car1 part2 < Car1 parts < Vehicle parts: 7200*3

Car1 part3 < Car1 parts < Vehicle parts: 5100*3

Car2 part1 < Car2 parts < Vehicle parts: 7900*3

Car2 part2 < Car2 parts < Vehicle parts: 6800*3

Car2 part3 < Car2 parts < Vehicle parts: 4900*3

Car3 part1 < Car3 parts < Vehicle parts: 7500*3

Car3 part2 < Car3 parts < Vehicle parts: 6400*3

Car3 part3 < Car3 parts < Vehicle parts: 4700*3

Computer server1 part1 < Computer server parts < Computer parts: 600*4

Computer server1 part2 < Computer server parts < Computer parts: 400*4

Computer server2 part1 < Computer server parts < Computer parts: 540*4

Computer server2 part2 < Computer server parts < Computer parts: 380*4

Computer1 part1 < Computer parts: 360*14

Computer1 part2 < Computer parts: 310*14

Computer2 part1 < Computer parts: 320*14

Computer2 part2 < Computer parts: 290*14

Computer3 part1 < Computer parts: 280*14

Computer3 part2 < Computer parts: 260*14

Computer4 part1 < Computer parts: 250*14

Computer4 part2 < Computer parts: 240*14

The multi-subaccount name of the Cash account and three transaction sub-equations respectively are:

88-654307-t-suppliers < Cash payments to suppliers < Operating activities

Cash (1): -15000 + Inventory (1): 8300*3 + Inventory (1): 7200*3 + Inventory (1): 5100*3 + Inventory (1): 7900*3 + Inventory (1): 6800*3 + Inventory (1): 4900*3 + Inventory (1): 7500*3 + Inventory (1): 6400*3 = Account payable (2): 147300

Inventory (1): 4700*3 + Inventory (1): 600*4 + Inventory (1): 400*4 + Inventory (1): 540*4 + Inventory (1): 380*4 + Inventory (1): 360*14+ Inventory (1): 310*14 + Inventory (1): 320*14 + Inventory (1): 290*14 = Account payable (2): 39700

Inventory (1): 280*14 + Inventory (1): 260*14 + Inventory (1): 250*14 + Inventory (1): 240*14 = Account payable (2): 14420

- On May 1, 2016, the Company1 purchases following inventories $50,800 from the Company3 (phone number: 123456082) on credit.

  Inven111 < Inven11 < Inven1: 10*300

  Inven112 < Inven11 < Inven1: 40*200

  Inven121 < Inven12 < Inven1: 0.8*6000

  Inven122 < Inven12 < Inven1: 50*200

  Inven21 < Inven2: 30*300

  Inven221 < Inven22 < Inven2: 30*200

  Inven222 < Inven22 < Inven2: 50*100

  PPUK parts < ASD parts < Inven2: 40*100

  PPGH parts < ASD parts < Inven2: 2*500

  The multi-subaccount name of the Cash account and the transaction sub-equation respectively are:

    88-654308-t-suppliers < Cash payments to suppliers < Operating activities

Inventory (1): 10*300 + Inventory (1): 40*200 + Inventory (1): 0.8*6000 + Inventory (1): 50*200 + Inventory (1): 30*300 + Inventory (1): 30*200 + Inventory (1): 50*100 + Inventory (1): 40*100 + Inventory (1): 2*500 = Account payable (2): 50800

- On May 1, 2016, the Company1 purchases following inventories $23,250 from the Proprietorship1 (phone number: 123456081) for -$3,250 cash and other on credit.

  Inven31 < Inven3: 10*150

  Inven32 < Inven3: 50*150

  Inven331 < Inven33 < Inven3: 20*150

  Inven332 < Inven33 < Inven3: 45*150

  HGFCVB parts < QASXC parts < Inven3: 10*150

  PPGHUP parts < ASDUP parts < Inven3: 20*150

  The multi-subaccount name of the Cash account and the transaction sub-equation respectively are:

    88-654309-t-suppliers < Cash payments to suppliers < Operating activities

    Cash (1): -3250 + Inventory (1): 10*150 + Inventory (1): 50*150 + Inventory (1): 20*150 + Inventory (1): 45*150 + Inventory (1): 10*150 + Inventory (1): 20*150 = Account payable (2): 20000

- On May 1, 2016, the Company1 purchases following inventories $6,350 from the Proprietorship2 (phone number: 123456080) for -$2,300 cash and other on credit.

  Inven411 < Inven41 < Inven4: 5*100

  Inven412 < Inven41 < Inven4: 18.5*100

  TTTCU parts < TTT parts < Inven4: 20*100

  RRRHJK parts < Inven4: 20*100

  The multi-subaccount name of the Cash account and the transaction sub-equation respectively are:

    88-654310-t-suppliers < Cash payments to suppliers < Operating activities

Cash (1): -2300 + Inventory (1): 5*100 + Inventory (1): 18.5*100 + Inventory (1): 20*100 + Inventory (1): 20*100 = Account payable (2): 4050

- On May 2, 2016, the Company1 transfers the supplies $2,800 to the Cost of goods manufactured to satisfy the need of producing. The transaction sub-equation is:

  Supplies (1): -2800 = Cost of goods manufactured (5): -2800

- On May 2, 2016, the Company1 transfers the following inventories $403,050 to the Cost of goods manufactured account (its subaccount: General parts expenses) to satisfy the producing need.

  Inven111 < Inven11 < Inven1: -10*300

  Inven112 < Inven11 < Inven1: -40*200

  Inven121 < Inven12 < Inven1: -0.8*6000

  Inven122 < Inven12 < Inven1: -50*200

  Inven21 < Inven2: -30*300

  Inven221 < Inven22 < Inven2: -30*200

  Inven222 < Inven22 < Inven2: -50*100

  PPUK parts < ASD parts < Inven2: -40*100

  PPGH parts < ASD parts < Inven2: -2*500

  Inven31 < Inven3: -10*150

  Inven32 < Inven3: -50*150

  Inven331 < Inven33 < Inven3: -20*150

  Inven332 < Inven33 < Inven3: -45*150

  HGFCVB parts < QASXC parts < Inven3: -10*150

  PPGHUP parts < ASDUP parts < Inven3: -20*150

  Inven411 < Inven41 < Inven4: -5*100

  Inven412 < Inven41 < Inven4: -18.5*100

  TTTCU parts < TTT parts < Inven4: -20*100

RRRHJK parts < Inven4: -20*100

Truck1 part1 < Truck1 parts < Vehicle parts: -8700*1

Truck1 part2 < Truck1 parts < Vehicle parts: -7600*1

Truck1 part3 < Truck1 parts < Vehicle parts: -5800*1

Truck2 part1 < Truck2 parts < Vehicle parts: -8500*1

Truck2 part2 < Truck2 parts < Vehicle parts: -7200*1

Truck2 part3 < Truck2 parts < Vehicle parts: -5400*1

Car1 part1 < Car1 parts < Vehicle parts: -8300*4

Car1 part2 < Car1 parts < Vehicle parts: -7200*4

Car1 part3 < Car1 parts < Vehicle parts: -5100*4

Car2 part1 < Car2 parts < Vehicle parts: -7900*4

Car2 part2 < Car2 parts < Vehicle parts: -6800*4

Car2 part3 < Car2 parts < Vehicle parts: -4900*4

Car3 part1 < Car3 parts < Vehicle parts: -7500*4

Car3 part2 < Car3 parts < Vehicle parts: -6400*4

Car3 part3 < Car3 parts < Vehicle parts: -4700*4

Computer server1 part1 < Computer server parts < Computer parts: -600*5

Computer server1 part2 < Computer server parts < Computer parts: -400*5

Computer server2 part1 < Computer server parts < Computer parts: -540*5

Computer server2 part2 < Computer server parts < Computer parts: -380*5

Computer1 part1 < Computer parts: -360*15

Computer1 part2 < Computer parts: -310*15

Computer2 part1 < Computer parts: -320*15

Computer2 part2 < Computer parts: -290*15

Computer3 part1 < Computer parts: -280*15

Computer3 part2 < Computer parts: -260*15

Computer4 part1 < Computer parts: -250*15

Computer4 part2 < Computer parts: -240*15

The six transaction sub-equations are respectively:

Inventory (1): - 10*300 + Inventory (1): - 40*200 + Inventory (1): - 0.8*6000 + Inventory (1): - 50*200 + Inventory (1): - 30*300 + Inventory (1): - 30*200 + Inventory (1): - 50*100 + Inventory (1): - 40*100 + Inventory (1): - 2*500 = Cost of goods manufactured (5): -50800

Inventory (1): -10*150 + Inventory (1): -50*150 + Inventory (1): -20*150 + Inventory (1): -45*150 + Inventory (1): -10*150 + Inventory (1): -20*150 + Inventory (1): -5*100 + Inventory (1): -18.5*100 + Inventory (1): -20*100 = Cost of goods manufactured (5): -27600

Inventory (1): -20*100 + Inventory (1): -8700*1 + Inventory (1): -7600*1 + Inventory (1): -5800*1 + Inventory (1): -8500*1 + Inventory (1): -7200*1 + Inventory (1): -5400*1 + Inventory (1): -8300*4 + Inventory (1): -7200*4 = Cost of goods manufactured (5): -107200

Inventory (1): - 5100*4 + Inventory (1): - 7900*4 + Inventory (1): - 6800*4 + Inventory (1): - 4900*4 + Inventory (1): - 7500*4 + Inventory (1): - 6400*4 + Inventory (1): - 4700*4 + Inventory (1): - 600*5+ Inventory (1): - 400*5 = Cost of goods manufactured (5): -178200

Inventory (1): - 540*5 + Inventory (1): - 380*5 + Inventory (1): - 360*15 + Inventory (1): - 310*15 + Inventory (1): - 320*15 + Inventory (1): - 290*15 + Inventory (1): - 280*15 + Inventory (1): - 260*15 = Cost of goods manufactured (5): -31900

Inventory (1): - 250*15 + Inventory (1): - 240*15 = Cost of goods manufactured (5): -7350

- On May 24, 2016, the Company1 pays -$623.75 cash to A13 (SIN: 909876513) for the Travelling expenses (travel allowance) $220.75 and the Other expenses (meals:

food111: $10*10 + food123: $15*10 + food312: $24*3 + food321: $27*3) $403.

- On May 31, 2016, the Company1 pays three employees' salary expenses for cash - $8,400 repeatedly.

- On May 31, 2016, the Company1 records the Amortization expenses $1,125 of a computer server2 ($562.5, five months), a computer3 ($291.67, five months), and a computer4 ($270.83, five months). The transaction sub-equation is:

  Accumulated amortization: Computer (1): -562.5 + Accumulated amortization: Computer (1): -291.67 + Accumulated amortization: Computer (1): -270.83 = Amortization expenses (5): -562.5 + Amortization expenses (5): -291.67 + Amortization expenses (5): -270.83

- On May 31, 2016, the Company1 cancels the balances of the Computer account and the Accumulated amortization: Computer account because these computers have used for two years. The transaction sub-equation is:

  Computer (1): -2700 + Computer (1): -1400 + Computer (1): -1300 + Accumulated amortization: Computer (1): 2700 + Accumulated amortization: Computer (1): 1400 + Accumulated amortization: Computer (1): 1300 = 0

- On June 1, 2016, the Company1 purchases a new Computer server1, a new Computer1, and a new Computer2 from the Company1 itself. Meanwhile, the Company1 also sells these computers to itself. The two transactions can be merged as a transaction. The balance of the Cash account does not change, so transaction sub-equation is:

  Computer (1): 2800 + Computer (1): 1600 + Computer (1): 1500 + Inventory (1): -1600 + Inventory (1): -1000 + Inventory (1): -920 = Sale (4): 5900 + Cost of goods sold (5): -3520

- On June 1, 2016, the Company1 sells one Computer server1 $2,800, one Computer1

$1,600, and one Computer2 $1,500 for sales $5,900 to the Company3 (phone number: 123456782) for cash $3,000 and other on credit. The multi-subaccount name of the Cash account and transaction sub-equation respectively are:

88-654308-c-customers < Cash receipts from customers < Operating activities

Cash (1): 3000 + Account receivable (1): 2900 + Inventory (1): -1600 + Inventory (1): -1000+ Inventory (1): -920 = Sales (4): 5900 + Cost of goods sold (5): -3520

- On June 10, 2016, the Company1 pays -$15,000 cash to the Company3 (phone number: 123456082) with the General ID 67. The multi-subaccount name of the Cash account and transaction sub-equation respectively are:

  88-654308-t-suppliers < Cash payments to suppliers < Operating activities

- On June 12, 2016, the Company1 pays -$64,000 cash to the Company2 (phone number: 123456083) with the General ID 64. The multi-subaccount name of the Cash account is:

  88-654307-t-suppliers < Cash payments to suppliers < Operating activities

- On June 23, 2016, the Company1 pays -$580.91 cash to A13 (SIN: 909876513) for the Travelling expenses (travel allowance) $270.91 and the Other expenses (meals: food112: $11*10 + food211: $8*10 + food311: $20*6) $310.

- On June 30, 2016, the Company1 pays three employees' salary expenses for cash -$8,400 repeatedly.

- On July 7, 2016, the Company1 pays -$442.56 cash to A14 (SIN: 909876514) for the Travelling expenses (travel allowance) $262.56 and the Other expenses (meals: food123: $15*6 + food322: $30*3) $180.

- On July 19, 2016, the Company1 sells one Computer4 to A8 (SIN: 909876508) for cash $1300. The multi-subaccount name of the Cash account and transaction sub-equation respectively are:

  909876508-c-customers < Cash receipts from customers < Operating activities

Cash (1): 1300 + Inventory (1): -770 = Sales (4): 1300 + Cost of goods sold (5): -770

- On July 25, 2016, the Company1 pays -$487.84 cash to A13 (SIN: 909876513) for the Travelling expenses (travel allowance) $185.84 and the Other expenses (meals: food211: $8*10 + food212: $9*10 + food311: $20*3 + food312: $24*3) $302.

- On July 31, 2016, the Company1 pays three employees' salary expenses for cash - $8,400 repeatedly.

- On August 1, 2016, the Company1 sells one Computer server1 $2,800 (cost: $1,600), one Computer1 $1,600 (cost: $1,000), and one Computer2 $1,500 (cost: $920) for sales $5,900 to the Business Bank1 (phone number: 123456786) for cash $5,000 and other on credit. The multi-subaccount name of the Cash account and transaction sub-equation respectively are:

  88-654304-c-customers < Cash receipts from customers < Operating activities

  Cash (1): 5000 + Account receivable (1): 900 + Inventory (1): -1600 + Inventory (1): -1000 + Inventory (1): -920 = Sales (4): 5900 + Cost of goods sold (5): -3520

- On August 1, 2016, the Company1 sells one Car3 $38,000 to A16 and A23 for cash $38,000. A16 pays cash -$10,000 with the primary account in the Business Bank1 and cash -$11,000 with the second account in the Business Bank2. A23 pays cash - $5,500 with the primary account in the Business Bank2 and cash -$11,500 with the second account in the Business Bank1. The multi-subaccount names of the Cash account and transaction sub-equation respectively are:

  909876516-c-customers < Cash receipts from customers < Operating activities
  909876516-c-customers < Cash receipts from customers < Operating activities
  909876523-c-customers < Cash receipts from customers < Operating activities
  909876523-c-customers < Cash receipts from customers < Operating activities

  Cash (1): 10000 + Cash (1): 11000 + Cash (1): 5500 + Cash (1): 11500 +

Inventory (1): -26000 = Sales (4): 38000 + Cost of goods sold (5): -26000

- On August 1, 2016, the Company1 sells one Computer server1 $2,800 (cost: $1,600), one Computer1 $1,600 (cost: $1,000), and one Computer2 $1,500 (cost: $920) for sales $5,900 to the Company2 (phone number: 123456783) for cash $3,000 and other on credit. The multi-subaccount name of the Cash account is:

  88-654307-c-customers < Cash receipts from customers < Operating activities

- On August 2, 2016, the Company1 sells one Computer1 to A1 (SIN: 909876501) for cash $1600. The multi-subaccount name of the Cash account and transaction sub-equation respectively are:

  909876501-c-customers < Cash receipts from customers < Operating activities

  Cash (1): 1600 + Inventory (1): -1000 = Sales (4): 1600 + Cost of goods sold (5): -1000

- On August 3, 2016, the Company1 pays -$12,000 cash to the Company2 (phone number: 123456083) with the General ID 64. The multi-subaccount name of the Cash account is:

  88-654307-t-suppliers < Cash payments to suppliers < Operating activities

- On August 10, 2016, the Company1 sells one Computer2 to A11 (SIN: 909876511) for cash $1,500. The multi-subaccount name of the Cash account and transaction sub-equation respectively are:

  909876511-c-customers < Cash receipts from customers < Operating activities

  Cash (1): 1500 + Inventory (1): -920 = Sales (4): 1500 + Cost of goods sold (5): -920

- On August 14, 2016, the Company1 sells one Truck1- Service package1 and one Car1- Service package3 to the Central Bank (phone number: 123456789) for cash $1040. The multi-subaccount name of the Cash account and transaction sub-equation respectively are:

88-654301-c-customers < Cash receipts from customers < Operating activities

Cash (1): 1040 = Service package incomes (4): 550 + Service package incomes (4): 490

- On August 17, 2016, the Company1 pays -$386.36 cash to A15 (SIN: 909876515) for the Travelling expenses (travel allowance) $263.36 and the Other expenses (meals: food522: $13*3 + food622: $28*3) $123.

- On August 25, 2016, the Company1 pays -$501.22 cash to A13 (SIN: 909876513) for the Travelling expenses (travel allowance) $189.22 and the Other expenses (meals: food211: $8*10 + food213: $10*10 + food311: $20*3 + food312: $24*3) $312.

- On August 31, 2016, the Company1 pays three employees' salary expenses for cash -$8,400 repeatedly.

- On September 2, 2016, the Company1 sells one Car3 to the Proprietorship2 (phone number: 123456780) for cash $18000 and other on credit. The multi-subaccount name of the Cash account and transaction sub-equation respectively are:

88-654310-c-customers < Cash receipts from customers < Operating activities

Cash (1): 18000 + Account receivable (1): 20000 + Inventory (1): -26000 = Sales (4): 38000 + Cost of goods sold (5): -26000

- On September 12, 2016, the Company1 receives $18,000 cash from the Business Bank1 (phone number: 123456786) with the General ID 30.

- On September 13, 2016, the Company1 pays -$25,000 cash to the Company3 (phone number: 123456082) with General ID 3 ($1,000) and the General ID 67 ($24,000). The multi-subaccount name of the Cash account and transaction sub-equation respectively are:

88-654308-t-suppliers < Cash payments to suppliers < Operating activities

- On September 14, 2016, the Company1 pays -$10,000 cash to the Company2 (phone number: 123456083) with the General ID 64.

- On September 26, 2016, the Company1 receives $17,000 cash from the Business Bank2 (phone number: 123456785) with the General ID 41.

- On September 26, 2016, the Company1 pays -$8,000 cash to the Company3 (phone number: 123456082) with the General ID 67.

- On September 28, 2016, the Company1 pays -$658.33 cash to A13 (SIN: 909876513) for the Travelling expenses (travel allowance) $207.33 and the Other expenses (meals: food221: $12*10 + food23: $16*10 + food321: $27*3 + food322: $30*3) $451.

- On September 30, 2016, the Company1 pays three employees' salary expenses for cash $8,400 repeatedly.

- On October 1, 2016, the Company1 sells one Computer server1 $2,800 (cost: $1,600), one Computer1 $1,600 (cost: $1,000), and one Computer2 $1,500 (cost: $920) to the Tax Bureau (phone number: 123456787) for cash $2400 and other on credit. The multi-subaccount name of the Cash account and transaction sub-equation respectively are:

  88-654303-c-customers < Cash receipts from customers < Operating activities

  Cash (1): 2400 + Account receivable (1): 3500 + Inventory (1): -1600 + Inventory (1): -1000 + Inventory (1): -920 = Sales (4): 5900 + Cost of goods sold (5): -3520

- On October 1, 2016, the Company1 sells one Computer server1 $2,800 (cost: $1,600), one Computer1 $1,600 (cost: $1,000), and one Computer2 $1,500 (cost: $920) for sales $5,900 to the Business Bank2 (phone number: 123456785) for cash $5,000 and other on credit. The multi-subaccount name of the Cash account is:

  88-654305-c-customers < Cash receipts from customers < Operating activities

- On October 1, 2016, the Company1 sells one Computer server1, one Computer1, and one Computer2 to the Proprietorship1 (phone number: 123456781) for cash $5,500 and other on credit. The multi-subaccount name of the Cash account is:

88-654309-c-customers < Cash receipts from customers < Operating activities

- On October 3, 2016, the Company1 sells one Truck2- Service package2 and one Car1- Service package3 to the Governrmnt1 (phone number: 123456788) for cash $990. The multi-subaccount name of the Cash account and transaction sub-equation respectively are:

  88-654302-c-customers < Cash receipts from customers < Operating activities

  Cash (1): 990 = Service package incomes (4): 500 + Service package incomes (4): 490

- On October 5, 2016, the Company1 sells one Car2 $39,000 to A13 and A25 for cash $39,000. A13 pays cash -$10,000 with the primary account in the Business Bank1 and cash -$11,500 with the second account in the Business Bank2. A25 pays cash -$10,500 with the primary account in the Business Bank1 and cash -$7,000 with the second account in the Business Bank2. The multi-subaccount names of the Cash account and transaction sub-equation respectively are:

  909876513-c-customers < Cash receipts from customers < Operating activities
  909876513-c-customers < Cash receipts from customers < Operating activities
  909876525-c-customers < Cash receipts from customers < Operating activities
  909876525-c-customers < Cash receipts from customers < Operating activities

  Cash (1): 10000 + Cash (1): 11500 + Cash (1): 10500 + Cash (1): 7000 + Inventory (1): -27000 = Sales (4): 39000 + Cost of goods sold (5): -27000

- On October 7, 2016, the Company1 pays -$392.36 cash to A15 (SIN: 909876515) for the Travelling expenses (travel allowance) $263.36 and the Other expenses (meals: food522: $13*3 + food614: $30*3) $129.

- On October 27, 2016, the Company1 pays -$607.57 cash to A13 (SIN: 909876513) for the Travelling expenses (travel allowance) $224.57 and the Other expenses (meals: food113: $12*10 + food214: $11*10 + food312: $24*3 + food321: $27*3)

$383.

- On October 31, 2016, the Company1 pays three employees' salary expenses for cash -$8,400 repeatedly.

- On November 5, 2016, the Company1 receives $2,900 cash from the Company3 (phone number: 123456782) with the General ID 82. The multi-subaccount name of the Cash account is:

  88-654308-c-customers < Cash receipts from customers < Operating activities

- On November 19, 2016, the Company1 pays -$551.13 cash to A13 (SIN: 909876513) for the Travelling expenses (travel allowance) $190.13 and the Other expenses (meals: food111: $10*10 + food113: $12*10 + food311: $20*3 + food321: $27*3) $361.

- On November 19, 2016, the Company1 sells one Truck2- Service package2, one Car1- Service package3, and one Car3- Service package5 to the Tax Bank (phone number: 123456787) for cash $1400. The multi-subaccount name of the Cash account and transaction sub-equation respectively are:

  88-654303-c-customers < Cash receipts from customers < Operating activities

  Cash (1): 1400 = Service package incomes (4): 500 + Service package incomes (4): 490 + Service package incomes (4): 410

- On November 19, 2016, the Company1 pays -$401.13 cash to A15 (SIN: 909876515) for the Travelling expenses (travel allowance) $269.13 and the Other expenses (meals: food53: $16*3 + food622: $28*3) $132.

- On November 21, 2016, the Company1 completed all products ($68,300) of the Computer account and transfers the balance of the Cost of goods manufactured account to the Inventory account. The Cost of goods manufactured account has four subaccounts of the "Supplies expenses", the "909876513-salary < Sales department-salary < Salary expenses", the "909876515-salary < Product department-salary < Salary expenses", and the "General parts expenses". Their amounts, which are used in the products of the Computer, are estimated and are $800, $13,000, $5,000, and

$ 49,500 respectively. The transaction sub-equation is:

Inventory (1): 1600*5 + Inventory (1): 1500*5 + Inventory (1): 1000*15 + Inventory (1): 920*15 + Inventory (1): 830*15 + Inventory (1): 770*15 = Cost of goods manufactured (5): 800 + Cost of goods manufactured (5): 13000 + Cost of goods manufactured (5): 5000 + Cost of goods manufactured (5): 49500

- On November 29, 2016, the Company1 pays -$14,420 cash to the Company2 (phone number: 123456083) with the General ID 66. The multi-subaccount name of the Cash account and transaction sub-equation respectively are:

  88-654307-t-suppliers < Cash payments to suppliers < Operating activities

- On November 29, 2016, the Company1 pays -$3,000 cash to the Company3 (phone number: 123456082) with the General ID 67. The multi-subaccount name of the Cash account and transaction sub-equation respectively are:

  88-654308-t-suppliers < Cash payments to suppliers < Operating activities

- On November 29, 2016, the Company1 sells one Computer2 to A4 (SIN: 909876504) for cash $1,500. The multi-subaccount name of the Cash account and transaction sub-equation respectively are:

  909876504-c-customers < Cash receipts from customers < Operating activities

  Cash (1): 1500 + Inventory (1): -920 = Sales (4): 1500 + Cost of goods sold (5): -920

- On November 30, 2016, the Company1 sells one Computer2 $1,500 (cost: $920) to A18 (SIN: 909876518) for cash $1,500. The multi-subaccount name of the Cash account is:

  909876518-c-customers < Cash receipts from customers < Operating activities

- On November 30, 2016, the Company1 sells one Computer4 $1,300 (cost: $770) to A6 (SIN: 909876506) for cash $1,300. The multi-subaccount name of the Cash account is:

  909876506-c-customers < Cash receipts from customers < Operating activities

- On November 30, 2016, the Company1 pays three employees' salary expenses for cash -$8,400 repeatedly.

- On December 1, 2016, the Company1 sells one Computer server1, one Computer1, and one Computer2 to the Proprietorship2 (phone number: 123456780) for cash $5,000 and other on credit. The multi-subaccount name of the Cash account and transaction sub-equation respectively are:

  88-654310-c-customers < Cash receipts from customers < Operating activities

  Cash (1): 5000 + Account receivable (1): 900 + Inventory (1): -1600 + Inventory (1): -1000+ Inventory (1): -920 = Sales (4): 5900 + Cost of goods sold (5): -3520

- On December 10, 2016, the Company1 sells one Computer1 $1,600 (cost: $1,000) to A24 (SIN: 909876524) for cash $1,600. The multi-subaccount name of the Cash account is:

  909876524-c-customers < Cash receipts from customers < Operating activities

- On December 11, 2016, the Company1 receives $1,500 cash from the Business Bank1 (phone number: 123456786) with the General ID 30. The multi-subaccount name of the Cash account is:

  88-654304-c-customers < Cash receipts from customers < Operating activities

- On December 16, 2016, the Company1 pays -$638.34 cash to A13 (SIN: 909876513) for the Travelling expenses (travel allowance) $225.34 and the Other expenses (meals: food112: $11*10 + food123: $15*10 + food312: $24*3 + food321: $27*3) $413.

- On December 19, 2016, the Company1 sells one Computer1 $1,600 (cost: $1,000) to A22 (SIN: 909876522) for cash $1,600. The multi-subaccount name of the Cash account is:

  909876522-c-customers < Cash receipts from customers < Operating activities

- On December 19, 2016, the Company1 receives $2,800 cash from the Business Bank2 (phone number: 123456785) with the General ID 41. The multi-subaccount name of the Cash account is:

88-654305-c-customers < Cash receipts from customers < Operating activities

- On December 22, 2016, the Company1 sells one Computer3 $1,400 (cost: $830) to A2 (SIN: 909876502) for cash $1,400. The multi-subaccount name of the Cash account is:

  909876502-c-customers < Cash receipts from customers < Operating activities

- On December 23, 2016, the Company1 pays -$444.45 cash to A14 (SIN: 909876514) for the Travelling expenses (travel allowance) $282.45 and the Other expenses (meals: food621: $26*3 + food622: $28*3) $162.

- On December 23, 2016, the Company1 pays -$5,500 cash to the Proprietorship2 (phone number: 123456080) with the General ID 51 ($2,000) and the General ID 69 ($3,500). The multi-subaccount name of the Cash account and transaction sub-equation respectively are:

  88-654310-t-suppliers < Cash payments to suppliers < Operating activities

- On December 23, 2016, the Company1 pays -$18,000 cash to the Proprietorship1 (phone number: 123456081) with the General ID 68. The multi-subaccount name of the Cash account and transaction sub-equation respectively are:

  88-654309-t-suppliers < Cash payments to suppliers < Operating activities

- On December 29, 2016, the Company1 receives $2,400 cash from the Tax Bureau (phone number: 123456787) with the General ID 110. The multi-subaccount name of the Cash account is:

  88-654303-c-customers < Cash receipts from customers < Operating activities

- On December 29, 2016, the Company1 receives $10,000 cash from the Proprietorship1 (phone number: 123456781) with the General ID 32. The multi-subaccount name of the Cash account is:

  88-654309-c-customers < Cash receipts from customers < Operating activities

- On December 29, 2016, the Company1 receives $27,000 cash from the Proprietorship2 (phone number: 123456780) with the General ID 33 ($8,000) and General ID 102 ($19,000). The multi-subaccount name of the Cash account is:

  88-654310-c-customers < Cash receipts from customers < Operating activities

- On December 29, 2016, the Company1 pays $39,700 cash to the Company2 (phone number: 123456083) with the General ID 65. The multi-subaccount name of the Cash account is:

  88-654307-t-suppliers < Cash payments to suppliers < Operating activities

- On December 30, 2016, the Company1 receives $2,000 cash from the Government1 (phone number: 123456788) with the General ID 63. The multi-subaccount name of the Cash account is:

  88-654302-c-customers < Cash receipts from customers < Operating activities

- On December 30, 2016, the Company1 receives $1,400 cash from the Business Bank1 (phone number: 123456786) with the General ID 30 ($500) the General ID 92 ($900). The multi-subaccount name of the Cash account is:

  88-654304-c-customers < Cash receipts from customers < Operating activities

- On December 31, 2016, the Company1 receives $3,500 cash from the Central Bank (phone number: 123456789) with the General ID 62. The multi-subaccount name of the Cash account is:

  88-654301-c-customers < Cash receipts from customers < Operating activities

- On December 31, 2016, the Company1 sells one Car1 $40,000 to A7 for cash $40,000. The multi-subaccount name of the Cash account and transaction sub-equation respectively are:

  909876507-c-customers < Cash receipts from customers < Operating activities

  Cash (1): 40000 + Inventory (1): -28000 = Sales (4): 40000 + Cost of goods sold (5): -28000

- On December 31, 2016, the Company1 sells one Car1 $40,000 (cost: $28,000) to A10 for cash $40,000. The multi-subaccount name of the Cash account is:
  909876510-c-customers < Cash receipts from customers < Operating activities

- On December 31, 2016, the Company1 pays three employees' salary expenses for cash -$8,400 repeatedly.

- On December 31, 2016, the Company1 transfers the balance of the Cost of goods manufactured account (products of vehicle) to the Working-in-process inventory account. The Cost of goods manufactured account has four subaccounts of the "Supplies expenses", the "909876513-salary < Sales department-salary < Salary expenses", the "909876515-salary < Product department-salary < Salary expenses", and the "General parts expenses". Their balances are -$2,000, -$7,800, -$18,200, and -$353,550 respectively. The transaction sub-equation is:

Working-in-process inventory (1): 32650*1 + Working-in-process inventory (1): 29700*1 + Working-in-process inventory (1): 27600*4 + Working-in-process inventory (1): 26600*4 + Working-in-process inventory (1): 25600*4 = Cost of goods manufactured (5): 2000 + Cost of goods manufactured (5): 7800 + Cost of goods manufactured (5): 18200 + Cost of goods manufactured (5): 353550

- On the same day, 2016, the Company1 sells one Car3 $38,000 (cost: $26,000) to A24 for cash $38,000. The multi-subaccount name of the Cash account is:

  909876524-c-customers < Cash receipts from customers < Operating activities

- On the same day, 2016, the Company1 pays -$55,000 cash to the Company2 (phone number: 123456083) with the General ID 64. The multi-subaccount name of the Cash account is:

  88-654307-t-suppliers < Cash payments to suppliers < Operating activities

- On the same day, the Company1 pays -$38,650 cash to the Business Bank1 for the Note interest expenses of the Note11 $22,500 ($250,000, one-level subaccount "Note11-interest") and the Note15 $16,150 ($170,000, one-level subaccount "Note15-interest"). The multi-subaccount name of the Cash account and the transaction sub-equation respectively are:

  88-654304-t-note interest < Cash payments to business banks < Operating activities

  Cash (1): -38650 = Note interest expenses (5): -22500 + Note interest expenses (5): -16150

- On the same day, the Company1 pays -$19,800 cash to the Business Bank2 for the Note interest expenses of the Note21 ($140,000, one-level subaccount "Note21-interest"). The multi-subaccount name of the Cash account and the transaction sub-equation respectively are:

  88-654305-t-note interest < Cash payments to business banks < Operating activities

  Cash (1): -19800 = Note interest expenses (5): -19800

- On the same day, the Company1 pays -$2,300 cash to the bond holders for the Bond interest expenses of the Bond31 (one-level subaccount "Bond31-interest"). The multi-subaccount names of the Cash account and the transaction sub-equations respectively are:

  88-654305-t-bond interest < Cash payments to bond holders < Operating activities
  909876501-t-bond interest < Cash payments to bond holders < Operating activities
  909876502-t-bond interest < Cash payments to bond holders < Operating activities
  909876508-t-bond interest < Cash payments to bond holders < Operating activities
  909876511-t-bond interest < Cash payments to bond holders < Operating activities
  909876514-t-bond interest < Cash payments to bond holders < Operating activities
  909876516-t-bond interest < Cash payments to bond holders < Operating activities
  909876518-t-bond interest < Cash payments to bond holders < Operating activities
  909876521-t-bond interest < Cash payments to bond holders < Operating activities
  909876522-t-bond interest < Cash payments to bond holders < Operating activities
  909876524-t-bond interest < Cash payments to bond holders < Operating activities
  909876525-t-bond interest < Cash payments to bond holders < Operating activities

  Cash (1): -230 + Cash (1): -138 + Cash (1): -276 + Cash (1): -230 + Cash (1): -322 + Cash (1): -92 = Bond interest expenses (5): -1288

  Cash (1): -184 + Cash (1): -92 + Cash (1): -138 + Cash (1): -230 + Cash (1): -138 + Cash (1): -230 = Bond interest expenses (5): -1012

- On the same day, the Company1 receives cash $400 for investment interest of the Bond11and cash $135 for investment interest of the Bond13 from the Business Bank1. The multi-subaccount name of the Cash account and transaction sub-equation respectively are:

  88-654304-c-investment income < Cash receipts from investments < Investing activities

  Cash (1): 400 + Cash (1): 135 = Investment incomes (4):400 + Investment incomes (4):135

- On the same day, the Company1 receives cash $369 for investment interest of the Bond21 from the Business Bank2. The multi-subaccount name of the Cash account and transaction sub-equation respectively are:

  88-654305-c-investment income < Cash receipts from investments < Investing activities

  Cash (1): 369 = Investment incomes (4): 369

- On the same day, the Company1 receives cash $120 from the Business Bank1 for primary deposit interest. The multi-subaccount name of the Cash account and transaction sub-equation respectively are:

  88-654304-c-deposit interest income < Cash receipts from deposit interest < Financial activities

  Cash (1): 120 = Deposit interest incomes (4):120

- On the same day, the Company1 records the Office supplies expenses -$2,332.13. The transaction sub-equation is:

  Supplies (1): -2332.13 = Office supplies expenses (5): -2332.13

- On the same day, the Company1 records the Vehicle's amortization expenses - $24,200 one year (5 years, straight line). The transaction sub-equation is:

  Accumulated amortization: Vehicle (1): -9000 + Accumulated amortization: Vehicle (1): -8000 + Accumulated amortization: Vehicle (1): -7200 = Amortization expenses (5): -9000 + Amortization expenses (5): -8000 + Amortization expenses (5): -7200

- On the same day, the Company1 records the Computer's amortization expenses $1,720.84 seven months (2 years, straight line) which includes a new computer server1 ($816.67), a new computer1 ($466.67), and a new computer2 ($437.5). Please pay attention here. The new computers are different cancelled computers. Total balance of the amortization expenses is equal to the sum of the cancelled computers' amortization expenses and the new computers' amortization expenses. The transaction sub-equation is:

  Accumulated amortization: Computer (1): -816.67 + Accumulated amortization: Computer (1): -466.67 + Accumulated amortization: Computer (1): -437.5 = Amortization expenses (5): -816.67 + Amortization expenses (5): -466.67 + Amortization expenses (5): -437.5

- On December 31, 2016, the Company1 records the Tax expenses -$8,694.39 and the Tax payable $8,694.39. The multi-subaccount name forms of the Tax expenses and the Tax payable accounts all are the 'n'. The transaction sub-equation is:

  0 = Tax payable (2): 8694.39 + Tax expenses (5): -8694.39

So far, I have entered all transactions of the Company1 in the fiscal year 2016. After getting the Income Statement and clicking the "Yes" button for new fiscal year, I can get the Balance Sheet of the Company1.

In the new fiscal year, the Company1 will record the following transaction.

- On January 2, 2017, the Company1 pays the balance $8,694.39 of the Tax payable account to the Tax Bureau. The multi-subaccount name of the Cash account and transaction sub-equation respectively are:

    88-654303-n-tax < Cash payments to Tax Bureau < Operating activities

    Cash (1): -8694.39 = Tax payable (2): -8694.39

3.6.2 Brief Summary of the Company1

The Figure 3.6-2 shows two sums and all cash transactions of the Company1 by using of SQL Server query. As a closed system based on the MathAccounting software, the sum0 should be equal to zero. However, the individuals are not responsible for recording any transaction, so the sum0 (-$56,106.27) is the sum of the amounts that individuals paid to the Company1. The opposite value ($38,933.25) of the sum1 (-$38,933.25) is the balance of the Cash account of the Company1 on December 31, 2016. It is also the balance of the deposits of the Company1 in the Business Bak1 on December 31, 2016.

The Figure 3.6-3 to the Figure 3.6-6 on page 408 to 411 show the four tables of the cash flows statement, the cash account, the income statement, and the balance sheet respectively.

```
SQLQuery1.sql - LIU...SS.dcj100 (sa (52))*  ×
 use dcj100
  select sum(amount) as sum0 from CashByMembers where IDM='88-654306' and TransDate between '2016-01-01' and '2016-12-31'
  select sum(amount) as sum1 from CashByMembers where IDM='88-654306' and Symbol = 'd'
 select * from CashByMembers where Recorder='88-654306' and TransDate between '2016-01-01' and '2016-12-31'
          order by TransDate
100 %   ▾
```

 Results   Messages

	sum0
1	-56106.27

	sum1
1	-38933.25

	IDM	Amount	Symbol	MultiSubaccount	Recorder	TransDate
1	88-654310	500.00	t	88-654310-t-supplies < Cash payments for operating expenses < Operating activities	88-654306	2016-01-02
2	88-654303	-60.00	c	88-654303-c-customers < Cash receipts from customers < Operating activities	88-654306	2016-01-13
3	88-654307	11000.00	t	88-654307-t-suppliers < Cash payments to suppliers < Operating activities	88-654306	2016-01-14
4	88-654308	8000.00	t	88-654308-t-suppliers < Cash payments to suppliers < Operating activities	88-654306	2016-01-14
5	909876513	415.67	n	909876513-n-operating expenses < Cash payments for operating expenses < Operating activities	88-654306	2016-01-15
6	909876515	42.12	n	909876515-n-operating expenses < Cash payments for operating expenses < Operating activities	88-654306	2016-01-16
7	88-654309	2040.00	t	88-654309-t-suppliers < Cash payments to suppliers < Operating activities	88-654306	2016-01-31
8	88-654310	1000.00	t	88-654310-t-suppliers < Cash payments to suppliers < Operating activities	88-654306	2016-01-31
9	909876514	2900.00	t	909876514-t-salary < Cash payments for operating expenses < Operating activities	88-654306	2016-01-31
10	909876513	2600.00	t	909876513-t-CGM < Cash payments for operating expenses < Operating activities	88-654306	2016-01-31
11	909876515	2900.00	t	909876515-t-CGM < Cash payments for operating expenses < Operating activities	88-654306	2016-01-31
12	88-654304	-19000.00	c	88-654304-c-customers < Cash receipts from customers < Operating activities	88-654306	2016-02-01
13	88-654309	-28000.00	c	88-654309-c-customers < Cash receipts from customers < Operating activities	88-654306	2016-02-01
14	88-654310	-30000.00	c	88-654310-c-customers < Cash receipts from customers < Operating activities	88-654306	2016-02-01
15	909876514	49.68	n	909876514-n-operating expenses < Cash payments for operating expenses < Operating activities	88-654306	2016-02-01
16	88-654303	-500.00	c	88-654303-c-customers < Cash receipts from customers < Operating activities	88-654306	2016-02-02
17	88-654301	-800.00	c	88-654301-c-customers < Cash receipts from customers < Operating activities	88-654306	2016-02-13
18	909876513	557.83	n	909876513-n-operating expenses < Cash payments for operating expenses < Operating activities	88-654306	2016-02-20

	IDM	Amount	Symbol	MultiSubaccount	Recorder	TransDate
19	88-654307	-600.00	c	88-654307-c-customers < Cash receipts from customers < Operating activities	88-654306	2016-02-25
20	88-654308	-900.00	c	88-654308-c-customers < Cash receipts from customers < Operating activities	88-654306	2016-02-27
21	909876514	2900.00	t	909876514-t-salary < Cash payments for operating expenses < Operating activities	88-654306	2016-02-28
22	909876513	2600.00	t	909876513-t-CGM < Cash payments for operating expenses < Operating activities	88-654306	2016-02-28
23	909876515	2900.00	t	909876515-t-CGM < Cash payments for operating expenses < Operating activities	88-654306	2016-02-28
24	88-654305	-19000.00	c	88-654305-c-customers < Cash receipts from customers < Operating activities	88-654306	2016-03-01
25	88-654308	1600.00	t	88-654308-t-suppliers < Cash payments to suppliers < Operating activities	88-654306	2016-03-04
26	88-654307	2400.00	t	88-654307-t-suppliers < Cash payments to suppliers < Operating activities	88-654306	2016-03-05
27	88-654309	-1000.00	c	88-654309-c-customers < Cash receipts from customers < Operating activities	88-654306	2016-03-06
28	88-654310	-2000.00	c	88-654310-c-customers < Cash receipts from customers < Operating activities	88-654306	2016-03-09
29	909876513	516.37	n	909876513-n-operating expenses < Cash payments for operating expenses < Operating activities	88-654306	2016-03-23
30	88-654301	-600.00	c	88-654301-c-customers < Cash receipts from customers < Operating activities	88-654306	2016-03-25
31	909876514	239.73	n	909876514-n-operating expenses < Cash payments for operating expenses < Operating activities	88-654306	2016-03-30
32	909876514	2900.00	t	909876514-t-salary < Cash payments for operating expenses < Operating activities	88-654306	2016-03-31
33	909876513	2600.00	t	909876513-t-CGM < Cash payments for operating expenses < Operating activities	88-054306	2016-03-31
34	909876515	2900.00	t	909876515-t-CGM < Cash payments for operating expenses < Operating activities	88-654306	2016-03-31
35	88-654310	1000.00	t	88-654310-t-supplies < Cash payments for operating expenses < Operating activities	88-654306	2016-04-12
36	909876513	717.38	n	909876513-n-operating expenses < Cash payments for operating expenses < Operating activities	88-654306	2016-04-28
37	88-654310	1000.00	t	88-654310-t-suppliers < Cash payments to suppliers < Operating activities	88-654306	2016-04-29
38	88-654302	-60.00	c	88-654302-c-customers < Cash receipts from customers < Operating activities	88-654306	2016-04-30
39	909876514	2900.00	t	909876514-t-salary < Cash payments for operating expenses < Operating activities	88-654306	2016-04-30
40	909876513	2600.00	t	909876513-t-CGM < Cash payments for operating expenses < Operating activities	88-654306	2016-04-30
41	909876515	2900.00	t	909876515-t-CGM < Cash payments for operating expenses < Operating activities	88-654306	2016-04-30
42	88-654301	-1900.00	c	88-654301-c-customers < Cash receipts from customers < Operating activities	88-654306	2016-05-01
43	88-654302	-8000.00	c	88-654302-c-customers < Cash receipts from customers < Operating activities	88-654306	2016-05-01
44	88-654307	15000.00	t	88-654307-t-suppliers < Cash payments to suppliers < Operating activities	88-654306	2016-05-01
45	88-654309	3250.00	t	88-654309-t-suppliers < Cash payments to suppliers < Operating activities	88-654306	2016-05-01
46	88-654310	2300.00	t	88-654310-t-suppliers < Cash payments to suppliers < Operating activities	88-654306	2016-05-01

Figure 3.6-2   Company1 Cash Received or Paid by Other Members (Continue)

	IDM	Amount	Symbol	MultiSubaccount	Recorder	TransDate
47	909876513	623.75	n	909876513-n-operating expenses < Cash payments for operating expenses < Operating activities	88-654306	2016-05-24
48	909876514	2900.00	t	909876514-t-salary < Cash payments for operating expenses < Operating activities	88-654306	2016-05-31
49	909876513	2600.00	t	909876513-t-CGM < Cash payments for operating expenses < Operating activities	88-654306	2016-05-31
50	909876515	2900.00	t	909876515-t-CGM < Cash payments for operating expenses < Operating activities	88-654306	2016-05-31
51	88-654308	-3000.00	c	88-654308-c-customers < Cash receipts from customers < Operating activities	88-654306	2016-06-01
52	88-654308	15000.00	t	88-654308-t-suppliers < Cash payments to suppliers < Operating activities	88-654306	2016-06-10
53	88-654307	64000.00	t	88-654307-t-suppliers < Cash payments to suppliers < Operating activities	88-654306	2016-06-12
54	909876513	580.91	n	909876513-n-operating expenses < Cash payments for operating expenses < Operating activities	88-654306	2016-06-23
55	909876514	2900.00	t	909876514-t-salary < Cash payments for operating expenses < Operating activities	88-654306	2016-06-30
56	909876513	2600.00	t	909876513-t-CGM < Cash payments for operating expenses < Operating activities	88-654306	2016-06-30
57	909876515	2900.00	t	909876515-t-CGM < Cash payments for operating expenses < Operating activities	88-654306	2016-06-30
58	909876514	442.56	n	909876514-n-operating expenses < Cash payments for operating expenses < Operating activities	88-654306	2016-07-07
59	909876508	-1300.00	c	909876508-c-customers < Cash receipts from customers < Operating activities	88-654306	2016-07-19
60	909876513	487.84	n	909876513-n-operating expenses < Cash payments for operating expenses < Operating activities	88-654306	2016-07-25
61	909876514	2900.00	t	909876514-t-salary < Cash payments for operating expenses < Operating activities	88-654306	2016-07-31
62	909876513	2600.00	t	909876513-t-CGM < Cash payments for operating expenses < Operating activities	88-654306	2016-07-31
63	909876515	2900.00	t	909876515-t-CGM < Cash payments for operating expenses < Operating activities	88-654306	2016-07-31
64	88-654304	-5000.00	c	88-654304-c-customers < Cash receipts from customers < Operating activities	88-654306	2016-08-01
65	909876516	-10000.00	c	909876516-c-customers < Cash receipts from customers < Operating activities	88-654306	2016-08-01
66	909876516	-11000.00	c	909876516-c-customers < Cash receipts from customers < Operating activities	88-654306	2016-08-01
67	909876523	-5500.00	c	909876523-c-customers < Cash receipts from customers < Operating activities	88-654306	2016-08-01
68	909876523	-11500.00	c	909876523-c-customers < Cash receipts from customers < Operating activities	88-654306	2016-08-01
69	88-654307	-3000.00	c	88-654307-c-customers < Cash receipts from customers < Operating activities	88-654306	2016-08-01
70	909876501	-1600.00	c	909876501-c-customers < Cash receipts from customers < Operating activities	88-654306	2016-08-02
71	88-654307	12000.00	t	88-654307-t-suppliers < Cash payments to suppliers < Operating activities	88-654306	2016-08-03
72	909876511	-1500.00	c	909876511-c-customers < Cash receipts from customers < Operating activities	88-654306	2016-08-10
73	88-654301	-1040.00	c	88-654301-c-customers < Cash receipts from customers < Operating activities	88-654306	2016-08-14
74	909876515	386.36	n	909876515-n-operating expenses < Cash payments for operating expenses < Operating activities	88-654306	2016-08-17

	IDM	Amount	Symbol	MultiSubaccount	Recorder	TransDate
75	909876513	501.22	n	909876513-n-operating expenses < Cash payments for operating expenses < Operating activities	88-654306	2016-08-25
76	909876514	2900.00	t	909876514-t-salary < Cash payments for operating expenses < Operating activities	88-654306	2016-08-31
77	909876513	2600.00	t	909876513-t-CGM < Cash payments for operating expenses < Operating activities	88-654306	2016-08-31
78	909876515	2900.00	t	909876515-t-CGM < Cash payments for operating expenses < Operating activities	88-654306	2016-08-31
79	88-654310	-18000.00	c	88-654310-c-customers < Cash receipts from customers < Operating activities	88-654306	2016-09-02
80	88-654304	-18000.00	c	88-654304-c-customers < Cash receipts from customers < Operating activities	88-654306	2016-09-12
81	88-654308	25000.00	t	88-654308-t-suppliers < Cash payments to suppliers < Operating activities	88-654306	2016-09-13
82	88-654307	10000.00	t	88-654307-t-suppliers < Cash payments to suppliers < Operating activities	88-654306	2016-09-14
83	88-654305	-17000.00	c	88-654305-c-customers < Cash receipts from customers < Operating activities	88-654306	2016-09-26
84	88-654308	8000.00	t	88-654308-t-suppliers < Cash payments to suppliers < Operating activities	88-654306	2016-09-26
85	909876513	658.33	n	909876513-n-operating expenses < Cash payments for operating expenses < Operating activities	88-654306	2016-09-28
86	909876514	2900.00	t	909876514-t-salary < Cash payments for operating expenses < Operating activities	88-654306	2016-09-30
87	909876513	2600.00	t	909876513-t-CGM < Cash payments for operating expenses < Operating activities	88-654306	2016-09-30
88	909876515	2900.00	t	909876515-t-CGM < Cash payments for operating expenses < Operating activities	88-654306	2016-09-30
89	88-654303	-2400.00	c	88-654303-c-customers < Cash receipts from customers < Operating activities	88-654306	2016-10-01
90	88-654304	-5000.00	c	88-654304-c-customers < Cash receipts from customers < Operating activities	88-654306	2016-10-01
91	88-654309	-5500.00	c	88-654309-c-customers < Cash receipts from customers < Operating activities	88-654306	2016-10-01
92	88-654304	5000.00	c	88-654304-c-customers < Cash receipts from customers < Operating activities	88-654306	2016-10-01
93	88-654305	-5000.00	c	88-654305-c-customers < Cash receipts from customers < Operating activities	88-654306	2016-10-01
94	88-654302	-990.00	c	88-654302-c-customers < Cash receipts from customers < Operating activities	88-654306	2016-10-03
95	909876513	-10000.00	c	909876513-c-customers < Cash receipts from customers < Operating activities	88-654306	2016-10-05
96	909876513	-11500.00	c	909876513-c-customers < Cash receipts from customers < Operating activities	88-654306	2016-10-05
97	909876525	-7000.00	c	909876525-c-customers < Cash receipts from customers < Operating activities	88-654306	2016-10-05
98	909876525	-10500.00	c	909876525-c-customers < Cash receipts from customers < Operating activities	88-654306	2016-10-05
99	909876515	392.36	n	909876515-n-operating expenses < Cash payments for operating expenses < Operating activities	88-654306	2016-10-07
100	88-654310	5500.00	t	88-654310-t-suppliers < Cash payments to suppliers < Operating activities	88-654306	2016-10-23
101	909876513	607.57	n	909876513-n-operating expenses < Cash payments for operating expenses < Operating activities	88-654306	2016-10-27
102	909876514	2900.00	t	909876514-t-salary < Cash payments for operating expenses < Operating activities	88-654306	2016-10-31

Figure 3.6-2   Company1 Cash Received or Paid by Other Members (Continue)

	IDM	Amount	Symbol	MultiSubaccount	Recorder	TransDate
103	909876513	2600.00	t	909876513-t-CGM < Cash payments for operating expenses < Operating activities	88-654306	2016-10-31
104	909876515	2900.00	t	909876515-t-CGM < Cash payments for operating expenses < Operating activities	88-654306	2016-10-31
105	88-654308	-2900.00	c	88-654308-c-customers < Cash receipts from customers < Operating activities	88-654306	2016-11-05
106	909876513	551.13	n	909876513-n-operating expenses < Cash payments for operating expenses < Operating activities	88-654306	2016-11-19
107	88-654303	-1400.00	c	88-654303-c-customers < Cash receipts from customers < Operating activities	88-654306	2016-11-19
108	909876515	401.13	n	909876515-n-operating expenses < Cash payments for operating expenses < Operating activities	88-654306	2016-11-19
109	88-654307	14420.00	t	88-654307-t-suppliers < Cash payments to suppliers < Operating activities	88-654306	2016-11-29
110	88-654308	3000.00	t	88-654308-t-suppliers < Cash payments to suppliers < Operating activities	88-654306	2016-11-29
111	909876504	-1500.00	c	909876504-c-customers < Cash receipts from customers < Operating activities	88-654306	2016-11-29
112	909876518	-1500.00	c	909876518-c-customers < Cash receipts from customers < Operating activities	88-654306	2016-11-30
113	909876506	-1300.00	c	909876506-c-customers < Cash receipts from customers < Operating activities	88-654306	2016-11-30
114	909876514	2900.00	t	909876514-t-salary < Cash payments for operating expenses < Operating activities	88-654306	2016-11-30
115	909876513	2600.00	t	909876513-t-CGM < Cash payments for operating expenses < Operating activities	88-654306	2016-11-30
116	909876515	2900.00	t	909876515-t-CGM < Cash payments for operating expenses < Operating activities	88-654306	2016-11-30
117	88-654310	-5000.00	c	88-654310-c-customers < Cash receipts from customers < Operating activities	88-654306	2016-12-01
118	909876524	-1600.00	c	909876524-c-customers < Cash receipts from customers < Operating activities	88-654306	2016-12-10
119	88-654304	-1500.00	c	88-654304-c-customers < Cash receipts from customers < Operating activities	88-654306	2016-12-11
120	909876513	638.34	n	909876513-n-operating expenses < Cash payments for operating expenses < Operating activities	88-654306	2016-12-16
121	909876522	-1600.00	c	909876522-c-customers < Cash receipts from customers < Operating activities	88-654306	2016-12-19
122	88-654305	-2800.00	c	88-654305-c-customers < Cash receipts from customers < Operating activities	88-654306	2016-12-19
123	909876502	-1400.00	c	909876502-c-customers < Cash receipts from customers < Operating activities	88-654306	2016-12-22
124	909876514	444.45	n	909876514-n-operating expenses < Cash payments for operating expenses < Operating activities	88-654306	2016-12-23
125	88-654309	18000.00	t	88-654309-t-suppliers < Cash payments to suppliers < Operating activities	88-654306	2016-12-23
126	88-654303	-2400.00	c	88-654303-c-customers < Cash receipts from customers < Operating activities	88-654306	2016-12-29
127	88-654309	-10000.00	c	88-654309-c-customers < Cash receipts from customers < Operating activities	88-654306	2016-12-29
128	88-654310	-27000.00	c	88-654310-c-customers < Cash receipts from customers < Operating activities	88-654306	2016-12-29
129	88-654307	39700.00	t	88-654307-t-suppliers < Cash payments to suppliers < Operating activities	88-654306	2016-12-29
130	88-654302	-2000.00	c	88-654302-c-customers < Cash receipts from customers < Operating activities	88-654306	2016-12-30

	IDM	Amount	Symbol	MultiSubaccount	Recorder	TransDate
130	88-654302	-2000.00	c	88-654302-c-customers < Cash receipts from customers < Operating activities	88-654306	2016-12-30
131	88-654304	-1400.00	c	88-654304-c-customers < Cash receipts from customers < Operating activities	88-654306	2016-12-30
132	88-654301	-3500.00	c	88-654301-c-customers < Cash receipts from customers < Operating activities	88-654306	2016-12-31
133	909876507	-40000.00	c	909876507-c-customers < Cash receipts from customers < Operating activities	88-654306	2016-12-31
134	909876524	-38000.00	c	909876524-c-customers < Cash receipts from customers < Operating activities	88-654306	2016-12-31
135	88-654304	38650.00	t	88-654304-t-note interest < Cash payments to business banks < Operating activities	88-654306	2016-12-31
136	88-654305	19800.00	t	88-654305-t-note interest < Cash payments to business banks < Operating activities	88-654306	2016-12-31
137	88-654305	230.00	t	88-654305-t-bond interest < Cash payments to bond holders < Operating activities	88-654306	2016-12-31
138	909876501	138.00	t	909876501-t-bond interest < Cash payments to bond holders < Operating activities	88-654306	2016-12-31
139	909876502	276.00	t	909876502-t-bond interest < Cash payments to bond holders < Operating activities	88-654306	2016-12-31
140	909876508	230.00	t	909876508-t-bond interest < Cash payments to bond holders < Operating activities	88-654306	2016-12-31
141	909876511	322.00	t	909876511-t-bond interest < Cash payments to bond holders < Operating activities	88-654306	2016-12-31
142	909876514	92.00	t	909876514-t-bond interest < Cash payments to bond holders < Operating activities	88-654306	2016-12-31
143	909876516	184.00	t	909876516-t-bond interest < Cash payments to bond holders < Operating activities	88-654306	2016-12-31
144	909876518	92.00	t	909876518-t-bond interest < Cash payments to bond holders < Operating activities	88-654306	2016-12-31
145	909876521	138.00	t	909876521-t-bond interest < Cash payments to bond holders < Operating activities	88-654306	2016-12-31
146	909876522	230.00	t	909876522-t-bond interest < Cash payments to bond holders < Operating activities	88-654306	2016-12-31
147	909876524	138.00	t	909876524-t-bond interest < Cash payments to bond holders < Operating activities	88-654306	2016-12-31
148	909876525	230.00	t	909876525-t-bond interest < Cash payments to bond holders < Operating activities	88-654306	2016-12-31
149	88-654304	-400.00	c	88-654304-c-investment income < Cash receipts from investments < Investing activities	88-654306	2016-12-31
150	88-654304	-135.00	c	88-654304-c-investment income < Cash receipts from investments < Investing activities	88-654306	2016-12-31
151	88-654305	-369.00	c	88-654305-c-investment income < Cash receipts from investments < Investing activities	88-654306	2016-12-31
152	88-654304	-120.00	c	88-654304-c-deposit interest income < Cash receipts from deposit interest < Financial activities	88-654306	2016-12-31
153	88-654307	55000.00	t	88-654307-t-suppliers < Cash payments to suppliers < Operating activities	88-654306	2016-12-31
154	909876510	-40000.00	c	909876510-c-customers < Cash receipts from customers < Operating activities	88-654306	2016-12-31
155	909876514	2900.00	t	909876514-t-salary < Cash payments for operating expenses < Operating activities	88-654306	2016-12-31
156	909876513	2600.00	t	909876513-t-CGM < Cash payments for operating expenses < Operating activities	88-654306	2016-12-31
157	909876515	2900.00	t	909876515-t-CGM < Cash payments for operating expenses < Operating activities	88-654306	2016-12-31

Query executed successfully.

Figure 3.6-2   Company1 Cash Received or Paid by Other Members

Cash Flow Statement

Cash Flows Statement Year Ended 2016-12-31	
Operating activities	
Cash payments for operating expenses	-$111,554.73
Cash payments to bond holders	-$2,300.00
Cash payments to business banks	-$58,450.00
Cash payments to suppliers	-$317,210.00
Cash receipts from customers	$459,550.00
Net cash provided by Operating activities	-$29,964.73
Investing activities	
Cash receipts from investments	$904.00
Net cash provided by Investing activities	$904.00
Financial activities	
Cash receipts from deposit interest	$120.00
Net cash provided by Financial activities	$120.00
Net change in cash	-$28,940.73
Cash, Begining	$67,873.98
Cash, Ending	$38,933.25

Figure 3.6-3   Company1 Cash Flows Statement

Cash

ID	Multi-Name	Amount	Balance	General ID	Transaction Date
47	Cash payments for operating expenses < Operating activities	-$19,538.91	$67,873.98	16	2015-12-31
48	88-654310-t-supplies < Cash payments for operating expenses < Oper...	-$500.00	$67,373.98	17	2016-01-02
49	88-654303-c-customers < Cash receipts from customers < Operating a...	$60.00	$67,433.98	22	2016-01-13
50	88-654307-t-suppliers < Cash payments to suppliers < Operating activit...	-$11,000.00	$56,433.98	23	2016-01-14
51	88-654308-t-suppliers < Cash payments to suppliers < Operating activit...	-$8,000.00	$48,433.98	24	2016-01-14
52	909876513-n-operating expenses < Cash payments for operating expe...	-$415.67	$48,018.31	25	2016-01-15
53	909876515-n-operating expenses < Cash payments for operating expe...	-$42.12	$47,976.19	26	2016-01-16
54	88-654309-t-suppliers < Cash payments to suppliers < Operating activit...	-$2,040.00	$45,936.19	27	2016-01-31
55	88-654310-t-suppliers < Cash payments to suppliers < Operating activit...	-$1,000.00	$44,936.19	28	2016-01-31
56	909876514-t-salary < Cash payments for operating expenses < Operati...	-$2,900.00	$42,036.19	29	2016-01-31
57	909876513-t-CGM < Cash payments for operating expenses < Operati...	-$2,600.00	$39,436.19	29	2016-01-31
58	909876515-t-CGM < Cash payments for operating expenses < Operati...	-$2,900.00	$36,536.19	29	2016-01-31
59	88-654304-c-customers < Cash receipts from customers < Operating a...	$19,000.00	$55,536.19	30	2016-02-01
60	88-654309-c-customers < Cash receipts from customers < Operating a...	$28,000.00	$83,536.19	32	2016-02-01
61	88-654310-c-customers < Cash receipts from customers < Operating a...	$30,000.00	$113,536.19	33	2016-02-01
62	909876514-n-operating expenses < Cash payments for operating expe...	-$49.68	$113,486.51	34	2016-02-01
63	88-654303-c-customers < Cash receipts from customers < Operating a...	$500.00	$113,986.51	35	2016-02-02
64	88-654301-c-customers < Cash receipts from customers < Operating a...	$800.00	$114,786.51	36	2016-02-13
65	909876513-n-operating expenses < Cash payments for operating expe...	-$557.83	$114,228.68	37	2016-02-20
66	88-654307-c-customers < Cash receipts from customers < Operating a...	$600.00	$114,828.68	38	2016-02-25
67	88-654308-c-customers < Cash receipts from customers < Operating a...	$900.00	$115,728.68	39	2016-02-27
68	909876514-t-salary < Cash payments for operating expenses < Operati...	-$2,900.00	$112,828.68	40	2016-02-28
69	909876513-t-CGM < Cash payments for operating expenses < Operati...	-$2,600.00	$110,228.68	40	2016-02-28
70	909876515-t-CGM < Cash payments for operating expenses < Operati...	-$2,900.00	$107,328.68	40	2016-02-28
183	909876524-c-customers < Cash receipts from customers < Operating a...	$38,000.00	$153,659.25	152	2016-12-31
184	88-654304-t-note interest < Cash payments to business banks < Operat...	-$38,650.00	$115,009.25	153	2016-12-31
185	88-654305-t-note interest < Cash payments to business banks < Operat...	-$19,800.00	$95,209.25	154	2016-12-31
186	88-654305-t-bond interest < Cash payments to bond holders < Operati...	-$230.00	$94,979.25	155	2016-12-31
187	909876501-t-bond interest < Cash payments to bond holders < Operati...	-$138.00	$94,841.25	155	2016-12-31
188	909876502-t-bond interest < Cash payments to bond holders < Operati...	-$276.00	$94,565.25	155	2016-12-31
189	909876508-t-bond interest < Cash payments to bond holders < Operati...	-$230.00	$94,335.25	155	2016-12-31
190	909876511-t-bond interest < Cash payments to bond holders < Operati...	-$322.00	$94,013.25	155	2016-12-31
191	909876514-t-bond interest < Cash payments to bond holders < Operati...	-$92.00	$93,921.25	155	2016-12-31
192	909876516-t-bond interest < Cash payments to bond holders < Operati...	-$184.00	$93,737.25	156	2016-12-31
193	909876518-t-bond interest < Cash payments to bond holders < Operati...	-$92.00	$93,645.25	156	2016-12-31
194	909876521-t-bond interest < Cash payments to bond holders < Operati...	-$138.00	$93,507.25	156	2016-12-31
195	909876522-t-bond interest < Cash payments to bond holders < Operati...	-$230.00	$93,277.25	156	2016-12-31
196	909876524-t-bond interest < Cash payments to bond holders < Operati...	-$138.00	$93,139.25	156	2016-12-31
197	909876525-t-bond interest < Cash payments to bond holders < Operati...	-$230.00	$92,909.25	156	2016-12-31
198	88-654304-c-investment income < Cash receipts from investments < In...	$400.00	$93,309.25	157	2016-12-31
199	88-654304-c-investment income < Cash receipts from investments < In...	$135.00	$93,444.25	157	2016-12-31
200	88-654305-c-investment income < Cash receipts from investments < In...	$369.00	$93,813.25	158	2016-12-31
201	88-654304-c-deposit interest income < Cash receipts from deposit inter...	$120.00	$93,933.25	159	2016-12-31
202	88-654307-t-suppliers < Cash payments to suppliers < Operating activit...	-$55,000.00	$38,933.25	163	2016-12-31
203	88-654304-c-customers < Cash receipts from customers < Operating a...	-$5,000.00	$33,933.25	164	2016-10-01
204	88-654305-c-customers < Cash receipts from customers < Operating a...	$5,000.00	$38,933.25	164	2016-10-01

Figure 3.6-4   Company1 Cash Account Table

Income Statement

	Year ended: 12/31/2016	
Revenues		
Sales		$493,400.00
Cost		
Cost of goods sold		-$334,810.00
Gross Margin		$158,590.00
Operating and administrative expenses		
Travelling expenses		-$4,187.73
Other expenses		-$5,067.00
Salary expenses		-$34,800.00
Cost of goods manufactured		$0.00
Bond interest expenses		-$2,300.00
Note interest expenses		-$58,450.00
Office supplies expenses		-$2,332.13
Amortization expenses		-$27,045.84
Other income		
Investment incomes		$904.00
Deposit interest incomes		$120.00
Service package incomes		$3,550.00
Earnings Before Income Taxes		$28,981.30
Tax		
Tax expenses		-$8,694.39
Net Earnings		$20,286.91
Retained Earnings,Begining		$0.00
Retained Earnings,Ending		$20,286.91

Figure 3.6-5   Company1 Income Statement

	As at 12/31/2016
ASSETS	
Current assets	
Cash	$38,933.25
Supplies	$2,410.31
Account receivable	$37,900.00
Inventory	$375,238.00
Working-in-process inventory	$381,550.00
	$836,031.56
Long term investments	
Bonds	$22,000.00
Share	$32,000.00
	$54,000.00
Equipment	
Vehicle	$121,000.00
Accumulated amortization: Vehicle	-$73,033.33
Computer	$5,900.00
Accumulated amortization: Computer	-$1,720.84
	$52,145.83
Total Assets	$942,177.39
LIABILITIES	
Current liabilities	
Account payable	$9,650.00
Tax payable	$8,694.39
	$18,344.39

Long term liabilities	
Bonds payable	$50,000.00
Notes payable	$640,000.00
	$690,000.00
Total Liability	$708,344.39
SHAREHOLDERS' EQUITY	
Owners capital	
Share capital	$200,000.00
Retained earnings (conversion)	$13,546.09
	$213,546.09
Retined earnings	$20,286.91
Accumulated other comprehensive income	$0.00
Total Shareholders' Equity	$233,833.00
Total Liabilities and Shareholders' Equity	$942,177.39

Figure 3.6-6   Company1 Balance Sheet Statement

3.7 Company2

3.7.1 An Accounting Fiscal Year of the Company2

In the new fiscal year, the Company2 occurs the following transactions.

- On January 2, 2016, the Company2 purchases the supplies $880 ($14*40 + $16*20) from the Proprietorship2 (phone number: 123456080) for cash -$500 and other on credit. The multi-subaccount name of the Cash account and transaction sub-equation respectively are:

  88-654310-t-supplies < Cash payments for operating expenses < Operating activities

  Cash (1): -500 + Supplies (1): 880 = Account payable (2): 380

- On January 2, 2016, the Company2 transfers the supplies $1,000 to the Cost of goods manufactured to satisfy the need of producing. The transaction sub-equation is:

  Supplies (1): -1000 = Cost of goods manufactured (5): -1000

- On January 2, 2016, the Company2 transfers the following inventories -$17,580 to the Cost of goods manufactured account to satisfy the need of producing.

  Inven111 < Inven11 < Inven1: -10*50

  Inven112 < Inven11 < Inven1: -40*40

  Inven121 < Inven12 < Inven1: -0.8*100

  Inven122 < Inven12 < Inven1: -50*30

  Inven21 < Inven2: -30*30

  Inven221 < Inven22 < Inven2: -30*50

  Inven222 < Inven22 < Inven2: -50*20

  PPUK parts < ASD parts < Inven2: -40*30

  PPGH parts < ASD parts < Inven2: -2*100

  Inven51 < Inven5: -10*75

  Inven52 < Inven5: -50*30

Inven531 < Inven53 < Inven5: -25*50

Inven532 < Inven53 < Inven5: -35*50

Inven541 < Inven54 < Inven5: -12*50

Inven542 < Inven54 < Inven5: -15*40

Inven611 < Inven61 < Inven6: -6.5*50

Inven612 < Inven61 < Inven6: -12.5*50

Inven621 < Inven62 < Inven6: -18*50

Inven63 < Inven6: -16*50

The three transaction sub-equations are respectively:

Inventory (1): -10*50 + Inventory (1): -40*40 + Inventory (1): -0.8*100 + Inventory (1): -50*30 + Inventory (1): -30*30 + Inventory (1): -30*50 + Inventory (1): -50*20 + Inventory (1): -40*30 + Inventory (1): -2*100 = Cost of goods manufactured (5): -8480

Inventory (1): -10*75 + Inventory (1): -50*30+ Inventory (1): -25*50 + Inventory (1): -35*50 + Inventory (1): -12*50+ Inventory (1): -15*40 + Inventory (1): -6.5*50 + Inventory (1): -12.5*50 = Cost of goods manufactured (5): -7400

Inventory (1): -18*50 + Inventory (1): -16*50 = Cost of goods manufactured (5): -1700

- On January 12, 2016, the Company2 sells one Computer1 part1 to A25 (SIN: 909876525) for cash $360. The multi-subaccount name of the Cash account and transaction sub-equation respectively are:

  909876525-c-customers < Cash receipts from customers < Operating activities

  Cash (1): 360 + Inventory (1): -235 = Sales (4): 360 + Cost of goods sold (5): -235

- On January 14, 2016, the Company2 receives $11,000 cash from the Company1 (phone number: 123456784) with the General ID 3. The multi-subaccount name of the Cash account is:

88-654306-c-customers < Cash receipts from customers < Operating activities

- On January 15, 2016, the Company2 pays -$5,000 cash to the Company3 (phone number: 123456082) with the General ID 3. The multi-subaccount name of the Cash account is:

88-654308-t-suppliers < Cash payments to suppliers < Operating activities

- On January 15, 2016, the Company2 pays -$411.32 cash to A16 (SIN: 909876516) for the Travelling expenses (travel allowance) $219.32 and the Other expenses (meals: food221: $12*8 + food312: $24*4) $192. The multi-subaccount name of the Cash account and the transaction sub-equation respectively are:

909876516-n-operating expenses < Cash payments for operating expenses < Operating activities

Cash (1): -411.32 = Travelling expenses (5): -219.32 + other expenses (5): -192

- On January 18, 2016, the Company2 pays -$112.57 cash to A17 (SIN: 909876517) for the Travelling expenses (travel allowance) $68.57 and the Other expenses (meals: food311: $20*1 + food312: 24*1) $44.

- On January 24, 2016, the Company2 receives $600 cash from the Company3 (phone number: 123456782) with the General ID 3. The multi-subaccount name of the Cash account is:

88-654308-c-customers < Cash receipts from customers < Operating activities

- On January 27, 2016, the Company2 receives $250 cash from the Proprietorship1 (phone number: 123456781) with the General ID 3. The multi-subaccount name of the Cash account is:

88-654309-c-customers < Cash receipts from customers < Operating activities

- On January 28, 2016, the Company2 sells one Truck1 part2 $7,600 (cost: $4,950) and Truck2part3 $5,400 (cost: $3500) for sales $13,000 to the Company3 (phone number: 123456782) for cash $7,000 and other on credit. The multi-subaccount name of the Cash account and transaction sub-equation respectively are:

88-654308-c-customers < Cash receipts from customers < Operating activities

Cash (1): 7000 + Account receivable (1): 6000 + Inventory (1): -4950 + Inventory (1): -3500 = Sales (4): 13000 + Cost of goods sold (5): -8450

- On January 30, 2016, the Company2 pays -$379.78 cash to A18 (SIN: 909876518) for the Travelling expenses (travel allowance) $235.78 and the Other expenses (meals: food312: $24*6) $144.

- On January 30, 2016, the Company2 pays -$500 cash to the Proprietorship1 (phone number: 123456081) with the General ID 3. The multi-subaccount name of the Cash account is:

88-654309-t-suppliers < Cash payments to suppliers < Operating activities

- On January 30, 2016, the Company2 pays -$300 cash to the Proprietorship2 (phone number: 123456080) with the General ID 3. The multi-subaccount name of the Cash account is:

88-654310-t-suppliers < Cash payments to suppliers < Operating activities

- On January 31, 2016, the Company2 pays three employees' salary expenses for cash -$8,380. The two multi-subaccount names of the Cash account and the transaction sub-equation respectively are:

909876517-t-salary < Cash payments for operating expenses < Operating activities
909876516-t-CGM < Cash payments for operating expenses < Operating activities
909876518-t-CGM < Cash payments for operating expenses < Operating activities

Cash (1): -2890 + Cash (1): -2610 + Cash (1): -2880 = Salary expenses (5): -2890 + Cost of goods manufactured (5): -2610 + Cost of goods manufactured (5): -2880

- On February 11, 2016, the Company2 receives $400 cash from the Tax Bureau (phone number: 123456787) with the General ID 3. The multi-subaccount name of the Cash account is:

88-654303-c-customers < Cash receipts from customers < Operating activities

- On February 20, 2016, the Company2 pays -$557.83 cash to A16 (SIN: 909876516) for the Travelling expenses (travel allowance) $247.83 and the Other expenses (meals: food53: $16*10 + food614: $30*5) $310. The multi-subaccount name of the Cash account and the transaction sub-equation respectively are:

  909876516-n-operating expenses < Cash payments for operating expenses < Operating activities

  Cash (1): -557.83 = Travelling expenses (5): -247.83 + other expenses (5): -310

- On February 21, 2016, the Company2 receives $500 cash from the Government1 (phone number: 123456788) with the General ID 3. The multi-subaccount name of the Cash account is:

  88-654302-c-customers < Cash receipts from customers < Operating activities

- On February 25, 2016, the Company2 pays -$600 cash to the Company1 (phone number: 123456084) with the General ID 3. The multi-subaccount name of the Cash account is:

  88-654306-t- suppliers < Cash payments to suppliers < Operating activities

- On February 26, 2016, the Company2 sells one Car1 part2 to the Business Bank1 (phone number: 123456786) for cash $5200 and other on credit. The multi-subaccount name of the Cash account and transaction sub-equation respectively are:

  88-654304-c-customers < Cash receipts from customers < Operating activities

  Cash (1): 5200 + Account receivable (1): 2000 + Inventory (1): -4650 = Sales (4): 7200 + Cost of goods sold (5): -4650

- On February 28, 2016, the Company2 pays three employees' salary expenses for cash -$8,380. The two multi-subaccount names of the Cash account and the transaction sub-equation respectively are:

  909876517-t-salary < Cash payments for operating expenses < Operating activities

909876516-t-CGM < Cash payments for operating expenses < Operating activities

909876518-t-CGM < Cash payments for operating expenses < Operating activities

Cash (1): -2890 + Cash (1): -2610 + Cash (1): -2880 = Salary expenses (5): -2890 + Cost of goods manufactured (5): -2610 + Cost of goods manufactured (5): -2880

- On March 1, 2016, the Company2 pays -$221.16 cash to A18 (SIN: 909876518) for the Travelling expenses (travel allowance) $119.16 and the Other expenses (meals: food312: $24*2 + food321: 27*2) $102.

- On March 4, 2016, the Company2 receives $2,400 cash from the Company1 (phone number: 123456784) with the General ID 3. The multi-subaccount name of the Cash account is:

  88-654306-c-customers < Cash receipts from customers < Operating activities

- On March 23, 2016, the Company2 pays -$347.65 cash to A16 (SIN: 909876516) for the Travelling expenses (travel allowance) $216.65 and the Other expenses (meals: food44: $15*5 + food622: $28*2) $131.

- On March 26, 2016, the Company2 pays -$253.93 cash to A17 (SIN: 909876517) for the Travelling expenses (travel allowance) $166.93 and the Other expenses (meals: food522: $13*3 + food612: $24*2) $87.

- On March 30, 2016, the Company2 pays -$700 cash to the Company3 (phone number: 123456082) with the General ID 3. The multi-subaccount name of the Cash account is:

  88-654308-t-suppliers < Cash payments to suppliers < Operating activities

- On March 31, 2016, the Company2 pays three employees' salary expenses for cash -$8,380 repeatedly.

- On April 12, 2016, the Company2 sells one Computer1 part2 to A1 (SIN: 909876501) for cash $310. The multi-subaccount name of the Cash account and transaction sub-equation respectively are:

  909876501-c-customers < Cash receipts from customers < Operating activities

Cash (1): 310 + Inventory (1): -202 = Sales (4): 310 + Cost of goods sold (5): -202

- On April 26, 2016, the Company2 pays -$369.88 cash to A16 (SIN: 909876516) for the Travelling expenses (travel allowance) $213.88 and the Other expenses (meals: food312: $24*3 +food321: $27*2 + food322: $30*1) $156.

- On April 29, 2016, the Company2 sells one Truck2 part2 $4,660 for sales $7,200 to the Proprietorship1 (phone number: 123456781) for cash $5000 and other on credit. The multi-subaccount name of the Cash account and transaction sub-equation respectively are:

    88-654309-c-customers < Cash receipts from customers < Operating activities

    Cash (1): 5000 + Account receivable (1): 2200 + Inventory (1): -4660 = Sales (4): 7200 + Cost of goods sold (5): -4660

- On April 30, 2016, the Company2 pays three employees' salary expenses for cash -$8,380 repeatedly.

- On May 1, 2016, the Company2 sells the following inventories $140,192 for sales $216,420 to the Company1 (phone number: 123456784) for $15,000 cash and other on credit.

    Car1 part1 < Car1 parts < Vehicle parts: -5380*3

    Car1 part2 < Car1 parts < Vehicle parts: -4650*3

    Car1 part3 < Car1 parts < Vehicle parts: -3300*3

    Car2 part1 < Car2 parts < Vehicle parts: -5100*3

    Car2 part2 < Car2 parts < Vehicle parts: -4400*3

    Car2 part3 < Car2 parts < Vehicle parts: -3170*3

    Car3 part1 < Car3 parts < Vehicle parts: -4850*3

    Car3 part2 < Car3 parts < Vehicle parts: -4150*3

    Car3 part3 < Car3 parts < Vehicle parts: -3050*3

    Computer server1 part1 < Computer server parts < Computer parts: -390*4

Computer server1 part2 < Computer server parts < Computer parts: -260*4

Computer server2 part1 < Computer server parts < Computer parts: -350*4

Computer server2 part2 < Computer server parts < Computer parts: -250*4

Computer1 part1 < Computer parts: -235*14

Computer1 part2 < Computer parts: -202*14

Computer2 part1 < Computer parts: -208*14

Computer2 part2 < Computer parts: -189*14

Computer3 part1 < Computer parts: -182*14

Computer3 part2 < Computer parts: -169*14

Computer4 part1 < Computer parts: -162*14

Computer4 part2 < Computer parts: -156*14

The multi-subaccount name of the Cash account and four transaction sub-equations respectively are:

88-654306-c-customers < Cash receipts from customers < Operating activities

Cash (1): 15000 + Account receivable (1): 46800 + Inventory (1): -5380*3 + Inventory (1): -4650*3 + Inventory (1): -3300*3 = Sales (4): 61800 + Cost of goods sold (5): -16140 + Cost of goods sold (5): -13950 + Cost of goods sold (5): -9900

Account receivable (1): 114600 + Inventory (1): -5100*3 + Inventory (1): -4400*3 + Inventory (1): -3170*3 + Inventory (1): -4850*3 + Inventory (1): -4150*3 + Inventory (1): -3050*3 = Sales (4): 114600 + Cost of goods sold (5): -74160

Account receivable (1): 17060 + Inventory (1): -390*4 + Inventory (1): -260*4 + Inventory (1): -350*4 + Inventory (1): -250*4 + Inventory (1): -235*14 + Inventory (1): -202*14 = Sales (4): 17060 + Cost of goods sold (5): -11118

Account receivable (1): 22960 + Inventory (1): -208*14 + Inventory (1): -189*14 + Inventory (1): -182*14 + Inventory (1): -169*14 + Inventory (1): -162*14 +

Inventory (1): -156*14 = Sales (4): 22960 + Cost of goods sold (5): -14924

In fact, the Cost of goods sold account has not any subaccount and its multi-subaccount name is the "n", so the items of the "Cost of goods sold (5): xx" in the above transaction sub-equations can be merged. Later, I will merge the items of the "Cost of goods sold (5): xx" in a transaction sub-equation.

- On May 2, 2016, the Company2 pays -$307.09 cash to A18 (SIN: 909876518) for the Travelling expenses (travel allowance) $217.09 and the Other expenses (meals: food213: $10*3 + food311: $20*3) $90.

- On May 3, 2016, the Company2 sells one Computer2 part2 (cost: $189) to A13 (SIN: 909876513) for cash $290. The multi-subaccount name of the Cash account is:

  909876513-c-customers < Cash receipts from customers < Operating activities

- On May 24, 2016, the Company2 pays -$366.59 cash to A16 (SIN: 909876516) for the Travelling expenses (travel allowance) $211.59 and the Other expenses (meals: food111: $10*8 + food312: $24*2 + food321: $27*1) $155.

- On May 31, 2016, the Company2 pays three employees' salary expenses for cash -$8,380 repeatedly.

- On June 12, 2016, the Company2 receives $64,000 cash from the Company1 (phone number: 123456784) with the General ID 51 ($46,800), the General ID 52 ($140), and General ID 53 ($17,060). The multi-subaccount name of the Cash account and transaction sub-equation respectively are:

  88-654306-c-customers < Cash receipts from customers < Operating activities

  Cash (1): -64000 + Account receivable (2): -46800 + Account receivable (2): -140 + Account receivable (2): -17060 = 0

- On June 14, 2016, the Company2 pays -$255.54 cash to A17 (SIN: 909876517) for the Travelling expenses (travel allowance) $187.54 and the Other expenses (meals: food611: $20*2 + food622: $28*1) $68.

- On June 23, 2016, the Company2 pays -$362.81 cash to A16 (SIN: 909876516) for the Travelling expenses (travel allowance) $199.81 and the Other expenses (meals: food113: $12*5 + food214: $11*5 + food312: $24*2) $163.

- On June 30, 2016, the Company2 pays three employees' salary expenses for cash - $8,380 repeatedly.

- On July 11, 2016, the Company2 sells one Computer2 part2 (cost: $189) for sales $290 to A5 (SIN: 909876505) for cash $290. The multi-subaccount name of the Cash account and transaction sub-equation respectively are:

  909876505-c-customers < Cash receipts from customers < Operating activities

  Cash (1): 290 + Inventory (1): -189 = Sales (4): 290 + Cost of goods sold (5): -189

- On July 13, 2016, the Company2 sells one Computer2 part1 ($208) for sales $320 to A7 (SIN: 909876507) for cash $320. The multi-subaccount name of the Cash account is:

  909876507-c-customers < Cash receipts from customers < Operating activities

- On July 27, 2016, the Company2 pays -$307.41 cash to A16 (SIN: 909876516) for the Travelling expenses (travel allowance) $189.41 and the Other expenses (meals: food212: $9*6 + food311: $20*2 + food312: $24*1) $118.

- On July 31, 2016, the Company2 records the Amortization expenses $1,720.84 of a computer server1 ($816.67, seven months), a computer1 ($466.67, seven months), and a computer2 ($437.5, seven months). The transaction sub-equation is:

  Accumulated amortization: Computer (1): -816.67 + Accumulated amortization: Computer (1): -466.67 + Accumulated amortization: Computer (1): -437.5 = Amortization expenses (5): -816.67 + Amortization expenses (5): -466.67 + Amortization expenses (5): -437.5

- On July 31, 2016, the Company2 cancels the balances of the Computer account and the Accumulated amortization: Computer account because these computers have used for two years. The transaction sub-equation is:

Computer (1): -2800 + Computer (1): -1600 + Computer (1): -1500 +
Accumulated amortization: Computer (1): 2800 + Accumulated amortization:
Computer (1): 1600 + Accumulated amortization: Computer (1): 1500 = 0

- On July 31, 2016, the Company2 pays three employees' salary expenses for cash -
  $8,380 repeatedly.

- On August 1, 2016, the Company2 purchases one Computer server1, one Computer1,
  and one Computer2 from the Company1 (phone number: 123456084) for cash -
  $3,000 and other on credit. The multi-subaccount name of the Cash account and
  transaction sub-equation respectively are:

  88-654306-t-suppliers < Cash payments to suppliers < Operating activities

  Cash (1): -3000 + Computer (1): 2800 + Computer (1): 1600 + Computer (1):
  1500 = Account payable (2): 2900

- On August 3, 2016, the Company2 receives $12,000 cash from the Company1
  (phone number: 123456784) with the General ID 52. The multi-subaccount name of
  the Cash account is:

  88-654306-c-customers < Cash receipts from customers < Operating activities

- On August 13, 2016, the Company2 sells one Computer1 part1 (cost: $235) to A11
  (SIN: 909876511) for cash $360. The multi-subaccount name of the Cash account is:

  909876511-c-customers < Cash receipts from customers < Operating activities

- On August 16, 2016, the Company2 pays -$373.77 cash to A17 (SIN: 909876517)
  for the Travelling expenses (travel allowance) $253.77 and the Other expenses
  (meals: food123: $15*4 + food322: $30*2) $120.

- On August 23, 2016, the Company2 pays -$392.33 cash to A16 (SIN: 909876516)
  for the Travelling expenses (travel allowance) $230.33 and the Other expenses
  (meals: food213: $10*6 + food312: $24*3 + food322: $30*1) $162.

- On August 31, 2016, the Company2 pays three employees' salary expenses for cash

-$8,380 repeatedly.

- On September 3, 2016, the Company2 sells one Computer1 part2 (cost: $202) for sales $310 to A19 (SIN: 909876519) for cash $310. The multi-subaccount name of the Cash account is:

  909876519-c-customers < Cash receipts from customers < Operating activities

- On September 10, 2016, the Company2 sells one Computer2 part1 ($208) for sales $320 to A22 (SIN: 909876522) for cash $320. The multi-subaccount name of the Cash account is:

  909876522-c-customers < Cash receipts from customers < Operating activities

- On September 12, 2016, the Company2 receives $4,000 cash from the Company3 (phone number: 123456782) with the General ID 30.

- On September 14, 2016, the Company2 pays -$380 cash to the Proprietorship2 (phone number: 123456080) with the General ID 18. The multi-subaccount name of the Cash account is:

  88-654310-t-suppliers < Cash payments to suppliers < Operating activities

- On September 14, 2016, the Company2 receives $10,000 cash from the Company1 (phone number: 123456784) with the General ID 52.

- On September 26, 2016, the Company2 receives $1,800 cash from the Proprietorship1 (phone number: 123456781) with the General ID 49. The multi-subaccount name of the Cash account is:

  88-654309-c-customers < Cash receipts from customers < Operating activities

- On September 28, 2016, the Company2 pays -$410.89 cash to A16 (SIN: 909876516) for the Travelling expenses (travel allowance) $227.89 and the Other expenses (meals: food23: $16*6 + food311: $20*3 + food321: $27*1) $183.

- On September 30, 2016, the Company2 pays three employees' salary expenses for cash -$8,380 repeatedly.

- On October 3, 2016, the Company2 sells one Truck2 part1 (cost: $5,500) for sales $8,500 to the Tax Bureau (phone number: 123456787) for cash $4500 and other on credit. The multi-subaccount name of the Cash account and transaction sub-equation respectively are:

88-654303-c-customers < Cash receipts from customers < Operating activities

Cash (1): 4500 + Account receivable (1): 4000 + Inventory (1): -5500 = Sales (4): 8500 + Cost of goods sold (5): -5500

- On October 6, 2016, the Company2 pays -$377.63 cash to A18 (SIN: 909876518) for the Travelling expenses (travel allowance) $260.63 and the Other expenses (meals: food522: $13*3 + food613: $26*3) $117.

- On October 27, 2016, the Company2 pays -$396.27 cash to A16 (SIN: 909876516) for the Travelling expenses (travel allowance) $222.27 and the Other expenses (meals: food113: $12*6 + food312: $24*3 + food322: $30*1) $174.

- On October 31, 2016, the Company2 pays three employees' salary expenses for cash -$8,380 repeatedly.

- On November 19, 2016, the Company2 pays -$399.28 cash to A16 (SIN: 909876516) for the Travelling expenses (travel allowance) $215.28 and the Other expenses (meals: food111: $10*7 + food311: $20*3 + food321: $27*2) $184.

- On November 20, 2016, the Company2 sells one Computer1 part1 (cost: $235) for sales $360 to A18 (SIN: 909876518) for cash $360. The multi-subaccount name of the Cash account is:

909876518-c-customers < Cash receipts from customers < Operating activities

- On November 20, 2016, the Company2 completed all computer products ($37,560) and transfers the balance of the Cost of goods manufactured account to the Inventory account. The Cost of goods manufactured account has four subaccounts of the "Supplies expenses", the "909876516-salary < Sales department-salary < Salary expenses", the "909876518-salary < Product department-salary < Salary expenses", and the "General parts expenses". Their amounts, which are used in the products of the computer products, are estimated and are $300, $22,000, $5,000, and $10,260 respectively. The two transaction sub-equations are:

Inventory account (1): 390*6 + Inventory account (1): 260*6 + Inventory account (1): 350*6 + Inventory account (1): 250*6 + Inventory account (1): 235*20 + Inventory account (1): 202*20 = Cost of goods manufactured (5): 300 + Cost of goods manufactured (5): 680 + Cost of goods manufactured (5): 5000 + Cost of goods manufactured (5): 10260

Inventory account (1): 208*20 + Inventory account (1): 189*20 + Inventory account (1): 182*20 + Inventory account (1): 169*20 + Inventory account (1): 162*20 + Inventory account (1): 156*20 = Cost of goods manufactured (5): 21320

- On November 28, 2016, the Company2 transfers the supplies $50 to the Cost of goods manufactured to satisfy the producing need. The transaction sub-equation is:

  Supplies (1): -50 = Cost of goods manufactured (5): -50

- On November 29, 2016, the Company2 receives $14,420 cash from the Company1 (phone number: 123456784) with the General ID 52. The multi-subaccount name of the Cash account is:

  88-654306-c-customers < Cash receipts from customers < Operating activities
- On November 30, 2016, the Company2 pays three employees' salary expenses for cash -$8,380 repeatedly.
- On December 17, 2016, the Company2 pays -$395.88 cash to A16 (SIN: 909876516) for the Travelling expenses (travel allowance) $221.88 and the Other expenses (meals: food111: $10*6 + food123: $15*4 + food321: $27*2) $174.
- On December 20, 2016, the Company2 pays -$424.37 cash to A18 (SIN: 909876518) for the Travelling expenses (travel allowance) $280.37 and the Other expenses (meals: food611: $20*3 + food622: $28*3) $144.
- On December 29, 2016, the Company2 receives $39,700 cash from the Company1 (phone number: 123456784) with the General ID 52.
- On December 30, 2016, the Company2 purchases the Inven611 (Inven611< Inven61

< Inven6) $1300 ($6.5*200) from the Company3 (phone number: 123456082) for cash -$600 and other on credit. The multi-subaccount name of the Cash account and transaction sub-equation respectively are:

88-654308-t-supplies < Cash payments for operating expenses < Operating activities

Cash (1): -600 + Inventory (1): 1300 = Account payable (2): 700

- On December 31, 2016, the Company2 receives $55,000 cash from the Company1 (phone number: 123456784) with the General ID 52 ($32,040) and the General ID 54 ($22,960).

- On December 31, 2016, the Company2 pays three employees' salary expenses for cash -$8,380 repeatedly.

- On the same day, the Company2 pays -$35,600 cash to the Business Bank1 for the Note interest expenses of the Note12 ($140,000, one-level subaccount "Note12-interest") and the Note14 ($250,000, one-level subaccount "Note14-interest"). The multi-subaccount name of the Cash account and the transaction sub-equation respectively are:

88-654304-t-note interest < Cash payments to business banks < Operating activities

Cash (1): -35600 = Note interest expenses (5): -12600 + Note interest expenses (5): -23000

- On the same day, the Company2 pays -$21,600 cash to the Business Bank2 for the Note interest expenses of the Note22 ($240,000, one-level subaccount "Note22-interest"). The multi-subaccount name of the Cash account and the transaction sub-equation respectively are:

88-654305-t-note interest < Cash payments to business banks < Operating activities

Cash (1): 21600 = Note interest expenses (5): -21600

- On the same day, the Company2 pays -$1,880 cash to the bond holders for the Bond interest expenses of the Bond41 (one-level subaccount "Bond41-interest"). The multi-subaccount names of the Cash account and the transaction sub-equations respectively are:

  88-654305-t-bond interest< Cash payments to bond holders < Operating activities

  909876504-t-bond interest< Cash payments to bond holders < Operating activities

  909876505-t-bond interest< Cash payments to bond holders < Operating activities

  909876506-t-bond interest< Cash payments to bond holders < Operating activities

  909876510-t-bond interest< Cash payments to bond holders < Operating activities

  909876513-t-bond interest< Cash payments to bond holders < Operating activities

  909876515-t-bond interest< Cash payments to bond holders < Operating activities

  909876519-t-bond interest< Cash payments to bond holders < Operating activities

  909876520-t-bond interest< Cash payments to bond holders < Operating activities

  909876523-t-bond interest< Cash payments to bond holders < Operating activities

  909876524-t-bond interest< Cash payments to bond holders < Operating activities

  909876525-t-bond interest< Cash payments to bond holders < Operating activities

  Cash (1): -376 + Cash (1): -188 + Cash (1): -94 + Cash (1): -47 + Cash (1): -141 + Cash (1): -235 = Bond interest expenses (5): -1081

  Cash (1): -94 + Cash (1): -141 + Cash (1): -94 + Cash (1): -141 + Cash (1): -235 + Cash (1): -94 = Bond interest expenses (5): -799

- On the same day, the Company2 receives cash $336 for investment interest of the Bond12 from the Business Bank1. The multi-subaccount name of the Cash account and transaction sub-equation respectively are:

  88-654304-c-investment income < Cash receipts from investments < Investing activities

  Cash (1): 336 = Investment incomes (4):336

- On the same day, the Company2 receives cash $264 for investment interest of the Bond22 from the Business Bank2. The multi-subaccount name of the Cash account and transaction sub-equation respectively are:

  88-654305-c-investment income < Cash receipts from investments < Investing activities

  Cash (1): 264 = Investment incomes (4): 264

- On the same day, the Company2 receives cash $120 from the Business Bank2 for primary deposit interest. The multi-subaccount name of the Cash account and transaction sub-equation respectively are:

  88-654305-c-deposit interest income < Cash receipts from deposit interest < Financial activities

  Cash (1): 120 = Deposit interest incomes (4):120

- On the same day, the Company2 records the Office supplies expenses -$. The transaction sub-equation is:

  Supplies (1): -21.02 = Office supplies expenses (5): -21.02

- On the same day, the Company2 records the Vehicle's amortization expenses - $24,200 one year (5 years, straight line). The transaction sub-equation is:

  Accumulated amortization: Vehicle (1): -9000 + Accumulated amortization: Vehicle (1): -8000 + Accumulated amortization: Vehicle (1): -8000 = Amortization expenses (5): -9000 + Amortization expenses (5): -8000 + Amortization expenses (5): -8000

- On the same day, the Company2 records the Computer's amortization expenses $1,229.16 five months (2 years, straight line) which includes a new computer server1 (-$583.33), a new computer1 (-$333.33), and a new computer2 (-$312.5). The transaction sub-equation is:

Accumulated amortization: Computer (1): -583.33 + Accumulated amortization: Computer (1): -333.33 + Accumulated amortization: Computer (1): -312.5 = Amortization expenses (5): -583.33 + Amortization expenses (5): -333.33 + Amortization expenses (5): -312.5

- On December 31, 2016, the Company2 transfers the balance of the Cost of goods manufactured account (products of vehicle) to the Working-in-process inventory account. The Cost of goods manufactured account has four subaccounts of the "Supplies expenses", the "909876516-salary < Sales department-salary < Salary expenses", the "909876518-salary < Product department-salary < Salary expenses", and the "General parts expenses". Their balances are -$750, -$9,320, -$29,560, and -$7,320 respectively. The three transaction sub-equations respectively are:

Working-in-process inventory (1): 600*5 + Working-in-process inventory (1): 600*5 + Working-in-process inventory (1): 600*5 + Working-in-process inventory (1): 600*5 + Working-in-process inventory (1): 600*5 = Cost of goods manufactured (5): 750 + Cost of goods manufactured (5): 9,320 + Cost of goods manufactured (5): 4930

Working-in-process inventory (1): 600*5+ Working-in-process inventory (1): 600*5+ Working-in-process inventory (1): 600*5 + Working-in-process inventory (1): 600*5 + Working-in-process inventory (1): 600*5 = Cost of goods manufactured (5): 15000

Working-in-process inventory (1): 600*5 + Working-in-process inventory (1): 600*5 + Working-in-process inventory (1): 600*6 + Working-in-process inventory (1): 600*6 + Working-in-process inventory (1): 625*6 = Cost of goods manufactured (5): 9630 + Cost of goods manufactured (5): 7320

- On December 31, 2016, the Company2 records the Tax expenses $0 and the Tax payable $0. The multi-subaccount name forms of the Tax expenses and the Tax payable accounts all are the 'n'. The transaction sub-equation is:

$$0 = \text{Tax payable (2): } 0 + \text{Tax expenses (5): } 0$$

So far, I have entered all transactions of the Company2 in the fiscal year 2016. After getting the Income Statement and clicking the "Yes" button for new fiscal year, I can get the Balance Sheet of the Company2.

3.7.2 Brief Summary of the Company2

The Figure 3.7-1 shows two sums and all cash transactions of the Company2 by using of SQL Server query. As a closed system based on the MathAccounting software, the sum0 should be equal to zero. However, the individuals are not responsible for recording any transaction, so the sum0 ($106,567.98) is the sum of the amounts that the individuals received from the Company2. If the sum0 is negative, then it is sum of the amounts that individuals paid to the Company2. The opposite value ($125,159.21) of the sum1 (-$125,159.21) is the balance of the Cash account of the Company2 on December 31, 2016. It is also the balance of the deposits of the Company2 in the Business Bak2 on December 31, 2016.

The Figure 3.7-2 to the Figure 3.7-5 on page 434 to page 436 show the four tables of the cash flows statement, the cash account, the income statement, and the balance sheet respectively.

```
SQLQuery1.sql - LIU...SS.dcj100 (sa (52))*  ×
 use dcj100
 select sum(amount) as sum0 from CashByMembers where IDM='88-654307' and TransDate between '2016-01-01' and '2016-12-31'
 select sum(amount) as sum1 from CashByMembers where IDM='88-654307' and Symbol = 'd'
 select * from CashByMembers where Recorder='88-654307' and TransDate between '2016-01-01' and '2016-12-31'
        order by TransDate
```

100 %   ▾

Results   Messages

	sum0
1	106567.98

	sum1
1	-125159.21

	IDM	Amount	Symbol	MultiSubaccount	Recorder	TransDate
1	88-654310	500.00	t	88-654310-t-supplies < Cash payments for operating expenses < Operating	88-654307	2016-01-02
2	909876525	-360.00	c	909876525-c-customers < Cash receipts from customers < Operating activities	88-654307	2016-01-12
3	88-654306	-11000.00	c	88-654306-c-customers < Cash receipts from customers < Operating activities	88-654307	2016-01-14
4	88-654308	5000.00	t	88-654308-t-suppliers < Cash payments to suppliers < Operating activities	88-654307	2016-01-15
5	909876516	411.32	n	909876516-n-operating expenses < Cash payments for operating expenses < Operating acti...	88-654307	2016-01-15
6	909876517	112.57	n	909876517-n-operating expenses < Cash payments for operating expenses < Operating acti...	88-654307	2016-01-18
7	88-654308	-600.00	c	88-654308-c-customers < Cash receipts from customers < Operating activities	88-654307	2016-01-24
8	88-654309	-250.00	c	88-654309-c-customers < Cash receipts from customers < Operating activities	88-654307	2016-01-27
9	88-654308	-7000.00	c	88-654308-c-customers < Cash receipts from customers < Operating activities	88-654307	2016-01-28
10	909876518	379.78	n	909876518-n-operating expenses < Cash payments for operating expenses < Operating acti...	88-654307	2016-01-30
11	88-654309	500.00	t	88-654309-t-suppliers < Cash payments to suppliers < Operating activities	88-654307	2016-01-30
12	88-654310	300.00	t	88-654310-t-suppliers < Cash payments to suppliers < Operating activities	88-654307	2016-01-30
13	909876517	2890.00	t	909876517-t-salary < Cash payments for operating expenses < Operating activities	88-654307	2016-01-31
14	909876516	2610.00	t	909876516-t-CGM < Cash payments for operating expenses < Operating activities	88-654307	2016-01-31
15	909876518	2880.00	t	909876518-t-CGM < Cash payments for operating expenses < Operating activities	88-654307	2016-01-31
16	88-654302	-500.00	c	88-654302-c-customers < Cash receipts from customers < Operating activities	88-654307	2016-02-02
17	88-654303	-400.00	c	88-654303-c-customers < Cash receipts from customers < Operating activities	88-654307	2016-02-11
18	909876516	557.83	n	909876516-n-operating expenses < Cash payments for operating expenses < Operating acti...	88-654307	2016-02-20
19	88-654306	600.00	t	88-654306-t- suppliers < Cash payments to suppliers < Operating activities	88-654307	2016-02-25
20	88-654304	-5200.00	c	88-654304-c-customers < Cash receipts from customers < Operating activities	88-654307	2016-02-26
21	909876517	2890.00	t	909876517-t-salary < Cash payments for operating expenses < Operating activities	88-654307	2016-02-28
22	909876516	2610.00	t	909876516-t-CGM < Cash payments for operating expenses < Operating activities	88-654307	2016-02-28
23	909876518	2880.00	t	909876518-t-CGM < Cash payments for operating expenses < Operating activities	88-654307	2016-02-28
24	909876518	221.16	n	909876518-n-operating expenses < Cash payments for operating expenses < Operating acti...	88-654307	2016-03-01
25	88-654306	-2400.00	c	88-654306-c-customers < Cash receipts from customers < Operating activities	88-654307	2016-03-04
26	909876516	347.65	n	909876516-n-operating expenses < Cash payments for operating expenses < Operating acti...	88-654307	2016-03-23
27	909876517	253.93	n	909876517-n-operating expenses < Cash payments for operating expenses < Operating acti...	88-654307	2016-03-26
28	88-654308	700.00	t	88-654308-t-suppliers < Cash payments to suppliers < Operating activities	88-654307	2016-03-30
29	909876517	2890.00	t	909876517-t-salary < Cash payments for operating expenses < Operating activities	88-654307	2016-03-31
30	909876516	2610.00	t	909876516-t-CGM < Cash payments for operating expenses < Operating activities	88-654307	2016-03-31
31	909876518	2880.00	t	909876518-t-CGM < Cash payments for operating expenses < Operating activities	88-654307	2016-03-31
32	909876501	-310.00	c	909876501-c-customers < Cash receipts from customers < Operating activities	88-654307	2016-04-12
33	909876516	369.88	n	909876516-n-operating expenses < Cash payments for operating expenses < Operating acti...	88-654307	2016-04-26
34	88-654309	-5000.00	c	88-654309-c-customers < Cash receipts from customers < Operating activities	88-654307	2016-04-29
35	909876517	2890.00	t	909876517-t-salary < Cash payments for operating expenses < Operating activities	88-654307	2016-04-30
36	909876516	2610.00	t	909876516-t-CGM < Cash payments for operating expenses < Operating activities	88-654307	2016-04-30
37	909876518	2880.00	t	909876518-t-CGM < Cash payments for operating expenses < Operating activities	88-654307	2016-04-30
38	88-654306	-15000.00	c	88-654306-c-customers < Cash receipts from customers < Operating activities	88-654307	2016-05-01
39	909876518	307.09	n	909876518-n-operating expenses < Cash payments for operating expenses < Operating acti...	88-654307	2016-05-02
40	909876513	-290.00	c	909876513-c-customers < Cash receipts from customers < Operating activities	88-654307	2016-05-03
41	909876516	366.59	n	909876516-n-operating expenses < Cash payments for operating expenses < Operating acti...	88-654307	2016-05-24
42	909876517	2890.00	t	909876517-t-salary < Cash payments for operating expenses < Operating activities	88-654307	2016-05-31
43	909876516	2610.00	t	909876516-t-CGM < Cash payments for operating expenses < Operating activities	88-654307	2016-05-31
44	909876518	2880.00	t	909876518-t-CGM < Cash payments for operating expenses < Operating activities	88-654307	2016-05-31
45	88-654306	-64000.00	c	88-654306-c-customers < Cash receipts from customers < Operating activities	88-654307	2016-06-12
46	909876517	255.54	n	909876517-n-operating expenses < Cash payments for operating expenses < Operating acti...	88-654307	2016-06-14
47	909876516	362.81	n	909876516-n-operating expenses < Cash payments for operating expenses < Operating acti...	88-654307	2016-06-23
48	909876517	2890.00	t	909876517-t-salary < Cash payments for operating expenses < Operating activities	88-654307	2016-06-30
49	909876516	2610.00	t	909876516-t-CGM < Cash payments for operating expenses < Operating activities	88-654307	2016-06-30
50	909876518	2880.00	t	909876518-t-CGM < Cash payments for operating expenses < Operating activities	88-654307	2016-06-30
51	909876505	-290.00	c	909876505-c-customers < Cash receipts from customers < Operating activities	88-654307	2016-07-11

Figure 3.7-1   Company2 Cash Received or Paid by Other Members (Continue)

	IDM	Amount	Symbol	MultiSubaccount	Recorder	TransDate
52	909876507	-320.00	c	909876507-c-customers < Cash receipts from customers < Operating activities	88-654307	2016-07-13
53	909876516	307.41	n	909876516-n-operating expenses < Cash payments for operating expenses < Operating acti...	88-654307	2016-07-27
54	909876517	2890.00	t	909876517-t-salary < Cash payments for operating expenses < Operating activities	88-654307	2016-07-31
55	909876516	2610.00	t	909876516-t-CGM < Cash payments for operating expenses < Operating activities	88-654307	2016-07-31
56	909876518	2880.00	t	909876518-t-CGM < Cash payments for operating expenses < Operating activities	88-654307	2016-07-31
57	88-654306	3000.00	t	88-654306-t-suppliers < Cash payments to suppliers < Operating activities	88-654307	2016-08-01
58	88-654306	-12000.00	c	88-654306-c-customers < Cash receipts from customers < Operating activities	88-654307	2016-08-03
59	909876511	-360.00	c	909876511-c-customers < Cash receipts from customers < Operating activities	88-654307	2016-08-13
60	909876517	373.77	n	909876517-n-operating expenses < Cash payments for operating expenses < Operating acti...	88-654307	2016-08-16
61	909876516	392.33	n	909876516-n-operating expenses < Cash payments for operating expenses < Operating acti...	88-654307	2016-08-23
62	909876517	2890.00	t	909876517-t-salary < Cash payments for operating expenses < Operating activities	88-654307	2016-08-31
63	909876516	2610.00	t	909876516-t-CGM < Cash payments for operating expenses < Operating activities	88-654307	2016-08-31
64	909876518	2880.00	t	909876518-t-CGM < Cash payments for operating expenses < Operating activities	88-654307	2016-08-31
65	909876519	-310.00	c	909876519-c-customers < Cash receipts from customers < Operating activities	88-654307	2016-09-03
66	909876522	-320.00	c	909876522-c-customers < Cash receipts from customers < Operating activities	88-654307	2016-09-10
67	88-654308	-4000.00	c	88-654308-c-customers < Cash receipts from customers < Operating activities	88-654307	2016-09-12
68	88-654310	380.00	t	88-654310-t-suppliers < Cash payments to suppliers < Operating activities	88-654307	2016-09-14
69	88-654306	-10000.00	c	88-654306-c-customers < Cash receipts from customers < Operating activities	88-654307	2016-09-14
70	88-654309	-1800.00	c	88-654309-c-customers < Cash receipts from customers < Operating activities	88-654307	2016-09-26
71	909876516	410.89	n	909876516-n-operating expenses < Cash payments for operating expenses < Operating acti...	88-654307	2016-09-28
72	909876517	2890.00	t	909876517-t-salary < Cash payments for operating expenses < Operating activities	88-654307	2016-09-30
73	909876516	2610.00	t	909876516-t-CGM < Cash payments for operating expenses < Operating activities	88-654307	2016-09-30
74	909876518	2880.00	t	909876518-t-CGM < Cash payments for operating expenses < Operating activities	88-654307	2016-09-30
75	88-654303	-4500.00	c	88-654303-c-customers < Cash receipts from customers < Operating activities	88-654307	2016-10-03
76	909876518	377.63	n	909876518-n-operating expenses < Cash payments for operating expenses < Operating acti...	88-654307	2016-10-06
77	909876516	396.27	n	909876516-n-operating expenses < Cash payments for operating expenses < Operating acti...	88-654307	2016-10-27
78	909876517	2890.00	t	909876517-t-salary < Cash payments for operating expenses < Operating activities	88-654307	2016-10-31
79	909876516	2610.00	t	909876516-t-CGM < Cash payments for operating expenses < Operating activities	88-654307	2016-10-31

	IDM	Amount	Symbol	MultiSubaccount	Recorder	TransDate
80	909876518	2880.00	t	909876518-t-CGM < Cash payments for operating expenses < Operating activities	88-654307	2016-10-31
81	909876516	399.28	n	909876516-n-operating expenses < Cash payments for operating expenses < Operating acti...	88-654307	2016-11-19
82	909876518	-360.00	c	909876518-c-customers < Cash receipts from customers < Operating activities	88-654307	2016-11-20
83	88-654306	-14420.00	c	88-654306-c-customers < Cash receipts from customers < Operating activities	88-654307	2016-11-29
84	909876517	2890.00	t	909876517-t-salary < Cash payments for operating expenses < Operating activities	88-654307	2016-11-30
85	909876516	2610.00	t	909876516-t-CGM < Cash payments for operating expenses < Operating activities	88-654307	2016-11-30
86	909876518	2880.00	t	909876518-t-CGM < Cash payments for operating expenses < Operating activities	88-654307	2016-11-30
87	909876516	395.88	n	909876516-n-operating expenses < Cash payments for operating expenses < Operating acti...	88-654307	2016-12-17
88	909876518	424.37	n	909876518-n-operating expenses < Cash payments for operating expenses < Operating acti...	88-654307	2016-12-20
89	88-654308	600.00	t	88-654308-t-supplies < Cash payments for operating expenses < Operating activities	88-654307	2016-12-30
90	88-654306	-55000.00	c	88-654306-c-customers < Cash receipts from customers < Operating activities	88-654307	2016-12-31
91	88-654305	376.00	t	88-654305-t-bond interest < Cash payments to bond holders < Operating activities	88-654307	2016-12-31
92	909876517	2890.00	t	909876517-t-salary < Cash payments for operating expenses < Operating activities	88-654307	2016-12-31
93	909876516	2610.00	t	909876516-t-CGM < Cash payments for operating expenses < Operating activities	88-654307	2016-12-31
94	909876518	2880.00	t	909876518-t-CGM < Cash payments for operating expenses < Operating activities	88-654307	2016-12-31
95	88-654304	35600.00	t	88-654304-t-note interest < Cash payments to business banks < Operating activities	88-654307	2016-12-31
96	88-654305	21600.00	t	88-654305-t-note interest < Cash payments to business banks < Operating activities	88-654307	2016-12-31
97	909876504	178.00	t	909876504-t-bond interest < Cash payments to bond holders < Operating activities	88-654307	2016-12-31
98	909876505	94.00	t	909876505-t-bond interest < Cash payments to bond holders < Operating activities	88-654307	2016-12-31
99	909876506	47.00	t	909876506-t-bond interest < Cash payments to bond holders < Operating activities	88-654307	2016-12-31
100	909876510	141.00	t	909876510-t-bond interest < Cash payments to bond holders < Operating activities	88-654307	2016-12-31
101	909876513	235.00	t	909876513-t-bond interest < Cash payments to bond holders < Operating activities	88-654307	2016-12-31
102	909876504	10.00	t	909876504-t-bond interest < Cash payments to bond holders < Operating activities	88-654307	2016-12-31
103	909876515	94.00	t	909876515-t-bond interest < Cash payments to bond holders < Operating activities	88-654307	2016-12-31
104	909876519	141.00	t	909876519-t-bond interest < Cash payments to bond holders < Operating activities	88-654307	2016-12-31
105	909876520	94.00	t	909876520-t-bond interest < Cash payments to bond holders < Operating activities	88-654307	2016-12-31
106	909876523	141.00	t	909876523-t-bond interest < Cash payments to bond holders < Operating activities	88-654307	2016-12-31
107	909876524	235.00	t	909876524-t-bond interest < Cash payments to bond holders < Operating activities	88-654307	2016-12-31

Figure 3.7-1   Company2 Cash Received or Paid by Other Members (Continue)

108	909876525	94.00	t	909876525-t-bond interest < Cash payments to bond holders < Operating activities	88-654307	2016-12-31
109	88-654304	-336.00	c	88-654304-c-investment income < Cash receipts from investments < Investing activities	88-654307	2016-12-31
110	88-654305	-264.00	c	88-654305-c-investment income < Cash receipts from investments < Investing activities	88-654307	2016-12-31
111	88-654304	-120.00	c	88-654304-c-deposit interest income < Cash receipts from deposit interest < Financial activities	88-654307	2016-12-31
112	88-654304	120.00	c	88-654304-c-deposit interest income < Cash receipts from deposit interest < Financial activities	88-654307	2016-12-31
113	88-654305	-120.00	c	88-654305-c-deposit interest income < Cash receipts from deposit interest < Financial activities	88-654307	2016-12-31

Query executed successfully.

Figure 3.7-1   Company2 Cash Received or Paid by Other Members

Cash Flow Statement

Cash Flows Statement Year Ended 2016-12-31	
Operating activities	
Cash payments for operating expenses	-$109,083.98
Cash payments to bond holders	-$1,880.00
Cash payments to business banks	-$57,200.00
Cash payments to suppliers	-$10,480.00
Cash receipts from customers	$255,690.00
Net cash provided by Operating activities	$77,046.02
Investing activities	
Cash receipts from investments	$600.00
Net cash provided by Investing activities	$600.00
Financial activities	
Cash receipts from deposit interest	$120.00
Net cash provided by Financial activities	$120.00
Net change in cash	$77,766.02
Cash, Begining	$47,393.19
Cash, Ending	$125,159.21

Figure 3.7-2   Company2 Cash Flows Statement

Cash

ID	Multi-Name	Amount	Balance	General ID	Transaction Date
41	88-654303-n-tax < Cash payments for operating expenses < Operating ...	-$71,318.63	$47,393.19	14	2015-12-31
42	88-654310-t-supplies < Cash payments for operating expenses < Oper...	-$500.00	$46,893.19	18	2016-01-02
43	909876525-c-customers < Cash receipts from customers < Operating a...	$360.00	$47,253.19	23	2016-01-12
44	88-654306-c-customers < Cash receipts from customers < Operating a...	$11,000.00	$58,253.19	24	2016-01-14
45	88-654308-t-suppliers < Cash payments to suppliers < Operating activiti...	-$5,000.00	$53,253.19	25	2016-01-15
46	909876516-n-operating expenses < Cash payments for operating expe...	-$411.32	$52,841.87	26	2016-01-15
47	909876517-n-operating expenses < Cash payments for operating expe...	-$112.57	$52,729.30	27	2016-01-18
48	88-654308-c-customers < Cash receipts from customers < Operating a...	$600.00	$53,329.30	28	2016-01-24
49	88-654309-c-customers < Cash receipts from customers < Operating a...	$250.00	$53,579.30	29	2016-01-27
50	88-654308-c-customers < Cash receipts from customers < Operating a...	$7,000.00	$60,579.30	30	2016-01-28
51	909876518-n-operating expenses < Cash payments for operating expe...	-$379.78	$60,199.52	31	2016-01-30
52	88-654309-t-suppliers < Cash payments to suppliers < Operating activiti...	-$500.00	$59,699.52	32	2016-01-30
53	88-654310-t-suppliers < Cash payments to suppliers < Operating activiti...	-$300.00	$59,399.52	33	2016-01-30
54	909876517-t-salary < Cash payments for operating expenses < Operati...	-$2,890.00	$56,509.52	34	2016-01-31
55	909876516-t-CGM < Cash payments for operating expenses < Operatin...	-$2,610.00	$53,899.52	34	2016-01-31
56	909876518-t-CGM < Cash payments for operating expenses < Operatin...	-$2,880.00	$51,019.52	34	2016-01-31
57	88-654302-c-customers < Cash receipts from customers < Operating a...	$500.00	$51,519.52	35	2016-02-02
58	88-654303-c-customers < Cash receipts from customers < Operating a...	$400.00	$51,919.52	36	2016-02-11
59	909876516-n-operating expenses < Cash payments for operating expe...	-$557.83	$51,361.69	37	2016-02-20
60	88-654306-t- suppliers < Cash payments to suppliers < Operating activit...	-$600.00	$50,761.69	38	2016-02-25
61	88-654304-c-customers < Cash receipts from customers < Operating a...	$5,200.00	$55,961.69	39	2016-02-26
62	909876517-t-salary < Cash payments for operating expenses < Operati...	-$2,890.00	$53,071.69	40	2016-02-28
63	909876516-t-CGM < Cash payments for operating expenses < Operatin...	-$2,610.00	$50,461.69	40	2016-02-28
64	909876518-t-CGM < Cash payments for operating expenses < Operatin...	-$2,880.00	$47,581.69	40	2016-02-28
134	909876516-t-CGM < Cash payments for operating expenses < Operatin...	-$2,610.00	$186,399.21	99	2016-12-31
135	909876518-t-CGM < Cash payments for operating expenses < Operatin...	-$2,880.00	$183,519.21	99	2016-12-31
136	88-654304-t-note interest < Cash payments to business banks < Operat...	-$35,600.00	$147,919.21	100	2016-12-31
137	88-654305-t-note interest < Cash payments to business banks < Operat...	-$21,600.00	$126,319.21	101	2016-12-31
138	88-654305-t-bond interest < Cash payments to bond holders < Operatin...	-$376.00	$125,943.21	102	2016-12-31
139	909876504-t-bond interest < Cash payments to bond holders < Operati...	-$178.00	$125,765.21	102	2016-12-31
140	909876505-t-bond interest < Cash payments to bond holders < Operati...	-$94.00	$125,671.21	102	2016-12-31
141	909876506-t-bond interest < Cash payments to bond holders < Operati...	-$47.00	$125,624.21	102	2016-12-31
142	909876510-t-bond interest < Cash payments to bond holders < Operati...	-$141.00	$125,483.21	102	2016-12-31
143	909876513-t-bond interest < Cash payments to bond holders < Operati...	-$235.00	$125,248.21	102	2016-12-31
144	909876504-t-bond interest < Cash payments to bond holders < Operati...	-$10.00	$125,238.21	102	2016-12-31
145	909876515-t-bond interest < Cash payments to bond holders < Operati...	-$94.00	$125,144.21	103	2016-12-31
146	909876519-t-bond interest < Cash payments to bond holders < Operati...	-$141.00	$125,003.21	103	2016-12-31
147	909876520-t-bond interest < Cash payments to bond holders < Operati...	-$94.00	$124,909.21	103	2016-12-31
148	909876523-t-bond interest < Cash payments to bond holders < Operati...	-$141.00	$124,768.21	103	2016-12-31
149	909876524-t-bond interest < Cash payments to bond holders < Operati...	-$235.00	$124,533.21	103	2016-12-31
150	909876525-t-bond interest < Cash payments to bond holders < Operati...	-$94.00	$124,439.21	103	2016-12-31
151	88-654304-c-investment income < Cash receipts from investments < Inv...	$336.00	$124,775.21	104	2016-12-31
152	88-654305-c-investment income < Cash receipts from investments < Inv...	$264.00	$125,039.21	105	2016-12-31
153	88-654304-c-deposit interest income < Cash receipts from deposit inter...	$120.00	$125,159.21	106	2016-12-31
154	88-654304-c-deposit interest income < Cash receipts from deposit inter...	-$120.00	$125,039.21	113	2016-12-31
155	88-654305-c-deposit interest income < Cash receipts from deposit inter...	$120.00	$125,159.21	113	2016-12-31

Figure 3.7-3   Company2 Cash Account Table

Income Statement

	Year ended: 12/31/2016
Revenues	
Sales	$255,240.00
Cost	
Cost of goods sold	-$165,355.00
Gross Margin	$89,885.00
Operating and administrative expenses	
Travelling expenses	-$4,405.98
Other expenses	-$3,018.00
Salary expenses	-$34,680.00
Cost of goods manufactured	$0.00
Bond interest expenses	-$1,880.00
Note interest expenses	-$57,200.00
Office supplies expenses	-$21.02
Amortization expenses	-$27,950.00
Other income	
Investment incomes	$600.00
Deposits interest incomes	$120.00
Earnings Before Income Taxes	-$38,550.00
Tax	
Tax expenses	$0.00
Net Earnings	-$38,550.00
Retained Earnings,Begining	$0.00
Retained Earnings,Ending	-$38,550.00

Figure 3.7-4   Company2 Income Statement

Balance Sheet

	As at 12/31/2016	
ASSETS		
Current assets		
Cash		$125,159.21
Supplies		$1.43
Account receivable		$14,700.00
Inventory		$262,895.00
Working-in-process inventory		$356,035.02
		$758,790.66
Long term investments		
Bonds		$14,000.00
Equipment		
Vehicle		$125,000.00
Accumulated amortization: Vehicle		-$69,083.33
Computer		$5,900.00
Accumulated amortization: Computer		-$1,229.16
		$60,587.51
Total Assets		$833,378.17
LIABILITIES		
Current liabilities		
Account payable		$3,900.00
Tax payable		$0.00
		$3,900.00
Long term liabilities		
Bonds payable		$40,000.00
Notes payable		$630,000.00
		$670,000.00
Total Liability		$673,900.00
SHAREHOLDERS' EQUITY		
Owners capital		
Share capital		$180,000.00
Retained earnings (conversion)		$18,028.17
		$198,028.17
Retined earnings		-$38,550.00
Accumulated other comprehensive income		$0.00
Total Shareholders' Equity		$159,478.17
Total Liabilities and Shareholders' Equity		$833,378.17

Figure 3.7-5   Company2 Balance Sheet Statement

3.8 Company3

3.8.1 An Accounting Fiscal Year of the Company3

In the new fiscal year, the Company3 occurs the following transactions.

- On January 2, 2016, the Company3 purchases the supplies $760 ($14*30 + $16*40) from the Proprietorship2 (phone number: 123456080) for cash -$400 and other on credit. The multi-subaccount name of the Cash account and transaction sub-equation respectively are:

  88-654310-t-supplies < Cash payments for operating expenses < Operating activities

  Cash (1): -400 + Supplies (1): 1060 = Account payable (2): 660

- On January 2, 2016, the Company3 sells the following inventories $94,830 for sales $161,468 to the Proprietorship1 (phone number: 123456781) for $10,000 cash and other on credit.

  Inven51 < Inven5: -6*500

  Inven52 < Inven5: -30*250

  Inven531 < Inven53 < Inven5: -15*500

  Inven532 < Inven53 < Inven5: -21*500

  Inven541 < Inven54 < Inven5: -7.2*500

  Inven542 < Inven54 < Inven5: -7.5*500

  Inven611 < Inven61 < Inven6: -4*600

  Inven612 < Inven61 < Inven6: -7.5*500

  Inven621 < Inven62 < Inven6: -10*400

  Inven63 < Inven6: -8*500

  Inven711 < Inven71 < Inven7: -21.6*200

  Inven712 < Inven71 < Inven7: -18.6*50

  Inven721 < Inven72 < Inven7: -12.5*344

  Inven722 < Inven72 < Inven7: -12*300

Inven731 < Inven73 < Inven7: -10.8*300

Inven732 < Inven73 < Inven7: -9.6*500

Inven811 < Inven81 < Inven8: -15*300

Inven812 < Inven81 < Inven8: -14.4*300

Inven813 < Inven81 < Inven8: -13.8*300

Inven82 < Inven8: -12*300

Inven831 < Inven83 < Inven8: -10.8*300

Inven832 < Inven83 < Inven8: -9.6*400

The multi-subaccount name of the Cash account and four transaction sub-equations respectively are:

88-654309-c-customers < Cash receipts from customers < Operating activities

Cash (1): 10000 + Account receivable (1): 51000 + Inventory (1): -6*500 + Inventory (1): -30*250 + Inventory (1): -15*500 + Inventory (1): -21*500 + Inventory (1): -7.2*500 + Inventory (1): -7.5*500 = Sales (4): 61000 + Cost of goods sold (5): -35850

Account receivable (1): 34100 + Inventory (1): -4*600 + Inventory (1): -7.5*500 + Inventory (1): -10*400 + Inventory (1): -8*500 + Inventory (1): -21.6*200 + Inventory (1): -18.6*50 = Sales (4): 34100 + Cost of goods sold (5): -19400

Account receivable (1): 41668 + Inventory (1): -12.5*344 + Inventory (1): -12*300 + Inventory (1): -10.8*300 + Inventory (1): -9.6*500 + Inventory (1): -15*300 + Inventory (1): -14.4*300 = Sales (4): 41668 + Cost of goods sold (5): -24760

Account receivable (1): 24700 + Inventory (1): -13.8*300 + Inventory (1): -12*300 + Inventory (1): -10.8*300 + Inventory (1): -9.6*400 = Sales (4): 24700 + Cost of goods sold (5): -14820

- On January 2, 2016, the Company3 sells the following inventories $99,090 for sales

$168,750 to the Proprietorship2 (phone number: 123456780) for $8,000 cash and other on credit.

Inven51 < Inven5: -6*500

Inven52 < Inven5: -30*250

Inven531 < Inven53 < Inven5: -15*500

Inven532 < Inven53 < Inven5: -21*500

Inven541 < Inven54 < Inven5: -7.2*500

Inven542 < Inven54 < Inven5: -7.5*500

Inven611 < Inven61 < Inven6: -4*700

Inven612 < Inven61 < Inven6: -7.5*500

Inven621 < Inven62 < Inven6: -10*500

Inven63 < Inven6: -8*500

Inven711 < Inven71 < Inven7: -21.6*300

Inven712 < Inven71 < Inven7: -18.6*50

Inven721 < Inven72 < Inven7: -12.5*400

Inven722 < Inven72 < Inven7: -12*300

Inven731 < Inven73 < Inven7: -10.8*300

Inven732 < Inven73 < Inven7: -9.6*500

Inven811 < Inven81 < Inven8: -15*300

Inven812 < Inven81 < Inven8: -14.4*300

Inven813 < Inven81 < Inven8: -13.8*300

Inven82 < Inven8: -12*300

Inven831 < Inven83 < Inven8: -10.8*300

Inven832 < Inven83 < Inven8: -9.6*400

The multi-subaccount name of the Cash account and four transaction sub-equations respectively are:

88-654310-c-customers < Cash receipts from customers < Operating activities

Cash (1): 8000 + Account receivable (1): 53000 + Inventory (1): -6*500 + Inventory (1): -30*250 + Inventory (1): -15*500 + Inventory (1): -21*500 +

Inventory (1): -7.2*500 + Inventory (1): -7.5*500 = Sales (4): 61000 + Cost of goods sold (5): -35850

Account receivable (1): 40150 + Inventory (1): -4*700 + Inventory (1): -7.5*500 + Inventory (1): -10*500 + Inventory (1): -8*500 + Inventory (1): -21.6*300 + Inventory (1): -18.6*50 = Sales (4): 40150 + Cost of goods sold (5): -22960

Account receivable (1): 42900 + Inventory (1): -12.5*400 + Inventory (1): -12*300 + Inventory (1): -10.8*300 + Inventory (1): -9.6*500 + Inventory (1): -15*300 + Inventory (1): -14.4*300 = Sales (4): 42900 + Cost of goods sold (5): -25460

Account receivable (1): 24700 + Inventory (1): -13.8*300 + Inventory (1): -12*300 + Inventory (1): -10.8*300 + Inventory (1): -9.6*400 = Sales (4): 24700 + Cost of goods sold (5): -14820

- On January 3, 2016, the Company3 purchases the following inventories $34,800 from the Proprietorship1 (phone number: 123456081) with the General ID 29 for cash -$9,300 and other on credit.

  Inven31 < Inven3: 10*260

  Inven32 < Inven3: 50*150

  Inven331 < Inven33 < Inven3: 20*260

  Inven332 < Inven33 < Inven3: 45*260

  HGFCVB parts < QASXC parts < Inven3: 10*260

  PPGHUP parts < ASDUP parts < Inven3: 20*260

  The multi-subaccount name of the Cash account and transaction sub-equation respectively are:

  88-654309-t-suppliers < Cash payments to suppliers < Operating activities

  Cash (1): -9300 + Inventory (1): 10*260 + Inventory (1): 50*150 + Inventory (1): 20*260 + Inventory (1): 45*260 + Inventory (1): 10*260 + Inventory (1): 20*260

= Account payable (2): 25500

- On January 3, 2016, the Company3 purchases the following inventories $19,050 from the Proprietorship2 (phone number: 123456080) with the General ID 30 for cash -$6,000 and other on credit.

  Inven411 < Inven41 < Inven4: 5*300

  Inven412 < Inven41 < Inven4: 18.5*300

  TTTCU parts < TTT parts < Inven4: 20*300

  RRRHJK parts < Inven4: 20*300

  The multi-subaccount name of the Cash account and transaction sub-equation respectively are:

  88-654310-t-suppliers < Cash payments to suppliers < Operating activities

  Cash (1): -6000 + Inventory (1): 5*300 + Inventory (1): 18.5*300 + Inventory (1): 20*300 + Inventory (1): 20*300 = Account payable (2): 13050

- On January 3, 2016, the Company3 transfers the supplies $920 to the Cost of goods manufactured to satisfy the need of producing. The transaction sub-equation is:

  Supplies (1): -920 = Cost of goods manufactured (5): -920

- On January 3, 2016, the Company3 transfers the following inventories $75,700 to the Cost of goods manufactured account to satisfy the need of producing.

  Inven31 < Inven3: -10*360

  Inven32 < Inven3: -50*250

  Inven331 < Inven33 < Inven3: -20*360

  Inven332 < Inven33 < Inven3: -45*360

  HGFCVB parts < QASXC parts < Inven3: -10*360

  PPGHUP parts < ASDUP parts < Inven3: -20*360

  Inven411 < Inven41 < Inven4: -5*400

  Inven412 < Inven41 < Inven4: -18.5*400

TTTCU parts < TTT parts < Inven4: -20*400

RRRHJK parts < Inven4: -20*400

The two transaction sub-equations are respectively:

Inventory (1): -10*360 + Inventory (1): -50*250 + Inventory (1): -20*360 + Inventory (1): -45*360 + Inventory (1): -10*360 + Inventory (1): -20*360 = Cost of goods manufactured (5): -50300

Inventory (1): -5*400+ Inventory (1): -18.5*400 + Inventory (1): -20*400 + Inventory (1): -20*400 = Cost of goods manufactured (5): -25,400

- On January 13, 2016, the Company3 receives $150 cash from the Proprietorship1 (phone number: 123456781) with the General ID 4. The multi-subaccount name of the Cash account and transaction sub-equation respectively are:

  88-654309-c-customers < Cash receipts from customers < Operating activities

  Cash (1): 150 + Account receivable (1): -150 = 0

- On January 13, 2016, the Company3 sells the following inventories -$2,852 for sales $4,660 to the Business Bank1 (phone number: 123456786) with the General ID 35 for cash $2,000 and other on credit.

  Inven121 < Inven12 < Inven1: -0.4*200

  Inven122 < Inven12 < Inven1: -30*30

  Inven21 < Inven2: -20*30

  Inven221 < Inven22 < Inven2: -20*30

  PPUK parts < ASD parts < Inven2: -22.4*30

  The multi-subaccount name of the Cash account is:

  88-654304-c-customers < Cash receipts from customers < Operating activities

- On January 14, 2016, the Company3 receives $8,000 cash from the Company1 (phone number: 123456784) with the General ID 4. The multi-subaccount name of the Cash account is:

88-654306-c-customers < Cash receipts from customers < Operating activities

- On January 15, 2016, the Company3 receives $5,000 cash from the Company2 (phone number: 123456783) with the General ID 4. The multi-subaccount name of the Cash account is:

    88-654307-c-customers < Cash receipts from customers < Operating activities

- On January 18, 2016, the Company3 pays -$261.26 cash to A19 (SIN: 909876519) for the Travelling expenses (travel allowance) $139.26 and the Other expenses (meals: food514: $11*4 + food613: $26*3) $122. The multi-subaccount name of the Cash account and the transaction sub-equation respectively are:

    909876519-n-operating expenses < Cash payments for operating expenses < Operating activities

    Cash (1): -261.26 = Travelling expenses (5): -139.26 + other expenses (5): -122

- On January 19, 2016, the Company3 pays -$143.68 cash to A20 (SIN: 909876520) for the Travelling expenses (travel allowance) $92.68 and the Other expenses (meals: food312: $24*1 + food321: $27*1) $51.

- On January 23, 2016, the Company3 sells two Inven112s (-$25*2) and three Inven222s (-$27*3) to A22 (SIN: 909876522) for cash $230 ($40*2 + $50*3). The multi-subaccount name of the Cash account is:

    909876522-c-customers < Cash receipts from customers < Operating activities

- On January 24, 2016, the Company3 pays -$600 cash to the Company2 (phone number: 123456083) with the General ID 1. The multi-subaccount name of the Cash account and transaction sub-equation respectively are:

    88-654307-t-suppliers < Cash payments to suppliers < Operating activities

    Cash (1): -1300 = Account payable (2): -1300

- On January 26, 2016, the Company3 pays -$1,300 cash to the Proprietorship1 (phone number: 123456081) with the General ID 4. The multi-subaccount name of the Cash account is:

88-654309-t-suppliers < Cash payments to suppliers < Operating activities

- On January 26, 2016, the Company3 pays -$800 cash to the Proprietorship2 (phone number: 123456080) with the General ID 4. The multi-subaccount name of the Cash account is:

88-654310-t-suppliers < Cash payments to suppliers < Operating activities

- On January 28, 2016, the Company3 receives $200 cash from the Proprietorship2 (phone number: 123456780) with the General ID 4. The multi-subaccount name of the Cash account is:

88-654310-c-customers < Cash receipts from customers < Operating activities

- On January 28, 2016, the Company3 purchases $13,000 parts (one Truck1 part2 $7,600 and Truck2 part3 $5,400) from the Company2 (phone number: 123456083) for cash -$7,000 and other on credit. Here, the parts are recorded as the Vehicle part expenses for simplification. The multi-subaccount name of the Cash account and transaction sub-equation respectively are:

88-654307-t-suppliers < Cash payments to suppliers < Operating activities

Cash (1): -7000 = Account payable (2): 6000 + Vehicle part expenses (5): -13000

- On January 30, 2016, the Company3 pays -$143.33 cash to A21 (SIN: 909876521) for the Travelling expenses (travel allowance) $101.33 and the Other expenses (meals: Food 212: $9*2 + food312: $24*1) $42.

- On January 31, 2016, the Company3 sells ten Inven111s (-$6*10) and five Inven122s (-$30*5) to A6 (SIN: 909876506) for cash $350 ($10*10 + $50*5). The multi-subaccount name of the Cash account is:

909876506-c-customers < Cash receipts from customers < Operating activities

- On January 31, 2016, the Company3 pays three employees' salary expenses for cash -$8,370. The two multi-subaccount names of the Cash account and the transaction sub-equation respectively are:

909876520-t-salary < Cash payments for operating expenses< Operating activities

909876519-t-CGM < Cash payments for operating expenses< Operating activities

909876521-t-CGM < Cash payments for operating expenses< Operating activities

Cash (1): -2880 + Cash (1): -2700 + Cash (1): -2790 = Salary expenses (5): -2880 + Cost of goods manufactured (5): -2700 + Cost of goods manufactured (5): -2790

- On February 13, 2016, the Company3 receives $200 cash from the Central Bank (phone number: 123456789) with the General ID 4. The multi-subaccount name of the Cash account is:

    88-654301-c-customers < Cash receipts from customers < Operating activities

- On February 22, 2016, the Company3 sells the following inventories -$3,320 for sales $5,600 to the Central Bank (phone number: 123456789) for cash $3,600 and other on credit.

    Inven111 < Inven11 < Inven1: -6*40

    Inven112 < Inven11 < Inven1: -25*40

    Inven221 < Inven22 < Inven2: -20*40

    Inven222 < Inven22 < Inven2: -27*40

    PPGH parts < ASD parts < Inven2: -1*200

    The multi-subaccount name of the Cash account is:

    88-654301-c-customers < Cash receipts from customers < Operating activities

- On February 23, 2016, the Company3 receives $300 cash from the Tax Bureau (phone number: 123456787) with the General ID 4. The multi-subaccount name of the Cash account is:

    88-654303-c-customers < Cash receipts from customers < Operating activities

- On February 25, 2016, the Company3 pays -$339.49 cash to A19 (SIN: 909876519) for the Travelling expenses (travel allowance) $215.49 and the Other expenses (meals: food23: $16*4 + food322: $30*2) $124.

- On February 27, 2016, the Company3 pays -$900 cash to the Company1 (phone number: 123456084) with the General ID 4. The multi-subaccount name of the Cash account is:

    88-654306-t-suppliers < Cash payments to suppliers < Operating activities

- On February 27, 2016, the Company3 sells the Inven21s (-$20*15) and the Inven221s (-$20*20) to A23 (SIN: 909876523) for cash $1,050 ($30*15 + $30*20). The multi-subaccount name of the Cash account is:

  909876523-c-customers < Cash receipts from customers < Operating activities

- On February 28, 2016, the Company3 pays three employees' salary expenses for cash -$8,370. The two multi-subaccount names of the Cash account and the transaction sub-equation respectively are:

  909876520-t-salary < Cash payments for operating expenses< Operating activities

  909876519-t-CGM < Cash payments for operating expenses< Operating activities

  909876521-t-CGM < Cash payments for operating expenses< Operating activities

  Cash (1): -2880 + Cash (1): -2700 + Cash (1): -2790 = Salary expenses (5): -2880 + Cost of goods manufactured (5): -2700 + Cost of goods manufactured (5): -2790

- On March 1, 2016, the Company3 pays -$225.64 cash to A21 (SIN: 909876521) for the Travelling expenses (travel allowance) $123.64 and the Other expenses (meals: food312: $24*2 + food321: $27*2) $102.

- On March 4, 2016, the Company3 receives $1,600 cash from the Company1 (phone number: 123456784) with the General ID 4. The multi-subaccount name of the Cash account and transaction sub-equation respectively are:

  88-654306-c-customers < Cash receipts from customers < Operating activities

- On March 23, 2016, the Company3 pays -$198.56 cash to A19 (SIN: 909876519) for the Travelling expenses (travel allowance) $125.56 and the Other expenses (meals: food44: $15*3 + food622: $28*1) $73.

- On March 24, 2016, the Company3 sells the Inven21s (-$20*50) and the Inven222s (-$27*40) to A2 (SIN: 909876502) for cash $3,500 ($30*50 + $50*40). The multi-subaccount name of the Cash account is:

  909876502-c-customers < Cash receipts from customers < Operating activities

- On March 30, 2016, the Company3 receives $700 cash from the Company2 (phone number: 123456783) with the General ID 4. The multi-subaccount name of the Cash account is:

88-654307-c-customers < Cash receipts from customers < Operating activities

- On March 31, 2016, the Company3 pays three employees' salary expenses for cash -$8,370 repeatedly.

- On April 6, 2016, the Company3 sells the following inventories -$1,300 for sales $2,200 to the Business Bank2 (phone number: 123456785) for cash $1,500 and other on credit.

  Inven111 < Inven11 < Inven1: -6*10

  Inven112 < Inven11 < Inven1: -25*10

  Inven221 < Inven22 < Inven2: -20*20

  Inven222 < Inven22 < Inven2: -27*20

  PPGH parts < ASD parts < Inven2: -1*50

  The multi-subaccount name of the Cash account is:

  88-654305-c-customers < Cash receipts from customers < Operating activities

- On April 14, 2016, the Company3 sells the Inven112s (-$25*50), the Inven121s (-$0.4*200), and the PPUK parts (-$22.4*50) to A10 (SIN: 909876510) for cash $4,160 ($40*50 + $0.8*200 + $40*50). The multi-subaccount name of the Cash account is:

  909876510-c-customers < Cash receipts from customers < Operating activities

- On April 26, 2016, the Company3 pays -$236.37 cash to A19 (SIN: 909876519) for the Travelling expenses (travel allowance) $158.37 and the Other expenses (meals: food312: $24*2 + food322: $30*1) $78.

- On April 30, 2016, the Company3 pays three employees' salary expenses for cash -$8,370 repeatedly.

- On May 1, 2016, the Company3 sells the following inventories -$30,640 ($15,200 + $15,440) for sales $50,800 ($25,800 + $25,000) to the Company1 (phone number: 123456784) on credit.

  Inven111 < Inven11 < Inven1: -6*300

  Inven112 < Inven11 < Inven1: -25*200

Inven121 < Inven12 < Inven1: -0.4*6000

Inven122 < Inven12 < Inven1: -30*200

Inven21 < Inven2: -20*300

Inven221 < Inven22 < Inven2: -20*200

Inven222 < Inven22 < Inven2: -27*100

PPUK parts < ASD parts < Inven2: -22.4*100

PPGH parts < ASD parts < Inven2: -1*500

The transaction sub-equations are:

Account receivable (1): 25,800 + Inventory (1): -6*300 + Inventory (1): -25*200 + Inventory (1): -0.4*6000 + Inventory (1): -30*200 = Sales (4): 25,800 + Cost of goods sold (5): -15200

Account receivable (1): 25,000 + Inventory (1): -20*300 + Inventory (1): -20*200 + Inventory (1): -27*100 + Inventory (1): -22.4*100 + Inventory (1): -1*500 = Sales (4): 25,000 + Cost of goods sold (5): -15,440

- On May 2, 2016, the Company3 pays -$167.19 cash to A21 (SIN: 909876521) for the Travelling expenses (travel allowance) $117.19 and the Other expenses (meals: food213: $10*3 + food311: $20*1) $50.

- On May 3, 2016, the Company3 sells the Inven112s (-$25*20) and the Inven121s (-$0.4*100) for sales $880 ($40*20 + $0.8*100) to A14 (SIN: 909876514) for cash $880. The multi-subaccount name of the Cash account is:

  909876514-c-customers < Cash receipts from customers < Operating activities

- On May 24, 2016, the Company3 pays -$339.55 cash to A19 (SIN: 909876516) for the Travelling expenses (travel allowance) $201.55 and the Other expenses (meals: food111: $10*6 + food312: $24*2 + food322: $30*1) $138.

- On May 31, 2016, the Company3 pays three employees' salary expenses for cash -$8,370 repeatedly.

- On May 31, 2016, the Company3 records the Amortization expenses $1,125 of a computer server2 ($562.5, five months), a computer3 ($291.67, five months), and a computer4 ($270.83, five months). The transaction sub-equation is:

Accumulated amortization: Computer (1): -562.5 + Accumulated amortization: Computer (1): -291.67 + Accumulated amortization: Computer (1): -270.83 = Amortization expenses (5): -562.5 + Amortization expenses (5): -291.67 + Amortization expenses (5): -270.83

- On May 31, 2016, the Company3 cancels the balances of the Computer account and the Accumulated amortization: Computer account because these computers have used for two years. The transaction sub-equation is:

Computer (1): -2700 + Computer (1): -1400 + Computer (1): -1300 + Accumulated amortization: Computer (1): 2700 + Accumulated amortization: Computer (1): 1400 + Accumulated amortization: Computer (1): 1300 = 0

- On June 1, 2016, the Company3 purchases one Computer server1, one Computer1, and one Computer2 from the Company1 (phone number: 123456084) for cash - $3,000 and other on credit. The multi-subaccount name of the Cash account and transaction sub-equation respectively are:

88-654306-t-suppliers < Cash payments to suppliers < Operating activities

Cash (1): -3000 + Computer (1): 2800 + Computer (1): 1600 + Computer (1): 1500 = Account payable (2): 2900

- On June 10, 2016, the Company3 receives $15,000 cash from the Company1 (phone number: 123456784) with the General ID 65. The multi-subaccount name of the Cash account and transaction sub-equation respectively are:

88-654306-c-customers < Cash receipts from customers < Operating activities

Cash (1): 15000 + Account receivable (2): -15000 = 0

- On June 14, 2016, the Company3 pays -$193.49 cash to A20 (SIN: 909876520) for the Travelling expenses (travel allowance) $125.49 and the Other expenses (meals: food611: $20*2 + food622: $28*1) $68.

- On June 16, 2016, the Company3 pays -$300 cash to the Proprietorship1 (phone number: 123456081) with the General ID 4. The multi-subaccount name of the Cash account is:

  88-654309-t-suppliers < Cash payments to suppliers < Operating activities

- On June 23, 2016, the Company3 pays -$254.33 cash to A19 (SIN: 909876519) for the Travelling expenses (travel allowance) $146.33 and the Other expenses (meals: food113: $12*5 + food312: $24*2) $108.

- On June 29, 2016, the Company3 sells the following inventories -$2,892 for sales $4,740 to the Tax Bureau (phone number: 123456787) with the General ID 78 for cash $2,000 and other on credit.

  Inven121 < Inven12 < Inven1: -0.4*300

  Inven122 < Inven12 < Inven1: -30*30

  Inven21 < Inven2: -20*30

  Inven221 < Inven22 < Inven2: -20*30

  PPUK parts < ASD parts < Inven2: -22.4*30

  The multi-subaccount name of the Cash account is:

  88-654303-c-customers < Cash receipts from customers < Operating activities

- On June 30, 2016, the Company3 pays three employees' salary expenses for cash -$8,370 repeatedly.

- On July 3, 2016, the Company3 receives $53,000 cash from the Proprietorship2 (phone number: 123456780) with the General ID 25. The multi-subaccount name of the Cash account and transaction sub-equation respectively are:

  88-654310-c-customers < Cash receipts from customers < Operating activities

- On July 4, 2016, the Company3 receives $55,000 cash from the Proprietorship1 (phone number: 123456781) with the General ID 21 ($51,000) and the General ID 22 ($4,000). The multi-subaccount name of the Cash account and transaction sub-equation respectively are:

88-654309-c-customers < Cash receipts from customers < Operating activities

- On July 11, 2016, the Company3 sells the Inven111s (-$6*10) and the Inven221s (-$20*5) for sales $250 ($10*10 + $30*5) to A4 (SIN: 909876504) for cash $250. The multi-subaccount name of the Cash account is:

  909876504-c-customers < Cash receipts from customers < Operating activities

- On July 13, 2016, the Company3 sells the Inven112s (-$25*12) and the Inven222s (-$27*6) for sales $780 ($40*12 + $50*6) to A21 (SIN: 909876521) for cash $780. The multi-subaccount name of the Cash account is:

  909876521-c-customers < Cash receipts from customers < Operating activities

- On July 16, 2016, the Company3 pays -$13,000 cash to the Proprietorship2 (phone number: 123456080) with the General ID 20 ($660) and the General ID 30 ($12,340). The multi-subaccount name of the Cash account is:

  88-654310-t-suppliers < Cash payments to suppliers < Operating activities

- On July 27, 2016, the Company3 pays -$221.14 cash to A19 (SIN: 909876519) for the Travelling expenses (travel allowance) $133.14 and the Other expenses (meals: food311: $20*2 + food312: $24*2) $88.

- On July 31, 2016, the Company3 pays three employees' salary expenses for cash -$8,370 repeatedly.

- On August 3, 2016, the Company3 sells the Inven112s (-$25*10) and the Inven221s (-$20*5) for sales $550 ($40*10 + $30*5) to A17 (SIN: 909876517) for cash $550. The multi-subaccount name of the Cash account is:

  909876517-c-customers < Cash receipts from customers < Operating activities

- On August 13, 2016, the Company3 sells the Inven222s (-$27*10) and the PPGH parts (-$1*100) for sales $700 ($50*10 + $2*100) to A13 (SIN: 909876513) for cash $700. The multi-subaccount name of the Cash account is:

  909876513-c-customers < Cash receipts from customers < Operating activities

- On August 15, 2016, the Company3 receives $66,000 cash from the Proprietorship2 (phone number: 123456780) with the General ID 26 ($40,150), the General ID 27

($1,150) and the General ID 28 ($24,700). The multi-subaccount name of the Cash account and transaction sub-equation respectively are:

88-654310-c-customers < Cash receipts from customers < Operating activities

- On August 17, 2016, the Company3 receives $65,000 cash from the Proprietorship1 (phone number: 123456781) with the General ID 22 ($30,100) and the General ID 23 ($34,900). The multi-subaccount name of the Cash account and transaction sub-equation respectively are:

88-654309-c-customers < Cash receipts from customers < Operating activities

- On August 23, 2016, the Company3 pays -$208.31 cash to A19 (SIN: 909876519) for the Travelling expenses (travel allowance) $130.31 and the Other expenses (meals: food312: $24*2 + food322: $30*1) $78.

- On August 31, 2016, the Company3 pays three employees' salary expenses for cash -$8,370 repeatedly.

- On September 4, 2016, the Company3 sells the Inven221s (-$20*12) and the Inven121s (-$0.4*200) for sales $520 ($30*12 + $0.8*200) to A18 (SIN: 909876518) for cash $520. The multi-subaccount name of the Cash account is:

909876518-c-customers < Cash receipts from customers < Operating activities

- On September 10, 2016, the Company3 sells the Inven111s (-$6*15) and the Inven112s (-$25*10) for sales $550 ($10*15 + $40*10) to A23 (SIN: 909876523) for cash $550. The multi-subaccount name of the Cash account is:

909876523-c-customers < Cash receipts from customers < Operating activities

- On September 12, 2016, the Company3 pays -$4,000 cash to the Company2 (phone number: 123456083) with the General ID 12 The multi-subaccount name of the Cash account is:

88-654307-t-suppliers < Cash payments to suppliers < Operating activities

- On September 13, 2016, the Company3 receives $25,000 cash from the Company1 (phone number: 123456784) with the General ID 66. The multi-subaccount name of the Cash account and transaction sub-equation respectively are:

88-654306-c-customers < Cash receipts from customers < Operating activities

- On September 15, 2016, the Company3 pays -$300 cash to the Proprietorship1 (phone number: 123456081) with the General ID 29. The multi-subaccount name of the Cash account is:

  88-654309-t-suppliers < Cash payments to suppliers < Operating activities

- On September 25, 2016, the Company3 sells the following inventories -$2,490 for sales $4,200 to the Government1 (phone number: 123456788) for cash $3,200 and other on credit.

  Inven111 < Inven11 < Inven1: -6*30

  Inven112 < Inven11 < Inven1: -25*30

  Inven221 < Inven22 < Inven2: -20*30

  Inven222 < Inven22 < Inven2: -27*30

  PPGH parts < ASD parts < Inven2: -1*150

  The multi-subaccount name of the Cash account is:

  88-654302-c-customers < Cash receipts from customers < Operating activities

- On September 26, 2016, the Company3 receives $8,000 cash from the Company1 (phone number: 123456784) with the General ID 4 ($1,000) and the General ID 65 ($7,000). The multi-subaccount name of the Cash account and transaction sub-equation respectively are:

  88-654306-c-customers < Cash receipts from customers < Operating activities

- On September 28, 2016, the Company3 pays -$214.84 cash to A19 (SIN: 909876519) for the Travelling expenses (travel allowance) $127.84 and the Other expenses (meals: food311: $20*3 + food321: $27*1) $87.

- On September 30, 2016, the Company3 pays three employees' salary expenses for cash -$8,370 repeatedly.

- On October 3, 2016, the Company3 sells the Inven111s (-$6*15) and the Inven112s (-$25*10) for sales $550 ($10*15 + $40*10) to A15 (SIN: 909876515) for cash $550. The multi-subaccount name of the Cash account is:

  909876515-c-customers < Cash receipts from customers < Operating activities

- On October 8, 2016, the Company3 pays -$218.66 cash to A21 (SIN: 909876521)

for the Travelling expenses (travel allowance) $140.66 and the Other expenses (meals: food522: $13*2 + food613: $26*2) $78.

- On October 11, 2016, the Company3 receives $41,000 cash from the Proprietorship2 (phone number: 123456780) with the General ID 27 ($41,000). The multi-subaccount name of the Cash account and transaction sub-equation respectively are:

    88-654310-c-customers < Cash receipts from customers < Operating activities

- On October 12, 2016, the Company3 receives $31,000 cash from the Proprietorship1 (phone number: 123456781) with the General ID 23 ($6,300) and the General ID 24 ($24,700). The multi-subaccount name of the Cash account and transaction sub-equation respectively are:

    88-654309-c-customers < Cash receipts from customers < Operating activities

- On October 18, 2016, the Company3 receives $2,660 cash from the Business Bank1 (phone number: 123456786) with the General ID 35. The multi-subaccount name of the Cash account and transaction sub-equation respectively are:

    88-654304-c-customers < Cash receipts from customers < Operating activities

- On October 25, 2016, the Company3 pays -$25,000 cash to the Proprietorship1 (phone number: 123456081) with the General ID 29. The multi-subaccount name of the Cash account is:

    88-654309-t-suppliers < Cash payments to suppliers < Operating activities

- On October 27, 2016, the Company3 pays -$242.23 cash to A19 (SIN: 909876519) for the Travelling expenses (travel allowance) $152.23 and the Other expenses (meals: food113: $12*5 + food322: $30*1) $90.

- On October 31, 2016, the Company3 pays three employees' salary expenses for cash -$8,380 repeatedly.

- On November 5, 2016, the Company3 pays -$2,900 cash to the Company1 (phone number: 123456084) with the General ID 14. The multi-subaccount name of the Cash account is:

    88-654306-t-suppliers < Cash payments to suppliers < Operating activities

- On November 19, 2016, the Company3 pays -$223.61 cash to A19 (SIN: 909876519)

for the Travelling expenses (travel allowance) $136.61 and the Other expenses (meals: food311: $20*3 + food321: $27*1) $87.

- On November 20, 2016, the Company3 sells the Inven111s (-$6*14) and the Inven222s (-$27*10) for sales $640 ($10*14 + $50*10) to A6 (SIN: 909876506) for cash $640. The multi-subaccount name of the Cash account is:

  909876506-c-customers < Cash receipts from customers < Operating activities

- On November 29, 2016, the Company3 receives $3,000 cash from the Company1 (phone number: 123456784). The multi-subaccount name of the Cash account is:

  88-654306-c-customers < Cash receipts from customers < Operating activities

- On November 30, 2016, the Company3 pays three employees' salary expenses for cash -$8,370 repeatedly.

- On December 17, 2016, the Company3 pays -$272.78 cash to A19 (SIN: 909876519) for the Travelling expenses (travel allowance) $168.78 and the Other expenses (meals: food111: $10*5 + food321: $27*2) $104.

- On December 20, 2016, the Company3 pays -$248.53 cash to A21 (SIN: 909876521) for the Travelling expenses (travel allowance) $160.53 and the Other expenses (meals: food611: $20*3 + food622: $28*1) $88.

- On December 28, 2016, the Company3 receives $2,500 cash from the Tax Bureau (phone number: 123456787) with the General ID 78 ($2,000) and the General 109 ($500). The multi-subaccount name of the Cash account is:

  88-654303-c-customers < Cash receipts from customers < Operating activities

- On December 30, 2016, the Company3 sells the Inven611s -$800 (-$4*200) for sales $1,300 ($6.5*200) to the Company2 (phone number: 123456783) for cash $600 and other on credit. The multi-subaccount name of the Cash account and transaction sub-equation respectively are:

  88-654307-c-customers < Cash receipts from customers < Operating activities

  Cash (1): 600 + Account receivable (1): 700 + Inventory (1): -800 = Sales (4): 1300 + Cost of goods sold (5): -800

- On December 31, 2016, the Company3 pays three employees' salary expenses for cash -$8,370 repeatedly.

- On the same day, the Company3 pays -$18,000 cash to the Business Bank1 for the Note interest expenses of the Note13 ($200,000, one-level subaccount "Note13-interest"). The multi-subaccount name of the Cash account and the transaction sub-equation respectively are:

  88-654304-t-note interest< Cash payments to business banks< Operating activities

  Cash (1): -18000 = Note interest expenses (5): -18000

- On the same day, the Company3 pays -$34,400 cash to the business Bank2 for the Note interest expenses of the Note23 $16,200 ($180,000, one-level subaccount "Note23-interest") and Note24 $18,200 ($200,000, one-level subaccount "Note24-interest"). The multi-subaccount name of the Cash account and the transaction sub-equation respectively are:

  88-654305-t-note interest< Cash payments to business banks< Operating activities

  Cash (1): -34400 = Note interest expenses (5): -16200 + Note interest expenses (5): -18200

- On the same day, the Company3 pays -$3,840 cash to the bond holders for the Bond interest expenses of the Bond51 (one-level subaccount "Bond51-interest"). The multi-subaccount names of the Cash account and the transaction sub-equations respectively are:

  909876501-t-bond interest < Cash payments to bond holders< Operating activities
  909876502-t-bond interest < Cash payments to bond holders< Operating activities
  909876503-t-bond interest < Cash payments to bond holders< Operating activities
  909876507-t-bond interest < Cash payments to bond holders< Operating activities
  909876508-t-bond interest < Cash payments to bond holders< Operating activities
  909876509-t-bond interest < Cash payments to bond holders< Operating activities

909876511-t-bond interest < Cash payments to bond holders< Operating activities

909876512-t-bond interest < Cash payments to bond holders< Operating activities

909876514-t-bond interest < Cash payments to bond holders< Operating activities

909876516-t-bond interest < Cash payments to bond holders< Operating activities

909876517-t-bond interest < Cash payments to bond holders< Operating activities

909876518-t-bond interest < Cash payments to bond holders< Operating activities

909876521-t-bond interest < Cash payments to bond holders< Operating activities

909876522-t-bond interest < Cash payments to bond holders< Operating activities

Cash (1): -288 + Cash (1): -192 + Cash (1): -336 + Cash (1): -288 + Cash (1): -336 + Cash (1): -240 + Cash (1): -192 + Cash (1): -384 = Bond interest expenses (5): - 2256

Cash (1): -240 + Cash (1): -336 + Cash (1): -240 + Cash (1): -288 + Cash (1): -192 + Cash (1): -288 = Bond interest expenses (5): -1584

- On the same day, the Company3 receives cash $320 for investment interest of the Bond11 ($8,000) from the Business Bank1. The multi-subaccount name of the Cash account and transaction sub-equation respectively are:

  88-654304-c-investment income < Cash receipts from investments < Investing activities

  Cash (1): 320 = Investment incomes (4):320

- On the same day, the Company3 receives cash $492 for investment interest of the Bond21 ($12,000) from the Business Bank2. The multi-subaccount name of the Cash account and transaction sub-equation respectively are:

  88-654305-c-investment income < Cash receipts from investments < Investing activities

  Cash (1): 492 = Investment incomes (4): 492

- On the same day, the Company3 receives cash $120 from the Business Bank2 for primary deposit interest. The multi-subaccount name of the Cash account and transaction sub-equation respectively are:

  88-654305-c-deposit interest income < Cash receipts from deposit interest < Financial activities

  Cash (1): 120 = Deposit interest incomes (4):120

- On the same day, the Company3 records the Office supplies expenses -$288.75. The transaction sub-equation is:

  Supplies (1): -288.75 = Office supplies expenses (5): -288.75

- On the same day, the Company3 records the Vehicle's amortization expenses - $24,200 one year (5 years, straight line). The two transaction sub-equations are:

  Accumulated amortization: Vehicle (1): -9000 + Accumulated amortization: Vehicle (1): -9000 + Accumulated amortization: Vehicle (1): -8000 + Accumulated amortization: Vehicle (1): -8000 = Amortization expenses (5): -9000 + Amortization expenses (5): -9000 + Amortization expenses (5): -8000+ Amortization expenses (5): -8000

  Accumulated amortization: Vehicle (1): -7600 + Accumulated amortization: Vehicle (1): -7600 = Amortization expenses (5): -7600 + Amortization expenses (5): -7600

- On the same day, the Company3 records the Computer's amortization expenses $1,720.84 seven months (2 years, straight line) which includes a new computer server1 ($816.67), a new computer1 ($466.67), and a new computer2 ($437.5). The transaction sub-equation is:

  Accumulated amortization: Computer (1): -816.67 + Accumulated amortization:

Computer (1): -466.67 + Accumulated amortization: Computer (1): -437.5 =
Amortization expenses (5): -816.67 + Amortization expenses (5): -466.67 +
Amortization expenses (5): -437.5

- On December 31, 2016, the Company3 transfers the balance $142,500 of the Cost of goods manufactured account to the Working-in-process inventory account. The Cost of goods manufactured account has four subaccounts of the "Supplies expenses", the "909876519-salary < Sales department-salary < Salary expenses", the "909876521-salary < Product department-salary < Salary expenses", and the "General parts expenses". Their balances are -$920, -$32,400, -$33,480, and -$75,700 respectively. Here, the balance of the "General parts expenses" is divided to four parts. The four transaction sub-equations respectively are:

Working-in-process inventory (1): 1*1000 + Working-in-process inventory (1): 4*1000 + Working-in-process inventory (1): 0.19*10000 + Working-in-process inventory (1): 4.1*1000 + Working-in-process inventory (1): 5.5*1000 + Working-in-process inventory (1): 5.1*1000 + Working-in-process inventory (1): 1*1000 + Working-in-process inventory (1): 2*1000 = Cost of goods manufactured (5): 920 + Cost of goods manufactured (5): 23680

Working-in-process inventory (1): 0.1*6000 + Working-in-process inventory (1): 0.5*5000 + Working-in-process inventory (1): 5*1000 + Working-in-process inventory (1): 2*1000 + Working-in-process inventory (1): 3*1000 + Working-in-process inventory (1): 0.83*1000 + Working-in-process inventory (1): 0.29*1000 + Working-in-process inventory (1): 0.5*5000 = Cost of goods manufactured (5): 16720

Working-in-process inventory (1): 0.9*1000 + Working-in-process inventory (1): 1.1*1000 + Working-in-process inventory (1): 0.01*1000 + Working-in-process inventory (1): 10.87*1000 + Working-in-process inventory (1): 9.1*1000 +

Working-in-process inventory (1): 5.5*1000 + Working-in-process inventory (1): 5*1000 + Working-in-process inventory (1): 5.3*1000 = Cost of goods manufactured (5): 32400 + Cost of goods manufactured (5): 5380

Working-in-process inventory (1): 3.7*1000 + Working-in-process inventory (1): 7*1000 + Working-in-process inventory (1): 7*1000 + Working-in-process inventory (1): 6.53*1000 + Working-in-process inventory (1): 6.17*1000 + Working-in-process inventory (1): 6*3000 + Working-in-process inventory (1): 5*3000 = Cost of goods manufactured (5): 33480 + Cost of goods manufactured (5): 29920

- On December 31, 2016, the Company3 records the Tax expenses -$3,555.43 and the Tax payable $3,555.43. The multi-subaccount name forms of the Tax expenses and the Tax payable accounts all are the 'n'. The transaction sub-equation is:

  0 = Tax payable (2): 3555.43 + Tax expenses (5): -3555.43

So far, I have entered all transactions of the Company3 in the fiscal year 2016. After getting the Income Statement and clicking the "Yes" button for new fiscal year, I can get the Balance Sheet of the Company3.

In the new fiscal year, the Company3 will record the following transaction.

- On January 2, 2017, the Company3 pays the balance -$3,555.43 of the Tax payable account to the Tax Bureau. The multi-subaccount name of the Cash account and transaction sub-equation respectively are:

  88-654303-n-tax < Cash payments to Tax Bureau < Operating activities

  Cash (1): -3555.43 = Tax payable (2): -3555.43

3.8.2 Brief Summary of the Company3

The Figure 3.8-1 shows two sums and all cash transactions of the Company3 by using of

SQL Server query. As a closed system based on the MathAccounting software, the sum0 should be equal to zero. However, the individuals are not responsible for recording any transaction, so the sum0 ($91,562.99) is the sum of the amounts that the individuals received from the Company3. If the sum0 is negative, then it is sum of the amounts that individuals paid to the Company3. The opposite value ($204,679.37) of the sum1 (-$204,679.37) is the balance of the Cash account of the Company3 on December 31, 2016. It is also the sum $204,679.37 (= $3,906.47 + $200,772.90) of the balances of the deposits of the Company3 in the Business Bank1 and the Business Bak2 on December 31, 2016.

The Figure 3.8-2 to the Figure 3.8-5 on page 465 to page 468 show the four tables of the cash flows statement, the cash account, the income statement, and the balance sheet respectively.

SQLQuery1.sql - LIU...SS.dcj100 (sa (52))* ×

```
use dcj100
select sum(amount) as sum0 from CashByMembers where IDM='88-654308' and TransDate between '2016-01-01' and '2016-12-31'
select sum(amount) as sum1 from CashByMembers where IDM='88-654308' and Symbol = 'd'
select * from CashByMembers where Recorder='88-654308' and TransDate between '2016-01-01' and '2016-12-31'
    order by TransDate
```

100 % ▾

Results   Messages

	sum0
1	91562.99

	sum1
1	-204679.37

	IDM	Amount	Symbol	MultiSubaccount	Recorder	TransDate
1	88-654310	400.00	t	88-654310-t-supplies < Cash payments for operating expenses < Operating activities	88-654308	2016-01-02
2	88-654309	-10000.00	c	88-654309-c-customers < Cash receipts from customers < Operating activities	88-654308	2016-01-02
3	88-654310	-8000.00	c	88-654310-c-customers < Cash receipts from customers < Operating activities	88-654308	2016-01-02
4	88-654309	9300.00	t	88-654309-t-suppliers < Cash payments to suppliers < Operating activities	88-654308	2016-01-03
5	88-654310	6000.00	t	88-654310-t-suppliers < Cash payments to suppliers < Operating activities	88-654308	2016-01-03
6	88-654309	-150.00	c	88-654309-c-customers < Cash receipts from customers < Operating activities	88-654308	2016-01-13
7	88-654304	-2000.00	c	88-654304-c-customers < Cash receipts from customers < Operating activities	88-654308	2016-01-13
8	88-654306	-8000.00	c	88-654306-c-customers < Cash receipts from customers < Operating activities	88-654308	2016-01-14
9	88-654307	-5000.00	c	88-654307-c-customers < Cash receipts from customers < Operating activities	88-654308	2016-01-15
10	909876519	261.26	n	909876519-n-operating expenses < Cash payments for operating expenses < Operating act...	88-654308	2016-01-18
11	909876520	143.68	n	909876520-n-operating expenses < Cash payments for operating expenses < Operating act...	88-654308	2016-01-19
12	909876522	-230.00	c	909876522-c-customers < Cash receipts from customers < Operating activities	88-654308	2016-01-23
13	88-654307	600.00	t	88-654307-t-suppliers < Cash payments to suppliers < Operating activities	88-654308	2016-01-24
14	88-654309	1300.00	t	88-654309-t-suppliers < Cash payments to suppliers < Operating activities	88-654308	2016-01-26
15	88-654310	800.00	t	88-654310-t-suppliers < Cash payments to suppliers < Operating activities	88-654308	2016-01-26
16	88-654310	-200.00	c	88-654310-c-customers < Cash receipts from customers < Operating activities	88-654308	2016-01-28
17	88-654307	7000.00	t	88-654307-t-suppliers < Cash payments to suppliers < Operating activities	88-654308	2016-01-28
18	909876521	143.33	n	909876521-n-operating expenses < Cash payments for operating expenses < Operating act...	88-654308	2016-01-30
19	909876506	-350.00	c	909876506-c-customers < Cash receipts from customers < Operating activities	88-654308	2016-01-31
20	909876520	2880.00	t	909876520-t-salary < Cash payments for operating expenses< Operating activities	88-654308	2016-01-31
21	909876519	2700.00	t	909876519-t-CGM < Cash payments for operating expenses< Operating activities	88-654308	2016-01-31
22	909876521	2790.00	t	909876521-t-CGM < Cash payments for operating expenses< Operating activities	88-654308	2016-01-31
23	88-654301	-200.00	c	88-654301-c-customers < Cash receipts from customers < Operating activities	88-654308	2016-02-13

	IDM	Amount	Symbol	MultiSubaccount	Recorder	TransDate
24	88-654301	-1500.00	c	88-654301-c-customers < Cash receipts from customers < Operating activities	88-654308	2016-02-22
25	88-654301	-2100.00	c	88-654301-c-customers < Cash receipts from customers < Operating activities	88-654308	2016-02-22
26	88-654303	-300.00	c	88-654303-c-customers < Cash receipts from customers < Operating activities	88-654308	2016-02-23
27	909876519	339.49	n	909876519-n-operating expenses < Cash payments for operating expenses < Operating act...	88-654308	2016-02-25
28	88-654306	900.00	t	88-654306-t-suppliers < Cash payments to suppliers < Operating activities	88-654308	2016-02-27
29	909876523	-1050.00	c	909876523-c-customers < Cash receipts from customers < Operating activities	88-654308	2016-02-27
30	909876520	2880.00	t	909876520-t-salary < Cash payments for operating expenses< Operating activities	88-654308	2016-02-28
31	909876519	2700.00	t	909876519-t-CGM < Cash payments for operating expenses< Operating activities	88-654308	2016-02-28
32	909876521	2790.00	t	909876521-t-CGM < Cash payments for operating expenses< Operating activities	88-654308	2016-02-28
33	909876521	225.64	n	909876521-n-operating expenses < Cash payments for operating expenses < Operating act...	88-654308	2016-03-01
34	88-654306	-1600.00	c	88-654306-c-customers < Cash receipts from customers < Operating activities	88-654308	2016-03-04
35	909876519	198.56	n	909876519-n-operating expenses < Cash payments for operating expenses < Operating act...	88-654308	2016-03-23
36	909876502	-3500.00	c	909876502-c-customers < Cash receipts from customers < Operating activities	88-654308	2016-03-24
37	88-654307	-700.00	c	88-654307-c-customers < Cash receipts from customers < Operating activities	88-654308	2016-03-30
38	909876520	2880.00	t	909876520-t-salary < Cash payments for operating expenses< Operating activities	88-654308	2016-03-31
39	909876519	2700.00	t	909876519-t-CGM < Cash payments for operating expenses< Operating activities	88-654308	2016-03-31
40	909876521	2790.00	t	909876521-t-CGM < Cash payments for operating expenses< Operating activities	88-654308	2016-03-31
41	909876520	2880.00	t	909876520-t-salary < Cash payments for operating expenses< Operating activities	88-654308	2016-03-31
42	909876519	2700.00	t	909876519-t-CGM < Cash payments for operating expenses< Operating activities	88-654308	2016-03-31
43	909876521	2790.00	t	909876521-t-CGM < Cash payments for operating expenses< Operating activities	88-654308	2016-03-31
44	88-654305	-1500.00	c	88-654305-c-customers < Cash receipts from customers < Operating activities	88-654308	2016-04-06
45	909876510	-4160.00	c	909876510-c-customers < Cash receipts from customers < Operating activities	88-654308	2016-04-14
46	909876519	236.37	n	909876519-n-operating expenses < Cash payments for operating expenses < Operating act...	88-654308	2016-04-26
47	909876520	2880.00	t	909876520-t-salary < Cash payments for operating expenses< Operating activities	88-654308	2016-04-30
48	909876519	2700.00	t	909876519-t-CGM < Cash payments for operating expenses< Operating activities	88-654308	2016-04-30
49	909876521	2790.00	t	909876521-t-CGM < Cash payments for operating expenses< Operating activities	88-654308	2016-04-30
50	909876521	167.19	n	909876521-n-operating expenses < Cash payments for operating expenses < Operating act...	88-654308	2016-05-02
51	909876514	-880.00	c	909876514-c-customers < Cash receipts from customers < Operating activities	88-654308	2016-05-03

	IDM	Amount	Symbol	MultiSubaccount	Recorder	TransDate
52	909876519	339.55	n	909876519-n-operating expenses < Cash payments for operating expenses < Operating act...	88-654308	2016-05-24
53	909876520	2880.00	t	909876520-t-salary < Cash payments for operating expenses< Operating activities	88-654308	2016-05-31
54	909876519	2700.00	t	909876519-t-CGM < Cash payments for operating expenses< Operating activities	88-654308	2016-05-31
55	909876521	2790.00	t	909876521-t-CGM < Cash payments for operating expenses< Operating activities	88-654308	2016-05-31
56	88-654306	3000.00	t	88-654306-t-suppliers < Cash payments to suppliers < Operating activities	88-654308	2016-06-01
57	88-654306	-15000.00	c	88-654306-c-customers < Cash receipts from customers < Operating activities	88-654308	2016-06-10
58	909876520	193.49	n	909876520-n-operating expenses < Cash payments for operating expenses < Operating act...	88-654308	2016-06-14
59	88-654309	300.00	t	88-654309-t-suppliers < Cash payments to suppliers < Operating activities	88-654308	2016-06-16
60	909876519	254.33	n	909876519-n-operating expenses < Cash payments for operating expenses < Operating act...	88-654308	2016-06-23
61	88-654303	-2740.00	c	88-654303-c-customers < Cash receipts from customers < Operating activities	88-654308	2016-06-29
62	88-654303	740.00	c	88-654303-c-customers < Cash receipts from customers < Operating activities	88-654308	2016-06-29
63	909876520	2880.00	t	909876520-t-salary < Cash payments for operating expenses< Operating activities	88-654308	2016-06-30
64	909876519	2700.00	t	909876519-t-CGM < Cash payments for operating expenses< Operating activities	88-654308	2016-06-30
65	909876521	2790.00	t	909876521-t-CGM < Cash payments for operating expenses< Operating activities	88-654308	2016-06-30
66	88-654310	-53000.00	c	88-654310-c-customers < Cash receipts from customers < Operating activities	88-654308	2016-07-03
67	88-654309	-55000.00	c	88-654309-c-customers < Cash receipts from customers < Operating activities	88-654308	2016-07-04
68	909876504	-250.00	c	909876504-c-customers < Cash receipts from customers < Operating activities	88-654308	2016-07-11
69	909876521	-780.00	c	909876521-c-customers < Cash receipts from customers < Operating activities	88-654308	2016-07-13
70	88-654310	13000.00	t	88-654310-t-suppliers < Cash payments to suppliers < Operating activities	88-654308	2016-07-16
71	909876519	221.14	n	909876519-n-operating expenses < Cash payments for operating expenses < Operating act...	88-654308	2016-07-27
72	909876520	2880.00	t	909876520-t-salary < Cash payments for operating expenses< Operating activities	88-654308	2016-07-31
73	909876519	2700.00	t	909876519-t-CGM < Cash payments for operating expenses< Operating activities	88-654308	2016-07-31
74	909876521	2790.00	t	909876521-t-CGM < Cash payments for operating expenses< Operating activities	88-654308	2016-07-31
75	909876517	-550.00	c	909876517-c-customers < Cash receipts from customers < Operating activities	88-654308	2016-08-03
76	909876513	-700.00	c	909876513-c-customers < Cash receipts from customers < Operating activities	88-654308	2016-08-13
77	88-654310	-66000.00	c	88-654310-c-customers < Cash receipts from customers < Operating activities	88-654308	2016-08-15
78	88-654309	-65000.00	c	88-654309-c-customers < Cash receipts from customers < Operating activities	88-654308	2016-08-17
79	909876519	208.31	n	909876519-n-operating expenses < Cash payments for operating expenses < Operating act...	88-654308	2016-08-23

	IDM	Amount	Symbol	MultiSubaccount	Recorder	TransDate
80	909876518	-520.00	c	909876518-c-customers < Cash receipts from customers < Operating activities	88-654308	2016-09-04
81	909876523	-550.00	c	909876523-c-customers < Cash receipts from customers < Operating activities	88-654308	2016-09-10
82	88-654307	4000.00	t	88-654307-t-suppliers < Cash payments to suppliers < Operating activities	88-654308	2016-09-12
83	88-654306	-25000.00	c	88-654306-c-customers < Cash receipts from customers < Operating activities	88-654308	2016-09-13
84	88-654309	300.00	t	88-654309-t-suppliers < Cash payments to suppliers < Operating activities	88-654308	2016-09-15
85	88-654302	-3200.00	c	88-654302-c-customers < Cash receipts from customers < Operating activities	88-654308	2016-09-25
86	88-654306	-8000.00	c	88-654306-c-customers < Cash receipts from customers < Operating activities	88-654308	2016-09-26
87	909876519	214.84	n	909876519-n-operating expenses < Cash payments for operating expenses < Operating act...	88-654308	2016-09-28
88	909876520	2880.00	t	909876520-t-salary < Cash payments for operating expenses< Operating activities	88-654308	2016-09-30
89	909876519	2700.00	t	909876519-t-CGM < Cash payments for operating expenses< Operating activities	88-654308	2016-09-30
90	909876521	2790.00	t	909876521-t-CGM < Cash payments for operating expenses< Operating activities	88-654308	2016-09-30
91	909876515	-550.00	c	909876515-c-customers < Cash receipts from customers < Operating activities	88-654308	2016-10-03
92	909876521	218.66	n	909876521-n-operating expenses < Cash payments for operating expenses < Operating act...	88-654308	2016-10-08
93	88-654310	-41000.00	c	88-654310-c-customers < Cash receipts from customers < Operating activities	88-654308	2016-10-11
94	88-654304	-2660.00	c	88-654304-c-customers < Cash receipts from customers < Operating activities	88-654308	2016-10-18
95	88-654309	25000.00	t	88-654309-t-suppliers < Cash payments to suppliers < Operating activities	88-654308	2016-10-25
96	909876519	242.23	n	909876519-n-operating expenses < Cash payments for operating expenses < Operating act...	88-654308	2016-10-27
97	909876520	2880.00	t	909876520-t-salary < Cash payments for operating expenses< Operating activities	88-654308	2016-10-31
98	909876519	2700.00	t	909876519-t-CGM < Cash payments for operating expenses< Operating activities	88-654308	2016-10-31
99	909876521	2790.00	t	909876521-t-CGM < Cash payments for operating expenses< Operating activities	88-654308	2016-10-31
100	88-654306	2900.00	t	88-654306-t-suppliers < Cash payments to suppliers < Operating activities	88-654308	2016-11-05
101	88-654309	-31000.00	c	88-654309-c-customers < Cash receipts from customers < Operating activities	88-654308	2016-11-12
102	909876519	223.61	n	909876519-n-operating expenses < Cash payments for operating expenses < Operating act...	88-654308	2016-11-19
103	909876506	-640.00	c	909876506-c-customers < Cash receipts from customers < Operating activities	88-654308	2016-11-20
104	88-654306	-3000.00	c	88-654306-c-customers < Cash receipts from customers < Operating activities	88-654308	2016-11-29
105	909876520	2880.00	t	909876520-t-salary < Cash payments for operating expenses< Operating activities	88-654308	2016-11-30
106	909876519	2700.00	t	909876519-t-CGM < Cash payments for operating expenses< Operating activities	88-654308	2016-11-30
107	909876521	2790.00	t	909876521-t-CGM < Cash payments for operating expenses< Operating activities	88-654308	2016-11-30

Figure 3.8-1   Company3 Cash Received or Paid by Other Members (Continue)

	IDM	Amount	Symbol	MultiSubaccount	Recorder	TransDate
108	909876519	272.78	n	909876519-n-operating expenses < Cash payments for operating expenses < Operating act...	88-654308	2016-12-17
109	909876521	248.53	n	909876521-n-operating expenses < Cash payments for operating expenses < Operating act...	88-654308	2016-12-20
110	88-654303	-2500.00	c	88-654303-c-customers < Cash receipts from customers < Operating activities	88-654308	2016-12-28
111	88-654307	-600.00	c	88-654307-c-customers < Cash receipts from customers < Operating activities	88-654308	2016-12-30
112	909876520	2880.00	t	909876520-t-salary < Cash payments for operating expenses< Operating activities	88-654308	2016-12-31
113	909876519	2700.00	t	909876519-t-CGM < Cash payments for operating expenses< Operating activities	88-654308	2016-12-31
114	909876521	2790.00	t	909876521-t-CGM < Cash payments for operating expenses< Operating activities	88-654308	2016-12-31
115	88-654304	18000.00	t	88-654304-t-note interest< Cash payments to business banks< Operating activities	88-654308	2016-12-31
116	88-654305	34400.00	t	88-654305-t-note interest< Cash payments to business banks< Operating activities	88-654308	2016-12-31
117	909876501	288.00	t	909876501-t-bond interest < Cash payments to bond holders< Operating activities	88-654308	2016-12-31
118	909876502	192.00	t	909876502-t-bond interest < Cash payments to bond holders< Operating activities	88-654308	2016-12-31
119	909876503	336.00	t	909876503-t-bond interest < Cash payments to bond holders< Operating activities	88-654308	2016-12-31
120	909876507	288.00	t	909876507-t-bond interest < Cash payments to bond holders< Operating activities	88-654308	2016-12-31
121	909876508	192.00	t	909876508-t-bond interest < Cash payments to bond holders< Operating activities	88-654308	2016-12-31
122	909876509	240.00	t	909876509-t-bond interest < Cash payments to bond holders< Operating activities	88-654308	2016-12-31
123	909876511	192.00	t	909876511-t-bond interest < Cash payments to bond holders< Operating activities	88-654308	2016-12-31
124	909876512	384.00	t	909876512-t-bond interest < Cash payments to bond holders< Operating activities	88-654308	2016-12-31
125	909876514	240.00	t	909876514-t-bond interest < Cash payments to bond holders< Operating activities	88-654308	2016-12-31
126	909876516	336.00	t	909876516-t-bond interest < Cash payments to bond holders< Operating activities	88-654308	2016-12-31
127	909876517	240.00	t	909876517-t-bond interest < Cash payments to bond holders< Operating activities	88-654308	2016-12-31
128	909876518	288.00	t	909876518-t-bond interest < Cash payments to bond holders< Operating activities	88-654308	2016-12-31
129	909876521	192.00	t	909876521-t-bond interest < Cash payments to bond holders< Operating activities	88-654308	2016-12-31
130	909876522	288.00	t	909876522-t-bond interest < Cash payments to bond holders< Operating activities	88-654308	2016-12-31
131	88-654304	-320.00	c	88-654304-c-investment income < Cash receipts from investments < Investing activities	88-654308	2016-12-31
132	88-654305	-492.00	c	88-654305-c-investment income < Cash receipts from investments < Investing activities	88-654308	2016-12-31
133	88-654305	-120.00	c	88-654305-c-deposit interest income < Cash receipts from deposit interest < Financial activi...	88-654308	2016-12-31
134	909876508	144.00	t	909876508-t-bond interest < Cash payments to bond holders< Operating activities	88-654308	2016-12-31

Query executed successfully.

Figure 3.8-1   Company3 Cash Received or Paid by Other Members

Cash Flow Statement

	Cash Flows Statement Year Ended 2016-12-31	
Operating activities		
Cash payments for operating expenses		-$105,192.99
Cash payments to bond holders		-$3,840.00
Cash payments to business banks		-$52,400.00
Cash payments to suppliers		-$74,400.00
Cash receipts from customers		$428,920.00
Net cash provided by Operating activities		$193,087.01
Investing activities		
Cash receipts from investments		$812.00
Net cash provided by Investing activities		$812.00
Financial activities		
Cash receipts from deposit interest		$120.00
Net cash provided by Financial activities		$120.00
Net change in cash		$194,019.01
Cash, Begining		$10,660.36
Cash, Ending		$204,679.37
*		

Figure 3.8-2   Company3 Cash Flows Statement

Cash

	ID	Multi-Name	Amount	Balance	General ID	Transaction Date
▶	48	88-654306-c-operating < Cash receipts from customers < Operating acti...	$1,000.00	$10,660.36	19	2015-12-31
	49	88-654310-t-supplies < Cash payments for operating expenses < Operat...	-$400.00	$10,260.36	20	2016-01-02
	50	88-654309-c-customers < Cash receipts from customers < Operating act...	$10,000.00	$20,260.36	21	2016-01-02
	51	88-654310-c-customers < Cash receipts from customers < Operating act...	$8,000.00	$28,260.36	25	2016-01-02
	52	88-654309-t-suppliers < Cash payments to suppliers < Operating activities	-$9,300.00	$18,960.36	29	2016-01-03
	53	88-654310-t-suppliers < Cash payments to suppliers < Operating activities	-$6,000.00	$12,960.36	30	2016-01-03
	54	88-654309-c-customers < Cash receipts from customers < Operating act...	$150.00	$13,110.36	34	2016-01-13
	55	88-654304-c-customers < Cash receipts from customers < Operating act...	$2,000.00	$15,110.36	35	2016-01-13
	56	88-654306-c-customers < Cash receipts from customers < Operating act...	$8,000.00	$23,110.36	36	2016-01-14
	57	88-654307-c-customers < Cash receipts from customers < Operating act...	$5,000.00	$28,110.36	37	2016-01-15
	58	909876519-n-operating expenses < Cash payments for operating expen...	-$261.26	$27,849.10	38	2016-01-18
	59	909876520-n-operating expenses < Cash payments for operating expen...	-$143.68	$27,705.42	39	2016-01-19
	60	909876522-c-customers < Cash receipts from customers < Operating ac...	$230.00	$27,935.42	40	2016-01-23
	61	88-654307-t-suppliers < Cash payments to suppliers < Operating activities	-$600.00	$27,335.42	41	2016-01-24
	62	88-654309-t-suppliers < Cash payments to suppliers < Operating activities	-$1,300.00	$26,035.42	42	2016-01-26
	63	88-654310-t-suppliers < Cash payments to suppliers < Operating activities	-$800.00	$25,235.42	43	2016-01-26
	64	88-654310-c-customers < Cash receipts from customers < Operating act...	$200.00	$25,435.42	44	2016-01-28
	65	88-654307-t-suppliers < Cash payments to suppliers < Operating activities	-$7,000.00	$18,435.42	45	2016-01-28
	66	909876521-n-operating expenses < Cash payments for operating expen...	-$143.33	$18,292.09	46	2016-01-30
	67	909876506-c-customers < Cash receipts from customers < Operating ac...	$350.00	$18,642.09	47	2016-01-31
	68	909876520-t-salary < Cash payments for operating expenses< Operatin...	-$2,880.00	$15,762.09	48	2016-01-31
	69	909876519-t-CGM < Cash payments for operating expenses< Operating ...	-$2,700.00	$13,062.09	48	2016-01-31
	70	909876521-t-CGM < Cash payments for operating expenses< Operating ...	-$2,790.00	$10,272.09	48	2016-01-31
	71	88-654301-c-customers < Cash receipts from customers < Operating act...	$200.00	$10,472.09	49	2016-02-13

	ID	Multi-Name	Amount	Balance	General ID	Transaction Date
	161	909876511-t-bond interest < Cash payments to bond holders< Operating...	-$192.00	-$71,900.63	115	2016-12-31
	162	909876512-t-bond interest < Cash payments to bond holders< Operating...	-$384.00	-$72,284.63	115	2016-12-31
	163	909876514-t-bond interest < Cash payments to bond holders< Operating...	-$240.00	-$72,524.63	116	2016-12-31
	164	909876516-t-bond interest < Cash payments to bond holders< Operating...	-$336.00	-$72,860.63	116	2016-12-31
	165	909876517-t-bond interest < Cash payments to bond holders< Operating...	-$240.00	-$73,100.63	116	2016-12-31
	166	909876518-t-bond interest < Cash payments to bond holders< Operating...	-$288.00	-$73,388.63	116	2016-12-31
	167	909876521-t-bond interest < Cash payments to bond holders< Operating...	-$192.00	-$73,580.63	116	2016-12-31
	168	909876522-t-bond interest < Cash payments to bond holders< Operating...	-$288.00	-$73,868.63	116	2016-12-31
	169	88-654304-c-investment income < Cash receipts from investments < Inv...	$320.00	-$73,548.63	117	2016-12-31
	170	88-654305-c-investment income < Cash receipts from investments < Inv...	$492.00	-$73,056.63	118	2016-12-31
	171	88-654305-c-deposit interest income < Cash receipts from deposit intere...	$120.00	-$72,936.63	119	2016-12-31
	172	88-654310-c-customers < Cash receipts from customers < Operating act...	$53,000.00	-$19,936.63	130	2016-07-03
	173	88-654309-c-customers < Cash receipts from customers < Operating act...	$55,000.00	$35,063.37	131	2016-07-04
	174	88-654310-c-customers < Cash receipts from customers < Operating act...	$66,000.00	$101,063.37	132	2016-08-15
	175	88-654309-c-customers < Cash receipts from customers < Operating act...	$65,000.00	$166,063.37	133	2016-08-17
	176	88-654310-c-customers < Cash receipts from customers < Operating act...	$41,000.00	$207,063.37	134	2016-10-11
	177	88-654309-c-customers < Cash receipts from customers < Operating act...	$31,000.00	$238,063.37	135	2016-11-12
	178	88-654304-c-customers < Cash receipts from customers < Operating act...	$2,660.00	$240,723.37	136	2016-10-18
	179	88-654310-t-suppliers < Cash payments to suppliers < Operating activities	-$13,000.00	$227,723.37	137	2016-07-16
	180	88-654309-t-suppliers < Cash payments to suppliers < Operating activities	-$25,000.00	$202,723.37	138	2016-10-25
	181	909876508-t-bond interest < Cash payments to bond holders< Operating...	-$144.00	$202,579.37	139	2016-12-31
	182	88-654301-c-customers < Cash receipts from customers < Operating act...	$2,100.00	$204,679.37	140	2016-02-22

Figure 3.8-3   Company3 Cash Account Table

Income Statement

Year ended: 12/31/2016	
Revenues	
Sales	$418,428.00
Cost	
Cost of goods sold	-$247,021.00
Gross Margin	$171,407.00
Operating and administrative expenses	
Travelling expenses	-$2,696.99
Other expenses	-$1,656.00
Salary expenses	-$34,560.00
Bond interest expenses	-$3,840.00
Office supplies expenses	-$288.75
Note interest expenses	-$52,400.00
Vehicle part expenses	-$13,000.00
Amortization expenses	-$52,045.84
Cost of goods manufactured	$0.00
Other income	
Investment incomes	$812.00
Deposit interest incomes	$120.00
Earnings Before Income Taxes	$11,851.42
Tax	
Tax expenses	-$3,555.43
Net Earnings	$8,295.99
Retained Earnings,Begining	$0.00
Retained Earnings,Ending	$8,295.99
*	

Figure 3.8-4   Company3 Income Statement

Balance Sheet

	As at 12/31/2016
ASSETS	
Current assets	
Cash	$204,679.37
Supplies	$61.13
Account receivable	$6,958.00
Inventory	$74,499.00
Working-in-process inventory	$507,610.00
	$793,807.50
Long term investments	
Bonds	$20,000.00
Equipment	
Vehicle	$246,000.00
Accumulated amortization: Vehicle	-$152,666.67
Computer	$5,900.00
Accumulated amortization: Computer	-$1,720.84
	$97,512.49
Total Assets	$911,319.99
LIABILITIES	
Current liabilities	
Account payable	$2,910.00
Tax payable	$3,555.43
	$6,465.43
Long term liabilities	
Bonds payable	$80,000.00
Notes payable	$580,000.00
	$660,000.00
Total Liability	$666,465.43
SHAREHOLDERS' EQUITY	
Owners capital	
Share capital	$220,000.00
Retained earnings (Conversion)	$16,558.57
	$236,558.57
Retined earnings	$8,295.99
Accumulated other comprehensive income	$0.00
Total Shareholders' Equity	$244,854.56
Total Liabilities and Shareholders' Equity	$911,319.99

Figure 3.8-5   Company3 Balance Sheet Statement

3.9 Proprietorship1

3.9.1 An Accounting Fiscal Year of the Proprietorship1

Because the Proprietorship1 mainly sells foods to individuals, it has many transactions every day. For simplification, I assume that an individual only buy foods (exception of business meal foods) two times for one year. Therefore, in the new fiscal year, the Proprietorship1 occurs the following transactions.

- On January 2, 2016, the Proprietorship1 purchases the supplies $750 ($14*35 + $16*35) from the Proprietorship2 (phone number: 123456080) for cash -$450 and other on credit. The multi-subaccount name of the Cash account and transaction sub-equation respectively are:

  88-654310-t-supplies < Cash payments for operating expenses < Operating activities

  Cash (1): -450 + Supplies (1): 1050 = Account payable (2): 600

- On January 2, 2016, the Proprietorship1 purchases the following inventories $161,468 from the Company3 (phone number: 123456082) for -$10,000 cash and other on credit.

  Inven51 < Inven5: 10*500

  Inven52 < Inven5: 50*250

  Inven531 < Inven53 < Inven5: 25*500

  Inven532 < Inven53 < Inven5: 35*500

  Inven541 < Inven54 < Inven5: 12*500

  Inven542 < Inven54 < Inven5: 15*500

  Inven611 < Inven61 < Inven6: 6.5*600

  Inven612 < Inven61 < Inven6: 12.5*500

  Inven621 < Inven62 < Inven6: 18*400

  Inven63 < Inven6: 16*500

  Inven711 < Inven71 < Inven7: 36*200

Inven712 < Inven71 < Inven7: 31*50

Inven721 < Inven72 < Inven7: 22*344

Inven722 < Inven72 < Inven7: 20*300

Inven731 < Inven73 < Inven7: 18*300

Inven732 < Inven73 < Inven7: 16*500

Inven811 < Inven81 < Inven8: 25*300

Inven812 < Inven81 < Inven8: 24*300

Inven813 < Inven81 < Inven8: 23*300

Inven82 < Inven8: 20*300

Inven831 < Inven83 < Inven8: 18*300

Inven832 < Inven83 < Inven8: 16*400

The multi-subaccount name of the Cash account and three transaction sub-equations respectively are:

88-654308-t-suppliers < Cash payments to suppliers < Operating activities

Cash (1): -10000 + Inventory (1): 10*500 + Inventory (1): 50*250 + Inventory (1): 25*500 + Inventory (1): 35*500 + Inventory (1): 12*500 + Inventory (1): 15*500 + Inventory (1): 6.5*600 + Inventory (1): 12.5*500 = Account Payable (2): 61150

Inventory (1): 18*400 + Inventory (1): 16*500 + Inventory (1): 36*200 + Inventory (1): 31*50 + Inventory (1): 22*344 + Inventory (1): 20*300 + Inventory (1): 18*300 + Inventory (1): 16*500 + Inventory (1): 25*300 = Account Payable (2): 58418

Inventory (1): 24*300 + Inventory (1): 23*300 + Inventory (1): 20*300 + Inventory (1): 18*300 + Inventory (1): 16*400 = Account Payable (2): 31900

- On January 3, 2016, the Proprietorship1 sells the following inventories -$20,360 for sales $34,800 to the Company3 (phone number: 123456782) for cash $9,300 and other on credit.

Inven31 < Inven3: -6*260

Inven32 < Inven3: -30*150

Inven331 < Inven33 < Inven3: -10*260

Inven332 < Inven33 < Inven3: -27*260

HGFCVB parts < QASXC parts < Inven3: -6*260

PPGHUP parts < ASDUP parts < Inven3: -12*260

The multi-subaccount name of the Cash account and transaction sub-equation respectively are:

88-654308-c-customers < Cash receipts from customers < Operating activities

Cash (1): 9300 + Account receivable (1): 25500 + Inventory (1): -6*260 + Inventory (1): -30*150 + Inventory (1): -10*260 + Inventory (1): -27*260 + Inventory (1): -6*260 + Inventory (1): -12*260 = Sales (4): 34,800 + Cost of goods sold (5): -20360

- On January 3, 2016, the Proprietorship1 transfers the supplies $900 to the Cost of goods manufactured to satisfy the need of producing. The transaction sub-equation is:

Supplies (1): -900 = Cost of goods manufactured (5): -900

- On January 3, 2016, the Proprietorship1 transfers the following inventories $6,350 to the Cost of goods manufactured account to satisfy the need of producing.

Inven411 < Inven41 < Inven4: -5*100

Inven412 < Inven41 < Inven4: -18.5*100

TTTCU parts < TTT parts < Inven4: -20*100

RRRHJK parts < Inven4: -20*100

The transaction sub-equations is:

Inventory (1): -5*100 + Inventory (1): -18.5*100 + Inventory (1): -20*100 +

Inventory (1): -20*100 = Cost of goods manufactured (5): -6350

- On January 3, 2016, the Proprietorship1 transfers the following inventories $48,370 to the Cost of goods manufactured account to satisfy the need of producing.

Inven51 < Inven5: -10*150

Inven52 < Inven5: -50*75

Inven531 < Inven53 < Inven5: -25*150

Inven532 < Inven53 < Inven5: -35*150

Inven541 < Inven54 < Inven5: -12*150

Inven542 < Inven54 < Inven5: -15*150

Inven611 < Inven61 < Inven6: -6.5*180

Inven612 < Inven61 < Inven6: -12.5*150

Inven621 < Inven62 < Inven6: -18*120

Inven63 < Inven6: -16*150

Inven711 < Inven71 < Inven7: -36*60

Inven712 < Inven71 < Inven7: -31*15

Inven721 < Inven72 < Inven7: -22*100

Inven722 < Inven72 < Inven7: -20*90

Inven731 < Inven73 < Inven7: -18*90

Inven732 < Inven73 < Inven7: -16*150

Inven811 < Inven81 < Inven8: -25*90

Inven812 < Inven81 < Inven8: -24*90

Inven813 < Inven81 < Inven8: -23*90

Inven82 < Inven8: -20*90

Inven831 < Inven83 < Inven8: -18*90

Inven832 < Inven83 < Inven8: -16*120

The three transaction sub-equations are respectively:

Inventory (1): -10*150 + Inventory (1): -50*75 + Inventory (1): -25*150 +

Inventory (1): -35*150 + Inventory (1): -12*150 + Inventory (1): -15*150 +

Inventory (1): -6.5*180 + Inventory (1): -12.5*150 + Inventory (1): -18*120 = Cost of goods manufactured (5): -23505

Inventory (1): -16*150 + Inventory (1): -36*60 + Inventory (1): -31*15 + Inventory (1): -22*100 + Inventory (1): -20*90 + Inventory (1): -18*90 + Inventory (1): -16*150 + Inventory (1): -25*90 + Inventory (1): -24*90 = Cost of goods manufactured (5): -17455

Inventory (1): -23*90 + Inventory (1): -20*90 + Inventory (1): -18*90 + Inventory (1): -16*120 = Cost of goods manufactured (5): -7410

- On January 6, 2016, the Proprietorship1 sells the Food113 $12*4 (cost: -$6*4) and the Food 322 $30*2 (cost: -$13*2) to A3 (SIN: 909876503) for cash $108. The multi-subaccount name of the Cash account is:

  909876503-c-customers < Cash receipts from customers < Operating activities

- On January 10, 2016, the Proprietorship1 sells the Food214 $11*4 (cost: -$5.5*4) and the Food321 $27*2 (cost: -$12*2) to A5 (SIN: 909876505) for cash $98. The multi-subaccount name of the Cash account is:

  909876505-c-customers < Cash receipts from customers < Operating activities

- On January 10, 2016, the Proprietorship1 sells the Food112 $11*4 (cost: -$5.5*4) and the Food23 $16*3 (cost: -$7.5*3) to A6 (SIN: 909876506) for cash $92. The multi-subaccount name of the Cash account is:

  909876506-c-customers < Cash receipts from customers < Operating activities

- On January 13, 2016, the Proprietorship1 pays -$150 cash to the Company3 (phone number: 123456082) with the General ID 2. The multi-subaccount name of the Cash account and transaction sub-equation respectively are:

  88-654308-t-supplies < Cash payments for operating expenses < Operating activities

  Cash (1): -150 = Account payable (2): -150

- On January 13, 2016, the Proprietorship1 sells the Food311: $20*1 (cost: -$8.5*1) to A15 (SIN: 909876515) for cash $20. The multi-subaccount name of the Cash account is:

  909876515-c-customers < Cash receipts from customers < Operating activities

- On January 13, 2016, the Proprietorship1 sells the Food221 $12*8 (cost: -$6*8) and the Food312 $24*4 (cost: -$11*4) to A16 (SIN: 909876516) for cash $192. The multi-subaccount name of the Cash account is:

  909876516-c-customers < Cash receipts from customers < Operating activities

- On January 16, 2016, the Proprietorship1 sells the Food321 $27*1 (cost: -$12*1) and the Food322 $30*1 (cost: -$13*1) to A8 (SIN: 909876508) for cash $57. The multi-subaccount name of the Cash account is:

  909876508-c-customers < Cash receipts from customers < Operating activities

- On January 16, 2016, the Proprietorship1 sells the Food311 $20*1 (cost: -$8.5*1) and the Food312 $24*1 (cost: -$11*1) to A17 (SIN: 909876517) for cash $44. The multi-subaccount name of the Cash account is:

  909876517-c-customers < Cash receipts from customers < Operating activities

- On January 18, 2016, the Proprietorship1 sells the Food312 $24*1 (cost: -$11*1) and the Food321 $27*1 (cost: -$12*1) to A20 (SIN: 909876520) for cash $51. The multi-subaccount name of the Cash account is:

  909876520-c-customers < Cash receipts from customers < Operating activities

- On January 18, 2016, the Proprietorship1 pays -$153.87 cash to A22 (SIN: 909876522) for the Travelling expenses (travel allowance) $105.87 and the Other expenses (meals: food514: $11*2 + food613: $26*1) $48. The multi-subaccount name of the Cash account and the transaction sub-equation respectively are:

  909876522-n-operating expenses < Cash payments for operating expenses < Operating activities

  Cash (1): -153.87 = Travelling expenses (5): -105.87 + other expenses (5): -48

- On January 19, 2016, the Proprietorship1 sells the Food321 $27*1 (cost: -$12*1) and

the Food322 $30*1 (cost: -$13*1) to A25 (SIN: 909876525) for cash $57. The multi-subaccount name of the Cash account is:

909876525-c-customers < Cash receipts from customers < Operating activities

- On January 25, 2016, the Proprietorship1 sells the Food311 $20*2 (cost: -$8.5*2) and the Food322 $30*2 (cost: -$13*2) to A9 (SIN: 909876509) for cash $100. The multi-subaccount name of the Cash account is:

909876509-c-customers < Cash receipts from customers < Operating activities

- On January 26, 2016, the Proprietorship1 receives $1,300 cash from the Company3 (phone number: 123456782) with the General ID 2. The multi-subaccount name of the Cash account is:

88-654308-c-customers < Cash receipts from customers < Operating activities

- On January 27, 2016, the Proprietorship1 pays -$250 cash to the Company2 (phone number: 123456083) with the General ID 2. The multi-subaccount name of the Cash account is:

88-654307-t-suppliers < Cash payments to suppliers < Operating activities

- On January 27, 2016, the Proprietorship1 sells the Food321 $27*1 (cost: -$12*1) and the Food322 $30*1 (cost: -$13*1) to A10 (SIN: 909876510) for cash $57. The multi-subaccount name of the Cash account is:

909876510-c-customers < Cash receipts from customers < Operating activities

- On January 28, 2016, the Proprietorship1 sells the Food312 $24*6 (cost: -$11*6) to A18 (SIN: 909876518) for cash $144. The multi-subaccount name of the Cash account is:

909876518-c-customers < Cash receipts from customers < Operating activities

- On January 28, 2016, the Proprietorship1 sells the Food212 $9*2 (cost: -$4.5*2) and the Food312 $24*1 (cost: -$11*1) to A21 (SIN: 909876521) for cash $42. The multi-subaccount name of the Cash account is:

909876521-c-customers < Cash receipts from customers < Operating activities

- On January 28, 2016, the Proprietorship1 sells the Food213 $10*2 (cost: -$5*2) and

the Food312 $24*1 (cost: -$11*1) to A23 (SIN: 909876523) for cash $44. The multi-subaccount name of the Cash account is:

909876523-c-customers < Cash receipts from customers < Operating activities

- On January 30, 2016, the Proprietorship1 receives $500 cash from the Company2 (phone number: 123456783) with the General ID 2. The multi-subaccount name of the Cash account is:

88-654307-c-customers < Cash receipts from customers < Operating activities

- On January 30, 2016, the Proprietorship1 pays $145.54 cash to A23 (SIN: 909876523) for the Travelling expenses (travel allowance) $101.54 and the Other expenses (meals: Food213: $10*2 + food312: $24*1) $44.

- On January 31, 2016, the Proprietorship1 receives $2,040 cash from the Company1 (phone number: 123456784) with the General ID 2. The multi-subaccount name of the Cash account is:

88-654306-c-customers < Cash receipts from customers < Operating activities

- On January 31, 2016, the Proprietorship1 pays two employees' salary expenses for cash -$5,670. The two multi-subaccount names of the Cash account and the transaction sub-equation respectively are:

909876522-t-salary < Cash payments for operating expenses < Operating activities

909876523-t-CGM < Cash payments for operating expenses < Operating activities

Cash (1): -2870 + Cash (1): -2800 = Salary expenses (5): -2870 + Cost of goods manufactured (5): -2800

- On January 31, 2016, the Proprietorship1 sells the following inventories -$5,200 for sales $10,400 to A12A20 (SIN: 909876528), who uses his (or her) father A12's (or mother A12's) secondary card of the Business Bank1, for cash $10,400.

Food111 < Food11 < Food1: -5*130

Food113 < Food11 < Food1: -6*130

Food121 < Food12 < Food1: -6.5*130

Food122 < Food12 < Food1: -7*130

Food211 < Food21 < Food2: -4*130

Food213 < Food21 < Food2: -5*130

Food222 < Food22 < Food2: -6.5*130

The multi-subaccount name of the Cash account is:

  909876512-c-customers < Cash receipts from customers < Operating activities

- On January 31, 2016, the Proprietorship1 sells the following inventories -$6,890 for sales $14,560 to A1 (SIN: 909876501) for cash $14,560.

Food112 < Food11 < Food1: -5.5*130

Food113 < Food11 < Food1: -6*130

Food121 < Food12 < Food1: -6.5*130

Food122 < Food12 < Food1: -7*130

Food123 < Food12 < Food1: -7.5*130

Food311 < Food31 < Food3: -8.5*130

Food321 < Food32 < Food3: -12*130

The multi-subaccount name of the Cash account is:

  909876501-c-customers < Cash receipts from customers < Operating activities

- On January 31, 2016, the Proprietorship1 sells the following inventories -$6,370 for sales $13,000 to A2 (SIN: 909876502) for cash $13,000.

Food112 < Food11 < Food1: -5.5*130

Food113 < Food11 < Food1: -6*130

Food121 < Food12 < Food1: -6.5*130

Food122 < Food12 < Food1: -7*130

Food123 < Food12 < Food1: -7.5*130

Food214 < Food21 < Food2: -5.5*130

Food312 < Food31 < Food3: -11*130

The multi-subaccount name of the Cash account is:

  909876502-c-customers < Cash receipts from customers < Operating activities

- On January 31, 2016, the Proprietorship1 sells the following inventories -$6,305 for sales $13,130 to A3 (SIN: 909876503) for cash $13,130.

  Food111 < Food11 < Food1: -5*130

  Food112 < Food11 < Food1: -5.5*130

  Food113 < Food11 < Food1: -6*130

  Food221 < Food22 < Food2: -6*130

  Food222 < Food22 < Food2: -6.5*130

  Food23 < Food2: -7.5*130

  Food321 < Food32 < Food3: -12*130

  The multi-subaccount name of the Cash account is:

  909876503-c-customers < Cash receipts from customers < Operating activities

- On January 31, 2016, the Proprietorship1 sells the following inventories -$6,825 for sales $14,430 to A4 (SIN: 909876504) for cash $14,430.

  Food111 < Food11 < Food1: -5*130

  Food113 < Food11 < Food1: -6*130

  Food121 < Food12 < Food1: -6.5*130

  Food122 < Food12 < Food1: -7*130

  Food123 < Food12 < Food1: -7.5*130

  Food311 < Food31 < Food3: -8.5*130

  Food321 < Food32 < Food3: -12*130

  The multi-subaccount name of the Cash account is:

  909876504-c-customers < Cash receipts from customers < Operating activities

- On January 31, 2016, the Proprietorship1 sells the following inventories -$6,760 for sales $14,170 to A5 (SIN: 909876505) for cash $14,170.

  Food112 < Food11 < Food1: -5.5*130

  Food113 < Food11 < Food1: -6*130

  Food121 < Food12 < Food1: -6.5*130

  Food122 < Food12 < Food1: -7*130

  Food123 < Food12 < Food1: -7.5*130

Food311 < Food31 < Food3: -8.5*130

Food312 < Food31 < Food3: -11*130

The multi-subaccount name of the Cash account is:

909876505-c-customers < Cash receipts from customers < Operating activities

- On January 31, 2016, the Proprietorship1 sells the following inventories -$6,045 for sales $12,610 to A6 (SIN: 909876506) for cash $12,610.

Food111 < Food11 < Food1: -5*130

Food113 < Food11 < Food1: -6*130

Food121 < Food12 < Food1: -6.5*130

Food122 < Food12 < Food1: -7*130

Food211 < Food21 < Food2: -4*130

Food213 < Food21 < Food2: -5*130

Food322 < Food32 < Food3: -13*130

The multi-subaccount name of the Cash account is:

909876506-c-customers < Cash receipts from customers < Operating activities

- On January 31, 2016, the Proprietorship1 sells the following inventories -$5,930 for sales $12,400 to A7 (SIN: 909876507) for cash $12,400.

Food112 < Food11 < Food1: -5.5*130

Food113 < Food11 < Food1: -6*130

Food121 < Food12 < Food1: -6.5*130

Food122 < Food12 < Food1: -7*130

Food123 < Food12 < Food1: -7.5*130

Food311 < Food31 < Food3: -8.5*130

Food321 < Food32 < Food3: -12*50

The multi-subaccount name of the Cash account is:

909876507-c-customers < Cash receipts from customers < Operating activities

- On January 31, 2016, the Proprietorship1 sells the following inventories -$6,305 for sales $13,000 to A8 (SIN: 909876508) for cash $13,000.

Food112 < Food11 < Food1: -5.5*130

Food113 < Food11 < Food1: -6*130

Food121 < Food12 < Food1: -6.5*130

Food122 < Food12 < Food1: -7*130

Food123 < Food12 < Food1: -7.5*130

Food211 < Food21 < Food2: -4*130

Food321 < Food32 < Food3: -12*130

The multi-subaccount name of the Cash account is:

909876508-c-customers < Cash receipts from customers < Operating activities

- On January 31, 2016, the Proprietorship1 sells the following inventories -$8,385 for sales $18,460 to A9 (SIN: 909876509) for cash $18,460.

Food221 < Food22 < Food2: -6*130

Food222 < Food22 < Food2: -6.5*130

Food23 < Food2: -7.5*130

Food311 < Food31 < Food3: -8.5*130

Food312 < Food31 < Food3: -11*130

Food321 < Food32 < Food3: -12*130

Food322 < Food32 < Food3: -13*130

The multi-subaccount name of the Cash account is:

909876509-c-customers < Cash receipts from customers < Operating activities

- On January 31, 2016, the Proprietorship1 sells the following inventories -$7,345 for sales $13,900 to A10 (SIN: 909876510) for cash $13,900.

Food221 < Food22 < Food2: -6*130

Food222 < Food22 < Food2: -6.5*130

Food23 < Food2: -7.5*130

Food311 < Food31 < Food3: -8.5*130

Food312 < Food31 < Food3: -11*130

Food321 < Food32 < Food3: -12*50

Food322 < Food32 < Food3: -13*50

The multi-subaccount name of the Cash account is:

909876510-c-customers < Cash receipts from customers < Operating activities

- On January 31, 2016, the Proprietorship1 sells the following inventories -$6,825 for sales $14,430 to A11 (SIN: 909876511) for cash $14,430.

  Food111 < Food11 < Food1: -5*130

  Food113 < Food11 < Food1: -6*130

  Food121 < Food12 < Food1: -6.5*130

  Food122 < Food12 < Food1: -7*130

  Food123 < Food12 < Food1: -7.5*130

  Food311 < Food31 < Food3: -8.5*130

  Food321 < Food32 < Food3: -12*130

  The multi-subaccount name of the Cash account is:

  909876511-c-customers < Cash receipts from customers < Operating activities

- On January 31, 2016, the Proprietorship1 sells the following inventories -$6,890 for sales $14,560 to A12 (SIN: 909876512) for cash $14,560.

  Food112 < Food11 < Food1: -5.5*130

  Food113 < Food11 < Food1: -6*130

  Food121 < Food12 < Food1: -6.5*130

  Food122 < Food12 < Food1: -7*130

  Food123 < Food12 < Food1: -7.5*130

  Food311 < Food31 < Food3: -8.5*130

  Food321 < Food32 < Food3: -12*130

  The multi-subaccount name of the Cash account is:

  909876512-c-customers < Cash receipts from customers < Operating activities

- On January 31, 2016, the Proprietorship1 sells the following inventories -$8,385 for sales $18,460 to A13 (SIN: 909876513) for cash $18,460.

  Food221 < Food22 < Food2: -6*130

  Food222 < Food22 < Food2: -6.5*130

  Food23 < Food2: -7.5*130

  Food311 < Food31 < Food3: -8.5*130

Food312 < Food31 < Food3: -11*130

Food321 < Food32 < Food3: -12*130

Food322 < Food32 < Food3: -13*130

The multi-subaccount name of the Cash account is:

909876513-c-customers < Cash receipts from customers < Operating activities

- On February 1, 2016, the Proprietorship1 purchases one Car3 $38,000 from the Company1 (phone number: 123456084) for cash -$28,000 and other on credit. The multi-subaccount name of the Cash account and transaction sub-equation respectively are:

88-654306-t-machinery < Cash payments for machinery < Operating activities

Cash (1): -28000 + Vehicle (1): 38000 = Account payable (2): 10000

- On February 17, 2016, the Proprietorship1 sells the Food23 $16*10 (cost: -$7.5*10) and the Food 322 $30*5 (cost: -$13*5) to A13 (SIN: 909876513) for cash $310. The multi-subaccount name of the Cash account is:

909876513-c-customers < Cash receipts from customers < Operating activities

- On February 20, 2016, the Proprietorship1 receives $400 cash from the Proprietorship2 (phone number: 123456780) with the General ID 2. The multi-subaccount name of the Cash account is:

88-654310-c-customers < Cash receipts from customers < Operating activities

- On February 21, 2016, the Proprietorship1 pays -$300 cash to the Proprietorship2 (phone number: 123456080) with the General ID 2. The multi-subaccount name of the Cash account is:

88-654310-t-suppliers < Cash payments to suppliers < Operating activities

- On February 23, 2016, the Proprietorship1 sells the Food23 $16*4 (cost: -$7.5*4) and the Food322 $30*2 (cost: -$13*2) to A19 (SIN: 909876519) for cash $124. The multi-subaccount name of the Cash account is:

909876519-c-customers < Cash receipts from customers < Operating activities

- On February 24, 2016, the Proprietorship1 sells the Food122 $ 14*4 (cost: -$7*4)

and the Food321 \$27*2 (cost: -\$12*2) to A5 (SIN: 909876505) for cash \$110. The multi-subaccount name of the Cash account is:

909876505-c-customers < Cash receipts from customers < Operating activities

- On February 25, 2016, the Proprietorship1 sells the Food123 \$15*3 (cost: -\$7.5*3) and the Food321 \$27*2 (cost: -\$12*2) to A3 (SIN: 909876503) for cash \$99. The multi-subaccount name of the Cash account is:

909876503-c-customers < Cash receipts from customers < Operating activities

- On February 28, 2016, the Proprietorship1 sells the Food312 \$24*2 (cost: -\$11*2) and the Food321 \$27*2 (cost: -\$12*2) to A18 (SIN: 909876518) for cash \$102. The multi-subaccount name of the Cash account is:

909876518-c-customers < Cash receipts from customers < Operating activities

- On February 28, 2016, the Proprietorship1 sells the Food312 \$24*2 (cost: -\$11*2) and the Food321 \$27*2 (cost: -\$12*2) to A21 (SIN: 909876521) for cash \$102. The multi-subaccount name of the Cash account is:

909876521-c-customers < Cash receipts from customers < Operating activities

- On February 28, 2016, the Proprietorship1 pays two employees' salary expenses for cash -\$5,670. The two multi-subaccount names of the Cash account and the transaction sub-equation respectively are:

909876522-t-salary < Cash payments for operating expenses < Operating activities

909876523-t-CGM < Cash payments for operating expenses < Operating activities

Cash (1): -2870 + Cash (1): -2800 = Salary expenses (5): -2870 + Cost of goods manufactured (5): -2800

- On March 6, 2016, the Proprietorship1 pays -\$1,000 cash to the Company1 (phone number: 123456084) with the General ID 2. The multi-subaccount name of the Cash account is:

88-654306-t-suppliers < Cash payments to suppliers < Operating activities

- On March 7, 2016, the Proprietorship1 sells the Food312 $24*2 (cost: -$11*2) and the Food322 $30*1 (cost: -$13*1) to A25 (SIN: 909876525) for cash $78. The multi-subaccount name of the Cash account is:

  909876525-c-customers < Cash receipts from customers < Operating activities

- On March 10, 2016, the Proprietorship1 sells the Food214 $11*3 (cost: -$5.5*3) and the Food322 $30*3 (cost: -$13*3) to A6 (SIN: 909876506) for cash $123. The multi-subaccount name of the Cash account is:

  909876506-c-customers < Cash receipts from customers < Operating activities

- On March 11, 2016, the Proprietorship1 sells the Food111 $10*2 (cost: -$5*2) and the Food322 $30*1 (cost: -$13*1) to A11 (SIN: 909876511) for cash $50. The multi-subaccount name of the Cash account is:

  909876511-c-customers < Cash receipts from customers < Operating activities

- On March 19, 2016, the Proprietorship1 sells the Food112 $11*2 (cost: -$5.5*2), the Food213 $10*3 (cost: -$5*3), and the Food 322 $30*4 (cost: -$13*4) to A4 (SIN: 909876504) for cash $172. The multi-subaccount name of the Cash account is:

  909876504-c-customers < Cash receipts from customers < Operating activities

- On March 23, 2016, the Proprietorship1 pays -$159.45 cash to A22 (SIN: 909876522) for the Travelling expenses (travel allowance) $101.45 and the Other expenses (meals: food44: $15*2 + food622: $28*1) $58.

- On March 26, 2016, the Proprietorship1 sells the Food111 $10*1 (cost: -$5*1), the Food214 $11*1 (cost: -$5.5*1), the Food312 $24*1 (cost: -$11*1), and the Food 321 $27*1 (cost: -$12*1) to A2 (SIN: 909876502) for cash $72. The multi-subaccount name of the Cash account is:

  909876502-c-customers < Cash receipts from customers < Operating activities

- On March 27, 2016, the Proprietorship1 sells the Food312 $24*1 (cost: -$11*1) and the Food321 $27*1 (cost: -$12*1) to A8 (SIN: 909876508) for cash $51. The multi-subaccount name of the Cash account is:

  909876508-c-customers < Cash receipts from customers < Operating activities

- On March 31, 2016, the Proprietorship1 pays two employees' salary expenses for cash -$5,670 repeatedly.

- On April 13, 2016, the Proprietorship1 sells the Food222 $13*3 (cost: -$6.5*3) and the Food322 $30*1 (cost: -$13*1) to A11 (SIN: 909876511) for cash $69. The multi-subaccount name of the Cash account is:

  909876511-c-customers < Cash receipts from customers < Operating activities

- On April 22, 2016, the Proprietorship1 sells the Food312 $24*2 (cost: -$11*2) and the Food321 $27*1 (cost: -$12*1) to A24 (SIN: 909876524) for cash $75. The multi-subaccount name of the Cash account is:

  909876524-c-customers < Cash receipts from customers < Operating activities

- On April 24, 2016, the Proprietorship1 sells the Food312 $24*3 (cost: -$11*3), the Food321 $27*2 (cost: -$12*2), and the Food322 $30*1 (cost: -$13*1) to A16 (SIN: 909876516) for cash $156. The multi-subaccount name of the Cash account is:

  909876516-c-customers < Cash receipts from customers < Operating activities

- On April 24, 2016, the Proprietorship1 sells the Food312 $24*2 (cost: -$11*2) and the Food322 $30*1 (cost: -$13*1) to A19 (SIN: 909876519) for cash $78. The multi-subaccount name of the Cash account is:

  909876519-c-customers < Cash receipts from customers < Operating activities

- On April 27, 2016, the Proprietorship1 sells the Food312 $24*2 (cost: -$11*2) and the Food321 $27*2 (cost: -$12*2) to A7 (SIN: 909876507) for cash $102. The multi-subaccount name of the Cash account is:

  909876507-c-customers < Cash receipts from customers < Operating activities

- On April 29, 2016, the Proprietorship1 purchases one Truck2 part2 $7,200 from the Company2 for cash -$5,000 and other on credit. The multi-subaccount name of the Cash account is:

  88-654307-t-supplies < Cash payments for operating expenses < Operating activities

- On April 30, 2016, the Proprietorship1 pays two employees' salary expenses for cash -$5,670 repeatedly.

- On April 30, 2016, the Proprietorship1 has completed all products of the Working-in-process inventory account. If the all general parts have just been consumed and the supplies has the rest $40, the rest supplies must be returned to the Supplies account from the Cost of goods manufactured account. The transaction sub-equation is:

Supplies (1): 40 = Cost of goods manufactured (5): 40

- On April 30, 2016, the Proprietorship1 transfers the balance of the Cost of goods manufactured account to the Working-in-process inventory account. The Cost of goods manufactured account has three subaccounts of the "Supplies expenses", the "909876523-salary < Product department-salary < Salary expenses", and the "General parts expenses". Their balances are -$860, -$11,200, and -$54,720 (-$48,370 - $6,350) respectively. Here, the balance of the subaccount "General parts expenses" will be divided to three parts which are used in three transaction sub-equations respectively. The three transaction sub-equations are:

Working-in-process inventory (1): 3*600 + Working-in-process inventory (1): 16*600 + Working-in-process inventory (1): 5*600 + Working-in-process inventory (1): 14*600 + Working-in-process inventory (1): 3*600 + Working-in-process inventory (1): 6*600 + Working-in-process inventory (1): 2.6*600 = Cost of goods manufactured (5): 860 + Cost of goods manufactured (5): 11200 + Cost of goods manufactured (5): 17700

Working-in-process inventory (1): 3*600 + Working-in-process inventory (1): 3*600 + Working-in-process inventory (1): 3.6*600 + Working-in-process inventory (1): 4*600 + Working-in-process inventory (1): 4*600 + Working-in-process inventory (1): 2*600 + Working-in-process inventory (1): 2.5*600 + Working-in-process inventory (1): 2.8*600 = Cost of goods manufactured (5): 14940

Working-in-process inventory (1): 3*600 + Working-in-process inventory (1):

3*600 + Working-in-process inventory (1): 3.4*600 + Working-in-process inventory (1): 4*600 + Working-in-process inventory (1): 4.4*600 + Working-in-process inventory (1): 6*600 + Working-in-process inventory (1): 6*600 + Working-in-process inventory (1): 7*600 = Cost of goods manufactured (5): 22080

- On April 30, 2016, the Proprietorship1 transfers the balance of the Working-in-process inventory account to the Inventory account. The five transaction sub-equations respectively are:

Working-in-process inventory (1): -6*600 + Working-in-process inventory (1): -30*600 + Working-in-process inventory (1): -10*600 + Working-in-process inventory (1): -27*600 + Working-in-process inventory (1): -6*600 + Inventory (1): 30*600 + Inventory (1): 10*600 + Inventory (1): 27*600 + Inventory (1): 6*600 = 0

Working-in-process inventory (1): -12*600 + Working-in-process inventory (1): -5*600 + Working-in-process inventory (1): -5.5*600 + Working-in-process inventory (1): -6*600 + Working-in-process inventory (1): -6.5*600 + Inventory (1): 12*600 + Inventory (1): 5*600 + Inventory (1): 5.5*600 + Inventory (1): 6*600 + Inventory (1): 6.5*600 = 0

Working-in-process inventory (1): -7*600 + Working-in-process inventory (1): -7.5*600 + Working-in-process inventory (1): -4*600 + Working-in-process inventory (1): -4.5*600 + Working-in-process inventory (1): -5*600 + Inventory (1): 7*600 + Inventory (1): 7.5*600 + Inventory (1): 4*600 + Inventory (1): 4.5*600 + Inventory (1): 5*600 = 0

Working-in-process inventory (1): -5.5*600 + Working-in-process inventory (1): -6*600 + Working-in-process inventory (1): -6.5*600 + Working-in-process inventory (1): -7.5*600 + Working-in-process inventory (1): -8.5*600 + Inventory

(1): 5.5*600 + Inventory (1): 6*600 + Inventory (1): 6.5*600 + Inventory (1): 7.5*600 + Inventory (1): 8.5*600 = 0

Working-in-process inventory (1): -11*600 + Working-in-process inventory (1): -12*600 + Working-in-process inventory (1): -13*600 + Inventory (1): 11*600 + Inventory (1): 12*600 + Inventory (1): 13*600 = 0

- On May 1, 2016, the Proprietorship 1 plans to produce the following products in the Figure 3.9-1.

Order	Product (the Lowest-level Subaccount) Names	Multi-subaccount Names	Costs	Amount
1	Food111	Food111 < Food11 < Food1	5.00	1200
2	Food112	Food112 < Food11 < Food1	5.50	1200
3	Food113	Food113 < Food11 < Food1	6.00	1200
4	Food121	Food121 < Food12 < Food1	6.50	1200
5	Food122	Food122 < Food12 < Food1	7.00	1200
6	Food123	Food123 < Food12 < Food1	7.50	1200
7	Food211	Food211 < Food21 < Food2	4.00	1200
8	Food212	Food212 < Food21 < Food2	4.50	1200
9	Food213	Food213 < Food21 < Food2	5.00	1200
10	Food214	Food214 < Food21 < Food2	5.50	1200
11	Food221	Food221 < Food22 < Food2	6.00	1200
12	Food222	Food222 < Food22 < Food2	6.50	1200
13	Food23	Food23 < Food2	7.50	1200
14	Food311	Food311 < Food31 < Food3	8.50	1200
15	Food312	Food312 < Food31 < Food3	11.00	1200
16	Food321	Food321 < Food32 < Food3	12.00	1200
17	Food322	Food322 < Food32 < Food3	13.00	1200

Figure 3.9-1   Producing Plan Table

Therefore, the Proprietorship1 purchases the supplies $1,500 ($14*50 + $16*50) from the Proprietorship2 (phone number: 123456080) for cash -$800 and other on credit. The multi-subaccount name of the Cash account and transaction sub-equation respectively are:

88-654310-t-supplies < Cash payments for operating expenses < Operating activities

Cash (1): -800 + Supplies (1): 1500 = Account payable (2): 700

- On May 1, 2016, the Proprietorship1 purchases the following inventories $8,255 from the Proprietorship2 (phone number: 123456080) for -$5,000 cash and other on credit.

Inven411 < Inven41 < Inven4: 5*130

Inven412 < Inven41 < Inven4: 18.5*130

TTTCU parts < TTT parts < Inven4: 20*130

RRRHJK parts < Inven4: 20*130

The multi-subaccount name of the Cash account and four transaction sub-equations respectively are:

88-654310-t-suppliers < Cash payments to suppliers < Operating activities

Cash (1): -5000 + Inventory (1): 5*130 + Inventory (1): 18.5*130 + Inventory (1): 20*130 + Inventory (1): 20*130 = Account Payable (2): 3255

- On May 1, 2016, the Proprietorship1 sells the following inventories -$13,650 for sales $23,250 to the Company1 (phone number: 123456784) for cash $3,250 and other on credit.

Inven31 < Inven3: -6*150

Inven32 < Inven3: -30*150

Inven331 < Inven33 < Inven3: -10*150

Inven332 < Inven33 < Inven3: -27*150

HGFCVB parts < QASXC parts < Inven3: -6*150

PPGHUP parts < ASDUP parts < Inven3: -12*150

The multi-subaccount name of the Cash account and the transaction sub-equation respectively are:

88-654306-c-customers < Cash receipts from customers < Operating activities

Cash (1): 3250 + Account receivable (1): 20,000 + Inventory (1): -6*150 + Inventory (1): -30*150 + Inventory (1): -10*150 + Inventory (1): -27*150 + Inventory (1): -12*150 + Inventory (1): = Sales (4): 23,250 + Cost of goods sold (5): -13650

- On May 1, 2016, the Proprietorship1 sells the following inventories -$13,650 for sales $23,250 to the Proprietorship2 (phone number: 123456780) for cash $9,000 and other on credit.

Inven31 < Inven3: -6*150

Inven32 < Inven3: -30*150

Inven331 < Inven33 < Inven3: -10*150

Inven332 < Inven33 < Inven3: -27*150

HGFCVB parts < QASXC parts < Inven3: -6*150

PPGHUP parts < ASDUP parts < Inven3: -12*150

The multi-subaccount name of the Cash account and the transaction sub-equation respectively are:

88-654310-c-customers < Cash receipts from customers < Operating activities

Cash (1): 9000 + Account receivable (1): 14,250 + Inventory (1): -6*150 + Inventory (1): -30*150 + Inventory (1): -10*150 + Inventory (1): -27*150 + Inventory (1): -12*150 + Inventory (1): = Sales (4): 23,250 + Cost of goods sold (5): -13650

- On May 1, 2016, the Proprietorship1 sells the Food213 $10*3 (cost: -$5*3) and the Food311 $20*3 (cost: -$8.5*3) to A18 (SIN: 909876518) for cash $90. The multi-subaccount name of the Cash account is:

909876518-c-customers < Cash receipts from customers < Operating activities

- On May 1, 2016, the Proprietorship1 sells the Food213 $10*3 (cost: -$5*3) and the

Food311 $20*1 (cost: -$8.5*1) to A21 (SIN: 909876521) for cash $50. The multi-subaccount name of the Cash account is:

909876521-c-customers < Cash receipts from customers < Operating activities

- On May 2, 2016, the Proprietorship1 transfers the supplies $1,500 to the Cost of goods manufactured account to satisfy the need of producing. The transaction sub-equation is:

  Supplies (1): -1500 = Cost of goods manufactured (5): -1500

- On May 2, 2016, the Proprietorship1 transfers the following inventories -$8,255 to the Cost of goods manufactured account to satisfy the need of producing.
  Inven411 < Inven41 < Inven4: -5*130
  Inven412 < Inven41 < Inven4: -18.5*130
  TTTCU parts < TTT parts < Inven4: -20*130
  RRRHJK parts < Inven4: -20*130
  The transaction sub-equations is:

  Inventory (1): -5*130 + Inventory (1): -18.5*130 + Inventory (1): -20*130 + Inventory (1): -20*130 = Cost of goods manufactured (5): -8255

- On May 2, 2016, the Proprietorship1 transfers the following inventories -$113,098 to the Cost of goods manufactured account to satisfy the need of producing.
  Inven51 < Inven5: -10*350
  Inven52 < Inven5: -50*175
  Inven531 < Inven53 < Inven5: -25*350
  Inven532 < Inven53 < Inven5: -35*350
  Inven541 < Inven54 < Inven5: -12*350
  Inven542 < Inven54 < Inven5: -15*350
  Inven611 < Inven61 < Inven6: -6.5*420
  Inven612 < Inven61 < Inven6: -12.5*350

Inven621 < Inven62 < Inven6: -18*280

Inven63 < Inven6: -16*350

Inven711 < Inven71 < Inven7: -36*140

Inven712 < Inven71 < Inven7: -31*35

Inven721 < Inven72 < Inven7: -22*244

Inven722 < Inven72 < Inven7: -20*210

Inven731 < Inven73 < Inven7: -18*210

Inven732 < Inven73 < Inven7: -16*350

Inven811 < Inven81 < Inven8: -25*210

Inven812 < Inven81 < Inven8: -24*210

Inven813 < Inven81 < Inven8: -23*210

Inven82 < Inven8: -20*210

Inven831 < Inven83 < Inven8: -18*210

Inven832 < Inven83 < Inven8: -16*280

The three transaction sub-equations are respectively:

Inventory (1): -10*350 + Inventory (1): -50*175 + Inventory (1): -25*350 + Inventory (1): -35*350 + Inventory (1): -12*350 + Inventory (1): -15*350 + Inventory (1): -6.5*420 + Inventory (1): -12.5*350 + Inventory (1): 18*280 = Cost of goods manufactured (5): -54845

Inventory (1): -16*350 + Inventory (1): -36*140 + Inventory (1): -31*35 + Inventory (1): -22*244 + Inventory (1): -20*210 + Inventory (1): -18*210 + Inventory (1): -16*350 + Inventory (1): -25*210 + Inventory (1): -24*210 = Cost of goods manufactured (5): -40963

Inventory (1): -23*210 + Inventory (1): -20*210 + Inventory (1): -18*210 + Inventory (1): -16*280 = Cost of goods manufactured (5): -17290

- On May 12, 2016, the Proprietorship1 sells the Food222 $13*4 (cost: -$6.5*4) and the Food311 $20*3 (cost: -$8.5*3) to A9 (SIN: 909876509) for cash $112. The multi-subaccount name of the Cash account is:

909876509-c-customers < Cash receipts from customers < Operating activities

- On May 12, 2016, the Proprietorship1 sells the Food213 $10*3 (cost: -$5*3) and the Food311 $20*1 (cost: -$8.5*1) to A23 (SIN: 909876523) for cash $50. The multi-subaccount name of the Cash account is:

909876523-c-customers < Cash receipts from customers < Operating activities

- On May 13, 2016, the Proprietorship1 sells the Food121 $13*4 (cost: -$5.5*3) and the Food311 $20*3 (cost: -$8.5*3) to A6 (SIN: 909876506) for cash $112. The multi-subaccount name of the Cash account is:

909876506-c-customers < Cash receipts from customers < Operating activities

- On May 14, 2016, the Proprietorship1 pays -$166.23 cash to A23 (SIN: 909876523) for the Travelling expenses (travel allowance) $116.23 and the Other expenses (meals: food213: $10*3 + food311: $20*1) $50.

- On May 14, 2016, the Proprietorship1 sells the Food123 $15*3 (cost: -$7.5*3) and the Food311 $20*3 (cost: -$8.5*3) to A3 (SIN: 909876503) for cash $105. The multi-subaccount name of the Cash account is:

909876503-c-customers < Cash receipts from customers < Operating activities

- On May 20, 2016, the Proprietorship1 sells the Food121 $13*2 (cost: -$6.5*2) and the Food322 $30*1 (cost: -$13*1) to A11 (SIN: 909876511) for cash $56. The multi-subaccount name of the Cash account is:

909876511-c-customers < Cash receipts from customers < Operating activities

- On May 22, 2016, the Proprietorship1 sells the Food111 $10*10 (cost: -$5*10), the Food123 $15*10 (cost: -$7.5*10), the Food312 $24*3 (cost: -$11*3), and the Food321 $27*3 (cost: -$12*3) to A13 (SIN: 909876513) for cash $403. The multi-subaccount name of the Cash account is:

909876513-c-customers < Cash receipts from customers < Operating activities

- On May 22, 2016, the Proprietorship1 sells the Food111 $10*8 (cost: -$5*8), the Food312 $24*2 (cost: -$11*2), and the Food321 $27*1 (cost: -$12*1) to A16 (SIN:

909876516) for cash $155. The multi-subaccount name of the Cash account is:

909876516-c-customers < Cash receipts from customers < Operating activities

- On May 22, 2016, the Proprietorship1 sells the Food111 $10*6 (cost: -$5*6), the Food312 $24*2 (cost: -$11*2), and the Food322 $30*1 (cost: -$13*1) to A19 (SIN: 909876519) for cash $138. The multi-subaccount name of the Cash account is:

909876519-c-customers < Cash receipts from customers < Operating activities

- On May 24, 2016, the Proprietorship1 pays $176.95 cash to A22 (SIN: 909876522) for the Travelling expenses (travel allowance) $120.95 and the Other expenses (meals: food513: $10*3 + food621: $26*1) $56.

- On May 31, 2016, the Proprietorship1 pays two employees' salary expenses for cash $5,670 repeatedly.

- On June 14, 2016, the Proprietorship1 sells the Food23 $16*3 (cost: -$7.5*3) and the Food312 $24*2 (cost: -$11*2) to A9 (SIN: 909876509) for cash $96. The multi-subaccount name of the Cash account is:

909876509-c-customers < Cash receipts from customers < Operating activities

- On June 16, 2016, the Proprietorship1 receives cash $300 from the Company3 (phone number: 123456782) with the General ID 2. The multi-subaccount name of the Cash account is:

88-654308-c-customers < Cash receipts from customers < Operating activities

- On June 18, 2016, the Proprietorship1 sells the Food214 $11*5 (cost: -$5.5*5) and the Food321 $27*2 (cost: -$12*2) to A12 (SIN: 909876512) for cash $109. The multi-subaccount name of the Cash account is:

909876512-c-customers < Cash receipts from customers < Operating activities

- On June 20, 2016, the Proprietorship1 sells the Food112 $11*10 (cost: -$5.5*10), the Food211 $8*10 (cost: -$4*10), and the Food311 $20*6 (cost: -$8.5*6) to A13 (SIN: 909876513) for cash $310. The multi-subaccount name of the Cash account is:

909876513-c-customers < Cash receipts from customers < Operating activities

- On June 20, 2016, the Proprietorship1 sells the Food113 $12*5 (cost: -$6*5), the Food214 $11*5 (cost: -$5.5*2), and the Food312 $24*2 (cost: -$11*2) to A16 (SIN:

909876516) for cash $163. The multi-subaccount name of the Cash account is:

909876516-c-customers < Cash receipts from customers < Operating activities

- On June 21, 2016, the Proprietorship1 sells the Food113 $12*5 (cost: -$6*5) and the Food312 $24*2 (cost: -$11*2) to A19 (SIN: 909876519) for cash $108. The multi-subaccount name of the Cash account is:

909876519-c-customers < Cash receipts from customers < Operating activities

- On June 23, 2016, the Proprietorship1 pays -$157.37 cash to A22 (SIN: 909876522) for the Travelling expenses (travel allowance) $109.37 and the Other expenses (meals: food521: $12*2 + food612: $24*1) $48.

- On June 30, 2016, the Proprietorship1 pays two employees' salary expenses for cash -$5,670 repeatedly.

- On July 4, 2016, the Proprietorship1 pays -$55,000 cash to the Company3 (phone number: 123456082) with the General ID 16. The multi-subaccount name of the Cash account and transaction sub-equation respectively are:

88-654308-t-suppliers < Cash payments to suppliers < Operating activities

- On July 5, 2016, the Proprietorship1 sells the Food123 $15*6 (cost: -$7.5*6) and the Food322 $30*3 (cost: -$13*3) to A14 (SIN: 909876514) for cash $180. The multi-subaccount name of the Cash account is:

909876514-c-customers < Cash receipts from customers < Operating activities

- On July 16, 2016, the Proprietorship1 sells the Food211 $8*6 (cost: -$4*6) and the Food 23 $16*4 (cost: -$7.5*4) to A4 (SIN: 909876504) for cash $112. The multi-subaccount name of the Cash account is:

909876504-c-customers < Cash receipts from customers < Operating activities

- On July 21, 2016, the Proprietorship1 sells the Food222 $13*5 (cost: -$6.5*5) and the Food322 $30*2 (cost: -$13*2) to A12 (SIN: 909876512) for cash $125. The multi-subaccount name of the Cash account is:

909876512-c-customers < Cash receipts from customers < Operating activities

- On July 22, 2016, the Proprietorship1 sells the Food211 $8*10 (cost: -$4*10), the Food212 $9*10 (cost: -$4.5*10), the Food311 $20*3 (cost: -$8.5*3), and the

Food312 $24*3 (cost: -$11*3) to A13 (SIN: 909876513) for cash $302. The multi-subaccount name of the Cash account is:

909876513-c-customers < Cash receipts from customers < Operating activities

- On July 22, 2016, the Proprietorship1 sells the Food212 $9*5 (cost: -$4.5*5) and the Food311 $20*3 (cost: -$8.5*3) to A5 (SIN: 909876505) for cash $105. The multi-subaccount name of the Cash account is:

909876505-c-customers < Cash receipts from customers < Operating activities

- On July 25, 2016, the Proprietorship1 sells the Food212 $9*6 (cost: -$4.5*6), the Food311 $20*2 (cost: -$8.5*2), and the Food312 $24*1 (cost: -$11*1) to A16 (SIN: 909876516) for cash $118. The multi-subaccount name of the Cash account is:

909876516-c-customers < Cash receipts from customers < Operating activities

- On July 25, 2016, the Proprietorship1 sells the Food311 $20*2 (cost: -$8.5*2) and the Food312 $24*2 (cost: -$11*2) to A19 (SIN: 909876519) for cash $88. The multi-subaccount name of the Cash account is:

909876519-c-customers < Cash receipts from customers < Operating activities

- On July 25, 2016, the Proprietorship1 sells the Food311 $20*2 (cost: -$8.5*2) and the Food312 $24*1 (cost: -$11*1) to A23 (SIN: 909876523) for cash $64. The multi-subaccount name of the Cash account is:

909876523-c-customers < Cash receipts from customers < Operating activities

- On July 27, 2016, the Proprietorship1 pays $187.55 cash to A23 (SIN: 909876523) for the Travelling expenses (travel allowance) $123.55 and the Other expenses (meals: food311: $20*2 + food312: $24*1) $64.

- On July 31, 2016, the Proprietorship1 pays two employees' salary expenses for cash $5,670 repeatedly.

- On July 31, 2016, the Proprietorship1 sells the following inventories -$5,135 for sales $10,270 to A1A8 (SIN: 909876526), who uses his (or her) father A1's (or motherA1's) secondary card of the Business Bank2, for cash $10,270.

Food111 < Food11 < Food1: -5*130

Food112 < Food11 < Food1: -5.5*130

Food121 < Food12 < Food1: -6.5*130

Food122 < Food12 < Food1: -7*130

Food211 < Food21 < Food2: -4*130

Food213 < Food21 < Food2: -5*130

Food222 < Food22 < Food2: -6.5*130

The multi-subaccount name of the Cash account is:

  909876501-c-customers < Cash receipts from customers < Operating activities

- On July 31, 2016, the Proprietorship1 sells the following inventories -$8,385 for sales $18,460 to A14 (SIN: 909876514) for cash $18,460.

Food221 < Food22 < Food2: -6*130

Food222 < Food22 < Food2: -6.5*130

Food23 < Food2: -7.5*130

Food311 < Food31 < Food3: -8.5*130

Food312 < Food31 < Food3: -11*130

Food321 < Food32 < Food3: -12*130

Food322 < Food32 < Food3: -13*130

The multi-subaccount name of the Cash account is:

  909876514-c-customers < Cash receipts from customers < Operating activities

- On July 31, 2016, the Proprietorship1 sells the following inventories -$8,255 for sales $18,200 to A15 (SIN: 909876515) for cash $18,200.

Food111 < Food11 < Food1: -5*130

Food222 < Food22 < Food2: -6.5*130

Food23 < Food2: -7.5*130

Food311 < Food31 < Food3: -8.5*130

Food312 < Food31 < Food3: -11*130

Food321 < Food32 < Food3: -12*130

Food322 < Food32 < Food3: -13*130

The multi-subaccount name of the Cash account is:

  909876515-c-customers < Cash receipts from customers < Operating activities

- On July 31, 2016, the Proprietorship1 sells the following inventories -$8,515 for sales $18,720 to A16 (SIN: 909876516) for cash $18,720.

  Food122 < Food12 < Food1: -7*130

  Food222 < Food22 < Food2: -6.5*130

  Food23 < Food2: -7.5*130

  Food311 < Food31 < Food3: -8.5*130

  Food312 < Food31 < Food3: -11*130

  Food321 < Food32 < Food3: -12*130

  Food322 < Food32 < Food3: -13*130

  The multi-subaccount name of the Cash account is:

    909876516-c-customers < Cash receipts from customers < Operating activities

- On July 31, 2016, the Proprietorship1 sells the following inventories -$8,125 for sales $17,940 to A17 (SIN: 909876517) for cash $17,940.

  Food211 < Food21 < Food2: -4*130

  Food222 < Food22 < Food2: -6.5*130

  Food23 < Food2: -7.5*130

  Food311 < Food31 < Food3: -8.5*130

  Food312 < Food31 < Food3: -11*130

  Food321 < Food32 < Food3: -12*130

  Food322 < Food32 < Food3: -13*130

  The multi-subaccount name of the Cash account is:

    909876517-c-customers < Cash receipts from customers < Operating activities

- On July 31, 2016, the Proprietorship1 sells the following inventories -$8,385 for sales $18,460 to A18 (SIN: 909876518) for cash $18,460.

  Food113 < Food11 < Food1: -6*130

  Food222 < Food22 < Food2: -6.5*130

  Food23 < Food2: -7.5*130

  Food311 < Food31 < Food3: -8.5*130

  Food312 < Food31 < Food3: -11*130

Food321 < Food32 < Food3: -12*130

Food322 < Food32 < Food3: -13*130

The multi-subaccount name of the Cash account is:

909876518-c-customers < Cash receipts from customers < Operating activities

- On July 31, 2016, the Proprietorship1 sells the following inventories -$8,450 for sales $18,590 to A19 (SIN: 909876519) for cash $18,590.

Food121 < Food12 < Food1: -6.5*130

Food222 < Food22 < Food2: -6.5*130

Food23 < Food2: -7.5*130

Food311 < Food31 < Food3: -8.5*130

Food312 < Food31 < Food3: -11*130

Food321 < Food32 < Food3: -12*130

Food322 < Food32 < Food3: -13*130

The multi-subaccount name of the Cash account is:

909876519-c-customers < Cash receipts from customers < Operating activities

- On July 31, 2016, the Proprietorship1 sells the following inventories -$5,200 for sales $10,400 to A20 (SIN: 909876520) for cash $10,400.

Food121 < Food12 < Food1: -6.5*130

Food122 < Food12 < Food1: -7*130

Food123 < Food12 < Food1: -7.5*130

Food211 < Food21 < Food2: -4*130

Food212 < Food21 < Food2: -4.5*130

Food213 < Food21 < Food2: -5*130

Food214 < Food21 < Food2: -5.5*130

The multi-subaccount name of the Cash account is:

909876520-c-customers < Cash receipts from customers < Operating activities

- On July 31, 2016, the Proprietorship1 sells the following inventories -$5,330 for sales $10,660 to A21 (SIN: 909876521) for cash $10,660.

Food121 < Food12 < Food1: -6.5*130

Food122 < Food12 < Food1: -7*130

Food123 < Food12 < Food1: -7.5*130

Food211 < Food21 < Food2: -4*130

Food212 < Food21 < Food2: -4.5*130

Food213 < Food21 < Food2: -5*130

Food222 < Food22 < Food2: -6.5*130

The multi-subaccount name of the Cash account is:

909876521-c-customers < Cash receipts from customers < Operating activities

- On July 31, 2016, the Proprietorship1 sells the following inventories -$5,265 for sales $10,530 to A22 (SIN: 909876522) for cash $10,530.

Food121 < Food12 < Food1: -6.5*130

Food122 < Food12 < Food1: -7*130

Food123 < Food12 < Food1: -7.5*130

Food211 < Food21 < Food2: -4*130

Food212 < Food21 < Food2: -4.5*130

Food213 < Food21 < Food2: -5*130

Food221 < Food22 < Food2: -6*130

The multi-subaccount name of the Cash account is:

909876522-c-customers < Cash receipts from customers < Operating activities

- On July 31, 2016, the Proprietorship1 sells the following inventories -$5,460 for sales $11,050 to A23 (SIN: 909876523) for cash $11,050.

Food121 < Food12 < Food1: -6.5*130

Food122 < Food12 < Food1: -7*130

Food123 < Food12 < Food1: -7.5*130

Food211 < Food21 < Food2: -4*130

Food212 < Food21 < Food2: -4.5*130

Food213 < Food21 < Food2: -5*130

Food23 < Food2: -7.5*130

The multi-subaccount name of the Cash account is:

- On July 31, 2016, the Proprietorship1 sells the following inventories -$5,590 for sales $11,570 to A24 (SIN: 909876524) for cash $11,570.

  Food121 < Food12 < Food1: -6.5*130

  Food122 < Food12 < Food1: -7*130

  Food123 < Food12 < Food1: -7.5*130

  Food211 < Food21 < Food2: -4*130

  Food212 < Food21 < Food2: -4.5*130

  Food213 < Food21 < Food2: -5*130

  Food311 < Food31 < Food3: -8.5*130

  The multi-subaccount name of the Cash account is:

  909876524-c-customers < Cash receipts from customers < Operating activities

- On July 31, 2016, the Proprietorship1 sells the following inventories -$5,915 for sales $12,090 to A25 (SIN: 909876525) for cash $12,090.

  Food121 < Food12 < Food1: -6.5*130

  Food122 < Food12 < Food1: -7*130

  Food123 < Food12 < Food1: -7.5*130

  Food211 < Food21 < Food2: -4*130

  Food212 < Food21 < Food2: -4.5*130

  Food213 < Food21 < Food2: -5*130

  Food312 < Food31 < Food3: -11*130

  The multi-subaccount name of the Cash account is:

  909876525-c-customers < Cash receipts from customers < Operating activities

- On August 10, 2016, the Proprietorship1 sells the Food212 $9*6 (cost: -$4.5*6) and the Food312 $24*4 (cost: -$11*4) to A3 (SIN: 909876503) for cash $150. The multi-subaccount name of the Cash account is:

  909876503-c-customers < Cash receipts from customers < Operating activities

- On August 14, 2016, the Proprietorship1 sells the Food123 $15*4 (cost: -$7.5*4) and the Food322 $30*2 (cost: -$13*2) to A17 (SIN: 909876517) for cash $120. The multi-subaccount name of the Cash account is:

909876517-c-customers < Cash receipts from customers < Operating activities

- On August 17, 2016, the Proprietorship1 pays -$65,000 cash to the Company3 (phone number: 123456082) with the General ID 16 (-$6,150), the General ID 17 (-$26,950), and the General ID 18(-$31,900). The multi-subaccount name of the Cash account and transaction sub-equation respectively are:

88-654308-t-suppliers < Cash payments to suppliers < Operating activities

- On August 17, 2016, the Proprietorship1 sells the Food221 $12*3 (cost: -$6*3) and the Food321 $27*1 (cost: -$12*1) to A10 (SIN: 909876510) for cash $63. The multi-subaccount name of the Cash account is:

909876510-c-customers < Cash receipts from customers < Operating activities

- On August 20, 2016, the Proprietorship1 sells the Food213 $10*6 (cost: -$5*6), the Food312 $24*3 (cost: -$11*3), and the Food322 $30*1 (cost: -$13*1) to A16 (SIN: 909876516) for cash $162. The multi-subaccount name of the Cash account is:

909876516-c-customers < Cash receipts from customers < Operating activities

- On August 21, 2016, the Proprietorship1 sells the Food312 $24*2 (cost: -$11*2) and the Food322 $30*1 (cost: -$13*1) to A19 (SIN: 909876519) for cash $78. The multi-subaccount name of the Cash account is:

909876519-c-customers < Cash receipts from customers < Operating activities

- On August 22, 2016, the Proprietorship1 sells the Food23 $16*4 (cost: -$7.5*4) and the Food312 $24*2 (cost: -$11*2) to A12 (SIN: 909876512) for cash $112. The multi-subaccount name of the Cash account is:

909876512-c-customers < Cash receipts from customers < Operating activities

- On August 22, 2016, the Proprietorship1 sells the Food211 $8*10 (cost: -$4*10), the Food213 $10*10 (cost: -$5*10), the Food311 $20*3 (cost: -$8.5*3), and the Food312 $24*3 (cost: -$11*3) to A13 (SIN: 909876513) for cash $312. The multi-subaccount name of the Cash account is:

909876513-c-customers < Cash receipts from customers < Operating activities

- On August 23, 2016, the Proprietorship1 pays -$166.18 cash to A22 (SIN:

909876522) for the Travelling expenses (travel allowance) $110.18 and the Other expenses (meals: food522: $13*2 + food614: $30*1) $56.

- On August 31, 2016, the Proprietorship1 pays two employees' salary expenses for cash -$5,670 repeatedly.

- On September 15, 2016, the Proprietorship1 receives $300 cash from the Company3 (phone number: 123456782) with the General ID 19. The multi-subaccount name of the Cash account is:

  88-654302-c-customers < Cash receipts from customers < Operating activities

- On September 17, 2016, the Proprietorship1 sells the Food222 $13*4 (cost: -$6.5*4) and the Food322 $30*2 (cost: -$13*2) to A9 (SIN: 909876509) for cash $112. The multi-subaccount name of the Cash account is:

  909876509-c-customers < Cash receipts from customers < Operating activities

- On September 17, 2016, the Proprietorship1 sells the Food213 $10*5 (cost: -$5*5) and the Food321 $27*2 (cost: -$12*2) to A12 (SIN: 909876512) for cash $104. The multi-subaccount name of the Cash account is:

  909876512-c-customers < Cash receipts from customers < Operating activities

- On September 19, 2016, the Proprietorship1 sells the Food312 $24*3 (cost: -$11*3) and the Food321 $27*1 (cost: -$12*1) to A24 (SIN: 909876524) for cash $99. The multi-subaccount name of the Cash account is:

  909876524-c-customers < Cash receipts from customers < Operating activities

- On September 26, 2016, the Proprietorship1 sells the Food221 $12*10 (cost: -$6*10), the Food23 $16*10 (cost: -$7.5*10), the Food321 $27*3 (cost: -$12*3), and the Food322 $30*3 (cost: -$13*3) to A13 (SIN: 909876513) for cash $451. The multi-subaccount name of the Cash account is:

  909876513-c-customers < Cash receipts from customers < Operating activities

- On September 26, 2016, the Proprietorship1 pays -$1,800 cash to the Company2 (phone number: 123456083) with the General ID 80. The multi-subaccount name of the Cash account is:

  88-654307-t-suppliers < Cash payments to suppliers < Operating activities

- On September 26, 2016, the Proprietorship1 sells the Food23 $16*6 (cost: -$7.5*6), the Food311 $20*3 (cost: -$8.5*3), and the Food321 $27*1 (cost: -$12*1) to A16 (SIN: 909876516) for cash $183. The multi-subaccount name of the Cash account is:

  909876516-c-customers < Cash receipts from customers < Operating activities

- On September 26, 2016, the Proprietorship1 sells the Food311 $20*3 (cost: -$8.5*3) and the Food321 $27*1 (cost: -$12*1) to A19 (SIN: 909876519) for cash $87. The multi-subaccount name of the Cash account is:

  909876519-c-customers < Cash receipts from customers < Operating activities

- On September 30, 2016, the Proprietorship1 pays two employees' salary expenses for cash -$5,670 repeatedly.

- On September 30, 2016, the Proprietorship1 records the Amortization expenses $2,025 of a computer server2 ($1,012.5, nine months), a computer3 ($525, nine months), and a computer4 ($487.5, nine months). The transaction sub-equation is:

  Accumulated amortization: Computer (1): -1,012.5+ Accumulated amortization: Computer (1): -525 + Accumulated amortization: Computer (1): -487.5 = Amortization expenses (5): -1,012.5 + Amortization expenses (5): -525 + Amortization expenses (5): -487.5

- On September 30, 2016, the Proprietorship1 cancels the balances of the Computer account and the Accumulated amortization: Computer account because these computers have used for two years. The transaction sub-equation is:

  Computer (1): -2700 + Computer (1): -1400 + Computer (1): -1300 + Accumulated amortization: Computer (1): 2700 + Accumulated amortization: Computer (1): 1400 + Accumulated amortization: Computer (1): 1300 = 0

- On October 1, 2016, the Proprietorship1 purchases one Computer server1, one Computer1, and one Computer2 from the Company1 (phone number: 123456084) for cash $5,500 and other on credit. The multi-subaccount name of the Cash account and transaction sub-equation respectively are:

88-654306-t-machinery < Cash payments for machinery < Operating activities

Cash (1): -5500 + Computer (1): 2800 + Computer (1): 1600 + Computer (1): 1500 = Account payable (2): 400

- On October 8, 2016, the Proprietorship1 pays -$168.73 cash to A22 (SIN: 909876522) for the Travelling expenses (travel allowance) $114.73 and the Other expenses (meals: food521: $12*2 + food614: $30*1) $54.

- On October 12, 2016, the Proprietorship1 pays -$31,000 cash to the Company3 (phone number: 123456082) with the General ID 17. The multi-subaccount name of the Cash account and transaction sub-equation respectively are:

  88-654308-t-suppliers < Cash payments to suppliers < Operating activities

- On October 16, 2016, the Proprietorship1 sells the Food123 $15*4 (cost: -$7.5*4) and the Food23 $16*3 (cost: -$7.5*3) to A12 (SIN: 909876512) for cash $108. The multi-subaccount name of the Cash account is:

  909876512-c-customers < Cash receipts from customers < Operating activities

- On October 21, 2016, the Proprietorship1 sells the Food213 $ 10*4 (cost: -$5*4) and the Food321 $27*3 (cost: -$12*3) to A3 (SIN: 909876503) for cash $121. The multi-subaccount name of the Cash account is:

  909876503-c-customers < Cash receipts from customers < Operating activities

- On October 22, 2016, the Proprietorship1 sells the Food214 $11*4 (cost: -$5.5*4) and the Food312 $24*3 (cost: -$11*3) to A5 (SIN: 909876505) for cash $116. The multi-subaccount name of the Cash account is:

  909876505-c-customers < Cash receipts from customers < Operating activities

- On October 22, 2016, the Proprietorship1 sells the Food123 $15*4 (cost: -$7.5*4) and the Food321 $27*2 (cost: -$12*2) to A9 (SIN: 909876509) for cash $114. The multi-subaccount name of the Cash account is:

  909876509-c-customers < Cash receipts from customers < Operating activities

- On October 24, 2016, the Proprietorship1 sells the Food113 $12*10 (cost: -$6*10), the Food214 $11*10 (cost: -$5.5*10), the Food312 $24*3 (cost: -$11*3), and the Food321 $27*3 (cost: -$12*3) to A13 (SIN: 909876513) for cash $383. The multi-subaccount name of the Cash account is:

909876513-c-customers < Cash receipts from customers < Operating activities

- On October 25, 2016, the Proprietorship1 receives $25,000 cash from the Company3 (phone number: 123456782) with the General ID 19. The multi-subaccount name of the Cash account is:

88-654308-c-customers < Cash receipts from customers < Operating activities

- On October 25, 2016, the Proprietorship1 sells the Food113 $12*6 (cost: -$6*6), the Food312 $24*3 (cost: -$11*3), and the Food322 $30*1 (cost: -$13*1) to A16 (SIN: 909876516) for cash $174. The multi-subaccount name of the Cash account is:

909876516-c-customers < Cash receipts from customers < Operating activities

- On October 25, 2016, the Proprietorship1 sells the Food113 $12*5 (cost: -$6*5) and the Food322 $30*1 (cost: -$13*1) to A19 (SIN: 909876519) for cash $90. The multi-subaccount name of the Cash account is:

909876519-c-customers < Cash receipts from customers < Operating activities

- On October 31, 2016, the Proprietorship1 pays two employees' salary expenses for cash -$5,670 repeatedly.

- On November 15, 2016, the Proprietorship1 sells the Food121 $13*3 (cost: -$6.5*3) and the Food321 $27*2 (cost: -$12*2) to A6 (SIN: 909876506) for cash $93. The multi-subaccount name of the Cash account is:

909876506-c-customers < Cash receipts from customers < Operating activities

- On November 15, 2016, the Proprietorship1 sells the Food111 $10*10 (cost: -$5*10), the Food113 $12*10 (cost: -$6*10), the Food311 $20*3 (cost: -$8.5*3), and the Food321 $27*3 (cost: -$12*3) to A13 (SIN: 909876513) for cash $361. The multi-subaccount name of the Cash account is:

909876513-c-customers < Cash receipts from customers < Operating activities

- On November 17, 2016, the Proprietorship1 sells the Food111 $10*7 (cost: -$5*7), the Food311 $20*3 (cost: -$8.5*3), and the Food321 $27*2 (cost: -$12*2) to A16

(SIN: 909876516) for cash $184. The multi-subaccount name of the Cash account is:

909876516-c-customers < Cash receipts from customers < Operating activities

- On November 17, 2016, the Proprietorship1 sells the Food311 $20*3 (cost: -$8.5*3) and the Food321 $27*1 (cost: -$12*1) to A19 (SIN: 909876519) for cash $87. The multi-subaccount name of the Cash account is:

909876519-c-customers < Cash receipts from customers < Operating activities

- On November 19, 2016, the Proprietorship1 sells the Food113 $12*5 (cost: -$6*5) and the Food311 $20*2 (cost: -$8.5*2) to A12 (SIN: 909876512) for cash $100. The multi-subaccount name of the Cash account is:

909876512-c-customers < Cash receipts from customers < Operating activities

- On November 19, 2016, the Proprietorship1 pays -$177.16 cash to A22 (SIN: 909876522) for the Travelling expenses (travel allowance) $120.16 and the Other expenses (meals: food412: $11*3 + food612: $24*1) $57.

- On November 30, 2016, the Proprietorship1 pays two employees' salary expenses for cash -$5,670 repeatedly.

- On November 30, 2016, the Proprietorship1 has completed all products of the Working-in-process inventory account. If the all general parts have just been consumed and the supplies has the rest $53, the rest supplies must be returned to the Supplies account from the Cost of goods manufactured account. The transaction sub-equation is:

Supplies (1): 53 = Cost of goods manufactured (5): 53

- On November 30, 2016, the Proprietorship1 transfers the balance of the Cost of goods manufactured account to the Working-in-process inventory account. The Cost of goods manufactured account has three subaccounts of the "Supplies expenses", the "909876523-salary < Product department-salary < Salary expenses", and the "General parts expenses". Their balances are -$1,447, -$22,400, and -$113,098 respectively. Here, the balance of the subaccount "909876523-salary < Product department-salary < Salary expenses" is the sum of the eight months' salary expenses because the Proprietorship1 will not produce any product and only do some maintenance of the equipment in December 2016. In addition, the balance of the subaccount "General parts expenses" will be divided to three parts which are used in three transaction sub-equations respectively. The three transaction sub-equations respectively are:

Working-in-process inventory (1): 5*1200 + Working-in-process inventory (1): 5.5*1200 + Working-in-process inventory (1): 6*1200 + Working-in-process inventory (1): 6.5*1200 + Working-in-process inventory (1): 7*1200 + Working-in-process inventory (1): 7.5*1200 + Working-in-process inventory (1): 4*1200 = Cost of goods manufactured (5): 1447 + Cost of goods manufactured (5): 22400 + Cost of goods manufactured (5): 25953

Working-in-process inventory (1): 4.5*1200 + Working-in-process inventory (1): 5*1200 + Working-in-process inventory (1): 5.5*1200 + Working-in-process inventory (1): 6*1200 + Working-in-process inventory (1): 6.5*1200 + Working-in-process inventory (1): 7.5*1200 + Working-in-process inventory (1): 8.5*1200 + Working-in-process inventory (1): 11*1200 = Cost of goods manufactured (5): 65400

Working-in-process inventory (1): 12*1200 + Working-in-process inventory (1): 13*1200 = Cost of goods manufactured (5): 30000

- On November 30, 2016, the proprietorship1 transfers the balance of the Working-in-process inventory account to the Inventory account. The four transaction sub-equations respectively are:

Working-in-process inventory (1): -5*1200 + Working-in-process inventory (1): -5.5*1200 + Working-in-process inventory (1): -6*1200 + Working-in-process inventory (1): -6.5*1200 + Working-in-process inventory (1): -7*1200 + Inventory (1): 5*1200 + Inventory (1): 5.5*1200 + Inventory (1): 6*1200 +

Inventory (1): 6.5*1200 + Inventory (1): 7*1200 = 0

Working-in-process inventory (1): -7.5*1200 + Working-in-process inventory (1): -4*1200 + Working-in-process inventory (1): -4.5*1200 + Working-in-process inventory (1): -5*1200 + Working-in-process inventory (1): -5.5*1200 + Inventory (1): 7.5*1200 + Inventory (1): 4*1200 + Inventory (1): 4.5*1200 + Inventory (1): 5*1200 + Inventory (1): 5.5*1200 = 0

Working-in-process inventory (1): -6*1200 + Working-in-process inventory (1): -6.5*1200 + Working-in-process inventory (1): -7.5*1200 + Working-in-process inventory (1): -8.5*1200 + Working-in-process inventory (1): -11*1200 + Inventory (1): 6*1200 + Inventory (1): 6.5*1200 + Inventory (1): 7.5*1200 + Inventory (1): 8.5*1200 + Inventory (1): 11*1200 = 0

Working-in-process inventory (1): -12*1200 + Working-in-process inventory (1): -13*1200 + Inventory (1): 12*1200 + Inventory (1): 13*1200 = 0

- On December 13, 2016, the Proprietorship1 sells the Food112 $11*10 (cost: -$5.5*10), the Food123 $15*10 (cost: -$7.5*10), the Food312 $24*3 (cost: -$11*3), and the Food321 $27*3 (cost: -$12*3) to A13 (SIN: 909876513) for cash $413. The multi-subaccount name of the Cash account is:

  909876513-c-customers < Cash receipts from customers < Operating activities
- On December 15, 2016, the Proprietorship1 sells the Food222 $13*3 (cost: -$6.5*3) and the Food311 $20*3 (cost: -$8.5*3) to A9 (SIN: 909876509) for cash $99. The multi-subaccount name of the Cash account is:

  909876509-c-customers < Cash receipts from customers < Operating activities
- On December 15, 2016, the Proprietorship1 sells the Food111 $10*5 (cost: -$5*5) and the Food321 $27*2 (cost: -$12*2) to A19 (SIN: 909876519) for cash $104. The multi-subaccount name of the Cash account is:

  909876519-c-customers < Cash receipts from customers < Operating activities

- On December 15, 2016, the Proprietorship1 sells the Food111 $10*2 (cost: -$5*2) and the Food321 $27*2 (cost: -$12*2) to A23 (SIN: 909876523) for cash $74. The multi-subaccount name of the Cash account is:

  909876523-c-customers < Cash receipts from customers < Operating activities

- On December 15, 2016, the Proprietorship1 sells the Food111 $10*6 (cost: -$5*6), the Food123 $15*4 (cost: -$7.5*4), and the Food321 $27*2 (cost: -$12*2) to A16 (SIN: 909876516) for cash $174. The multi-subaccount name of the Cash account is:

  909876516-c-customers < Cash receipts from customers < Operating activities

- On December 17, 2016, the Proprietorship1 pays -$207.52 cash to A23 (SIN: 909876523) for the Travelling expenses (travel allowance) $133.52 and the Other expenses (meals: food111: $10*2 + food321: $27*2) $74.

- On December 19, 2016, the Proprietorship1 pays -$198.35 cash to A22 (SIN: 909876522) for the Travelling expenses (travel allowance) $130.35 and the Other expenses (meals: food611: $20*2 + food622: $28*1) $68.

- On December 20, 2016, the Proprietorship1 sells the Food221 $12*3 (cost: -$6*3), Food222 $13*3 (cost: -$6.5*3), and the Food321 $27*2 (cost: -$12*2) to A3 (SIN: 909876503) for cash $129. The multi-subaccount name of the Cash account is:

  909876503-c-customers < Cash receipts from customers < Operating activities

- On December 23, 2016, the Proprietorship1 receives $18,000 cash from the Company1 (phone number: 123456784) with the General ID 93. The multi-subaccount name of the Cash account is:

  88-654306-c-customers < Cash receipts from customers < Operating activities

- On December 26, 2016, the Proprietorship1 sells the Food111 $10*6 (cost: -$5*6), Food213 $10*6 (cost: -$5*6), and the Food312 $24*3 (cost: -$11*3) to A5 (SIN: 909876505) for cash $192. The multi-subaccount name of the Cash account is:

  909876505-c-customers < Cash receipts from customers < Operating activities

- On December 26, 2016, the Proprietorship1 sells the Food113 $12*6 (cost: -$6*6), Food214 $11*6 (cost: -$5.5*6), and the Food311 $20*3 (cost: -$8.5*3) to A6 (SIN: 909876506) for cash $198. The multi-subaccount name of the Cash account is:

909876506-c-customers < Cash receipts from customers < Operating activities

- On December 27, 2016, the Proprietorship1 sells the Food222 $13*5 (cost: -$6.5*5) and the Food322 $30*2 (cost: -$13*2) to A12 (SIN: 909876512) for cash $125. The multi-subaccount name of the Cash account is:

909876512-c-customers < Cash receipts from customers < Operating activities

- On December 29, 2016, the Proprietorship1 pays -$10,000 cash to the Company1 (phone number: 123456084) with the General ID 60. The multi-subaccount name of the Cash account is:

88-654306-t-suppliers < Cash payments to suppliers < Operating activities

- On December 31, 2016, the Proprietorship1 pays -$4,300 cash to the Proprietorship2 (phone number: 123456080) with the General ID 15 ($600), the General ID 91 ($700), and the General ID 92 ($3,000). The multi-subaccount name of the Cash account is:

88-654310-t-suppliers < Cash payments to suppliers < Operating activities

- On December 31, 2016, the Proprietorship1 pays two employees' salary expenses for cash -$5,670 repeatedly.

- On the same day, the Proprietorship1 pays -$11,280 cash to the business Bank2 for the Note interest expenses of the Note25 ($120,000, one-level subaccount "Note25-interest"). The multi-subaccount name of the Cash account and the transaction sub-equation respectively are:

88-654305-t-note interest < Cash payments to business banks < Operating activities

Cash (1): -11,280 = Note interest expenses (5): -11,280

- On the same day, the Proprietorship1 pays -$2,500 cash to the bond holders for the Bond interest expenses of the Bond61 (one-level subaccount "Bond61-interest"). The multi-subaccount names of the Cash account and the transaction sub-equations respectively are:

909876504-t-bond interest < Cash payments to bond holders < Operating

activities

909876505-t-bond interest < Cash payments to bond holders < Operating activities

909876506-t-bond interest < Cash payments to bond holders < Operating activities

909876508-t-bond interest < Cash payments to bond holders < Operating activities

909876510-t-bond interest < Cash payments to bond holders < Operating activities

909876513-t-bond interest < Cash payments to bond holders < Operating activities

909876515-t-bond interest < Cash payments to bond holders < Operating activities

909876516-t-bond interest < Cash payments to bond holders < Operating activities

909876517-t-bond interest < Cash payments to bond holders < Operating activities

909876518-t-bond interest < Cash payments to bond holders < Operating activities

909876519-t-bond interest < Cash payments to bond holders < Operating activities

909876520-t-bond interest < Cash payments to bond holders < Operating activities

909876521-t-bond interest < Cash payments to bond holders < Operating activities

909876522-t-bond interest < Cash payments to bond holders < Operating activities

Cash (1): -150 + Cash (1): -200 + Cash (1): -250 + Cash (1): -100 + Cash (1): -150 + Cash (1): -250 + Cash (1): -200 + Cash (1): -100 = Bond interest expenses

(5): -1400

Cash (1): -250 + Cash (1): -150 + Cash (1): -250 + Cash (1): -150 + Cash (1): -200 + Cash (1): -100 = Bond interest expenses (5): -1100

- On the same day, the Proprietorship1 receives cash $416 ($200 + $126 + $90) for investment interest of the Bond11 ($5,000), the Bond12 ($3,000), and the Bond13 ($2,000) from the Business Bank1. The multi-subaccount name of the Cash account and transaction sub-equation respectively are:

  88-654304-c-investment income < Cash receipts from investments < Investing activities

  Cash (1): 416 = Investment incomes (4):200 + Investment incomes (4): 126 + Investment incomes (4): 90

- On the same day, the Proprietorship1 receives cash $352 for investment interest of the Bond22 ($8,000) from the Business Bank2. The multi-subaccount name of the Cash account and transaction sub-equation respectively are:

  88-654305-c-investment income < Cash receipts from investments < Investing activities

  Cash (1): 352 = Investment incomes (4): 352

- On the same day, the Proprietorship1 receives cash $120 from the Business Bank1 for primary deposit interest. The multi-subaccount name of the Cash account and transaction sub-equation respectively are:

  88-654304-c-deposit interest income < Cash receipts from deposit interest < Financial activities

  Cash (1): 120 = Deposit interest incomes (4):120

- On the same day, the Proprietorship1 records the Office supplies expenses -$. The transaction sub-equation is:

Supplies (1): -321.57 = Office supplies expenses (5): -321.57

- On the same day, the Proprietorship1 records the Vehicle's amortization expenses - $14,966.67 one year (5 years, straight line). The two transaction sub-equations are:

Accumulated amortization: Vehicle (1): -8000 = Amortization expenses (5): -8000

- On the same day, the Proprietorship1 records the Computer's amortization expenses $737.5 three months (2 years, straight line) which includes a new computer server1 ($350), a new computer1 ($200), and a new computer2 ($187.5). The transaction sub-equation is:

Accumulated amortization: Computer (1): -350 + Accumulated amortization: Computer (1): -200 + Accumulated amortization: Computer (1): -187.5 = Amortization expenses (5): -350 + Amortization expenses (5): -200 + Amortization expenses (5): -187.5

- On December 31, 2016, the Proprietorship1 records the Tax expenses -$34,827.41 and the Tax payable $34,827.41. The multi-subaccount name forms of the Tax expenses and the Tax payable accounts all are the 'n'. The transaction sub-equation is:

0 = Tax payable (2): 34827.41 + Tax expenses (5): -34827.41

So far, I have entered all transactions of the Proprietorship1 in the fiscal year 2016. After getting the Income Statement and clicking the "Yes" button for new fiscal year, I can get the Balance Sheet of the Proprietorship1.

In the new fiscal year, the Proprietorship1 will record the following transaction.

- On January 2, 2017, the Proprietorship1 pays the balance -$34,827.41 of the Tax payable account to the Tax Bureau. The multi-subaccount name of the Cash account and transaction sub-equation respectively are:

88-654303-n-tax < Cash payments to Tax Bureau < Operating activities

Cash (1): -34827.41 = Tax payable (2): -34827.41

3.9.2 Brief Summary of the Proprietorship1

The Figure 3.9-2 on the next page shows two sums and all cash transactions of the Proprietorship1 by using of SQL Server query. As a closed system based on the MathAccounting software, the sum0 should be equal to zero. However, the individuals are not responsible for recording any transaction, so the sum0 (-$323,447.10) is the sum of the amounts that individuals paid to the Proprietorship1. The opposite value ($177,678.88) of the sum1 (-$177,678.88) is the balance of the Cash account of the Proprietorship1 on December 31, 2016. It is also the balance of the deposit of the Proprietorship1 in the Business Bak1 on December 31, 2016.

The Figure 3.9-3 to the Figure 3.9-6 on page 520 to page 523 show the four tables of the cash flows statement, the cash account, the income statement, and the balance sheet respectively.

```
SQLQuery1.sql - LIU...SS.dcj100 (sa (52))*  ×
  use dcj100
  select sum(amount) as sum0 from CashByMembers where IDM='88-654309' and TransDate between '2016-01-01' and '2016-12-31'
  select sum(amount) as sum1 from CashByMembers where IDM='88-654309' and Symbol = 'd'
  select * from CashByMembers where Recorder='88-654309' and TransDate between '2016-01-01' and '2016-12-31'
          order by TransDate
100 %   ▾
  Results   Messages
```

	sum0
1	-323447.10

	sum1
1	-177678.88

	IDM	Amount	Symbol	MultiSubaccount	Recorder	TransDate
1	88-654310	450.00	t	88-654310-t-supplies < Cash payments for operating expenses < Operating activities	88-654309	2016-01-02
2	88-654308	10000.00	t	88-654308-t-suppliers < Cash payments to suppliers < Operating activities	88-654309	2016-01-02
3	88-654308	-9300.00	c	88-654308-c-customers < Cash receipts from customers < Operating activities	88-654309	2016-01-03
4	909876503	-108.00	c	909876503-c-customers < Cash receipts from customers < Operating activities	88-654309	2016-01-06
5	909876505	-98.00	c	909876505-c-customers < Cash receipts from customers < Operating activities	88-654309	2016-01-10
6	909876506	-92.00	c	909876506-c-customers < Cash receipts from customers < Operating activities	88-654309	2016-01-10
7	88-654308	150.00	t	88-654308-t-supplies < Cash payments for operating expenses < Operating activities	88-654309	2016-01-13
8	909876515	-20.00	c	909876515-c-customers < Cash receipts from customers < Operating activities	88-654309	2016-01-13
9	909876516	-192.00	c	909876516-c-customers < Cash receipts from customers < Operating activities	88-654309	2016-01-13
10	909876517	-44.00	c	909876517-c-customers < Cash receipts from customers < Operating activities	88-654309	2016-01-16
11	909876508	-57.00	c	909876508-c-customers < Cash receipts from customers < Operating activities	88-654309	2016-01-16
12	909876520	-51.00	c	909876520-c-customers < Cash receipts from customers < Operating activities	88-654309	2016-01-18
13	909876522	153.87	n	909876522-n-operating expenses < Cash payments for operating expenses < Operating activities	88-654309	2016-01-18
14	909876525	-57.00	c	909876525-c-customers < Cash receipts from customers < Operating activities	88-654309	2016-01-19
15	909876509	-100.00	c	909876509-c-customers < Cash receipts from customers < Operating activities	88-654309	2016-01-25
16	88-654308	-1300.00	c	88-654308-c-customers < Cash receipts from customers < Operating activities	88-654309	2016-01-26
17	88-654307	250.00	t	88-654307-t-suppliers < Cash payments to suppliers < Operating activities	88-654309	2016-01-27
18	909876510	-57.00	c	909876510-c-customers < Cash receipts from customers < Operating activities	88-654309	2016-01-27
19	909876518	-144.00	c	909876518-c-customers < Cash receipts from customers < Operating activities	88-654309	2016-01-28
20	909876521	-42.00	c	909876521-c-customers < Cash receipts from customers < Operating activities	88-654309	2016-01-28
21	909876523	-44.00	c	909876523-c-customers < Cash receipts from customers < Operating activities	88-654309	2016-01-28
22	88-654307	-500.00	c	88-654307-c-customers < Cash receipts from customers < Operating activities	88-654309	2016-01-30
23	909876523	145.54	n	909876523-n-operating expenses < Cash payments for operating expenses < Operating activities	88-654309	2016-01-30

	IDM	Amount	Symbol	MultiSubaccount	Recorder	TransDate
24	88-654306	-2040.00	c	88-654306-c-customers < Cash receipts from customers < Operating activities	88-654309	2016-01-31
25	909876522	2870.00	t	909876522-t-salary < Cash payments for operating expenses < Operating activities	88-654309	2016-01-31
26	909876523	2800.00	t	909876523-t-CGM < Cash payments for operating expenses < Operating activities	88-654309	2016-01-31
27	909876512	-10400.00	c	909876512-c-customers < Cash receipts from customers < Operating activities	88-654309	2016-01-31
28	909876501	-14560.00	c	909876501-c-customers < Cash receipts from customers < Operating activities	88-654309	2016-01-31
29	909876502	-13000.00	c	909876502-c-customers < Cash receipts from customers < Operating activities	88-654309	2016-01-31
30	909876503	-13130.00	c	909876503-c-customers < Cash receipts from customers < Operating activities	88-654309	2016-01-31
31	909876504	-14430.00	c	909876504-c-customers < Cash receipts from customers < Operating activities	88-654309	2016-01-31
32	909876505	-14170.00	c	909876505-c-customers < Cash receipts from customers < Operating activities	88-654309	2016-01-31
33	909876506	-12610.00	c	909876506-c-customers < Cash receipts from customers < Operating activities	88-654309	2016-01-31
34	909876507	-12400.00	c	909876507-c-customers < Cash receipts from customers < Operating activities	88-654309	2016-01-31
35	909876508	-13000.00	c	909876508-c-customers < Cash receipts from customers < Operating activities	88-654309	2016-01-31
36	909876509	-18460.00	c	909876509-c-customers < Cash receipts from customers < Operating activities	88-654309	2016-01-31
37	909876510	-13900.00	c	909876510-c-customers < Cash receipts from customers < Operating activities	88-654309	2016-01-31
38	909876511	-14430.00	c	909876511-c-customers < Cash receipts from customers < Operating activities	88-654309	2016-01-31
39	909876512	-14560.00	c	909876512-c-customers < Cash receipts from customers < Operating activities	88-654309	2016-01-31
40	909876513	-18460.00	c	909876513-c-customers < Cash receipts from customers < Operating activities	88-654309	2016-01-31
41	88-654306	28000.00	t	88-654306-t-machinery < Cash payments for machinery < Operating activities	88-654309	2016-02-01
42	909876513	-310.00	c	909876513-c-customers < Cash receipts from customers < Operating activities	88-654309	2016-02-17
43	88-654310	-400.00	c	88-654310-c-customers < Cash receipts from customers < Operating activities	88-654309	2016-02-20
44	88-654310	300.00	t	88-654310-t-suppliers < Cash payments to suppliers < Operating activities	88-654309	2016-02-21
45	909876519	-124.00	c	909876519-c-customers < Cash receipts from customers < Operating activities	88-654309	2016-02-23
46	909876505	-110.00	c	909876505-c-customers < Cash receipts from customers < Operating activities	88-654309	2016-02-24
47	909876503	-99.00	c	909876503-c-customers < Cash receipts from customers < Operating activities	88-654309	2016-02-25
48	909876518	-102.00	c	909876518-c-customers < Cash receipts from customers < Operating activities	88-654309	2016-02-28
49	909876521	-102.00	c	909876521-c-customers < Cash receipts from customers < Operating activities	88-654309	2016-02-28
50	000070522	2870.00	t	909876522-t-salary < Cash payments for operating expenses < Operating activities	88-654309	2016-02-28
51	909876523	2800.00	t	909876523-t-CGM < Cash payments for operating expenses < Operating activities	88-654309	2016-02-28

Figure 3.9-2 Proprietorship1 Cash Received or Paid by Other Members (Continue)

	IDM	Amount	Symbol	MultiSubaccount	Recorder	TransDate
52	88-654306	1000.00	t	88-654306-t-suppliers < Cash payments to suppliers < Operating activities	88-654309	2016-03-06
53	909876525	-78.00	c	909876525-c-customers < Cash receipts from customers < Operating activities	88-654309	2016-03-07
54	909876506	-123.00	c	909876506-c-customers < Cash receipts from customers < Operating activities	88-654309	2016-03-10
55	909876511	-50.00	c	909876511-c-customers < Cash receipts from customers < Operating activities	88-654309	2016-03-11
56	909876504	-172.00	c	909876504-c-customers < Cash receipts from customers < Operating activities	88-654309	2016-03-19
57	909876522	159.45	n	909876522-n-operating expenses < Cash payments for operating expenses < Operating activities	88-654309	2016-03-23
58	909876502	-72.00	c	909876502-c-customers < Cash receipts from customers < Operating activities	88-654309	2016-03-26
59	909876508	-51.00	c	909876508-c-customers < Cash receipts from customers < Operating activities	88-654309	2016-03-27
60	909876522	2870.00	t	909876522-t-salary < Cash payments for operating expenses < Operating activities	88-654309	2016-03-31
61	909876523	2800.00	t	909876523-t-CGM < Cash payments for operating expenses < Operating activities	88-654309	2016-03-31
62	909876511	-69.00	c	909876511-c-customers < Cash receipts from customers < Operating activities	88-654309	2016-04-13
63	909876524	-75.00	c	909876524-c-customers < Cash receipts from customers < Operating activities	88-654309	2016-04-22
64	909876516	-156.00	c	909876516-c-customers < Cash receipts from customers < Operating activities	88-654309	2016-04-24
65	909876519	-78.00	c	909876519-c-customers < Cash receipts from customers < Operating activities	88-654309	2016-04-24
66	909876507	-102.00	c	909876507-c-customers < Cash receipts from customers < Operating activities	88-654309	2016-04-27
67	88-654307	5000.00	t	88-654307-t-supplies < Cash payments for operating expenses < Operating activities	88-654309	2016-04-29
68	909876522	2870.00	t	909876522-t-salary < Cash payments for operating expenses < Operating activities	88-654309	2016-04-30
69	909876523	2800.00	t	909876523-t-CGM < Cash payments for operating expenses < Operating activities	88-654309	2016-04-30
70	88-654310	800.00	t	88-654310-t-supplies < Cash payments for operating expenses < Operating activities	88-654309	2016-05-01
71	88-654310	5000.00	t	88-654310-t-suppliers < Cash payments to suppliers < Operating activities	88-654309	2016-05-01
72	88-654306	-3250.00	c	88-654306-c-customers < Cash receipts from customers < Operating activities	88-654309	2016-05-01
73	88-654310	-9000.00	c	88-654310-c-customers < Cash receipts from customers < Operating activities	88-654309	2016-05-01
74	909876518	-90.00	c	909876518-c-customers < Cash receipts from customers < Operating activities	88-654309	2016-05-01
75	909876521	-50.00	c	909876521-c-customers < Cash receipts from customers < Operating activities	88-654309	2016-05-01
76	909876523	-50.00	c	909876523-c-customers < Cash receipts from customers < Operating activities	88-654309	2016-05-12
77	909876509	-112.00	c	909876509-c-customers < Cash receipts from customers < Operating activities	88-654309	2016-05-12
78	909876506	-112.00	c	909876506-c-customers < Cash receipts from customers < Operating activities	88-654309	2016-05-13
79	909876523	166.23	n	909876523-n-operating expenses < Cash payments for operating expenses < Operating activities	88-654309	2016-05-14

	IDM	Amount	Symbol	MultiSubaccount	Recorder	TransDate
80	909876503	-105.00	c	909876503-c-customers < Cash receipts from customers < Operating activities	88-654309	2016-05-14
81	909876511	-56.00	c	909876511-c-customers < Cash receipts from customers < Operating activities	88-654309	2016-05-20
82	909876513	-403.00	c	909876513-c-customers < Cash receipts from customers < Operating activities	88-654309	2016-05-22
83	909876516	-155.00	c	909876516-c-customers < Cash receipts from customers < Operating activities	88-654309	2016-05-22
84	909876519	-138.00	c	909876519-c-customers < Cash receipts from customers < Operating activities	88-654309	2016-05-22
85	909876522	176.95	n	909876522-n-operating expenses < Cash payments for operating expenses < Operating activities	88-654309	2016-05-24
86	909876522	2870.00	t	909876522-t-salary < Cash payments for operating expenses < Operating activities	88-654309	2016-05-31
87	909876523	2800.00	t	909876523-t-CGM < Cash payments for operating expenses < Operating activities	88-654309	2016-05-31
88	909876509	-96.00	c	909876509-c-customers < Cash receipts from customers < Operating activities	88-654309	2016-06-14
89	88-654308	-300.00	c	88-654308-c-customers < Cash receipts from customers < Operating activities	88-654309	2016-06-16
90	909876512	-109.00	c	909876512-c-customers < Cash receipts from customers < Operating activities	88-654309	2016-06-18
91	909876513	-310.00	c	909876513-c-customers < Cash receipts from customers < Operating activities	88-654309	2016-06-20
92	909876516	-163.00	c	909876516-c-customers < Cash receipts from customers < Operating activities	88-654309	2016-06-20
93	909876519	-108.00	c	909876519-c-customers < Cash receipts from customers < Operating activities	88-654309	2016-06-21
94	909876522	157.37	n	909876522-n-operating expenses < Cash payments for operating expenses < Operating activities	88-654309	2016-06-23
95	909876522	2870.00	t	909876522-t-salary < Cash payments for operating expenses < Operating activities	88-654309	2016-06-30
96	909876523	2800.00	t	909876523-t-CGM < Cash payments for operating expenses < Operating activities	88-654309	2016-06-30
97	88-654308	55000.00	t	88-654308-t-suppliers < Cash payments to suppliers < Operating activities	88-654309	2016-07-04
98	909876514	-180.00	c	909876514-c-customers < Cash receipts from customers < Operating activities	88-654309	2016-07-05
99	909876504	-112.00	c	909876504-c-customers < Cash receipts from customers < Operating activities	88-654309	2016-07-16
100	909876512	-125.00	c	909876512-c-customers < Cash receipts from customers < Operating activities	88-654309	2016-07-21
101	909876513	-302.00	c	909876513-c-customers < Cash receipts from customers < Operating activities	88-654309	2016-07-22
102	909876505	-105.00	c	909876505-c-customers < Cash receipts from customers < Operating activities	88-654309	2016-07-22
103	909876516	-118.00	c	909876516-c-customers < Cash receipts from customers < Operating activities	88-654309	2016-07-25
104	909876519	-88.00	c	909876519-c-customers < Cash receipts from customers < Operating activities	88-654309	2016-07-25
105	909876523	-64.00	c	909876523-c-customers < Cash receipts from customers < Operating activities	88-654309	2016-07-25
106	909876523	187.55	n	909876523-n-operating expenses < Cash payments for operating expenses < Operating activities	88-654309	2016-07-27
107	909876522	2870.00	t	909876522-t-salary < Cash payments for operating expenses < Operating activities	88-654309	2016-07-31

Figure 3.9-2　Proprietorship1 Cash Received or Paid by Other Members (Continue)

	IDM	Amount	Symbol	MultiSubaccount	Recorder	TransDate
108	909876523	2800.00	t	909876523-t-CGM < Cash payments for operating expenses < Operating activities	88-654309	2016-07-31
109	909876501	-10270.00	c	909876501-c-customers < Cash receipts from customers < Operating activities	88-654309	2016-07-31
110	909876514	-18460.00	c	909876514-c-customers < Cash receipts from customers < Operating activities	88-654309	2016-07-31
111	909876515	-18200.00	c	909876515-c-customers < Cash receipts from customers < Operating activities	88-654309	2016-07-31
112	909876516	-18720.00	c	909876516-c-customers < Cash receipts from customers < Operating activities	88-654309	2016-07-31
113	909876517	-17940.00	c	909876517-c-customers < Cash receipts from customers < Operating activities	88-654309	2016-07-31
114	909876518	-18460.00	c	909876518-c-customers < Cash receipts from customers < Operating activities	88-654309	2016-07-31
115	909876519	-18590.00	c	909876519-c-customers < Cash receipts from customers < Operating activities	88-654309	2016-07-31
116	909876520	-10400.00	c	909876520-c-customers < Cash receipts from customers < Operating activities	88-654309	2016-07-31
117	909876521	-10660.00	c	909876521-c-customers < Cash receipts from customers < Operating activities	88-654309	2016-07-31
118	909876522	-10530.00	c	909876522-c-customers < Cash receipts from customers < Operating activities	88-654309	2016-07-31
119	909876523	-11050.00	c	909876523-c-customers < Cash receipts from customers < Operating activities	88-654309	2016-07-31
120	909876524	-11570.00	c	909876524-c-customers < Cash receipts from customers < Operating activities	88-654309	2016-07-31
121	909876525	-12090.00	c	909876525-c-customers < Cash receipts from customers < Operating activities	88-654309	2016-07-31
122	909876503	-150.00	c	909876503-c-customers < Cash receipts from customers < Operating activities	88-654309	2016-08-10
123	909876517	-120.00	c	909876517-c-customers < Cash receipts from customers < Operating activities	88-654309	2016-08-14
124	88-654308	65000.00	t	88-654308-t-suppliers < Cash payments to suppliers < Operating activities	88-654309	2016-08-17
125	909876510	-63.00	c	909876510-c-customers < Cash receipts from customers < Operating activities	88-654309	2016-08-17
126	909876516	-162.00	c	909876516-c-customers < Cash receipts from customers < Operating activities	88-654309	2016-08-20
127	909876519	-78.00	c	909876519-c-customers < Cash receipts from customers < Operating activities	88-654309	2016-08-21
128	909876513	-312.00	c	909876513-c-customers < Cash receipts from customers < Operating activities	88-654309	2016-08-22
129	909876512	-112.00	c	909876512-c-customers < Cash receipts from customers < Operating activities	88-654309	2016-08-22
130	909876522	166.18	n	909876522-n-operating expenses < Cash payments for operating expenses < Operating activities	88-654309	2016-08-23
131	909876522	2870.00	t	909876522-t-salary < Cash payments for operating expenses < Operating activities	88-654309	2016-08-31
132	909876523	2800.00	t	909876523-t-CGM < Cash payments for operating expenses < Operating activities	88-654309	2016-08-31
133	88-654302	-300.00	c	88-654302-c-customers < Cash receipts from customers < Operating activities	88-654309	2016-09-15
134	909876512	-104.00	c	909876512-c-customers < Cash receipts from customers < Operating activities	88-654309	2016-09-17
135	909876509	-112.00	c	909876509-c-customers < Cash receipts from customers < Operating activities	88-654309	2016-09-17

	IDM	Amount	Symbol	MultiSubaccount	Recorder	TransDate
136	909876524	-99.00	c	909876524-c-customers < Cash receipts from customers < Operating activities	88-654309	2016-09-19
137	909876513	-451.00	c	909876513-c-customers < Cash receipts from customers < Operating activities	88-654309	2016-09-26
138	88-654307	1800.00	t	88-654307-t-suppliers < Cash payments to suppliers < Operating activities	88-654309	2016-09-26
139	909876516	-183.00	c	909876516-c-customers < Cash receipts from customers < Operating activities	88-654309	2016-09-26
140	909876519	-87.00	c	909876519-c-customers < Cash receipts from customers < Operating activities	88-654309	2016-09-26
141	909876522	2870.00	t	909876522-t-salary < Cash payments for operating expenses < Operating activities	88-654309	2016-09-30
142	909876523	2800.00	t	909876523-t-CGM < Cash payments for operating expenses < Operating activities	88-654309	2016-09-30
143	88-654306	5500.00	t	88-654306-t-machinery < Cash payments for machinery < Operating activities	88-654309	2016-10-01
144	909876522	168.73	n	909876522-n-operating expenses < Cash payments for operating expenses < Operating activities	88-654309	2016-10-08
145	88-654308	31000.00	t	88-654308-t-suppliers < Cash payments to suppliers < Operating activities	88-654309	2016-10-12
146	909876512	-108.00	c	909876512-c-customers < Cash receipts from customers < Operating activities	88-654309	2016-10-16
147	909876503	-121.00	c	909876503-c-customers < Cash receipts from customers < Operating activities	88-654309	2016-10-21
148	909876505	-116.00	c	909876505-c-customers < Cash receipts from customers < Operating activities	88-654309	2016-10-22
149	909876509	-114.00	c	909876509-c-customers < Cash receipts from customers < Operating activities	88-654309	2016-10-22
150	909876513	-383.00	c	909876513-c-customers < Cash receipts from customers < Operating activities	88-654309	2016-10-24
151	88-654308	-25000.00	c	88-654308-c-customers < Cash receipts from customers < Operating activities	88-654309	2016-10-25
152	909876516	-174.00	c	909876516-c-customers < Cash receipts from customers < Operating activities	88-654309	2016-10-25
153	909876519	-90.00	c	909876519-c-customers < Cash receipts from customers < Operating activities	88-654309	2016-10-25
154	909876522	2870.00	t	909876522-t-salary < Cash payments for operating expenses < Operating activities	88-654309	2016-10-31
155	909876523	2800.00	t	909876523-t-CGM < Cash payments for operating expenses < Operating activities	88-654309	2016-10-31
156	909876506	-93.00	c	909876506-c-customers < Cash receipts from customers < Operating activities	88-654309	2016-11-15
157	909876513	-361.00	c	909876513-c-customers < Cash receipts from customers < Operating activities	88-654309	2016-11-15
158	909876516	-184.00	c	909876516-c-customers < Cash receipts from customers < Operating activities	88-654309	2016-11-17
159	909876519	-87.00	c	909876519-c-customers < Cash receipts from customers < Operating activities	88-654309	2016-11-17
160	909876522	177.16	n	909876522-n-operating expenses < Cash payments for operating expenses < Operating activities	88-654309	2016-11-19
161	909876512	-100.00	c	909876512-c-customers < Cash receipts from customers < Operating activities	88-654309	2016-11-19
162	909876522	2870.00	t	909876522-t-salary < Cash payments for operating expenses < Operating activities	88-654309	2016-11-30
163	909876523	2800.00	t	909876523-t-CGM < Cash payments for operating expenses < Operating activities	88-654309	2016-11-30

Figure 3.9-2   Proprietorship1 Cash Received or Paid by Other Members (Continue)

	IDM	Amount	Symbol	MultiSubaccount	Recorder	TransDate
164	909876513	-413.00	c	909876513-c-customers < Cash receipts from customers < Operating activities	88-654309	2016-12-13
165	909876519	-104.00	c	909876519-c-customers < Cash receipts from customers < Operating activities	88-654309	2016-12-15
166	909876523	-74.00	c	909876523-c-customers < Cash receipts from customers < Operating activities	88-654309	2016-12-15
167	909876516	-174.00	c	909876516-c-customers < Cash receipts from customers < Operating activities	88-654309	2016-12-15
168	909876509	-99.00	c	909876509-c-customers < Cash receipts from customers < Operating activities	88-654309	2016-12-15
169	909876523	207.52	n	909876523-n-operating expenses < Cash payments for operating expenses < Operating activities	88-654309	2016-12-17
170	909876522	198.35	n	909876522-n-operating expenses < Cash payments for operating expenses < Operating activities	88-654309	2016-12-19
171	909876503	-129.00	c	909876503-c-customers < Cash receipts from customers < Operating activities	88-654309	2016-12-20
172	88-654306	-18000.00	c	88-654306-c-customers < Cash receipts from customers < Operating activities	88-654309	2016-12-23
173	909876505	-192.00	c	909876505-c-customers < Cash receipts from customers < Operating activities	88-654309	2016-12-26
174	909876506	-198.00	c	909876506-c-customers < Cash receipts from customers < Operating activities	88-654309	2016-12-26
175	909876512	-125.00	c	909876512-c-customers < Cash receipts from customers < Operating activities	88-654309	2016-12-27
176	88-654306	10000.00	t	88-654306-t-suppliers < Cash payments to suppliers < Operating activities	88-654309	2016-12-29
177	909876522	2870.00	t	909876522-t-salary < Cash payments for operating expenses < Operating activities	88-654309	2016-12-31
178	909876523	2800.00	t	909876523-t-CGM < Cash payments for operating expenses < Operating activities	88-654309	2016-12-31
179	88-654305	11280.00	t	88-654305-t-note interest < Cash payments to business banks < Operating activities	88-654309	2016-12-31
180	909876504	150.00	t	909876504-t-bond interest < Cash payments to bond holders < Operating activities	88-654309	2016-12-31
181	909876505	200.00	t	909876505-t-bond interest < Cash payments to bond holders < Operating activities	88-654309	2016-12-31
182	909876506	250.00	t	909876506-t-bond interest < Cash payments to bond holders < Operating activities	88-654309	2016-12-31
183	909876508	100.00	t	909876508-t-bond interest < Cash payments to bond holders < Operating activities	88-654309	2016-12-31
184	909876510	150.00	t	909876510-t-bond interest < Cash payments to bond holders < Operating activities	88-654309	2016-12-31
185	909876513	250.00	t	909876513-t-bond interest < Cash payments to bond holders < Operating activities	88-654309	2016-12-31
186	909876515	200.00	t	909876515-t-bond interest < Cash payments to bond holders < Operating activities	88-654309	2016-12-31
187	909876516	100.00	t	909876516-t-bond interest < Cash payments to bond holders < Operating activities	88-654309	2016-12-31
188	909876517	250.00	t	909876517-t-bond interest < Cash payments to bond holders < Operating activities	88-654309	2016-12-31
189	909876518	150.00	t	909876518-t-bond interest < Cash payments to bond holders < Operating activities	88-654309	2016-12-31
190	909876519	250.00	t	909876519-t-bond interest < Cash payments to bond holders < Operating activities	88-654309	2016-12-31
191	909876520	150.00	t	909876520-t-bond interest < Cash payments to bond holders < Operating activities	88-654309	2016-12-31
192	909876521	200.00	t	909876521-t-bond interest < Cash payments to bond holders < Operating activities	88-654309	2016-12-31
193	909876522	100.00	t	909876522-t-bond interest < Cash payments to bond holders < Operating activities	88-654309	2016-12-31
194	88-654304	-416.00	c	88-654304-c-investment income < Cash receipts from investments < Investing activities	88-654309	2016-12-31
195	88-654305	-352.00	c	88-654305-c-investment income < Cash receipts from investments < Investing activities	88-654309	2016-12-31
196	88-654305	-120.00	c	88-654305-c-deposit interest income < Cash receipts from deposit interest < Financial activities	88-654309	2016-12-31
197	88-654310	4300.00	t	88-654310-t-suppliers < Cash payments to suppliers < Operating activities	88-654309	2016-12-31
198	88-654305	120.00	c	88-654305-c-deposit interest income < Cash receipts from deposit interest < Financial activities	88-654309	2016-12-31
199	88-654304	-120.00	c	88-654304-c-deposit interest income < Cash receipts from deposit interest < Financial activities	88-654309	2016-12-31

Query executed successfully.

Figure 3.9-2   Proprietorship1 Cash Received or Paid by Other Members

Cash Flow Statement

Cash Flows Statement Year Ended 2016-12-31	
Operating activities	
Cash payments for machinery	-$33,500.00
Cash payments for operating expenses	-$76,504.90
Cash payments to bond holders	-$2,500.00
Cash payments to business banks	-$11,280.00
Cash payments to suppliers	-$183,650.00
Cash receipts from customers	$465,442.00
Net cash provided by Operating activities	$158,007.10
Investing activities	
Cash receipts from investments	$768.00
Net cash provided by Investing activities	$768.00
Financial activities	
Cash receipts from deposit interest	$120.00
Net cash provided by Financial activities	$120.00
Net change in cash	$158,895.10
Cash, Begining	$18,783.78
Cash, Ending	$177,678.88

Figure 3.9-3 Proprietorship1 Cash Flows Statement

Cash

ID	Multi-Name	Amount	Balance	General ID	Transaction Date
37	88-654303-n-tax < Cash payments for operating expenses < Operating a...	-$20,752.91	$18,783.78	12	2015-12-31
38	88-654310-t-supplies < Cash payments for operating expenses < Operati...	-$450.00	$18,333.78	15	2016-01-02
39	88-654308-t-suppliers < Cash payments to suppliers < Operating activities	-$10,000.00	$8,333.78	16	2016-01-02
40	88-654308-c-customers < Cash receipts from customers < Operating acti...	$9,300.00	$17,633.78	19	2016-01-03
41	909876503-c-customers < Cash receipts from customers < Operating act...	$108.00	$17,741.78	26	2016-01-06
42	909876505-c-customers < Cash receipts from customers < Operating act...	$98.00	$17,839.78	27	2016-01-10
43	909876506-c-customers < Cash receipts from customers < Operating act...	$92.00	$17,931.78	28	2016-01-10
44	88-654308-t-supplies < Cash payments for operating expenses < Operati...	-$150.00	$17,781.78	29	2016-01-13
45	909876515-c-customers < Cash receipts from customers < Operating act...	$20.00	$17,801.78	30	2016-01-13
46	909876516-c-customers < Cash receipts from customers < Operating act...	$192.00	$17,993.78	31	2016-01-13
47	909876517-c-customers < Cash receipts from customers < Operating act...	$44.00	$18,037.78	32	2016-01-16
48	909876520-c-customers < Cash receipts from customers < Operating act...	$51.00	$18,088.78	33	2016-01-18
49	909876522-n-operating expenses < Cash payments for operating expen...	-$153.87	$17,934.91	34	2016-01-18
50	909876525-c-customers < Cash receipts from customers < Operating act...	$57.00	$17,991.91	35	2016-01-19
51	88-654308-c-customers < Cash receipts from customers < Operating acti...	$1,300.00	$19,291.91	36	2016-01-26
52	88-654307-t-suppliers < Cash payments to suppliers < Operating activities	-$250.00	$19,041.91	37	2016-01-27
53	909876518-c-customers < Cash receipts from customers < Operating act...	$144.00	$19,185.91	38	2016-01-28
54	909876521-c-customers < Cash receipts from customers < Operating act...	$42.00	$19,227.91	39	2016-01-28
55	909876523-c-customers < Cash receipts from customers < Operating act...	$44.00	$19,271.91	40	2016-01-28
56	88-654307-c-customers < Cash receipts from customers < Operating acti...	$500.00	$19,771.91	41	2016-01-30
57	909876523-n-operating expenses < Cash payments for operating expen...	-$145.54	$19,626.37	42	2016-01-30
58	88-654306-c-customers < Cash receipts from customers < Operating acti...	$2,040.00	$21,666.37	43	2016-01-31
59	909876522-t-salary < Cash payments for operating expenses < Operatin...	-$2,870.00	$18,796.37	44	2016-01-31
60	909876523-t-CGM < Cash payments for operating expenses < Operating...	-$2,800.00	$15,996.37	44	2016-01-31
215	909876509-c-customers < Cash receipts from customers < Operating act...	$100.00	$175,914.88	207	2016-01-25
216	909876508-c-customers < Cash receipts from customers < Operating act...	$51.00	$175,965.88	208	2016-03-27
217	909876507-c-customers < Cash receipts from customers < Operating act...	$102.00	$176,067.88	209	2016-04-27
218	909876509-c-customers < Cash receipts from customers < Operating act...	$112.00	$176,179.88	210	2016-05-12
219	909876509-c-customers < Cash receipts from customers < Operating act...	$96.00	$176,275.88	211	2016-06-14
220	909876509-c-customers < Cash receipts from customers < Operating act...	$112.00	$176,387.88	212	2016-09-17
221	909876509-c-customers < Cash receipts from customers < Operating act...	$114.00	$176,501.88	213	2016-10-22
222	909876509-c-customers < Cash receipts from customers < Operating act...	$99.00	$176,600.88	214	2016-12-15
223	909876510-c-customers < Cash receipts from customers < Operating act...	$57.00	$176,657.88	215	2016-01-27
224	909876511-c-customers < Cash receipts from customers < Operating act...	$50.00	$176,707.88	216	2016-03-11
225	909876511-c-customers < Cash receipts from customers < Operating act...	$69.00	$176,776.88	217	2016-04-13
226	909876511-c-customers < Cash receipts from customers < Operating act...	$56.00	$176,832.88	218	2016-05-20
227	909876512-c-customers < Cash receipts from customers < Operating act...	$109.00	$176,941.88	219	2016-06-18
228	909876512-c-customers < Cash receipts from customers < Operating act...	$125.00	$177,066.88	220	2016-07-21
229	909876510-c-customers < Cash receipts from customers < Operating act...	$63.00	$177,129.88	221	2016-08-17
230	909876512-c-customers < Cash receipts from customers < Operating act...	$112.00	$177,241.88	222	2016-08-22
231	909876512-c-customers < Cash receipts from customers < Operating act...	$104.00	$177,345.88	223	2016-09-17
232	909876512-c-customers < Cash receipts from customers < Operating act...	$108.00	$177,453.88	224	2016-10-16
233	909876512-c-customers < Cash receipts from customers < Operating act...	$100.00	$177,553.88	225	2016-11-19
234	909876512-c-customers < Cash receipts from customers < Operating act...	$125.00	$177,678.88	226	2016-12-27
235	88-654305-c-deposit interest income < Cash receipts from deposit intere...	-$120.00	$177,558.88	227	2016-12-31
236	88-654304-c-deposit interest income < Cash receipts from deposit intere...	$120.00	$177,678.88	227	2016-12-31

Figure 3.9-4   Proprietorship1 Cash Account Table

Income Statement

Year ended: 12/31/2016	
Revenues	'
Sales	$477,352.00
Cost	
Cost of goods sold	-$235,534.00
Gross Margin	$241,818.00
Operating and administrative expenses	
Travelling expenses	-$1,387.90
Other expenses	-$677.00
Salary expenses	-$34,440.00
Bond interest expenses	-$2,500.00
Note interest expenses	-$11,280.00
Vehicle part expenses	-$7,200.00
Amortization expenses	-$10,762.50
Cost of goods manufactured	$0.00
Office supplies expenses	-$321.57
Other income	
Investment incomes	$768.00
Deposit interest incomes	$120.00
Earnings Before Income Taxes	$174,137.03
Tax	
Tax expenses	-$34,827.41
Net Earnings	$139,309.62
Retained Earnings.Begining	$0.00
Retained Earnings.Ending	$139,309.62

Figure 3.9-5   Proprietorship1 Income Statement

Balance Sheet

	As at 12/31/2016
ASSETS	
Current assets	
Cash	$177,678.88
Supplies	$76.88
Account receivable	$16,450.00
Inventory	$248,866.00
Working-in-process inventory	$0.00
	$443,071.76
Long term investments	
Bonds	$18,000.00
Equipment	
Vehicle	$78,000.00
Accumulated amortization: Vehicle	-$26,000.00
Computer	$5,900.00
Accumulated amortization: Computer	-$737.50
	$57,162.50
Total Assets	$518,234.26
LIABILITIES	
Current liabilities	
Account payable	$1,523.00
Tax payable	$34,827.41
	$36,350.41
Long term liabilities	
Bonds payable	$50,000.00
Notes payable	$120,000.00
	$170,000.00
Total Liability	$206,350.41
SHAREHOLDERS' EQUITY	
Owners capital	
Share capital	$160,000.00
Retained earnings (Conversion)	$12,574.23
	$172,574.23
Retined earnings	$139,309.62
Accumulated other comprehensive income	$0.00
Total Shareholders' Equity	$311,883.85
Total Liabilities and Shareholders' Equity	$518,234.26

Figure 3.9-6   Proprietorship1 Balance Sheet Statement

3.10 Proprietorship2

3.10.1 An Accounting Fiscal Year of the Proprietorship2

Because the Proprietorship2 mainly sells foods to individuals, it has many transactions every day. For simplification, I assume that an individual only buy foods (exception of business foods) two times for one year. Therefore, in the new fiscal year, the Proprietorship2 occurs the following transactions.

- On January 2, 2016, the Proprietorship2 purchases the supplies $600 ($14*20 + $16*20) from the Proprietorship2 itself (phone number: 123456780). The balance of the Cash account does not have any change, so merged the transaction sub-equation is:

    Supplies (1): 600 + Inventory (1): -140 + Inventory (1): -160 = Sales (4): 600 + Cost of goods sold (5): -300

- On January 2, 2016, the Proprietorship2 sells the Supplies1 $14*7 (cost: -$7*7) and the Supplies2 $16*4 (cost: -$8*4) for sales $162 to the Business Bank1 (phone number: 123456786) for cash $162. The multi-subaccount name of the Cash account is:

    88-654304-c-customers < Cash receipts from customers < Operating activities

- On January 2, 2016, the Proprietorship2 sells the Supplies1 $14*3 (cost: -$7*3) and the Supplies2 $16*9 (cost: -$8*9) for sales $186 to the Business Bank2 (phone number: 123456785) for cash $186. The multi-subaccount name of the Cash account is:

    88-654305-c-customers < Cash receipts from customers < Operating activities

- On January 2, 2016, the Proprietorship2 sells the Supplies1 $14*30 (cost: -$7*30) and the Supplies2 $16*40 (cost: -$8*40) for sales $1,060 to the Company3 (phone number: 123456782) for cash $400 and other on credit. The multi-subaccount name of the Cash account is:

    88-654308-c-customers < Cash receipts from customers < Operating activities

- On January 2, 2016, the Proprietorship2 sells the Supplies1 $14*40 (cost: -$7*40) and the Supplies2 $16*20 (cost: -$8*20) for sales $880 to the Company2 (phone number: 123456783) for cash $500 and other on credit. The multi-subaccount name of the Cash account is:

  88-654307-c-customers < Cash receipts from customers < Operating activities

- On January 2, 2016, the Proprietorship2 sells the Supplies1 $14*35 (cost: -$7*35) and the Supplies2 $16*35 (cost: -$8*35) for sales $1,050 to the Proprietorship 1 (phone number: 123456781) for cash $450 and other on credit. The multi-subaccount name of the Cash account is:

  88-654309-c-customers < Cash receipts from customers < Operating activities

- On January 2, 2016, the Proprietorship2 purchases the following inventories $168,750 From the Company3 (phone number: 123456082) for -$8,000 cash and other on credit.

  Inven51 < Inven5: 10*500

  Inven52 < Inven5: 50*250

  Inven531 < Inven53 < Inven5: 25*500

  Inven532 < Inven53 < Inven5: 35*500

  Inven541 < Inven54 < Inven5: 12*500

  Inven542 < Inven54 < Inven5: 15*500

  Inven611 < Inven61 < Inven6: 6.5*700

  Inven612 < Inven61 < Inven6: 12.5*500

  Inven621 < Inven62 < Inven6: 18*500

  Inven63 < Inven6: 16*500

  Inven711 < Inven71 < Inven7: 36*300

  Inven712 < Inven71 < Inven7: 31*50

  Inven721 < Inven72 < Inven7: 22*400

  Inven722 < Inven72 < Inven7: 20*300

  Inven731 < Inven73 < Inven7: 18*300

  Inven732 < Inven73 < Inven7: 16*500

Inven811 < Inven81 < Inven8: 25*300

Inven812 < Inven81 < Inven8: 24*300

Inven813 < Inven81 < Inven8: 23*300

Inven82 < Inven8: 20*300

Inven831 < Inven83 < Inven8: 18*300

Inven832 < Inven83 < Inven8: 16*400

The multi-subaccount name of the Cash account and four transaction sub-equations respectively are:

88-654308-t-suppliers < Cash payments to suppliers < Operating activities

Cash (1): -8000 + Inventory (1): 10*500 + Inventory (1): 50*250 + Inventory (1): 25*500 + Inventory (1): 35*500 + Inventory (1): 12*500 + Inventory (1): 15*500 + Inventory (1): 6.5*700 + Inventory (1): 12.5*500 = Account Payable (2): 63800

Inventory (1): 18*500 + Inventory (1): 16*500 + Inventory (1): 36*300 + Inventory (1): 31*50 + Inventory (1): 22*400 + Inventory (1): 20*300 + Inventory (1): 18*300 + Inventory (1): 16*500 + Inventory (1): 25*300 = Account Payable (2): 65050

Inventory (1): 24*300 + Inventory (1): 23*300 + Inventory (1): 20*300 + Inventory (1): 18*300 + Inventory (1): 16*400 = Account Payable (2): 31900

- On January 2, 2016, the Proprietorship2 sells the Supplies1 $14*50 (cost: -$7*50) and the Supplies2 $16*50 (cost: -$8*50) for sales $1,500 to the Company1 (phone number: 123456784) for cash $500 and other on credit. The multi-subaccount name of the Cash account is:

  88-654306-c-customers < Cash receipts from customers < Operating activities

- On January 3, 2016, the Proprietorship2 sells the following inventories -$11,430 for sales $19,050 to the Company3 (phone number: 123456782) for cash $6,000 and other on credit.

Inven411 < Inven41 < Inven4: -3*300

Inven412 < Inven41 < Inven4: -11.1*300

TTTCU parts < TTT parts < Inven4: -12*300

RRRHJK parts < Inven4: -12*300

The multi-subaccount name of the Cash account and transaction sub-equation respectively are:

88-654308-c-customers < Cash receipts from customers < Operating activities

Cash (1): 6000 + Account receivable (1): 13050 + Inventory (1): -3*300 + Inventory (1): -11.1*300 + Inventory (1): -12*300 + Inventory (1): -12*300 = Sales (4): 19050 + Cost of goods sold (5): -11430

- On January 3, 2016, the Proprietorship2 transfers the supplies $720 ($14*24 + $16*24) to the Cost of goods manufactured to satisfy the need of producing. The transaction sub-equation is:

Supplies (1): -720 = Cost of goods manufactured (5): -720

- On January 3, 2016, the Proprietorship2 transfers the following inventories $15,500 to the Cost of goods manufactured account to satisfy the need of producing.

Inven31 < Inven3: -10*100

Inven32 < Inven3: -50*100

Inven331 < Inven33 < Inven3: -20*100

Inven332 < Inven33 < Inven3: -45*100

HGFCVB parts < QASXC parts < Inven3: -10*100

PPGHUP parts < ASDUP parts < Inven3: -20*100

The transaction sub-equations is:

Inventory (1): -10*100 + Inventory (1): -50*100 + Inventory (1): -20*100 + Inventory (1): -45*100 + Inventory (1): -10*100 + Inventory (1): -20*100 = Cost of goods manufactured (5): -15500

- On January 3, 2016, the Proprietorship2 transfers the following inventories -$33,750 to the Cost of goods manufactured account to satisfy the need of producing.

Inven51 < Inven5: -10*100

Inven52 < Inven5: -50*50

Inven531 < Inven53 < Inven5: -25*100

Inven532 < Inven53 < Inven5: -35*100

Inven541 < Inven54 < Inven5: -12*100

Inven542 < Inven54 < Inven5: -15*100

Inven611 < Inven61 < Inven6: -6.5*140

Inven612 < Inven61 < Inven6: -12.5*100

Inven621 < Inven62 < Inven6: -18*100

Inven63 < Inven6: -16*100

Inven711 < Inven71 < Inven7: -36*60

Inven712 < Inven71 < Inven7: -31*10

Inven721 < Inven72 < Inven7: -22*80

Inven722 < Inven72 < Inven7: -20*60

Inven731 < Inven73 < Inven7: -18*60

Inven732 < Inven73 < Inven7: -16*100

Inven811 < Inven81 < Inven8: -25*60

Inven812 < Inven81 < Inven8: -24*60

Inven813 < Inven81 < Inven8: -23*60

Inven82 < Inven8: -20*60

Inven831 < Inven83 < Inven8: -18*60

Inven832 < Inven83 < Inven8: -16*80

The three transaction sub-equations are respectively:

Inventory (1): -10*100 + Inventory (1): -50*50 + Inventory (1): -25*100 +

Inventory (1): -35*100 + Inventory (1): -12*100 + Inventory (1): -15*100 +

Inventory (1): -6.5*140 + Inventory (1): -12.5*100 + Inventory (1): -18*100 =

Cost of goods manufactured (5): -16160

Inventory (1): -16*100 + Inventory (1): -36*60 + Inventory (1): -31*10 + Inventory (1): -22*80 + Inventory (1): -20*60 + Inventory (1): -18*60 + Inventory (1): -16*100 + Inventory (1): -25*60 + Inventory (1): -24*60 = Cost of goods manufactured (5): -12650

Inventory (1): -23*60 + Inventory (1): -20*60 + Inventory (1): -18*60 + Inventory (1): -16*80 = Cost of goods manufactured (5): - 4940

- On January 12, 2016, the Proprietorship2 sells the Food513 $10*4 (cost: -$5*4) and the Food613 $26*3 (cost: -$13*3) to A24 (SIN: 909876524) for cash $118. The multi-subaccount name of the Cash account is:

  909876524-c-customers < Cash receipts from customers < Operating activities

- On January 13, 2016, the Proprietorship2 sells the Food514 $11*8 (cost: -$5.5*8) and the Food614 $30*4 (cost: -$15*4) to A13 (SIN: 909876513) for cash $208. The multi-subaccount name of the Cash account is:

  909876513-c-customers < Cash receipts from customers < Operating activities

- On January 14, 2016, the Proprietorship2 pays -$255.37 cash to A24 (SIN: 909876524) for the Travelling expenses (travel allowance) $133.37 and the Other expenses (meals: food514: $10*4 + food613: $26*3) $122. The multi-subaccount name of the Cash account and the transaction sub-equation respectively are:

  909876524-n-operating expenses < Cash payments for operating expenses < Operating activities

  Cash (1): -255.37 = Travelling expenses (5): -133.37 + other expenses (5): -122

- On January 15, 2016, the Proprietorship2 sells the Food621 $26*1 (cost: -$13*1) and the Food622 $28*1 (cost: -$14*1) to A11 (SIN: 909876511) for cash $54. The multi-subaccount name of the Cash account is:

  909876511-c-customers < Cash receipts from customers < Operating activities

- On January 16, 2016, the Proprietorship2 sells the Food514 $11*4 (cost: -$5.5*4) and the Food613 $26*3 (cost: -$13*3) to A19 (SIN: 909876519) for cash $122. The multi-subaccount name of the Cash account is:

  909876519-c-customers < Cash receipts from customers < Operating activities

- On January 16, 2016, the Proprietorship2 sells the Food514 $11*2 (cost: -$5.5*2) and the Food613 $26*1 (cost: -$13*1) to A22 (SIN: 909876522) for cash $48. The multi-subaccount name of the Cash account is:

  909876522-c-customers < Cash receipts from customers < Operating activities

- On January 18, 2016, the Proprietorship2 sells the Food422 $13*1 (cost: -$6.5*1) and the Food613 $26*1 (cost: -$13*1) to A1 (SIN: 909876501) for cash $39. The multi-subaccount name of the Cash account is:

  909876501-c-customers < Cash receipts from customers < Operating activities

- On January 20, 2016, the Proprietorship2 sells the Food613 $26*2 (cost: -$13*2) and the Food614 $30*1 (cost: -$15*1) to A7 (SIN: 909876507) for cash $82. The multi-subaccount name of the Cash account is:

  909876507-c-customers < Cash receipts from customers < Operating activities

- On January 21, 2016, the Proprietorship2 pays -$149.65 cash to A25 (SIN: 909876525) for the Travelling expenses (travel allowance) $92.65 and the Other expenses (meals: food321: $27*1 + food322: $30*1) $57.

- On January 22, 2016, the Proprietorship2 sells the Food53 $16*4 (cost: -$8*4) and the Food622 $28*2 (cost: -$14*2) to A12 (SIN: 909876512) for cash $120. The multi-subaccount name of the Cash account is:

  909876512-c-customers < Cash receipts from customers < Operating activities

- On January 26, 2016, the Proprietorship2 receives $800 cash from the Company3 (phone number: 123456782) with the General ID 3. The multi-subaccount name of the Cash account is:

  88-654308-c-customers < Cash receipts from customers < Operating activities

- On January 28, 2016, the Proprietorship2 pays -$200 cash to the Company3 (phone number: 123456082) with the General ID 3. The multi-subaccount name of the Cash account is:

88-654308-t-suppliers < Cash payments to suppliers < Operating activities

- On January 30 2016, the Proprietorship2 receives $300 cash from the Company2 (phone number: 123456783) with the General ID 3. The multi-subaccount name of the Cash account is:

88-654307-c-customers < Cash receipts from customers < Operating activities

- On January 31, 2016, the Proprietorship2 receives $1,000 cash from the Company1 (phone number: 123456784) with the General ID 3. The multi-subaccount name of the Cash account is:

88-654306-c-customers < Cash receipts from customers < Operating activities

- On January 31, 2016, the Proprietorship2 sells the Food612 $24*1 (cost: -$12*1) to A14 (SIN: 909876514) for cash $24. The multi-subaccount name of the Cash account is:

909876514-c-customers < Cash receipts from customers < Operating activities

- On January 31, 2016, the Proprietorship2 pays two employees' salary expenses for cash -$5,660. The two multi-subaccount names of the Cash account and the transaction sub-equation respectively are:

909876524-t-salary < Cash payments for operating expenses < Operating activities

909876525-t-CGM < Cash payments for operating expenses < Operating activities

Cash (1): -2870 + Cash (1): -2790 = Salary expenses (5): -2870 + Cost of goods manufactured (5): -2790

- On January 31, 2016, the Proprietorship2 sells the following inventories -$5,395 for sales $10,790 to A1A8 (SIN: 909876526), who uses his (or her) father A1's (or mother A1's) secondary card of the Business Bank2, for cash $10,790.

Food411 < Food41 < Food4: -5*130

Food412 < Food41 < Food4: -5.5*130

Food421 < Food42 < Food4: -6*130

Food422 < Food42 < Food4: -6.5*130

Food43 < Food4: -7*130

Food44 < Food4: -7.5*130

Food511 < Food51 < Food5: -4*130

The multi-subaccount name of the Cash account is:

909876501-c-customers < Cash receipts from customers < Operating activities

- On January 31, 2016, the Proprietorship2 sells the following inventories -$5,460 for sales $10,920 to A14 (SIN: 909876514) for cash $10,920.

Food411 < Food41 < Food4: -5*130

Food412 < Food41 < Food4: -5.5*130

Food421 < Food42 < Food4: -6*130

Food422 < Food42 < Food4: -6.5*130

Food43 < Food4: -7*130

Food44 < Food4: -7.5*130

Food512 < Food51 < Food5: -4.5*130

The multi-subaccount name of the Cash account is:

909876514-c-customers < Cash receipts from customers < Operating activities

- On January 31, 2016, the Proprietorship2 sells the following inventories -$5,525 for sales $11,050 to A15 (SIN: 909876515) for cash $11,050.

Food411 < Food41 < Food4: -5*130

Food412 < Food41 < Food4: -5.5*130

Food421 < Food42 < Food4: -6*130

Food422 < Food42 < Food4: -6.5*130

Food43 < Food4: -7*130

Food44 < Food4: -7.5*130

Food513 < Food51 < Food5: -5*130

The multi-subaccount name of the Cash account is:

909876515-c-customers < Cash receipts from customers < Operating activities

- On January 31, 2016, the Proprietorship2 sells the following inventories -$5,590 for sales $11,180 to A16 (SIN: 909876516) for cash $11,180.

  Food411 < Food41 < Food4: -5*130

  Food412 < Food41 < Food4: -5.5*130

  Food421 < Food42 < Food4: -6*130

  Food422 < Food42 < Food4: -6.5*130

  Food43 < Food4: -7*130

  Food44 < Food4: -7.5*130

  Food514 < Food51 < Food5: -5.5*130

  The multi-subaccount name of the Cash account is:

    909876516-c-customers < Cash receipts from customers < Operating activities

- On January 31, 2016, the Proprietorship2 sells the following inventories -$5,135 for sales $10,270 to A17 (SIN: 909876517) for cash $10,270.

  Food511 < Food51 < Food5: -4*130

  Food512 < Food51 < Food5: -4.5*130

  Food513 < Food51 < Food5: -5*130

  Food514 < Food51 < Food5: -5.5*130

  Food521 < Food52 < Food5: -6*130

  Food522 < Food52 < Food5: -6.5*130

  Food53 < Food5: -8*130

  The multi-subaccount name of the Cash account is:

    909876517-c-customers < Cash receipts from customers < Operating activities

- On January 31, 2016, the Proprietorship2 sells the following inventories -$5,915 for sales $11,830 to A18 (SIN: 909876518) for cash $11,830.

  Food511 < Food51 < Food5: -4*130

  Food512 < Food51 < Food5: -4.5*130

  Food513 < Food51 < Food5: -5*130

  Food514 < Food51 < Food5: -5.5*130

  Food521 < Food52 < Food5: -6*130

Food522 < Food52 < Food5: -6.5*130

Food622 < Food62 < Food6: -14*130

The multi-subaccount name of the Cash account is:

909876518-c-customers < Cash receipts from customers < Operating activities

- On January 31, 2016, the Proprietorship2 sells the following inventories -$5,785 for sales $11,570 to A19 (SIN: 909876519) for cash $11,570.

Food511 < Food51 < Food5: -4*130

Food512 < Food51 < Food5: -4.5*130

Food513 < Food51 < Food5: -5*130

Food514 < Food51 < Food5: -5.5*130

Food521 < Food52 < Food5: -6*130

Food522 < Food52 < Food5: -6.5*130

Food621 < Food62 < Food6: -13*130

The multi-subaccount name of the Cash account is:

909876519-c-customers < Cash receipts from customers < Operating activities

- On January 31, 2016, the Proprietorship2 sells the following inventories -$6,045 for sales $12,090 to A20 (SIN: 909876520) for cash $12,090.

Food511 < Food51 < Food5: -4*130

Food512 < Food51 < Food5: -4.5*130

Food513 < Food51 < Food5: -5*130

Food514 < Food51 < Food5: -5.5*130

Food521 < Food52 < Food5: -6*130

Food522 < Food52 < Food5: -6.5*130

Food614 < Food61 < Food6: -15*130

The multi-subaccount name of the Cash account is:

909876520-c-customers < Cash receipts from customers < Operating activities

- On January 31, 2016, the Proprietorship2 sells the following inventories -$6,435 for sales $12,870 to A21 (SIN: 909876521) for cash $12,870.

Food411 < Food41 < Food4: -5*130

Food412 < Food41 < Food4: -5.5*130

Food421 < Food42 < Food4: -6*130

Food422 < Food42 < Food4: -6.5*130

Food43 < Food4: -7*130

Food44 < Food4: -7.5*130

Food612 < Food61 < Food6: -12*130

The multi-subaccount name of the Cash account is:

909876521-c-customers < Cash receipts from customers < Operating activities

- On January 31, 2016, the Proprietorship2 sells the following inventories -$5,395 for sales $10,790 to A22 (SIN: 909876522) for cash $10,790.

Food511 < Food51 < Food5: -4*130

Food512 < Food51 < Food5: -4.5*130

Food513 < Food51 < Food5: -5*130

Food514 < Food51 < Food5: -5.5*130

Food521 < Food52 < Food5: -6*130

Food522 < Food52 < Food5: -6.5*130

Food611 < Food61 < Food6: -10*130

The multi-subaccount name of the Cash account is:

909876522-c-customers < Cash receipts from customers < Operating activities

- On January 31, 2016, the Proprietorship2 sells the following inventories -$6,175 for sales $12,350 to A23 (SIN: 909876523) for cash $12,350.

Food411 < Food41 < Food4: -5*130

Food412 < Food41 < Food4: -5.5*130

Food421 < Food42 < Food4: -6*130

Food511 < Food51 < Food5: -4*130

Food521 < Food52 < Food5: -6*130

Food53 < Food5: -8*130

Food613 < Food61 < Food6: -13*130

The multi-subaccount name of the Cash account is:

909876523-c-customers < Cash receipts from customers < Operating activities

- On January 31, 2016, the Proprietorship2 sells the following inventories -$5,005 for sales $10,010 to A24 (SIN: 909876524) for cash $10,010.

  Food43 < Food4: -7*130

  Food511 < Food51 < Food5: -4*130

  Food512 < Food51 < Food5: -4.5*130

  Food513 < Food51 < Food5: -5*130

  Food514 < Food51 < Food5: -5.5*130

  Food521 < Food52 < Food5: -6*130

  Food522 < Food52 < Food5: -6.5*130

  The multi-subaccount name of the Cash account is:

  909876524-c-customers < Cash receipts from customers < Operating activities

- On January 31, 2016, the Proprietorship2 sells the following inventories -$5,135 for sales $10,270 to A25 (SIN: 909876525) for cash $10,270.

  Food412 < Food41 < Food4: -5.5*130

  Food421 < Food42 < Food4: -6*130

  Food422 < Food42 < Food4: -6.5*130

  Food511 < Food51 < Food5: -4*130

  Food512 < Food51 < Food5: -4.5*130

  Food513 < Food51 < Food5: -5*130

  Food53 < Food5: -8*130

  The multi-subaccount name of the Cash account is:

  909876525-c-customers < Cash receipts from customers < Operating activities

- On February 1, 2016, the Proprietorship2 purchases one Car3 $38,000 from the Company1 (phone number: 123456084) for cash -$30,000 and other on credit. The multi-subaccount name of the Cash account and transaction sub-equation respectively are:

  88-654306-t-machinery < Cash payments for machinery < Operating activities

Cash (1): -30000 + Vehicle (1): 38000 = Account payable (2): 8000

- On February 6, 2016, the Proprietorship2 sells the Food611 $20*3 (cost: -$10*3) and the Food622 $28*2 (cost: -$14*2) to A12 (SIN: 909876512, using secondary card of the Business Bank1) for cash $116. The multi-subaccount name of the Cash account is:

  909876512-c-customers < Cash receipts from customers < Operating activities

- On February 17, 2016, the Proprietorship2 sells the Food53 $16*10 (cost: -$8*10) and the Food614 $30*5 (cost: -$15*5) to A16 (SIN: 909876516) for cash $310. The multi-subaccount name of the Cash account is:

  909876516-c-customers < Cash receipts from customers < Operating activities

- On February 19, 2016, the Proprietorship2 sells the Food611 $20*3 (cost: -$10*3) and the Food621 $26*2 (cost: -$13*2) to A9 (SIN: 909876509) for cash $112. The multi-subaccount name of the Cash account is:

  909876509-c-customers < Cash receipts from customers < Operating activities

- On February 20, 2016, the Proprietorship2 pays -$400 cash to the Proprietorship1 (phone number: 123456081) with the General ID 3. The multi-subaccount name of the Cash account is:

  88-654309-t-suppliers < Cash payments to suppliers < Operating activities

- On February 21, 2016, the Proprietorship2 receives $300 cash from the Proprietorship1 (phone number: 123456781) with the General ID 3. The multi-subaccount name of the Cash account is:

  88-654309-c-customers < Cash receipts from customers < Operating activities

- On February 22, 2016, the Proprietorship2 sells the Food611 $20*2 (cost: -$10*2) and the Food622 $28*2 (cost: -$14*2) to A8 (SIN: 909876508) for cash $96. The multi-subaccount name of the Cash account is:

  909876508-c-customers < Cash receipts from customers < Operating activities

- On February 23, 2016, the Proprietorship2 sells the Food53 $16*2 (cost: -$8*2) and the Food614 $30*1 (cost: -$15*1) to A24 (SIN: 909876524) for cash $62. The multi-subaccount name of the Cash account is:

909876524-c-customers < Cash receipts from customers < Operating activities

- On February 25, 2016, the Proprietorship2 pays -$187.84 cash to A24 (SIN: 909876524) for the Travelling expenses (travel allowance) $125.84 and the Other expenses (meals: food53: $16*2 + food614: $30*1) $62. The multi-subaccount name of the Cash account and the transaction sub-equation respectively is:

909876524-n-operaing expenses < Cash payments for operating expenses < Operating activities

- On February 28, 2016, the Proprietorship2 pays two employees' salary expenses for cash -$5,660. The two multi-subaccount names of the Cash account and the transaction sub-equation respectively are:

909876524-t-salary < Cash payments for operating expenses < Operating activities

909876525-t-CGM < Cash payments for operating expenses < Operating activities

Cash (1): -2870 + Cash (1): -2790 = Salary expenses (5): -2870 + Cost of goods manufactured (5): -2790

- On March 7, 2016, the Proprietorship2 sells the Food521 $12*4 (cost: -$6*4) and the Food621 $26*2 (cost: -$13*2) to A12 (SIN: 909876512) for cash $100. The multi-subaccount name of the Cash account is:

909876512-c-customers < Cash receipts from customers < Operating activities

- On March 7, 2016, the Proprietorship2 pays -$201.66 cash to A25 (SIN: 909876525) for the Travelling expenses (travel allowance) $123.66 and the Other expenses (meals: food312: $24*2 + food322: $30*1) $78.

- On March 9, 2016, the Proprietorship2 pays -$2,000 cash to the Company1 (phone number: 123456084) with the General ID 3. The multi-subaccount name of the Cash account is:

88-654306-t-suppliers < Cash payments to suppliers < Operating activities

- On March 18, 2016, the Proprietorship2 sells the Food53 $16*3 (cost: -$8*3) and the Food622 $28*2 (cost: -$14*2) to A9 (SIN: 909876509) for cash $104. The multi-subaccount name of the Cash account is:

  909876509-c-customers < Cash receipts from customers < Operating activities

- On March 20, 2016, the Proprietorship2 sells the Food44 $15*10 (cost: -$7.5*10) and the Food622 $28*5 (cost: -$14*5) to A13 (SIN: 909876513) for cash $290. The multi-subaccount name of the Cash account is:

  909876513-c-customers < Cash receipts from customers < Operating activities

- On March 20, 2016, the Proprietorship2 sells the Food44 $15*5 (cost: -$7.5*5) and the Food622 $28*2 (cost: -$14*2) to A16 (SIN: 909876516) for cash $131. The multi-subaccount name of the Cash account is:

  909876516-c-customers < Cash receipts from customers < Operating activities

- On March 21, 2016, the Proprietorship2 sells the Food44 $15*3 (cost: -$7.5*3) and the Food622 $28*1 (cost: -$14*1) to A19 (SIN: 909876519) for cash $73. The multi-subaccount name of the Cash account is:

  909876519-c-customers < Cash receipts from customers < Operating activities

- On March 21, 2016, the Proprietorship2 sells the Food44 $15*2 (cost: -$7.5*2) and the Food622 $28*1 (cost: -$14*1) to A22 (SIN: 909876522) for cash $58. The multi-subaccount name of the Cash account is:

  909876522-c-customers < Cash receipts from customers < Operating activities

- On March 22, 2016, the Proprietorship2 sells the Food611 $20*2 (cost: -$10*2) and the Food622 $28*2 (cost: -$14*2) to A7 (SIN: 909876507) for cash $96. The multi-subaccount name of the Cash account is:

  909876507-c-customers < Cash receipts from customers < Operating activities

- On March 24, 2016, the Proprietorship2 sells the Food522 $13*3 (cost: -$6.5*3) and the Food612 $24*2 (cost: -$12*2) to A17 (SIN: 909876517) for cash $87. The multi-subaccount name of the Cash account is:

  909876517-c-customers < Cash receipts from customers < Operating activities

- On March 25, 2016, the Proprietorship2 sells the Food43 $14*3 (cost: -$7*2) and

the Food622 $28*1 (cost: -$14*1) to A25 (SIN: 909876525) for cash $70. The multi-subaccount name of the Cash account is:

909876525-c-customers < Cash receipts from customers < Operating activities

- On March 27, 2016, the Proprietorship2 pays -$191.43 cash to A25 (SIN: 909876525) for the Travelling expenses (travel allowance) $121.43 and the Other expenses (meals: food43: $14*3 + food622: $28*1) $70.

- On March 28, 2016, the Proprietorship2 sells the Food521 $12*3 (cost: -$6*3) and the Food612 $24*2 (cost: -$12*2) to A14 (SIN: 909876514) for cash $84. The multi-subaccount name of the Cash account is:

909876514-c-customers < Cash receipts from customers < Operating activities

- On March 31, 2016, the Proprietorship2 pays two employees' salary expenses for cash $5,660 repeatedly.

- On April 1, 2016, the Proprietorship2 purchases the supplies $750 ($14*25 + $16*25) from the Proprietorship2 itself (phone number: 123456780). The balance of the Cash account does not have any change, so the merged transaction sub-equation is:

Supplies (1): 750 + Inventory (1): -175 + Inventory (1): -200 = Sales (4): 750 + Cost of goods sold (5): -375

- On April 1, 2016, the Proprietorship2 transfers the supplies $90 ($14*3 + $16*3) to the Cost of goods manufactured to satisfy the need of producing. The transaction sub-equation is:

Supplies (1): -90 = Cost of goods manufactured (5): -90

- On April 6, 2016, the Proprietorship2 sells the Food613 $26*2 (cost: -$13*2) and the Food622 $28*2 (cost: -$14*2) to A9 (SIN: 909876509) for cash $108. The multi-subaccount name of the Cash account is:

909876509-c-customers < Cash receipts from customers < Operating activities

- On April 12, 2016, the Proprietorship2 sells the Supplies1 $14*100 (cost: -$7*100)

and the Supplies2 $16*100 (cost: -$8*100) for sales $3000 to the Company1 (phone number: 123456784) for cash $1,000 and other on credit. The multi-subaccount name of the Cash account is:

88-654306-c-customers < Cash receipts from customers < Operating activities

- On April 13, 2016, the Proprietorship2 sells the Food613 $26*2 (cost: -$13*2) and the Food614 $30*2 (cost: -$15*2) to A5 (SIN: 909876505) for cash $112. The multi-subaccount name of the Cash account is:

909876505-c-customers < Cash receipts from customers < Operating activities

- On April 15, 2016, the Proprietorship2 sells the Food611 $20*1 (cost: -$10*1) and the Food614 $30*1 (cost: -$15*1) to A2 (SIN: 909876502) for cash $50. The multi-subaccount name of the Cash account is:

909876502-c-customers < Cash receipts from customers < Operating activities

- On April 17, 2016, the Proprietorship2 sells the Food53 $16*4 (cost: -$8*4) and the Food622 $28*2 (cost: -$14*2) to A12 (SIN: 909876512) for cash $120. The multi-subaccount name of the Cash account is:

909876512-c-customers < Cash receipts from customers < Operating activities

- On April 20, 2016, the Proprietorship2 sells the Food612 $24*2 (cost: -$12*2) and the Food621 $26*2 (cost: -$13*2) to A4 (SIN: 909876502) for cash $100. The multi-subaccount name of the Cash account is:

909876504-c-customers < Cash receipts from customers < Operating activities

- On April 24, 2016, the Proprietorship2 pays -$236.37 cash to A24 (SIN: 909876524) for the Travelling expenses (travel allowance) $161.37 and the Other expenses (meals: food312: $24*2 + food321: $27*1) $75.

- On April 26, 2016, the Proprietorship2 sells the Food422 $13*10 (cost: -$6.5*10), the Food612 $24*5 (cost: -$12*5), the Food613 $26*5 (cost: -$13*5), and the Food614 $30*3 (cost: -$15*3) to A13 (SIN: 909876513) for cash $470. The multi-subaccount name of the Cash account is:

909876513-c-customers < Cash receipts from customers < Operating activities

- On April 29, 2016, the Proprietorship2 receives $1,000 cash from the Company1 (phone number: 123456784) with the General ID 24. The multi-subaccount name of the Cash account is:

88-654306-c-customers < Cash receipts from customers < Operating activities

- On April 30, 2016, the Proprietorship2 sells the Supplies1 $14*11 (cost: -$7*11) and the Supplies2 $16*11 (cost: -$8*11) for sales $330 to the Government1 (phone number: 123456788) for cash $330. The multi-subaccount name of the Cash account is:

88-654302-c-customers < Cash receipts from customers < Operating activities

- On April 30, 2016, the Proprietorship2 pays three employees' salary expenses for cash -$5,660 repeatedly.

- On April 30, 2016, the Proprietorship2 has completed all products of the Working-in-process inventory account. If the all general parts have just been consumed and the supplies has the rest $70, the rest supplies must be returned to the Supplies account from the Cost of goods manufactured account. The transaction sub-equation is:

Supplies (1): 70 = Cost of goods manufactured (5): 70

- On April 30, 2016, the Proprietorship2 transfers the balance of the Cost of goods manufactured account to the Working-in-process inventory account. The Cost of goods manufactured account has three subaccounts of the "Supplies expenses", the "909876525-salary < Product department-salary < Salary expenses", and the "General parts expenses". Their balances are -$740, -$11,160, and -$49,250 (-$33,750 - $15,500) respectively. Here, the balance of the subaccount "General parts expenses" will be divided to three parts which are used in three transaction sub-equations respectively. The three transaction sub-equations are:

Working-in-process inventory (1): 1*1000 + Working-in-process inventory (1): 5*1000 + Working-in-process inventory (1): 5.5*1000 + Working-in-process inventory (1): 5*1000 + Working-in-process inventory (1): 2*1000 + Working-in-process inventory (1): 2.25*1000 + Working-in-process inventory (1): 3*1000 = Cost of goods manufactured (5): 740 + Cost of goods manufactured (5): 11160 + Cost of goods manufactured (5): 11850

Working-in-process inventory (1): 3*1000 + Working-in-process inventory (1): 3*1000 + Working-in-process inventory (1): 4*1000 + Working-in-process inventory (1): 2*1000 + Working-in-process inventory (1): 2*1000 + Working-in-process inventory (1): 2*1000 + Working-in-process inventory (1): 2*1000 + Working-in-process inventory (1): 3*1000 + Working-in-process inventory (1): 3*1000 = Cost of goods manufactured (5): 24000

Working-in-process inventory (1): 4*1000 + Working-in-process inventory (1): 5*200 + Working-in-process inventory (1): 6*200 + Working-in-process inventory (1): 6.5*200 + Working-in-process inventory (1): 7.5*200 + Working-in-process inventory (1): 7*200 + Working-in-process inventory (1): 7*200 + Working-in-process inventory (1): 4*200 + Working-in-process inventory (1): 4*200 = Cost of goods manufactured (5): 13400

- On April 30, 2016, the Proprietorship2 transfers the balance of the Working-in-process inventory account to the Inventory account. The five transaction sub-equations respectively are:

Working-in-process inventory (1): -3*1000 + Working-in-process inventory (1): -11.1*1000 + Working-in-process inventory (1): -12*1000 + Working-in-process inventory (1): -12*1000 + Working-in-process inventory (1): -5*1000 + Inventory (1): 3*1000 + Inventory (1): 11.1*1000 + Inventory (1): 12*1000 + Inventory (1): 12*1000 + Inventory (1): 5*1000 = 0

Working-in-process inventory (1): -5.5*1000 + Working-in-process inventory (1): -6*1000 + Working-in-process inventory (1): -6.5*1000 + Working-in-process inventory (1): -7*1000 + Working-in-process inventory (1): -7.5*1000 +

Inventory (1): 5.5*1000 + Inventory (1): 6*1000 + Inventory (1): 6.5*1000 + Inventory (1): 7*1000 + Inventory (1): 7.5*1000 = 0

Working-in-process inventory (1): -4*1000 + Working-in-process inventory (1): -4.5*1000 + Working-in-process inventory (1): -5*1000 + Working-in-process inventory (1): -5.5*1000 + Working-in-process inventory (1): -6*1000 + Inventory (1): 4*1000 + Inventory (1): 4.5*1000 + Inventory (1): 5*1000 + Inventory (1): 5.5*1000 + Inventory (1): 6*1000 = 0

Working-in-process inventory (1): -6.5*1000 + Working-in-process inventory (1): -8*1000 + Working-in-process inventory (1): -10*200 + Working-in-process inventory (1): -12*200 + Working-in-process inventory (1): -13*200 + Inventory (1): 6.5*1000 + Inventory (1): 8*1000 + Inventory (1): 10*200 + Inventory (1): 12*200 + Inventory (1): 13*200 = 0

Working-in-process inventory (1): -15*200 + Working-in-process inventory (1): -13*200 + Working-in-process inventory (1): -14*200 + Working-in-process inventory (1): -7*200 + Working-in-process inventory (1): -8*200 + Inventory (1): 15*200 + Inventory (1): 13*200 + Inventory (1): 14*200 + Inventory (1): 7*200 + Inventory (1): 8*200 = 0

- On May 1, 2016, the Proprietorship2 plans to produce the following products in the Figure 3.10-1.

Order	Product (the Lowest-level Subaccount) Names	Multi-subaccount Names	Costs	Amounts
1	Food411	Food411 < Food41 < Food4	5.00	1200
2	Food412	Food412 < Food41 < Food4	5.50	1200
3	Food421	Food421 < Food42 < Food4	6.00	1200
4	Food422	Food422 < Food42 < Food4	6.50	1200
5	Food43	Food43 < Food4	7.00	1200
6	Food44	Food44 < Food4	7.50	1200
7	Food511	Food511 < Food51 < Food5	4.00	1200
8	Food512	Food512 < Food51 < Food5	4.50	1200

9	Food513	Food513 < Food51 < Food5	5.00	1200
10	Food514	Food514 < Food51 < Food5	5.50	1200
11	Food521	Food521 < Food52 < Food5	6.00	1200
12	Food522	Food522 < Food52 < Food5	6.50	1200
13	Food53	Food53 < Food5	8.00	1200
14	Food611	Food611 < Food61 < Food6	10.00	1000
15	Food612	Food612 < Food61 < Food6	12.00	1000
16	Food613	Food613 < Food61 < Food6	13.00	1000
17	Food614	Food614 < Food61 < Food6	15.00	1000
18	Food621	Food621 < Food62 < Food6	13.00	1000
19	Food622	Food622 < Food62 < Food6	14.00	1000
20	Supplies1	Supplies1	7.00	800
21	Supplies2	Supplies2	8.00	800

Figure 3.10-1   Producing Plan Table

Therefore, the Proprietorship2 purchases the supplies $900 ($14*30 + $16*30) from the Proprietorship2 itself (phone number: 123456080). The balance of the Cash account does not change, so the merged transaction sub-equation is:

Supplies (1): 900 + Inventory (1): -450 = Sales (4): 900 + Cost of goods sold (5): -450

- On May 1, 2016, the Proprietorship2 purchases the following inventories $23,250 from the Proprietorship1 (phone number: 123456081) for -$9,000 cash and other on credit.

Inven31 < Inven3: 10*150

Inven32 < Inven3: 50*150

Inven331 < Inven33 < Inven3: 20*150

Inven332 < Inven33 < Inven3: 45*150

HGFCVB parts < QASXC parts < Inven3: 10*150

PPGHUP parts < ASDUP parts < Inven3: 20*150

The multi-subaccount name of the Cash account and four transaction sub-equations respectively are:

88-654309-t-suppliers < Cash payments to suppliers < Operating activities

Cash (1): -9000 + Inventory (1): 10*150 + Inventory (1): 50*150 + Inventory (1): 20*150 + Inventory (1): 45*150 + Inventory (1): 10*150 + Inventory (1): 20*150 = Account Payable (2): 14250

- On May 1, 2016, the Proprietorship2 sells the following inventories -$3,810 for sales $6,350 to the Company1 (phone number: 123456784) for cash $2,300 and other on credit.

Inven411 < Inven41 < Inven4: -3*100

Inven412 < Inven41 < Inven4: -11.1*100

TTTCU parts < TTT parts < Inven4: -12*100

RRRHJK parts < Inven4: -12*100

The multi-subaccount name of the Cash account and the transaction sub-equation respectively are:

88-654306-c-customers < Cash receipts from customers < Operating activities

Cash (1): 2300 + Account receivable (1): 4050 + Inventory (1): -3*100 + Inventory (1): -11.1*100 + Inventory (1): -12*100 + Inventory (1): -12*100 = Sales (4): 6350 + Cost of goods sold (5): -3810

- On May 1, 2016, the Proprietorship2 sells the following inventories -$4,953 for sales $8,255 to the Proprietorship1 (phone number: 123456781) for cash $5,000 and other on credit.

Inven411 < Inven41 < Inven4: -3*130

Inven412 < Inven41 < Inven4: -11.1*130

TTTCU parts < TTT parts < Inven4: -12*130

RRRHJK parts < Inven4: -12*130

The multi-subaccount name of the Cash account and the transaction sub-equation respectively are:

88-654309-c-customers < Cash receipts from customers < Operating activities

Cash (1): 5000 + Account receivable (1): 3255 + Inventory (1): -3*130 + Inventory (1): -11.1*130 + Inventory (1): -12*130 + Inventory (1): -12*130 = Sales (4): 8255 + Cost of goods sold (5): -4953

- On May 1, 2016, the Proprietorship2 sells the Supplies1 $14*50 (cost: -$7*50) and the Supplies2 $16*50 (cost: -$8*50) for sales $1,500 to the Proprietorship1 (phone number: 123456781) for cash $800 and other on credit. The multi-subaccount name of the Cash account is:

  88-654309-c-customers < Cash receipts from customers < Operating activities

- On May 2, 2016, the Proprietorship2 transfers the supplies $920 to the Cost of goods manufactured account to satisfy the need of producing. The transaction sub-equation is:

  Supplies (1): -920 = Cost of goods manufactured (5): -920

- On May 2, 2016, the Proprietorship2 transfers the following inventories -$23,250 to the Cost of goods manufactured account to satisfy the need of producing.

  Inven31 < Inven3: -10*150

  Inven32 < Inven3: -50*150

  Inven331 < Inven33 < Inven3: -20*150

  Inven332 < Inven33 < Inven3: -45*150

  HGFCVB parts < QASXC parts < Inven3: -10*150

  PPGHUP parts < ASDUP parts < Inven3: -20*150

  The transaction sub-equations is:

  Inventory (1): -10*150 + Inventory (1): -50*150 + Inventory (1): -20*150 + Inventory (1): -45*150 + Inventory (1): 10*150 + Inventory (1): 20*150 = Cost of goods manufactured (5): -23,250

- On May 2, 2016, the Proprietorship2 transfers the following inventories -$135,000 to the Cost of goods manufactured account to satisfy the need of producing.

Inven51 < Inven5: -10*400

Inven52 < Inven5: -50*200

Inven531 < Inven53 < Inven5: -25*400

Inven532 < Inven53 < Inven5: -35*400

Inven541 < Inven54 < Inven5: -12*400

Inven542 < Inven54 < Inven5: -15*400

Inven611 < Inven61 < Inven6: -6.5*560

Inven612 < Inven61 < Inven6: -12.5*400

Inven621 < Inven62 < Inven6: -18*400

Inven63 < Inven6: -16*400

Inven711 < Inven71 < Inven7: -36*240

Inven712 < Inven71 < Inven7: -31*40

Inven721 < Inven72 < Inven7: -22*320

Inven722 < Inven72 < Inven7: -20*240

Inven731 < Inven73 < Inven7: -18*240

Inven732 < Inven73 < Inven7: -16*400

Inven811 < Inven81 < Inven8: -25*240

Inven812 < Inven81 < Inven8: -24*240

Inven813 < Inven81 < Inven8: -23*240

Inven82 < Inven8: -20*240

Inven831 < Inven83 < Inven8: -18*240

Inven832 < Inven83 < Inven8: -16*320

The three transaction sub-equations are respectively:

Inventory (1): -10*400 + Inventory (1): -50*200 + Inventory (1): -25*400 +

Inventory (1): -35*400 + Inventory (1): -12*400 + Inventory (1): -15*400 +

Inventory (1): -6.5*560 + Inventory (1): -12.5*400 + Inventory (1): 18*400 =

Cost of goods manufactured (5): -64640

Inventory (1): -16*400 + Inventory (1): -36*240 + Inventory (1): -31*40 + Inventory (1): -22*320 + Inventory (1): -20*240 + Inventory (1): -18*240 + Inventory (1): -16*400 + Inventory (1): -25*240 + Inventory (1): -24*240 = Cost of goods manufactured (5): -50600

Inventory (1): -23*240 + Inventory (1): -20*240 + Inventory (1): -18*240 + Inventory (1): -16*320 = Cost of goods manufactured (5): -19760

- On May 8, 2016, the Proprietorship2 sells the Supplies1 $14*10 (cost: -$7*10) and the Supplies2 $16*10 (cost: -$8*10) for sales $300 to the Tax Bureau (phone number: 123456787) for cash $300. The multi-subaccount name of the Cash account is:

  88-654303-c-customers < Cash receipts from customers < Operating activities

- On May 15, 2016, the Proprietorship2 sells the Food613 $26*2 (cost: -$13*2) and the Food621 $26*1 (cost: -$13*1) to A24 (SIN: 909876524) for cash $78. The multi-subaccount name of the Cash account is:

  909876524-c-customers < Cash receipts from customers < Operating activities

- On May 16, 2016, the Proprietorship2 sells the Supplies1 $14*10 (cost: -$7*10) and the Supplies2 $16*11 (cost: -$8*11) for sales $316 to the Central Bank (phone number: 123456789) for cash $316. The multi-subaccount name of the Cash account is:

  88-654301-c-customers < Cash receipts from customers < Operating activities

- On May 17, 2016, the Proprietorship2 pays -$210.77 cash to A24 (SIN: 909876524) for the Travelling expenses (travel allowance) $132.77 and the Other expenses (meals: food613: $26*2 + food621: $26*1) $78.

- On May 22, 2016, the Proprietorship2 sells the Food513 $10*3 (cost: -$5*3) and the Food621 $26*1 (cost: -$13*1) to A22 (SIN: 909876522) for cash $56. The multi-subaccount name of the Cash account is:

  909876522-c-customers < Cash receipts from customers < Operating activities

- On May 24, 2016, the Proprietorship2 sells the Food522 $13*4 (cost: -$6.5*4) and the Food622 $28*2 (cost: -$14*2) to A12 (SIN: 909876512) for cash $108. The multi-subaccount name of the Cash account is:

  909876512-c-customers < Cash receipts from customers < Operating activities

- On May 31, 2016, the Proprietorship2 pays two employees' salary expenses for cash -$5,660 repeatedly.

- On June 3, 2016, the Proprietorship2 sells the Food613 $26*1 (cost: -$13*1) and the Food622 $28*1 (cost: -$14*1) to A8 (SIN: 909876508) for cash $54. The multi-subaccount name of the Cash account is:

  909876508-c-customers < Cash receipts from customers < Operating activities

- On June 12, 2016, the Proprietorship2 sells the Food611 $20*2 (cost: -$10*2) and the Food622 $28*1 (cost: -$14*1) to A17 (SIN: 909876517) for cash $68. The multi-subaccount name of the Cash account is:

  909876517-c-customers < Cash receipts from customers < Operating activities

- On June 12, 2016, the Proprietorship2 sells the Food611 $20*2 (cost: -$10*2) and the Food622 $28*1 (cost: -$14*1) to A20 (SIN: 909876520) for cash $68. The multi-subaccount name of the Cash account is:

  909876520-c-customers < Cash receipts from customers < Operating activities

- On June 15, 2016, the Proprietorship2 sells the Food44 $15*3 (cost: -$7.5*3) and the Food53 $16*3 (cost: -$8*3) to A3 (SIN: 909876503) for cash $93. The multi-subaccount name of the Cash account is:

  909876503-c-customers < Cash receipts from customers < Operating activities

- On June 17, 2016, the Proprietorship2 sells the Food514 $11*3 (cost: -$5.5*3) and the Food611 $20*3 (cost: -$10*3) to A5 (SIN: 909876505) for cash $93. The multi-subaccount name of the Cash account is:

  909876505-c-customers < Cash receipts from customers < Operating activities

- On June 17, 2016, the Proprietorship2 sells the Food513 $10*3 (cost: -$5*3) and the Food611 $20*3 (cost: -$10*3) to A6 (SIN: 909876506) for cash $90. The multi-subaccount name of the Cash account is:

909876506-c-customers < Cash receipts from customers < Operating activities

- On June 17, 2016, the Proprietorship2 sells the Food612 $24*2 (cost: -$12*2) and the Food613 $26*1 (cost: -$13*1) to A24 (SIN: 909876524) for cash $74. The multi-subaccount name of the Cash account is:

  909876524-c-customers < Cash receipts from customers < Operating activities

- On June 18, 2016, the Proprietorship2 sells the Food522 $13*4 (cost: -$6.5*4) and the Food622 $28*3 (cost: -$14*3) to A2 (SIN: 909876502) for cash $136. The multi-subaccount name of the Cash account is:

  909876502-c-customers < Cash receipts from customers < Operating activities

- On June 19, 2016, the Proprietorship2 pays -$196.83 cash to A24 (SIN: 909876524) for the Travelling expenses (travel allowance) $122.83 and the Other expenses (meals: food612: $24*2 + food613: $26*1) $74.

- On June 21, 2016, the Proprietorship2 sells the Food521 $12*2 (cost: -$6*2) and the Food612 $24*1 (cost: -$12*1) to A22 (SIN: 909876522) for cash $48. The multi-subaccount name of the Cash account is:

  909876522-c-customers < Cash receipts from customers < Operating activities

- On June 30, 2016, the Proprietorship2 pays two employees' salary expenses for cash -$5,660 repeatedly.

- On July 2, 2016, the Proprietorship2 sells the Food44 $15*3 (cost: -$7.5*3) and the Food612 $24*3 (cost: -$12*3) to A9 (SIN: 909876509) for cash $117. The multi-subaccount name of the Cash account is:

  909876509-c-customers < Cash receipts from customers < Operating activities

- On July 3, 2016, the Proprietorship2 pays -$53,000 cash to the Company3 (phone number: 123456082) with the General ID 21 (-$21,100) and the General ID 23(-$31,900). The multi-subaccount name of the Cash account and transaction sub-equation respectively are:

  88-654308-t-suppliers < Cash payments to suppliers < Operating activities

- On July 9, 2016, the Proprietorship2 sells the Food612 $24*2 (cost: -$12*2) and the Food621 $26*1 (cost: -$13*1) to A11 (SIN: 909876511) for cash $74. The multi-subaccount name of the Cash account is:

909876511-c-customers < Cash receipts from customers < Operating activities

- On July 16, 2016, the Proprietorship2 receives $13,000 cash from the Company3 (phone number: 123456782) with the General ID 18 (-$660) and the General ID 25 (-$12,340). The multi-subaccount name of the Cash account is:

88-654308-c-customers < Cash receipts from customers < Operating activities

- On July 21, 2016, the Proprietorship2 sells the Food621 $26*2 (cost: -$13*2) and the Food622 $28*2 (cost: -$14*2) to A25 (SIN: 909876525) for cash $108. The multi-subaccount name of the Cash account is:

909876525-c-customers < Cash receipts from customers < Operating activities

- On July 23, 2016, the Proprietorship2 pays -$251.19 cash to A25 (SIN: 909876525) for the Travelling expenses (travel allowance) $143.19 and the Other expenses (meals: food621: $26*2 + food622: $28*2) $108.

- On July 31, 2016, the Proprietorship2 pays two employees' salary expenses for cash -$5,660 repeatedly.

- On July 31, 2016, the Proprietorship2 sells the following inventories -$5,460 for sales $10,920 to A12A20 (SIN: 909876528), who uses his (or her) father A12's (or mother A12's) secondary card of the Business Bank1, for cash $10,920.

Food411 < Food41 < Food4: -5*130

Food412 < Food41 < Food4: -5.5*130

Food421 < Food42 < Food4: -6*130

Food422 < Food42 < Food4: -6.5*130

Food43 < Food4: -7*130

Food44 < Food4: -7.5*130

Food512 < Food51 < Food5: -4.5*130

The multi-subaccount name of the Cash account is:

909876512-c-customers < Cash receipts from customers < Operating activities

- On July 31, 2016, the Proprietorship2 sells the following inventories -$5,525 for sales $11,050 to A1 (SIN: 909876501) for cash $11,050.

Food411 < Food41 < Food4: -5*130

Food412 < Food41 < Food4: -5.5*130

Food421 < Food42 < Food4: -6*130

Food422 < Food42 < Food4: -6.5*130

Food43 < Food4: -7*130

Food44 < Food4: -7.5*130

Food513 < Food51 < Food5: -5*130

The multi-subaccount name of the Cash account is:

909876501-c-customers < Cash receipts from customers < Operating activities

- On July 31, 2016, the Proprietorship2 sells the following inventories -$5,590 for sales $11,180 to A2 (SIN: 909876502) for cash $11,180.

Food411 < Food41 < Food4: -5*130

Food412 < Food41 < Food4: -5.5*130

Food421 < Food42 < Food4: -6*130

Food422 < Food42 < Food4: -6.5*130

Food43 < Food4: -7*130

Food44 < Food4: -7.5*130

Food514 < Food51 < Food5: -5.5*130

The multi-subaccount name of the Cash account is:

909876502-c-customers < Cash receipts from customers < Operating activities

- On July 31, 2016, the Proprietorship2 sells the following inventories -$5,655 for sales $11,310 to A3 (SIN: 909876503) for cash $11,310.

Food411 < Food41 < Food4: -5*130

Food412 < Food41 < Food4: -5.5*130

Food421 < Food42 < Food4: -6*130

Food422 < Food42 < Food4: -6.5*130

Food43 < Food4: -7*130

Food44 < Food4: -7.5*130

Food521 < Food52 < Food5: -6*130

The multi-subaccount name of the Cash account is:

909876503-c-customers < Cash receipts from customers < Operating activities

- On July 31, 2016, the Proprietorship2 sells the following inventories -$5,720 for sales $11,440 to A4 (SIN: 909876504) for cash $11,440.

Food411 < Food41 < Food4: -5*130

Food412 < Food41 < Food4: -5.5*130

Food421 < Food42 < Food4: -6*130

Food422 < Food42 < Food4: -6.5*130

Food43 < Food4: -7*130

Food44 < Food4: -7.5*130

Food522 < Food52 < Food5: -6.5*130

The multi-subaccount name of the Cash account is:

909876504-c-customers < Cash receipts from customers < Operating activities

- On July 31, 2016, the Proprietorship2 sells the following inventories -$5,915 for sales $11,830 to A5 (SIN: 909876505) for cash $11,830.

Food411 < Food41 < Food4: -5*130

Food412 < Food41 < Food4: -5.5*130

Food421 < Food42 < Food4: -6*130

Food422 < Food42 < Food4: -6.5*130

Food43 < Food4: -7*130

Food44 < Food4: -7.5*130

Food53 < Food5: -8*130

The multi-subaccount name of the Cash account is:

909876505-c-customers < Cash receipts from customers < Operating activities

- On July 31, 2016, the Proprietorship2 sells the following inventories -$5,395 for sales $10,790 to A6 (SIN: 909876506) for cash $10,790.

Food511 < Food51 < Food5: -4*130

Food512 < Food51 < Food5: -4.5*130

Food513 < Food51 < Food5: -5*130

Food514 < Food51 < Food5: -5.5*130

Food521 < Food52 < Food5: -6*130

Food522 < Food52 < Food5: -6.5*130

Food611 < Food61 < Food6: -10*130

The multi-subaccount name of the Cash account is:

909876506-c-customers < Cash receipts from customers < Operating activities

- On July 31, 2016, the Proprietorship2 sells the following inventories -$5,655 for sales $11,310 to A7 (SIN: 909876507) for cash $11,310.

Food511 < Food51 < Food5: -4*130

Food512 < Food51 < Food5: -4.5*130

Food513 < Food51 < Food5: -5*130

Food514 < Food51 < Food5: -5.5*130

Food521 < Food52 < Food5: -6*130

Food522 < Food52 < Food5: -6.5*130

Food612 < Food61 < Food6: -12*130

The multi-subaccount name of the Cash account is:

909876507-c-customers < Cash receipts from customers < Operating activities

- On July 31, 2016, the Proprietorship2 sells the following inventories -$5,785 for sales $11,570 to A8 (SIN: 909876508) for cash $11,570.

Food511 < Food51 < Food5: -4*130

Food512 < Food51 < Food5: -4.5*130

Food513 < Food51 < Food5: -5*130

Food514 < Food51 < Food5: -5.5*130

Food521 < Food52 < Food5: -6*130

Food522 < Food52 < Food5: -6.5*130

Food613 < Food61 < Food6: -13*130

The multi-subaccount name of the Cash account is:

909876508-c-customers < Cash receipts from customers < Operating activities

- On July 31, 2016, the Proprietorship2 sells the following inventories -$6,045 for sales $12,090 to A9 (SIN: 909876509) for cash $12,090.

Food511 < Food51 < Food5: -4*130

Food512 < Food51 < Food5: -4.5*130

Food513 < Food51 < Food5: -5*130

Food514 < Food51 < Food5: -5.5*130

Food521 < Food52 < Food5: -6*130

Food522 < Food52 < Food5: -6.5*130

Food614 < Food61 < Food6: -15*130

The multi-subaccount name of the Cash account is:

909876509-c-customers < Cash receipts from customers < Operating activities

- On July 31, 2016, the Proprietorship2 sells the following inventories -$5,785 for sales $11,570 to A10 (SIN: 909876510) for cash $11,570.

Food511 < Food51 < Food5: -4*130

Food512 < Food51 < Food5: -4.5*130

Food513 < Food51 < Food5: -5*130

Food514 < Food51 < Food5: -5.5*130

Food521 < Food52 < Food5: -6*130

Food522 < Food52 < Food5: -6.5*130

Food621 < Food62 < Food6: -13*130

The multi-subaccount name of the Cash account is:

909876510-c-customers < Cash receipts from customers < Operating activities

- On July 31, 2016, the Proprietorship2 sells the following inventories -$5,135 for sales $10,270 to A11 (SIN: 909876511) for cash $10,270.

Food412 < Food41 < Food4: -5.5*130

Food511 < Food51 < Food5: -4*130

Food512 < Food51 < Food5: -4.5*130

Food513 < Food51 < Food5: -5*130

Food521 < Food52 < Food5: -6*130

Food522 < Food52 < Food5: -6.5*130

Food53 < Food5: -8*130

The multi-subaccount name of the Cash account is:

909876511-c-customers < Cash receipts from customers < Operating activities

- On July 31, 2016, the Proprietorship2 sells the following inventories -$5,915 for sales $11,830 to A12 (SIN: 909876512) for cash $11,830.

Food511 < Food51 < Food5: -4*130

Food512 < Food51 < Food5: -4.5*130

Food513 < Food51 < Food5: -5*130

Food514 < Food51 < Food5: -5.5*130

Food521 < Food52 < Food5: -6*130

Food522 < Food52 < Food5: -6.5*130

Food622 < Food62 < Food6: -14*130

The multi-subaccount name of the Cash account is:

909876512-c-customers < Cash receipts from customers < Operating activities

- On July 31, 2016, the Proprietorship2 sells the following inventories -$5,915 for sales $11,830 to A13 (SIN: 909876513) for cash $11,830.

Food411 < Food41 < Food4: -5*130

Food412 < Food41 < Food4: -5.5*130

Food43 < Food4: -7*130

Food44 < Food4: -7.5*130

Food521 < Food52 < Food5: -6*130

Food522 < Food52 < Food5: -6.5*130

Food53 < Food5: -8*130

The multi-subaccount name of the Cash account is:

909876513-c-customers < Cash receipts from customers < Operating activities

- On August 9, 2016, the Proprietorship2 sells the Food513 $10*5 (cost: -$5*5) and the Food53 $16*4 (cost: -$8*4) to A6 (SIN: 909876506) for cash $114. The multi-subaccount name of the Cash account is:

909876506-c-customers < Cash receipts from customers < Operating activities

- On August 12, 2016, the Proprietorship2 sells the Food611 $20*2 (cost: -$10*2) and the Food621 $26*3 (cost: -$13*3) to A9 (SIN: 909876509) for cash $118. The multi-subaccount name of the Cash account is:

  909876509-c-customers < Cash receipts from customers < Operating activities

- On August 14, 2016, the Proprietorship2 sells the Food522 $13*3 (cost: -$6.5*3) and the Food622 $28*3 (cost: -$14*3) to A15 (SIN: 909876515) for cash $123. The multi-subaccount name of the Cash account is:

  909876515-c-customers < Cash receipts from customers < Operating activities

- On August 15, 2016, the Proprietorship2 pays -$66,000 cash to the Company3 (phone number: 123456082) with the General ID 21 (-$950) and the General ID 22 (-$65,050). The multi-subaccount name of the Cash account and transaction sub-equation respectively are:

  88-654308-t-suppliers < Cash payments to suppliers < Operating activities

- On August 15, 2016, the Proprietorship2 sells the Food514 $11*2 (cost: -$5.5*2) and the Food614 $30*1 (cost: -$15*1) to A8 (SIN: 909876508) for cash $52. The multi-subaccount name of the Cash account is:

  909876508-c-customers < Cash receipts from customers < Operating activities

- On August 16, 2016, the Proprietorship2 sells the Food612 $24*2 (cost: -$12*2) and the Food621 $26*1 (cost: -$13*1) to A24 (SIN: 909876524) for cash $74. The multi-subaccount name of the Cash account is:

  909876524-c-customers < Cash receipts from customers < Operating activities

- On August 18, 2016, the Proprietorship2 pays -$203.47 cash to A24 (SIN: 909876524) for the Travelling expenses (travel allowance) $129.47 and the Other expenses (meals: food612: $24*2 + food621: $26*1) $74.

- On August 21, 2016, the Proprietorship2 sells the Food522 $13*2 (cost: -$6.5*2) and the Food614 $30*1 (cost: -$15*1) to A22 (SIN: 909876522) for cash $56. The multi-subaccount name of the Cash account is:

  909876522-c-customers < Cash receipts from customers < Operating activities

- On August 31, 2016, the Proprietorship2 pays two employees' salary expenses for cash -$5,660 repeatedly.

- On September 2, 2016, the Proprietorship2 purchases one Car3 $38,000 from the Company1 (phone number: 123456084) for cash -$18,000 and other on credit. The multi-subaccount name of the Cash account is:

    88-654306-t-machinery < Cash payments for machinery < Operating activities

- On September 5, 2016, the Proprietorship2 sells the Food514 $11*3 (cost: -$5.5*3) and the Food621 $26*1 (cost: -$13*1) to A2 (SIN: 909876502) for cash $59. The multi-subaccount name of the Cash account is:

    909876502-c-customers < Cash receipts from customers < Operating activities

- On September 5, 2016, the Proprietorship2 sells the Food513 $10*3 (cost: -$5*3) and the Food622 $28*2 (cost: -$14*2) to A4 (SIN: 909876504) for cash $86. The multi-subaccount name of the Cash account is:

    909876504-c-customers < Cash receipts from customers < Operating activities

- On September 7, 2016, the Proprietorship2 sells the Food43 $14*3 (cost: -$7*3) and the Food612 $24*2 (cost: -$12*2) to A7 (SIN: 909876507) for cash $90. The multi-subaccount name of the Cash account is:

    909876507-c-customers < Cash receipts from customers < Operating activities

- On September 14, 2016, the Proprietorship2 receives $380 cash from the Company2 (phone number: 123456783) with the General ID 19. The multi-subaccount name of the Cash account is:

    88-654307-c-customers < Cash receipts from customers < Operating activities

- On September 15, 2016, the Proprietorship2 sells the Food514 $11*3 (cost: -$5.5*3) and the Food612 $24*3 (cost: -$12*3) to A6 (SIN: 909876506) for cash $105. The multi-subaccount name of the Cash account is:

    909876506-c-customers < Cash receipts from customers < Operating activities

- On September 21, 2016, the Proprietorship2 pays -$256.18 cash to A24 (SIN: 909876524) for the Travelling expenses (travel allowance) $157.18 and the Other expenses (meals: food312: $24*3 + food321: $27*1) $99.

- On September 30, 2016, the Proprietorship2 pays two employees' salary expenses for cash -$5,660 repeatedly.

- On October 3, 2016, the Proprietorship2 sells the Food522 $13*3 (cost: -$6.5*3) and the Food614 $30*3 (cost: -$15*3) to A15 (SIN: 909876515) for cash $129. The multi-subaccount name of the Cash account is:

  909876515-c-customers < Cash receipts from customers < Operating activities

- On October 4, 2016, the Proprietorship2 sells the Food522 $13*3 (cost: -$6.5*3) and the Food613 $26*3 (cost: -$13*3) to A18 (SIN: 909876518) for cash $117. The multi-subaccount name of the Cash account is:

  909876518-c-customers < Cash receipts from customers < Operating activities

- On October 6, 2016, the Proprietorship2 sells the Food522 $13*2 (cost: -$6.5*2) and the Food613 $26*2 (cost: -$13*2) to A21 (SIN: 909876521) for cash $78. The multi-subaccount name of the Cash account is:

  909876521-c-customers < Cash receipts from customers < Operating activities

- On October 6, 2016, the Proprietorship2 sells the Food521 $12*2 (cost: -$6*2) and the Food614 $30*1 (cost: -$15*1) to A22 (SIN: 909876522) for cash $54. The multi-subaccount name of the Cash account is:

  909876522-c-customers < Cash receipts from customers < Operating activities

- On October 8, 2016, the Proprietorship2 sells the Food511 $8*3 (cost: -$4*3) and the Food53 $16*2 (cost: -$8*2) to A8 (SIN: 909876508) for cash $56. The multi-subaccount name of the Cash account is:

  909876508-c-customers < Cash receipts from customers < Operating activities

- On October 11, 2016, the Proprietorship2 pays -$41,000 cash to the Company3 (phone number: 123456082) with the General ID 21. The multi-subaccount name of the Cash account and transaction sub-equation respectively are:

  88-654308-t-suppliers < Cash payments to suppliers < Operating activities

- On October 16, 2016, the Proprietorship2 sells the Food522 $13*2 (cost: -$6.5*2) and the Food614 $30*2 (cost: -$15*2) to A24 (SIN: 909876524) for cash $86. The multi-subaccount name of the Cash account is:

909876524-c-customers < Cash receipts from customers < Operating activities

- On October 18, 2016, the Proprietorship2 pays -$228.66 cash to A24 (SIN: 909876524) for the Travelling expenses (travel allowance) $142.66 and the Other expenses (meals: food522: $13*2 + food614: $30*2) $86.

- On October 31, 2016, the Proprietorship2 pays two employees' salary expenses for cash -$5,660 repeatedly.

- On November 1, 2016, the Proprietorship2 sells the Food514 $11*3 (cost: -$5.5*3) and the Food622 $28*1 (cost: -$14*1) to A11 (SIN: 909876511) for cash $61. The multi-subaccount name of the Cash account is:

  909876511-c-customers < Cash receipts from customers < Operating activities

- On November 11, 2016, the Proprietorship2 sells the Food514 $11*3 (cost: -$5.5*3) and the Food613 $26*2 (cost: -$13*2) to A4 (SIN: 909876504) for cash $85. The multi-subaccount name of the Cash account is:

  909876504-c-customers < Cash receipts from customers < Operating activities

- On November 16, 2016, the Proprietorship2 sells the Food53 $16*4 (cost: -$8*4) and the Food614 $30*2 (cost: -$15*2) to A9 (SIN: 909876509) for cash $124. The multi-subaccount name of the Cash account is:

  909876509-c-customers < Cash receipts from customers < Operating activities

- On November 16, 2016, the Proprietorship2 sells the Food53 $16*3 (cost: -$8*3) and the Food622 $28*3 (cost: -$14*3) to A15 (SIN: 909876515) for cash $132. The multi-subaccount name of the Cash account is:

  909876515-c-customers < Cash receipts from customers < Operating activities

- On November 18, 2016, the Proprietorship2 sells the Food611 $20*3 (cost: -$10*3) and the Food621 $26*1 (cost: -$13*1) to A24 (SIN: 909876524) for cash $86. The multi-subaccount name of the Cash account is:

  909876524-c-customers < Cash receipts from customers < Operating activities

- On November 20, 2016, the Proprietorship2 pays -$204.61 cash to A24 (SIN: 909876524) for the Travelling expenses (travel allowance) $118.61 and the Other expenses (meals: food611: $20*3 + food621: $26*1) $86.

- On November 30, 2016, the Proprietorship2 pays two employees' salary expenses for cash -$5,660 repeatedly.

- On November 30, 2016, the Proprietorship2 records the Amortization expenses $2,475 of a computer server2 (-$1,237.5, eleven months), a computer3 (-$641.67, eleven months), and a computer4 (-$595.83, eleven months). The transaction sub-equation is:

Accumulated amortization: Computer (1): -1237.5 + Accumulated amortization: Computer (1): -641.67 + Accumulated amortization: Computer (1): -595.83 = Amortization expenses (5): -1237.5 + Amortization expenses (5): -641.67 + Amortization expenses (5): -595.83

- On November 30, 2016, the Proprietorship2 cancels the balances of the Computer account and the Accumulated amortization: Computer account because these computers have used for two years. The transaction sub-equation is:

Computer (1): -2700 + Computer (1): -1400 + Computer (1): -1300 + Accumulated amortization: Computer (1): 2700 + Accumulated amortization: Computer (1): 1400 + Accumulated amortization: Computer (1): 1300 = 0

- On November 30, 2016, the Proprietorship2 has completed all products of the Working-in-process inventory account. If the all general parts have just been consumed and the supplies has the rest $90, the rest supplies must be returned to the Supplies account from the Cost of goods manufactured account. The transaction sub-equation is:

Supplies (1): 90 = Cost of goods manufactured (5): 90

- On November 30, 2016, the Proprietorship2 transfers the balance of the Cost of goods manufactured account to the Working-in-process inventory account. The Cost of goods manufactured account has three subaccounts of the "Supplies expenses", the "909876525-salary < Product department-salary < Salary expenses", and the "General parts expenses". Their balances are -$830, -$22,320, and -$158,250 (-$135,000 - $23,250) respectively. Here, the balance of the subaccount "909876525-salary < Product department-salary < Salary expenses" is the sum of the eight months' salary expenses because the Proprietorship2 will not produce any product and only do some maintenance of the equipment in December 2016. In addition, the balance of the subaccount "General parts expenses" will be divided to three parts which are used in three transaction sub-equations respectively. The three transaction sub-equations respectively are:

Working-in-process inventory (1): 5*1200 + Working-in-process inventory (1): 5.5*1200 + Working-in-process inventory (1): 6*1200 + Working-in-process inventory (1): 6.5*1200 + Working-in-process inventory (1): 7*1200 + Working-in-process inventory (1): 7.5*1200 + Working-in-process inventory (1): 4*1200 = Cost of goods manufactured (5): 830 + Cost of goods manufactured (5): 22320 + Cost of goods manufactured (5): 26650

Working-in-process inventory (1): 4.5*1200 + Working-in-process inventory (1): 5*1200 + Working-in-process inventory (1): 5.5*1200 + Working-in-process inventory (1): 6*1200 + Working-in-process inventory (1): 6.5*1200 + Working-in-process inventory (1): 8*1200 + Working-in-process inventory (1): 10*1000 + Working-in-process inventory (1): 12*1000 + Working-in-process inventory (1): 13*1000 = Cost of goods manufactured (5): 77600

Working-in-process inventory (1): 15*1000 + Working-in-process inventory (1): 13*1000 + Working-in-process inventory (1): 14*1000 + Working-in-process inventory (1): 7*800 + Working-in-process inventory (1): 8*800 = Cost of goods manufactured (5): 54000

- On November 30, 2016, the proprietorship2 transfers the balance of the Working-in-process inventory account to the Inventory account. The five transaction sub-equations respectively are:

Working-in-process inventory (1): -5*1200 + Working-in-process inventory (1): -5.5*1200 + Working-in-process inventory (1): -6*1200 + Working-in-process inventory (1): -6.5*1200 + Working-in-process inventory (1): -7*1200 + Inventory (1): 5*1200 + Inventory (1): 5.5*1200 + Inventory (1): 6*1200 + Inventory (1): 6.5*1200 + Inventory (1): 7*1200 = 0

Working-in-process inventory (1): -7.5*1200 + Working-in-process inventory (1): -4*1200 + Working-in-process inventory (1): -4.5*1200 + Working-in-process inventory (1): -5*1200 + Working-in-process inventory (1): -5.5*1200 + Inventory (1): 7.5*1200 + Inventory (1): 4*1200 + Inventory (1): 4.5*1200 + Inventory (1): 5*1200 + Inventory (1): 5.5*1200 = 0

Working-in-process inventory (1): -6*1200 + Working-in-process inventory (1): -6.5*1200 + Working-in-process inventory (1): -8*1200 + Working-in-process inventory (1): -10*1000 + Working-in-process inventory (1): -12*1000 + Inventory (1): 6*1200 + Inventory (1): 6.5*1200 + Inventory (1): 8*1200 + Inventory (1): 10*1000 + Inventory (1): 12*1000 = 0

Working-in-process inventory (1): -13*1000 + Working-in-process inventory (1): -15*1000 + Working-in-process inventory (1): -13*1000 + Working-in-process inventory (1): -14*1000 + Inventory (1): 13*1000 + Inventory (1): 15*1000 + Inventory (1): 13*1000 + Inventory (1): 14*1000 = 0

Working-in-process inventory (1): -7*800 + Working-in-process inventory (1): -8*800 + Inventory (1): 7*800 + Inventory (1): 8*800 − 0

- On December 1, 2016, the Proprietorship2 purchases one Computer server1, one Computer1, and one Computer2 from the Company1 (phone number: 123456084) for cash -$5,000 and other on credit. The multi-subaccount name of the Cash account and transaction sub-equation respectively are:

  88-654306-t-machinery < Cash payments for machinery < Operating activities

  Cash (1): -5000 + Computer (1): 2800 + Computer (1): 1600 + Computer (1): 1500 = Account payable (2): 900

- On December 2, 2016, the Proprietorship2 sells the Food612 $24*2 (cost: -$12*2) and the Food622 $28*1 (cost: -$14*1) to A10 (SIN: 909876510) for cash $76. The multi-subaccount name of the Cash account is:

  909876510-c-customers < Cash receipts from customers < Operating activities

- On December 8, 2016, the Proprietorship2 sells the Food43 $14*3 (cost: -$7*3), the Food44 $15*2 (cost: -$7.5*2), and the Food612 $24*2 (cost: -$12*2) to A1 (SIN: 909876501) for cash $120. The multi-subaccount name of the Cash account is:

  909876501-c-customers < Cash receipts from customers < Operating activities

- On December 15, 2016, the Proprietorship2 sells the Food613 $26*3 (cost: -$13*3) and the Food614 $30*1 (cost: -$15*1) to A24 (SIN: 909876524) for cash $108. The multi-subaccount name of the Cash account is:

  909876524-c-customers < Cash receipts from customers < Operating activities

- On December 17, 2016, the Proprietorship2 pays -$277.93 cash to A24 (SIN: 909876524) for the Travelling expenses (travel allowance) $169.93 and the Other expenses (meals: food613: $26*3 + food614: $30*1) $108.

- On December 17, 2016, the Proprietorship2 sells the Food611 $20*2 (cost: -$10*2) and the Food622 $28*1 (cost: -$14*1) to A22 (SIN: 909876522) for cash $68. The multi-subaccount name of the Cash account is:

  909876522-c-customers < Cash receipts from customers < Operating activities

- On December 18, 2016, the Proprietorship2 sells the Food611 $20*3 (cost: -$10*3) and the Food622 $28*3 (cost: -$14*3) to A18 (SIN: 909876518) for cash $144. The multi-subaccount name of the Cash account is:

909876518-c-customers < Cash receipts from customers < Operating activities

- On December 18, 2016, the Proprietorship2 sells the Food611 $20*3 (cost: -$10*3) and the Food622 $28*1 (cost: -$14*1) to A21 (SIN: 909876521) for cash $88. The multi-subaccount name of the Cash account is:

909876521-c-customers < Cash receipts from customers < Operating activities

- On December 18, 2016, the Proprietorship2 sells the Food612 $24*3 (cost: -$12*3) and the Food613 $26*1 (cost: -$13*1) to A25 (SIN: 909876525) for cash $98. The multi-subaccount name of the Cash account is:

909876525-c-customers < Cash receipts from customers < Operating activities

- On December 20, 2016, the Proprietorship2 sells the Food621 $26*3 (cost: -$13*3) and the Food622 $28*3 (cost: -$14*3) to A14 (SIN: 909876514) for cash $162. The multi-subaccount name of the Cash account is:

909876514-c-customers < Cash receipts from customers < Operating activities

- On December 20, 2016, the Proprietorship2 pays -$249.51 cash to A25 (SIN: 909876525) for the Travelling expenses (travel allowance) $151.51 and the Other expenses (meals: food612: $24*3 + food613: $26*1) $98.

- On December 23, 2016, the Proprietorship2 receives $5,500 cash from the Company1 (phone number: 123456784) with the General ID 85 ($2,000) and the General ID 110 ($3,500). The multi-subaccount name of the Cash account is:

88-654306-c-customers < Cash receipts from customers < Operating activities

- On December 26, 2016, the Proprietorship2 sells the Food53 $16*3 (cost: -$8*3) and the Food614 $30*2 (cost: -$15*2) to A7 (SIN: 909876507) for cash $108. The multi-subaccount name of the Cash account is:

909876507-c-customers < Cash receipts from customers < Operating activities

- On December 29, 2016, the Proprietorship2 pays -$27,000 cash to the Company1 (phone number: 123456084) with the General ID 8 (-$8,000) and the General ID 165 (-$19,000). The multi-subaccount name of the Cash account is:

88-654306-t-machinery < Cash payments for machinery < Operating activities

- On December 31, 2016, the Proprietorship2 receives $4,300 cash from the Proprietorship1 (phone number: 123456781) with the General ID 111 ($3,600) and the General ID 112 ($700). The multi-subaccount name of the Cash account is:

  88-654309-c-customers < Cash receipts from customers < Operating activities

- On December 31, 2016, the Proprietorship2 pays two employees' salary expenses for cash -$5,660 repeatedly.

- On the same day, the Proprietorship2 pays -$3,640 cash to the bond holders for the Bond interest expenses of the Bond71 (one-level subaccount "Bond71-interest"). The multi-subaccount names of the Cash account and the transaction sub-equations respectively are:

  909876501-t-bond interest < Cash payments to bond holders < Operating activities

  909876502-t-bond interest < Cash payments to bond holders < Operating activities

  909876504-t-bond interest < Cash payments to bond holders < Operating activities

  909876507-t-bond interest < Cash payments to bond holders < Operating activities

  909876509-t-bond interest < Cash payments to bond holders < Operating activities

  909876511-t-bond interest < Cash payments to bond holders < Operating activities

  909876512-t-bond interest < Cash payments to bond holders < Operating activities

  909876516-t-bond interest < Cash payments to bond holders < Operating activities

  909876517-t-bond interest < Cash payments to bond holders < Operating activities

  909876518-t-bond interest < Cash payments to bond holders < Operating

activities

909876519-t-bond interest < Cash payments to bond holders < Operating activities

909876520-t-bond interest < Cash payments to bond holders < Operating activities

Cash (1): -364 + Cash (1): -312 + Cash (1): -260 + Cash (1): -312 + Cash (1): -312 + Cash (1): -260 + Cash (1): -208 + Cash (1): -364 = Bond interest expenses (5): -2392

Cash (1): -260 + Cash (1): -312 + Cash (1): -260 + Cash (1): -416 = Bond interest expenses (5): -1248

- On the same day, the Proprietorship2 pays -$2,750 cash to the bond holders for the Bond interest expenses of the Bond72 (one-level subaccount "Bond72-interest"). The multi-subaccount names of the Cash account and the transaction sub-equations respectively are:

909876504-t-bond interest < Cash payments to bond holders < Operating activities

909876505-t-bond interest < Cash payments to bond holders < Operating activities

909876506-t-bond interest < Cash payments to bond holders < Operating activities

909876508-t-bond interest < Cash payments to bond holders < Operating activities

909876510-t-bond interest < Cash payments to bond holders < Operating activities

909876513-t-bond interest < Cash payments to bond holders < Operating activities

909876515-t-bond interest < Cash payments to bond holders < Operating

activities

909876516-t-bond interest < Cash payments to bond holders < Operating activities

909876517-t-bond interest < Cash payments to bond holders < Operating activities

909876518-t-bond interest < Cash payments to bond holders < Operating activities

Cash (1): -220 + Cash (1): -275 + Cash (1): -330 + Cash (1): -275 + Cash (1): -330 + Cash (1): -220 + Cash (1): -275 + Cash (1): -330 = Bond interest expenses (5): -2255

Cash (1): -275 + Cash (1): -220 = Bond interest expenses (5): -495

- On the same day, the Proprietorship2 receives cash $252 for investment interest of the Bond12 ($6,000) from the Business Bank1. The multi-subaccount name of the Cash account and transaction sub-equation respectively are:

  88-654304-c-investment income < Cash receipts from investments < Investing activities

  Cash (1): 252 = Investment incomes (4):252

- On the same day, the Proprietorship2 receives cash $463 for investment interest of the Bond21 ($7,000) and the Bond22 ($4,000) from the Business Bank2. The multi-subaccount name of the Cash account and transaction sub-equation respectively are:

  88-654305-c-investment income < Cash receipts from investments < Investing activities

  Cash (1): 463 = Investment incomes (4): 287 + Investment incomes (4): 176

- On the same day, the Proprietorship2 receives cash $120 from the Business Bank2 for primary deposit interest. The multi-subaccount name of the Cash account and transaction sub-equation respectively are:

88-654305-c-deposit interest income < Cash receipts from deposit interest < Financial activities

Cash (1): 120 = Deposit interest incomes (4):120

- On the same day, the Proprietorship2 records the Office supplies expenses -$677.53. The transaction sub-equation is:

Supplies (1): -677.53 = Office supplies expenses (5): -677.53

- On the same day, the Proprietorship2 records the Vehicle's amortization expenses - $14,966.67 one year (5 years, straight line). The two transaction sub-equations are:

Accumulated amortization: Vehicle (1): -8000 + Accumulated amortization: Vehicle (1): -6966.67 + Accumulated amortization: Vehicle (1): -2533.33 = Amortization expenses (5): -8000 + Amortization expenses (5): -6966.67 + Amortization expenses (5): -2533.33

- On the same day, the Proprietorship2 records the Computer's amortization expenses $245.84 one months (2 years, straight line) which includes a new computer server1 ($116.67), a new computer1 ($66.67), and a new computer2 ($62.5). The transaction sub-equation is:

Accumulated amortization: Computer (1): -116.67 + Accumulated amortization: Computer (1): -66.67 + Accumulated amortization: Computer (1): -62.5 = Amortization expenses (5): -116.67 + Amortization expenses (5): -66.67 + Amortization expenses (5): -62.5

- On December 31, 2016, the Proprietorship2 records the Tax expenses -$22,373.43 and the Tax payable $22,373.43. The multi-subaccount name forms of the Tax expenses and the Tax payable accounts all are the 'n'. The transaction sub-equation is:

$$0 = \text{Tax payable (2): } 22373.43 + \text{Tax expenses (5): } -22373.43$$

So far, I have entered all transactions of the Proprietorship2 in the fiscal year 2016. After getting the Income Statement and clicking the "Yes" button for new fiscal year, I can get the Balance Sheet of the Proprietorship2.

In the new fiscal year, the Proprietorship2 will record the following transaction.

- On January 2, 2017, the Proprietorship2 pays the balance -$22,373.43 of the Tax payable account to the Tax Bureau. The multi-subaccount name of the Cash account and transaction sub-equation respectively are:

  88-654303-n-tax < Cash payments to Tax Bureau < Operating activities

  $$\text{Cash (1): } -22373.43 = \text{Tax payable (2): } -22373.43$$

3.10.2 Brief Summary of the Proprietorship2

The Figure 3.10-2 shows two sums and all cash transactions of the Proprietorship2 by using of SQL Server query. As a closed system based on the MathAccounting software, the sum0 should be equal to zero. However, the individuals are not responsible for recording any transaction, so the sum0 (-$235,054.43) is the sum of the amounts that individuals paid to the Proprietorship2. The opposite value ($29,882.22) of the sum1 (-$29,882.22) is the balance of the Cash account of the Proprietorship2 on December 31, 2016. It is also the balance of the deposit of the Proprietorship2 in the Business Bak2 on December 31, 2016.

The Figure 3.10-3 to the Figure 3.10-6 on page 575 to page 578 show the four tables of the cash flows statement, the cash account, the income statement, and the balance sheet respectively.

```
use dcj100
select sum(amount) as sum0 from CashByMembers where IDM='88-654310' and TransDate between '2016-01-01' and '2016-12-31'
select sum(amount) as sum1 from CashByMembers where IDM='88-654310' and Symbol = 'd'
select * from CashByMembers where Recorder='88-654310' and TransDate between '2016-01-01' and '2016-12-31'
        order by TransDate
```

100 % ▾

Results   Messages

	sum0
1	-235054.53

	sum1
1	-29882.22

	IDM	Amount	Symbol	MultiSubaccount	Recorder	TransDate
1	88-654308	-400.00	c	88-654308-c-customers < Cash receipts from customers < Operating activities	88-654310	2016-01-02
2	88-654307	-500.00	c	88-654307-c-customers < Cash receipts from customers < Operating activities	88-654310	2016-01-02
3	88-654309	-450.00	c	88-654309-c-customers < Cash receipts from customers < Operating activities	88-654310	2016-01-02
4	88-654308	8000.00	t	88-654308-t-suppliers < Cash payments to suppliers < Operating activities	88-654310	2016-01-02
5	88-654306	-500.00	c	88-654306-c-customers < Cash receipts from customers < Operating activities	88-654310	2016-01-02
6	88-654304	-162.00	c	88-654304-c-customers < Cash receipts from customers < Operating activities	88-654310	2016-01-02
7	88-654305	-186.00	c	88-654305-c-customers < Cash receipts from customers < Operating activities	88-654310	2016-01-02
8	88-654308	-6000.00	c	88-654308-c-customers < Cash receipts from customers < Operating activities	88-654310	2016-01-03
9	909876524	-118.00	c	909876524-c-customers < Cash receipts from customers < Operating activities	88-654310	2016-01-12
10	909876513	-208.00	c	909876513-c-customers < Cash receipts from customers < Operating activities	88-654310	2016-01-13
11	909876524	255.37	n	909876524-n-operating expenses < Cash payments for operating expenses < Operating activities	88-654310	2016-01-14
12	909876511	-54.00	c	909876511-c-customers < Cash receipts from customers < Operating activities	88-654310	2016-01-15
13	909876519	-122.00	c	909876519-c-customers < Cash receipts from customers < Operating activities	88-654310	2016-01-16
14	909876522	-48.00	c	909876522-c-customers < Cash receipts from customers < Operating activities	88-654310	2016-01-16
15	909876501	-39.00	c	909876501-c-customers < Cash receipts from customers < Operating activities	88-654310	2016-01-18
16	909876507	-82.00	c	909876507-c-customers < Cash receipts from customers < Operating activities	88-654310	2016-01-20
17	909876525	149.65	n	909876525-n-operating expenses < Cash payments for operating expenses < Operating activities	88-654310	2016-01-21
18	909876512	-120.00	c	909876512-c-customers < Cash receipts from customers < Operating activities	88-654310	2016-01-22
19	88-654308	-800.00	c	88-654308-c-customers < Cash receipts from customers < Operating activities	88-654310	2016-01-26
20	88-654308	200.00	t	88-654308-t-suppliers < Cash payments to suppliers < Operating activities	88-654310	2016-01-28
21	88-654307	-300.00	c	88-654307-c-customers < Cash receipts from customers < Operating activities	88-654310	2016-01-30
22	88-654306	-1000.00	c	88-654306-c-customers < Cash receipts from customers < Operating activities	88-654310	2016-01-31
23	909876514	-24.00	c	909876514-c-customers < Cash receipts from customers < Operating activities	88-654310	2016-01-31

	IDM	Amount	Symbol	MultiSubaccount	Recorder	TransDate
24	909876524	2870.00	t	909876524-t-salary < Cash payments for operating expenses < Operating activities	88-654310	2016-01-31
25	909876525	2790.00	t	909876525-t-CGM < Cash payments for operating expenses < Operating activities	88-654310	2016-01-31
26	909876501	-10790.00	c	909876501-c-customers < Cash receipts from customers < Operating activities	88-654310	2016-01-31
27	909876514	-10920.00	c	909876514-c-customers < Cash receipts from customers < Operating activities	88-654310	2016-01-31
28	909876515	-11050.00	c	909876515-c-customers < Cash receipts from customers < Operating activities	88-654310	2016-01-31
29	909876516	-11180.00	c	909876516-c-customers < Cash receipts from customers < Operating activities	88-654310	2016-01-31
30	909876517	-10270.00	c	909876517-c-customers < Cash receipts from customers < Operating activities	88-654310	2016-01-31
31	909876518	-11830.00	c	909876518-c-customers < Cash receipts from customers < Operating activities	88-654310	2016-01-31
32	909876519	-11570.00	c	909876519-c-customers < Cash receipts from customers < Operating activities	88-654310	2016-01-31
33	909876520	-12090.00	c	909876520-c-customers < Cash receipts from customers < Operating activities	88-654310	2016-01-31
34	909876521	-12870.00	c	909876521-c-customers < Cash receipts from customers < Operating activities	88-654310	2016-01-31
35	909876522	-10790.00	c	909876522-c-customers < Cash receipts from customers < Operating activities	88-654310	2016-01-31
36	909876523	-12350.00	c	909876523-c-customers < Cash receipts from customers < Operating activities	88-654310	2016-01-31
37	909876524	-10010.00	c	909876524-c-customers < Cash receipts from customers < Operating activities	88-654310	2016-01-31
38	909876525	-10270.00	c	909876525-c-customers < Cash receipts from customers < Operating activities	88-654310	2016-01-31
39	88-654306	30000.00	t	88-654306-t-machinery < Cash payments for machinery < Operating activities	88-654310	2016-02-01
40	909876512	-116.00	c	909876512-c-customers < Cash receipts from customers < Operating activities	88-654310	2016-02-06
41	909876516	-310.00	c	909876516-c-customers < Cash receipts from customers < Operating activities	88-654310	2016-02-17
42	909876509	-112.00	c	909876509-c-customers < Cash receipts from customers < Operating activities	88-654310	2016-02-19
43	88-654309	400.00	t	88-654309-t-suppliers < Cash payments to suppliers < Operating activities	88-654310	2016-02-20
44	88-654309	-300.00	c	88-654309-c-customers < Cash receipts from customers < Operating activities	88-654310	2016-02-21
45	909876508	-96.00	c	909876508-c-customers < Cash receipts from customers < Operating activities	88-654310	2016-02-22
46	909876524	-62.00	c	909876524-c-customers < Cash receipts from customers < Operating activities	88-654310	2016-02-23
47	909876524	187.84	n	909876524-n-operating expenses < Cash payments for operating expenses < Operating activities	88-654310	2016-02-25
48	909876524	2870.00	t	909876524-t-salary < Cash payments for operating expenses < Operating activities	88-654310	2016-02-28
49	909876525	2790.00	t	909876525-t-CGM < Cash payments for operating expenses < Operating activities	88-654310	2016-02-28
50	909876512	-100.00	c	909876512-c-customers < Cash receipts from customers < Operating activities	88-654310	2016-03-07
51	909876525	201.66	n	909876525-n-operating expenses < Cash payments for operating expenses < Operating activities	88-654310	2016-03-07

Figure 3.10-2   Proprietorship2 Cash Received or Paid by Other Members (Continue)

	IDM	Amount	Symbol	MultiSubaccount	Recorder	TransDate
52	88-654306	2000.00	t	88-654306-t-suppliers < Cash payments to suppliers < Operating activities	88-654310	2016-03-09
53	909876509	-104.00	c	909876509-c-customers < Cash receipts from customers < Operating activities	88-654310	2016-03-18
54	909876513	-290.00	c	909876513-c-customers < Cash receipts from customers < Operating activities	88-654310	2016-03-20
55	909876516	-131.00	c	909876516-c-customers < Cash receipts from customers < Operating activities	88-654310	2016-03-20
56	909876519	-73.00	c	909876519-c-customers < Cash receipts from customers < Operating activities	88-654310	2016-03-21
57	909876522	-58.00	c	909876522-c-customers < Cash receipts from customers < Operating activities	88-654310	2016-03-21
58	909876507	-96.00	c	909876507-c-customers < Cash receipts from customers < Operating activities	88-654310	2016-03-22
59	909876517	-87.00	c	909876517-c-customers < Cash receipts from customers < Operating activities	88-654310	2016-03-24
60	909876525	-70.00	c	909876525-c-customers < Cash receipts from customers < Operating activities	88-654310	2016-03-25
61	909876525	191.43	n	909876525-n-operating expenses < Cash payments for operating expenses < Operating activities	88-654310	2016-03-27
62	909876514	-84.00	c	909876514-c-customers < Cash receipts from customers < Operating activities	88-654310	2016-03-28
63	909876524	2870.00	t	909876524-t-salary < Cash payments for operating expenses < Operating activities	88-654310	2016-03-31
64	909876525	2790.00	t	909876525-t-CGM < Cash payments for operating expenses < Operating activities	88-654310	2016-03-31
65	909876509	-108.00	c	909876509-c-customers < Cash receipts from customers < Operating activities	88-654310	2016-04-06
66	88-654306	-1000.00	c	88-654306-c-customers < Cash receipts from customers < Operating activities	88-654310	2016-04-12
67	909876505	-112.00	c	909876505-c-customers < Cash receipts from customers < Operating activities	88-654310	2016-04-13
68	909876502	-50.00	c	909876502-c-customers < Cash receipts from customers < Operating activities	88-654310	2016-04-15
69	909876512	-120.00	c	909876512-c-customers < Cash receipts from customers < Operating activities	88-654310	2016-04-17
70	909876524	236.37	n	909876524-n-operating expenses < Cash payments for operating expenses < Operating activities	88-654310	2016-04-24
71	909876513	-470.00	c	909876513-c-customers < Cash receipts from customers < Operating activities	88-654310	2016-04-26
72	88-654306	-1000.00	c	88-654306-c-customers < Cash receipts from customers < Operating activities	88-654310	2016-04-29
73	88-654302	-330.00	c	88-654302-c-customers < Cash receipts from customers < Operating activities	88-654310	2016-04-30
74	909876524	2870.00	t	909876524-t-salary < Cash payments for operating expenses < Operating activities	88-654310	2016-04-30
75	909876525	2790.00	t	909876525-t-CGM < Cash payments for operating expenses < Operating activities	88-654310	2016-04-30
76	909876504	-100.00	c	909876504-c-customers < Cash receipts from customers < Operating activities	88-654310	2016-04-30
77	88-654309	9000.00	t	88-654309-t-suppliers < Cash payments to suppliers < Operating activities	88-654310	2016-05-01
78	88-654306	-2300.00	c	88-654306-c-customers < Cash receipts from customers < Operating activities	88-654310	2016-05-01
79	88-654309	-5000.00	c	88-654309-c-customers < Cash receipts from customers < Operating activities	88-654310	2016-05-01

	IDM	Amount	Symbol	MultiSubaccount	Recorder	TransDate
80	88-654309	-800.00	c	88-654309-c-customers < Cash receipts from customers < Operating activities	88-654310	2016-05-01
81	88-654303	-300.00	c	88-654303-c-customers < Cash receipts from customers < Operating activities	88-654310	2016-05-08
82	909876524	-78.00	c	909876524-c-customers < Cash receipts from customers < Operating activities	88-654310	2016-05-15
83	88-654301	-316.00	c	88-654301-c-customers < Cash receipts from customers < Operating activities	88-654310	2016-05-16
84	909876524	210.77	n	909876524-n-operating expenses < Cash payments for operating expenses < Operating activities	88-654310	2016-05-17
85	909876522	-56.00	c	909876522-c-customers < Cash receipts from customers < Operating activities	88-654310	2016-05-22
86	909876512	-108.00	c	909876512-c-customers < Cash receipts from customers < Operating activities	88-654310	2016-05-24
87	909876524	2870.00	t	909876524-t-salary < Cash payments for operating expenses < Operating activities	88-654310	2016-05-31
88	909876525	2790.00	t	909876525-t-CGM < Cash payments for operating expenses < Operating activities	88-654310	2016-05-31
89	909876508	-54.00	c	909876508-c-customers < Cash receipts from customers < Operating activities	88-654310	2016-06-03
90	909876517	-68.00	c	909876517-c-customers < Cash receipts from customers < Operating activities	88-654310	2016-06-12
91	909876520	-68.00	c	909876520-c-customers < Cash receipts from customers < Operating activities	88-654310	2016-06-12
92	909876503	-93.00	c	909876503-c-customers < Cash receipts from customers < Operating activities	88-654310	2016-06-15
93	909876505	-93.00	c	909876505-c-customers < Cash receipts from customers < Operating activities	88-654310	2016-06-17
94	909876506	-90.00	c	909876506-c-customers < Cash receipts from customers < Operating activities	88-654310	2016-06-17
95	909876524	-74.00	c	909876524-c-customers < Cash receipts from customers < Operating activities	88-654310	2016-06-17
96	909876502	-136.00	c	909876502-c-customers < Cash receipts from customers < Operating activities	88-654310	2016-06-18
97	909876524	196.83	n	909876524-n-operating expenses < Cash payments for operating expenses < Operating activities	88-654310	2016-06-19
98	909876522	-48.00	c	909876522-c-customers < Cash receipts from customers < Operating activities	88-654310	2016-06-21
99	909876524	2870.00	t	909876524-t-salary < Cash payments for operating expenses < Operating activities	88-654310	2016-06-30
100	909876525	2790.00	t	909876525-t-CGM < Cash payments for operating expenses < Operating activities	88-654310	2016-06-30
101	909876509	-117.00	c	909876509-c-customers < Cash receipts from customers < Operating activities	88-654310	2016-07-02
102	88-654308	53000.00	t	88-654308-t-suppliers < Cash payments to suppliers < Operating activities	88-654310	2016-07-03
103	909876511	-74.00	c	909876511-c-customers < Cash receipts from customers < Operating activities	88-654310	2016-07-09
104	909876505	-11830.00	c	909876505-c-customers < Cash receipts from customers < Operating activities	88-654310	2016-07-15
105	88-654308	-13000.00	c	88-654308-c-customers < Cash receipts from customers < Operating activities	88-654310	2016-07-16
106	909876525	-108.00	c	909876525-c-customers < Cash receipts from customers < Operating activities	88-654310	2016-07-21
107	909876525	251.19	n	909876525-n-operating expenses < Cash payments for operating expenses < Operating activities	88-654310	2016-07-23

Figure 3.10-2 Proprietorship2 Cash Received or Paid by Other Members (Continue)

	IDM	Amount	Symbol	MultiSubaccount	Recorder	TransDate
108	909876524	2870.00	t	909876524-t-salary < Cash payments for operating expenses < Operating activities	88-654310	2016-07-31
109	909876525	2790.00	t	909876525-t-CGM < Cash payments for operating expenses < Operating activities	88-654310	2016-07-31
110	909876512	-10920.00	c	909876512-c-customers < Cash receipts from customers < Operating activities	88-654310	2016-07-31
111	909876501	-11050.00	c	909876501-c-customers < Cash receipts from customers < Operating activities	88-654310	2016-07-31
112	909876502	-11180.00	c	909876502-c-customers < Cash receipts from customers < Operating activities	88-654310	2016-07-31
113	909876503	-11310.00	c	909876503-c-customers < Cash receipts from customers < Operating activities	88-654310	2016-07-31
114	909876504	-11440.00	c	909876504-c-customers < Cash receipts from customers < Operating activities	88-654310	2016-07-31
115	909876506	-10790.00	c	909876506-c-customers < Cash receipts from customers < Operating activities	88-654310	2016-07-31
116	909876507	-11310.00	c	909876507-c-customers < Cash receipts from customers < Operating activities	88-654310	2016-07-31
117	909876508	-11570.00	c	909876508-c-customers < Cash receipts from customers < Operating activities	88-654310	2016-07-31
118	909876509	-12090.00	c	909876509-c-customers < Cash receipts from customers < Operating activities	88-654310	2016-07-31
119	909876510	-11570.00	c	909876510-c-customers < Cash receipts from customers < Operating activities	88-654310	2016-07-31
120	909876511	-10270.00	c	909876511-c-customers < Cash receipts from customers < Operating activities	88-654310	2016-07-31
121	909876512	-11830.00	c	909876512-c-customers < Cash receipts from customers < Operating activities	88-654310	2016-07-31
122	909876513	-11830.00	c	909876513-c-customers < Cash receipts from customers < Operating activities	88-654310	2016-07-31
123	909876506	-114.00	c	909876506-c-customers < Cash receipts from customers < Operating activities	88-654310	2016-08-09
124	909876509	-118.00	c	909876509-c-customers < Cash receipts from customers < Operating activities	88-654310	2016-08-12
125	909876515	-123.00	c	909876515-c-customers < Cash receipts from customers < Operating activities	88-654310	2016-08-14
126	88-654308	66000.00	t	88-654308-t-suppliers < Cash payments to suppliers < Operating activities	88-654310	2016-08-15
127	909876508	-52.00	c	909876508-c-customers < Cash receipts from customers < Operating activities	88-654310	2016-08-15
128	909876524	-74.00	c	909876524-c-customers < Cash receipts from customers < Operating activities	88-654310	2016-08-16
129	909876524	203.47	n	909876524-n-operating expenses < Cash payments for operating expenses < Operating activities	88-654310	2016-08-18
130	909876522	-56.00	c	909876522-c-customers < Cash receipts from customers < Operating activities	88-654310	2016-08-21
131	909876524	2870.00	t	909876524-t-salary < Cash payments for operating expenses < Operating activities	88-654310	2016-08-31
132	909876525	2790.00	t	909876525-t-CGM < Cash payments for operating expenses < Operating activities	88-654310	2016-08-31
133	88-654306	18000.00	t	88-654306-t-machinery < Cash payments for machinery < Operating activities	88-654310	2016-09-02
134	909876502	-59.00	c	909876502-c-customers < Cash receipts from customers < Operating activities	88-654310	2016-09-05
135	909876504	-86.00	c	909876504-c-customers < Cash receipts from customers < Operating activities	88-654310	2016-09-05

	IDM	Amount	Symbol	MultiSubaccount	Recorder	TransDate
136	909876507	-90.00	c	909876507-c-customers < Cash receipts from customers < Operating activities	88-654310	2016-09-07
137	88-654307	-380.00	c	88-654307-c-customers < Cash receipts from customers < Operating activities	88-654310	2016-09-14
138	909876506	-105.00	c	909876506-c-customers < Cash receipts from customers < Operating activities	88-654310	2016-09-15
139	909876524	256.18	n	909876524-n-operating expenses < Cash payments for operating expenses < Operating activities	88-654310	2016-09-21
140	909876524	2870.00	t	909876524-t-salary < Cash payments for operating expenses < Operating activities	88-654310	2016-09-30
141	909876525	2790.00	t	909876525-t-CGM < Cash payments for operating expenses < Operating activities	88-654310	2016-09-30
142	909876515	-129.00	c	909876515-c-customers < Cash receipts from customers < Operating activities	88-654310	2016-10-03
143	909876518	-117.00	c	909876518-c-customers < Cash receipts from customers < Operating activities	88-654310	2016-10-04
144	909876521	-78.00	c	909876521-c-customers < Cash receipts from customers < Operating activities	88-654310	2016-10-06
145	909876522	-54.00	c	909876522-c-customers < Cash receipts from customers < Operating activities	88-654310	2016-10-06
146	909876508	-56.00	c	909876508-c-customers < Cash receipts from customers < Operating activities	88-654310	2016-10-08
147	88-654308	41000.00	t	88-654308-t-suppliers < Cash payments to suppliers < Operating activities	88-654310	2016-10-11
148	909876524	-86.00	c	909876524-c-customers < Cash receipts from customers < Operating activities	88-654310	2016-10-16
149	909876524	228.66	n	909876524-n-operating expenses < Cash payments for operating expenses < Operating activities	88-654310	2016-10-18
150	909876524	2870.00	t	909876524-t-salary < Cash payments for operating expenses < Operating activities	88-654310	2016-10-31
151	909876525	2790.00	t	909876525-t-CGM < Cash payments for operating expenses < Operating activities	88-654310	2016-10-31
152	909876511	-61.00	c	909876511-c-customers < Cash receipts from customers < Operating activities	88-654310	2016-11-01
153	909876504	-85.00	c	909876504-c-customers < Cash receipts from customers < Operating activities	88-654310	2016-11-11
154	909876509	-124.00	c	909876509-c-customers < Cash receipts from customers < Operating activities	88-654310	2016-11-16
155	909876515	-132.00	c	909876515-c-customers < Cash receipts from customers < Operating activities	88-654310	2016-11-16
156	909876524	-86.00	c	909876524-c-customers < Cash receipts from customers < Operating activities	88-654310	2016-11-18
157	909876524	204.61	n	909876524-n-operating expenses < Cash payments for operating expenses < Operating activities	88-654310	2016-11-20
158	909876524	2870.00	t	909876524-t-salary < Cash payments for operating expenses < Operating activities	88-654310	2016-11-30
159	909876525	2790.00	t	909876525-t-CGM < Cash payments for operating expenses < Operating activities	88-654310	2016-11-30
160	88-654306	5000.00	t	88-654306-t-machinery < Cash payments for machinery < Operating activities	88-654310	2016-12-01
161	909876510	-76.00	c	909876510-c-customers < Cash receipts from customers < Operating activities	88-654310	2016-12-02
162	909876501	-120.00	c	909876501-c-customers < Cash receipts from customers < Operating activities	88-654310	2016-12-08
163	909876524	-108.00	c	909876524-c-customers < Cash receipts from customers < Operating activities	88-654310	2016-12-15

Figure 3.10-2   Proprietorship2 Cash Received or Paid by Other Members (Continue)

	IDM	Amount	Symbol	MultiSubaccount	Recorder	TransDate
164	909876524	277.93	n	909876524-n-operating expenses < Cash payments for operating expenses < Operating activities	88-654310	2016-12-17
165	909876522	-68.00	c	909876522-c-customers < Cash receipts from customers < Operating activities	88-654310	2016-12-17
166	909876518	-144.00	c	909876518-c-customers < Cash receipts from customers < Operating activities	88-654310	2016-12-18
167	909876521	-88.00	c	909876521-c-customers < Cash receipts from customers < Operating activities	88-654310	2016-12-18
168	909876525	-98.00	c	909876525-c-customers < Cash receipts from customers < Operating activities	88-654310	2016-12-18
169	909876514	-162.00	c	909876514-c-customers < Cash receipts from customers < Operating activities	88-654310	2016-12-20
170	909876525	249.51	n	909876525-n-operating expenses < Cash payments for operating expenses < Operating activities	88-654310	2016-12-20
171	88-654306	-5500.00	c	88-654306-c-customers < Cash receipts from customers < Operating activities	88-654310	2016-12-23
172	909876507	-108.00	c	909876507-c-customers < Cash receipts from customers < Operating activities	88-654310	2016-12-29
173	88-654306	27000.00	t	88-654306-t-machinery < Cash payments for machinery < Operating activities	88-654310	2016-12-29
174	88-654309	-4300.00	c	88-654309-c-customers < Cash receipts from customers < Operating activities	88-654310	2016-12-31
175	909876524	2870.00	t	909876524-t-salary < Cash payments for operating expenses < Operating activities	88-654310	2016-12-31
176	909876525	2790.00	t	909876525-t-CGM < Cash payments for operating expenses < Operating activities	88-654310	2016-12-31
177	909876501	364.00	t	909876501-t-bond interest < Cash payments to bond holders < Operating activities	88-654310	2016-12-31
178	909876502	312.00	t	909876502-t-bond interest < Cash payments to bond holders < Operating activities	88-654310	2016-12-31
179	909876504	260.00	t	909876504-t-bond interest < Cash payments to bond holders < Operating activities	88-654310	2016-12-31
180	909876507	312.00	t	909876507-t-bond interest < Cash payments to bond holders < Operating activities	88-654310	2016-12-31
181	909876509	312.00	t	909876509-t-bond interest < Cash payments to bond holders < Operating activities	88-654310	2016-12-31
182	909876511	260.00	t	909876511-t-bond interest < Cash payments to bond holders < Operating activities	88-654310	2016-12-31
183	909876512	208.00	t	909876512-t-bond interest < Cash payments to bond holders < Operating activities	88-654310	2016-12-31
184	909876516	364.00	t	909876516-t-bond interest < Cash payments to bond holders < Operating activities	88-654310	2016-12-31
185	909876517	260.00	t	909876517-t-bond interest < Cash payments to bond holders < Operating activities	88-654310	2016-12-31
186	909876518	312.00	t	909876518-t-bond interest < Cash payments to bond holders < Operating activities	88-654310	2016-12-31
187	909876519	260.00	t	909876519-t-bond interest < Cash payments to bond holders < Operating activities	88-654310	2016-12-31
188	909876520	416.00	t	909876520-t-bond interest < Cash payments to bond holders < Operating activities	88-654310	2016-12-31
189	909876504	220.00	t	909876504-t-bond interest < Cash payments to bond holders < Operating activities	88-654310	2016-12-31
190	909876505	275.00	t	909876505-t-bond interest < Cash payments to bond holders < Operating activities	88-654310	2016-12-31
191	909876506	330.00	t	909876506-t-bond interest < Cash payments to bond holders < Operating activities	88-654310	2016-12-31
192	909876508	275.00	t	909876508-t-bond interest < Cash payments to bond holders < Operating activities	88-654310	2016-12-31
193	909876510	330.00	t	909876510-t-bond interest < Cash payments to bond holders < Operating activities	88-654310	2016-12-31
194	909876513	220.00	t	909876513-t-bond interest < Cash payments to bond holders < Operating activities	88-654310	2016-12-31
195	909876515	275.00	t	909876515-t-bond interest < Cash payments to bond holders < Operating activities	88-654310	2016-12-31
196	909876516	330.00	t	909876516-t-bond interest < Cash payments to bond holders < Operating activities	88-654310	2016-12-31
197	909876517	275.00	t	909876517-t-bond interest < Cash payments to bond holders < Operating activities	88-654310	2016-12-31
198	909876518	220.00	t	909876518-t-bond interest < Cash payments to bond holders < Operating activities	88-654310	2016-12-31
199	88-654304	-252.00	c	88-654304-c-investment income < Cash receipts from investments < Investing activities	88-654310	2016-12-31
200	88-654305	-463.00	c	88-654305-c-investment income < Cash receipts from investments < Investing activities	88-654310	2016-12-31
201	88-654305	-120.00	c	88-654305-c-deposit interest income < Cash receipts from deposit interest < Financial activities	88-654310	2016-12-31

Query executed successfully.

Figure 3.10-2   Proprietorship2 Cash Received or Paid by Other Members

Cash Flow Statement

Cash Flows Statement Year Ended 2016-12-31	
Operating activities	
Cash payments for machinery	-$80,000.00
Cash payments for operating expenses	-$71,221.47
Cash payments to bond holders	-$6,390.00
Cash payments to suppliers	-$179,600.00
Cash receipts from customers	$357,490.00
Net cash provided by Operating activities	$20,278.53
Investing activities	
Cash receipts from investments	$715.00
Net cash provided by Investing activities	$715.00
Financial activities	
Cash receipts from deposit interest	$120.00
Net cash provided by Financial activities	$120.00
Net change in cash	$21,113.53
Cash, Begining	$8,768.69
Cash, Ending	$29,882.22

Figure 3.10-3   Proprietorship2 Cash Flows Statement

Cash

ID	Multi-Name	Amount	Balance	General ID	Transaction Date
43	88-654303-n-tax < Cash payments for operating expenses < Operating a...	-$10,079.23	$8,768.69	15	2015-12-31
44	88-654308-c-customers < Cash receipts from customers < Operating act...	$400.00	$9,168.69	18	2016-01-02
45	88-654307-c-customers < Cash receipts from customers < Operating act...	$500.00	$9,668.69	19	2016-01-02
46	88-654309-c-customers < Cash receipts from customers < Operating act...	$450.00	$10,118.69	20	2016-01-02
47	88-654308-t-suppliers < Cash payments to suppliers < Operating activities	-$8,000.00	$2,118.69	21	2016-01-02
48	88-654306-c-customers < Cash receipts from customers < Operating act...	$500.00	$2,618.69	24	2016-01-02
49	88-654308-c-customers < Cash receipts from customers < Operating act...	$6,000.00	$8,618.69	25	2016-01-03
50	909876524-c-customers < Cash receipts from customers < Operating ac...	$118.00	$8,736.69	31	2016-01-12
51	909876513-c-customers < Cash receipts from customers < Operating ac...	$208.00	$8,944.69	32	2016-01-13
52	909876524-n-operating expenses < Cash payments for operating expen...	-$255.37	$8,689.32	33	2016-01-14
53	909876511-c-customers < Cash receipts from customers < Operating ac...	$54.00	$8,743.32	34	2016-01-15
54	909876519-c-customers < Cash receipts from customers < Operating ac...	$122.00	$8,865.32	35	2016-01-16
55	909876522-c-customers < Cash receipts from customers < Operating ac...	$48.00	$8,913.32	36	2016-01-16
56	909876501-c-customers < Cash receipts from customers < Operating ac...	$39.00	$8,952.32	37	2016-01-18
57	909876507-c-customers < Cash receipts from customers < Operating ac...	$82.00	$9,034.32	38	2016-01-20
58	909876525-n-operating expenses < Cash payments for operating expen...	-$149.65	$8,884.67	39	2016-01-21
59	909876512-c-customers < Cash receipts from customers < Operating ac...	$120.00	$9,004.67	40	2016-01-22
60	88-654308-c-customers < Cash receipts from customers < Operating act...	$800.00	$9,804.67	41	2016-01-26
61	88-654308-t-suppliers < Cash payments to suppliers < Operating activities	-$200.00	$9,604.67	42	2016-01-28
62	88-654307-c-customers < Cash receipts from customers < Operating act...	$300.00	$9,904.67	43	2016-01-30
63	88-654306-c-customers < Cash receipts from customers < Operating act...	$1,000.00	$10,904.67	44	2016-01-31
64	909876514-c-customers < Cash receipts from customers < Operating ac...	$24.00	$10,928.67	45	2016-01-31
65	909876524-t-salary < Cash payments for operating expenses < Operatin...	-$2,870.00	$8,058.67	46	2016-01-31
66	909876525-t-CGM < Cash payments for operating expenses < Operating...	-$2,790.00	$5,268.67	46	2016-01-31
223	909876511-t-bond interest < Cash payments to bond holders < Operatin...	-$260.00	$33,269.22	218	2016-12-31
224	909876512-t-bond interest < Cash payments to bond holders < Operatin...	-$208.00	$33,061.22	218	2016-12-31
225	909876516-t-bond interest < Cash payments to bond holders < Operatin...	-$364.00	$32,697.22	218	2016-12-31
226	909876517-t-bond interest < Cash payments to bond holders < Operatin...	-$260.00	$32,437.22	219	2016-12-31
227	909876518-t-bond interest < Cash payments to bond holders < Operatin...	-$312.00	$32,125.22	219	2016-12-31
228	909876519-t-bond interest < Cash payments to bond holders < Operatin...	-$260.00	$31,865.22	219	2016-12-31
229	909876520-t-bond interest < Cash payments to bond holders < Operatin...	-$416.00	$31,449.22	219	2016-12-31
230	909876504-t-bond interest < Cash payments to bond holders < Operatin...	-$220.00	$31,229.22	220	2016-12-31
231	909876505-t-bond interest < Cash payments to bond holders < Operatin...	-$275.00	$30,954.22	220	2016-12-31
232	909876506-t-bond interest < Cash payments to bond holders < Operatin...	-$330.00	$30,624.22	220	2016-12-31
233	909876508-t-bond interest < Cash payments to bond holders < Operatin...	-$275.00	$30,349.22	220	2016-12-31
234	909876510-t-bond interest < Cash payments to bond holders < Operatin...	-$330.00	$30,019.22	220	2016-12-31
235	909876513-t-bond interest < Cash payments to bond holders < Operatin...	-$220.00	$29,799.22	220	2016-12-31
236	909876515-t-bond interest < Cash payments to bond holders < Operatin...	-$275.00	$29,524.22	220	2016-12-31
237	909876516-t-bond interest < Cash payments to bond holders < Operatin...	-$330.00	$29,194.22	220	2016-12-31
238	909876517-t-bond interest < Cash payments to bond holders < Operatin...	-$275.00	$28,919.22	221	2016-12-31
239	909876518-t-bond interest < Cash payments to bond holders < Operatin...	-$220.00	$28,699.22	221	2016-12-31
240	88-654304-c-investment income < Cash receipts from investments < Inv...	$252.00	$28,951.22	222	2016-12-31
241	88-654305-c-investment income < Cash receipts from investments < Inv...	$463.00	$29,414.22	223	2016-12-31
242	88-654305-c-deposit interest income < Cash receipts from deposit intere...	$120.00	$29,534.22	224	2016-12-31
243	88-654304-c-customers < Cash receipts from customers < Operating act...	$162.00	$29,696.22	228	2016-01-02
244	88-654305-c-customers < Cash receipts from customers < Operating act...	$186.00	$29,882.22	229	2016-01-02

Figure 3.10-4   Proprietorship2 Cash Account Table

Income Statement

Year ended: 12/31/2016	
Revenues	
Sales	$358,855.00
Cost	
Cost of goods sold	-$182,793.00
Gross Margin	$176,062.00
Operating and administrative expenses	
Travelling expenses	-$2,026.47
Other expenses	-$1,275.00
Salary expenses	-$34,440.00
Bond interest expenses	-$6,390.00
Office supplies expenses	-$677.53
Amortization expenses	-$20,220.84
Cost of goods manufactured	$0.00
Other income	
Investment incomes	$715.00
Deposit interest incomes	$120.00
Earnings Before Income Taxes	$111,867.16
Tax	
Tax expenses	-$22,373.43
Net Earnings	$89,493.73
Retained Earnings.Begining	$0.00
Retained Earnings.Ending	$89,493.73

Figure 3.10-5   Proprietorship2 Income Statement

Balance Sheet

	As at 12/31/2016	
ASSETS		
Current assets		
Cash		$29,882.22
Supplies		$170.32
Account receivable		$1,515.00
Inventory		$265,607.00
WIP Inventory		$0.00
		$297,174.54
Long term investments		
Bonds		$17,000.00
Equipment		
Vehicle		$116,000.00
Accumulated amortization: Vehicle		-$30,833.33
Computer		$5,900.00
Accumulated amortization: Computer		-$245.84
		$90,820.83
Total Assets		$404,995.37
LIABILITIES		
Current liabilities		
Account payable		$16,900.00
Tax payable		$22,373.43
		$39,273.43
Long term liabilities		
Bonds payable		$120,000.00
Total Liability		$159,273.43
SHAREHOLDERS' EQUITY		
Owners capital		
Share capital		$150,000.00
Retained earnings (Conversion)		$6,228.21
		$156,228.21
Retined earnings		$89,493.73
Accumulated other comprehensive income		$0.00
Total Shareholders' Equity		$245,721.94
Total Liabilities and Shareholders' Equity		$404,995.37

Figure 3.10-6   Proprietorship2 Balance Sheet Statement

3.11 Analysis and Conclusion

Based on the database dcj100, the Tax Bureau can automatically get cash, investment, and taxation information of all social members, including all organizations and all individuals, by using of a special software in the future. Moreover, the financial information is not provided by one social member himself, but is provided by other social members. However, I do not programme the special software now. In this book, the following all information is gotten by using of SQL Server query in the database dcj100. Please pay attention here. All information of an organization or an individual are provided by other organizations. The information must be correct and reliable. Therefore, drawing up false accounts, tax evasion, and money laundering will be impossible to occur.

3.11.1 Cash Balances of all Members

The following Figure 3.11-1 shows the detail information of the 10 organizations or companies on December 31, 2016. The data can be gotten by using of SQL Server query, seeing the page 237.

Order	Business No.	Name	Phone number	Tax rate	Business Bank1	Business Bank2	Balance	Primary Account
1	88-654300	Cash Management Center	123456700	0	758,814.45	0	758,814.45	Business Bank1
2	88-654301	Central Bank	123456789	0	0	2,527.17	2,527.17	Business Bank2
3	88-654302	Government1	123456788	0	146.31	10.08	156.39	Business Bank1
4	88-654303	Tax Bureau	123456787	0	933.59	1,117.96	2,051.55	Business Bank1
5	88-654304	Business Bank1	123456786	0.3	-	0	0	Business Bank1
6	88-654305	Business Bank2	123456785	0.3	0	-	0	Business Bank2
7	88-654306	Company1	123456784	0.3	38,933.25	0	38,933.25	Business Bank1
8	88-654307	Company2	123456783	0.3	0	125,159.21	125,159.21	Business Bank2
9	88-654308	Company3	123456782	0.3	3,906.47	200,772.90	204,679.37	Business Bank2
10	88-654309	Proprietorship1	123456781	0.2	177,678.88	0	177,678.88	Business Bank1
11	88-654310	Proprietorship2	123456780	0.2	0	29,882.22	29,882.22	Business Bank2
12	Total	-	-	-	980,412.95	359469.54	1,339,882.49	-

Figure 3.11-1   Organizations Information after One Year Table

The Figure 3.11-2 on this page and next page shows the detail information of the 30 persons (including five children) on December 31, 2016. From the Figure 3.11-2, the individual A10 (SIN: 909876510) overdraws -$3,812.

Order	SIN	Name	Employer Name	Business Bank1	Business Bank2	Balance	Primary Account
1	909876501	A1	Central Bank	13,870.03	940.15	14,810.18	Business Bank1
2	909876502	A2	Central Bank	19,516.91	16,500.55	36,017.46	Business Bank1
3	909876503	A3	Government1	24,129.69	16,260.10	40,389.79	Business Bank1
4	909876504	A4	Government1	26,733.62	11,400.61	38,134.23	Business Bank1
5	909876505	A5	Tax Bureau	26,127.31	11,970.23	38,097.54	Business Bank1
6	909876506	A6	Tax Bureau	29,585.55	11,100.54	40,686.09	Business Bank1
7	909876507	A7	Business Bank1	2,492.39	0	2,492.39	Business Bank1
8	909876508	A8	Business Bank1	26,343.83	11,000.11	37,343.94	Business Bank1
9	909876509	A9	Business Bank1	33,316.89	0	33,316.89	Business Bank1
10	909876510	A10	Business Bank2	0	-3,812.00	-3,812.00	Business Bank2
11	909876511	A11	Business Bank2	11,656.41	24,871.27	36,527.68	Business Bank2
12	909876512	A12	Business Bank2	7,184.23	8,218.65	15,402.88	Business Bank2
13	909876513	A13	Company1	10,141.69	310.18	10,451.87	Business Bank1
14	909876514	A14	Company1	23,943.83	12,200.45	36,144.28	Business Bank1
15	909876515	A15	Company1	33,137.24	0	33,137.24	Business Bank1
16	909876516	A16	Company2	14,460.72	300.74	14,761.46	Business Bank1
17	909876517	A17	Company2	0	34,117.69	34,117.69	Business Bank2
18	909876518	A18	Company2	22,703.66	10,510.99	33,214.65	Business Bank1
19	909876519	A19	Company3	11,230.11	21,849.39	33,079.50	Business Bank2
20	909876520	A20	Company3	11,082.23	29,604.68	40,686.91	Business Bank2
21	909876521	A21	Company3	0	37,305.53	37,305.53	Business Bank2
22	909876522	A22	Proprietorship1	16,456.03	24,652.20	41,108.23	Business Bank2
23	909876523	A23	Proprietorship1	460.84	18,986.05	19,446.89	Business Bank2
24	909876524	A24	Proprietorship2	3,251.28	0	3,251.28	Business Bank1
25	909876525	A25	Proprietorship2	12,566.76	9,150.25	21,717.01	Business Bank1
26	909876526	A1A8	Child of A1 and A8	0	0	0	A1: Business Bank2
27	909876527	A1A8	Child of A1 and A8	0	0	0	A8: -
28	909876528	A12A20	Child of A12 and A20	0	0	0	A12: Business Bank1
29	909876529	A13A25	Child of A13 and A25	0	0	0	A13: -
30	909876530	A16A23	Child of A16 and A23	0	0	0	A16: -
31	Total			380,391.25	307438.36	687,829.61	-

Figure 3.11-2   Individuals Information after One Year Table

The following Figure 3.11-3 shows the cash detail information of the Business Bank1 and the Business Bank2.

Order	Name	Balance	Self-Cash	Total Deposits	Companies Deposits	Individuals Deposits
1	Business Bank1	1,364,039.73	3,235.53	1,360,804.20	980,412.95	380,391.25
2	Business Bank2	635,960.27	-30,947.63	666,907.90	359,469.54	307438.36
3	**Total**	**2000000.00**	**-27,712.10**	**2,027,712.10**	**1,339,882.49**	**687,829.61**

Figure 3.11-3   Two Business Banks Information Table

3.11.2 Perfect Financial Information of all Individuals

3.11.2.1 Taxation Information of all Individuals

The following Figure 3.11-4 shows taxable incomes $34,920 of the individual A1 (SIN: 909876501) in this fiscal year.

Figure 3.11-4   A1 Taxable Incomes

By using of the same method, I can get other 24 individuals' taxable incomes information.

The Figure 3.11-5 shows taxable incomes $33,924 of the individual A25 (SIN: 909876525).

```
SQLQuery1.sqi - LIU...SS.dcj100 (sa (52))*  ×
 use dcj100

 select sum(amount) as sum1t from CashByMembers where IDM='909876525' and Symbol='t'
        and TransDate between '2016-01-01' and '2016-12-31'

 select * from CashByMembers where IDM='909876525' and Symbol='t'
        and TransDate between '2016-01-01' and '2016-12-31'
```

100 % ▾

Results   Messages

	sum1t
1	33924.00

	IDM	Amount	Symbol	MultiSubaccount	Recorder	TransDate
1	909876525	230.00	t	909876525-t-bond interest < Cash payments to bond holders < Operating activities	88-654306	2016-12-31
2	909876525	94.00	t	909876525-t-bond interest < Cash payments to bond holders < Operating activities	88-654307	2016-12-31
3	909876525	2790.00	t	909876525-t-CGM < Cash payments for operating expenses < Operating activities	88-654310	2016-01-31
4	909876525	2790.00	t	909876525-t-CGM < Cash payments for operating expenses < Operating activities	88-654310	2016-02-28
5	909876525	2790.00	t	909876525-t-CGM < Cash payments for operating expenses < Operating activities	88-654310	2016-03-31
6	909876525	2790.00	t	909876525-t-CGM < Cash payments for operating expenses < Operating activities	88-654310	2016-04-30
7	909876525	2790.00	t	909876525-t-CGM < Cash payments for operating expenses < Operating activities	88-654310	2016-05-31
8	909876525	2790.00	t	909876525-t-CGM < Cash payments for operating expenses < Operating activities	88-654310	2016-06-30
9	909876525	2790.00	t	909876525-t-CGM < Cash payments for operating expenses < Operating activities	88-654310	2016-07-31
10	909876525	2790.00	t	909876525-t-CGM < Cash payments for operating expenses < Operating activities	88-654310	2016-08-31
11	909876525	2790.00	t	909876525-t-CGM < Cash payments for operating expenses < Operating activities	88-654310	2016-09-30
12	909876525	2790.00	t	909876525-t-CGM < Cash payments for operating expenses < Operating activities	88-654310	2016-10-31
13	909876525	2790.00	t	909876525-t-CGM < Cash payments for operating expenses < Operating activities	88-654310	2016-11-30
14	909876525	2790.00	t	909876525-t-CGM < Cash payments for operating expenses < Operating activities	88-654310	2016-12-31
15	909876525	120.00	t	909876525-t-deposit interest expenses < Cash payments for operating expenses < Operating act...	88-654304	2016-12-31

Figure 3.11-5   A25 Taxable Incomes

Based on the above information, I design a table which includes 25 individuals' taxable incomes information, seeing the Figure 3.11-6. If the taxable income is in the $30,000 to $35,000, the tax rate is 10% for total taxable incomes. If the taxable income is over the $35,000, the tax rate is 20% for the difference between the taxable income and the $35,000. From the Figure 3.11-6, the total taxation of all individuals is the $89,014.80.

Order	SIN	Name	Employer Name	Taxable Incomes	Taxation1	Taxation2	Total taxation
1	909876501	A1	Central Bank	34,920.00	3492.00	0	3492.00
2	909876502	A2	Central Bank	35,384.00	3500.00	76.80	3576.80
3	909876503	A3	Government1	34,910.00	3491.00	0	3491.00
4	909876504	A4	Government1	35,740.00	3500.00	148.00	3648.00
5	909876505	A5	Tax Bureau	34,589.00	3458.90	0	3458.90
6	909876506	A6	Tax Bureau	35,646.00	3500.00	129.20	3629.20
7	909876507	A7	Business Bank1	37,444.00	3500.00	488.80	3988.80

8	909876508	A8	Business Bank1	35,981.00	3500.00	196.20	3696.20
9	909876509	A9	Business Bank1	34,358.00	3435.80	0	3435.80
10	909876510	A10	Business Bank2	36,941.00	3500.00	388.20	3888.20
11	909876511	A11	Business Bank2	36,246.00	3500.00	249.20	3749.20
12	909876512	A12	Business Bank2	33,792.00	3379.20	0	3379.20
13	909876513	A13	Company1	32,268.00	3226.80	0	3226.80
14	909876514	A14	Company1	35,497.00	3500.00	99.40	3599.40
15	909876515	A15	Company1	35,869.00	3500.00	173.80	3673.80
16	909876516	A16	Company2	32,954.00	3295.40	0	3295.40
17	909876517	A17	Company2	36,050.00	3500.00	210.00	3710.00
18	909876518	A18	Company2	36,000.00	3500.00	200.00	3700.00
19	909876519	A19	Company3	33,573.00	3357.30	0	3357.30
20	909876520	A20	Company3	35,976.00	3500.00	195.20	3695.20
21	909876521	A21	Company3	34,762.00	3476.20	0	3476.20
22	909876522	A22	Proprietorship1	35,378.00	3500.00	75.60	3575.60
23	909876523	A23	Proprietorship1	33,861.00	3386.10	0	3386.10
24	909876524	A24	Proprietorship2	34,933.00	3493.30	0	3493.30
25	909876525	A25	Proprietorship2	33,924.00	3392.40	0	3392.40
26	Total			876,996.00	86,384.40	2,630.40	89,014.80

Figure 3.11-6   25 Individuals Taxable taxations

3.11.2.2 Investment Information of all Individuals

There is not any individual who makes investment in this fiscal year. However, I can get the investment information prior to this fiscal year by using of SQL Server query. The Figure 3.11-7 on the next page shows investment balance $696,000 of the individual A7 (SIN: 909876507) on December 31, 2016 and other detail information. By using of the same method, I can get other 24 individuals' investment information. The Figure 3.11-8 on the next pages shows all investment information of the 25 individuals. From the Figure 3.11-8, the total investment is -$2,990,000. This balance and other class investment balances can also be gotten by using of SQL Server query, seeing the Figure 3.11-9 which follows the Figure 3.11-8.

```
SQLQuery1.sql - LIU...SS.dcj100 (sa (52))* ×

use dcj100

select sum(amount) as sum1t from CashByMembers where IDM='909876507' and Symbol='i'

select * from CashByMembers where IDM='909876507' and Symbol='i'
```

100 % ▾

Results | Messages

	sum1t
1	-696000.00

	IDM	Amount	Symbol	MultiSubaccount	Recorder	TransDate
1	909876507	-4000.00	i	909876507-i-bond21 < Cash receipts from issued bonds < Financial activities	88-654305	2015-12-31
2	909876507	-5000.00	i	909876507-i-bond01 < Cash receipts from issued bonds < Financial activities	88-654300	2015-12-31
3	909876507	-9000.00	i	909876507-i-bond11 < Cash receipts from issued bonds < Financial activities	88-654304	2015-12-31
4	909876507	-117439.99	i	909876507-i-owners < Cash receipts from owners < Financial activities	88-654304	2015-12-31
5	909876507	-482560.01	i	909876507-i-owners < Cash receipts from owners < Financial activities	88-654304	2015-12-31
6	909876507	-66000.00	i	909876507-i-owners < Cash receipts from owners < Financial activities	88-654308	2015-12-31
7	909876507	-6000.00	i	909876507-i-bond51 < Cash receipts from issued bonds < Financial activities	88-654308	2015-12-31
8	909876507	-6000.00	i	909876507-i-bond71 < Cash receipts from issued bonds < Financial activities	88-654310	2015-12-31

Figure 3.11-7   A7 Investment Information

Order	SIN	Name	Employer Name	Investment Class	Date	Balance (Class)
1	909876501	A1	Central Bank	Bond	2015-12-31	-26,000.00
2	909876502	A2	Central Bank	Bond	2015-12-31	-23,000.00
3	909876503	A3	Government1	Bond	2015-12-31	-24,000.00
4	909876504	A4	Government1	Bond	2015-12-31	-30,000.00
5	909876505	A5	Tax Bureau	Bond	2015-12-31	-15,000.00
6	909876506	A6	Tax Bureau	Bond	2015-12-31	-25,000.00
7	909876507	A7	Business Bank1	Bond	2015-12-31	-30,000.00
8	909876507	A7	Business Bank1	Open company	2015-12-31	-666,000.00
9	909876508	A8	Business Bank1	Bond	2015-12-31	-19,000.00
10	909876509	A9	Business Bank1	Bond	2015-12-31	-28,000.00
11	909876509	A9	Business Bank1	Open company	2015-12-31	-400,000.00
12	909876510	A10	Business Bank2	Bond	2015-12-31	-17,000.00
13	909876511	A11	Business Bank2	Bond	2015-12-31	-29,000.00
14	909876511	A11	Business Bank2	Open company	2015-12-31	-360,000.00
15	909876512	A12	Business Bank2	Bond	2015-12-31	-17,000.00
16	909876512	A12	Business Bank2	Open company	2015-12-31	-80,000.00
17	909876513	A13	Company1	Bond	2015-12-31	-20,000.00
18	909876513	A13	Company1	Open company	2015-12-31	-90,000.00
19	909876514	A14	Company1	Bond	2015-12-31	-13,000.00
20	909876514	A14	Company1	Open company	2015-12-31	-54,000.00
21	909876515	A15	Company1	Bond	2015-12-31	-20,000.00
22	909876515	A15	Company1	Open company	2015-12-31	-70,000.00

23	909876516	A16	Company2	Bond	2015-12-31	-31,000.00
24	909876517	A17	Company2	Bond	2015-12-31	-25,000.00
25	909876517	A17	Company2	Open company	2015-12-31	-291,000.00
26	909876518	A18	Company2	Bond	2015-12-31	-27,000.00
27	909876518	A18	Company2	Open company	2015-12-31	-50,000.00
28	909876519	A19	Company3	Bond	2015-12-31	-22,000.00
29	909876519	A19	Company3	Open company	2015-12-31	-88,000.00
30	909876520	A20	Company3	Bond	2015-12-31	-21,000.00
31	909876521	A21	Company3	Bond	2015-12-31	-33,000.00
32	909876522	A22	Proprietorship1	Bond	2015-12-31	-18,000.00
33	909876522	A22	Proprietorship1	Open company	2015-12-31	-160,000.00
34	909876523	A23	Proprietorship1	Bond	2015-12-31	-3,000.00
35	909876524	A24	Proprietorship2	Bond	2015-12-31	-8,000.00
36	909876524	A24	Proprietorship2	Open company	2015-12-31	-150,000.00
37	909876525	A25	Proprietorship2	Bond	2015-12-31	-7,000.00
38	**Total**					**-2,990,000.00**

Figure 3.11-8   25 Individuals Investment Information

Figure 3.11-9   Total Investment Balance and Class Investment Balances

From Figure 3.11-9, the total investment balance of the 25 individuals is also -$2,990,000. The bonds' investment balance of some individuals is -$531,000. The companies' investment balance of some individuals is -$2,459,000.

3.11.2.3 Consuming Information of all Individuals

The following Figure 3.11-10 shows consuming balance -$48,739 of the individual A1 (SIN: 909876501) in this fiscal year.

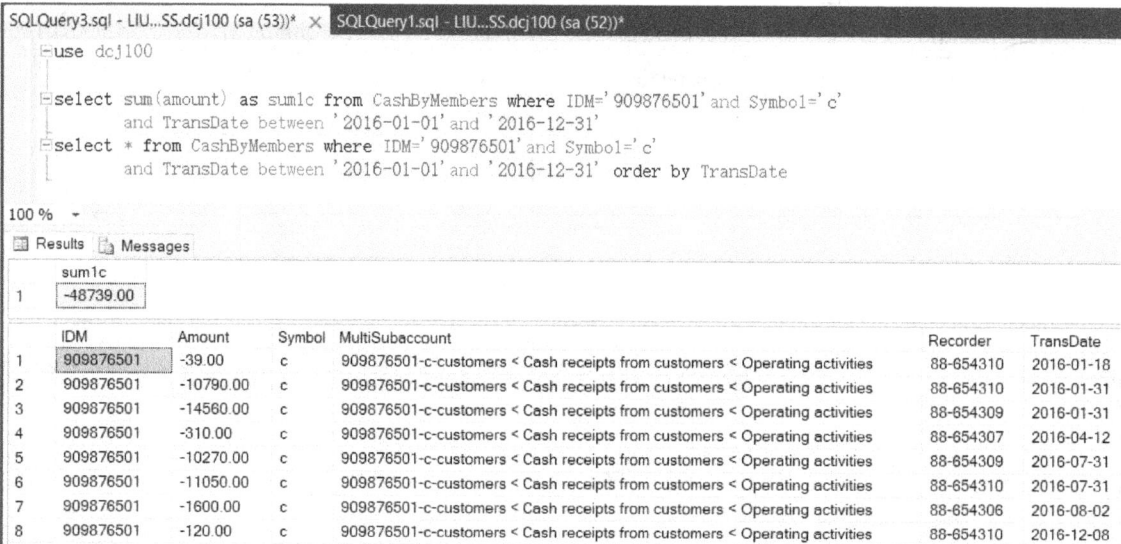

Figure 3.11-9   A1 Consuming Information

By using of the same method, I can get other 24 individuals' consuming balance information. The Figure 3.11-11 on this page and the next pages shows consuming balance information of the 25 individuals. From the Figure 3.11-11, the total consuming balance is -$934,648. This total consuming balance of 25 individuals can also be gotten by using of SQL Server query, seeing the Figure 3.11-12 which follows the Figure 3.11-11. It is -$934,648 too.

Order	SIN	Name	Employer Name	Consuming Balance
1	909876501	A1	Central Bank	-48739.00
2	909876502	A2	Central Bank	-29,397.00
3	909876503	A3	Government1	-25,245.00
4	909876504	A4	Government1	-28,175.00

5	909876505	A5	Tax Bureau	-27,116.00
6	909876506	A6	Tax Bureau	-26,617.00
7	909876507	A7	Business Bank1	-64,508.00
8	909876508	A8	Business Bank1	-26,236.00
9	909876509	A9	Business Bank1	-31,866.00
10	909876510	A10	Business Bank2	-69,826.00
11	909876511	A11	Business Bank2	-26,924.00
12	909876512	A12	Business Bank2	-49,057.00
13	909876513	A13	Company1	-56,993.00
14	909876514	A14	Company1	-30,710.00
15	909876515	A15	Company1	-30,204.00
16	909876516	A16	Company2	-53,002.00
17	909876517	A17	Company2	-29,079.00
18	909876518	A18	Company2	-33,267.00
19	909876519	A19	Company3	-31,647.00
20	909876520	A20	Company3	-22,609.00
21	909876521	A21	Company3	-24,670.00
22	909876522	A22	Proprietorship1	-23,858.00
23	909876523	A23	Proprietorship1	-42,232.00
24	909876524	A24	Proprietorship2	-62,040.00
25	909876525	A25	Proprietorship2	-40,631.00
26	**Total**			**-934,648.00**

Figure 3.11-11   25 Individuals Consuming Information

```
use dcj100
select sum(amount) as sum1c from CashByMembers where IDM not like '%-%' and Symbol='c' and
    TransDate between '2016-01-01' and '2016-12-31'
select * from CashByMembers where IDM not like '%-%' and Symbol='c' and TransDate between '2016-01-01' and '2016-12-31'
    order by IDM
```

	sum1c
1	-934648.00

	IDM	Amount	Symbol	MultiSubaccount	Recorder	TransDate
1	909876501	-1600.00	c	909876501-c-customers < Cash receipts from customers < Operating activities	88-654306	2016-08-02
2	909876501	-310.00	c	909876501-c-customers < Cash receipts from customers < Operating activities	88-654307	2016-04-12
3	909876501	-14560.00	c	909876501-c-customers < Cash receipts from customers < Operating activities	88-654309	2016-01-31
4	909876501	-10270.00	c	909876501-c-customers < Cash receipts from customers < Operating activities	88-654309	2016-07-31
5	909876501	-10790.00	c	909876501-c-customers < Cash receipts from customers < Operating activities	88-654310	2016-01-31
6	909876501	-39.00	c	909876501-c-customers < Cash receipts from customers < Operating activities	88-654310	2016-01-18
7	909876501	-11050.00	c	909876501-c-customers < Cash receipts from customers < Operating activities	88-654310	2016-07-31
8	909876501	-120.00	c	909876501-c-customers < Cash receipts from customers < Operating activities	88-654310	2016-12-08
9	909876502	-11180.00	c	909876502-c-customers < Cash receipts from customers < Operating activities	88-654310	2016-07-31
10	909876502	-136.00	c	909876502-c-customers < Cash receipts from customers < Operating activities	88-654310	2016-06-18
11	909876502	-59.00	c	909876502-c-customers < Cash receipts from customers < Operating activities	88-654310	2016-09-05

Figure 3.11-12   Total Consuming Information

3.11.2.4 No Taxable incomes Information of all Individuals

The following Figure 3.11-13 shows no taxable incomes' balance $3,124.78 of the individual A9 (SIN: 909876509) in this fiscal year.

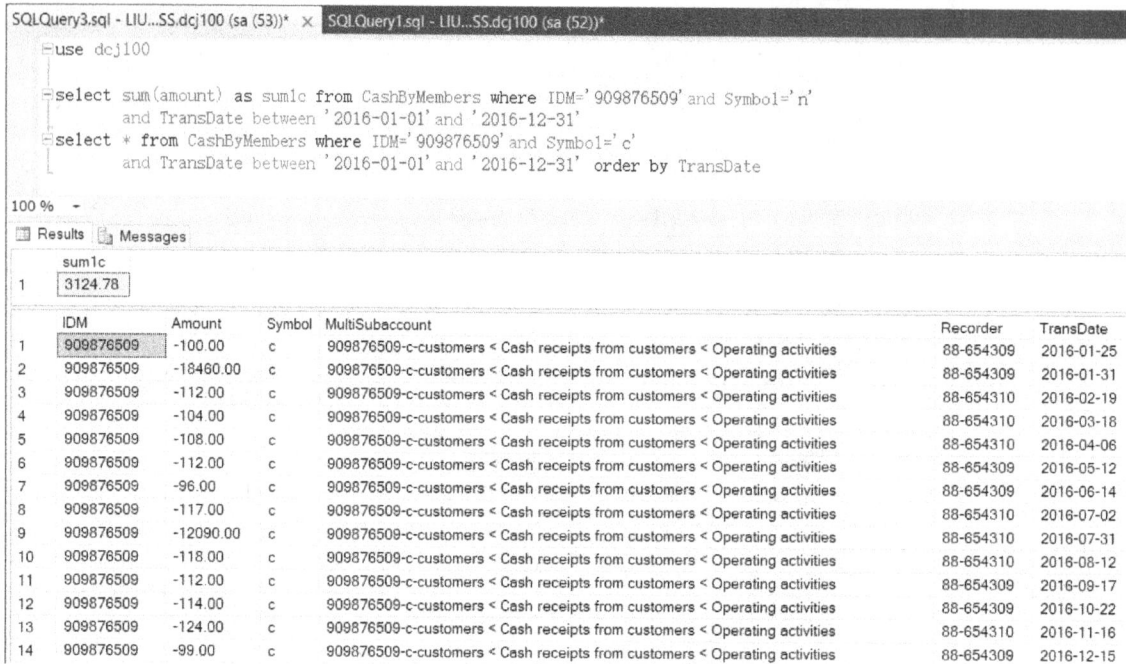

Figure 3.11-13   A9 no Taxable Incomes Information

By using of the same method, I can get other 24 individuals' no taxable incomes balance information. The Figure 3.11-14 on this page and the next pages shows no taxable incomes balance information of the 25 individuals. From the Figure 3.11-14, the total no taxable incomes balance is $48,983.36. This total no taxable incomes balance of 25 individuals can also be gotten by using of SQL Server query, seeing the Figure 3.11-15 which follows the Figure 3.11-14. It is also the $48,983.36 in this fiscal year.

Order	SIN	Name	Employer Name	Consuming Balance
1	909876501	A1	Central Bank	728.93
2	909876502	A2	Central Bank	1,329.80
3	909876503	A3	Government1	2,664.46
4	909876504	A4	Government1	1,938.59
5	909876505	A5	Tax Bureau	2,693.35

6	909876506	A6	Tax Bureau	3,356.03
7	909876507	A7	Business Bank1	1,056.36
8	909876508	A8	Business Bank1	978.18
9	909876509	A9	Business Bank1	3,124.78
10	909876510	A10	Business Bank2	472.79
11	909876511	A11	Business Bank2	974.71
12	909876512	A12	Business Bank2	3,267.31
13	909876513	A13	Company1	6,856.34
14	909876514	A14	Company1	1,176.42
15	909876515	A15	Company1	1,221.97
16	909876516	A16	Company2	4,718.14
17	909876517	A17	Company2	995.81
18	909876518	A18	Company2	1,710.03
19	909876519	A19	Company3	3,012.47
20	909876520	A20	Company3	337.17
21	909876521	A21	Company3	1,003.35
22	909876522	A22	Proprietorship1	1,358.06
23	909876523	A23	Proprietorship1	706.84
24	909876524	A24	Proprietorship2	2,258.03
25	909876525	A25	Proprietorship2	1,043.44
26	**Total**			**48,983.36**

Figure 3.11-14   25 Individuals no Taxable Incomes Information

Figure 3.11-15   Total no Taxable Incomes Information

3.11.3 Cash Flows Statement of Three Organizations

3.11.3.1 Individuals Transactions

Because individual is not responsible to record any transaction, there is a missing part in the closed system. The relationship between the organizations and the individuals can be divided two classes: employers and individuals, and other organizations and individuals. The following Figure 3.11-16 shows the relationship of received or paid cash between the organizations and the individuals.

Order	Class	Symbol	Employers and Individuals	Other Organizations and Individuals
1	Received Cash from Individuals (-$*-1)	i	Cash receipts from issued bonds < Financial activities	Cash receipts from issued bonds < Financial activities
2	Received Cash from Individuals (-$*-1)	c	Cash receipts from customers < Operating activities	Cash receipts from customers < Operating activities
3	Received Cash from Individuals (-$*-1)	d	-	-
4	Paid Cash to Individuals (+$*-1)	t	Cash payments for operating expenses < Operating activities	Cash payments to bond holders < Financial activities
5	Paid Cash to Individuals (+$*-1)	n	Cash payments for operating expenses < Operating activities	Cash payments for operating expenses < Operating activities

Figure 3.11-16   Relationship of Received or Paid Cash

By using of SQL Server query, I can get three balances received or paid cash by the Cash Management Center (Business No. 88-654300), the Company2 (Business No. 88-654307), and the Proprietorship1 (Business No. 88-654309), seeing the following Figure 3.11-17.

Figure 3.11-17   Received or Paid Cash Balances of two Organizations

For getting detail information of the three organizations' balance in the Figure 3.11-17, I must look for the multi-subaccount information in the records of the three organizations themselves. The following Figure 3.11-18 shows the detail information of cash balance received or paid by the Cash Management Center.

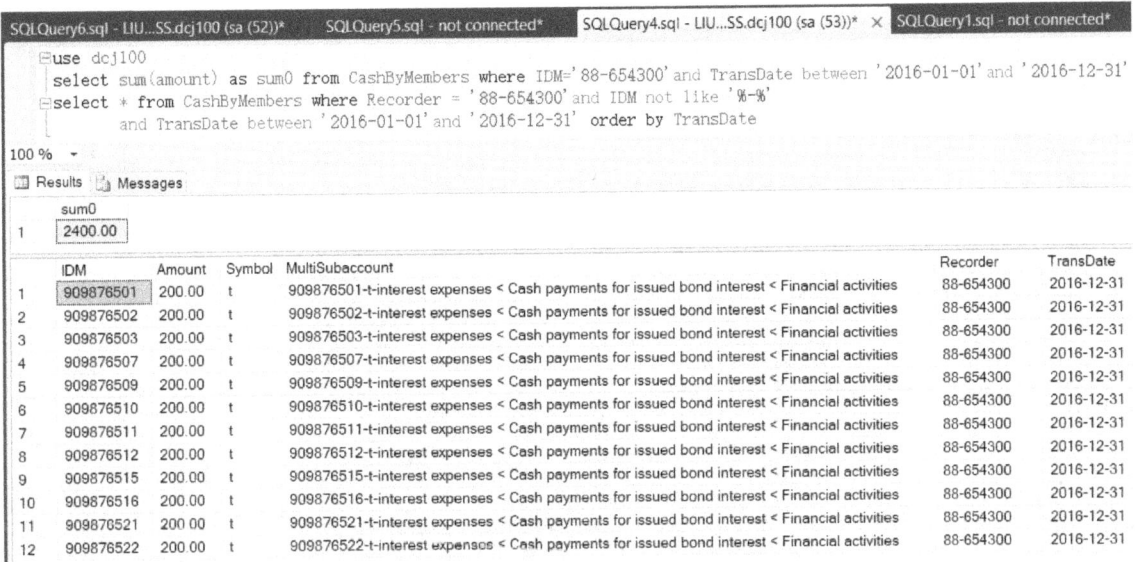

```
SQLQuery6.sql - LIU...SS.dcj100 (sa (52))*    SQLQuery5.sql - not connected*    SQLQuery4.sql - LIU...SS.dcj100 (sa (53))*  ×  SQLQuery1.sql - not connected*
┌use dcj100
│  select sum(amount) as sum0 from CashByMembers where IDM='88-654300' and TransDate between '2016-01-01' and '2016-12-31'
├select * from CashByMembers where Recorder = '88-654300' and IDM not like '%-%'
│          and TransDate between '2016-01-01' and '2016-12-31' order by TransDate
100 %  ▼
```

Results   Messages

	sum0
1	2400.00

	IDM	Amount	Symbol	MultiSubaccount	Recorder	TransDate
1	909876501	200.00	t	909876501-t-interest expenses < Cash payments for issued bond interest < Financial activities	88-654300	2016-12-31
2	909876502	200.00	t	909876502-t-interest expenses < Cash payments for issued bond interest < Financial activities	88-654300	2016-12-31
3	909876503	200.00	t	909876503-t-interest expenses < Cash payments for issued bond interest < Financial activities	88-654300	2016-12-31
4	909876507	200.00	t	909876507-t-interest expenses < Cash payments for issued bond interest < Financial activities	88-654300	2016-12-31
5	909876509	200.00	t	909876509-t-interest expenses < Cash payments for issued bond interest < Financial activities	88-654300	2016-12-31
6	909876510	200.00	t	909876510-t-interest expenses < Cash payments for issued bond interest < Financial activities	88-654300	2016-12-31
7	909876511	200.00	t	909876511-t-interest expenses < Cash payments for issued bond interest < Financial activities	88-654300	2016-12-31
8	909876512	200.00	t	909876512-t-interest expenses < Cash payments for issued bond interest < Financial activities	88-654300	2016-12-31
9	909876515	200.00	t	909876515-t-interest expenses < Cash payments for issued bond interest < Financial activities	88-654300	2016-12-31
10	909876516	200.00	t	909876516-t-interest expenses < Cash payments for issued bond interest < Financial activities	88-654300	2016-12-31
11	909876521	200.00	t	909876521-t-interest expenses < Cash payments for issued bond interest < Financial activities	88-654300	2016-12-31
12	909876522	200.00	t	909876522-t-interest expenses < Cash payments for issued bond interest < Financial activities	88-654300	2016-12-31

Figure 3.11-18   Received or Paid Cash by CMC

From the Figure 3.11-18, the balance $2,400 all belongs to the multi-subaccount name of the "Cash payments for issued bond interest < Financial activities" for the Cash Management Center (Business No. 88-654300). Here, positive balance is that the Cash Management Center paid cash to the individuals.

Based on the above information, I can get the Cash Management Center's multi-subaccount names of the Cash account for these individuals' transactions, seeing the Figure 3.11-19.

Order	Symbol	Multi-subaccount Name	Balance
1	t	Cash payments for issued bond interest < Financial activities	-2,400.00
2	Total	-	-2,400.00

Figure 3.11-19   Company2 Multi-subaccount Names

The Figure 3.11-20 on the next pages shows the detail information of cash balance received or paid by the Company2. Here, the negative balance is that the Company2 received cash from the individuals.

```
use dcj100
select sum(amount) as sum0 from CashByMembers where IDM='88-654307' and TransDate between '2016-01-01' and '2016-12-31'
select * from CashByMembers where Recorder = '88-654307' and IDM not like '%-%'
        and TransDate between '2016-01-01' and '2016-12-31' order by TransDate
```

100 %   ▾

Results   Messages

	sum0
1	106567.98

	IDM	Amount	Symbol	MultiSubaccount	Recorder	TransDate
1	909876525	-360.00	c	909876525-c-customers < Cash receipts from customers < Operating activities	88-654307	2016-01-12
2	909876516	411.32	n	909876516-n-operating expenses < Cash payments for operating expenses < Operating activities	88-654307	2016-01-15
3	909876517	112.57	n	909876517-n-operating expenses < Cash payments for operating expenses < Operating activities	88-654307	2016-01-18
4	909876518	379.78	n	909876518-n-operating expenses < Cash payments for operating expenses < Operating activities	88-654307	2016-01-30
5	909876517	2890.00	t	909876517-t-salary < Cash payments for operating expenses < Operating activities	88-654307	2016-01-31
6	909876516	2610.00	t	909876516-t-CGM < Cash payments for operating expenses < Operating activities	88-654307	2016-01-31
7	909876518	2880.00	t	909876518-t-CGM < Cash payments for operating expenses < Operating activities	88-654307	2016-01-31
8	909876516	557.83	n	909876516-n-operating expenses < Cash payments for operating expenses < Operating activities	88-654307	2016-02-20
9	909876517	2890.00	t	909876517-t-salary < Cash payments for operating expenses < Operating activities	88-654307	2016-02-28
10	909876516	2610.00	t	909876516-t-CGM < Cash payments for operating expenses < Operating activities	88-654307	2016-02-28
11	909876518	2880.00	t	909876518-t-CGM < Cash payments for operating expenses < Operating activities	88-654307	2016-02-28
12	909876518	221.16	n	909876518-n-operating expenses < Cash payments for operating expenses < Operating activities	88-654307	2016-03-01
13	909876516	347.65	n	909876516-n-operating expenses < Cash payments for operating expenses < Operating activities	88-654307	2016-03-23
14	909876517	253.93	n	909876517-n-operating expenses < Cash payments for operating expenses < Operating activities	88-654307	2016-03-26
15	909876517	2890.00	t	909876517-t-salary < Cash payments for operating expenses < Operating activities	88-654307	2016-03-31
16	909876516	2610.00	t	909876516-t-CGM < Cash payments for operating expenses < Operating activities	88-654307	2016-03-31
17	909876518	2880.00	t	909876518-t-CGM < Cash payments for operating expenses < Operating activities	88-654307	2016-03-31
18	909876501	-310.00	c	909876501-c-customers < Cash receipts from customers < Operating activities	88-654307	2016-04-12
19	909876516	369.88	n	909876516-n-operating expenses < Cash payments for operating expenses < Operating activities	88-654307	2016-04-26
20	909876517	2890.00	t	909876517-t-salary < Cash payments for operating expenses < Operating activities	88-654307	2016-04-30
21	909876516	2610.00	t	909876516-t-CGM < Cash payments for operating expenses < Operating activities	88-654307	2016-04-30
22	909876518	2880.00	t	909876518-t-CGM < Cash payments for operating expenses < Operating activities	88-654307	2016-04-30
23	909876518	307.09	n	909876518-n-operating expenses < Cash payments for operating expenses < Operating activities	88-654307	2016-05-02
24	909876513	-290.00	c	909876513-c-customers < Cash receipts from customers < Operating activities	88-654307	2016-05-03
25	909876516	366.59	n	909876516-n-operating expenses < Cash payments for operating expenses < Operating activities	88-654307	2016-05-24
26	909876517	2890.00	t	909876517-t-salary < Cash payments for operating expenses < Operating activities	88-654307	2016-05-31
27	909876516	2610.00	t	909876516-t-CGM < Cash payments for operating expenses < Operating activities	88-654307	2016-05-31
28	909876518	2880.00	t	909876518-t-CGM < Cash payments for operating expenses < Operating activities	88-654307	2016-05-31
29	909876517	255.54	n	909876517-n-operating expenses < Cash payments for operating expenses < Operating activities	88-654307	2016-06-14
30	909876516	362.81	n	909876516-n-operating expenses < Cash payments for operating expenses < Operating activities	88-654307	2016-06-23
31	909876517	2890.00	t	909876517-t-salary < Cash payments for operating expenses < Operating activities	88-654307	2016-06-30
32	909876516	2610.00	t	909876516-t-CGM < Cash payments for operating expenses < Operating activities	88-654307	2016-06-30
33	909876518	2880.00	t	909876518-t-CGM < Cash payments for operating expenses < Operating activities	88-654307	2016-06-30
34	909876505	-290.00	c	909876505-c-customers < Cash receipts from customers < Operating activities	88-654307	2016-07-11
35	909876507	-320.00	c	909876507-c-customers < Cash receipts from customers < Operating activities	88-654307	2016-07-13
36	909876516	307.41	n	909876516-n-operating expenses < Cash payments for operating expenses < Operating activities	88-654307	2016-07-27
37	909876517	2890.00	t	909876517-t-salary < Cash payments for operating expenses < Operating activities	88-654307	2016-07-31
38	909876516	2610.00	t	909876516-t-CGM < Cash payments for operating expenses < Operating activities	88-654307	2016-07-31
39	909876518	2880.00	t	909876518-t-CGM < Cash payments for operating expenses < Operating activities	88-654307	2016-07-31
40	909876511	-360.00	c	909876511-c-customers < Cash receipts from customers < Operating activities	88-654307	2016-08-13
41	909876517	373.77	n	909876517-n-operating expenses < Cash payments for operating expenses < Operating activities	88-654307	2016-08-16
42	909876516	392.33	n	909876516-n-operating expenses < Cash payments for operating expenses < Operating activities	88-654307	2016-08-23
43	909876517	2890.00	t	909876517-t-salary < Cash payments for operating expenses < Operating activities	88-654307	2016-08-31
44	909876516	2610.00	t	909876516-t-CGM < Cash payments for operating expenses < Operating activities	88-654307	2016-08-31
45	909876518	2880.00	t	909876518-t-CGM < Cash payments for operating expenses < Operating activities	88-654307	2016-08-31
46	909876519	-310.00	c	909876519-c-customers < Cash receipts from customers < Operating activities	88-654307	2016-09-03
47	909876522	-320.00	c	909876522-c-customers < Cash receipts from customers < Operating activities	88-654307	2016-09-10
48	909876516	410.89	n	909876516-n-operating expenses < Cash payments for operating expenses < Operating activities	88-654307	2016-09-28
49	909876517	2890.00	t	909876517-t-salary < Cash payments for operating expenses < Operating activities	88-654307	2016-09-30
50	909876516	2610.00	t	909876516-t-CGM < Cash payments for operating expenses < Operating activities	88-654307	2016-09-30
51	909876518	2880.00	t	909876518-t-CGM < Cash payments for operating expenses < Operating activities	88-654307	2016-09-30
52	909876518	377.63	n	909876518-n-operating expenses < Cash payments for operating expenses < Operating activities	88-654307	2016-10-06
53	909876516	396.27	n	909876516-n-operating expenses < Cash payments for operating expenses < Operating activities	88-654307	2016-10-27
54	909876517	2890.00	t	909876517-t-salary < Cash payments for operating expenses < Operating activities	88-654307	2016-10-31
55	909876516	2610.00	t	909876516-t-CGM < Cash payments for operating expenses < Operating activities	88-654307	2016-10-31
56	909876518	2880.00	t	909876518-t-CGM < Cash payments for operating expenses < Operating activities	88-654307	2016-10-31

Figure 3.11-20   Received or Paid Cash by Company2 (Continue)

57	909876516	399.28	n	909876516-n-operating expenses < Cash payments for operating expenses < Operating activities	88-654307	2016-11-19
58	909876518	-360.00	c	909876518-c-customers < Cash receipts from customers < Operating activities	88-654307	2016-11-20
59	909876517	2890.00	t	909876517-t-salary < Cash payments for operating expenses < Operating activities	88-654307	2016-11-30
60	909876516	2610.00	t	909876516-t-CGM < Cash payments for operating expenses < Operating activities	88-654307	2016-11-30
61	909876518	2880.00	t	909876518-t-CGM < Cash payments for operating expenses < Operating activities	88-654307	2016-11-30
62	909876516	395.88	n	909876516-n-operating expenses < Cash payments for operating expenses < Operating activities	88-654307	2016-12-17
63	909876518	424.37	n	909876518-n-operating expenses < Cash payments for operating expenses < Operating activities	88-654307	2016-12-20
64	909876517	2890.00	t	909876517-t-salary < Cash payments for operating expenses < Operating activities	88-654307	2016-12-31
65	909876516	2610.00	t	909876516-t-CGM < Cash payments for operating expenses < Operating activities	88-654307	2016-12-31
66	909876518	2880.00	t	909876518-t-CGM < Cash payments for operating expenses < Operating activities	88-654307	2016-12-31
67	909876504	178.00	t	909876504-t-bond interest < Cash payments to bond holders < Operating activities	88-654307	2016-12-31
68	909876505	94.00	t	909876505-t-bond interest < Cash payments to bond holders < Operating activities	88-654307	2016-12-31
69	909876506	47.00	t	909876506-t-bond interest < Cash payments to bond holders < Operating activities	88-654307	2016-12-31
70	909876510	141.00	t	909876510-t-bond interest < Cash payments to bond holders < Operating activities	88-654307	2016-12-31
71	909876513	235.00	t	909876513-t-bond interest < Cash payments to bond holders < Operating activities	88-654307	2016-12-31
72	909876504	10.00	t	909876504-t-bond interest < Cash payments to bond holders < Operating activities	88-654307	2016-12-31
73	909876515	94.00	t	909876515-t-bond interest < Cash payments to bond holders < Operating activities	88-654307	2016-12-31
74	909876519	141.00	t	909876519-t-bond interest < Cash payments to bond holders < Operating activities	88-654307	2016-12-31
75	909876520	94.00	t	909876520-t-bond interest < Cash payments to bond holders < Operating activities	88-654307	2016-12-31
76	909876523	141.00	t	909876523-t-bond interest < Cash payments to bond holders < Operating activities	88-654307	2016-12-31
77	909876524	235.00	t	909876524-t-bond interest < Cash payments to bond holders < Operating activities	88-654307	2016-12-31
78	909876525	94.00	t	909876525-t-bond interest < Cash payments to bond holders < Operating activities	88-654307	2016-12-31

Query executed successfully.

Figure 3.11-20   Received or Paid Cash by Company2

From the Figure 3.11-20, there are three symbols of the "t", the "n", and "c" for these individuals' transactions. Therefore, I must get the three sums of the transactions with the three symbols. The following Figure 3.11-21 shows the three class of transactions' results for the Company2.

```
use dcj100
select sum(amount) as sum0 from CashByMembers where IDM='88-654307' and TransDate between '2016-01-01' and '2016-12-31'
select sum(amount) as sumt from CashByMembers where Recorder = '88-654307' and IDM not like '%-%'
    and TransDate between '2016-01-01' and '2016-12-31'  and Symbol='t'
select sum(amount) as sumn from CashByMembers where Recorder = '88-654307' and IDM not like '%-%'
    and TransDate between '2016-01-01' and '2016-12-31'  and Symbol='n'
select sum(amount) as sumc from CashByMembers where Recorder = '88-654307' and IDM not like '%-%'
    and TransDate between '2016-01-01' and '2016-12-31'  and Symbol='c'
```

100 %

Results   Messages

	sum0
1	106567.98

	sumt
1	102064.00

	sumn
1	7423.98

	sumc
1	-2920.00

Figure 3.11-21   Company2 Sums of Three Class of Transactions

Based on the Figure 3.11-19 and the Figure 3.11-21, I can get the Company2's multi-subaccount names of the Cash account for these individuals' transactions, seeing the Figure 3.11-22.

Order	Symbol	Multi-subaccount Name	Balance
1	t	Cash payments for operating expenses < Operating activities	-102,064.00
2	n	Cash payments for operating expenses < Operating activities	-7,423.98
3	c	Cash receipts from customers < Operating activities	2,920.00
12	**Total**	-	**-106,567.98**

Figure 3.11-22   Company2 Multi-subaccount Names

The Figure 3.11-23 on the next pages shows the detail information of cash balance received or paid by the Proprietorship1. Here, the negative balance is that the Proprietorship1 received cash from the individuals.

```
use dcj100
select sum(amount) as sum0 from CashByMembers where IDM='88-654309' and TransDate between '2016-01-01' and '2016-12-31'
select * from CashByMembers where Recorder = '88-654309' and IDM not like '%-%'
        and TransDate between '2016-01-01' and '2016-12-31' order by TransDate
```

100 %   ▾

Results   Messages

	sum0
1	-323447.10

	IDM	Amount	Symbol	MultiSubaccount	Recorder	TransDate
1	909876503	-108.00	c	909876503-c-customers < Cash receipts from customers < Operating activities	88-654309	2016-01-06
2	909876505	-98.00	c	909876505-c-customers < Cash receipts from customers < Operating activities	88-654309	2016-01-10
3	909876506	-92.00	c	909876506-c-customers < Cash receipts from customers < Operating activities	88-654309	2016-01-10
4	909876515	-20.00	c	909876515-c-customers < Cash receipts from customers < Operating activities	88-654309	2016-01-13
5	909876516	-192.00	c	909876516-c-customers < Cash receipts from customers < Operating activities	88-654309	2016-01-13
6	909876517	-44.00	c	909876517-c-customers < Cash receipts from customers < Operating activities	88-654309	2016-01-16
7	909876508	-57.00	c	909876508-c-customers < Cash receipts from customers < Operating activities	88-654309	2016-01-16
8	909876520	-51.00	c	909876520-c-customers < Cash receipts from customers < Operating activities	88-654309	2016-01-18
9	909876522	153.87	n	909876522-n-operating expenses < Cash payments for operating expenses < Operating activit...	88-654309	2016-01-18
10	909876525	-57.00	c	909876525-c-customers < Cash receipts from customers < Operating activities	88-654309	2016-01-19
11	909876509	-100.00	c	909876509-c-customers < Cash receipts from customers < Operating activities	88-654309	2016-01-25
12	909876510	-57.00	c	909876510-c-customers < Cash receipts from customers < Operating activities	88-654309	2016-01-27
13	909876518	-144.00	c	909876518-c-customers < Cash receipts from customers < Operating activities	88-654309	2016-01-28
14	909876521	-42.00	c	909876521-c-customers < Cash receipts from customers < Operating activities	88-654309	2016-01-28
15	909876523	-44.00	c	909876523-c-customers < Cash receipts from customers < Operating activities	88-654309	2016-01-28
16	909876523	145.54	n	909876523-n-operating expenses < Cash payments for operating expenses < Operating activit...	88-654309	2016-01-30
17	909876522	2870.00	t	909876522-t-salary < Cash payments for operating expenses < Operating activities	88-654309	2016-01-31
18	909876523	2800.00	t	909876523-t-CGM < Cash payments for operating expenses < Operating activities	88-654309	2016-01-31
19	909876512	-10400.00	c	909876512-c-customers < Cash receipts from customers < Operating activities	88-654309	2016-01-31
20	909876501	-14560.00	c	909876501-c-customers < Cash receipts from customers < Operating activities	88-654309	2016-01-31
21	909876502	-13000.00	c	909876502-c-customers < Cash receipts from customers < Operating activities	88-654309	2016-01-31
22	909876503	-13130.00	c	909876503-c-customers < Cash receipts from customers < Operating activities	88-654309	2016-01-31
23	909876504	-14430.00	c	909876504-c-customers < Cash receipts from customers < Operating activities	88-654309	2016-01-31
24	909876505	-14170.00	c	909876505-c-customers < Cash receipts from customers < Operating activities	88-654309	2016-01-31
25	909876506	-12610.00	c	909876506-c-customers < Cash receipts from customers < Operating activities	88-654309	2016-01-31
26	909876507	-12400.00	c	909876507-c-customers < Cash receipts from customers < Operating activities	88-654309	2016-01-31

	IDM	Amount	Symbol	MultiSubaccount	Recorder	TransDate
27	909876508	-13000.00	c	909876508-c-customers < Cash receipts from customers < Operating activities	88-654309	2016-01-31
28	909876509	-18460.00	c	909876509-c-customers < Cash receipts from customers < Operating activities	88-654309	2016-01-31
29	909876510	-13900.00	c	909876510-c-customers < Cash receipts from customers < Operating activities	88-654309	2016-01-31
30	909876511	-14430.00	c	909876511-c-customers < Cash receipts from customers < Operating activities	88-654309	2016-01-31
31	909876512	-14560.00	c	909876512-c-customers < Cash receipts from customers < Operating activities	88-654309	2016-01-31
32	909876513	-18460.00	c	909876513-c-customers < Cash receipts from customers < Operating activities	88-654309	2016-01-31
33	909876513	-310.00	c	909876513-c-customers < Cash receipts from customers < Operating activities	88-654309	2016-02-17
34	909876519	-124.00	c	909876519-c-customers < Cash receipts from customers < Operating activities	88-654309	2016-02-23
35	909876505	-110.00	c	909876505-c-customers < Cash receipts from customers < Operating activities	88-654309	2016-02-24
36	909876503	-99.00	c	909876503-c-customers < Cash receipts from customers < Operating activities	88-654309	2016-02-25
37	909876518	-102.00	c	909876518-c-customers < Cash receipts from customers < Operating activities	88-654309	2016-02-28
38	909876521	-102.00	c	909876521-c-customers < Cash receipts from customers < Operating activities	88-654309	2016-02-28
39	909876522	2870.00	t	909876522-t-salary < Cash payments for operating expenses < Operating activities	88-654309	2016-02-28
40	909876523	2800.00	t	909876523-t-CGM < Cash payments for operating expenses < Operating activities	88-654309	2016-02-28
41	909876525	-78.00	c	909876525-c-customers < Cash receipts from customers < Operating activities	88-654309	2016-03-07
42	909876506	-123.00	c	909876506-c-customers < Cash receipts from customers < Operating activities	88-654309	2016-03-10
43	909876511	-50.00	c	909876511-c-customers < Cash receipts from customers < Operating activities	88-654309	2016-03-11
44	909876504	-172.00	c	909876504-c-customers < Cash receipts from customers < Operating activities	88-654309	2016-03-19
45	909876522	159.45	n	909876522-n-operating expenses < Cash payments for operating expenses < Operating activit...	88-654309	2016-03-23
46	909876502	-72.00	c	909876502-c-customers < Cash receipts from customers < Operating activities	88-654309	2016-03-26
47	909876508	-51.00	c	909876508-c-customers < Cash receipts from customers < Operating activities	88-654309	2016-03-27
48	909876522	2870.00	t	909876522-t-salary < Cash payments for operating expenses < Operating activities	88-654309	2016-03-31
49	909876523	2800.00	t	909876523-t-CGM < Cash payments for operating expenses < Operating activities	88-654309	2016-03-31
50	909876511	-69.00	c	909876511-c-customers < Cash receipts from customers < Operating activities	88-654309	2016-04-13
51	909876524	-75.00	c	909876524-c-customers < Cash receipts from customers < Operating activities	88-654309	2016-04-22
52	909876516	-156.00	c	909876516-c-customers < Cash receipts from customers < Operating activities	88-654309	2016-04-24

Figure 3.11-23   Received or Paid Cash by Proprietorship1 (Continue)

	IDM	Amount	Symbol	MultiSubaccount	Recorder	TransDate
53	909876519	-78.00	c	909876519-c-customers < Cash receipts from customers < Operating activities	88-654309	2016-04-24
54	909876507	-102.00	c	909876507-c-customers < Cash receipts from customers < Operating activities	88-654309	2016-04-27
55	909876522	2870.00	t	909876522-t-salary < Cash payments for operating expenses < Operating activities	88-654309	2016-04-30
56	909876523	2800.00	t	909876523-t-CGM < Cash payments for operating expenses < Operating activities	88-654309	2016-04-30
57	909876518	-90.00	c	909876518-c-customers < Cash receipts from customers < Operating activities	88-654309	2016-05-01
58	909876521	-50.00	c	909876521-c-customers < Cash receipts from customers < Operating activities	88-654309	2016-05-01
59	909876523	-50.00	c	909876523-c-customers < Cash receipts from customers < Operating activities	88-654309	2016-05-12
60	909876509	-112.00	c	909876509-c-customers < Cash receipts from customers < Operating activities	88-654309	2016-05-12
61	909876506	-112.00	c	909876506-c-customers < Cash receipts from customers < Operating activities	88-654309	2016-05-13
62	909876523	166.23	n	909876523-n-operating expenses < Cash payments for operating expenses < Operating activit...	88-654309	2016-05-14
63	909876503	-105.00	c	909876503-c-customers < Cash receipts from customers < Operating activities	88-654309	2016-05-14
64	909876511	-56.00	c	909876511-c-customers < Cash receipts from customers < Operating activities	88-654309	2016-05-20
65	909876513	-403.00	c	909876513-c-customers < Cash receipts from customers < Operating activities	88-654309	2016-05-22
66	909876516	-155.00	c	909876516-c-customers < Cash receipts from customers < Operating activities	88-654309	2016-05-22
67	909876519	-138.00	c	909876519-c-customers < Cash receipts from customers < Operating activities	88-654309	2016-05-22
68	909876522	176.95	n	909876522-n-operating expenses < Cash payments for operating expenses < Operating activit...	88-654309	2016-05-24
69	909876522	2870.00	t	909876522-t-salary < Cash payments for operating expenses < Operating activities	88-654309	2016-05-31
70	909876523	2800.00	t	909876523-t-CGM < Cash payments for operating expenses < Operating activities	88-654309	2016-05-31
71	909876509	-96.00	c	909876509-c-customers < Cash receipts from customers < Operating activities	88-654309	2016-06-14
72	909876512	-109.00	c	909876512-c-customers < Cash receipts from customers < Operating activities	88-654309	2016-06-18
73	909876513	-310.00	c	909876513-c-customers < Cash receipts from customers < Operating activities	88-654309	2016-06-20
74	909876516	-163.00	c	909876516-c-customers < Cash receipts from customers < Operating activities	88-654309	2016-06-20
75	909876519	-108.00	c	909876519-c-customers < Cash receipts from customers < Operating activities	88-654309	2016-06-21
76	909876522	157.37	n	909876522-n-operating expenses < Cash payments for operating expenses < Operating activit...	88-654309	2016-06-23
77	909876522	2870.00	t	909876522-t-salary < Cash payments for operating expenses < Operating activities	88-654309	2016-06-30
78	909876523	2800.00	t	909876523-t-CGM < Cash payments for operating expenses < Operating activities	88-654309	2016-06-30
79	909876514	-180.00	c	909876514-c-customers < Cash receipts from customers < Operating activities	88-654309	2016-07-05
80	909876504	-112.00	c	909876504-c-customers < Cash receipts from customers < Operating activities	88-654309	2016-07-16
81	909876512	-125.00	c	909876512-c-customers < Cash receipts from customers < Operating activities	88-654309	2016-07-21
82	909876513	-302.00	c	909876513-c-customers < Cash receipts from customers < Operating activities	88-654309	2016-07-22

	IDM	Amount	Symbol	MultiSubaccount	Recorder	TransDate
83	909876505	-105.00	c	909876505-c-customers < Cash receipts from customers < Operating activities	88-654309	2016-07-22
84	909876516	-118.00	c	909876516-c-customers < Cash receipts from customers < Operating activities	88-654309	2016-07-25
85	909876519	-88.00	c	909876519-c-customers < Cash receipts from customers < Operating activities	88-654309	2016-07-25
86	909876523	-64.00	c	909876523-c-customers < Cash receipts from customers < Operating activities	88-654309	2016-07-25
87	909876523	187.55	n	909876523-n-operating expenses < Cash payments for operating expenses < Operating activit...	88-654309	2016-07-27
88	909876522	2870.00	t	909876522-t-salary < Cash payments for operating expenses < Operating activities	88-654309	2016-07-31
89	909876523	2800.00	t	909876523-t-CGM < Cash payments for operating expenses < Operating activities	88-654309	2016-07-31
90	909876501	-10270.00	c	909876501-c-customers < Cash receipts from customers < Operating activities	88-654309	2016-07-31
91	909876514	-18460.00	c	909876514-c-customers < Cash receipts from customers < Operating activities	88-654309	2016-07-31
92	909876515	-18200.00	c	909876515-c-customers < Cash receipts from customers < Operating activities	88-654309	2016-07-31
93	909876516	-18720.00	c	909876516-c-customers < Cash receipts from customers < Operating activities	88-654309	2016-07-31
94	909876517	-17940.00	c	909876517-c-customers < Cash receipts from customers < Operating activities	88-654309	2016-07-31
95	909876518	-18460.00	c	909876518-c-customers < Cash receipts from customers < Operating activities	88-654309	2016-07-31
96	909876519	-18590.00	c	909876519-c-customers < Cash receipts from customers < Operating activities	88-654309	2016-07-31
97	909876520	-10400.00	c	909876520-c-customers < Cash receipts from customers < Operating activities	88-654309	2016-07-31
98	909876521	-10660.00	c	909876521-c-customers < Cash receipts from customers < Operating activities	88-654309	2016-07-31
99	909876522	-10530.00	c	909876522-c-customers < Cash receipts from customers < Operating activities	88-654309	2016-07-31
100	909876523	-11050.00	c	909876523-c-customers < Cash receipts from customers < Operating activities	88-654309	2016-07-31
101	909876524	-11570.00	c	909876524-c-customers < Cash receipts from customers < Operating activities	88-654309	2016-07-31
102	909876525	-12090.00	c	909876525-c-customers < Cash receipts from customers < Operating activities	88-654309	2016-07-31
103	909876503	-150.00	c	909876503-c-customers < Cash receipts from customers < Operating activities	88-654309	2016-08-10
104	909876517	-120.00	c	909876517-c-customers < Cash receipts from customers < Operating activities	88-654309	2016-08-14
105	909876510	-63.00	c	909876510-c-customers < Cash receipts from customers < Operating activities	88-654309	2016-08-17
106	909876516	-162.00	c	909876516-c-customers < Cash receipts from customers < Operating activities	88-654309	2016-08-20
107	909876519	-78.00	c	909876519-c-customers < Cash receipts from customers < Operating activities	88-654309	2016-08-21
108	909876513	-312.00	c	909876513-c-customers < Cash receipts from customers < Operating activities	88-654309	2016-08-22
109	909876512	-112.00	c	909876512-c-customers < Cash receipts from customers < Operating activities	88-654309	2016-08-22
110	909876522	166.18	n	909876522-n-operating expenses < Cash payments for operating expenses < Operating activit...	88-654309	2016-08-23
111	909876522	2870.00	t	909876522-t-salary < Cash payments for operating expenses < Operating activities	88-654309	2016-08-31
112	909876523	2800.00	t	909876523-t-CGM < Cash payments for operating expenses < Operating activities	88-654309	2016-08-31

Figure 3.11-23   Received or Paid Cash by Proprietorship1 (Continue)

	IDM	Amount	Symbol	MultiSubaccount	Recorder	TransDate
113	909876512	-104.00	c	909876512-c-customers < Cash receipts from customers < Operating activities	88-654309	2016-09-17
114	909876509	-112.00	c	909876509-c-customers < Cash receipts from customers < Operating activities	88-654309	2016-09-17
115	909876524	-99.00	c	909876524-c-customers < Cash receipts from customers < Operating activities	88-654309	2016-09-19
116	909876513	-451.00	c	909876513-c-customers < Cash receipts from customers < Operating activities	88-654309	2016-09-26
117	909876516	-183.00	c	909876516-c-customers < Cash receipts from customers < Operating activities	88-654309	2016-09-26
118	909876519	-87.00	c	909876519-c-customers < Cash receipts from customers < Operating activities	88-654309	2016-09-26
119	909876522	2870.00	t	909876522-t-salary < Cash payments for operating expenses < Operating activities	88-654309	2016-09-30
120	909876523	2800.00	t	909876523-t-CGM < Cash payments for operating expenses < Operating activities	88-654309	2016-09-30
121	909876522	168.73	n	909876522-n-operating expenses < Cash payments for operating expenses < Operating activit...	88-654309	2016-10-08
122	909876512	-108.00	c	909876512-c-customers < Cash receipts from customers < Operating activities	88-654309	2016-10-16
123	909876503	-121.00	c	909876503-c-customers < Cash receipts from customers < Operating activities	88-654309	2016-10-21
124	909876505	-116.00	c	909876505-c-customers < Cash receipts from customers < Operating activities	88-654309	2016-10-22
125	909876509	-114.00	c	909876509-c-customers < Cash receipts from customers < Operating activities	88-654309	2016-10-22
126	909876513	-383.00	c	909876513-c-customers < Cash receipts from customers < Operating activities	88-654309	2016-10-24
127	909876516	-174.00	c	909876516-c-customers < Cash receipts from customers < Operating activities	88-654309	2016-10-25
128	909876519	-90.00	c	909876519-c-customers < Cash receipts from customers < Operating activities	88-654309	2016-10-25
129	909876522	2870.00	t	909876522-t-salary < Cash payments for operating expenses < Operating activities	88-654309	2016-10-31
130	909876523	2800.00	t	909876523-t-CGM < Cash payments for operating expenses < Operating activities	88-654309	2016-10-31
131	909876506	-93.00	c	909876506-c-customers < Cash receipts from customers < Operating activities	88-654309	2016-11-15
132	909876513	-361.00	c	909876513-c-customers < Cash receipts from customers < Operating activities	88-654309	2016-11-15
133	909876516	-184.00	c	909876516-c-customers < Cash receipts from customers < Operating activities	88-654309	2016-11-17
134	909876519	-87.00	c	909876519-c-customers < Cash receipts from customers < Operating activities	88-654309	2016-11-17
135	909876522	177.16	n	909876522-n-operating expenses < Cash payments for operating expenses < Operating activit...	88-654309	2016-11-19
136	909876512	-100.00	c	909876512-c-customers < Cash receipts from customers < Operating activities	88-654309	2016-11-19
137	909876522	2870.00	t	909876522-t-salary < Cash payments for operating expenses < Operating activities	88-654309	2016-11-30
138	909876523	2800.00	t	909876523-t-CGM < Cash payments for operating expenses < Operating activities	88-654309	2016-11-30
139	909876513	-413.00	c	909876513-c-customers < Cash receipts from customers < Operating activities	88-654309	2016-12-13
140	909876519	-104.00	c	909876519-c-customers < Cash receipts from customers < Operating activities	88-654309	2016-12-15
141	909876523	-74.00	c	909876523-c-customers < Cash receipts from customers < Operating activities	88-654309	2016-12-15
142	909876516	-174.00	c	909876516-c-customers < Cash receipts from customers < Operating activities	88-654309	2016-12-15
143	909876509	-99.00	c	909876509-c-customers < Cash receipts from customers < Operating activities	88-654309	2016-12-15
144	909876523	207.52	n	909876523-n-operating expenses < Cash payments for operating expenses < Operating activit...	88-654309	2016-12-17
145	909876522	198.35	n	909876522-n-operating expenses < Cash payments for operating expenses < Operating activit...	88-654309	2016-12-19
146	909876503	-129.00	c	909876503-c-customers < Cash receipts from customers < Operating activities	88-654309	2016-12-20
147	909876505	-192.00	c	909876505-c-customers < Cash receipts from customers < Operating activities	88-654309	2016-12-26
148	909876506	-198.00	c	909876506-c-customers < Cash receipts from customers < Operating activities	88-654309	2016-12-26
149	909876512	-125.00	c	909876512-c-customers < Cash receipts from customers < Operating activities	88-654309	2016-12-27
150	909876522	2870.00	t	909876522-t-salary < Cash payments for operating expenses < Operating activities	88-654309	2016-12-31
151	909876523	2800.00	t	909876523-t-CGM < Cash payments for operating expenses < Operating activities	88-654309	2016-12-31
152	909876504	150.00	t	909876504-t-bond interest < Cash payments to bond holders < Operating activities	88-654309	2016-12-31
153	909876505	200.00	t	909876505-t-bond interest < Cash payments to bond holders < Operating activities	88-654309	2016-12-31
154	909876506	250.00	t	909876506-t-bond interest < Cash payments to bond holders < Operating activities	88-654309	2016-12-31
155	909876508	100.00	t	909876508-t-bond interest < Cash payments to bond holders < Operating activities	88-654309	2016-12-31
156	909876510	150.00	t	909876510-t-bond interest < Cash payments to bond holders < Operating activities	88-654309	2016-12-31
157	909876513	250.00	t	909876513-t-bond interest < Cash payments to bond holders < Operating activities	88-654309	2016-12-31
158	909876515	200.00	t	909876515-t-bond interest < Cash payments to bond holders < Operating activities	88-654309	2016-12-31
159	909876516	100.00	t	909876516-t-bond interest < Cash payments to bond holders < Operating activities	88-654309	2016-12-31
160	909876517	250.00	t	909876517-t-bond interest < Cash payments to bond holders < Operating activities	88-654309	2016-12-31
161	909876518	150.00	t	909876518-t-bond interest < Cash payments to bond holders < Operating activities	88-654309	2016-12-31
162	909876519	250.00	t	909876519-t-bond interest < Cash payments to bond holders < Operating activities	88-654309	2016-12-31
163	909876520	150.00	t	909876520-t-bond interest < Cash payments to bond holders < Operating activities	88-654309	2016-12-31
164	909876521	200.00	t	909876521-t-bond interest < Cash payments to bond holders < Operating activities	88-654309	2016-12-31
165	909876522	100.00	t	909876522-t-bond interest < Cash payments to bond holders < Operating activities	88-654309	2016-12-31

Query executed successfully.

Figure 3.11-23   Received or Paid Cash by Proprietorship1

From the Figure 3.11-23, there are three symbols of the "t", the "n", and "c" for these individuals' transactions. Therefore, I must get the three sums of the transactions with the three symbols. The following Figure 3.11-24 shows the three class of transactions' results for the Proprietorship1.

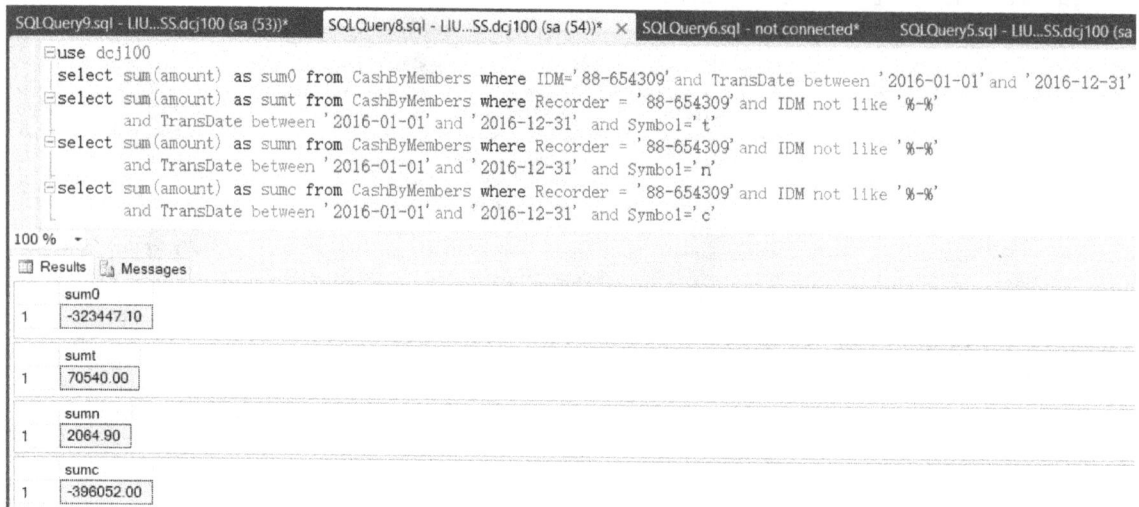

```
SQLQuery9.sql - LIU...SS.dcj100 (sa (53))*     SQLQuery8.sql - LIU...SS.dcj100 (sa (54))*  ×  SQLQuery6.sql - not connected*     SQLQuery5.sql - LIU...SS.dcj100 (sa
use dcj100
select sum(amount) as sum0 from CashByMembers where IDM='88-654309' and TransDate between '2016-01-01' and '2016-12-31'
select sum(amount) as sumt from CashByMembers where Recorder = '88-654309' and IDM not like '%-%'
    and TransDate between '2016-01-01' and '2016-12-31' and Symbol='t'
select sum(amount) as sumn from CashByMembers where Recorder = '88-654309' and IDM not like '%-%'
    and TransDate between '2016-01-01' and '2016-12-31' and Symbol='n'
select sum(amount) as sumc from CashByMembers where Recorder = '88-654309' and IDM not like '%-%'
    and TransDate between '2016-01-01' and '2016-12-31' and Symbol='c'
```

100 % ▾

Results | Messages

	sum0
1	-323447.10

	sumt
1	70540.00

	sumn
1	2064.90

	sumc
1	-396052.00

Figure 3.11-24   Proprietorship1 Sums of Three Class of Transactions

Based on the Figure 3.11-23 and the Figure 3.11-24, I can get the multi-subaccount names of the Cash account for these individuals' transactions, seeing the Figure 3.11-25.

Order	Symbol	Multi-subaccount Name	Balance
1	t	Cash payments for operating expenses < Operating activities	-70,540.00
2	n	Cash payments for operating expenses < Operating activities	-2,064.90
3	c	Cash receipts from customers < Operating activities	396,052.00
12	Total	-	323,447.10

Figure 3.11-25   Proprietorship1 Multi-subaccount Names

3.11.3.2 Beginning Cash Balance of Three Organizations

By using of SQL Server query, I can get the beginning cash balance of three Organizations on January 1, 2016, seeing the Figure 3.11-26 on the next page.

```
SQLQuery4.sql - LIU...SS.dcj100 (sa (54))*    SQLQuery10.sql - LI...ESS.dcj100 (sa (55))*  ×   SQLQuery9.sql - LIU...SS.dcj100 (sa (53))*    SQLQuery8.sql - LIU...SS.dcj100
  use dcj100
  select sum(amount) as sum0 from CashByMembers where Recorder ='88-654300' and TransDate between' 2015-01-01' and' 2015-12-31'
  select sum(amount) as sum7 from CashByMembers where Recorder ='88-654307' and TransDate between' 2015-01-01' and' 2015-12-31'
  select sum(amount) as sum9 from CashByMembers where Recorder ='88-654309' and TransDate between' 2015-01-01' and' 2015-12-31'
100 %  ▾
  Results    Messages
      sum0
1   -1058058.20

      sum7
1   -47393.19

      sum9
1   -18783.78
```

Figure 3.11-26   Beginning Cash Balance of Three Organizations

3.11.3.3 Three Organizations Transactions

The transactions, which occurred between the organizations, have been recorded by the two sides of the transactions. Therefore, I can get the records of one organization's transactions by using of other organizations' transactions records.

The following Figure 3.11-27 shows the relationship of received or paid cash between one organization and the other organizations.

Order	Class	Symbol	One Organization Multi-subaccount Names	Other Organizations Multi-subaccount Names
1	Paid Cash to Other Organizations (-$)	i	Cash payments for investments < Investing activities	Cash receipts from issued bonds < Financial activities
2	Paid Cash to Other Organizations (-$)	c	Cash payments for machinery < Operating activities	Cash receipts from customers < Operating activities
3	Paid Cash to Other Organizations (-$)	c	Cash payments to suppliers < Operating activities	Cash receipts from customers < Operating activities
4	Paid Cash to Other Organizations (-$)	c	Cash payments to Banks < Operating activities	Cash receipts from customers < Operating activities
5	Paid Cash to Other Organizations (-$)	c	Cash payments for investment < Operating activities	Cash receipts from investments < Investing activities
6	Paid Cash to Other Organizations (-$)	c	Cash payments to governments < Operating activities	Cash receipts from national budgets < Financial activities
7	Received Cash from Other Organizations (+$)	t	Cash receipts from investments < Investing activities	Cash payments to bond holders < Financial activities
8	Received Cash from Other Organizations (+$)	t	Cash receipts from customers < Operating activities	Cash payments to suppliers < Operating activities
9	Received Cash from Other Organizations (+$)	n	Cash receipts from banks < Financial activities	Cash payments to note lenders < Operating activities

Figure 3.11-27   Relationship of Received or Paid Cash between Organizations

From the Figure 3.11-26, the one organization with the symbol "c" has four possible multi-subaccount names. Based on the related organization' product or the related organization' class, I can decide what the multi-subaccount name is.

3.11.3.3.1 Cash Management Center Transactions

The following Figure 3.11-28 shows the detail information of the other organizations' transactions, which are related to the Cash Management Center, with the symbol "t". Here, the positive balance is that the Cash Management Center received cash from the other organizations.

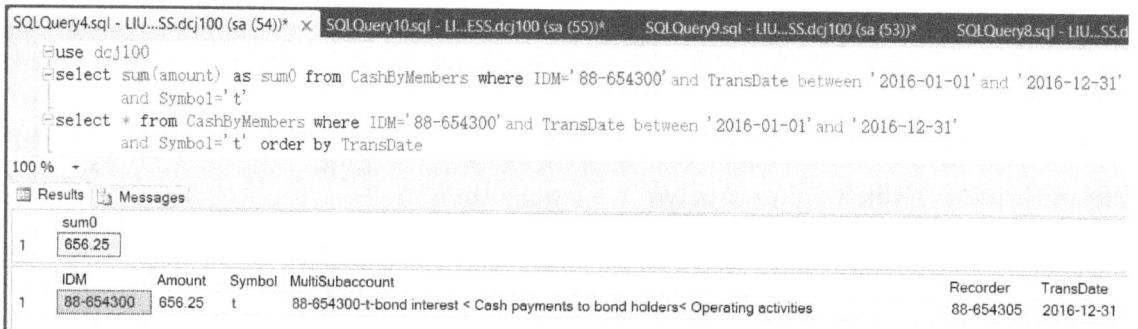

	IDM	Amount	Symbol	MultiSubaccount		Recorder	TransDate
1	88-654300	656.25	t	88-654300-t-bond interest < Cash payments to bond holders< Operating activities		88-654305	2016-12-31

Figure 3.11-28   CMC Sum and Detail of Transactions with Symbol t

The following Figure 3.11-29 shows the detail information of the other organizations' transactions, which are related to the Cash Management Center, with the symbol "n". There is not any transaction with the symbol "n" in this fiscal year.

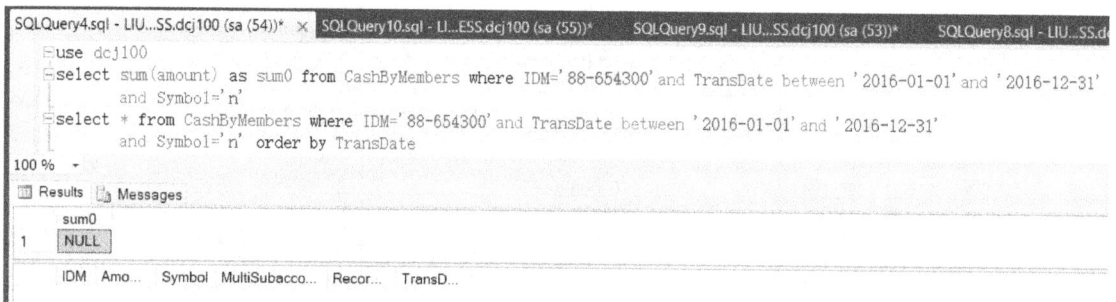

Figure 3.11-29   CMC Sum and Detail of Transactions with Symbol n

The Figure 3.11-30 on the next page shows the detail information of the other organizations' transactions, which are related to the Cash Management Center, with the symbol "i". Here, the negative balance is that the Cash Management Center paid cash to the other organizations.

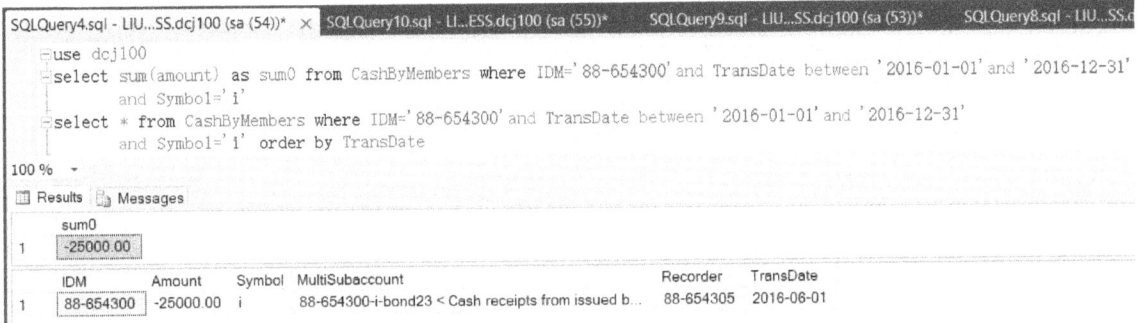

Figure 3.11-30   CMC Sum and Detail of Transactions with Symbol i

The following Figure 3.11-31 shows the detail information of the other organizations' transactions, which are related to the Cash Management Center, with the symbol "c". Here, the negative balance is that the Cash Management Center paid cash to the other organizations.

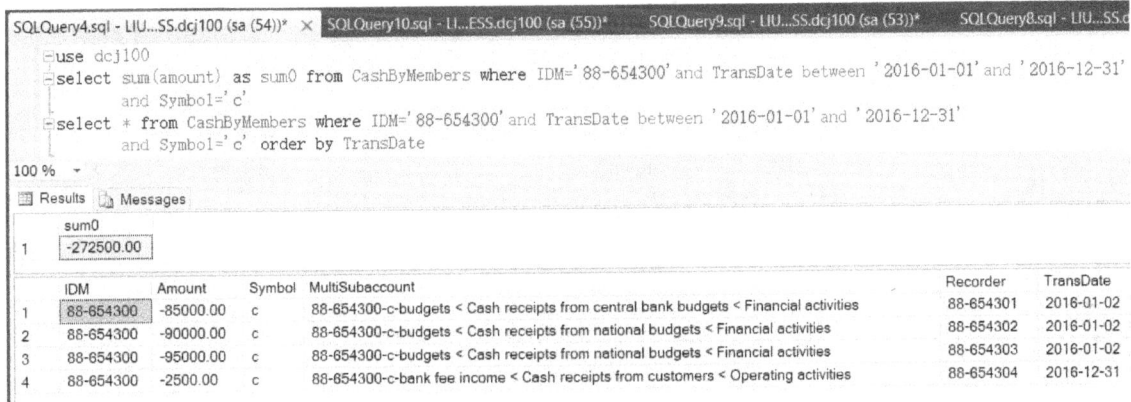

Figure 3.11-31   CMC Sum and Detail of Transactions with Symbol c

Based on the Figure 3.11-27 to the Figure 3.11-31, I can get the Cash Management Center's multi-subaccount names of the Cash account for the other organizations' transactions, seeing the Figure 3.11-32 on next page.

Order	Symbol	Multi-subaccount Name	Balance
1	t	Cash receipts from investments < Investing activities	656.25
2	i	Cash payments for investments < Investing activities	-25,000.00
3	c	Cash payments to Banks < Operating activities	-2,500.00
4	c	Cash payments to governments < Operating activities	-270,000.00
5	Total	-	**-296,843.75**

Figure 3.11-32   CMC Multi-subaccount Names

3.11.3.3.2 Company2 Transactions

The following Figure 3.11-33 shows the detail information of the other organizations' transactions, which are related to the Company2, with the symbol "t". Here, the positive balance is that the Company2 received cash from the other organizations.

```
SQLQuery4.sql - LIU...SS.dcj100 (sa (54))*   ×   SQLQuery10.sql - LI...ESS.dcj100 (sa (55))*      SQLQuery9.sql - LIU...SS.dcj100 (sa (53))*      SQLQuery8.sql - LIU...SS.dc
use dcj100
select sum(amount) as sum0 from CashByMembers where IDM='88-654307' and TransDate between '2016-01-01' and '2016-12-31'
    and Symbol='t'
select * from CashByMembers where IDM='88-654307' and TransDate between '2016-01-01' and '2016-12-31'
    and Symbol='t' order by TransDate
100 %  -
```

Results   Messages

	sum0
1	253490.00

	IDM	Amount	Symbol	MultiSubaccount	Recorder	TransDate
1	88-654307	11000.00	t	88-654307-t-suppliers < Cash payments to suppliers < Operating activities	88-654306	2016-01-14
2	88-654307	600.00	t	88-654307-t-suppliers < Cash payments to suppliers < Operating activities	88-654308	2016-01-24
3	88-654307	250.00	t	88-654307-t-suppliers < Cash payments to suppliers < Operating activities	88-654309	2016-01-27
4	88-654307	7000.00	t	88-654307-t-suppliers < Cash payments to suppliers < Operating activities	88-654308	2016-01-28
5	88-654307	400.00	t	88-654307-t-machinery < Cash payments for machinery < Operating activities	88-654303	2016-02-11
6	88-654307	500.00	t	88-654307-t-machinery < Cash payments for machinery < Operating activities	88-654302	2016-02-21
7	88-654307	5200.00	t	88-654307-t-supplies < Cash payments for operating expenses < Operating activities	88-654304	2016-02-26
8	88-654307	2400.00	t	88-654307-t-suppliers < Cash payments for operating expenses < Operating activities	88-654306	2016-03-05
9	88-654307	5000.00	t	88-654307-t-supplies < Cash payments for operating expenses < Operating activities	88-654309	2016-04-29
10	88-654307	15000.00	t	88-654307-t-suppliers < Cash payments to suppliers < Operating activities	88-654306	2016-05-01
11	88-654307	64000.00	t	88-654307-t-suppliers < Cash payments to suppliers < Operating activities	88-654306	2016-06-12
12	88-654307	12000.00	t	88-654307-t-suppliers < Cash payments to suppliers < Operating activities	88-654308	2016-08-03
13	88-654307	4000.00	t	88-654307-t-suppliers < Cash payments to suppliers < Operating activities	88-654308	2016-09-12
14	88-654307	10000.00	t	88-654307-t-suppliers < Cash payments to suppliers < Operating activities	88-654306	2016-09-14
15	88-654307	1800.00	t	88-654307-t-suppliers < Cash payments to suppliers < Operating activities	88-654309	2016-09-26
16	88-654307	4500.00	t	88-654307-t- part activities < Cash payments for operating activities < Operating activities	88-654303	2016-10-03
17	88-654307	14420.00	t	88-654307-t-suppliers < Cash payments to suppliers < Operating activities	88-654306	2016-11-29
18	88-654307	39700.00	t	88-654307-t-suppliers < Cash payments to suppliers < Operating activities	88-654306	2016-12-29
19	88-654307	55000.00	t	88-654307-t-suppliers < Cash payments to suppliers < Operating activities	88-654306	2016-12-31
20	88-654307	336.00	t	88-654307-t-bond interest < Cash payments to bond holders< Operating activities	88-654304	2016-12-31
21	88-654307	264.00	t	88-654307-t-bond interest< Cash payments to bond holders< Operating activities	88-654305	2016-12-31
22	88-654307	120.00	t	88-654307-t-deposit interest expenses < Cash payments for operating expenses < Operating acti...	88-654305	2016-12-31

Figure 3.11-33   Company2 Sum and Detail of Transactions with Symbol t

From the Figure 3.11-33, the cash received by the Company2 can be divided three class of the "Cash receipts from customers < Operating activities", the "Cash receipts from banks < Financial activities", and the "Cash receipts from investments < Investing activities". The balance with the "Cash receipts from banks < Financial activities" is $120, so I must get the sum of the transactions with the multi-subaccount name "Cash receipts from investments < Investing activities". The following Figure 3.11-34 shows the result $600. The rest is $252,770 (= $253,490 - $600 -$120).

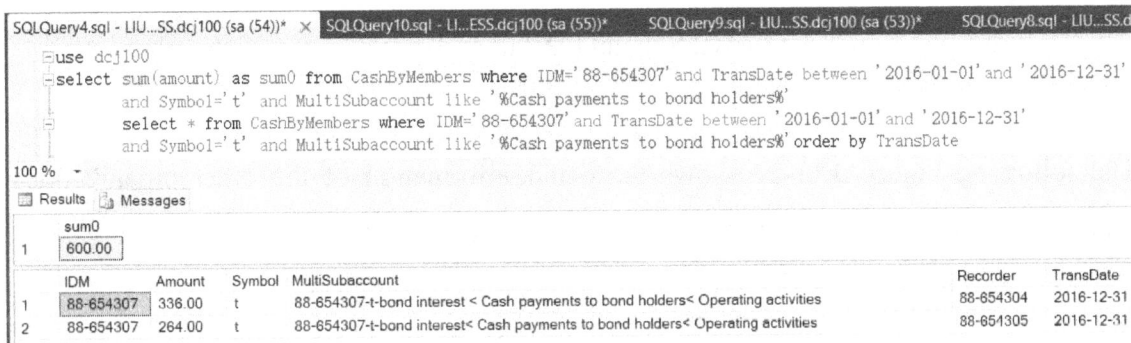

Figure 3.11-34   Company2 Sum of Investment Transactions

The following Figure 3.11-35 shows the detail information of the other organizations' transactions, which are related to the Company2, with the symbol "n". There is not any transaction with the symbol "n" in this fiscal year.

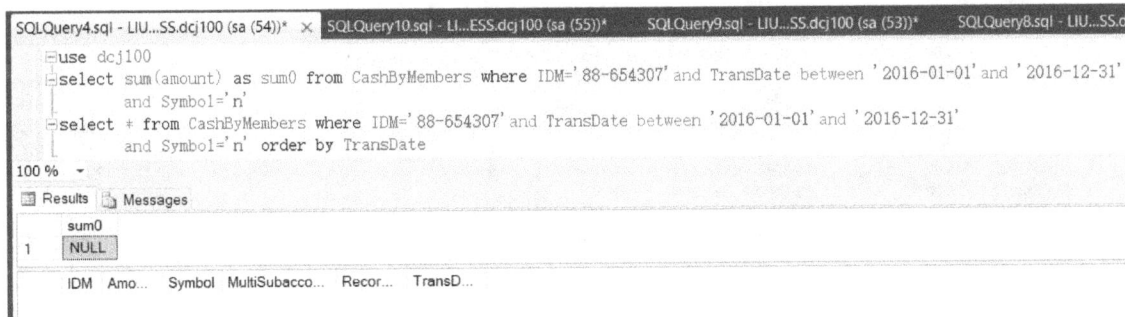

Figure 3.11-35   Company2 Sum and Detail of Transactions with Symbol n

The Figure 3.11-36 on the next page shows the detail information of the other organizations' transactions, which are related to the Company2, with the symbol "i". There is not any transaction with the symbol "n" in this fiscal year.

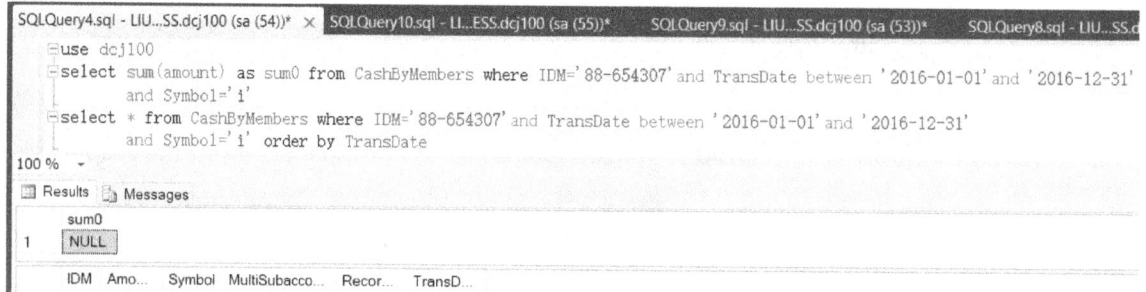

Figure 3.11-36   Company2 Sum and Detail of Transactions with Symbol i

The following Figure 3.11-37 shows the detail information of the other organizations' transactions, which are related to the Company2, with the symbol "c". Here, the negative balance is that the Company2 paid cash to the other organizations.

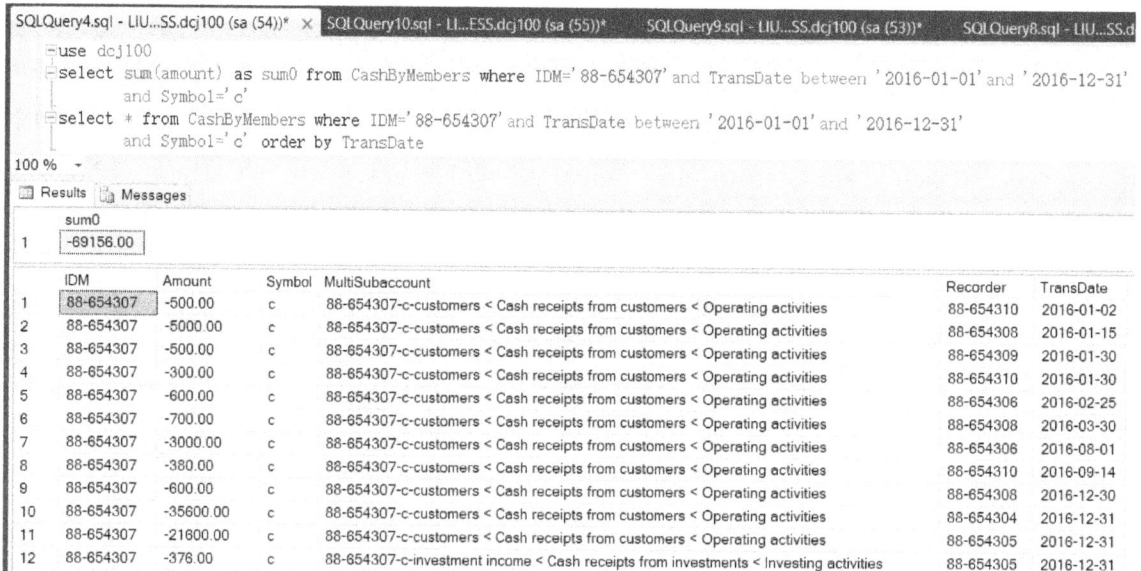

Figure 3.11-37   Company2 Sum and Detail of Transactions with Symbol c

From the Figure 3.11-37, there is a transaction whose multi-subaccount name should be the "Cash payments for investments < Investing activities" and there is other two transactions whose multi-subaccount name should be the "Cash payments to Banks < Operating activities". Their balances are -$376 and -$57,200 (= -$35,600 -$21,600) respectively.

Based on the Figure 3.11-33 to the Figure 3.11-37, I can get the Company2's multi-subaccount names of the Cash account for the other organizations' transactions, seeing the following Figure 3.11-38.

Order	Symbol	Multi-subaccount Name	Balance
1	t	Cash receipts from banks < Financial activities	120.00
2	t	Cash receipts from investments < Investing activities	600.00
3	t	Cash receipts from customers < Operating activities	252,770.00
4	c	Cash payments to Banks < Operating activities	-57,200.00
5	c	Cash payments to suppliers < Operating activities	-11,580.00
6	c	Cash payments for investment < Operating activities	-376.00
7	Total	-	184,334.00

Figure 3.11-38   Company2 Multi-subaccount Names

3.11.3.3.3 Proprietorship1 Transactions

The following Figure 3.11-39 on the next page shows the detail information of the other organizations' transactions, which are related to the Proprietorship1, with the symbol "t". Here, the positive balance is that the Proprietorship1 received cash from the other organizations.

From the Figure 3.11-39 on the next page, the cash received by the Proprietorship1 can be divided three class of the "Cash receipts from customers < Operating activities", the "Cash receipts from banks < Financial activities", and the "Cash receipts from investments < Investing activities". The balance with the "Cash receipts from banks < Financial activities" is $120, so I must get the sum of the transactions with the multi-subaccount name "Cash receipts from investments < Investing activities" by using of SQL Server query. The Figure 3.11-40 on the next page shows the result $768. Therefore, the rest is $69,390 (= $70,278 - $768 -$120).

Figure 3.11-39   Proprietorship1 Sum and Detail of Transactions with Symbol t

Figure 3.11-40   Proprietorship1 Sum of Investment Transactions

The Figure 3.11-41 on the next page shows the detail information of the other organizations' transactions, which are related to the Proprietorship1, with the symbol "n". There is not any transaction with the symbol "n" in this fiscal year.

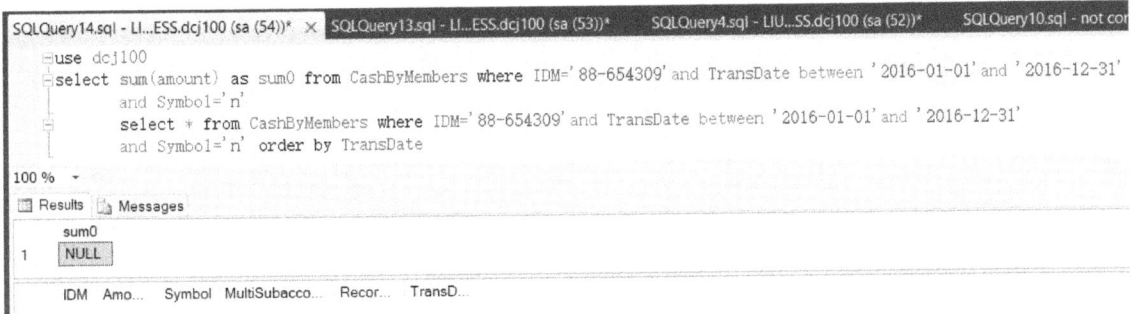

Figure 3.11-41 Proprietorship1 Sum and Detail of Transactions with Symbol n

The following Figure 3.11-42 shows the detail information of the other organizations' transactions, which are related to the Proprietorship1, with the symbol "i". There is not any transaction with the symbol "n" in this fiscal year.

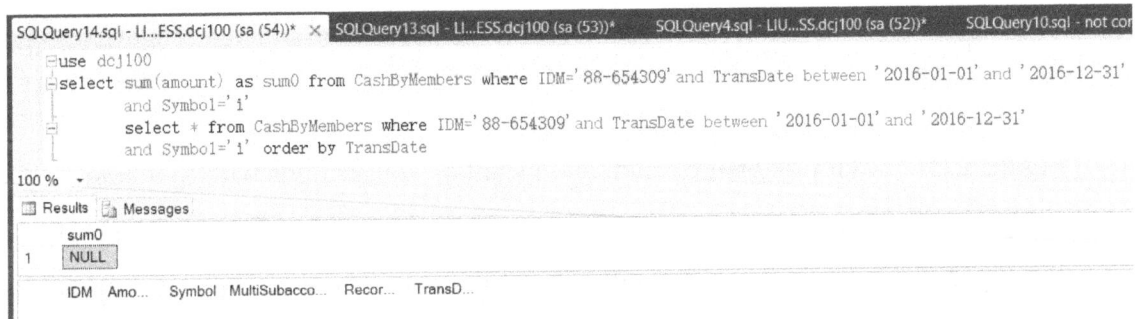

Figure 3.11-42 Proprietorship1 Sum and Detail of Transactions with Symbol i

The Figure 3.11-43 on the next page shows the detail information of the other organizations' transactions, which are related to the Proprietorship1, with the symbol "c". Here, the negative balance is that the Proprietorship1 paid cash to the other organizations.

```
use dcj100
select sum(amount) as sum0 from CashByMembers where IDM='88-654309' and TransDate between '2016-01-01' and '2016-12-31'
       and Symbol='c'
       select * from CashByMembers where IDM='88-654309' and TransDate between '2016-01-01' and '2016-12-31'
       and Symbol='c' order by TransDate
```

100 %

Results Messages

	sum0
1	-234830.00

	IDM	Amount	Symbol	MultiSubaccount	Recorder	TransDate
1	88-654309	-10000.00	c	88-654309-c-customers < Cash receipts from customers < Operating activities	88-654308	2016-01-02
2	88-654309	-450.00	c	88-654309-c-customers < Cash receipts from customers < Operating activities	88-654310	2016-01-02
3	88-654309	-150.00	c	88-654309-c-customers < Cash receipts from customers < Operating activities	88-654308	2016-01-13
4	88-654309	-250.00	c	88-654309-c-customers < Cash receipts from customers < Operating activities	88-654307	2016-01-27
5	88-654309	-28000.00	c	88-654309-c-customers < Cash receipts from customers < Operating activities	88-654306	2016-02-01
6	88-654309	-300.00	c	88-654309-c-customers < Cash receipts from customers < Operating activities	88-654310	2016-02-21
7	88-654309	-1000.00	c	88-654309-c-customers < Cash receipts from customers < Operating activities	88-654306	2016-03-06
8	88-654309	-5000.00	c	88-654309-c-customers < Cash receipts from customers < Operating activities	88-654307	2016-04-29
9	88-654309	-5000.00	c	88-654309-c-customers < Cash receipts from customers < Operating activities	88-654310	2016-05-01
10	88-654309	-800.00	c	88-654309-c-customers < Cash receipts from customers < Operating activities	88-654310	2016-05-01
11	88-654309	-55000.00	c	88-654309-c-customers < Cash receipts from customers < Operating activities	88-654308	2016-07-04
12	88-654309	-65000.00	c	88-654309-c-customers < Cash receipts from customers < Operating activities	88-654308	2016-08-17
13	88-654309	-1800.00	c	88-654309-c-customers < Cash receipts from customers < Operating activities	88-654307	2016-09-26
14	88-654309	-5500.00	c	88-654309-c-customers < Cash receipts from customers < Operating activities	88-654306	2016-10-01
15	88-654309	-31000.00	c	88-654309-c-customers < Cash receipts from customers < Operating activities	88-654308	2016-11-12
16	88-654309	-10000.00	c	88-654309-c-customers < Cash receipts from customers < Operating activities	88-654306	2016-12-29
17	88-654309	-4300.00	c	88-654309-c-customers < Cash receipts from customers < Operating activities	88-654310	2016-12-31
18	88-654309	-11280.00	c	88-654309-c-customers < Cash receipts from customers < Operating activities	88-654305	2016-12-31

Figure 3.11-43   Proprietorship1 Sum and Detail of Transactions with Symbol c

From the Figure 3.11-43, there is only one class of the transactions. However, their multi-subaccount name may be the "Cash payments to suppliers < Operating activities" or the "Cash payments for machinery < Operating activities". Because the products of the Company1 (Business No. 88-654306) are the vehicles and the computers, the multi-subaccount name of the cash that is paid to the Company1 is the "Cash payments for machinery < Operating activities". Therefore, I must get the sum of the transactions with the multi-subaccount name "Cash payments for machinery < Operating activities" (query condition: Recorder = '88-654306'). The Figure 3.11-44 on the next page shows that the result is -$44,500. In addition, there is an organization that is the Business Bank2 (Business No. 88-654305), so I must get the sum of the transactions with the multi-subaccount name "Cash payments to Banks < Operating activities" (query condition: Recorder = '88-654305'). The Figure 3.11-45 on the next page shows the result -$44,500. The rest balance is -$179,050 (= -$234,830 + $44,500 + $11,280).

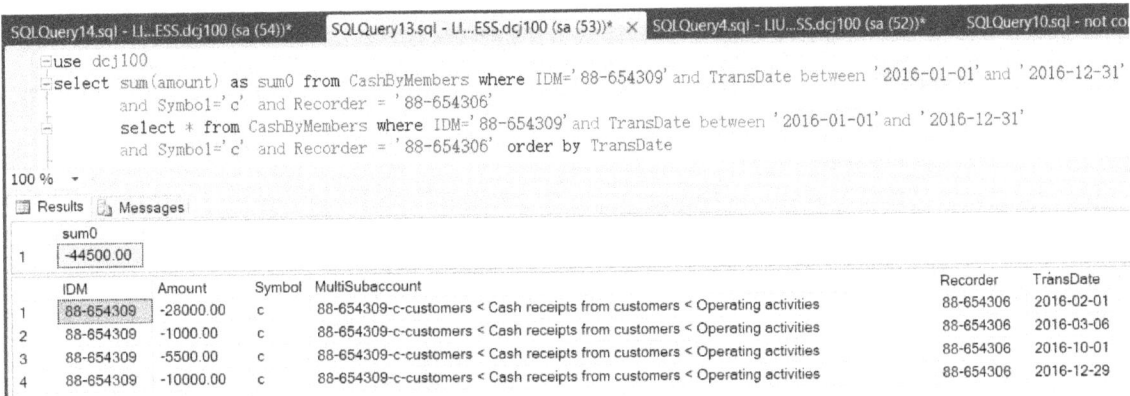

Figure 3.11-44　Proprietorship1 Sum of Machinery Transactions

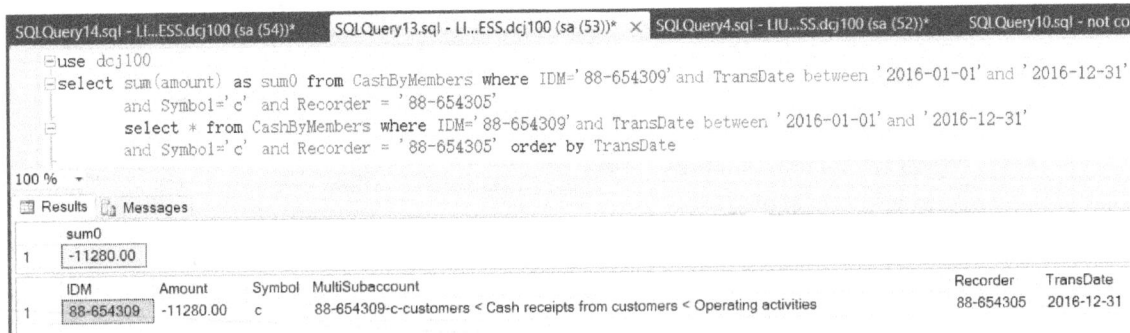

Figure 3.11-45　Proprietorship1 Sum of Bank Transactions

Based on the Figure 3.11-39 to the Figure 3.11-45, I can get the Proprietorship1's multi-subaccount names of the Cash account for the other organizations' transactions, seeing the following Figure 3.11-46.

Order	Symbol	Multi-subaccount Name	Balance
1	t	Cash receipts from banks < Financial activities	120.00
2	t	Cash receipts from investments < Investing activities	768.00
3	t	Cash receipts from customers < Operating activities	69,390.00
4	c	Cash payments to Banks < Operating activities	-11,280.00
5	c	Cash payments for machinery < Operating activities	-44,500.00
6	c	Cash payments to suppliers < Operating activities	-179,050.00
7	Total	-	-164,552.00

Figure 3.11-46　Proprietorship1 Multi-subaccount Names

3.11.3.5 Cash Flows Statement of Three Organizations

Merging the Figure 3.11-19 on the page 591 and Figure 3.11-32 on the page 602 together, I can get the Cash Flows Statement of the Cash Management Center, seeing the following Figure 3.11-50. You can compare the cash flows statement with the Figure 3.1-3 on the page 224 in this Chapter.

Cash Flows Statement, Year ended 2016-12-31	
Operating activities	
Cash payments to Banks < Operating activities	-2,500.00
Cash payments to governments < Operating activities	-270,000.00
Net cash provided by Operating activities	-272,500.00
Investing activities	
Cash receipts from investments < Investing activities	656.25
Cash payments for investments < Investing activities	-25,000.00
Net cash provided by Investing activities	-24,343.75
Financial activities	
Cash payments for issued bond interest < Financial activities	-2,400.00
Net cash provided by Financial activities	-2,400.00
Net change in cash	-299,243.75
Cash, Beginning	1,058,058.20
Cash, Ending	$758,814.45

Figure 3.11-50   CMC Cash Flows Statement

Merging the Figure 3.11-22 on the page 594 and Figure 3.11-38 on the page 605 together, I can get the Cash Flows Statement of the Company2, seeing the Figure 3.11-51 on the next page. You can compare the cash flows statement with the Figure 3.7-2 on the page 433 in this Chapter. There is some difference of the Operating activities in the two cash flow statements. The reason is that some individuals cash of the Cash payments to bond holders

(Here, it is the Cash payments for investment) is put in the Cash payments for operating expenses and the Cash payments to suppliers.

Cash Flows Statement, Year ended 2016-12-31	
Operating activities	
Cash payments for operating expenses < Operating activities	-109,487.98
Cash payments to suppliers < Operating activities	-11,580.00
Cash payments to Banks < Operating activities	-57,200.00
Cash payments for investment < Operating activities	-376.00
Cash receipts from customers < Operating activities	255,690.00
Net cash provided by Operating activities	77,046.02
Investing activities	
Cash receipts from investments < Investing activities	600.00
Net cash provided by Investing activities	600.00
Financial activities	
Cash receipts from banks < Financial activities	120.00
Net cash provided by Financial activities	120.00
Net change in cash	77,766.02
Cash, Beginning	47,393.19
Cash, Ending	125,159.21

Figure 3.11-51   Company2 Cash Flows Statement

Merging the Figure 3.11-25 on the page 598 and Figure 3.11-46 on the page 609 together, I can get the Cash Flows Statement of the Proprietorship1, seeing the Figure 3.11-52 on the next page. You can compare the cash flows statement with the Figure 3.9-3 on the page 519 in this Chapter. There is some difference between the two cash flows statements. The reason is only that some cash is put in the different category of the Operating activities.

Cash Flows Statement, Year ended 2016-12-31	
Operating activities	
Cash payments for operating expenses < Operating activities	-72,604.90
Cash payments to suppliers < Operating activities	-179,050.00
Cash payments for machinery < Operating activities	-44,500.00
Cash payments to Banks < Operating activities	-11,280.00
Cash receipts from customers < Operating activities	465,442.00
Net cash provided by Operating activities	158,007.10
Investing activities	
Cash receipts from investments < Investing activities	768.00
Net cash provided by Investing activities	768.00
Financial activities	
Cash receipts from banks < Financial activities	120.00
Net cash provided by Financial activities	120.00
Net change in cash	158,895.10
Cash, Beginning	18,783.78
Cash, Ending	177,678.88

Figure 3.11-52   Proprietorship1 Cash Flows Statement

3.11.4 Investment Information of Organizations

By using of SQL Server query, I can get the detail investment information for all organization in this fiscal year. The Figure 3.11-53 on the next page shows the detail investment information of the Tax Bureau (Business No. 88-654303) in this fiscal year. By using of the same method, I can get other organizations' investment information. From the Figure 3.11-53, there is only an investment transaction on June 1, 2016.

```
SQLQuery14.sql - not connected*    SQLQuery13.sql - LI...ESS.dcj100 (sa (52))*  ×  SQLQuery4.sql - not connected*    SQLQuery10.sql - not connected*    SQ

use dcj100
select sum(amount) as sum0 from CashByMembers where IDM='88-654303' and TransDate between '2016-01-01' and '2016-12-31'
    and Symbol='i'
    select * from CashByMembers where IDM='88-654303' and TransDate between '2016-01-01' and '2016-12-31'
    and Symbol='i' order by TransDate
100 %  ▾
Results  Messages
    sum0
1   -5000.00

    IDM         Amount    Symbol  MultiSubaccount                                                              Recorder    TransDate
1   88-654303   -5000.00  i       88-654303-i-bond23 < Cash receipts from issued bonds < Financial activities  88-654305   2016-06-01
```

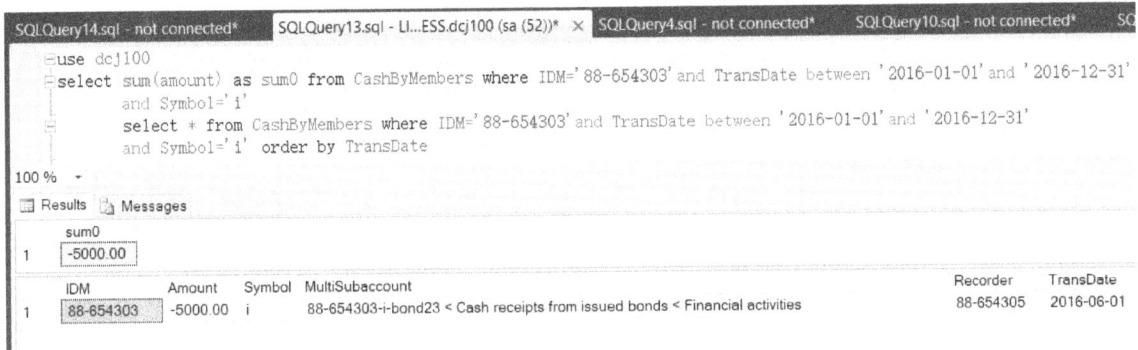

Figure 3.11-52   Tax Bureau Investment Information

3.11.5 Taxation information of Organizations

Because the revenue recognition principle is not the standard of the received cash, I can only get part of the taxable incomes by using of SQL Server query in this book now. Seeing the Figure 3.11-39 on the page 606, the balance $70,278 is the part of the taxable incomes for the Proprietorship1.

From theory, the total incomes' balance, which is equal to sum of the balance of the Sales account and the balance of the other incomes, is equal to the sum of balance of the Cash account with the symbol "t" and the increased amount of the Account receivable account in one fiscal year. Please pay attention here. The purpose of the digital currency is that one organization' tax information is gotten by using of the other organizations providing information. However, the Account receivable account is different from the Cash account in process of using digital currency. The other side of a transaction including the Cash account is also the Cash account, while the other side of the transaction including the Account receivable account is the Account payable accounts of many organizations, seeing the Figure 3.11-53 on the next page.

For getting correct the total incomes' balance, I must add a two-level subaccount name to the multi-subaccount name of the Account payable account. The new form of the multi-subaccount name of the Account payable account is the "Social member ID-x-xxx < Phone number". The sum of the changed amount of the Cash account with the symbol "t" and the changed amount of the Account payable account with the symbol "t" is the balance of the total incomes in one fiscal year. I will do the work in my next book.

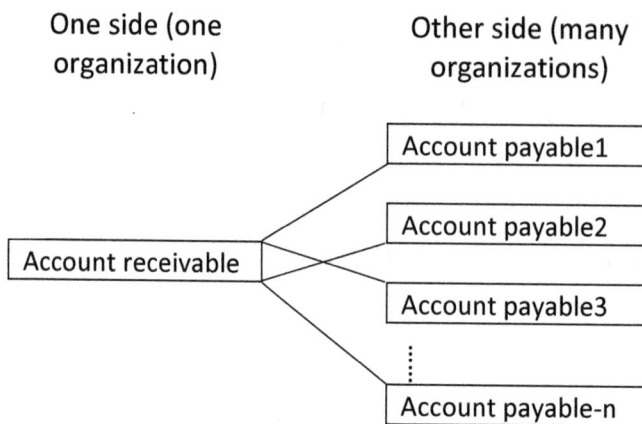

One side (one organization)   Other side (many organizations)

```
                                    ┌──────────────────────┐
                                    │  Account payable1     │
                                    └──────────────────────┘

                                    ┌──────────────────────┐
                                    │  Account payable2     │
┌──────────────────────┐           └──────────────────────┘
│  Account receivable   │
└──────────────────────┘           ┌──────────────────────┐
                                    │  Account payable3     │
                                    └──────────────────────┘
                                              ⋮
                                    ┌──────────────────────┐
                                    │  Account payable-n    │
                                    └──────────────────────┘
```

Figure 3.11-53   Two Sides of One Transaction

Chapter 4

Mixed Digital Currency Model

The mixed digital currency means that there is some paper money in the process of money circulation. In this situation, the MathAccounting software is also a good solution and the possibility of drawing up false accounts, tax evasion, and money laundering is very small. Moreover, taking some measures and doing analysis can prevent them to occur.

4.1 Introduction of Mixed Digital Currency Model

Compared with the simple (pure) digital currency model, the only change is that there is 30% paper money of the issued money $2,000,000 in the Mixed Digital Currency Model. For making the Mixed Digital Currency Model work normally, building three parent accounts of the Paper cash, the Paper cash payable, and the Paper cash receivable is necessary in the MathAccounting software. For this purpose, the Business Bank, which distributes the paper money to all social members, must be responsible for recording detail information. When a social member deposits some paper money into his (or her) account or withdraws some paper money from his (or her) account, the Business Bank must record this twin transaction of the Paper cash account except for recording deposit changes. The multi-subaccount names of the Paper cash account and this transaction sub-equations respectively are:

Social member ID-p-deposit < Paper cash receipts from customers deposits < Operating activities

Paper cash (1): xxx = Paper cash payable (2): -xxx (deposit into bank)

Or

Social member ID-w-withdraw < Paper cash payments to customers withdraw < Operating activities

Cash (1): -xxx + Paper cash receivable (1): xxx = 0 (withdraw from bank)

In fact, these related twin transactions of the Business Bank can be recorded automatically by using of the various smart bank cards.

For other organizations, every paper cash transaction must be recorded as a twin transaction. The multi-subaccount name of the Paper cash account and this twin transaction sub-equation respectively are:

Social member ID-p-customer < Paper cash receipts from customers < Operating activities

Paper cash (1): xxx = Paper cash payable (2): xxx

When the organizations deposits the paper cash into the Business bank, they must record another twin transaction. The multi-subaccount name of the Paper cash account and this twin transaction sub-equation respectively are:

Social member ID-p-customer < Paper cash receipts from customers < Operating activities

Paper cash (1): -xxx = Paper cash payable (2): -xxx

For tax evasion or other purpose, some organizations may do not record these paper cash transactions. In this situation, the Tax Bureau can get one social member's three balances of the Cash account with the symbol "t", the Cash account with the symbol "p", and the Cash account with the symbol "w" from the database dcj100 in this fiscal year. The balance of the Cash account with the symbol "p" must be less the sum of the balances of the Cash account with the symbol "t" and the Cash account with the symbol "w" in one fiscal year. The more discussion and analysis will be done in my next book.

4.2 Forecast and Conclusion

The simple digital currency model is based on a closed society, so all transactions occurred in this society has also constructed a closed system. However, there are many different societies (countries), which use the different currencies, in the world. Moreover, there are many transactions between these different societies (countries) every day, seeing the following Figure 4.2-1.

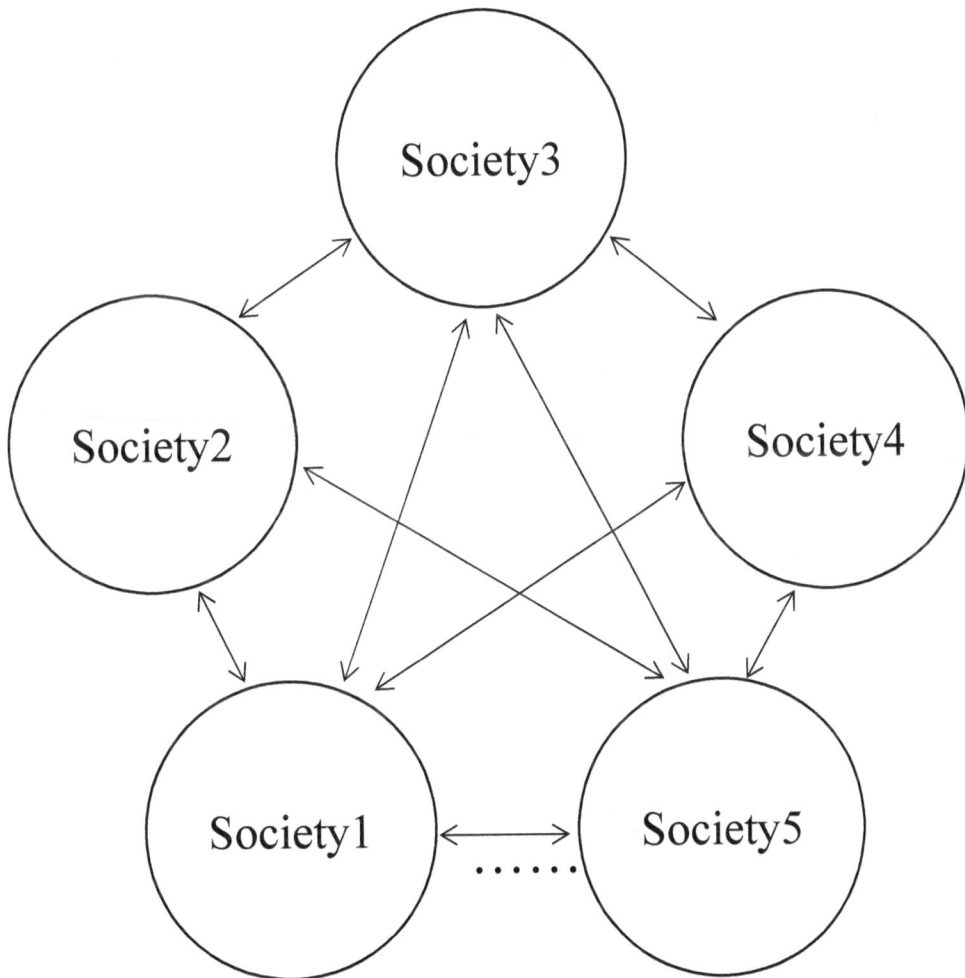

Figure 4.2-1   Great Closed System of World

In this situation, the closed system in a society is missing a part and the simple digital currency model will not work normally. For solving this problem, every society must found an organization of the Foreign Currency Management Center. While the Foreign Currency Management Center begins to record the cash (foreign currency) paid to the other societies (countries) or received form the other societies (countries), the simple digital currency model will normally work again. Of course, when each Foreign Currency Management Center records a transaction, the three-level subaccount of the Cash account is the "Local social member ID-x-xxx". All closed society systems will construct a great closed system of a world. It is future of the Accounting, the Auditing, the Taxation, and the Finance.

REFERENCES

[JIE] Guoping Jie, *A Mathematical Accounting Model and its MathAccounting Software* First Edition. Guoping Jie Press. Ontario, 2016.

[JIE] Guoping Jie, *A Mathematical Accounting Model and its MathAccounting Software* Second Edition. Guoping Jie Press. Ontario, 2017.

www.ingramcontent.com/pod-product-compliance
Lightning Source LLC
Chambersburg PA
CBHW080652220326

41598CB00033B/5184

* 9 7 8 0 9 9 5 8 2 0 3 3 3 *